W9-BGY-069

what is the short story?

Revised

Elizabeth Ross

212 - 228
229 - 250

Usher

1810

P 6

Characters
authors,
nat - critical
comments

simile
metaphor

Gothic

MLA
251-266

Auction #26

what is the short story?

Revised

Eugene Current-García and Walton R. Patrick
Auburn University

Scott, Foresman and Company
Glenview, Illinois   Brighton, England

Cover illustration: "Nagare III" by Kay Sekimachi, 1968, from
"Objects: USA, the Johnson Collection of Contemporary Crafts."

Library of Congress Catalog Card Number: 73–85422
ISBN: 0–673–07886–8

Copyright © 1974, 1961 Scott, Foresman and Company, Glenview, Illinois.
Philippines Copyright 1974 Scott, Foresman and Company.
All Rights Reserved.
Printed in the United States of America.

Regional offices of Scott, Foresman and Company are located in
Dallas, Texas; Glenview, Illinois; Oakland, New Jersey; Palo
Alto, California; Tucker, Georgia; and Brighton, England.

Read 320–324 Kafka
        341 – 350 Lardner
* Bibliography + term paper ~~project~~ topic

preface

The aim of this revised edition of *What Is the Short Story?* is the same as that of the earlier edition: to provide source materials for the study of the short story as a distinctive literary genre. The two-part structure, consisting first of critical statements which broadly represent historical trends and second of stories, has been retained, but a number of changes have been made in both parts as well as in the editorial materials throughout the volume. The critical part, for example, has been consolidated into three sections and some of the older critical statements have been replaced by five more recent ones. Furthermore, three introductory essays, especially written for this edition, have been added to each of the critical sections. Each essay provides an historical background against which the critical theories and short stories can be read, understood, and analyzed. Seven new stories, including ones by James Joyce, Ernest Hemingway, William Faulkner, Ernest J. Gaines, and Joyce Carol Oates, have been added. The biographical sketches have been revised, wherever possible, and the bibliography has been updated by the selective addition of articles and books which have appeared since the first edition was published.

The critical theory comprising the first section of the book purposely reflects the often contradictory, widely diversified range of opinions and beliefs which the short story has evoked ever since writers and critics began experimenting with it in the early nineteenth century. Some of these critical statements were written by recognized masters of the short story; others, by critics, literary historians, and journalists who have concerned themselves in some special way with the short story as a literary form. In order to clarify the shift of critical emphasis from age to age, we have arranged the statements chronologically and grouped them under three headings which we believe will most readily reveal the developing concepts they represent. Arranged thus, this small but representative core of the large body of critical theory the short story has stimulated over the past century and a half can provide the student with both an historical and analytical approach to the short story. The inclusion where possible of a statement by a writer who is also represented in the story section permits the student to compare a particular author's theory of the short-story art with his or her actual practice of that art.

Professor Henry Seidel Canby's remark that "men of genius" have found in the short story "a new voice" aptly suggests that a significant quantity of the best literature produced both in America and abroad during the nineteenth and twentieth centuries has appeared in the short-story form. To understand the artistry of this form (or any other literary form) requires an awareness of the range of conflicting ideas about it and an ability to discriminate wisely among them. The critical statements in this book have therefore been carefully selected to awaken such discrimination—that is, to aid in answering such closely related questions as What is the short story? What are its aims? Its special characteristics? Its materials? Its methods? What is the difference between it and other literary forms? The underlying assumption is that students who can reason well on basic questions of this sort will approach the reading of short stories with deeper insights and a fuller appreciation than they would otherwise possess.

With a similar view in mind, the stories in the second part of the book have also been arranged in the order of their publication to show how major changes in practice and technique have altered and extended the art of the short story from time to time and to afford a convenient means of studying the relationships existing between the practice and the critical theory. The general questions following each of the main sections in Part One are designed to bring this study of interrelationships into play, as well as to provide topics for discussion and for short compositions. In addition, the brief questions following each of the critical statements and each of the stories are intended as aids to the reading, understanding, and analysis of these individual pieces, while the broader topics listed at the end of the book are intended to suggest approaches toward the preparation of longer discussions and term papers. Many of the questions and topics have been revised, while a number of new ones have been added.

Bibliographical references are given at the bottom of the first page on which each critical statement and short story begins. Miss Florence Blakely and Miss Mary Frances Morris of the Duke University Library, and Dr. Ruth Fourier and Mrs. Helen Peet of the Auburn University Library have given valuable assistance in locating first publication dates and sources.

Eugene Current-García
Walton R. Patrick

contents

Historical Trends
and Critical Theories

Short Stories

Author, title, characters

Margarine daw
Easter Eve
Tryst
shut
good man is hard to find
Strength of god
How I contemplated the world
mrs. billingsby's wine
a tree of nite

historical
trends
and
critical
theories

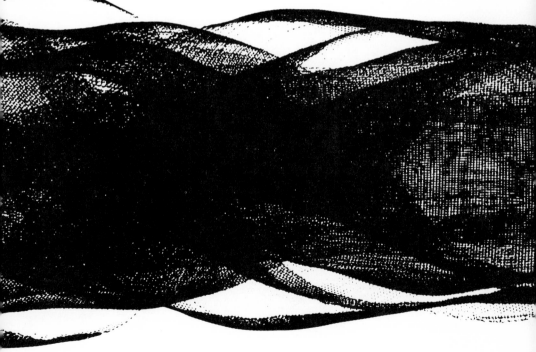

I

BEGINNINGS:
DEFINITIONS AND THE SEARCH FOR FORM

Short fiction is a very old form of writing, its recorded history going back to a collection of Egyptian stories entitled The Tales of the Magicians, *which may have been composed as long ago as 4000 B.C. Subsequently, the tradition of short fiction in prose and verse brought forth such notable collections as* The Thousand and One Nights *(tenth century A.D.), Boccaccio's* Decameron *(1352), Chaucer's* Canterbury Tales *(c. 1397), and Malory's* Morte d'Arthur *(1485), to name only a few. Embracing an endless variety of forms and aims, short fiction thus is as old as literature itself.*

Yet, the form of short fiction we know today as the short story is essentially a product of the nineteenth century, for it was during the early decades of the 1800s that writers in various major countries of the Western world first began to recognize and talk about the short story as a particular literary genre in its own right, sharply distinguishable from other forms of short fiction such as the tale, sketch, brief narrative, anecdote, and so on. As the critical statements in the following section will show, early nineteenth-century writers even disagreed about a proper name for the genre: Irving, Poe, and Hawthorne variously termed it "the tale," "the short prose tale," or "the sketch." They also differed considerably about the aims, purposes, and methods of writing the short story: Irving wanted to entertain and amuse; Poe, to achieve "a totality of effect"; Hawthorne, "to open up an intercourse with the world"—that is, to treat serious themes. Despite these differences and uncertainties about what to call the form, all three of these writers clearly realized that they were working with a separate literary entity requiring "a nicety of execution," a finesse in style, and a completeness and a unity which made it a distinctive work of art. From the stories included in this book by Pushkin (a Russian) and Balzac (a Frenchman), we must conclude that their ideas on short story form were as clearly defined as those of their American counterparts, Irving, Hawthorne, and Poe.

As we ponder not only the critical statements of these early nineteenth-century writers but also the conscious artistry implicit in their stories, we may wonder what influences at work in their different countries caused them to grasp almost simultaneously the concept of the short story as a distinctive literary genre. One possible explanation is that the growing artistic maturity of the novel in the period led story writers (who often also wrote novels) to discover richer possibilities in short fiction than had been seen earlier. A more significant explanation, however, is that the rapid spread of magazines and newspapers created a wider outlet than had ever before existed for the publication of short pieces of fiction complete in a single issue. Competition among writers desiring to sell their stories to this steadily expanding market stimulated them to greater and greater artistic effort. By Poe's own testimony, for example, he deliberately set out to write horror stories superior to those he found in the current magazines. As the century advanced and the number of periodicals increased—in 1885, 3,300 were published in the United States alone—magazine editors competed more and more vigorously for compact, fast-paced, and forcibly written stories.

It is in the context of this quickening emphasis on short-story form that we can view both the statements and the stories of later nineteenth-century masters such as Chekhov, James, and Maupassant, as well as the perhaps greatly oversimplified critical dogmas of such critics as Brander Matthews. The problem for the story writer became that of pruning away every nonessential word or phrase, of driving straight for the story climax with all possible economy of means. Chekhov described his own approach to story writing when he advised another writer metaphorically "to slough off at one stroke all that is useless"; and then added: "To make a face from marble means to remove from the slab everything which is not the face." Even though Henry James seldom succeeded in holding down the length of his stories to the goal he usually established in advance, he aimed to make "The Real Thing" a tremendously succinct story, "with a very short pulse or rhythm—and the closest selection of detail. . . ." James, like many other modern writers, greatly admired Maupassant's uncanny ability to compress, to abbreviate, to reduce a story to its basic dramatic and pictorial essentials.

By the end of the nineteenth century, although the short story was a well-established, highly popular literary form, some critics were still concerned about both its name and its critical definition. One of them, Brander Matthews, insisted that a capital letter and a hyphen should be used to distinguish the "Short-story" from the story which is "merely short." The same critic took pains to make sharper distinctions between the short story and other literary forms than had been made before and to establish a number of qualities such as conciseness, compression, originality, and ingenuity as the sine qua non of short-story form. Later critics have disparaged Matthews' viewpoint for being too narrow, too closely oriented toward one type of story form. But the significant fact is that by around 1900, approximately three-quarters of a century after Irving, the short story had evolved into a well-defined, perhaps even overdefined literary form.

WASHINGTON IRVING

ON STYLE AND PURPOSE IN THE SHORT STORY

(From a letter to Henry Brevoort, December 1824*)
I fancy much of what I value myself upon in writing, escapes the observation of the great mass of my readers, who are intent more upon the story than the way in which it is told. For my part, I consider a story merely as a frame on which to stretch my materials. It is the play of thought, and sentiment, and language; the weaving in of characters, lightly, yet expressively delineated; the familiar and faithful exhibition of scenes in common life; and the half-concealed vein of humor that is often playing through the whole,—these are among what I aim at, and upon which I felicitate myself in proportion as I think I succeed. I have preferred adopting the mode of sketches and short tales rather than long works, because I choose to take a line of writing peculiar to myself, rather than fall into the manner or school of any other writer; and there is a constant activity of thought and a nicety of execution required in writings of the kind, more than the world appears to imagine. It is comparatively easy to swell a story to any size when you have once the scheme and the characters in your mind; the mere interest of the story, too, carries the reader on through pages and pages of careless writing, and the author may often be dull for half a volume at a time, if he has some striking scene at the end of it; but in these shorter writings, every page must have its merit. The author must be continually piquant; woe to him if he makes an awkward sentence or writes a stupid page; the critics are sure to pounce upon it. Yet if he succeed, the very variety and piquancy of his writings—nay, their very brevity, make them frequently recurred to, and when the mere interest of the story is exhausted, he begins to get credit for his touches of pathos or humor; his points of wit or turns of language. I give these as some of the reasons that have induced me to keep on thus far in the way I had opened for myself. . . .

---

*Reprinted here from *The Life and Letters of Washington Irving,* condensed editions, ed. Pierre M. Irving (New York: G. P. Putnam's Sons, 1869), Vol. II.

(From Irving's preface to Tales of a Traveller, *1824*)*
 . . . As I know this to be a story-telling and a story-reading age, and
that the world is fond of being taught by apologue, I have digested the
instruction I would convey into a number of tales. They may not possess
the power of amusement, which the tales told by many of my contemporaries possess; but then I value myself on the sound moral which
each of them contains. This may not be apparent at first, but the reader
will be sure to find it out in the end. I am for curing the world by gentle
alternatives, not by violent doses; indeed, the patient should never be
conscious that he is taking a dose. I have learnt this much from
experience under the hands of the worthy Hippocrates of Mentz.

I am not, therefore, for those barefaced tales which carry their moral
on the surface, staring one in the face; they are enough to deter the
squeamish reader. On the contrary, I have often hid my moral from
sight, and disguised it as much as possible by sweets and spices, so that
while the simple reader is listening with open mouth to a ghost or a love
story, he may have a bolus of sound morality popped down his throat,
and be never the wiser for the fraud. . . .

---

*Reprinted here from *The Works of Washington Irving*, new edition, revised (New York:
G. P. Putnam's Sons, 1860), Vol. VII.

For Study and Discussion

1. What does Irving mean when he calls the story "a frame on which to
   stretch my materials"?

2. Pick out and discuss the six specific elements which he says require "a
   nicety of execution" if they are to be successfully combined in a short
   tale or sketch.

3. Look up the term *apologue*, used by Irving. Is he serious or whimsical
   when he says that each of his tales contains a "sound moral"? What is
   his attitude toward the practice of moralizing in the fiction of his time?
   What moral, if any, can you find disguised by means of "sweets and
   spices" in his story "The Spectre Bridegroom"?

EDGAR ALLAN POE

ON THE AIM AND TECHNIQUE OF THE SHORT STORY

The tale proper, in our opinion, affords unquestionably the fairest field for the exercise of the loftiest talent, which can be afforded by the wide domains of mere prose. Were we bidden to say how the highest genius could be most advantageously employed for the best display of its own powers, we should answer, without hesitation—in the composition of a rhymed poem, not to exceed in length what might be perused in an hour. Within this limit alone can the highest order of true poetry exist. We need only here say, upon this topic, that, in almost all classes of composition, the unity of effect or impression is a point of the greatest importance. It is clear, moreover, that this unity cannot be thoroughly preserved in productions whose perusal cannot be completed at one sitting. We may continue the reading of a prose composition, from the very nature of prose itself, much longer than we can persevere, to any good purpose, in the perusal of a poem. This latter, if truly fulfilling the demands of the poetic sentiment, induces an exaltation of the soul which cannot be long sustained. All high excitements are necessarily transient. Thus a long poem is a paradox. And, without unity of impression, the deepest effects cannot be brought about. Epics were the offspring of an imperfect sense of Art, and their reign is no more. A poem *too* brief may produce a vivid, but never an intense or enduring impression. Without a certain continuity of effort—without a certain duration or repetition of purpose—the soul is never deeply moved. There must be the dropping of the water upon the rock. De Béranger has wrought brilliant things— pungent and spirit-stirring—but, like all immassive bodies, they lack *momentum*, and thus fail to satisfy the Poetic Sentiment. They sparkle and excite, but, from want of continuity, fail deeply to impress. Extreme brevity will degenerate into epigrammatism; but the sin of extreme length is even more unpardonable. *In medio tutissimus ibis.*

Were we called upon, however, to designate that class of composition

---

From a review, originally published in *Graham's Magazine*, May 1842, of Nathaniel Hawthorne's *Twice-Told Tales*. Reprinted here from *The Complete Works of Edgar Allan Poe*, ed. James A. Harrison (New York: Thomas Y. Crowell and Co., 1902), Vol. XI.

which, next to such a poem as we have suggested, should best fulfil the demands of high genius—should offer it the most advantageous field of exertion—we should unhesitatingly speak of the prose tale, as Mr. Hawthorne has here exemplified it. We allude to the short prose narrative, requiring from a half-hour to one or two hours in its perusal. The ordinary novel is objectionable, from its length, for reasons already stated in substance. As it cannot be read at one sitting, it deprives itself, of course, of the immense force derivable from *totality*. Worldly interests intervening during the pauses of perusal, modify, annul, or counteract, in a greater or less degree, the impressions of the book. But simple cessation in reading, would, of itself, be sufficient to destroy the true unity. In the brief tale, however, the author is enabled to carry out the fulness of his intention, be it what it may. During the hour of perusal the soul of the reader is at the writer's control. There are no external or extrinsic influences—resulting from weariness or interruption.

A skilful literary artist has constructed a tale. If wise, he has not fashioned his thoughts to accommodate his incidents; but having conceived, with deliberate care, a certain unique or single *effect* to be wrought out, he then invents such incidents—he then combines such events as may best aid him in establishing this preconceived effect. If his very initial sentence tend not to the outbringing of this effect, then he has failed in his first step. In the whole composition there should be no word written, of which the tendency, direct or indirect, is not to the one pre-established design. And by such means, with such care and skill, a picture is at length painted which leaves in the mind of him who contemplates it with a kindred art, a sense of the fullest satisfaction. The idea of the tale has been presented unblemished, because undisturbed; and this is an end unattainable by the novel. Undue brevity is just as exceptionable here as in the poem; but undue length is yet more to be avoided.

We have said that the tale has a point of superiority even over the poem. In fact, while the *rhythm* of this latter is an essential aid in the development of the poet's highest idea—the idea of the Beautiful—the artificialities of this rhythm are an inseparable bar to the development of all points of thought or expression which have their basis in *Truth*. But Truth is often, and in very great degree, the aim of the tale. Some of the finest tales are tales of ratiocination. Thus the field of this species of composition, if not in so elevated a region on the mountain of Mind, is a table-land of far vaster extent than the domain of the mere poem. Its products are never so rich, but infinitely more numerous, and more appreciable by the mass of mankind. The writer of the prose tale, in short, may bring to his theme a vast variety of modes or inflections of thought and expression—(the ratiocinative, for example, the sarcastic, or the humorous) which are not only antagonistical to the nature of the poem, but absolutely forbidden by one of its most peculiar and indispensable adjuncts; we allude, of course, to rhythm. It may be added here, *par parenthese*, that the author who aims at the purely beautiful in a prose tale is laboring at great disadvantage. For Beauty can be better treated in the poem. Not so with terror, or passion, or horror, or a multitude of such other points. And here it will be seen how full of prejudice are the usual animadversions against those *tales of effect*, many fine examples of which were found in the earlier numbers of Blackwood. The impressions produced were wrought in a legitimate sphere of action, and constituted a legitimate although sometimes an exaggerated interest. They were relished by every man of genius: although there were found many men of genius who condemned them without just ground. The true critic will but demand that the design intended be accomplished, to the fullest extent, by the means most advantageously applicable.

We have very few American tales of real merit—we may say, indeed, none, with the exception of "The Tales of a Traveller" of Washington Irving, and these "Twice-Told Tales" of Mr. Hawthorne. Some of the pieces of Mr. John Neal abound in vigor and originality; but in general, his compositions of this class are excessively diffuse, extravagant, and indicative of an imperfect sentiment of Art. Articles at random are, now and then, met with in our periodicals which might be advantageously compared with the best effusions of the British Magazines; but, upon the whole, we are far behind our progenitors in this department of literature.

Of Mr. Hawthorne's Tales we would say, emphatically, that they belong to the highest region of Art—an Art subservient to genius of a very lofty order. We had supposed, with good reason for so supposing, that he had been thrust into this present position by one of the impudent *cliques* which beset our literature, and whose pretensions it is our full purpose to expose at the earliest opportunity; but we have been most agreeably mistaken. We know of few compositions which the critic can more honestly commend than these "Twice-Told Tales." As Americans, we feel proud of the book.

Mr. Hawthorne's distinctive trait is invention, creation, imagination, originality—a trait which, in the literature of fiction, is positively worth all the rest. But the nature of originality, so far as regards its manifestation in letters, is but imperfectly understood. The inventive or original mind as frequently displays itself in novelty of *tone* as in novelty of matter. Mr. Hawthorne is original at *all* points.

It would be a matter of some difficulty to designate the best of these tales; we repeat that, without exception, they are beautiful. "Wakefield" is remarkable for the skill with which an old idea—a well-known incident—is worked up or discussed. A man of whims conceives the purpose of quitting his wife and residing *incognito*, for twenty years, in her immediate neighborhood. Something of this kind actually happened in London. The force of Mr. Hawthorne's tale lies in the analysis of the motives which must or might have impelled the husband to such folly, in the first instance, with the possible causes of his perseverance. Upon this thesis a sketch of singular power has been constructed.

"The Wedding Knell" is full of the boldest imagination—an imagination fully controlled by taste. The most captious critic could find no flaw in this production.

"The Minister's Black Veil" is a masterly composition of which the sole defect is that to the rabble its exquisite skill will be *caviare*. The *obvious* meaning of this article will be found to smother its insinuated one. The *moral* put into the mouth of the dying minister will be supposed to convey the *true* import of the narrative; and that a crime of dark dye, (having reference to the "young lady") has been committed, is a point which only minds congenial with that of the author will perceive.

"Mr. Higginbotham's Catastrophe" is vividly original and managed most dexterously.

"Dr. Heidegger's Experiment" is exceedingly well imagined, and executed with surpassing ability. The artist breathes in every line of it.

"The White Old Maid" is objectionable, even more than the "Minister's Black Veil," on the score of its mysticism. Even with the thoughtful and analytic, there will be much trouble in penetrating its entire import.

"The Hollow of the Three Hills" we would quote in full, had we space;—not as evincing higher talent than any of the other pieces, but as affording an excellent example of the author's peculiar ability. The subject is commonplace. A witch subjects the Distant and the Past to the view of a mourner. It has been the fashion to describe, in such cases, a mirror in which the images of the absent appear; or a cloud of smoke is made to arise, and thence the figures are gradually unfolded. Mr. Hawthorne has wonderfully heightened his effect by making the ear, in place of the eye, the medium by which the fantasy is conveyed. The head of the mourner is enveloped in the cloak of the witch, and within its magic folds there arise sounds which have an all-sufficient intelligence. Throughout this article also, the artist is conspicuous—not more in positive than in negative merits. Not only is all done that should be done, but (what perhaps is an end with more difficulty attained) there is nothing done which should not be. Every word *tells*, and there is not a word which does *not* tell. . . .

In the way of objection we have scarcely a word to say of these tales. There is, perhaps, a somewhat too general or prevalent *tone*—a tone of melancholy and mysticism. The subjects are insufficiently varied. There is not so much of *versatility* evinced as we might well be warranted in expecting from the high powers of Mr. Hawthorne. But beyond these trivial exceptions we have really none to make. The style is purity itself. Force abounds. High imagination gleams from every page. Mr. Hawthorne is a man of the truest genius. We only regret that the limits of our Magazine will not permit us to pay him that full tribute of commendation, which, under other circumstances, we should be so eager to pay.

(From "The Philosophy of Composition"*)

. . . Nothing is more clear than that every plot, worth the name, must be elaborated to its *dénouement* before anything be attempted with the pen. It is only with the *dénouement* constantly in view that we can give a plot its indispensable air of consequence, or causation, by making the incidents, and especially the tone at all points, tend to the development of the intention.

There is a radical error, I think, in the usual mode of constructing a story. Either history affords a thesis—or one is suggested by an incident of the day—or, at best, the author sets himself to work, in the combination of striking events to form merely the basis of his narrative—designing, generally, to fill in with description, dialogue, or autorial [*sic*] comment, whatever crevices of fact, or action, may, from page to page, render themselves apparent.

I prefer commencing with the consideration of an *effect*. Keeping originality *always* in view—for he is false to himself who ventures to dispense with so obvious and so easily attainable a source of interest—I say to myself, in the first place, "Of the innumerable effects, or impressions, of which the heart, the intellect, or (more generally) the soul is susceptible, what one shall I, on the present occasion, select?" Having chosen a novel, first, and secondly a vivid effect, I consider whether it can be best wrought by incident or tone—whether by ordinary incidents and peculiar tone, or the converse, or by peculiarity both of incident and tone—afterward looking about me (or rather within) for such combinations of event, or tone, as shall best aid me in the construction of the effect. . . .

(From Poe's "Tale Writing—Nathaniel Hawthorne"†)

In the preface to my sketches of New York Literati, while speaking of the broad distinction between the seeming public and real private opinion respecting our authors, I thus alluded to Nathaniel Hawthorne:

"For example, Mr. Hawthorne, the author of 'Twice-Told Tales,' is scarcely recognized by the press or by the public, and when noticed at all, is noticed merely to be damned by faint praise. Now, my opinion of him is, that although his walk is limited and he is fairly to be charged with mannerism, treating all subjects in a similar tone of dreamy *innuendo*,

---

*Originally published in *Graham's Magazine*, April 1846. Reprinted here from *Works*, Vol. XIV.

†Originally published in *Godey's Magazine and Lady's Book*, November 1847. This article was a revision and expansion of Poe's earlier review (1842) of Hawthorne's *Twice-Told Tales*. Reprinted here from *Works*, Vol. XIII.

yet in this walk he evinces extraordinary genius, having no rival either in America or elsewhere; and this opinion I have never heard gainsaid by any one literary person in the country. That this opinion, however, is a spoken and not a written one, is referable to the facts, first, that Mr. Hawthorne is a poor man, and, secondly, that he *is not* an ubiquitous quack."

The reputation of the author of "Twice-Told Tales" has been confined, indeed, until very lately, to literary society; and I have not been wrong, perhaps, in citing him as *the* example, *par excellence*, in this country, of the privately-admired and publicly-unappreciated man of genius. . . .

Beyond doubt, this inappreciation of him on the part of the public arose chiefly from the two causes to which I have referred—from the facts that he is neither a man of wealth nor a quack;—but these are insufficient to account for the whole effect. No small portion of it is attributable to the very marked idiosyncrasy of Mr. Hawthorne himself. In one sense, and in great measure, to be peculiar is to be original, and than the true originality there is no higher literary virtue. This true or commendable originality, however, implies not the uniform, but the continuous peculiarity—a peculiarity springing from ever-active vigor of fancy—better still if from ever-present force of imagination, giving its own hue, its own character to everything it touches, and, especially, *self impelled to touch everything.*

It is often said, inconsiderately, that very original writers always fail in popularity—that such and such persons are too original to be comprehended by the mass. "Too peculiar," should be the phrase, "too idiosyncratic." It is, in fact, the excitable, undisciplined and childlike popular mind which most keenly feels the original. . . .

The fact is, that if Mr. Hawthorne were really original, he could not fail of making himself felt by the public. But the fact is, he is *not* original in any sense. Those who speak of him as original, mean nothing more than that he differs in his manner or tone, and in his choice of subjects, from any author of their acquaintance—their acquaintance not extending to the German Tieck, whose manner, in *some* of his works, is absolutely identical with that *habitual* to Hawthorne. But it is clear that the element of the literary originality is novelty. The element of its appreciation by the reader is the reader's sense of the new. Whatever gives him a new and insomuch a pleasurable emotion, he considers original, and whoever frequently gives him such emotion, he considers an original writer. In a word, it is by the sum total of these emotions that he decides upon the writer's claim to originality. I may observe here, however, that there is clearly a point at which even novelty itself would cease to produce the legitimate originality, if we judge this originality, as we should, by the effect designed: this point is that at which *novelty becomes nothing novel;* and here the artist, *to preserve his originality*, will subside into the commonplace. . . .

These points properly understood, it will be seen that the critic (unacquainted with Tieck) who reads a single tale or essay by Hawthorne, may be justified in thinking him original; but the tone, or manner, or choice of subject, which induces in this critic the sense of the new, will—if not in a second tale, at least in a third and all subsequent ones—not only fail of inducing it, but bring about an exactly antagonistic impression. In concluding a volume, and more especially in concluding all the volumes of the author, the critic will abandon his first design of calling him "original," and content himself with styling him "peculiar."

With the vague opinion that to be original is to be unpopular, I could, indeed, agree, were I to adopt an understanding of originality which, to my surprise, I have known adopted by many who have a right to be called critical. They have limited, in a love for mere words, the literary to the metaphysical originality. They regard as original in letters, only such combinations of thought, of incident, and so forth, as are, in fact, absolutely novel. It is clear, however, not only that it is the novelty of *effect* alone which is worth consideration, but that this effect is *best* wrought, for the end of all fictitious composition, pleasure, by shunning rather than by seeking the absolute novelty of combination. Originality, thus understood, tasks and startles the intellect, and so brings into undue action the faculties to which, in the lighter literature, we least appeal. And thus understood, it cannot fail to prove unpopular with the masses, who, seeking in this literature amusement, are positively offended by instruction. But the true originality—true in respect of its purposes—is that which, in bringing out the half-formed, the reluctant, or the unexpressed fancies of mankind, or in exciting the more delicate pulses of the heart's passion, or in giving birth to some universal sentiment or instinct in embryo, thus combines with the pleasurable effect of *apparent* novelty, a real egoistic delight. The reader, in the case first supposed, (that of the absolute novelty,) is excited, but embarrassed, disturbed, in some degree even pained at his own want of perception, at his own folly in not having himself hit upon the idea. In the second case, his pleasure is doubled. He is filled with an intrinsic and extrinsic delight. He feels and intensely enjoys the seeming novelty of the thought, enjoys it as really novel, as absolutely original with the writer—*and himself*. They two, he fancies, have, alone of all men, thought thus. They two have, together, created this thing. Henceforward there is a bond of sympathy between them, a sympathy which irradiates every subsequent page of the book.

There is a species of writing which, with some difficulty, may be admitted as a lower degree of what I have called the true original. In its perusal, we say to ourselves, not "how original this is!" nor "here is an idea which I and the author have alone entertained," but "here is a charmingly obvious fancy," or sometimes even, "here is a thought which I am not sure has ever occurred to myself, but which, of course, has occurred to all the rest of the world." This kind of composition (which still appertains to a high order) is usually designated as "the natural." It has little external resemblance, but strong internal affinity to the true original, if, indeed, as I have suggested, it is not of this latter an inferior degree. It is best exemplified, among English writers, in Addison, Irving and *Hawthorne*. The "ease" which is so often spoken of as its distinguishing feature, it has been the fashion to regard as ease in appearance alone, as a point of really difficult attainment. This idea, however, must be received with some reservation. The natural style is difficult only to those who should never intermeddle with it—to the unnatural. It is but the result of writing with the understanding, or with the instinct, that the *tone,* in composition, should be that which, at any given point or upon any given topic, would be the tone of the great mass of humanity. The author who, after the manner of the North Americans, is merely at *all* times *quiet,* is, of course, upon *most* occasions, merely silly or stupid, and has no more right to be thought "easy" or "natural" than has a cockney exquisite or the sleeping beauty in the wax-works.

The "peculiarity" or sameness, or monotone of Hawthorne, would, in its mere character of "peculiarity," and without reference to what *is* the peculiarity, suffice to deprive him of all chance of popular appreciation. But at his failure to be appreciated, we can, *of course,* no longer wonder, when we find him monotonous at decidedly the worst of all possible points—at that point which, having the least concern with Nature, is the farthest removed from the popular intellect, from the popular sentiment and from the popular taste. I allude to the strain of allegory which completely overwhelms the greater number of his subjects, and which in some measure interferes with the direct conduct of absolutely all.

In defence of allegory, (however, or for whatever object, employed,) there is scarcely one respectable word to be said. Its best appeals are made to the fancy—that is to say, to our sense of adaptation, not of matters proper, but of matters improper for the purpose, of the real with the unreal; having never more of intelligible connection than has something with nothing, never half so much of effective affinity as has the substance for the shadow. The deepest emotion aroused within us by the happiest allegory, *as* allegory, is a very, very imperfectly satisfied sense of the writer's ingenuity in overcoming a difficulty we should have preferred his not having attempted to overcome. The fallacy of the idea that allegory, in any of its moods, can be made to enforce a truth—that metaphor, for example, may illustrate as well as embellish an argument—could be promptly demonstrated: the converse of the supposed fact might be shown, indeed, with very little trouble—but these are topics foreign to my present purpose. One thing is clear, that if allegory ever establishes a fact, it is by dint of overturning a fiction. Where the suggested meaning runs through the obvious one in a *very* profound under-current so as never to interfere with the upper one without our own volition, so as never to show itself unless *called* to the surface, there only, for the proper uses of fictitious narrative, is it available at all. Under the best circumstances, it must always interfere with that unity of effect which to the artist, is worth all the allegory in the world. Its vital injury, however, is rendered to the most vitally important point in fiction—that of earnestness or verisimilitude. . . .

The obvious causes, however, which have prevented Mr. Hawthorne's *popularity*, do not suffice to condemn him in the eyes of the few who belong properly to books, and to whom books, perhaps, do not quite so properly belong. These few estimate an author, not as do the public, altogether by what he does, but in great measure—indeed, even in the greatest measure—by what he evinces a capability of doing. In this view, Hawthorne stands among literary people in America much in the same light as did Coleridge in England. The few, also, through a certain warping of the taste, which long pondering upon books as books merely never fails to induce, are not in condition to view the errors of a scholar as errors altogether. At any time these gentlemen are prone to think the public not right rather than an educated author wrong. But the simple truth is that the writer who aims at impressing the people, is *always* wrong when he fails in forcing that people to receive the impression. How far Mr. Hawthorne has addressed the people at all, is, of course, not a question for me to decide. His books afford strong internal evidence of having been written to himself and his particular friends alone. . . .

He is peculiar and *not* original—unless in those detailed fancies and detached thoughts which his want of general originality will deprive of the appreciation due to them, in preventing them forever reaching the *public eye*. He is infinitely too fond of allegory, and can never hope for popularity so long as he persists in it. This he will not do, for allegory is at war with the whole tone of his nature, which disports itself never so well as when escaping from the mysticism of his Goodman Browns and White Old Maids into the hearty, genial, but still Indian-summer sunshine of his Wakefields and Little Annie's Rambles. Indeed *his* spirit of "metaphor run-mad" is clearly imbibed from the phalanx and phalanstery atmosphere in which he has been so long struggling for breath. He has not half the material for the exclusiveness of authorship that he possesses for its universality. He has the purest style, the finest taste, the most available scholarship, the most delicate humor, the most touching pathos, the most radiant imagination, the most consummate ingenuity; and with these varied good qualities he has done *well* as a mystic. But is there any one of these qualities which should prevent his doing doubly as well in a career of honest, upright, sensible, prehensible and comprehensible things? Let him mend his pen, get a bottle of visible ink, come out from the Old Manse, cut Mr. Alcott, hang (if possible) the editor of "The Dial," and throw out of the window to the pigs all his odd numbers of "The North American Review."

For Study and Discussion

1. On what grounds does Poe argue that the short story and the poem "best fulfil the demands of high genius"? What advantages does the short story have over the poem, and vice versa?

2. How is Poe's attitude toward "the ordinary novel" similar to and different from Irving's attitude?

3. According to Poe, what must the writer of short tales aim for if he wishes to become a successful literary artist? What exact steps should the writer take in order to fulfill that aim? Does this procedure sound reasonable?

4. What does Poe mean by "tales of ratiocination"? Why does he say that some of the finest tales belong in this category?

5. Which American writers, in Poe's view, had produced tales "of real merit"? On what grounds does he praise their work?

6. What evidence does Poe give to support his assertion that Hawthorne's stories "belong to the highest region of Art"? Which of Hawthorne's stories does he praise unreservedly? Which ones does he find "objectionable"? Why?

7. In his first review of Hawthorne's *Twice-Told Tales* (1842) Poe wrote, "Mr. Hawthorne is original at *all* points." Five years later, however, he said in "Tale Writing" that Hawthorne "is *not* original in any sense." Is this a flat contradiction? Compare these two critical judgments carefully and try to explain the reasons why Poe modified his opinion of Hawthorne's artistry (see Robert D. Jacobs, *Poe: Journalist and Critic*, 1969, pp. 391–94).

8. Explain Poe's use of the terms *originality* and *peculiarity*. Does the distinction he draws seem valid?

9. On what grounds does Poe disapprove of the use of allegory in fiction? Does he condemn allegory altogether? Under what conditions will he concede its usefulness in "fictitious narrative"?

NATHANIEL HAWTHORNE

SELF-CRITICISM

(From the author's introduction to "Rappaccini's Daughter"*)
His [the author's] writings, to do them justice, are not altogether
destitute of fancy and originality; they might have won him greater
reputation but for an inveterate love of allegory, which is apt to invest his
plots and characters with the aspect of scenery and people in the clouds,
and to steal away the human warmth out of his conceptions. His fictions
are sometimes historical, sometimes of the present day, and sometimes,
so far as can be discovered, have little or no reference either to time or
space. In any case, he generally contents himself with a very slight
embroidery of outward manners,—the faintest possible counterfeit of
real life,—and endeavors to create an interest by some less obvious
peculiarity of the subject. Occasionally a breath of Nature, a raindrop of
pathos and tenderness, or a gleam of humor, will find its way into the
midst of his fantastic imagery, and make us feel as if, after all, we were
yet within the limits of our native earth. . . .

(From the author's preface to the 1851 edition of Twice-Told Tales†*)*
The author of *Twice-Told Tales* has a claim to one distinction, which,
as none of his literary brethren will care about disputing it with him, he
need not be afraid to mention. He was, for a good many years, the
obscurest man of letters in America.

These stories were published in magazines and annuals, extending
over a period of ten or twelve years, and comprising the whole of the
writer's young manhood, without making (so far as he has ever been
aware) the slightest impression on the public. . . .

After a long while the first collected volume of the "Tales" was
published. By this time, if the Author had ever been greatly tormented by
literary ambition (which he does not remember or believe to have been
the case), it must have perished, beyond resuscitation, in the dearth of

---

*Originally published in the *Democratic Review*, December 1844. Reprinted here from
The Complete Works of Nathaniel Hawthorne, Riverside Edition, ed. George Parsons
Lathrop (Boston: Houghton, Mifflin Co., 1883), Vol. II.
†Reprinted here from *Works*, Vol. I.

nutriment. This was fortunate; for the success of the volume was not such as would have gratified a craving desire for notoriety. . . .

As he glances over these long-forgotten pages, and considers his way of life while composing them, the Author can very clearly discern why all this was so. After so many sober years, he would have reason to be ashamed if he could not criticise his own work as fairly as another man's; and, though it is little his business, and perhaps still less his interest, he can hardly resist a temptation to achieve something of the sort. If writers were allowed to do so, and would perform the task with perfect sincerity and unreserve, their opinions of their own productions would often be more valuable and instructive than the works themselves.

At all events, there can be no harm in the Author's remarking that he rather wonders how the *Twice-Told Tales* should have gained what vogue they did than that it was so little and so gradual. They have the pale tint of flowers that blossomed in too retired a shade—the coolness of a meditative habit, which diffuses itself through the feeling and observation of every sketch. Instead of passion there is sentiment, and, even in what purport to be pictures of actual life, we have allegory, not always so warmly dressed in its habiliments of flesh and blood as to be taken into the reader's mind without a shiver. Whether from lack of power, or an unconquerable reserve, the Author's touches have often an effect of tameness; the merriest man can hardly contrive to laugh at his broadest humor; the tenderest woman, one would suppose, will hardly shed warm tears at his deepest pathos. The book, if you would see anything in it, requires to be read in the clear, brown, twilight atmosphere in which it was written; if opened in the sunshine, it is apt to look exceedingly like a volume of blank pages.

With the foregoing characteristics, proper to the production of a person in retirement (which happened to be the Author's category at the time), the book is devoid of others that we should quite as naturally look for. The sketches are not, it is hardly necessary to say, profound; but it is rather more remarkable that they so seldom, if ever, show any design on the writer's part to make them so. They have none of the abstruseness of idea, or obscurity of expression, which mark the written communications of a solitary mind with itself. They never need translation. It is, in fact, the style of a man of society. Every sentence, so far as it embodies thought or sensibility, may be understood and felt by anybody who will give himself the trouble to read it, and will take up the book in a proper mood.

This statement of apparently opposite peculiarities leads us to a perception of what the sketches truly are. They are not the talk of a secluded man with his own mind and heart (had it been so, they could hardly have failed to be more deeply and permanently valuable), but his attempts, and very imperfectly successful ones, to open an intercourse with the world. . . .

For Study and Discussion

1. How closely does Hawthorne's criticism of his own short stories agree
   with Poe's criticism of them? On what specific points does Hawthorne's analysis of his early stories differ from Poe's judgment? Is
   his criticism more or less severe than Poe's?

2. What do you make of Hawthorne's concluding statement that his
   Twice-Told Tales were "not the talk of a secluded man with his own
   mind and heart . . . but his attempts . . . to open an intercourse with
   the world"? What does this statement tell us about Hawthorne's
   attitude toward his profession as a literary artist?

3. Does Hawthorne's "inveterate love of allegory" enhance or lessen the
   effectiveness of his story "The Birthmark"? Would it be an equally
   good story if its allegorical implications were omitted?

4. What is the main difference between Hawthorne's and Irving's
   attitudes toward the craft of fiction writing? Between Hawthorne's
   and Poe's?

ANTON CHEKHOV

ON PROBLEMS OF TECHNIQUE IN THE SHORT STORY

(From a letter to Alexander P. Chekhov, April 1883*)
You underscore trifles in your writings, and yet you are not a subjective writer by nature; it is an acquired trait in you. To give up this acquired subjectivity is as easy as to take a drink. One needs only to be more honest, to throw oneself overboard everywhere, not to obtrude oneself into the hero of one's own novel, to renounce oneself for at least a half hour. You have a story in which a young wedded couple kiss all through dinner, grieve without cause, weep oceans of tears. Not a single sensible word; nothing but *sentimentality*. And you did not write for the reader. You wrote because *you* like that sort of chatter. But suppose you were to describe the dinner, how they ate, what they ate, what the cook was like, how insipid your hero is, how content with his lazy happiness, how insipid your heroine is, how funny is her love for this napkin-bound, sated, overfed goose,—we all like to see happy, contented people, that is true,—but to describe them, what *they* said and how many times they kissed is not enough—you need something else: to free yourself from the personal expression that a placid honey-happiness produces upon everybody. . . . Subjectivity is a terrible thing. It is bad in this alone, that it reveals the author's hands and feet. I'll bet that all priests' daughters and clerks' wives who read your works are in love with you, and if you were a German you would get free beer in all the Bierhalle where the German women serve. If it were not for this subjectivity you would be the best of artists. You know how to laugh, sting, and ridicule, you possess a rounded style, you have experienced much, have seen so much,—alas! The material is all wasted. . . .

(From a letter to Alexander P. Chekhov, May 10, 1886)
In my opinion a true description of Nature should be very brief and have a character of relevance. Commonplaces such as, "the setting sun

*Reprinted here from *Letters on the Short Story, the Drama, and Other Literary Topics by Anton Chekhov*, ed. Louis S. Friedland. Translated by Constance Garnett (New York: Minton, Balch and Co., 1924). The letters reprinted below are also from the same volume.

bathing in the waves of the darkening sea, poured its purple gold, etc.,"—"the swallows flying over the surface of the water twittered merrily,"—such commonplaces one ought to abandon. In descriptions of Nature one ought to seize upon the little particulars, grouping them in such a way that, in reading, when you shut your eyes, you get a picture.

For instance, you will get the full effect of a moonlight night if you write that on the mill-dam a little glowing star-point flashed from the neck of a broken bottle, and the round, black shadow of a dog, or a wolf, emerged and ran, etc. Nature becomes animated if you are not squeamish about employing comparisons of her phenomena with ordinary human activities, etc.

In the sphere of psychology, details are also the thing. God preserve us from commonplaces. Best of all is it to avoid depicting the hero's state of mind; you ought to try to make it clear from the hero's actions. It is not necessary to portray many characters. The centre of gravity should be in two persons: him and her. . . .

I write this to you as a reader having a definite taste. Also, in order that you, when writing, may not feel alone. To be alone in work is a hard thing. Better poor criticism than none at all. Is it not so?

(From a letter to I. L. Shcheglov, January 22, 1888)

Oh, you of little faith,—you are interested to know what flaws I found in your "Mignon." Before I point them out I warn you that they have a technical rather than a critico-literary interest. Only a writer can appreciate them, but a reader not at all. Here they are. . . . I think that you, an author scrupulous and untrusting, afraid that your characters will not stand out clearly enough, are too much given to thoroughly detailed description. The result is an overwrought "motleyness" of effect that impairs the general impression.

In order to show how powerfully music can affect one at times, but distrustful of the reader's ability to understand you readily, you zealously set forth the psychology of your Feodrik; the psychology is successful, but then the interval between two such moments as "amari, morire" and the pistol-shot, is dragged out unduly, and the reader, before he reaches the suicide-scene, has had time to recover from the pain of "amari, morire." But you must give the reader no chance to recover: he must always be kept in suspense. These remarks would not apply if "Mignon" were a novel. Long, detailed works have their own peculiar aims, which require a most careful execution regardless of the total impression. But in short stories it is better to say not enough than to say too much, because,—because—I don't know why! . . .

(From a letter to A. S. Souvorin, October 27, 1888)

. . . You write that the hero of my "Party" is a character worth developing. Good Lord! I am not a senseless brute, you know; I understand that. I understand that I cut the throats of my characters and spoil them, and that I waste good material. . . . On my conscience, I would gladly have spent six months over the "Party"; I like taking things easy, and see no attraction in publishing in white-hot haste. I would willingly, with pleasure, with feeling, in a leisurely way, describe the *whole* of my hero, describe his state of mind while his wife was in labor, his trial, the unpleasant feeling he has after he is acquitted; I would describe the midwife and the doctors having tea in the middle of the night, I would describe the rain. . . . It would give me nothing but pleasure, because I like to take pains and dawdle. But what am I to do? I begin a story on September 10th with the thought that I must finish it by October 5th at the latest; if I don't I shall fail the editor and be left without money. I let myself go at the beginning and write with an easy mind; but by the time I get to the middle I begin to grow timid and to fear that my story will be too long: I have to remember that the *Sieverny Viestnik* has not much money, and that I am one of their expensive contributors. This is why the beginning of my stories is always very promising and looks as though I were starting on a novel, the middle is huddled and timid, and the end is, as in a short sketch, like fireworks. And so in planning a story one is bound to think first about its framework: from a crowd of leading or subordinate characters one selects one person only—wife or husband; one puts him on the canvas and paints him alone, making him prominent, while the others one scatters over the canvas like small coin, and the result is something like the vault of heaven: one big moon and a number of very small stars around it. But the moon is not a success, because it can only be understood if the stars too are intelligible, and the stars are not worked out. And so what I produce is not literature, but something like the patching of Trishka's coat. What am I to do? I don't know, I don't know. I must trust to time which heals all things.

Speaking on my conscience again, I have not yet begun my literary work, though I have received a literary prize. Subjects for five stories and two novels are languishing in my head. One of the novels was thought of long ago, and some of the characters have grown old without managing to get themselves written. In my head there is a whole army of people asking to be let out and waiting for the words of command. All that I have written so far is rubbish in comparison with what I should like to write and should write with rapture. It is all the same to me whether I write "The Party" or "Lights," or a vaudeville or a letter to a friend—it is all dull, spiritless, mechanical, and I get annoyed with critics who attach any importance to "Lights," for instance. I fancy that I deceive them with my work just as I deceive many people with my face, which looks serious or overcheerful. I don't like being successful; the subjects which sit in my head are annoyed, jealous of what has already been written. I am vexed that the rubbish has been done and the good things lie about in the lumber-room like old books. Of course, in thus lamenting I rather exaggerate, and much of what I say is only my fancy, but there is something of the truth in it, a good big part of it. What do I call good? The images which seem best to me, which I love and jealously guard lest I spend and spoil them for the sake of some "Party" written against time. . . . If my love is mistaken, I am wrong, but then it may not be mistaken! I am either a fool and a conceited fellow or I really am an organism capable of being a good writer. All that I now write displeases and bores me, but what sits in my head interests, excites, and moves me—from which I conclude that everybody does the wrong thing and I alone know the secret of doing the right one. Most likely all writers think that. But the devil himself would break his neck at these problems. . . .

(From a letter to A. S. Souvorin, April 1, 1890)
You abuse me for objectivity, calling it indifference to good and evil, lack of ideals and ideas, and so on. You would have me, when I describe horse-thieves, say: "Stealing horses is an evil." But that has been known for ages without my saying so. Let the jury judge them; it's my job simply to show what sort of people they are. I write: you are dealing with horse-thieves, so let me tell you that they are not beggars but well-fed people, that they are people of a special cult, and that horse-stealing is not simply theft but a passion. Of course it would be pleasant to combine art with a sermon, but for me personally it is extremely difficult and almost impossible, owing to the conditions of technique. You see, to depict horse-thieves in seven hundred lines I must all the time speak and think in their tone and feel in their spirit, otherwise, if I introduce subjectivity, the image becomes blurred and the story will not be as compact as all short stories ought to be. When I write, I reckon entirely upon the reader to add for himself the subjective elements that are lacking in the story.

(From a letter to E. M. Sh——, November 17, 1895)
I read your story with great pleasure. Your hand is acquiring firmness, and your style is improving. I like the whole story, except the ending, which appears to me to lack force. . . . But this is a matter of taste and not so important. If one is to talk about flaws one should not confine oneself to details. You have a defect and a very serious one. In my opinion it is this: you do not polish your things, and hence they seem frequently to be florid and overloaded. Your works lack the compactness that makes short things alive. There is skill in your stories; there is talent, literary sense, but very slight art. You put your characters together in the right way, but not plastically. You are either too lazy or you do not wish to slough off at one stroke all that is useless. To make a face from marble means to remove from the slab everything that is not the face. Do I make myself clear? Do you understand? There are two or three awkward expressions which I underlined.

(From a letter to Maxim Gorky, September 3, 1899)
. . . More advice: when reading the proofs, cross out a host of concrete nouns and other words. You have so many such nouns that the reader's mind finds it a task to concentrate on them, and he soon grows tired. You understand it at once when I say, "The man sat on the grass;" you understand it because it is clear and makes no demands on the attention. On the other hand, it is not easily understood, and it is difficult for the mind, if I write, "A tall, narrow-chested, middle-sized man, with a red beard, sat on the green grass, already trampled by pedestrians, sat silently, shyly, and timidly looked about him." That is not immediately grasped by the mind, whereas good writing should be grasped at once,—in a second. . . .

For Study and Discussion

1. What does Chekhov mean by the terms *subjectivity* and *sentimentality*? In his view how are these qualities related? Why does he consider them both bad for the short story?

2. On what grounds might Chekhov have criticized unfavorably either Poe's or Hawthorne's writing?

3. How do Chekhov's remarks about descriptions of nature fit in with his other advice on the art and technique of the short story? What does he mean by "a character of relevance" as opposed to "commonplaces"?

4. What were some of the problems that Chekhov had to face in trying to master the art of short-story writing? Compare his attitudes with those of Poe in regard to the planning of a story.

5. Chekhov says that "in planning a story one is bound to think first about its framework." What does he mean by "framework"? Is it the same thing that Irving meant by describing his story as a "frame" on which to stretch his materials?

6. What are the major flaws Chekhov identifies in the stories he mentions? Which flaws does he regard as the most serious or inexcusable?

7. Why is Chekhov opposed to the practice of sermonizing in fiction? Do you agree that his position is aesthetically sound?

8. In the writing of short stories Chekhov urges the need for clarity, compactness, and force. How does he suggest that these qualities can be attained? Would his advice apply as well to nonfiction prose?

9. On what basis does Chekhov distinguish between talent, literary sense, and art in the writing of fiction? Pick out and discuss the various striking images he employs to emphasize his points.

HENRY JAMES

ON THE GENESIS OF "THE REAL THING"

In pursuance of my plan of writing some very short tales—things of from 7000 to 10,000 words, the easiest length to 'place,' I began yesterday the little story that was suggested to me some time ago by an incident related to me by George du Maurier—the lady and gentleman who called upon him with a word from Frith, an oldish, faded, ruined pair—he an officer in the army—who unable to turn a penny in any other way, were trying to find employment as models. I was struck with the pathos, the oddity and typicalness of the situation—the little tragedy of good-looking gentlefolk, who had been all their life stupid and well-dressed, living, on a fixed income, at country-houses, watering places and clubs, like so many others of their class in England, and were now utterly unable to *do* anything, had no cleverness, no art nor craft to make use of as a *gagne-pain*—could only *show* themselves, clumsily, for the fine, clean, well-groomed animals that they were, only hope to make a little money by—in this manner—just simply *being.* I thought I saw a subject for very brief treatment in this *donnée*—and I think I do still; but to do anything worth while with it I must (as always, great Heavens!) be very clear as to what is in it and what I wish to get out of it. I tried a beginning yesterday, but I instantly became conscious that I must straighten out the little idea. It must be an idea—it can't be a 'story' in the vulgar sense of the word. It must be a picture; it must illustrate something. God knows that's enough—if the thing *does* illustrate. To make little anecdotes of this kind real *morceaux de vie* is a plan quite inspiring enough. *Voyons un peu*, therefore, what one can put into this one—I mean how much of life. One must put a little action—not a stupid, mechanical, arbitrary action, but something that is of the real essence of the subject. I thought of representing the husband as jealous of the wife—that is, jealous of the artist employing her, from the moment that, in point of fact, she begins to sit. But this is vulgar and obvious—worth

Notebook entry for February 22, 1891. Reprinted here from *The Notebooks of Henry James*, ed. F. O. Matthiessen and Kenneth B. Murdock (New York: Oxford University Press, 1947), by permission of the publisher. Copyright 1947 by Oxford University Press.

nothing. What I wish to represent is the baffled, ineffectual, incompetent character of their attempt, and how it illustrates once again the everlasting English amateurishness—the way superficial, untrained, unprofessional effort goes to the wall when confronted with trained, competitive, intelligent, *qualified* art—in whatever line it may be a question of. It is out of *that* element that my little action and movement must come; and now I begin to see just how—as one always *does*—Glory be to the Highest—when one begins to look at a thing hard and straight and seriously—to fix it—as I am so sadly lax and desultory about doing. What subjects I should find—for *everything*—if I could only achieve this more as a habit! Let my contrast and complication here come from the opposition—to my melancholy Major and his wife—of a couple of little vulgar professional people *who know*, with the consequent bewilderment, vagueness, depression of the former—their failure to understand how such people can be better than *they*—their failure, disappointment, disappearance—going forth into the vague again. *Il y a bien quelque chose a tirer de ca.* They have no pictorial sense. They are only clean and stiff and stupid. The others are dirty, even—the melancholy Major and his wife remark on it, wondering. The artist is beginning a big illustrated book, a new edition of a famous novel—say *Tom Jones:* and he is willing to try to work them in—for he takes an interest in their predicament, and feels—sceptically, but, with his flexible artistic sympathy—the appeal of their type. He is willing to give them a trial. Make it out that *he* himself is on trial—he is young and 'rising,' but he has still his golden spurs to win. He can't afford, *en somme*, to make many mistakes. He has regular work in drawing every week for a serial novel in an illustrated paper; but the great project—that of a big house—of issuing an illustrated Fielding promises him a big lift. He has been intrusted with (say) *Joseph Andrews*, experimentally; he will have to do this brilliantly in order to have the engagement for the rest confirmed. He has already 2 models in his service—the 'complication' must come from *them*. One is a common, clever, London girl, of the smallest origin and without conventional beauty, but of aptitude, of perceptions—knowing thoroughly *how*. She says 'lydy' and 'plice' but she has the pictorial sense; and can look like anything he wants her to look like. She poses, in short, in perfection. So does her colleague, a professional Italian, a little fellow—ill dressed, smelling of garlic, but admirably serviceable, quite universal. They must be contrasted, confronted, *juxtaposed* with the others; whom they take for people who *pay*, themselves, till they learn the truth when they are overwhelmed with derisive amazement. The denouncement simply that the melancholy Major and his wife won't do—they're not 'in it.' Their surprise—their helpless, proud assent—without other prospects: yet at the same time *their* degree of more silent amazement at the success of the two inferior people—who are so much less nice-looking than themselves. Frankly, however, is this contrast enough of a *story*, by itself? It seems to me Yes—for it's an IDEA—and how the deuce should I get *more* into 7000 words? It must be simply 50 pp. of my manuscript. The little tale of *The Servant (Brooksmith)* which I did the other day for *Black and White* and which I thought of at the same time as this, proved a very tight squeeze into the same tiny number of words, and I probably shall find that there is much more to be done with this than the compass will admit of. Make it tremendously succinct—with a very short pulse or rhythm—and the closest selection of detail—in other words *summarize* intensely and keep down the lateral development. It *should* be a little gem of bright, quick, vivid form. I shall get every grain of 'action' that the space admits of if I make something, for the artist, hang in the balance—depend on the way he does this particular work. It's when he finds that he shall lose his great opportunity if he keeps on with them, that he has to tell the gentlemanly couple, that, frankly, they won't serve his turn—and make them wander forth into the cold world again. I must keep them the age I've made them—50 and 40—because it's more touching; but I must bring up the age of the 2 real models to almost the same thing. That increases the incomprehensibility (to the amateurs) of their usefulness. Picture the immanence, in the latter, of the idle, provided-for, country-house habit—the blankness of their *manière d'être*. But in how tremendously few words I must do it. This is a lesson—a *magnificent* lesson—if I'm to do a good many. Something as admirably compact and *selected* as Maupassant.

For Study and Discussion

1. What does James mean by the term *donnée* in connection with his method of writing fiction? Paraphrase briefly the *donnée* which he says led to his plans for writing "The Real Thing."

2. What is the underlying theme or idea that James proposes to develop in this story? How does he plan to work up his material so as to make his subject both meaningful and interesting?

3. With what sorts of characters, action, and contrasts does he propose to dramatize the central situation that he wishes to represent?

4. How does he decide to focus his contrasts so that a sense of urgency and suspense may be aroused as the story unfolds? As a result of this decision, how important a role is to be played by his artist?

5. How does James plan to intensify the ironic effect of his story? Exactly what developments in the story does he say will contribute to its irony?

6. Why should he assume that it will be difficult for him to write his story in seven thousand words? How does he intend to meet this problem?

BRET HARTE

THE DEVELOPMENT OF THE AMERICAN SHORT STORY

The short story was familiar enough in form in America during the early half of the century; perhaps the proverbial haste of American life was some inducement to its brevity. It had been the medium through which some of the most characteristic work of the best American writers had won the approbation of the public. Poe—a master of the art, as yet unsurpassed—had written; Longfellow and Hawthorne had lent it the graces of the English classics. But it was not the American short story of to-day. It was not characteristic of American life, American habits, nor American thought. It was not vital and instinct with the experience and observation of the average American; it made no attempt to follow his reasoning or to understand his peculiar form of expression—which it was apt to consider vulgar; it had no sympathy with those dramatic contrasts and surprises which are the wonders of American civilisation; it took no account of the modifications of environment and of geographical limitations; indeed, it knew little of American geography. Of all that was distinctly American it was evasive—when it was not apologetic. And even when graced by the style of the best masters, it was distinctly provincial.

It would be easier to trace the causes which produced this than to assign any distinct occasion or period for the change. What was called American literature was still limited to English methods and [based] upon English models. The best writers either wandered far afield for their inspiration, or, restricted to home material, were historical or legendary; artistically contemplative of their own country, but seldom observant. Literature abode on a scant fringe of the Atlantic seaboard, gathering the drift from other shores, and hearing the murmur of other lands rather than the voices of its own; it was either expressed in an artificial treatment of life in the cities, or, as with Irving, was frankly satirical of provincial social ambition. There was much 'fine' writing; there were American Addisons, Steeles, and Lambs—there were provin-

From "The Rise of the 'Short Story,'" originally published in, and reprinted here from, the *Cornhill Magazine*, July 1899.

cial 'Spectators' and 'Tatlers.' The sentiment was English. Even Irving in the pathetic sketch of 'The Wife' echoed the style of 'Rosamond Grey.' There were sketches of American life in the form of the English Essayists, with no attempt to understand the American character. The literary man had little sympathy with the rough and half-civilised masses who were making his country's history; if he used them at all it was as a foil to bring into greater relief his hero of the unmistakable English pattern. In his slavish imitation of the foreigner, he did not, however, succeed in retaining the foreigner's quick appreciation of novelty. It took an Englishman to first develop the humour and picturesqueness of American or 'Yankee' dialect, but Judge Haliburton succeeded better in reproducing 'Sam Slick's' speech than his character. Dr. Judd's 'Margaret'—one of the early American stories—although a vivid picture of New England farm life and strongly marked with local color, was in incident and treatment a mere imitation of English rural tragedy. It would, indeed, seem that while the American people had shaken off the English yoke in government, politics, and national progression, while they had already startled the old world with invention and originality in practical ideas, they had never freed themselves from the trammels of English literary precedent. The old sneer 'Who reads an American book?' might have been answered by another: 'There are no *American* books.'

But while the American literary imagination was still under the influence of English tradition, an unexpected factor was developing to diminish its power. It was *Humour*—of a quality as distinct and original as the country and civilisation in which it was developed. It was at first noticeable in the anecdote or 'story,' and after the fashion of such beginnings, was orally transmitted. It was common in the barrooms, the gatherings in the 'country store,' and finally at public meetings in the mouths of 'stump orators.' Arguments were clenched, and political principles illustrated, by a 'funny story.' It invaded even the camp meeting and pulpit. It at last received the currency of the public press. But wherever met it was so distinctively original and novel, so individual and characteristic, that it was at once known and appreciated abroad as 'an American story.' Crude at first, it received a literary polish in the press, but its dominant quality remained. It was concise and condense [*sic*], yet suggestive. It was delightfully extravagant—or a miracle of understatement. It voiced not only the dialect, but the habits of thought of a people or locality. It gave a new interest to slang. From a paragraph of a dozen lines it grew into a half column, but always retaining its conciseness and felicity of statement. It was a foe to prolixity of any kind, it admitted no fine writing nor affectation of style. It went directly to the point. It was burdened by no conscientiousness; it was often irreverent; it was devoid of all moral responsibility—but it was original! By degrees it developed character with its incident, often, in a few lines gave a striking photograph of a community or a section, but always reached its conclusion without an unnecessary word. It became—and still exists—as an essential feature of newspaper literature. It was the parent of the American 'short story.'

But although these beginnings assumed more of a national character than American serious or polite literature, they were still purely comic, and their only immediate result was the development of a number of humourists in the columns of the daily press—all possessing the dominant national quality with a certain individuality of their own. For a while it seemed as if they were losing the faculty of story-telling in the elaboration of eccentric character—chiefly used as a vehicle for smart sayings, extravagant incident, or political satire. They were eagerly received by the public and, in their day, were immensely popular, and probably were better known at home and abroad than the more academic but less national humourists of New York or Boston. The national note was always struck even in their individual variations, and the admirable portraiture of the shrewd and humourous showman in 'Artemus Ward' survived his more mechanical bad spelling. Yet they did not invade the current narrative fiction; the short and long story-tellers went with their old-fashioned methods, their admirable morals, their well-worn sentiments, their colourless heroes and heroines of the first ranks of provincial society. Neither did social and political convulsions bring anything new in the way of Romance. . . .

The gold discovery had drawn to the Pacific slope of the continent a . . . heterogeneous and remarkable population. The immigration of 1849 and 1850 had taken farmers from the plow, merchants from their desks, and students from their books, while every profession was represented in the motley crowd of gold-seekers. Europe and her colonies had contributed to swell these adventurers—for adventurers they were whatever their purpose; the risks were great, the journey long and difficult—the nearest came from a distance of over a thousand miles; that the men were necessarily pre-equipped with courage, faith and endurance was a foregone conclusion. They were mainly young; a gray-haired man was a curiosity in the mines in the early days, and an object of rude respect and reverence. They were consequently free from the trammels of precedent or tradition in arranging their lives and making their rude homes. There was a singular fraternity in this ideal republic into which all men entered free and equal. Distinction of previous condition or advantages were unknown, even record and reputation for ill or good were of little benefit or embarrassment to the possessor; men were accepted for what they actually were, and what they could do in taking their part in the camp or settlement. The severest economy, the direst poverty, the most menial labour carried no shame or disgrace with it; individual success brought neither envy nor jealousy. What was one man's fortune to-day might be the luck of another to-morrow. Add to this Utopian simplicity of the people, the environment of magnificent scenery, a unique climate, and a vegetation that was marvelous in its proportions and spontaneity of growth; let it be further considered that the strongest relief was given to this picture by its setting among the crumbling ruins of early Spanish possession—whose monuments still existed in Mission and Presidio, and whose legitimate Castilian descendants still lived and moved in picturesque and dignified contrast to their energetic invaders—and it must be admitted that a condition of romantic and dramatic possibilities was created unrivaled in history.

But the earlier literature of the Pacific slope was, like that of the Atlantic seaboard, national and characteristic only in its humour. The local press sparkled with wit and satire, and, as in the East, developed its usual individual humourists. . . .

. . . [In 1868] the present writer was called upon to take the editorial control of the 'Overland Monthly,' a much more ambitious magazine venture than had yet appeared in California. The best writers had been invited to contribute to its pages. But in looking over his materials on preparing the first number, he was discouraged to find the same notable lack of characteristic fiction. There were good literary articles, sketches of foreign travel, and some essays in description of the natural resources of California—excellent from a commercial and advertising viewpoint. But he failed to discover anything of that wild and picturesque life which had impressed him, first as a truant schoolboy, and afterwards as a youthful schoolmaster among the mining population. In this perplexity he determined to attempt to make good the deficiency himself. He wrote 'The Luck of Roaring Camp.' However far short it fell of his ideal and his purpose, he conscientiously believed that he had painted much that 'he saw, and part of which he was,' that his subject and characters were distinctly Californian, as was equally his treatment of them. But an unexpected circumstance here intervened. The publication of the story was objected to by both printer and publisher, virtually for not being in the conventional line of subject, treatment, and morals! The introduction of the abandoned outcast mother of the foundling, 'Luck,' and the language used by the characters, received a serious warning and protest. The writer was obliged to use his right as editor to save his unfortunate contribution from oblivion. When it appeared at last, he saw with consternation that the printer and publisher had really voiced the local opinion; that the press of California was still strongly dominated by the old conservatism and conventionalism of the East, and that when 'The Luck of Roaring Camp' was not denounced as 'improper' and 'corrupting,' it was coldly received as being 'singular' and 'strange.' A still more extraordinary instance of the 'provincial note' was struck in the criticism of a religious paper that the story was strongly 'unfavourable to immigration' and decidedly unprovocative of the 'investment of foreign capital.' However, its instantaneous and cordial acceptance as a new departure by the critics of the Eastern States and Europe, enabled the writer to follow it with other stories of like character. More than that, he was gratified to find a disposition on the part of his contributors to shake off their conservative trammels, and in an admirable and original sketch of a wandering circus attendant called 'Centrepole Bill,' he was delighted to recognize and welcome a convert. The term 'Imitator,' often used by the critics who, as previously stated, had claimed for the present writer the invention of this kind of literature, could not fairly apply to those who had cut loose from conventional methods, and sought to honestly describe the life around them, and he can only claim to have shown them that it could be done. How well it has since been done, what charm of individual flavor and style has been brought to it by such writers as Harris, Cable, Page, Mark Twain in 'Huckleberry Finn,' the author of 'The Great Smoky Mountains,' and Miss Wilkins, the average reader need not be told. It would seem evident, therefore, that the secret of the American short story was the treatment of characteristic American life, with absolute knowledge of its peculiarities and sympathy with its methods; with no fastidious ignoring of its habitual expression, or the inchoate poetry that may be found even hidden in its slang; with no moral determination except that which may be the legitimate outcome of the story itself; with no more elimination than may be necessary for the artistic conception, and never from the fear of the 'fetish' of conventionalism. Of such is the American short story of to-day—the germ of American Literature to come.

For Study and Discussion

1. According to Harte, what important elements were missing from American stories written before 1860? Do you accept his assertion? If not, how would you refute it?

2. In Harte's view, what single element helped to bring about a genuinely American short story? Do you think he gives too much emphasis to this element? Why?

3. How did the discovery of gold in the West contribute to the development of the American short story? Did life on the Pacific coast simply provide fresh materials for fiction writers, or did it also tend to open up new ways of handling those materials? Explain.

4. What role does Harte say he himself played in liberating American stories from old-fashioned methods and attitudes? How successful was he?

5. Examine critically Harte's conclusion regarding "the secret of the American short story." Do his requirements necessarily exclude the stories by Irving, Poe, and Hawthorne?

BRANDER MATTHEWS

THE PHILOSOPHY OF THE SHORT-STORY

The difference between a Novel and a Novelet is one of length only; a Novelet is a brief Novel. But the difference between a Novel and a Short-story is a difference of kind. A true Short-story is something other and something more than a mere story which is short. A true Short-story differs from the Novel chiefly in its essential unity of impression. In a far more exact and precise use of the word, a Short-story has unity as a Novel cannot have it.* Often, it may be noted by the way, the Short-story fulfils the three false unities of the French classic drama: it shows one action, in one place, on one day. A Short-story deals with a single character, a single event, a single emotion, or the series of emotions called forth by a single situation. Poe's paradox that a poem cannot greatly exceed a hundred lines in length under penalty of ceasing to be one poem and breaking into a string of poems, may serve to suggest the precise difference between the Short-story and the Novel. The Short-story is the single effect, complete and self-contained, while the Novel is of necessity broken into a series of episodes. Thus the Short-story has, what the Novel cannot have, the effect of "totality," as Poe called it, the unity of impression.

Of a truth the Short-story is not only not a chapter out of a Novel, or an incident or an episode extracted from a longer tale, but at its best it impresses the reader with the belief that it would be spoiled if it were made larger, or if it were incorporated into a more elaborate work. The

---

Reprinted from Matthews' *The Philosophy of the Short-Story* (New York: Longmans, Green and Co., 1901). This text represents a slight modification of an essay by Matthews which first appeared, under the same title, in *Lippincott's Magazine*, October 1885. The core of Matthews' "philosophy" had been stated earlier in "Short Stories," a brief article published in the *London Saturday Review*, July 5, 1884.

*In a letter to a friend, Stevenson lays down the law with his usual directness: "Make another end to it? Ah, yes, but that's not the way I write; the whole tale is implied; I never use an effect when I can help it, unless it prepares the effects that are to follow; that's what a story consists in. To make another end, that is to make the beginning all wrong. The *dénouement* of a long story is nothing, it is just 'a full close,' which you may approach and accompany as you please—it is a coda, not an essential member in the rhythm; but the body and end of a short-story is bone of the bone and blood of the blood of the beginning." 'Vailima Letters,' vol. i., p. 147.

difference in spirit and in form between the Lyric and the Epic is scarcely greater than the difference between the Short-story and the Novel; and the 'Raven' and 'How we brought the good news from Ghent to Aix' are not more unlike the 'Lady of the Lake' and 'Paradise Lost,' in form and in spirit, than the 'Luck of Roaring Camp,' and the 'Man without a Country,' two typical Short-stories, are unlike 'Vanity Fair' and the 'Heart of Midlothian,' two typical Novels.

Another great difference between the Short-story and the Novel lies in the fact that the Novel, nowadays at least, must be a love-tale, while the Short-story need not deal with love at all. Although there are to be found by diligent search a few Novels which are not love-tales—and of course 'Robinson Crusoe' is the example that swims at once into recollection—yet the immense majority of Novels have the tender passion either as the motive power of their machinery or as the pivot on which their plots turn. Although 'Vanity Fair' was a Novel without a hero, nearly every other Novel has a hero and a heroine; and the novelist, however unwillingly, must concern himself in their love-affairs.

But the writer of Short-stories is under no bonds of this sort. Of course he may tell a tale of love if he choose, and if love enters into his tale naturally and to its enriching; but he need not bother with love at all unless he please. . . .

But other things are required of a writer of Short-stories which are not required of a writer of Novels. The novelist may take his time; he has abundant room to turn about. The writer of Short-stories must be concise, and compression, a vigorous compression, is essential. For him, more than for any one else, the half is more than the whole. Again, the novelist may be commonplace, he may bend his best energies to the photographic reproduction of the actual; if he show us a cross-section of real life we are content; but the writer of Short-stories must have originality and ingenuity. If to compression, originality, and ingenuity he add also a touch of fantasy, so much the better.

In fact, it may be said that no one has ever succeeded as a writer of Short-stories who had not ingenuity, originality, and compression; and that most of those who have succeeded in this line had also the touch of fantasy. But there are not a few successful novelists lacking, not only in fantasy and compression, but also in ingenuity and originality; they had other qualities, no doubt, but these they had not. If an example must be given, the name of Anthony Trollope will occur to all. Fantasy was a thing he abhorred; compression he knew not; and originality and ingenuity can be conceded to him only by a strong stretch of the ordinary meaning of the words. Other qualities he had in plenty, but not these. And, not having them, he was not a writer of Short-stories. Judging from his essay on Hawthorne,* one may even go so far as to say that Trollope did not know a good Short-story when he saw it.

*This critical paper of Trollope's on "The Genius of Nathaniel Hawthorne" was contributed to the *North American Review* for September 1879. Apparently, like many other of his essays, it has not been reprinted.

I have written "Short-stories" with a capital S and a hyphen because I wished to emphasise the distinction between the Short-story and the story which is merely short. The Short-story is a high and difficult department of fiction. The story which is short can be written by anybody who can write at all; and it may be good, bad, or indifferent; but at its best it is wholly unlike the Short-story. In 'An Editor's Tales' Trollope has given us excellent specimens of the story which is short; and the narratives which make up this book are amusing enough and clever enough, but they are wanting in the individuality and in the completeness of the genuine Short-story. Like the brief tales to be seen in the British monthly magazines and in the Sunday editions of American newspapers into which they are copied, they are, for the most part, either merely amplified anecdotes or else incidents which might have been used in a Novel just as well as not.

Now, it cannot be said too emphatically that the genuine Short-story abhors the idea of the Novel. It neither can be conceived as part of a Novel, nor can it be elaborated and expanded so as to form a Novel. A good Short-story is no more the synopsis of a Novel than it is an episode from a Novel.† A slight Novel, or a Novel cut down, is a Novelet: it is not a Short-story. Mr. Howells's 'Their Wedding Journey' and Miss Howard's 'One Summer' are Novelets,—little Novels. Mr. Anstey's 'Vice Versa,' Mr. Besant's 'Case of Mr. Lucraft,' Hugh Conway's 'Called Back,' Mr. Julian Hawthorne's 'Archibald Malmaison,' and Mr. Stevenson's 'Strange Case of Dr. Jekyll and Mr. Hyde' are Short-stories in conception, although they are without the compression which the Short-story requires.

It may be remembered that in the acute and learned essay on *vers de société** which he prefixed to his admirable 'Lyra Elegantiarum,' Mr. Frederick Locker declared that the two characteristics of the best *vers de société* were brevity and brilliancy, and that the 'Rape of the Lock' would be the type and model of the best *vers de société*—if it were not just a little too long. So it is with the 'Case of Mr. Lucraft,' with 'Vice Versa,' with 'Archibald Malmaison': they are just a little too long.

It is to be noted as a curious coincidence that there is no exact word in English to designate either *vers de société* or the Short-story, and yet in no language are there better *vers de société* or Short-stories than in English. It may be remarked also that there is a certain likeness between *vers de société* and Short-stories: for one thing, both seem easy to write

---

†In some rambling notes on "The Short-story" contributed to the *Nineteenth Century* for March 1898, Mr. Frederick Wedmore reiterates certain of the points made in this essay. For one thing, he declares that a good Short-story can never be "a novel in a nut-shell"; it "cannot possibly be a *précis*, a synopsis, a *scenario*, as it were, of a novel. It is a separate thing—as separate, almost, as the Sonnet is from the Epic,—it involves the exercise almost of a different art."

*Light verse dealing with contemporary fashions and foibles—Eds.

and are hard. And the typical qualifications of each may apply with almost equal force to the other: *vers de société* should reveal compression, ingenuity, and originality, and Short-stories should have brevity and brilliancy. In no class of writing are neatness of construction and polish of execution more needed than in the writing of *vers de société* and of Short-stories. The writer of Short-stories must have the sense of form, which has well been called "the highest and last attribute of a creative writer." The construction must always be logical, adequate, harmonious. . . .

But, although the sense of form and the gift of style are essential to the writing of a good Short-story, they are secondary to the idea, to the conception, to the subject. Those who hold, with a certain American novelist, that it is no matter what you have to say, but only how you say it, need not attempt the Short-story; for the Short-story, far more than the Novel even, demands a subject. The Short-story is nothing if there is no story to tell;—one might almost say that a Short-story is nothing if it has no plot,—except that "plot" may suggest to some readers a complication and an elaboration which are not really needful. But a plan—if this word is less liable to misconception than "plot"—a plan a Short-story must have, while it would be easy to cite Novels of eminence which are wholly amorphous—for example, 'Tristram Shandy.'

Whatever its length, the Novel, so Mr. Henry James told us not long ago, "is, in its broadest definition, a personal impression of life." The most powerful force in French fiction to-day is M. Émile Zola, chiefly known in America and England, I fear me greatly, by the dirt which masks and degrades the real beauty and firm strength not seldom concealed in his novels; and M. Émile Zola declares that the novelist of the future will not concern himself with the artistic evolution of a plot; he will take *une histoire quelconque*, any kind of a story, and make it serve his purpose,—which is to give elaborate pictures of life in all its most minute details.

It is needless to say that the acceptance of these theories is a negation of the Short-story. Important as are form and style, the subject of the Short-story is of more importance yet. What you have to tell is of greater interest than how you tell it. . . . [A] Short-story in which nothing happens at all is an absolute impossibility.

Perhaps the difference between a Short-story and a Sketch can best be indicated by saying that, while a Sketch may be still-life, in a Short-story something always happens. A Sketch may be an outline of character, or even a picture of a mood of mind, but in a Short-story there must be something done, there must be an action.* . . .

---

*This difference is considered briefly by Mr. F. B. Perkins in the characteristically clever preface to the volume of his ingenious Short-stories, which takes its title from the first and best—'Devil-Puzzlers' (New York: G. P. Putnam's Sons).

The more carefully we study the history of fiction the more clearly we perceive that the Novel and the Short-story are essentially different— that the difference between them is not one of mere length only, but fundamental. The Short-story seeks one set of effects in its own way, and the Novel seeks a wholly distinct set of effects in a wholly distinct way. We are led also to the conclusion that the Short-story—in spite of the fact that in our language it has no name of its own—is one of the few sharply defined literary forms. It is a *genre*, as M. Brunetière terms it, a species, as a naturalist might call it, as individual as the Lyric itself and as various. It is as distinct an entity as the Epic, as Tragedy, as Comedy. Now the Novel is not a form of the same sharply defined individuality; it is—or at least it may be—anything. It is the child of the Epic and the heir of the Drama; but it is a hybrid. And one of the foremost of living American novelists, who happens also to be one of the most acute and sympathetic of American critics, has told me that he was often distracted by the knowledge of this fact even while he was engaged in writing a novel.*

In the history of literature the Short-story was developed long before the Novel, which indeed is but a creature of yesterday, and which was not really established in popular esteem as a worthy rival of the drama until after the widespread success of the Waverly Novels in the early years of the nineteenth century. The Short-story also seems much easier of accomplishment than the Novel, if only because it is briefer. And yet the list of the masters of the Short-story is far less crowded than the list of the masters of the longer form. There are a score or more very great novelists recorded in the history of fiction; but there are scarcely more than half a score Short-story writers of an equal eminence.

From Chaucer and Boccaccio we must spring across the centuries until we come to Hawthorne and Poe almost without finding another name that insists upon enrolment. In these five hundred years there were great novelists not a few, but there was no great writer of Short-stories. A little later than Hawthorne and Poe, and indeed almost contemporaneous with them, are Mérimée and Turgenef, whose title to be recorded there is none to dispute. Now at the end of the nineteenth century we find two more that no competent critic would dare to omit,—Guy de Maupassant and Rudyard Kipling.

APPENDIX

So far as the author is aware, he had no predecessor in asserting that the Short-story differs from the Novel essentially,—and not merely in the matter of length. So far as he knows, it was in the present paper the suggestion was first made that the Short-story is in reality a *genre*, a

---

*This paragraph and the one following were not in the original essay—Eds.

separate kind, a genus by itself. But although this distinction may not have been made explicitly by any earlier critic, there is little doubt that Poe felt it, even if he did not formulate it in set terms. It seems to be implicit in more than one of his critical essays, more particularly in that on 'Hawthorne's Tales.' . . .

For Study and Discussion

1. Does Matthews support satisfactorily his assertion that "the difference between a Novel and a Short-story is a difference of kind" (p. 33)? What do you make of his next statement regarding "a true Short-story"?

2. Why, according to Matthews, can a short story have unity whereas a novel cannot? Do you agree or disagree with his distinction? Why?

3. What other specific characteristics does Matthews say the "true" short story should possess? How similar are these characteristics to the ones Poe advocated? Does Matthews' definition of the short story add anything significant to those of Poe and the other writers represented above?

4. Enumerate and explain the differences which, according to Matthews, distinguish the short story from (1) the novel, (2) the sketch. Which of these, if any, would you agree are valid distinctions?

5. Which similarities does Matthews find between the short story and *vers de société?* Do you think this is a useful comparison?

HENRY SEIDEL CANBY

ON THE SHORT STORY

The London "Academy" has seen fit recently to scoff at the critics who have been exercising themselves over the so-called art of the Short Story. The Short Story, the "Academy" thinks, is a short novel, and its art is distinguished by just one thing, and that is inferiority.

Perhaps there has seemed to be a greater outpouring of criticism and discussion than this literary fashion of the Short Story warrants, since in some respects it is a very old fashion indeed, and the story of Ruth, for instance, or the Paolo and Francesca incident in the "Inferno," differ from their modern prototypes only in certain characteristics of internal structure and external relation. But the new Short Story has gained more individuality. It supports the magazines and has invaded the newspapers. It gets itself bound into books and has made many authors famous. Is it a separate genus of literary expression, belonging to the narrative family, but distinct from the novel, or is it merely a variety of that well-recognized form? Professor Brander Matthews holds to the former view, and bases his opinion largely upon a certain "unity of impression," which he says is characteristic of the Short Story. Mr. Wedmore, the English critic, strenuously affirms the distinction between the two; and it may be assumed that Edgar Allan Poe held some such belief, for he says that "Terror, passion, horror, most fields but that of pure beauty, can be best treated in a tale."

Considerable evidence will be necessary before the Short Story can be proved deserving of a separate classification, and "unity of impression" needs some defining before it is ranked under this evidence. Poe used the phrase in argument, and thought mainly of the time element. A tale could be read at a sitting; a novel must be read in gulps, as it were, of a handful of chapters each, and the impression, which the unity of the tale should convey, naturally suffered. But Professor Matthews, wielding the same phrase, seems to refer to the effect of the design of the narrative upon the reader, whether read at one sitting or a dozen. A single vivid impression is to be the result of the Short Story; while many, diverse yet

---

Originally published in, and reprinted here from, the *Dial*, October 16, 1901.

harmonious, impressions are to follow upon the reading of a novel. Yet surely many novels, such as George Eliot's "Romola" or Meredith's "The Egoist," leave a unity of impression not essentially differing from that of which Professor Matthews speaks. In the first, the degeneration of the beautiful Greek is not only the central thread, but the digest of the whole story; as in the other book is the egoism of Willoughby. Neither this quality nor the unity gained by condensation is a completely sufficing reason for the separate classification of the Short Story.

There is another way of getting at this matter. The great difference between a poem, an historical essay, and a novel upon the same subject, lies in the point of view. The poem works through imagination and suggestion. The history deals with the facts that the poem almost neglects, and has to do with selection among these facts. The novel, supposing it to be historical, uses first the methods of the history, leavens the result with fancy, sets it forth suggestively, and, keeping in view the end of art instead of the necessity for truth, produces still other results. Compare, for instance, Carlyle's life of Cromwell, Milton's sonnet on Cromwell, and Scott's novel based upon the life of the same hero. It is such a distinction in the point of view which differentiates a novel from a Short Story.

From the eighteenth century downward, novelists have tried from their little Olympus to get the all-embracing view, to record the good and the bad, the thought and the action, the youthful deed and the aged penalty. Either by details, or, when that was not practicable, by suggestion, their transcription of life has been as full as they could make it. Their art is always to imitate the breadth and the fulness of living. At one extreme of this imitation is realism, and there the picture is somewhat photographic; at the other extreme is romance, where the reader's imagination is tickled into supplying much not plainly told by the author. In either case the life depicted in the books, like the life in the world, has many facets; though the multiplicity of actual experience may not be present, the suggestion of it will not be lacking, if the book is good. Thus the novel is natural, in so far as any artistic transfer of the real world into the world of imagination can be natural.

In the Short Story, as in the poem or the history, there is a different point of view, and *therefore* a different treatment. Just the reverse of this might be true if the story that Mr. Kipling writes is merely a variety of the longer form that Mr. Hardy uses. But the primal difference lies in the way the authors view their crude materials, which is to say the life about them. While the novel-writer aims at an eminently natural method of transcription, the author of the Short Story adopts a very artificial one. His endeavor is to give a striking narrative picture of one phase of the situation or the character, as the case may be. His aim is toward a strip lengthwise, disregarding much that a cross-section might show. He deals with a series of incidents, closely related to one another but not at all related to the by-play of life which, in reality, must accompany them. He treats of a mood always existing, but in the story supremely indicated; perhaps of an adventure or a catastrophe, which differs from the *dénouement* of a novel in that the interest is concentrated,—the cause in the hero's character, ready-made for the occasion, the results in the circumstances of the tale. If all narration amounts, as critics say, merely to a simplification of experience, imaginative or real, then a Short Story is simplification to the highest degree. We are selecting, far more than in a novel, and this because we are looking only for the chain of related incidents that go to make up one event. We are picking out the steps that make the tragedy, as in Maupassant's famous tale "La Parure," or in Bret Harte's "The Outcasts of Poker Flat"; we are looking only for what bears upon our narrow purpose, that the interest may be concentrated and the conception vivified beyond the power of a novel. The process is very artificial but very powerful: it is like turning a telescope upon one nebula in the heavens. Thus it is the standpoint of the author that makes the distinction between a short novel and a long Short Story. In the one the writer digests life histories, or portions of them; in the other he looks only for the episode, which, like the bubble on the stream, is part of and yet distinguished from the main current. Recognizing the futility in certain cases, and the needlessness in others, of expressing the whole truth, he succeeds much better with the half. He foregoes completeness and gains in force, and this by a change in the standpoint from which he views his world of fact and fancy.

There is a great deal of truth in the charge that this point of view means superficiality, provided the word be taken in its root sense. Of course the Short Story is superficial in this way; it is that which chiefly distinguishes the form. It is intended for surface work; it is meant to catch and record the striking things and make them more striking. It is a precipitate of the important things from the general solution, and these must be the most easily precipitated. There is no room for intricate subjectivity and plot in a dozen pages. The function of the Short Story is to be interesting, to convey vivid impressions; and therefore it must, to a degree, work with the evident and superficial things. Such an endeavor has produced its characteristic form, potential for the powerful expression of the daily facts about us. Thus, though the novel with a purpose is bad enough, the Short Story with a purpose beneath its expression of interesting fact or fancy, or which forsakes its natural field to delve deep into the mystery of things or the confusion of psychological character-subtleties, is usually a flat failure. Such are some of Hawthorne's tales,—good allegories but poor Short Stories.

New developments in literature do not arise nor become popular without reason. There are causes, artistic and otherwise, for the present blossoming of the Short Story, causes which in themselves differ from those which have made the novel flourish. In a time of much writing, tastes are quickly jaded, and the Short Story, because it is terse, striking, highly-colored, and somewhat new, meets with quick applause. Its length is of advantage, for many people can be made to swallow good literature in a pill who reject it in larger doses. But the class of readers thus gained accounts less for the literary development of the tale than for the vast number of poor Short Stories now breeding manifold. Such a *clientele* can increase the production, and will usually debase the quality, of any form of literary production, as the attitude of the prurient-minded populace of the Restoration increased and debased the output of the contemporary dramatists. Unintelligent appreciation is not likely to be responsible for a high development in art. That there has been an artistic advance, and a great one, in Short Story telling, needs for illustration only a comparison of a Blackwood's tale of the 30's and a Kipling Indian story.

The old desire for something new and more pungent would account for the encouragement which this new development has received. And there is an undoubted need, in a generation whose life is greatly varied by widely-diffused knowledge and extensive intercommunication, for the vivid expression of little things. This would add another impulse. But a literary structure which displays the greatest nicety of form to be found outside the domain of poetry indicates some more aesthetic cause than those so far mentioned. In simple truth the Short Story has attained a wonderful perfection because wonderful men have worked with and through it. It has just come into its own. In England of the 30's, publishers would not look upon anything less than a volume in fiction as a serious literary effort,—and they preferred three volumes. It was only in the 40's that Poe and Hawthorne in America began the cult of the tale. Coppée's search for the inevitable word and Maupassant's refinement of the *conte* came later still. The Short Story was adapted to the needs of the time and the tastes of the people. Men of genius found through it a new voice, and the attempt to perfect, to give laws and a form to the instrument, progressed because of the men who tried. In pre-Hawthornian times these authors employed the tale for the by-products of their minds; afterwards it has served to express some of the great conceptions of their genius. It is this which best accounts for the chastening of its form.

Except in one instance, which is the vivid expression of single incidents or detached movements in life, the Short Story is not to be chosen before the novel; but in its capabilities for perfection of structure, for nice discrimination in means, and for a satisfying exposition of the full power of words, it is much superior to the novel, and can rank only below the poem. But the novel, and the Short Story are distinct instruments, differently designed, for diverse needs. Perhaps if the "Academy" should itself take a different point of view, it might not be so unwilling to grant to the latter a separate use and classification.

For Study and Discussion

1. Why is Canby reluctant to accept Matthews' classification of the short story as an entity entirely separate from the novel?

2. What does Canby mean by his statement that "it is the standpoint of the author that makes the distinction between a short novel and a long Short Story"?

3. How does Canby distinguish between realism and romance in fiction? Does his distinction have any bearing on the art of the short story?

4. Why does he agree that the short story, as compared with the novel, is apt to be superficial?

5. In Canby's opinion, what is the proper function of the short story? Do you agree that "the Short Story with a purpose . . . is usually a flat failure"?

6. How does Canby account for the great "artistic advance" he says the short story has made between the 1830s and 1901 (the date of this essay)?

7. In what restricted sense is Canby willing to grant that the short story "is much superior to the novel"? Can you accept his distinction in this instance?

TOPICS FOR DISCUSSION AND WRITING

1. On what points do the eight writers in this section agree in their definitions of the short story? How do they differ? Which writer gives the clearest definition? The most comprehensive? The most satisfactory? Defend your choices in an essay.

2. To what extent do the writers disagree on what the *aim* of a short story should be? Would you say that the position taken by any one of the writers is more valid than that taken by the others? If so, why? Can a short story logically have more than one aim? Select two stories from among the first six in the text and compare and contrast them on the basis of their aim or aims.

3. In somewhat different terms, the authors of the statements emphasize the importance of *economy* and *precision of language* in the

short story. Irving, for example, speaks of "nicety of execution"; James refers to the need for being "tremendously succinct"; and Chekhov stresses the necessity "to slough off at one stroke all that is useless." Write an essay showing how economy and precise language have been used effectively in several stories, such as those by Pushkin, Turgenev, Harte, Maupassant.

4. Poe repeatedly stresses the importance of *unity* in the short story—unity of effect, tone, atmosphere, action, etc. Which of the other writers in this section appear to attach a similar importance to unity? What means do they suggest for achieving it? Which stories, among the first nine or ten in this collection, most obviously satisfy the requirements of unity? Write an essay to show how unity has been achieved in the stories you select.

5. What is meant by the *effect* of a story? How is the effect produced? Does it have anything to do with the theme of a story? With the writer's attitude? With the characters who are involved in the story? Write an essay comparing the effect produced by the stories of two or three of the following writers: Balzac, Aldrich, Chekhov, James.

6. How important is *humor* in the make-up of a short story? Is it an essential ingredient? By what various means can humor be injected into a story? Noting what writers in this section have to say about humor, write an essay on the use of humor in such stories as those by Irving, Harte, Aldrich, and James.

7. In his essay "On the Short Story," Canby asks, "Is it a separate genus of literary expression, belonging to the narrative family, but distinct from the novel, or is it merely a variety of that well-recognized form?" How does Canby himself answer this question? What position do the other writers in this section take on the issue? In your opinion, which presents the most logical argument? Taking into account the views expressed by these authors, write an essay defending or attacking the assertion that the novel and the short story are entirely separate literary forms.

8. Besides trying to define the relationship between the short story and the novel, most of the writers in this section compare the short story to, or distinguish it from, a number of shorter literary forms—the sketch, various types of poetry (the lyric, *vers de société*, etc.), the brief narrative, the tale. Which of these comparisons or distinctions do you find most tenuous? Most valid? Write an essay discussing the relationship you think exists between the short story and one other short literary form.

II

REVOLT AGAINST "RULES" AND
PRESCRIPTIVE DEFINITIONS

After the turn of the century the popularity of the short story stimulated and kept pace with the rapid spread of commercial journalism. Even more than in earlier decades, short fiction became the "darling" of the magazines as editors everywhere, especially in the United States, eagerly sought and paid handsome sums for stories which met their specifications for catching the public's fancy. In the face of increasing competition, however, these popular magazines established specifications that grew more and more technically exacting. The kind of story most in demand was fast-paced and action-centered, one which moved rapidly to a sharp climax and exploded in a "surprise" ending—qualifications illustrated in such stories as O. Henry's "The Gift of the Magi," Aldrich's "Marjorie Daw," and Jacobs' "The Monkey's Paw." Yet, however artificial they may seem today, it can be said that each of these stories, insofar as careful plotting, economy of language, and reversal of situation deserve consideration, was probably superior to most of those published in the popular magazines of the period. And even then, as noted by critics represented in the following essays, the virtually exclusive demand for this type of story tended to reduce story-writing technique to a stereotype, bringing to the fore what soon became widely known—and admired!—as the "magazine" or "formula" story.

The popular magazine, however, was not alone responsible for degrading the technique of the short story to the point which some of its critics labeled "senile," "pathological," and "decadent." A second, perhaps equally important influence, was the fiction manual or handbook. From 1900 to 1930 nearly forty such handbooks were published, some of which achieved widespread acclaim and a profitable income for their authors through many reprinted editions.* Designed as textbooks for use in home correspondence and college courses in story-writing, as well as for use by the independent writer, these books purported to give aspiring authors "points of information" or professional advice on every step in the production of short fiction

---

*As one example, J. Berg Esenwein's Writing the Short-Story: A Practical Handbook on the Rise, Structure, Writing, and Sale of the Modern Short-Story *(New York: Hinds, Noble and Eldredge, 1909) was so popular that it had entered its twelfth reprint by 1919.*

from the construction of suitable plots to the marketing of their finished manuscript. Since the sale of one's manuscript was the primary if not the exclusive end in view of these handbooks, most of their authors evidently held Brander Matthews' essay, "The Philosophy of the Short-Story," in higher esteem than did his anonymous reviewer in the London Academy *(see pp. 48–50); for their treatises echoed and re-echoed Matthews' critical viewpoint and thus helped indoctrinate still further in the popular mind a dogmatic approach to the writing of short fiction. By 1920, the "literature of the grim mechanics of story-writing," as one critic noted, appeared to be threatening to outstrip the production of stories themselves so that the timeliness of Ring Lardner's witty parody of a fiction manual in "How to Write Short Stories" no doubt struck his contemporaries more forcibly than it would today. In any case, it had long been obvious that the combined influence of the commercial magazine and the fiction manual had reduced the short story—at least in its typical, more popular form—to a sterile, overwrought product.*

As usual when a literary genre becomes rigidly standardized or stereotyped, both critics and authors revolt from the stereotype and begin seeking new directions and redefinitions. Thus, the censure and dissatisfaction reflected in the following essays are merely a small but representative fraction of the critical protest directed against the magazine or formula story during the second and third decades of the twentieth century. Some critics, such as Herbert Cory, simply sought to describe the plight of the short story as they saw it; others tended to blame a particular writer, as N. B. Fagin did, for the degradation into which the whole tradition of the short story seemed to have fallen. Still others, like Henry S. Canby and Sherwood Anderson, strove to redefine the direction of story development—one by calling for "free fiction" and holding up Chekhov as a model, the other by insisting that "form" rather than "plot" should be emphasized. Although standardized magazine fiction continued to flourish, nevertheless, by about 1930, the critics' prolonged outcry against stereotyped technique and ready-made, prescriptive approaches to story-writing was no longer needed. For in 1935, William Saroyan could ask—and triumphantly answer his own question, "What, if anything, is a story?" by saying, "frankly, I do not exactly know, and believe no one exactly knows. . . ." (p. 80).

Taken out of context, Saroyan's remarks seem to suggest that, in his view at least, the short story had relapsed into a formless, vaguely defined genre. But such is not true at all. On the contrary, while his essay argues that a story should have an organic form, the important point is contained in his description of and insistence upon a personal, individualized approach to story writing. The ultimate value of the revolt from the formula story, therefore, was precisely that it encouraged writers to seek their own personal solutions to story-writing. At the same time, the ever-increasing pressure of criticism directed toward the problems of short fiction had other beneficial effects: in seeking their own individual approaches to creating stories, writers worked with more self-conscious artistry than ever before so that the tradition of the short story during the 1920s and 1930s in the hands of such masters as Kipling, Joyce, Faulkner, Hemingway, and Katherine Anne Porter, to name only a few, displayed more brilliance than ever before.

These writers, to be sure, paid little if any attention to the more pre-scriptive requirements of handbook peddlers or magazine editors. Rather, as genuine artists, each feeling his own way innovatively toward the goal of imaginative creation, they resisted the lure of easy money and avoided the obvious paths leading toward the multiplicity of prefabricated formula stories, aiming instead to achieve high standards of craftsmanship in the art of short fiction. Often at first their progress was lonely and frustrating because their aims and methods were misunderstood or ignored; and yet, like the work of such earlier masters as Poe, Hawthorne, and James, the new subtleties they brought to bear in various ways of combining themes, imagery, characters, action, dialogue, etc., became in time the criteria for measuring excellence. In short, the stories they produced showed, eventual-ly, how much richer than any handbook suggested the form of modern short fiction could be.

ANONYMOUS

REVIEW OF MATTHEWS' *PHILOSOPHY OF THE SHORT-STORY*

In a tiny volume, *The Philosophy of the Short-story* (note well the hyphen, for it has a significance), by Prof. Brander Matthews, D.C.L., of Columbia University, published by Messrs. Longmans, the whole question of the short story is critically and historically "raised." The Professor is known in this country as an amiable *flâneur* of letters, and in America not only as an expert on dramatic literature, but also as a contributor of short stories to the magazines; it will be seen whether or not the present book is likely to substantiate the fabric of his reputation. His aim appears to be threefold: to define the short story, to give an outline of its history, and to prove that it differs essentially from the novel. "I have written 'Short-stories' with a capital S and a hyphen," he says, "because I wished to emphasise the distinction between the Short-story and the story which is merely short. The Short-story is a high and difficult department of fiction. The story which is short can be written by anybody who can write at all; and it may be good, bad, or indifferent; but at its best it is wholly unlike the Short-story." From this we must infer that every Short-story is good, and yet that it resembles the story which is short only when the latter is indifferent or bad. A Short-story, we are told, deals with a single character, a single event, a single emotion, or the series of emotions called forth by a single situation. "No one has ever succeeded as a writer of Short-stories who had not ingenuity, originality, and compression," and the successful have usually also had "the touch of fantasy"; by which Prof. Matthews means the supernatural. But "the successful novelist may be common-place." In the matter of form the Professor is somewhat vague. "The Short-story should not be void or without form, but its form may be whatever the author please." It is true that three pages later he says that the Short-story is "one of the few sharply defined literary forms," but he omits to define that form, sharply or otherwise. As regards subject, however, our philosopher hits the nail on the head with absolute precision: "The Short-story is nothing if there is no story to tell." Here is perhaps the sole incontrovertible statement in the book, and one regrets that its effectiveness should be impaired by

Originally published in, and reprinted here from, the London *Academy*, March 30, 1901.

another remark on the same page, "The Short-story, far more than the Novel even, demands a subject." . . . Lastly, "the sense of form and the gift of style are essential to the writer of a *good* Short-story" (then after all there are bad), and "the construction must always be logical, adequate, harmonious."

So much for what the Short-story is and the Short-story-writer must have. Turning to history, "from Chaucer and Boccaccio we must spring across the centuries until we come to Hawthorne and Poe." "In these five hundred years there were great novelists not a few, but there was no great writer of Short-stories." (What cheer, shade of Balzac, with your *Grande Bretêche?*) "A little later than Hawthorne and Poe . . . are Mérimée and Turgenef. . . . Now at the end of the nineteenth century we find two more that no competent critic would dare to omit—Guy de Maupassant and Rudyard Kipling." The history of the Short-story, *la voilà!* . . .

With only one portion of this careless and absurd compilation is it possible to deal at all seriously. In his appendix the Professor writes with naïve complacency: "So far as the author is aware, he had no predecessor in asserting that the Short-story differs from the Novel essentially— and not merely in the matter of length. So far as he knows, it was in the present paper the suggestion was first made that the Short-story is in reality a *genre*, a separate kind, a genus by itself." No doubt it was the obsession of this theory which caused him, after stating it briefly in an English weekly in 1884, to restate it at greater length in an American monthly in 1885, then to include that second statement in a volume of essays in 1888, and, finally, to issue it, revised and enlarged, as a separate brochure in 1901. The Professor says: "The difference between a Novel and a Novelet is one of length only: a Novelet is a brief novel; but the difference between a Novel and a Short-story is a difference of kind. A true Short-story is something other and something more than a mere story which is short. A true Short-story differs from the Novel chiefly in its unity of impression. In a far more exact and precise use of the word, a Short-story has unity as a Novel cannot have it." All this is wrong, a negligent utterance of negligent thought. How can a Short-story be "something other than" a short story? The answer is that it cannot. All that can be usefully asserted is that a *précis* of a long novel might make a bad short story. The whole difference between the Novel and the Short-story arises from the difference of length. It is because the short story is short that it usually deals with "a single episode," &c. But some short stories deal with many episodes; for instance, de Maupassant's *Odyssée d'une Fille*. If Prof. Matthews says that the *Odyssée d'une Fille* is not a Short-story, or is a bad Short-story, or is an inferior "mere" short story, or is a *précis* of a long novel, he is mistaken: that is all. It is an ancient game to fit facts into a theory by the device of arbitrarily limiting the significance of everyday words, but a very tiresome game; and no one will follow the Professor in his attempt to lay down a rule that short stories are not short stories unless they happen to be short stories of a particular sort. There is no difference whatever of *kind* between a Novel and a Short-story. The latter relates an episode, the former a succession of episodes: each is self-complete. "Of a truth," the Professor says again, "the Short-story is not only not a chapter out of a Novel . . . but (*sic*) at its best it impresses the reader with the belief that it would be spoiled if it were made larger, or if it were incorporated into a more elaborate work." Here is a platitude: every art work should be alterable only at the cost of its perfection. Not even in technique is there a difference between the two forms; the methods of narrative are the same for one episode as for a chain of episodes. And touching that alleged more absolute "Unity of impression" of the Short-story, what the Professor ought to mean is that the impression made by the Short-story is less complex, simpler (he might have added, less powerful) than that made by the Novel. But complexity does not exclude unity, nor need simplicity include it. The truth is that the Professor has excogitated this part of his theory from the well-known paradoxical essay in which Poe tries to demonstrate that there can be no such thing as a long poem, and that every so-called long poem is, in fact, a series of short ones. But perhaps the most astonishing of all the Professor's assertions is that "the difference *in spirit* and in form between the Lyric and the Epic is scarcely greater than the difference between the Short-story and the Novel."

For years past it has been a fashion among prattlers to prattle about "the art of the short story," as though it were something apart, high, and of unique difficulty. The short story is a smaller, simpler, easier, and less important form of the novel. Other things being equal, a short story can never have the force of a novel. As to the comparative difficulty of the two, ask any author who has written both fine novels and fine short stories.

For Study and Discussion

1. On what grounds does the reviewer find Matthews' *Philosophy* to be "a negligent utterance of negligent thought"? Do you agree or disagree? Why?

2. Does the reviewer successfully refute Matthews' contention regarding the unity of impression that can be achieved in the short story but not in the novel? If you think so, point out how he does it.

3. How does the reviewer define the short story? Would any other critics you have read agree with this definition?

4. Which of the reviewer's assertions would Canby be inclined to challenge?

HENRY SEIDEL CANBY

FREE FICTION

I

What impresses me most in the contemporary short story as I find it in American magazines, is its curious sophistication. Its bloom is gone. I have read through dozens of periodicals without finding one with fresh feeling and the easy touch of the writer who writes because his story urges him. And when with relief I do encounter a narrative that is not conventional in structure and mechanical in its effects, the name of the author is almost invariably that of a newcomer, or of one of our few uncorrupted masters of the art. Still more remarkable, the good short stories that I meet with in my reading are the trivial ones,—the sketchy, the anecdotal, the merely adventurous or merely picturesque; as they mount toward literature they seem to increase in artificiality and constraint; when they purport to interpret life they become machines, and nothing more, for the discharge of sensation, sentiment, or romance. And this is true, so far as I can discover, of the stories which most critics and more editors believe to be successful, the stories which are most characteristic of magazine narrative and of the output of American fiction in our times.

I can take my text from any magazine, from the most literary to the least. In the stories selected by all of them I find the resemblances greater than the differences and the latter seldom amount to more than a greater or a less excellence of workmanship and style. The 'literary' magazines, it is true, more frequently surprise one by a story told with original and consummate art; but then the 'popular' magazines balance this merit by their more frequent escape from mere prettiness. In both kinds, the majority of the stories come from the same mill, even though the hands that shape them may differ in refinement and in taste. Their range is narrow, and, what is more damning, their art seems constantly to verge upon artificiality.

Originally published in, and reprinted here from, the *Atlantic Monthly*, July 1915. Reprinted by permission of Edward Tatnall Canby.

These made-to-order stories (and this is certainly not too strong a term for the majority of them) are not interesting to a critical reader. He sticks to the novel, or, more frequently, goes to France, to Russia, or to England for his fiction, as the sales-list of any progressive publisher will show. And I do not believe that they are deeply interesting to an uncritical reader. He reads them to pass the time; and, to judge from the magazines themselves, gives his more serious attention to the 'write-ups' of politics, current events, new discoveries, and men in the public eye,—to reality, in other words, written as if it were fiction, and more interesting than the fiction that accompanies it, because, in spite of its enlivening garb, it is guaranteed by writer and editor to be true. I am not impressed by the perfervid letters published by the editor in praise of somebody's story as a 'soul-cure,' or the greatest of the decade. They were written, I suppose, but they are not typical. They do not insult the intelligence as do the ridiculous puffs which it is now the fashion to place like a sickly limelight at the head of a story; but they do not convince me of the story's success with the public. Actually, men and women, discussing these magazines, seldom speak of the stories. They have been interested,—in a measure. The 'formula,' as I shall show later, is bound to get that result. But they have dismissed the characters and forgotten the plots.

I do not deny that this supposedly successful short story is easy to read. It is—fatally easy. And here precisely is the trouble. To borrow a term from dramatic criticism, it is 'well made,' and that is what makes it so thin, so bloodless, and so unprofitable to remember, in spite of its easy narrative and its 'punch.' Its success as literature, curiously enough for a new literature and a new race like ours, is limited, not by crudity, or inexpressiveness, but by form, by the very rigidity of its carefully perfected form. Like other patent medicines, it is constructed by formula.

II

It is not difficult to construct an outline of the 'formula' by which thousands of current narratives are being whipped into shape. Indeed, by turning to the nearest textbook on 'Selling the Short Story,' I could find one ready-made. (There could be no clearer symptom of the disease I wish to diagnose than these many 'practical' textbooks, with their over-emphasis upon technique and their under-estimate of all else that makes literature.) The story *must* begin, it appears, with action or with dialogue. A mother packs her son's trunk while she gives him unheeded advice mingled with questions about shirts and socks; a corrupt and infuriated director pounds on the mahogany table at his board meeting, and curses the honest fool (hero of the story) who has got in his way; or, '"Where did Mary Worden get that curious gown?" inquired Mrs. Van Deming, glancing across the sparkling glass and silver of the hotel terrace.' Any one of these will serve as instance of the breakneck beginning which Kipling made obligatory. Once started, the narrative must move, move, move furiously, each action and every speech pointing directly toward the unknown climax. A pause is a confession of weakness. This Poe taught for a special kind of story; and this a later generation, with a servility which would have amazed that sturdy fighter, requires of all narrative. Then the climax, which must neatly, quickly, and definitely end the action for all time, either by a solution you have been urged to hope for by the wily author in every preceding paragraph, or in a way which is logically correct but never, never suspected. O. Henry is responsible for the vogue of the latter of these two alternatives,—and the strain of living up to his inventiveness has been frightful. Finally comes a last suspiration, usually in the advertising pages. Sometimes it is a beautiful descriptive sentence charged with sentiment, sometimes a smart epigram, according to the style of story, or the 'line' expected of the author. Try this, as the advertisements say, on your favorite magazine.

This formula, with variations which readers can supply for themselves or draw from textbooks on the short story, is not a wholly bad method of writing fiction. It is, I venture to assert, a very good one,—if you desire merely effective story-telling. It is probably the best way of making the short story a thoroughly efficient tool for the presentation of modern life. And there lies, I believe, the whole trouble. The short story, its course plotted and its form prescribed, has become too efficient. Now efficiency is all that we ask of a railroad, efficiency is half at least of what we ask of journalism; but efficiency is not the most, it is perhaps the least, important among the undoubted elements of good literature.

In order to make the short story efficient, the dialogue, the setting, the plot, the character development, have been squeezed and whittled and moulded until the means of telling the story fits the ends of the story-telling as neatly as hook fits eye. As one writer on how to manufacture short stories tells us in discussing character development, the aspirant must—

'Eliminate every trait or deed which does not help peculiarly to make the character's part in the particular story either intelligible or open to such sympathy as it merits';

'Paint in only the "high lights," that is . . . never qualify or elaborate a trait or episode, merely for the sake of preserving the effect of the character's full reality.'

And thus the story is to be subdued to the service of the climax as the body of man to his brain.

But what these writers upon the short story do not tell us is that efficiency of this order works backward as well as forward. If means are to correspond with ends, why then ends must be adjusted to means. Not only must the devices of the story-teller be directed with sincerity toward the tremendous effect he wishes to make with his climax upon you and me, his readers; but the interesting life which it is or should be his purpose to write about for our delectation must be manoeuvred, or must be chosen or rejected, not according to the limitation which small space—enough in all conscience—imposes, but with its suitability to the 'formula' in mind. In brief, if we are to have complete efficiency, the right kind of life and no other must be put into the short-story hopper. Nothing which cannot be told rapidly must be dropped in, lest it clog the 'formula's' smoothly spinning wheels. If it is a story of slowly developing incongruity in married life, the action must be speeded beyond probability, like a film in the moving pictures, before it is ready to be made into a short story. If it is a tale of disillusionment on a prairie farm, with the world and life flattening out together, some sharp climax must be provided nevertheless, because that is the only way in which to tell a story. Indeed it is easy to see the dangers which arise from sacrificing truth to a formula in the interests of efficiency.

This is the limitation by form; the limitation by subject is quite as annoying. American writers from Poe down have been fertile in plots. Especially since O. Henry took the place of Kipling as a literary master, ingenuity, inventiveness, cleverness in its American sense, have been squandered upon the short story. But plots do not make variety. Themes make variety. Human nature regarded in its multitudinous phases makes variety. There are only a few themes in current American short stories, —the sentimental theme from which breed ten thousand narratives; the theme of intellectual analysis and of moral psychology favored by the 'literary' magazines; the 'big-business' theme; the theme of American effrontery; the social-contrast theme; the theme of successful crime. Add a few more, and you will have them all. Read a hundred examples, and you will see how infallibly the authors—always excepting our few masters—limit themselves to conventional aspects of even these conventional themes. Reflect, and you will see how the first—the theme of sentiment—has overflowed its banks and washed over all the rest, so that, whatever else a story may be, it must somewhere, somehow, make the honest American heart beat more softly.

There is an obvious cause for this in the taste of the American public, which I do not propose to neglect. But here too we are in the grip of the 'formula,' of the idea that there is only one way to construct a short story—a swift succession of climaxes rising precipitously to a giddy eminence. For the formula is rigid, not plastic as life is plastic. It fails to grasp innumerable stories which break the surface of American life day by day and disappear uncaught. Stories of quiet homely life, events significant for themselves that never reach a burning climax, situations that end in irony, or doubt, or aspiration, it mars in the telling. The method which, as teachers of the short story tell us, makes story-telling easy, itself limits our variety.

Nothing brings home the artificiality and the narrowness of this American fiction so clearly as a comparison, for better and for worse, with the Russian short story. I have in mind the works of Anton Tchekoff, whose short stories have lately been translated into excellent English and published in two volumes. Fresh from a reading of these books, one feels, it is true, quite as inclined to criticize as to praise. Why are the characters therein depicted so persistently disagreeable, even in the lighter stories? Why are the women always freckled, the men predominantly red and watery in the eye? Why is the country so flat, so foggy, so desolate; and why are the peasants so lumpish and miserable? Russia cannot be quite so dreary as this; the prevailing grimness must be due to some mental obfuscation of her writers. I do not refer to the gloomy, powerful realism of the stories of hopeless misery. There, if one criticizes, it must be only the advisability of the choice of such subjects. One does not doubt the truth of the picture. I mean the needless dinginess of much of Russian fiction, and of many of these powerful short stories.

Nevertheless, when one has said his worst, and particularly when he has eliminated the dingier stories of the collection, he returns with an admiration, almost passionate, to the truth, the variety, above all to the freedom of these stories. I do not know Russia or the Russians, and yet I am as sure of the absolute truth of that unfortunate doctor in 'La Cigale,' who builds up his heroic life of self-sacrifice while his wife seeks selfishly elsewhere for a hero, as I am convinced of the essential unreality, except in dialect and manners, of the detectives, the 'dope-fiends,' the hard business men, the heroic boys and lovely girls that people most American short stories. As for variety,—the Russian does not handle numerous themes. He is obsessed with the dreariness of life, and his obsession is only occasionally lifted; he has no room to wander widely through human nature. And yet his work gives an impression of variety that the American magazine never attains. He is free to be various. When the mood of gloom is off him, he experiments at will, and often with consummate success. He seems to be sublimely unconscious that readers are supposed to like only a few kinds of stories; and as unaware of the taboo upon religious or reflective narrative as of the prohibition upon the ugly in fiction. As life in any manifestation becomes interesting in his eyes, his pen moves freely. And so he makes life interesting in many varieties, even when his Russian prepossessions lead him far away from our Western moods.

Freedom. That is the word here, and also in his method of telling these stories. No one seems to have said to Tchekoff, 'Your stories must move, move, move.' Sometimes, indeed, he pauses outright, as life pauses; sometimes he seems to turn aside, as life turns aside before its progress is resumed. No one has ever made clear to him that every word from the first of the story must point unerringly toward the solution and the effect of the plot. His paragraphs spring from the characters and the situation. They are led on to the climax by the story itself. They do not drag the panting reader down a rapid action, to fling him breathless upon the 'I told you so' of a conclusion prepared in advance.

I have in mind especially a story of Tchekoff's called 'The Night Before Easter.' It is a very interesting story; it is a very admirable story, conveying in a few pages much of Russian spirituality and more of universal human nature; but I believe that all, or nearly all, of our American magazines would refuse it; not because it lacks picturesqueness, or narrative suspense, or vivid characterization—all of these it has in large measure. They would reject it because it does not seem to move rapidly, or because it lacks a vigorous climax. The Goltva swollen in flood lies under the Easter stars. As the monk Jerome ferries the traveler over to where fire and cannon-shot and rocket announce the rising of Christ to the riotous monastery, he asks, 'Can you tell me, kind master, why it is that even in the presence of great happiness a man cannot forget his grief?' Deacon Nicholas is dead, who alone in the monastery could write prayers that touched the heart. And of them all, only Jerome read his 'akaphists.' 'He used to open the door of his cell and make me sit by him, and we used to read. . . . His face was compassionate and tender—' In the monastery the countryside is crowding to hear the Easter service. The choir sings 'Lift up thine eyes, O Zion, and behold.' But Nicholas is dead, and there is none to penetrate the meaning of the Easter canon, except Jerome who toils all night on the ferry because they had forgotten him. In the morning, the traveler recrosses the Goltva. Jerome is still on the ferry. He rests his dim, timid eyes upon them all, and then fixes his gaze on the rosy face of a merchant's wife. There is little of the man in that long gaze. He is seeking in the woman's face the sweet and gentle features of his lost friend.

The American editor refuses such a story. There is no plot here, he says, and no 'punch.' He is wrong, although an imperfect abstract like mine cannot convict him. For the narrative presents an unforgettable portrait of wistful hero-worship, set in the dim mists of a Russian river against the barbaric splendor of an Easter midnight mass. To force a climax upon this poignant story would be to spoil it. And when it appears, as it will, in reprint, in some periodical anthology of current fiction, it will not fail to impress American readers.

But the American editor must have a climax which drives home what he thinks the public wants. If it is not true, so much the worse for truth. If it falsifies the story, well, a lying story with a 'punch' is better than a true one that lacks a fire-spitting climax. The audience who judge a play by the effect of its 'curtain,' will not complain of a trifling illogicality in narrative, or a little juggling with what might happen if the story were life. Of what the editor wants I find a typical example in a recent number of a popular magazine. The story is well written; it is interesting until it begins to lie; moreover it is 'featured' as one of the best short stories of the year. An American girl, brought up in luxury, has fed her heart with romantic sentiment. The world is a Christmas tree. If you are good and pretty and 'nice,' you have only to wait until you get big enough to shake it, and then down will come some present—respect from one's friends and family, perhaps a lover. And then she wakes up. Her father points out that she is pinching him by her extravagance. Nobody seems to want her kind of 'niceness'; which indeed does no one much good. There is nothing that she can do that is useful in the world, for she has never learned. She begins to doubt the Christmas tree. There enters a man—a young electrical engineer, highly trained, highly ambitious, but caught in the wheels of a great corporation where he is merely a cog; wanting to live, wanting to love, wanting to be married, yet condemned to labor for many years more upon a salary which perhaps would little more than pay for her clothes. By an ingenious device they are thrown together in a bit of wild country near town, and are made to exchange confidences. So far, no one can complain of the truth of this story; and furthermore it is well told. Here are two products of our social machine, both true to type. Suppose they want to marry? What can we do about it? The story-teller has posed his question with a force not to be denied. But I wish we had had a Tchekoff to answer it. As for this author, he leads his characters to a conveniently deserted house, lights a fire on the hearth, sets water boiling for tea, and in a few pages of charming romance would persuade us that with a few economies in this rural residence, true love may have its course and a successful marriage crown the morning's adventure. Thus in one dazzling sweep, the greatest and most sugary plum of all drops from the very tip of the Christmas tree into the lap of the lady, who had just learned that happiness in the real world comes in no such haphazard and undeserved a fashion. Really! Have we degenerated from Lincoln's day? Is it easy now to fool all of us all of the time, so that a tale-teller dares to expose silly romance at the beginning of his story, and yet dose us with it at the end! Not that one objects to romance. It is as necessary as food, and almost as valuable. But romance that pretends to be realism, realism that fizzles out into sentimental romance—is there any excuse for that? Even if it provides 'heart interest' and an effective climax?

The truth is, of course, that the Russian stories are based upon life; the typical stories of the American magazines, for all their realistic details, are too often studied, not from American life but from literary convention. Even when their substance is fresh, their unfoldings and above all their solutions are second-hand. If the Russian authors could write American stories I believe that their work would be more truly popular than what we are now getting. They would be free to be interesting in any direction and by any method. The writer of the American short story is not free.

III

I should like to leave the subject here with a comparison that any reader can make for himself. But American pride recalls the past glory of our short story, and common knowledge indicates the present reality of a few authors—several of them women—who are writing fiction of which any race might be proud. The optimist cannot resist meditating on the way out for our enslaved short story.

The ultimate responsibility for its present position must fall, I suppose, upon our American taste, which, when taken by and large, is unquestionably crude, easily satisfied, and not sensitive to good things. American taste does not rebel against the 'formula.' If interest is pricked it does not inquire too curiously into the nature of the goad. American taste is partial to sentiment, and antagonistic to themes that fail to present the American in the light of optimistic romance. But our defects in taste are slowly but certainly being remedied. The schools are at work upon them; journalism, for all its noisy vulgarity, is at work upon them. Our taste in art, our taste in poetry, our taste in architecture, our taste in music go up, as our taste in fiction seems to go down.

But what are the writers of short stories and what are the editors and publishers doing to help taste improve itself until, as Henry James says, it acquires a keener relish than ever before?

It profits nothing to attack the American writer. He does, it may fairly be assumed, what he can, and I do not wish to discuss here the responsibility of the public for his deficiencies. The editor and the publisher, however, stand in a somewhat different relationship to the American short story. They may assert with much justice that they are public servants merely; nevertheless they *do* control the organs of literary expression, and it is through them that any positive influence on the side of restriction or proscription must be exerted, whatever may be its ultimate source. If a lack of freedom in method and in choice of subject is one reason for the sophistication of our short story, then the editorial policy of American magazines is a legitimate field for speculation.

I can reason only from the evidence of the product and the testimony of authors, successful and unsuccessful. Yet one conclusion springs to the eye, and is enough in itself to justify investigation. The critical basis upon which the American editor professes to build his magazine is of doubtful validity. I believe that it is unsound. His policy, as stated in 'editorial announcements' and confirmed by his advertisements of the material he selects, is first to find out what the public wants, and next to supply it. This is reasonable in appearance. It would seem to be good commercially, and, as a policy, I should consider it good for art, which must consult the popular taste or lose its vitality. But a pitfall lies between this theory of editorial selection and its successful practice. The editor must really know what the public wants. If he does not, he becomes a dogmatic critic of a very dangerous school.

Those who know the theatre and its playwrights, are agreed that the dramatic manager, at least in America, is a very poor judge of what the public desires. The percentage of bad guesses in every metropolitan season is said to be very high. Is the editor more competent? It would seem that he is, to judge from the stability of our popular magazines. But that he follows the public taste with any certainty of judgment is rendered unlikely, not only by inherent improbability, but also by three specific facts: the tiresome succession of like stories which follow unendingly in the wake of every popular success; the palpable fear of the editor to attempt innovation, experiment, or leadership; and the general complaint against 'magazine stories.' In truth, the American editor plays safe, constantly and from conviction; and playing safe in the short story means the adoption of the 'formula,' which is sure to be somewhat successful; it means restriction to a few safe themes. He swings from the detective story to the tale of the alien, from the 'heart-interest' story to the narrative of 'big business.' When, as has happened recently, a magazine experimented with eroticism, and found it successful, the initiative of its editor was felt to be worthy of general remark. . . .

In both our 'popular' and our 'literary' magazines, freer fiction would follow upon better criticism. The readers of the 'literary' magazines are already seeking foreign-made narratives, and neglecting the American short story built for them according to the standardized model of 1915. The readers of the 'popular' magazines want chiefly journalism (an utterly different thing from literature); and that they are getting in good measure in the non-fiction and part-fiction sections of the magazines. But they also seek, as all men seek, some literature. If, instead of imposing the 'formula' (which is, after all, a journalistic mechanism— and a good one—adapted for speedy and evanescent effects), if, instead of imposing the 'formula' upon all the subjects they propose to have turned into fiction, the editors of these magazines should also experiment, should release some subjects from the tyranny of the 'formula,' and admit others which its cult has kept out, the result might be surprising. It is true that the masses have no taste for literature,—as a steady diet; it is still more certain that not even the most mediocre of multitudes can be permanently hoodwinked by formula.

But the magazines can take care of themselves; it is the short story in which I am chiefly interested. Better criticism and greater freedom for fiction might vitalize our overabundant, unoriginal, unreal, unversatile, —everything but unformed short story. Its artifice might again become art. And when one thinks of the multitudinous situations, impressions, incidents in this fascinating whirl of modern life, incapable perhaps of presentation in a novel because of their very impermanence, admirably adapted to the short story because of their vividness and their deep if narrow significance, the voice of protest must go up against any artificial, arbitrary limitations upon the art. Freedom to make his appeal to the public with any subject not morbid or indecent, is all the writer can ask.

Freedom to publish sometimes what the editor likes and the public may like, instead of what the editor approves because the public has liked it, is all that he needs. There is plenty of blood in the American short story yet, though I have read through whole magazines without finding a drop of it.

When we give literature in America the same opportunity to invent, to experiment, that we have already given journalism, there will be more legitimate successors to Irving, to Hawthorne, to Poe and Bret Harte. There will be more writers, like O. Henry, who write stories to please themselves, and thus please the majority. There will be fewer writers, like O. Henry, who stop short of the final touch of perfection because American taste (and the American editor) puts no premium upon artistic work. There will be fewer stories, I trust, where sentiment is no longer a part, but the whole of life. Most of all, form, *the* form, the *formula*, will relax its grip upon the short story, will cease its endless tapping upon the door of interest, and its smug content when some underling (while the brain sleeps) answers its stereotyped appeal. And we may get more narratives like Mrs. Wharton's *Ethan Frome*, to make us feel that now as much as ever there is literary genius waiting in America.

For Study and Discussion

1. What does Canby mean when he says that the good short stories he has been reading are "the trivial ones"?

2. Consider Canby's brief description of the typical "formula" short story. Is his criticism valid? To which of the American stories you have read so far could it be applied?

3. Why does he feel that the short story has become too "efficient"?

4. According to Canby, what is the difference between "limitation by form" and "limitation by subject"? Why does he find both annoying?

5. Despite the dreariness of Russian life depicted in Chekhov's tales, why does Canby find them fresher and more interesting than the typical American magazine stories? How firmly does he support this criticism?

6. What, in Canby's view, makes Chekhov's story "Easter Eve" superior to the "well-written" American story he summarizes (pp. 56–57)? Why does he accuse the latter story of "lying"? Do you agree with his harsh judgment?

7. In asserting that "the writer of the American short story is not free," is Canby blaming the writer, the reader, or the magazine editor for this condition?

8. According to Canby, who besides the writer is ultimately responsible for improving the artistic quality of American short stories? What influence in particular may be expected to bring about this improvement?

9. Canby wrote this essay more than fifty years ago. Are his judgments still valid today? To what extent would you modify them?

HERBERT ELLSWORTH CORY

THE SENILITY OF THE SHORT-STORY

When one says that the short-story is on its last legs one may well appear to be courting the reputation of a voice in the wilderness to the point of perversity and absurdity. Everywhere, it would seem, such a prophecy must be confounded by the flaring covers on the news-stands. Yet it is precisely because the short-story was never more widely current that it begins to show the surest signs of degeneration. I do not say this because the short-story ministers to the mob. That might have been to its credit. I say it because the short-story ministers to the mob in its most capricious and hedonistic mood, and because the short-story is now produced by "the mob of gentlemen who write with ease."

The history of literature is, from one point of view, the history of the slow decay of *genres* when they have passed from the masters to the mob of servile imitators who have the receipt without the inspiration. I do not mean to imply that these *genres* sink down in eternal ruin. They simply lie fallow. Some master, in an age that has forgotten "the mob of gentlemen," regenerates the form. But all *genres*, particularly those of a highly wrought technique, must lie fallow for a time after small men have toyed with some great formal innovation of a master. Pope's satires, with their astonishing finish but obvious mannerisms, were subjected to an unjust depreciation, from which even now they have not altogether recovered, because the middle decades of the eighteenth century were sated by the shrill voices of his clever imitators, who had the receipt but not the inspiration. Tennyson developed a marvellously rich but a peculiarly self-conscious blank-verse. Open Stedman's "Victorian Anthology," and read at random among the scores of perfectly proper and cloying Tennysonians. Then you will see why the master complained that

Originally published in, and reprinted here from, the *Dial*, May 3, 1917, by permission of Anthony F. Cory and Mrs. Mary S. C. Rinehart, children of Herbert Ellsworth Cory.

Most can raise the flowers now,
　For all have got the seed.

And some are pretty enough,
　And some are poor indeed;
And now again the people
　Call it but a weed.

Most of the exaggerated depreciation of Tennyson to-day is but the result of the self-indulgence of the Tennysonians. It is a story of endless variations and analogues. Never, after his callow years, did Byron stoop to Byronism; but his followers seldom rose above it. So Thackeray and Carlyle, moved to ill-temper over the din of little voices, sneered and fulminated at Byron.

Now there never was a form or *genre* that had a more highly wrought technique than the short-story. Its chief masters, men like Poe and de Maupassant, are really virtuosi more than artists. Its technique is so much less difficult than that of the essay that high-school teachers find it facile material for their students. Nothing is more insidiously easy in America to-day than to become a popular teacher with the short-story as your medium. It is so much easier to write than the essay and so much more obviously attractive that hundreds of grub-streeters supply an artificially stimulated demand, obtuse undergraduate students of composition plunge their teachers into a premature literary dyspepsia, hundreds of languid and day-dreaming women make it possible for quack teachers to earn with private classes a plausible semblance of an honest living.

But the demand for the short-story is, I repeat, an artificially stimulated demand. We do not want the short-story—we *think* we want it. In our healthier moments we condemn our modern speed mania. In our healthier moments we desire the literature of cool reflection. The very technique of the short-story is pathological, and titillates our nerves in our pathological moments. The short-story is the blood kinsman of the quick-lunch, the vaudeville, and the joy-ride. It is the supreme art-form of those who believe in the philosophy of quick-results. Why is its technique pathological? In the first place, its unity is abnormally artificial and intense. Turn even to the high-water mark of the short-story, Poe's "Fall of the House of Usher." Every group of vowel sounds, every word-connotation, every descriptive and narrative atom is concentrated on that *crescendo* of nameless fear that makes the story seizing. It is well that we have had masters to do this for us. But is it well that we should gorge ourselves on a *genre* in which unity has become an obsession? Consider also the popular habit of truncating the short-story violently at the climax. Seldom are we healed by a *dénouement* in which we may find a *katharsis*,—in which we are allowed to realize that terror and pity or inextinguishable laughter have purged our souls. Consider, thirdly, the rapid action of the short-story. Life is made to whirl by, as we read, like the walls of a subway. Yet reality shows us that only at rare moments, even in the twentieth century, do men live like this. What, we might like to ask, is the significance of the lives of these puppets who are swept by us with frenzied haste? Ah, but this is an irrelevant question. The incessant readers of the short-story are sufferers from that same nervous irritability which marks alike the capitalist and the labor-agitator when they cry, "For Gawd's sake let's *do* something."

Tell an undergraduate or his father, the tired business man, that because the short-story is popular it is doomed. Say that the technique is pathological whether the content be tragic, morbid, comic, or sentimental. Warn your hearer that the short-story is the patent-medicine of contemporary art, which serves but to make the disorders of the age more deep-seated while it brings its factitious recreation. Point out that it is the literature not of healthy exhilaration but of feverish excitement. You are pretty sure to cause a smile—if your auditor happens to have a shred of the rare virtue of patience. You will become noted as a literary soap-boxer. It is so easy, in an age of drift, to seize upon fashions that pass in the night as eternal verities. But he who has any literary perspective at all will remember the time not long past when the public insisted on the leisurely "three-decker" novel whose demise Mr. Kipling celebrated with his characteristic superficiality,—the novel that threw its light into every cranny of human character, that paused again and again to reflect upon life genially or wistfully or acridly. The student of literature will remember that half a century before the "three-decker," Robert Southey, an excellent prose-writer and a lover of mellow prose, poured out reams of perfunctory verse because the public had an inordinate appetite for rather sentimental narrative poems of huge dimensions about an oriental Thalaba the Destroyer or a Roderick, the Last of the Goths. Let the provincial reader who thinks the nervous quick-step of modern journalistic prose the only manner that could ever have been widely popular open De Quincey's essay on style. There he will find to his amazement a man who himself wrote plesiosaurian sentences protesting against a public and a corps of popular journalists who doted on periodic sentences that uncoiled their enormous proportions like boa constrictors.

Seldom has the short-story, even in its prime in the last half of the nineteenth century, attained to high seriousness. And to-day there are few of its practitioners, whether their content be healthy or unhealthy, gay or sad, whose attitude toward life is not more or less vitiated by some tinge of the triviality, the egocentric mania, the commercialism, or the mere virtuosity that contaminate all petty or casual artists. The depths of our age, beneath a phantom surface of intermittent and delirious gaiety, cry out for a deeper art. There never was an age that was really in more deadly earnest, never an age more full of unorganized religious zeal. The international agony, the national bewilderments, the fearful social injustices, the heart-beat of our epical life—these can neither be described nor interpreted by the trivial and the hasty. The short-story is but a more delicate manifestation of that universal fever that has bankrupted mankind, and from which our deepest instincts of self-preservation urge us with tremendous pressure to arouse ourselves. From the depths, the most naïve and the most sophisticated of our readers yearn for new prophets like Carlyle and Ruskin, who came too soon. We would turn gladly from the prettily suggestive to the earnestly and beautifully explicit. We would be relieved to give up the contemplation of morbidly perfected miniatures for impetuous Rubens-like panorama with large perspectives. If a great artist would take subjects like "Poverty," "Immigration," "Violence and the Labor Movement," and treat them with thoroughness and eloquence in a form compounded of historical narrative and reflective essay, if he could unite in himself the dialectic of metaphysics with its concern over fundamental principles, the sense of the picturesque tempered by a sense of moral horror, an Emersonian or, better, a Fichtean fervor to edify, he would express the aspiration of the world to-day,—he would be our supreme artist. How passionately the public desires such an art is shown by the wide sale of books that approach this ideal in content and in form. We may attach, too, something more than a sinister significance to the public craving for the pseudo-propagandist American drama which traffics insincerely with social questions. The audiences which crowd the theatres may be prurient, yet their impulses can be readily sublimated by an art equally vivid, but more sober and more reflective. Such an art is sure to come. When such a deeply popular longing is so widespread, the artist already lies in the womb of the community. For the supreme artist is not one who concerns himself with "originality," at least not self-consciously. The self-conscious search for originality leads only to the rococo and the morbid. The great artist is so moved with a conviction that is extra-individual, the conviction of his community in its most spacious moods, in its most magnificent hopes, that he loses himself in these to save himself.

Whatever may be the content of the short-story, its technique has grown more and more self-conscious. And self-consciousness is the mortal foe of true originality. We may take comfort in the very fact that the short-story teems to-day on our news-stands. This is sure evidence of its garrulous senility. And the senility of the short-story augurs the sounds of voices more sonorous, the early appearance of a larger art.

For Study and Discussion

1. What signs of degeneration does Cory find in the modern short story? Is his argument the same as Canby's? If not, in what ways do these two critics differ?

2. Would you agree that the short story "is so much easier to write than the essay"? If not, how would you refute Cory's assertion?

3. What does Cory mean by saying that "the very technique of the short-story is pathological"? Why does he call the short story "the patent-medicine of contemporary art"?

4. What evidence does Cory offer in support of his criticism that the short story has seldom "attained to high seriousness"? Do you accept his argument?

5. What constructive suggestions for the improvement of the short story does Cory offer?

6. Are Cory's strictures directed more toward the content or toward the technique of typical American stories written in his time? Which of the stories in this collection, if any, do you think would satisfy his demand for "a larger art"? Defend your choices.

N. BRYLLION FAGIN

"O. HENRYISM"

Is it not a propitious time to attempt a revaluation of our short-story dogmas? What is the contribution of O. Henryism to our national letters and to the short story as a form of literary expression? How great an artist really was William Sidney Porter, the founder of the Cult? Is it sacrilege to attempt to answer these questions?

O. Henry left us more than two hundred and fifty stories. In the decade before his death he turned out an average of twenty-five stories a year. Mr. William Johnston, an editor of the New York *World*, relates the struggles of O. Henry in trying to live up to a three-year contract he had with that paper calling for a story a week. There were weeks when O. Henry would haunt the hotels and cafés of New York in a frantic search of material, and there were times when the stories could not be produced on time and O. Henry would sit down and write the most ingenious excuses. Needless to state that O. Henry's stories bear all the marks of this haste and anxiety. Nearly all of them are sketchy, reportorial, superficial, his gift of felicitous expression "camouflaging" the poverty of theme and character. The best of them lack depth and roundness, often disclosing a glint of a sharp idea unworked, untransmuted by thought and emotion.

Of his many volumes of stories, "The Four Million" is without doubt the one which is most widely known. It was his bold challenge to the world that he was the discoverer—even though he gave the census taker due credit—of four million people instead of four hundred in America's metropolis that first attracted attention and admiration. The implication was that he was imbued with the purpose of unbaring the lives of these four million and especially of the neglected lower classes. A truly admirable and ambitious self-assignment. And so we have "The Four Million." But to what extent was he successful in carrying out his assignment. How much of the surging, shifting, pale, rich, orderly, chaotic, and wholly incongruous life of New York is actually pulsating in the twenty-five little stories collected in the volume?

Reprinted from Fagin's *Short Story-Writing: An Art or a Trade?* (New York: Thomas Seltzer, Inc., 1923).

What is the first one, "Tobin's Palm," if not a mere long-drawn-out jest? Is it anything more than an anecdote exploiting palmistry as a "trait"—to use another technical term—or point? It isn't New York, nor Tobin, nor any other character, that makes this story interesting. It is O. Henry's trick at the end. The prophecy is fulfilled, after all, in such an unexpected way, and we are such satisfied children!

What is the second story, the famous "Gift of the Magi"? We have discussed it and analyzed it in our texts and lauded it everywhere. How much of the life of the four million does it hold up to us? It is better than the first story; yes, much better. But why is it a masterpiece? Not because it tries to take us into the home of a married couple attempting to exist in our largest city on the husband's income of $20 per week. No, that wouldn't make it famous. Much better stories of poverty have been written, much more faithful and poignant, and the great appreciative public does not even remember them. It is the wizard's mechanics, his stunning invention—that's the thing! Della sells her hair and buys a fob for hubby's watch; while at the same time hubby sells his watch and buys her a comb. But you don't know all this until they get together for the presentation of the gifts, and then you gasp. We call this working criss-cross, a plot of cross purposes. In this story we usually overlook entirely one little thing—the last paragraph. It really is superfluous and therefore constitutes a breech of technique. We preach against preaching. Tell your story, we say, and stop. "Story" is synonymous with *action*. O. Henry didn't stop—so that even he was sometimes a breaker of laws. But this uncomfortable thought doesn't really have to be noted! . . .

Thus an examination of O. Henry's work by any one not blinded by hero-worship and popular esteem, discloses at best an occasional brave peep at life, hasty, superficial and dazzlingly flippant; an idea, raw, unassimilated, timidly works its way to the surface only to be promptly suppressed by a hand skilled in producing sensational effects. At its worst, his work is no more than a series of cheap jokes renovated and expanded. But over all there is the unmistakable charm of a master trickster, of a facile player with incidents and words. . . .

Just how long O. Henry's stories will live and his influence predominate is a prediction no one can safely undertake to venture at this time. It depends upon how long we will permit his influence to predominate. The great mass of our reading public will continue to venerate any writer as long as our official censors continue to write panegyrics of him, and our colleges to hold him up as a model. The literary aspirants coming to us for instruction are recruited largely from among this indiscriminating public. Sooner or later, however, we must realize that the American Maupassant has not yet come and that those who foisted the misnomer upon William Sidney Porter have done the American short story a great injury. Before this most popular of our literary forms can come into its own the O. Henry cult must be demolished. O. Henry himself must be assigned his rightful position—among the tragic figures of America's potential artists whose genius was distorted and stifled by our prevailing commercial and infantile conception of literary values. Our short story itself must be cleansed; its paint and powder removed; its fluffy curls shorn—so that our complacent reader may be left to contemplate its "rag and a bone and a hank of hair."

When the great American short-story master finally does come, no titles borrowed from the French or any other nationality will be necessary and adequate. His own worth will forge his crown, and his worth will not be measured in tricks and stunts and puzzles and cleverness. His sole object will not be to spring effects upon his unwary reader. His will be sincere honest art—with due apologies for this obvious contradiction in terms, for art can be nothing but sincere!—a result of deep, genuine emotions and an overflowing imagination. His very soul will be imbued with the simple truth, so succinctly put by Mr. H. L. Mencken, that "the way to sure and tremendous effects is by the route of simplicity, naturalness, and ingenuousness."

For Study and Discussion

1. On what grounds does Fagin question the validity of O. Henry's popularity as a short-story artist?

2. Why does Fagin assert that the stories in O. Henry's *The Four Million* are an inadequate representation of life in New York City? How would you counter his argument?

3. Is O. Henry's "Gift of the Magi" a genuine masterpiece? What are its special virtues? Its weaknesses? Do its faults outweigh its virtues?

4. Is Fagin altogether fair in condemning O. Henry as "a master trickster" and comparing him unfavorably with Maupassant?

5. How valid for its time is Fagin's contention that the O. Henry cult must be demolished before the American short story can "come into its own"?

6. Fagin's essay was written in 1923. Has the O. Henry cult been demolished since then? Select and discuss three or four recent stories in this collection which might satisfy Fagin's demand for "sincere honest art."

SHERWOOD ANDERSON

FORM, NOT PLOT

I was walking in the street or sitting in a train and overheard a remark dropped from the lips of some man or woman. Out of a thousand such remarks, heard almost every day, one stayed in my head. I could not shake it out. And then people constantly told me tales and in the telling of them there was a sentence used that intoxicated. "I was lying on my back on the porch and the street lamp shone on my mother's face. What was the use? I could not say to her what was in my mind. She would not have understood. There was a man lived next door who kept going past the house and smiling at me. I got it into my head that he knew all that I could not tell mother."

A few such sentences in the midst of a conversation overheard or dropped into a tale someone told. These were the seeds of stories. How could one make them grow?

In telling tales of themselves people constantly spoiled the tale in telling. They had some notion of how a story should be told got from reading. Little lies crept in. They had done something mean and tried to justify some action that for the tale's sake did not need justification.

There was a notion that ran through all story-telling in America, that stories must be built about a plot and that absurd Anglo-Saxon notion that they must point a moral, uplift the people, make better citizens, etc. The magazines were filled with these plot stories and most of the plays on our stage were plot plays. "The Poison Plot," I called it in conversation with my friends as the plot notion did seem to me to poison all story-telling. What was wanted I thought was form, not plot, an altogether more elusive and difficult thing to come at.

The plots were frameworks about which the stories were to be constructed and editors were inordinately fond of them. One got "an idea for a story." What was meant was that a new trick had been thought out. Nearly all the adventure stories and the well-known American

Reprinted from *A Story Teller's Story* (New York: B. W. Huebsch, Inc., 1924) by permission of Harold Ober Associates, Inc. Copyright 1924 by B. W. Huebsch; copyright renewed 1951 by Eleanor Copenhaver Anderson.

western stories were so constructed. A man went into the redwood forests or into the deserts and took up land. He has been a rather mean, second-rate chap in civilization but in the new place a great change comes over him. Well, the writer had got him out where there was no one looking and could do as he pleased with the fellow. Never mind what he had been. The forests or the deserts had changed him completely. The writer could make a regular angel of him, have him rescue downtrodden women, catch horse thieves, exhibit any kind of bravery required to keep the reader excited and happy.

A word of good sense dropped in anywhere would have blown the whole thing to pieces but there was no danger. In all such writing all consideration for human beings was thrown aside. No one lived in such tales. Let such a writer begin to think of human beings, care a little for human beings, and his pasteboard world would melt before his eyes. The man in the desert or in the redwood forests was of course the same man he had been before he went there. He had the same problems to face. God knows we would all flee to the forests or the deserts at once if going there could so transform anyone. At least I know I should waste no time in getting there.

In the construction of these stories there was endless variation but in all of them human beings, the lives of human beings, were altogether disregarded. . . .

. . . In certain moods one became impregnated with the seeds of a hundred new tales in one day. The telling of the tales, to get them into form, to clothe them, find just the words and the arrangement of words that would clothe them—that was a quite different matter. . . .

For such men as myself you must understand there is always a great difficulty about telling the tale after the scent has been picked up. The tales that continually came to me in the way indicated above could of course not become tales until I had clothed them. Having, from a conversation overheard or in some other way, got the tone of a tale, I was like a woman who has just become impregnated. Something was growing inside me. At night when I lay in my bed I could feel the heels of the tale kicking against the walls of my body. Often as I lay thus every word of the tale came to me quite clearly but when I got out of bed to write it down the words would not come.

I had constantly to seek in roads new to me. Other men had felt what I had felt, had seen what I had seen—how had they met the difficulties I faced? My father when he told his tales walked up and down the room before his audience. He pushed out little experimental sentences and watched his audience narrowly. There was a dull-eyed old farmer sitting in a corner of the room. Father had his eyes on the fellow. "I'll get him," he said to himself. He watched the farmer's eyes. When the experimental sentence he had tried did not get anywhere he tried another and kept trying. Beside words he had—to help the telling of his tales—the advantage of being able to act out those parts for which he could find no words. He could frown, shake his fists, smile, let a look of pain or annoyance drift over his face.

These were his advantages that I had to give up if I was to write my tales rather than tell them and how often I had cursed my fate.

How significant words had become to me! At about this time an American woman living in Paris, Miss Gertrude Stein, had published a book called "Tender Buttons" and it had come into my hands. How it had excited me! Here was something purely experimental and dealing in words separated from sense—in the ordinary meaning of the word sense—an approach I was sure the poets must often be compelled to make. Was it an approach that would help me? I decided to try it.

A year or two before the time of which I am now writing an American painter, Mr. Felix Russman, had taken me one day into his workshop to show me his colors. He laid them out on a table before me and then his wife called him out of the room and he stayed for half an hour. It had been one of the most exciting moments of my life. I shifted the little pans of color about, laid one color against another. I walked away and came near. Suddenly there had flashed into my consciousness, for perhaps the first time in my life, the secret inner world of the painters. Before that time I had wondered often enough why certain paintings, done by the old masters, and hung in our Chicago Art Institute, had so strange an effect upon me. Now I thought I knew. The true painter revealed all of himself in every stroke of his brush. Titian made one feel so utterly the splendor of himself; from Fra Angelico and Sandro Botticelli there came such a deep human tenderness that on some days it fairly brought tears to the eyes; in a most dreadful way and in spite of all his skill Bouguereau gave away his own inner nastiness while Leonardo made one feel all of the grandeur of his mind just as Balzac had made his readers feel the universality and wonder of his mind.

Very well then, the words used by the tale-teller were as the colors used by the painter. Form was another matter. It grew out of the materials of the tale and the teller's reaction to them. It was the tale trying to take form that kicked about inside the tale-teller at night when he wanted to sleep.

And words were something else. Words were the surfaces, the clothes of the tale. I thought I had begun to get something a little clearer now. I had smiled to myself a little at the sudden realization of how little native American words had been used by American story-writers. When most American writers wanted to be very American they went in for slang. Surely we American scribblers had paid long and hard for the English blood in our veins. The English had got their books into our schools, their ideas of correct forms of expression were firmly fixed in our minds. Words as commonly used in our writing were in reality an army that marched in a certain array and the generals in command of the army were still English. One saw the words as marching, always just so—in books—and came to think of them so—in books.

But when one told a tale to a group of advertising men sitting in a barroom in Chicago or to a group of laborers by a factory door in Indiana one instinctively disbanded the army. There were moments then for what have always been called by our correct writers "unprintable words." One got now and then a certain effect by a bit of profanity. One dropped instinctively into the vocabulary of the men about, was compelled to do so to get the full effect sought for the tale. Was the tale he was telling not just the tale of a man named Smoky Pete and how he caught his foot in the trap set for himself?—or perhaps one was giving them the Mama Geigans story. The devil. What had the words of such a tale to do with Thackeray or Fielding? Did the men to whom one told the tale not know a dozen Smoky Petes and Mama Geigans? Had one ventured into the classic English models for tale-telling at that moment there would have been a roar. "What the devil! Don't you go high-toning us!"

And it was sure one did not always seek a laugh from his audience. Sometimes one wanted to move the audience, make them squirm with sympathy. Perhaps one wanted to throw an altogether new light on a tale the audience already knew.

Would the common words of our daily speech in shops and offices do the trick? Surely the Americans among whom one sat talking had felt everything the Greeks had felt, everything the English felt? Deaths came to them, the tricks of fate assailed their lives. I was certain none of them lived felt or talked as the average American novel made them live feel and talk and as for the plot short stories of the magazines—those bastard children of De Maupassant, Poe and O. Henry—it was certain there were no plot short stories ever lived in any life I had known anything about. . . .

For Study and Discussion

1. According to Anderson, what are the "seeds" of stories and where do they come from? In what ways might they differ from James' concept of the *donnée*?

2. Explain Anderson's hostility toward both the *plot* and the *moral* in typical American short stories. Is his criticism essentially the same as Canby's? How convincingly does he support it?

3. Does Anderson differentiate clearly between *form* and *plot* in the short story? In trying to achieve form in his own stories, what sort of problems did he encounter? With what sorts of methods or approaches did he experiment?

4. Does Anderson's analogy between painting and writing, between colors and words, help clarify the problem of form in fiction? In what ways does it help?

5. How can *words* alone assist in creating the form that Anderson was seeking? What kinds of words is he talking about?

6. Discuss the implications of Anderson's statement that form "grew out of the materials of the tale and the teller's reaction to them." Why does he imply that stories like Poe's or O. Henry's fail to meet this criterion?

RING LARDNER

HOW TO WRITE SHORT STORIES

A glimpse at the advertising columns of our leading magazines shows that whatever else this country may be shy of, there is certainly no lack of correspondence schools that learns you the art of short-story writing. The most notorious of these schools makes the boast that one of their pupils cleaned up $5000.00 and no hundreds dollars writing short stories according to the system learnt in their course, though it don't say if that amount was cleaned up in one year or fifty.

However, for some reason another when you skin through the pages of high class periodicals, you don't very often find them cluttered up with stories that was written by boys or gals who had win their phi beta skeleton keys at this or that story-writing college. In fact, the most of the successful authors of the short fiction of to-day never went to no kind of a college, or if they did, they studied piano tuning or the barber trade. They could of got just as far in what I call the literary game if they had of stayed home those four years and helped mother carry out the empty bottles.

The answer is that you can't find no school in operation up to date, whether it be a general institution of learning or a school that specializes in story writing, which can make a great author out of a born druggist.

But a little group of our deeper drinkers has suggested that maybe boys and gals who wants to take up writing as their life work would be benefited if some person like I was to give them a few hints in regards to the technic of the short story, how to go about planning it and writing it, when and where to plant the love interest and climax, and finally how to market the finished product without leaving no bad taste in the mouth.

Well, then, it seems to me like the best method to use in giving out these hints is to try and describe my own personal procedure from the time I get inspired till the time the manuscript is loaded on to the trucks.

The first thing I generally always do is try and get hold of a catchy title, like for instance, "Basil Hargrave's Vermifuge," or "Fun at the Incinerat-

Reprinted from the author's preface to *How to Write Short Stories (with Samples)* (New York: Charles Scribner's Sons, 1924) by permission of the publisher. Copyright 1924 by Charles Scribner's Sons.

ing Plant." Then I set down to a desk or flat table of any kind and lay out 3 or 4 sheets of paper with as many different colored pencils and look at them cock-eyed a few moments before making a selection.

How to begin—or, as we professionals would say, "how to commence"—is the next question. It must be admitted that the method of approach ("L'approchement") differs even among first class fictionists. For example, Blasco Ibañez usually starts his stories with a Spanish word, Jack Dempsey with an "I" and Charley Peterson with a couple of simple declarative sentences about his leading character, such as "Hazel Goodtree had just gone mah jong. She felt faint."

Personally it has been my observation that the reading public prefers short dialogue to any other kind of writing and I always aim to open my tale with two or three lines of conversation between characters—or, as I call them, my puppets—who are to play important roles. I have often found that something one of these characters says, words I have perhaps unconsciously put into his or her mouth, directs my plot into channels deeper than I had planned and changes, for the better, the entire sense of my story.

To illustrate this, let us pretend that I have laid out a plot as follows: Two girls, Dorothy Abbott and Edith Quaver, are spending the heated term at a famous resort. The Prince of Wales visits the resort, but leaves on the next train. A day or two later, a Mexican reaches the place and looks for accommodations, but is unable to find a room without a bath. The two girls meet him at the public filling station and ask him for a contribution to their autograph album. To their amazement, he utters a terrible oath, spits in their general direction and hurries out of town. It is not until years later that the two girls learn he is a notorious forger and realize how lucky they were after all.

Let us pretend that the above is the original plot. Then let us begin the writing with haphazard dialogue and see whither it leads:

"Where was you?" asked Edith Quaver.

"To the taxidermist's," replied Dorothy Abbott.

The two girls were spending the heated term at a famous watering trough. They had just been bathing and were now engaged in sorting dental floss.

"I am getting sick in tired of this place," went on Miss Quaver.

"It is mutual," said Miss Abbott, shying a cucumber at a passing paper-hanger.

There was a rap at their door and the maid's voice announced that company was awaiting them downstairs. The two girls went down and entered the music room. Garnett Whaledriver was at the piano and the girls tiptoed to the lounge.

The big Nordic, oblivious of their presence, allowed his fingers to form weird, fantastic minors before they strayed unconsciously into the first tones of Chopin's 121st Fugue for the Bass Drum.

From this beginning, a skilled writer could go most anywheres, but it would be my tendency to drop these three characters and take up the life of a mule in the Grand Canyon. The mule watches the train come in from the east, he watches the trains come in from the west, and keeps wondering who is going to ride him. But <u>she</u> never finds out.

The love interest and climax would come when a man and a lady, both strangers, got to talking together on the train going back east.

"Well," said Mrs. Croot, for it was she, "what did you think of the Canyon?"

"Some cave," replied her escort.

"What a funny way to put it!" replied Mrs. Croot. "And now play me something."

Without a word, Warren took his place on the piano bench and at first allowed his fingers to form weird, fantastic chords on the black keys. Suddenly and with no seeming intention, he was in the midst of the second movement of Chopin's Twelfth Sonata for Flute and <u>Cuspidor</u>. Mrs. Croot felt faint.

That will give young writers an idea of how an apparently trivial thing such as a line of dialogue will upset an entire plot and lead an author far from the path he had pointed for himself. It will also serve as a model for beginners to follow in regards to style and technic. I will not insult my readers by going on with the story to its obvious conclusion. That simple task they can do for themselves, and it will be good practice.

So much for the planning and writing. Now for the marketing of the completed work. A good many young writers make the mistake of enclosing a stamped, self-addressed envelope, big enough for the manuscript to come back in. This is too much of a temptation to the editor.

Personally I have found it a good scheme to not even sign my name to the story, and when I have got it sealed up in its envelope and stamped and addressed, I take it to some town where I don't live and mail it from there. The editor has no idea who wrote the story, so how can he send it back? He is in a quandary.

In conclusion let me warn my pupils never to write their stories—or, as we professionals call them, "yarns"—on used paper. And never to write them on a post-card. And never to send them by telegraph (Morse code). . . .

For Study and Discussion

1. In reading Lardner's essay, when do you first realize that he is spoofing? Point out specific evidence of his ridicule in the opening paragraphs.

2. What precisely is he satirizing? Does he have a serious underlying purpose? Is his purpose in any way similar to that of Anderson or Canby?

3. What other devices besides ungrammatical language does Lardner employ as a means of achieving ludicrous effects?

4. What is the point of Lardner's plot involving the two girls, Dorothy Abbott and Edith Quaver? What is the purpose of his repeated reference to "weird, fantastic chords"?

5. Is there any point to Lardner's last four paragraphs? How are they related to the central theme developed in the rest of the essay?

6. Lardner's essay might be more accurately entitled "How Not to Write Short Stories," but this title would detract from the essay's chief ingredient, sardonic humor. To what extent is the same ingredient present in his story "Haircut"?

WILLIAM SAROYAN

WHAT IS A STORY?

Whatever else art may be (such as revelation of nature, criticism of
civilization, commentary, propaganda, judgment, social or spiritual
history, or simply entertainment), art is primarily substance selected
accurately, for definite reasons, whether good or not good. Inevitably, of
course, mortality is the final limitation of every art form, and no matter
how wild or profound the imagination, it is no less nourished by the
elements of the earth, so that any thought, however elevated or abstract,
or any vision, however pure, is inevitably rooted in the concrete, and
therefore any perfection in art is no more than a *seeming* perfection, just
as any perfection in nature is tentative, having beginning and ending. In
nature, however, the repetition of perfection is reasonably assured and
the end of a thing is the cause of its beginning again: space and time;
earth, air, water, sun, and all the elements of life; seasons; growth; and
finally decay, dispersal, or death; and then seed, or birth, and growth
again, perfection again, and death again, endlessly: the four seasons, the
order of the universe. And since in nature man's reality is not greatly
different from the reality, let us say, of rodents, man's activity, even in
art, is helplessly the consequence of universal patterns and rhythms; and
therefore the repetition of perfection in art is no more than this same
repetition in nature, and the absolute ending of one is no less unlikely
than the absolute ending of the other. When the universe swallows itself
into nothing, art will swallow itself into nothing, not before.

Nevertheless, there is this truth: substance in art is unlike substance in
nature. The body of art, though closely related to the elements of the
earth and the rhythms of the universe, is a subtler body, composed of
subtler matter, and the rhythm of art is, while no more than an
intensification of universal rhythms (seasons, growth of plants, movements of rivers and seas), finally a different rhythm. It is inevitably the
man himself, and more besides: not simply the man as he would be

Originally published in, and reprinted here from, the *Saturday Review of Literature*,
January 5, 1935. Copyright 1935 by The Saturday Review Company, Inc. Copyright © 1962
by Saturday Review, Inc. Used with permission.

destined to be if he lived simply, innocently, unconsciously, but the man (and his rhythm) as he comes to live through the various stages of growth: disillusion, loss of innocence, creation of consciousness, and finally a return to the mystical and unknown, a new seeking after innocence (which if found now becomes a much nobler innocence than the innocence simply of not knowing, not being aware), and a constant employment of consciousness, imposing it on the whole of the earth, on all life, on every natural rhythm.

This, I think, is the nature of *being* one who creates art, and it is certainly not the nature of being one who simply imitates art, which is another story, and to me a boring one. Anybody can learn to write sentences, paragraphs, and books, and apparently *everybody* seems to have learned enough about writing sentences to want to write books. I doubt, however, if more than a dozen living people are trying to create art, and trying like the devil not to imitate it. In writing there are Joyce, and Stein, Jolas and Cummings and Williams. In drawing and painting there is Picasso; in sculpture Eric Gill and Brancusi and Mestrovic; in music (well, I don't know enough about music even to be able to name several, but certainly I would name American jazz as a whole); and, seriously, in journalism, in the day to day record of the sensational in life, I would name the slaves of William Randolph Hearst, for they are creating what must be identified as art, and then rejected as poor art. The same can even be said for some of the others I have named. I am now interested in the *trying*, and not in the question of whether or not the art created is good or bad. Even when *created* art is bad, it is somewhat good in that it is important, since bad is simply the opposite of good, and good can result from bad in time, and generally does.

What, if anything, is a story? Well, frankly, I do not exactly know, and believe no one exactly knows, and if anyone *does* exactly know, I believe this *knowing* isn't so terrifically important, and if it is important at all, I do not believe it is important enough to stand in the way of the growth of art, which is inevitably the growth of living, and if I myself am interested in anything at all, I am interested in growth, in keeping in motion, in expanding, in not standing still, however artfully. To be petrified, I suppose, is to be perfect after a fashion, but I would rather be wholly alive, in motion, and imperfect. I would certainly prefer to stop writing altogether than to be turned into a pillar of salt. The man who journeys should not turn back to look upon the road he has traveled.

Short, or short short, story or novel, are necessary terms, I suppose, but not too necessary not to be ignored, if need be, and I think need be. Art is not wholly duration, although duration is part of art. What it is mostly is integration, a making of wholeness. An egg is whole, and is an egg no less because it is small or large, ostrich or robin, white or spotted. The wholeness of a billiard ball is unlike the wholeness of an egg in that it cannot be eaten or hatched into a bird. The wholeness of a billiard ball is form alone: the shape round, the color white, the texture smooth, the density even and sustained: form alone. The egg is form AND substance. That is, living substance, mutability, substance growing.

So, if a creation of art is not large, it is no less a creation of art, and even if it is not a story, short or long, it is still a creation of art. I don't care *what* my stuff is called, just so I go on creating it. I don't even care if it is printed and read or not, just so I go on creating it, which is the beginning and the end of my part of the bargain. In a country where the art of ballyhoo is highly developed it is inevitable that even an important writer shall be so widely ballyhooed as to seem to be only another unimportant writer, and this is so because publication of a book, however important, is primarily a business risk, involving money, and the need to sell a book, even if it is great, makes ballyhoo essential, and too much ballyhoo rather amusingly upsets the balance of critics normally sound, and the result is that a great writer is interpreted in terms of the amount of ballyhoo surrounding him, which is critically idiotic, and has absolutely nothing to do with the works of the writer, and less to do with the writer himself. A thing is what it is, especially a created thing. An uncreated thing, an imitated thing, is not even what it is supposed to be, and is therefore largely nothing. It is not a question of whether or not a creation is a story, but a question of whether or not it *is* at all, and if it *is*, but is seemingly not a story, it *is* nevertheless and that's all there is to it.

For Study and Discussion

1. In his opening paragraphs, Saroyan makes several basic comparisons between nature and art. How are these two entities related in his thinking, and what has this relationship to do with the writing of stories?

2. What does Saroyan mean when he says that "man's activity, even in art, is helplessly the consequence of universal patterns and rhythms"?

3. In what sense are the substance and rhythm of art different from the substance and rhythm of nature?

4. If "anybody can learn to write sentences, paragraphs, and books," why does Saroyan doubt that "more than a dozen living people are trying to create art"? Is he being facetious, or is there a serious point at issue here?

5. Does Saroyan answer the question "What Is a Story?" If not, what does he have to say about it?

6. What is the point of his comparison between a billiard ball and an egg? How does this apply to the writing of short stories?

7. Does Saroyan offer any criterion for distinguishing between a "created thing" and an "imitated thing"? How would you judge his own story (p. 386) in the light of this distinction?

TOPICS FOR DISCUSSION AND WRITING

1. In one way or another, each of the writers in this section criticizes certain aspects of the contemporary short story. On what points do they agree? What are some of the significant differences in their thinking? How does each of them distinguish between good and bad stories? In an essay, compare and contrast the views of these writers with those of the critics in Section I.

2. In what ways are Poe, Maupassant, Harte, Kipling, and O. Henry responsible for the vogue of the "formula" story which Canby and others of these critics deplore? Are all "formula" stories necessarily poor stories? Select from the collection what seems to you to be a good example of the "formula" story, and write a detailed analysis of it, arriving at a definite conclusion about its merits or demerits.

3. Do any of the writers in this section offer definite suggestions for improving the techniques of short-story writing? What do they say is needed in order to "free" the art of the short story? To rid it of conventional stereotypes? To develop it into a higher art form? What forces will have to be overcome in bringing about such desired ends?

4. Which of the following stories would satisfy the demands made by this group of writers for free, genuine artistry: "A Hunger Artist," "The Daring Young Man on the Flying Trapeze," "The Fly," "The Strength of God"? Develop your views in an essay.

5. To what extent do these writers agree that the short story should make a valid commentary on real life? What specific suggestions do they offer for strengthening the content and intensifying the impact of short stories? What is the basis for their argument that the story of "form" makes a more valid commentary on life than does the story of "plot"? Write an essay comparing a story of "plot" with a story of "form"; take a position on the issue of whether the "plot notion" necessarily handicaps the writer who wants to make a serious commentary on life.

6. Among the first twenty-three stories in the book (Irving through Lawrence), which two or three do you think Brander Matthews would have found most praiseworthy? Matthews' reviewer? Canby? Anderson? Lardner? Saroyan? Write an essay in the form of an imaginary dialogue or interview between yourself and one of these critics in which your ideas and his regarding the best of these stories are set forth.

III

NEW DIRECTIONS:
FREEDOM AND FORM

As we noted in the introduction to Section II, writers in the 1920s and 1930s began developing the short story in many new ways. By revolting against the stereotyped "formula" story of the commercial magazines and handbooks, they established new standards of form and technique which, though initially often misunderstood or ignored, have now become broadly recognized as significant refinements in the art of short fiction. As a result of these pioneering efforts, stories written by younger contemporaries since the 1940s have appeared in an amazing variety of forms and types, ranging from straight narratives involving recognizable characters in plotted external action to highly stylized, ingenious explorations of mental processes, interior monologues, dream visions, and symbolic fantasies.*

Quite often these contemporary writers, when challenged to explain or justify the aims and directions implicit in their fiction, have turned critic and thus have added substantially to the growing body of critical theory devoted to the whys and wherefores of fiction writing in general as well as of their particular methods of achieving it. To the average reader or student—assuming even a casual interest on his part—the aggregate of these ideas may sometimes seem as bewildering an array of observations and opinions as are the strange and unfamiliar things going on in many of the modern stories. Yet, a careful and representative sampling of recent serious discussion of the contemporary short story will reveal that only a few basic ideas predominate in most of it—and that some of these ideas are surprisingly similar to those of earlier masters like Poe, Hawthorne, Chekhov, or James. In the following thirteen essays, for example, nine of which were written by preeminent artists of the short story in our time, perhaps four fundamental ideas stand out which help clarify the variety of modes exemplified in the thousands of short stories published during the past thirty years. Though but a smattering of recent critical theory, these

---

*Two other forces which have also contributed much during recent decades toward raising literary standards as well as to the volume of high-quality short fiction are the so-called little magazines (literary quarterlies) and the spread of creative writing courses in many of the larger universities—usually under the direction of a professional "writer-in-residence." As Herschel Brickell indicates in his essay, these two forces have worked together to stimulate an interest in creative writing for its own sake rather than for monetary reward.

ideas neatly summarize contemporary thought on the art of today's short fiction.

First of these four ideas is one that may be called inwardness; *that is, the recognition that contemporary fiction writers have tended more and more to focus upon the interaction of mental processes rather than upon external, overt conflicts. Bonaro Overstreet, for example, in the first essay in this section, explains this recent development in general terms by noting that twentieth-century writers, having abandoned two faiths firmly held by their predecessors, have necessarily felt impelled to penetrate ever deeper into human consciousness to account for the seeming chaos of human behavior. Because the "drama of our century," as she puts it, "is the drama of what goes on in the mind," our short-story writers have increasingly concerned themselves not with the logic "of dovetailed incidents that total up to a precise plot," but rather with "the complex logic of mental and emotional experience." Herschel Brickell reiterates this idea of inwardness by saying that the contemporary short story has become "a slice of the mind and the spirit rather than the body." Both he and Overstreet clearly imply—as do many other critics—that although twentieth-century writers, in their eagerness to plumb the mysteries of the subconscious, have had to throw overboard neat plots and happy endings, more has been gained than lost. For even at the cost of seeming distortion, illogicality, grotesqueness, and the absurd, the best modern stories provide a richer illumination of human motives—if not always pleasanter entertainment—than nine-teenth-century stories do because they are truer to life as we know it. Flannery O'Connor in "The Fiction Writer and His Country" defends this position quite ably in explaining the grotesque as a valid means of conveying repugnant distortions of modern life to an unbelieving au-dience—"to the hard of hearing you shout, and for the almost blind you draw large and startling figures"—as well as in her fine statement: "Art requires a delicate adjustment of the outer and inner worlds in such a way that, without changing their nature, they can be seen through each other."*

Granting the accuracy of Miss O'Connor's assertion, one must yet ask how the artist may work to secure that delicate adjustment of the outer and inner worlds. Here again, present-day critics and fiction writers substan-tially agree upon a second basic idea, though they may express it in various ways. It may be designated simply as individuality: *that is, an approach based on artistic integrity, or a need for complete honesty in confronting human experience, and a determination to present what one sees and feels in accordance with an unshakable faith in one's theme and point of view regardless of whether or not one's story is likely to ring the cash register. As Katherine Anne Porter derisively observes in her essay, you don't really need a plot or an O. Henry twist unless you want to make money; but if you want to become a respectable artist, you must "First, have faith in your theme, then get so well acquainted with your characters that they live and grow in your imagination exactly as if you saw them in the flesh; and finally, tell their story with all the truth and tenderness and severity you are capable of. . . ." Clearly implicit in this statement are all the various ideas similarly set forth by Eudora Welty on problems of form, plot, character-ization, sensitivity, and imagination in the creation of durable stories. When she says that every good story has mystery, "not the puzzle kind, but the mystery of allurement," and then goes on to point out why D. H. Lawrence's stories often possess this desirable quality, even though the characters in them may seem deranged, she underscores the values—and the beauty—which a forthright, independent imagination can infuse into a fictional treatment of human relationships. The same idea is again reem-phasized in V. S. Pritchett's brief commentary on the inescapable require-ment of personality—"without personality . . . the storyteller is sunk"— for he stresses the fact that good storytellers, however distinctive their methods or materials, know that they are "putting on a personal, individual act" and thus "owe the indispensable shock they give to the reader to their personality." Again, is there not simply another twist to the same idea in Joyce Carol Oates' beautiful definition of the short story as "a dream verbalized . . . some kind of manifestation of desire . . . the most interest-ing thing about [which] is its mystery"?*

A third idea commonly shared by these writers involves method— *the artist's management and combination of the materials he or she chooses to work with. Since each fiction writer sees life with a distinctive pair of eyes and wishes to place his own individual stamp on what he sees, there would presumably be no limit to the number of methods open to him—and perhaps they are infinitely varied. Yet, there is room for agreement here too. Brickell, for example, talks about "a straight line from the opening to the closing sentence"; and when he adds, in reference to the fascinating blend of the classical and the colloquial in Faulkner's and Welty's stories, that "there is no departure from the rule that the short story writer must proceed directly to where he says he is going," his words reecho Poe's precise utterance over a century ago. Similarly, James Joyce in defining the useful entity* epiphany, *which he contributed to the theory of short fiction, speaks in terms of an organized, climactic procedure involving analysis, synthesis, and the apprehension of symmetry and radiance. His strange sounding terms describe the familiar process of careful selectivity, putting first things first, shearing away everything that does not belong (as Chekhov advised), and heading straight for the climactic disclosure. Truman Capote puts it another way when he talks about realizing "the most natural way of telling the story. The test of whether or not a writer has divined the natural shape of his story is just this: after reading it, can you imagine it differently, or does it silence your imagination and seem to you absolute and final?" And finally, Frank O'Connor, reflecting on the skills and devices so masterfully concealed in the stories of Chekhov, Maupassant, Mansfield, and others, notes that the most important thing for him in the construction of his stories is also the design, "the thing that tells you there's a bad gap in the narrative* here and you really ought to fill that up in some way or another." Clearly, these writers, while insisting on the artist's need to find his own individual form and style, agree that a natural form and style based on the control of his materials must be found if his stories are to rise above mediocrity.

The fourth idea, though unstated, is clearly implicit in virtually everything the critics in this section have to say about the writing of short stories. It might be called the idea of responsibility or of integrity. Whatever it is called, it is simply another way of saying that the writer must be serious; that he must hang on to his self-respect at all costs and be willing to work hard at his craft, day after day, regardless of whether fame and fortune come early or late—or not at all. In Katherine Anne Porter's words: "Be as good a writer as you can, say what you think and feel, add a little something . . . and if you have any character of your own, you will have a style of your own; it grows, as your ideas grow, and as your knowledge of your craft increases." The key words here are character and knowledge, implying a forthright determination to confront life honestly and, knowing one's limitations, to work hard. Flannery O'Connor gives the idea another twist in saying that to know oneself is "also to know the world, and it is also, paradoxically, a form of exile from that world." Frank O'Connor, speaking of his own practice, admits that he finds it necessary to rewrite a story "Endlessly, endlessly, endlessly. And keep on rewriting" even after it has been published. And Truman Capote puts it even more bluntly in disposing of the question of devices for improving technique: "Work is the only device I know of. . . . Too many writers seem to consider the writing of short stories as a kind of finger exercise." As a prescription for success in the writing of short stories, perhaps what all of these authors have been saying is very much like the advice which Henry James long ago said he would offer to a novice in the art of fiction: "Try to be one of the people on whom nothing is lost!"

If one were to skim casually through any typical collection of recently published "best" short stories, one would be forced to conclude that the short story has come a long way since the time of Washington Irving's tentative experiments in this narrative form. And where it is going from here is anybody's guess. For as one perceptive artist has noted approvingly, some of the most fascinating contemporary stories are strange ones "that call attention to themselves as artificial constructions, daring us to believe in them." Given the broad freedom of expression which today's artist can claim, some of these stories are indeed bewildering, even at times irritating and repellent, since they may portray human actions, attitudes, and motives once thought of as unspeakable. And yet, if the experience of reading such stories, however odd or "unrealistic" their form, moves today's readers as strongly as Poe's tales of "the grotesque and arabesque" moved the readers of his day, it will be because today's artists—no less than Poe or Irving—have learned the secrets of a technique involving a "nicety of execution."

BONARO OVERSTREET

LITTLE STORY, WHAT NOW?

Is it really time to weave funeral wreaths for the short story? We gather that impression from various critics who tell us, dolefully, that this well-beloved form is not what it once was. But must all things die that are not what they once were?

The short story has had a peculiar history—and in this history lies a clue to why critics pronounce elegies over it whenever it shows an unfamiliar face. Most literary types belong to the ages. The short story belongs to the nineteenth century.

The short story that bears that trade-mark is, first of all, a story with a plot—a close-knit structure that can be seen steadily and whole. In the well-constructed story of plot, of incident and coincident, things happen —and nothing happens that does not push the story along toward its climax. The skillful writer of the nineteenth-century story had his materials as well in hand, as obedient to his organizing will, as had the strong man who spanned a continent with a railroad. He, too, in his own way, was a competent executive.

A respect for action and the fruits of action, however, is not an isolated phenomenon. Psychologically, it cannot be. It has to be underwritten by two basic faiths. Joined with these, action becomes an efficient means to an end. Without them, it becomes—as it became during the twenties of our own century—a frenetic means of escape from having to think about ends. These two faiths necessary to an eager respect for action permeated nineteenth-century thinking—and the nineteenth-century short story.

The first of these faiths was simply that it is possible—indeed, natural—for people to know the difference between right and wrong. The short story might have its villain—drunkard, thief, exploiter, snob, traitor, forecloser of a mortgage, or what not—but there was a clear assumption, accepted alike by author and public, that the behavior of

Originally published in, and reprinted here from, the *Saturday Review of Literature*, November 22, 1941. Copyright 1941 by The Saturday Review Company, Inc. Copyright © 1968 by Saturday Review, Inc. Used with permission.

such a villain went counter to something so fundamental in the scheme of things that he must repent or perish. The life of action, in fiction or out, can command respect when, and only when, the basic code of values is taken for granted—and rare indeed in the nineteenth century were stories of ethical *laissez faire*.

The second faith was that people are, for the most part, what they seem to be. They may be torn by temptations, but their struggles are above-board—part of their conscious, active experience. They may be afraid, but their fears attach to known causes in the objective world and can be overcome by fitting activity. They may be guilty of deceit, but scarcely of self-deceit: they know well enough what they are up to, and sooner or later they give themselves away by their conduct. Here, again, is a faith that must accompany an eager belief in action: for since men of action cannot be forever hunting out obscure motives and hidden clues, they have to assume a reliable correspondence between inner character and outward behavior. In the nineteenth century people commonly assumed such a correspondence. Story writers did likewise, and based their plots upon it.

What of the twentieth century? It is not, in the same sense as the nineteenth, marked by *eventfulness*. To say this may seem paradoxical—even absurd. For more things happen every day, every minute, than ever before. But *eventfulness* is a psychological as well as a physical matter—and the twentieth century is dog-tired of action: action that goes on because it cannot seem to stop; that is always having to go on to counterbalance other action that is likewise going on because it cannot stop.

What event, now—what physical discovery, or new mechanism—can stir the satiated, event-ridden imagination of man to visions of a brave new world? Our age-old Icarian dream took shape in the first clumsy aeroplane that lifted its wings from the earth; and within two decades the bombing plane was dumping its loads of death upon cities. If we take this as symbolic of what has happened to one after another of the machines and enterprises to which we attached our faith, we can say that the dropped bombs have ripped raw caverns not only in the streets of cities but in the hearts of men; they have reduced to rubble not only our houses but our hopes. It was a splendid thing for man to invent a plane that could conquer space. But what value is there in his inventing a plane that can merely hold its own against another death-dealing plane: hold its own, that is, until the enemy model is improved so that he will have to improve his own model to hold his own? Not by such a vicious circle as this can an eager faith in action be kept alive.

In the twentieth century, because we have lost the faiths that must underpin a confident life of action, we are being thrown back upon a study of human nature—human motives, fears, wants, prejudices. The drama of our century is the drama of what goes on in the mind. The outward action—whether it be the slightest gesture of a hand or the ruthless invasion of one nation by another—is significant only as it throws light upon the obscure mental and emotional states that have bred it.

The characteristic science of our century is psychology. It has naturalized in our speech such words and phrases as *inferiority complex, stream of consciousness, inhibition, the subconscious, frustration, rationalization.* These are not action-words. They reflect our growing need to understand what goes on in the hidden corners of our human nature.

What of the short story in our century? Its future is as unpredictable as that of all our other institutions. But this we can say: during the past several decades it has become a more and more expert medium for the expression of our deep concern about human moods and motives— moods and motives that have shown themselves to be far less transparent than we once thought they were.

Two protests commonly made against the current short story are, first, that it specializes in the unpleasant and abnormal and, second, that it is formless—has no plot. (Thus Irvin S. Cobb, in a recent interview in the *New York Times,* spoke the mind of disgruntled critics and public alike when he said, "I couldn't do these things they publish now, with no beginning and no end and a little incest in the middle.") Both of these charges against the short story can be maintained with a show of reason. But the sober critic who cares more about understanding the new than expressing his nostalgia for the old may choose to suspend judgment— may suspect that these faults are transition-faults. The nineteenth-century story-teller was a master of plot. His twentieth-century fellow, seeing that life was not made up of neatly parcelled collections of incidents, took his rebel stand: let his stream-of-consciousness dictate his words. The nineteenth-century writer—for reasons of common faith—wrought happy endings even out of situations that seemed logically to promise little happiness. The twentieth-century writer—for reasons of common cynicism—first turned to the unhappy and abnormal. Anyone, however, who makes an unbiased approach to the short stories being written today will realize, I think, that these are no longer either formless or swaggeringly dedicated to the sordid.

The twentieth-century story-teller is becoming, in his own way, a master of rigorous form. But to understand this form, we must recognize that it is dictated by psychological materials and processes, not primarily by events in the objective world. Its logic is not, and cannot be, that of dovetailed incidents that total up to a precise plot—a plot that any teacher of English can outline on a blackboard. Its logic is the complex logic of mental and emotional experience. Associate linkages, personal memories and fears and faiths, rationalized reasons for behavior, subsurface thinking that goes on in contradiction to surface talk—all these, and a multitude of other factors, must be recognized by the writer, today, as part of the deeper logic of any given situation. In determining its outcome, they may be far more important than are objective events.

Some readers complain that nothing happens in modern stories. But we all know from our own experience that a great deal can be happening—that volcanic changes in mind and mood can take place—when there is scarcely a surface ripple for the casual observer to detect. Objective events are necessary for drama in inverse proportion to the psychological charge that a situation carries. If little is thought or felt, much must happen; if much is thought and felt, no elaborate stacking-up of incidents is necessary for dramatic catharsis through pity and fear. The pity and fear of human thinking and feeling is what dictates the strict form which the twentieth-century story is learning to impose upon itself.

As for the complaint that stories are deliberately unpleasant, I think the answer must be that they are as unpleasant as sincerity makes them—neither more nor less. When first-rate nineteenth-century writers made a clear distinction between right and wrong, and provided in their plot for the triumph of the former, they were not insincere. They were not trying to be a good influence, nor to furnish their readers with an easy avenue of escape from ugliness. The confidence they expressed in the basic rationality of life was their own sincere confidence. The happy ending became a trivial formula only when genuine faith no longer gave it solid meaning. The twentieth-century rebellion has been against formulated insincerity, against stories that went on using the spent trappings of faith after the faith had gone. Moralists who now urge that writers should be purveyors of good cheer had best recognize the dubiousness of their own position: they are asking that writers practise a profound insincerity—and that is an odd thing for moralists to ask. The average man, today, does not go at life with confident faith. He does not believe all is well with the world, nor that providence insures a happy ending to all our human tangles. Is it probable that the writer, more sensitive than the average, can go through today's world clothed in a sense of glory?

The happy-ending story still exists as an avenue of escape for millions. But what kind of escape do we really want our writers to provide? Do we ask only that they provide us with a few moments of forgetfulness? Or do we ask that they, with their peculiar power to go beyond the obvious, so add to our own understanding of the life we live that we can become, because of our companionship with them, better equipped to see with our eyes and hear with our ears?

It seems to me that the short story, today, far from being in a state of decline, is approaching a state where it can rightly mean more than it has ever meant. As it becomes increasingly deft in its power to portray our individual and social complexity, it will offer a veritable treasure house of insight-materials not only to lay readers whose main preoccupation is living with their human fellows but to sociologists and psychologists. At a time when an understanding of human behavior seems the only alternative to racial suicide, we can thank our lucky stars that our short-story writers, with full sincerity, are at the job of trying to understand. If they ask us to face unpleasant realities, that is certainly not more than life itself is asking. And if they work to mature a form that is true to the intricate logic of their psychological materials, we would do ill to complain that their stories do not have a traditional array of incidents woven into a close-knit plot.

The short story has enjoyed one rich period of development. It is entering upon another period which, I believe, promises even greater richness, more subtle wisdom and beauty. In a changing world, this new development may be cut short by altered conditions. But if the twentieth-century story has a chance to mature along the lines of its present growth, it will make its own unique place in literary history.

For Study and Discussion

1. On what two faiths concerning human nature was the plot story of the nineteenth century based?

2. What has brought about the decline of these two faiths in the twentieth century? What marked changes in the content and technique of the short story has this decline precipitated?

3. What two protests are commonly made against the twentieth-century short story? How does Overstreet refute these protests? Are her arguments convincing? Apply them to several stories in the text such as those by Toomer, Saroyan, Capote, Flannery O'Connor, and Oates.

4. According to Overstreet, what dictates the form of the twentieth-century story? Compare her viewpoint on form with those of Anderson, Saroyan, and Welty.

5. Why does Overstreet believe that the twentieth-century story offers valuable insights not only to the general reader but also to the sociologist and psychologist?

HARRY SHAW

SOME CLINICAL NOTES

What has become of the good short stories? Fewer and fewer are appearing in the old quality and experimental periodicals; many of these magazines now carry no fiction at all. Is it time for the long-mourned personal essay to move over and make room for another obsolescent type? . . .

Is it "the temper of the times"? For more than twenty years, editors and writers have been declaring that the American reading public is "fact-hungry." Wars, rumors of wars, depression, recession, and labor upheavals have tended to make people "look at the record." And yet this country has known many periods of national unrest and anxiety in the past hundred years without an eclipse of short fiction; actually, in troubled times, the public has sought release and escape through fiction. Furthermore, fiction has usually been considered a more powerful and illuminating medium than non-fiction for the probing of problems. No, some other explanation is needed.

Another answer is that some of the better short-story writers have simply stopped contributing to the quality magazines and have turned to better-paying fields. This is true, to some extent, yet it is no new development; writers have been doing just that in this country for decades. But what has become of the custom of "arrived" authors, writing for the mass-circulation, big-paying magazines, the colossi, occasionally contributing a story to one of the quality periodicals because of the "prestige" involved? Perhaps the prestige of the qualities has faded somewhat and writers are increasingly more eager to take the cash and let the credit go. But some less partial, more valid explanation still seems needed.

Many short-story writers have gone to Hollywood, others now prepare radio scripts. It seems obvious, however, that most film and radio writers have been recruited from among "popular" authors, those who might best or most easily touch mass minds and mass emotions. Unquestionably the movies and the radio are competing with magazine stories for people's attention; but the competition logically, although not

Originally published in, and reprinted here from, the *Saturday Review of Literature*, November 22, 1941. Copyright 1941 by The Saturday Review Company, Inc. Copyright © 1968 by Saturday Review, Inc. Used with permission.

actually, is more severe in the field of mass-circulation magazines than among serious publications. Few authentic, talented short-story writers have worked regularly or for any extended period of time in either industry. The good writers are not in Hollywood and the broadcasting studios in significant numbers, nor are they lost in new media. How many original, outstanding scenarios or radio scripts have appeared to rival the great quality magazine stories of the past?

Some editors insist that very few good short stories are currently available. The commercial appeal of the standardized story has probably undermined the potential artistry of some writers, men and women who might have developed into significant figures. And yet, although authors must eat and all artists are profoundly influenced by their times, scores of fiction writers in the past have refused to be cheapened by prevailing trade winds. Since 1929, some experimental magazines—proving grounds for many authentic writers—have expired. But "little" magazines have always had a "now-you-see-them-now-you-don't" existence. Large numbers of them have appeared all through the past decade, quite enough to print the best output of the apprentice fictioneer. Today there are sufficient experimental and quality magazines, and quite enough intelligent, even astute editors to publish whatever significant, high-grade fiction is available. *Story*, for example, has been publishing consistently sound fiction for the past decade (although it, too, has frequently carried *novellas* in addition to short stories of "standard" length). Similarly, *Esquire* and *The New Yorker* have managed to publish considerable worthwhile short fiction during recent years. But, as has been remarked earlier, the quantitative fictional decline in the older quality magazines is far greater than the combined story output of these periodicals and other "recent arrivals."

The best explanation of the dearth of artistic, worthwhile short stories lies in the resurgence of another type of writing. The magazine article has come of age, technically and stylistically. Non-fiction writers have outstripped the field in the race for the coveted, limited space available in periodicals. Many of the potentially best short-story writers, if not sleeping, have at least been dozing at the switch. And a few, as already indicated, have been working for another railroad. While somnolent or absent, they have allowed article writers to steal many of the stylistic qualities and techniques which they themselves had developed and perfected. The best magazine articles today are more meaty than short stories and just as entertaining. Story technique, excellent though it has become, has tended to remain static, standardized, whereas article writing has reached new levels, sometimes artistic, sometimes tricky, but consistently appealing.

More and more editors and authors are learning that truth is not only stranger than fiction but that it can be made more entertaining. Thirty or twenty or even ten years ago, much periodical non-fiction was ponderous; "think-pieces" and philosophical essays appeared in polysyllabic and involved dullness. Quality magazines carried them because of their importance and to add "tone," but they relied upon short stories to furnish entertainment and sell copies. Not so today. A glance at the paid advertising of even big-circulation magazines such as *The Saturday Evening Post, Colliers, Liberty,* and some of the women's periodicals, will reveal that fact is more "featured" than fiction in luring prospective purchasers and advertisers. The article writer is in the saddle.

Today's editor knows that readers can flip pages, throw down the magazine, turn on the radio, or go to the movies. He sees to it that his readers are not bored. He recognizes that they have rights, presumably the major part of which is insurance against dullness. The successful article writer, realizing that virtually all readers have an exceptional capacity for resisting information, will delete whole chunks of laboriously acquired data, will "streamline" facts, cover them with chocolate, and present something which may be informative and significant but will certainly be palatable and entertaining.

In all popular and most quality magazines, today's article moves quickly and interestingly because of its "aids to interest," such as dialogue, incidents, characterization, anecdotes, and humor. Some fact writers use even the "flash-back" technique of the short story—beginning with some dramatic scene or incident and proceeding with the article logically and chronologically. They use the tested method of advertising writing: first, get the reader's attention; then arouse his interest; next, make him want to read further; finally, secure a positive reaction to the message presented.

One successful and important article writer always tells students that non-fiction for both quality and popular periodicals must sound like an intelligent conversation at dinner. "Assume," says he, "that your dinner partner has asked a question about some subject which you know pretty thoroughly. You would answer her simply and animatedly, not weigh her down with statistics nor talk like a walking encyclopedia. You would tell her first those things and facts which furnish the clearest possible picture of the subject, and the most authentic, and you would constantly remember that certain matters interesting to you might not appeal to her. Try to write the way you would talk. Don't be stuffy and don't be dull."

That hundreds of writers are following this advice is fully evident. Few non-fiction contributors today assume a pontifical pose, regardless of their authority. And readers are responding to these new attitudes and techniques. It's no longer difficult to read articles. Some intellectually snobbish readers, culture-thirsty, even congratulate themselves upon reading authoritative, meaty articles rather than "just another story."

What is happening is that increasing numbers of magazines are following the lead set twenty years ago by a few foresighted publications. As far back as 1920, and even before, the *Atlantic* was running many warmly human, highly individualistic travel sketches, personal experience articles, and even letters. These contributions, increasingly continued through the years, were essentially factual and yet obviously fictional in appeal. The magazine made no attempt then, as now, to differentiate between story and fact. The *Atlantic*, among others, realized twenty years ago that more important non-fiction is available for printing than significant short fiction. It is also worth noting that two of the three full-length books which the *Atlantic* serialized in 1940 were non-fiction. When unsuccessful attempts were being made to resuscitate *Scribner's* between 1936 and 1939, the editors tried desperately by means of correspondence, personal contacts, and contests to build up not the fiction content of the magazine but the widely popular and genuinely significant "Life in the United States" department. These practices were but straws in the wind, indicating that the important short story was not being produced in numbers, or not being recognized, or not wanted.

Today, some editors, many writers, and all "schools of writing" and writer's magazines seem blissfully unaware of what has happened. But the quality story's number is up, at least for the present, and unless something is done to scotch the slide, our ablest story writers are going to find it increasingly difficult to find a market. A few seem to have waked up: within recent months several worthwhile short narratives based upon careful research have appeared. They are so impregnated with facts about army camp life, armaments, or the Gestapo that they seem little different from articles except in the use of hypothetical situations and protagonists. They represent almost a new type—a "factual narrative"—capitulation to the now long-current mania for fact. The method is not entirely new, for *Liberty* experimented with factual narratives ten years ago, without notable success.

The facts seem plain: fewer and fewer short stories, more and more articles are appearing in the quality magazines. More non-fiction books are being serialized. Full-length novels are appearing in space formerly reserved for short stories. Every outstandingly successful magazine started in the past fifteen years has been devoted wholly or mainly to fact. Editors are not cheating readers of their due; important story writers have been overwhelmed by the *Panzer* divisions of an up-to-date army of factual writers.

American reading tastes have radically changed.

For Study and Discussion

1. Why does Shaw believe that "the quality story's number is up, at least for the present"? What reasons does he give for its decline?

2. What devices or techniques has the modern nonfiction writer "borrowed" from the fiction writer?

3. What does Shaw mean by the term "factual narrative"? Could this description be applied to any of the stories in this collection?

KATHERINE ANNE PORTER

NO PLOT, MY DEAR, NO STORY

This is a fable, children, of our times. There was a great big little magazine with four and one half million subscribers, or readers, I forget which; and the editors sat up nights thinking of new ways to entertain these people who bought their magazine and made a magnificent argument to convince advertisers that $3,794.36 an inch space-rates was a mere gift at the price. Look at all the buying-power represented. Look at all the money these subscribers must have if they can afford to throw it away on a magazine like the one we are talking about. So the subscribers subscribed and the readers read and the advertisers bought space and everything went on ring-around-the-rosy like that for God knows how long. In fact, it is going on right now.

So the editors thought up something beautiful and sent out alarms to celebrated authors and the agents of celebrated authors, asking every-body to think hard and remember the best story he had ever read, anywhere, anytime, and tell it over again in his own words, and he would be paid a simply appalling price for this harmless pastime.

By some mistake a penniless and only semi-celebrated author got on this list, and as it happened, that was the day the government had threatened to move in and sell the author's typewriter for taxes overdue, and a dentist had threatened to sue for a false tooth in the very front of the author's face; and there was also a grocery bill. So this looked as if Providence had decided to take a hand in the author's business, and he or she, it doesn't matter, sat down at once and remembered at least *one* of the most beautiful stories he or she had ever read anywhere.* It was all about three little country women finding a wounded man in a ditch, giving him cold water to drink out of his own cap, piling him into their cart and taking him off to a hospital, where the doctors said they might have saved their trouble for the man was as good as dead.

Originally published in *The Writer*, June 1942. Reprinted here from *The Collected Essays and Occasional Writings of Katherine Anne Porter* (New York: Delacorte Press, 1970) by permission of the publisher. Copyright 1942 by Katherine Anne Porter. A Seymour Lawrence Book/Delacorte Press.
*"Living Water" by C. Sergeev-Tzensky, *The Dial,* July 1929.

The little women were just silly enough to be happy anyway that they had found him, and he wasn't going to die by himself in a ditch, at any rate. So they went on to market.

A month later they went back to the hospital, each carrying a wreath to put on the grave of the man they had rescued and found him there still alive in a wheelchair; and they were so overcome with joy they couldn't think, but just dropped on their knees in gratitude that his life was saved; this in spite of the fact that he probably was not going to be of any use to himself or anybody else for a long time if ever. . . . It was a story about instinctive charity and selfless love. The style was fresh and clear as the living water of their tenderness.

You may say that's not much of a story, but I hope you don't for it would pain me to hear you agree with the editors of that magazine. They sent it back to the author's agent with a merry little note: "No plot, my dear—no *story*. Sorry."

So it looks as if the tax collector will get the author's typewriter, and the dentist the front tooth, and the crows may have the rest; and all because the poor creature was stupid enough to think that a short story needed *first* a *theme*, and then a point of view, a certain knowledge of human nature and strong feeling about it, and style—that is to say, his own special way of telling a thing that makes it precisely his own and no one else's. . . . The greater the theme and the better the style, the better the story, you might say.

You might say, and it would be nice to think you would. Especially if you are an author and write short stories. Now listen carefully: except in emergencies, when you are trying to manufacture a quick trick and make some easy money, you don't really need a plot. If you have one, all well and good, if you know what it means and what to do with it. If you are aiming to take up the writing *trade*, you need very different equipment from that which you will need for the *art*, or even just the *profession* of writing. There are all sorts of schools that can teach you exactly how to handle the 197 variations on any one of the 37 basic plots; how to take a parcel of characters you never saw before and muddle them up in some difficulty and get the hero or heroine out again, and dispose of the bad uns; they can teach you the O. Henry twist; the trick of "slanting" your stuff toward this market and that; you will learn what goes over big, what not so big, what doesn't get by at all; and you will learn for yourself, if you stick to the job, *why* all this happens. Then you are all set, maybe. After that you have only to buy a pack of "Add-a-Plot" cards (free ad.) and go ahead. Frankly, I wish you the luck you deserve. You have richly earned it.

But there are other and surer and much more honest ways of making money, and Mama advises you to look about and investigate them before leaping into such a gamble as mercenary authorhood. Any plan to make money is a gamble, but grinding out "slanted" stuff takes a certain knack, a certain willingness to lose all, including honor; you will need a cold heart and a very thick skin and an allowance from your parents while you are getting started toward the big money. You stand to lose your youth, your eyesight, your self-respect, and whatever potentialities you may have had in other directions, and if the worst comes to the worst, remember, nobody promised you anything. . . . Well, if you are going to throw all that, except the self-respect, into the ash can, you may as well, if you wish to write, be as good a writer as you can, say what you think and feel, add a little something, even if it is the merest fraction of an atom, to the sum of human achievement.

First, have faith in your theme, then get so well acquainted with your characters that they live and grow in your imagination exactly as if you saw them in the flesh; and finally, tell their story with all the truth and tenderness and severity you are capable of; and if you have any character of your own, you will have a style of your own; it grows, as your ideas grow, and as your knowledge of your craft increases.

You will discover after a great while that you are probably a writer. You may even make some money at it.

One word more: I have heard it said, boldly and with complete sincerity by persons who should know better, that the only authors who do not write for the high-paying magazines are those who have not been able to make the grade; that any author who professes to despise or even disapprove of such writing and such magazines is a hypocrite; that he would be too happy to appear in those pages if only he were invited.

To such effrontery I have only one answer, based on experience and certain knowledge. It is simply not true.

For Study and Discussion

1. In your opinion, is the story Porter summarizes "much of a story" or not?

2. What other elements of fiction does Porter place ahead of plot? Which two of these does she imply are the most important? Under what circumstances does a writer need a plot?

3. In Porter's view, what happens to the writer who approaches story writing as a *trade* rather than as an *art*? What is the clear distinction that she draws between writing as a trade or profession and writing as an art?

4. With which other critics does Porter's general viewpoint most closely agree? Anderson's? Saroyan's? Welty's?

5. Comment on the validity and force of Porter's concluding paragraphs. What do they tell you about her stature as a writer?

Be familiar w/ the parts we discussed in class

JAMES JOYCE

DEFINITION OF EPIPHANY

He [Stephen Hero] was passing through Eccles' St one evening, one misty evening, with all these thoughts dancing the dance of unrest in his brain when a trivial incident set him composing some ardent verses which he entitled a "Vilanelle of the Temptress." A young lady was standing on the steps of one of those brown brick houses which seem the very incarnation of Irish paralysis. A young gentleman was leaning on the rusty railings of the area. Stephen as he passed on his quest heard the following frag:ment of colloquy out of which he received an impression keen enough to afflict his sensitiveness very severely.

The Young Lady—(drawling discreetly) . . . O, yes . . . I was . . . at the . . . cha . . . pel . . .

The Young Gentleman—(inaudibly) . . . I . . . (again inaudibly) . . . I . . .

The Young Lady—(softly) . . . O . . . but you're . . . ve . . . ry . . . wick . . . ed . . .

This triviality made him think of collecting many such moments together in a book of epiphanies. By an epiphany he meant a sudden spiritual manifestation, whether in the vulgarity of speech or of gesture or in a memorable phase of the mind itself. He believed that it was for the man of letters to record these epiphanies with extreme care, seeing that they themselves are the most delicate and evanescent of moments. He told Cranly that the clock of the Ballast Office was capable of an epiphany. Cranly questioned the inscrutable dial of the Ballast Office with his no less inscrutable countenance:

—Yes, said Stephen. I will pass it time after time, allude to it, refer to it, catch a glimpse of it. It is only an item in the catalogue of Dublin's street furniture. Then all at once I see it and I know at once what it is: epiphany.

An excerpt originally published in James Joyce's *Stephen Hero*, edited by Theodore Spencer (New York: New Directions Press, 1944). Reprinted here from a new edition, eds. John J. Slocum and Herbert Cahoon (New York: New Directions Press, 1959), by permission of The Society of Authors as the literary representative of the Estate of James Joyce, the executors of the James Joyce Estate, the editor, and Jonathan Cape Ltd.

—What?

—Imagine my glimpses at that clock as the gropings of a spiritual eye which seeks to adjust its vision to an exact focus. The moment the focus is reached the object is epiphanised. It is just in this epiphany that I find the third, the supreme quality of beauty.

—Yes? said Cranly absently.

—No esthetic theory, pursued Stephen relentlessly, is of any value which investigates with the aid of the lantern of tradition. What we symbolise in black the Chinaman may symbolise in yellow: each has his own tradition. Greek beauty laughs at Coptic beauty and the American Indian derides them both. It is almost impossible to reconcile all tradition whereas it is by no means impossible to find the justification of every form of beauty which has ever been adored on the earth by an examination into the mechanism of esthetic apprehension whether it be dressed in red, white, yellow or black. We have no reason for thinking that the Chinaman has a different system of digestion from that which we have though our diets are quite dissimilar. The apprehensive faculty must be scrutinised in action.

—Yes . . .

—You know what Aquinas says: The three things requisite for beauty are, integrity, a wholeness, symmetry and radiance. Some day I will expand that sentence into a treatise. Consider the performance of your own mind when confronted with any object, hypothetically beautiful. Your mind to apprehend that object divides the entire universe into two parts, the object, and the void which is not the object. To apprehend it you must lift it away from everything else: and then you perceive that it is one integral thing, that is *a* thing. You recognise its integrity. Isn't that so?

—And then?

—That is the first quality of beauty: it is declared in a simple sudden synthesis of the faculty which apprehends. What then? Analysis then. The mind considers the object in whole and in part, in relation to itself and to other objects, examines the balance of its parts, contemplates the form of the object, traverses every cranny of the structure. So the mind receives the impression of the symmetry of the object. The mind recognises that the object is in the strict sense of the word, a *thing*, a definitely constituted entity. You see?

—Let us turn back, said Cranly.

They had reached the corner of Grafton St and as the footpath was overcrowded they turned back northwards. Cranly had an inclination to watch the antics of a drunkard who had been ejected from a bar in Suffolk St but Stephen took his arm summarily and led him away.

—Now for the third quality. For a long time I couldn't make out what Aquinas meant. He uses a figurative word (a very unusual thing for him) but I have solved it. *Claritas* is *quidditas*. After the analysis which discovers the second quality the mind makes the only logically possible synthesis and discovers the third quality. This is the moment which I call epiphany. First we recognise that the object is one integral thing, then we recognise that it is an organised composite structure, a *thing* in fact: finally, when the relation of the parts is exquisite, when the parts are adjusted to the special point, we recognise that it is *that* thing which it is. Its soul, its whatness, leaps to us from the vestment of its appearance. The soul of the commonest object, the structure of which is so adjusted, seems to us radiant. The object achieves its epiphany.

Having finished his argument Stephen walked on in silence. He felt Cranly's hostility and he accused himself of having cheapened the eternal images of beauty. For the first time, too, he felt slightly awkward in his friend's company and to restore a mood of flippant familiarity he glanced up at the clock of the Ballast Office and smiled:

—It has not epiphanised yet, he said.

For Study and Discussion

1. According to one scholar, Joyce's "Theory of epiphanies," presented in the conversation between Stephen Hero and his friend Cranly, is "central to our understanding of Joyce as an artist" (Theodore Spencer in his Introduction to *Stephen Hero*, 1963, p. 16). Is *epiphany* as Joyce uses the term synonymous with *revelation*? If not, how do the terms differ?

2. Why does Hero (Joyce's mouthpiece) believe that the writer should "record . . . epiphanies with extreme care"?

3. How could the clock on the Ballast Office become epiphanized?

4. Does Joyce's story "Araby" involve an epiphany? If so, where in the story does it occur, and what is its significance?

5. Do other modern story writers also make use of the epiphany principle? Examine such stories as Mansfield's "The Fly," K. A. Porter's "Theft," Capote's "A Tree of Night," and Taylor's "Mrs. Billingsby's Wine" and try to identify an epiphany in each of them.

EUDORA WELTY

THE READING AND WRITING OF SHORT STORIES

Experience teaches us that when we are in the act of writing we are alone and on our own, in a kind of absolute state of Do Not Disturb. And experience tells us further that each story is a specific thing, never a general thing—never. The words in the story we are writing now might as well never have been used before. They all shine; they are never smudged. Stories are *new* things, stories make words new; that is one of their illusions and part of their beauty. And of course the great stories of the world are the ones that seem new to their readers on and on, always new because they keep their power of revealing something.

But although all stories in the throes of being written seem new and although good stories are new and persist, there will always be some characteristics and some functions about them as old as time, as human nature itself, to keep them more or less alike, at least of a family; and there may be other things, undiscovered yet, in the language, in technique, in the world's body of knowledge, to change them out of our present recognition. Critics, historians, and scholars deal with these affairs—and keep good track of them—while for us, the practitioners, the writing of stories seems to simmer down—between stories—into some generalities that are worth talking about. . . .

How do we write a story? Our own way. Beyond that, I think it is hard to assign a process to it.

The mind in writing a story is in the throes of imagination, and it is not in the calculations of analysis. There is a Great Divide in the workings of the mind, shedding its energy in two directions: it creates in imagination, and it tears down in analysis. The two ways of working have a great way of worrying the life out of each other. But why can't they both go their ways in peace?

Let's not, to begin with, deny the powers and achievements of good criticism. That would be smug, ignorant, and blind. Story criticism can

Originally published in, and reprinted here from, the *Atlantic Monthly*, February 1949, and March 1949, by permission of Random House, Inc. Copyright 1949 by Eudora Welty.

seem blind itself, when it is ingrown and tedious; on the other hand, it can see things in large wholes and in subtle relationships we should be only stupid not to investigate. It can illuminate even though, in the face of all its achievements, its business is not: to tell *how*. There is the Great Divide.

I feel like saying as a friend, to beginning writers, Don't be unduly worried by the analyses of stories you may see in some textbooks or critical articles. They are brilliant, no doubt useful to their own ends, but should not be alarming, for in a practical sense they just do not bear in a practical way on writing. To use my own case, that being the only one I can rightly speak of, I have been baffled by analysis and criticism of some of my stories. When I see them analyzed—most usually, "reduced to elements"—sometimes I think, "This is none of me." Not that I am too proud to like being reduced, especially; but that I could not remember *starting* with those elements—with anything that I could so label. The fact that a story will reduce to elements, can be analyzed, does not necessarily mean it started with them—certainly not consciously. A story can start with a bird song.

Criticism, or more strictly, analysis, is an impossible way to learn how the story was written. Analysis is a one-way process, and is only good after the event. In the newsreel pictures when the dive is shown in reverse, a swimmer can come back out of the water; the splash is swallowed up, he rises in the air and is safe and dry back on the diving board. But in truth you can't come by way of analysis back to the starting point of inspiration; that's against some law of the universe, it might almost seem. I myself lack a scientific upbringing; I hear the arrow of time exists, and I feel quite certain, by every instinct, so does the arrow of creation.

. . . A story is not the same thing when it ends that it was when it began. Something happens—the writing of it. It *becomes.* And as a story becomes, I believe we as readers understand by becoming too—by enjoying.

Let's look at some short stories as writers of stories ourselves and people who like them; let's see a little how they are disposed, watch them in their motions, and enjoy them.

Luckily, we shall have none of the problems of *not* enjoying them. Putting a story in its place—we shall escape that. Putting a story in its place when its place has become the important thing means absolutely not giving over to the story. It also means taking oneself with proper seriousness, keeping close watch not to make a fool of oneself, and watching limbs, lest one go out on a few. Enjoying them, we can go out on many a limb. Yet there is really a tougher requirement for enjoying: flexibility and openness of the mind—of the pores, possibly. For heaven forbid we should feel disgrace in seeking understanding by way of pleasure.

We would be sure of this, I believe, if we asked ourselves, How would we wish a story of our own to be understood? By way of delight—by its being purely read, for the first fresh impact and the wonder attached; isn't this the honest answer? It seems to me too that almost the first hope we ever had, when we gave someone a story all fresh and new, was that the story would *read new*. And that's how we should read.

What bliss! Think how often this is denied us. That's why we think of childhood books so lovingly. But hasn't every writer the rightful wish to have his story so read? And isn't this wish implicit in the story itself? By reading secondhandedly, or obediently as taught, or by approaching a story without an open mind, we wrong its very first attribute—its uniqueness, with its sister attribute of freshness. We are getting to be old, jaded readers—instructed, advised readers, victims of summaries and textbooks; and if we write stories as victims of this attitude ourselves, what will happen to us? While we read and while we write, let's forget what we're being forever told and find the fresh world again—of enjoyment and pleasure and the story unspoiled, delighted in or hated for its own sake.

By enjoying, I don't mean to be *easy* on a story. Not all melted, the way William Saroyan at times requests readers to be. I mean only not to bother the story—not interrupt and interpret it on the side as if the conscience were at stake. To see it clear and itself, we must see it objectively.

After all, the constellations, patterns, we are used to seeing in the sky are purely subjective; it is because our combining things, our heroes, existed in the world almost as soon as we did that we were able long ago to see Perseus up there, and not a random scattering of little lights. Let's look at a particular story and see it solitary out in space, not part of some trend. It doesn't matter a bit for the moment who wrote it or when, or what magazine or book it appeared in or got rejected from, or how much or how little money the author got for it or whether he had an agent, or that he received letters in the mail when it was printed, saying, "It is found that your story does not reduce to the elements of a story." We're seeing this story as a little world in space, just as we can isolate one star in the sky by a concentrated vision.

The first thing we notice about our story is that we can't really see the solid outlines of it—it seems bathed in something of its own. It is wrapped in an atmosphere. This is what makes it shine, perhaps, as well as what initially obscures its plain, real shape.

We are bearing in mind that the atmosphere in a story may be its chief glory—and for another thing, that it may be giving us an impression altogether contrary to what lies under it. The brightness may be the result of whizzing in a circle. Some action stories fling off the brightest clouds of obscuring and dazzling light, like ours here. Our penetrating look brings us the suspicion finally that this busy object is quite dark within, for all its clouds of speed, those primary colors of red and yellow and blue. It looks like one of Ernest Hemingway's stories, and it is.

Now a story behaves, it goes through motions—that's part of it. Some stories leave a train of light behind them, meteorlike, so that much later than they strike our eye we may see their meaning like an after-effect. These wildly careening stories are in many ways among the most interesting of all—the kind of story sometimes called apocalyptic. I think of Faulkner's stories as being not meteors but comets; in a way still beyond their extravagance and unexpectedness and disregard of the steadier laws of time and space, Faulkner's stories are cometlike in that they do have a wonderful course of their own: they reappear, in their own time they reiterate their meaning, and by reiteration show a whole further story over and beyond their single significance.

If we have thought of Hemingway's stories, then, as being bare and solid as billiard balls, so scrupulously cleaned of adjectives, of every unneeded word as they are, of being plain throughout as a verb in itself is plain, we may come to think twice about it. The atmosphere that cloaks D. H. Lawrence's stories is of sensation, which is a pure but thick cover, a cloak of self-luminous air, but the atmosphere that surrounds Hemingway's stories is just as thick and to some readers less illuminating. Action can be inscrutable, more than sensation can be. It can be just as voluptuous, too, just as vaporous, and much more desperately concealing.

So the first thing we see about a story is its mystery. And in the best stories, we return at the last to see mystery again. Every good story has mystery—not the puzzle kind, but the mystery of allurement. As we understand the story better, it is likely that the mystery does not necessarily decrease; rather it simply grows more beautiful.

Now, of what is this story composed, the one we're sighting? What is the plot, in other words?

E. M. Forster in his book on the novel makes the acute distinction between plot and narrative thread. A story is a "narrative of events arranged in their time-sequence. A plot is also a narrative of events, the emphasis falling on causality." With a plot, instead of keeping on asking, What next? we ask, Why? . . .

As we all have observed, plot can throw its weight in any of several ways, varying in their complexity, flexibility, and interest: onto the narrative, or situation; onto the character; onto the interplay of characters; and onto some higher aspects of character, emotional states, and so on, which is where the rules leave off, if they've come with us this far, and the uncharted country begins. . . .

The plot of a short story in many instances is quite openly a projection of character. In a highly specialized instance, but a good example, the whole series of ghostly events in *The Turn of the Screw* may obviously be taken as a vision—a set of hallucinations of the governess who tells us the story. The story is a manufactured evidence against the leading character, in effect.

Not always does plot project character, even primarily. William Sansom, a young English writer, might be mentioned as one new writer who pays his highest respect to pure idea. Virginia Woolf too was at least as interested in a beam of light as she was in a tantrum.

In outward semblance, many stories have plots in common—which is of no more account than that many people have blue eyes. Plots are, indeed, what we see with. What's seen is what we're interested in. . . .

When plot, whatever it does or however it goes, becomes the outward manifestation of the very germ of the story, then it is purest—then the narrative thread is least objectionable, then it is not in the way. When it is identifiable in every motion and progression of its own with the motions and progression of simple revelation, then it is at its highest use. Plot can be made so beautifully to reveal character, reveal atmosphere and the breathing of it, reveal the secrets of hidden, inner (that is, "real") life, that its very unfolding is a joy. It is a subtle satisfaction—that comes from where? Probably it comes from a deep-seated perception we all carry in us of the beauty of organization—of that less strictly definable thing, of form.

Where does form come from—how do you "get it"? My guess is that form is evolved. It is the residue, the thrown-off shape, of the very act of writing, as I look at it. It is the work, its manifestation in addition to the characters, the plot, the sensory impressions—it is the result of these, which comes to more than their mathematical total. It is these plus something more. This something more springs from the whole. It pertains to the essence of the story. From the writer's point of view, we might say that form is somehow connected with the process of the story's work—that form *is* the work. From the reader's point of view, we might say that form is connected with recognition; it is what makes us know, in a story, what we are looking at, what unique thing we are for a length of time intensely contemplating. It does seem that the part of the mind which form speaks to and reaches is the memory.

In stories today, form, however acutely and definitely it may be felt, does not necessarily imply a formal structure. It is not accounted for by structure, rather. A story with a "pattern," an exact kind of design, may lack a more compelling over-all quality which we call form. Edgar Allan Poe and other writers whose ultimate aim depended on pattern, on a perfect and dovetailing structure (note the relation to puzzles and to detection and mystery here), might have felt real horror at a story by D. H. Lawrence first of all because of the unmitigated shapelessness of Lawrence's narrative. Lawrence's world of action and conversation is as far from the frozen perfection, the marblelike situations, of Poe as we can imagine; Lawrence's story world is a shambles—a world just let go, like a sketchy housekeeper's un-straightened-up room. More things are important than this dust! Lawrence would say, and he would be as right as the crier of that cry always is.

And what about his characters? Are they real, recognizable, neat men and women? Would you know them if you saw them? Not even, I think, if they began to speak on the street as they speak in the stories, in the very words—they would only appear as deranged people. For the truth seems to be that Lawrence's characters don't really speak their words—not conversationally, not to one another; they are *not* speaking on the street, but are playing like fountains or radiating like the moon or storming like the sea, or their silence is the silence of wicked rocks. It is borne home to us that Lawrence is writing of our human relationships on earth in terms of eternity, and these terms set Lawrence's form.

The author himself appears in authorship in phases like the moon, and sometimes blesses us and sometimes smites us while we stand there under him. But we see that his plots and his characters are alike sacrificed to something; there is something which Lawrence considers as transcending them both. Others besides him have thought that something does. But Lawrence alone, that I have knowledge of now, thinks the transcending thing is found direct through the senses. It is the world of the senses that Lawrence writes in, works in, thinks in, takes as his medium—and if that is strange to us, isn't the loss ours? Through this world he will send his story. It is the plot too; it is his story's reason for being, with sex the channel the senses most deeply, mysteriously, run through, cutting down through layers and centuries and country after country of hypocrisy. . . .

We all use the everyday world in our stories, and some of us feel inclined or even bound to give it at least a cursory glance and treatment, but Lawrence does not care. He feels no responsibility there at all. He does not care if the mechanics and props of everyday life suffer in his stories from distortion unto absurdity, if his narrative thins and frays away into silliness. Those things aren't what he's concerned with. His plots might remind you of some kind of tropical birds—that are awkward in structure and really impossible-looking when they're on the ground, and then when they take wing and fly, a miracle happens. All that clumsiness and outrageousness is gone; the bird's body becomes astonishingly functional, and iridescent in flight. . . .

A story's major emphasis may fall on the things that make it up—on character, on plot, on its physical or moral world, in sensory or symbolic form. And perhaps the way this emphasis is let fall may determine the value of the story; may determine not how well it is written, but the worth of its being written.

Of course fashion and the habits of understanding stories at given periods in history may play their parts, unconsciously or willfully. But mainly, I venture to think, the way emphasis falls, the value of a story, is the thing nearest dependent upon the individual and personal factor involved, the writer behind the writing.

The fine story writers seem to be in a sense obstructionists. As if they hold back their own best interests. It's a strange illusion. For if we look to the source of the deepest pleasure we receive from a writer, how surprising it seems that this very source is the quondam obstruction. The fact is, in seeking our source of pleasure we have entered another world again. We are speaking of beauty.

And beauty is not a blatant or promiscuous or obvious quality; indeed at her finest she is somehow associated with obstruction—with reticence of a number of kinds. . . . Time after time Lawrence refuses to get his story told, to let his characters talk in any natural way; the story is held up forever, and through so delaying and through such refusal on the author's part, we enter the magical world of pure sense, of evocation— the shortest cut known through the woods.

Could it be that one who carps at difficulties in a writer ("Why didn't he write it like this? Why didn't he write another story?"), at infringements of the rules and lack of performance of duty, fails to take note of beauty? And fails to see straight off that beauty springs from deviation, from desire not to comply but to act inevitably, as long as truth is in sight, whatever that inevitability may mean?

Where does beauty come from, in the short story? Beauty comes from form, from development of idea, from after-effect. It often comes from carefulness, lack of confusion, elimination of waste—and yes, those are the rules. But that can be on occasion a cold kind of beauty, when there are warm kinds. And beware of tidiness. Sometimes spontaneity is the most sparkling kind of beauty—Katherine Mansfield had it. It is a fortuitous circumstance attending the birth of some stories, like a fairy godmother that has—this time—accepted the standing invitation and come smiling in.

Beauty may be missed or forgotten sometimes by the analyzers because it is not a means, not a way of getting the story along, or furthering a thing in the world. For beauty is a result—as form is a result. It *comes*. We are lucky when beauty comes, for often we try, but then when the virtues of our story are counted, beauty is standing behind the door. I think it may be wrong to try for beauty; we should try for other things, and then hope.

Intensity and beauty are qualities that will come out of man's imagination and out of his passion—which use sensitivity for their finding and focusing power. (This can't beg the question quite so hopelessly as assigning the best stories to genius.) It seems to be true that for practical purposes, in writing a story, beauty is in greatest accord with sensitivity.

The two things that cannot be imitated, beauty and sensitivity, are or may be kin to each other. But there is only one of them we can strive for. Sensitivity in ourselves. It is our technique. In the end, our technique is sensitivity, and beauty may be our reward.

A short-story writer can try anything. He has tried anything—but presumably not everything. Variety is, has been, and no doubt will remain endless in possibilities, because the power and stirring of the mind never rests. It is what this power will try that will most pertinently define the short story. Not rules, not aesthetics, not problems and their solution. It is not rules as long as there is imagination; not aesthetics as long as there is passion; not success as long as there is intensity behind the effort that calls forth and communicates, that will try and try again.

And at the other end of the stories is the reader. There is no use really to fear "the reader." The surly old bugaboo who wants his money's worth out of a magazine—yes, he is there (or I suspect it is a she, still wanting her money's worth and having yet to be convinced she's got it); but there is another reader too, perhaps with more at stake.

Inescapably, this reader exists—the same as ourselves; the reader who is also a user of imagination and thought. This reader picks up a story, maybe our new story, and behold, sees it fresh, and meets it with a storehouse of hope and interest.

And, reader and writer, we can wish each other well. Don't we after all want the same thing? A story of beauty and passion and truth.

For Study and Discussion

1. What does Welty say is the "Great Divide" in the workings of the mind, and why is it that the two ways of working worry "the life out of each other"?

2. In Welty's view, why is it impossible to learn from a critical analysis how a story was written? How are stories meant to be read?

3. What does she mean by "atmosphere," and what importance does she attach to it? How does a story's atmosphere sometimes obscure "its plain, real shape"?

4. How does Welty distinguish between "plot" and "form" in the short story? What importance does she attach to each? Compare her conclusions with those of Sherwood Anderson.

5. What distinction does she make between the stories of Poe and those of D. H. Lawrence? What gives Lawrence's stories their form?

6. What does Welty mean by "beauty"? Where does it come from? What is the relationship between "beauty" and "sensitivity"? To the extent that it can be defined, what is the "beauty" of Welty's own story, "A Visit of Charity"? Lawrence's "Two Blue Birds"? Faulkner's "Mule in the Yard"? Flannery O'Connor's "A Good Man Is Hard to Find"? Gaines' "Just Like a Tree"?

HERSCHEL BRICKELL

WHAT HAPPENED TO THE SHORT STORY?

I

Those of us who keep a watchful eye on the short story—as I must, since I am charged with the responsibility of choosing some twenty stories each year for the O. Henry Memorial Award Prize Stories—have been aware that important things were happening to this form of literary expression in which American writers stand supreme.

At exactly what moment these things began to happen is not easy to say. Putting down pegs in literary matters is risky business at best, and if put down, they had better be placed loosely. It *is* possible to say, however, that the contemporary short story owes more to Hawthorne than to any other one person, and Hawthorne's first volume of *Twice-Told Tales*, most of which had been published in the popular Annuals of the period, was published in 1837.

Then Poe, ever the acute critic, in reviewing the Hawthorne collection, first formulated the rules for the short story, which still stand as a statement of fundamental principles. But Poe had still another important influence because of his effect on the symbolist poets of France, and the present-day short story owes much to symbolism.

As for foreign influences, there have been two—Chekhov and his New Zealand-born disciple, Katherine Mansfield. It was these two who disregarded most of the rules and made the short narrative take on new life, giving it depth and penetration. Our own Sherwood Anderson found a way further to relax the short story, to give it greater freedom.

And from Anderson's time on, we have seen writers of talent engaged in one of art's oldest battles, the attempt to break the picture free from the frame, to pour more water—or wine—into the bottle than it would seem to be able to hold. This they have been accomplishing with greater

Originally published in, and reprinted here from, the *Atlantic Monthly*, September 1951, by permission of Maxwell Aley Associates.

or less success for a matter of twenty-five years, but the trick has only just now been mastered to a degree where many writers with many points of view can work it effectively.

The way it is done is to draw the short story ever nearer to poetry, in the precise and beautiful use of language, so that no story of the present worth a second glance is without its overtones. In the main, the topics are subjective—one speaks here, of course, not at all of the commercial short story, which adheres pretty rigidly to formulae or it does not sell, but of the serious, or artistic, story.

To put it as simply as possible, the short story of the middle period was a story of doing, with action as its theme. Then it gradually moved inward, and in the hands of many people, almost all of whom had first written poetry—and this includes both Hemingway and Faulkner—it became "a slice of life," as we used to say of Maupassant, but a slice of the mind and the spirit rather than the body.

There are Chekhov and Mansfield tales that do not escape by much the designation "sketches," rather than stories. The distinction is not at all difficult to make, since the sketch is static and the story dynamic. But what has happened now to a striking degree is that the work of these masters has been improved upon, since the current story has dramatic conflict as well as form.

It does not wander so much as a millimeter from its objective. Anyone fond of making diagrams will find the material ready to hand in any good short story he cares to examine. There is a straight line from the opening to the closing sentence, and one may change the old saying "In my end was my beginning" to the precept "In my beginning *must* be my end." This does not mean that in the hands of such experts as Stephen Vincent Benét, William Faulkner, and Eudora Welty there may not be found a sensation of relaxation, as if there were plenty of time to talk and be listened to, which is a very old trick with the oral storyteller. Probably one of the oldest, since it involves the important element of suspense.

But in Faulkner's legends and in Miss Welty's curious style—a fascinating blend of the colloquial and the classical—there is no departure from the rule that the short story writer must proceed directly to where he says he is going. He wastes no words, because he has none to waste, but he does not mind letting the reader think that nobody is really in a hurry. It is pleasant not to feel hurried when listening to a good yarn, and the pleasure principle is just as important in the short story as it is in any other kind of writing.

This business about the relationship of the short story and poetry needs careful examination. It does not mean at all that good stories of the present are written in a "poetical" manner, because if they were, they would not really be any good. It was Goethe who said that in writing prose one must have something to say, but in writing lyric poetry it did not really matter. (A poem should not mean/But be, said Archibald

MacLeish.) I am sure Goethe smiled when he made the remark to Eckermann I have quoted, but whether he was in dead earnest or not, it is certain that there is no relationship at all between the short story and the lyric which does no more than sing.

In fact, the safest comparison is, perhaps, between the ballad and the short story, where one is on unimpeachable ground, since the ballad must tell a story, too. But the truth is that no matter how ontological Messrs. Goethe and MacLeish might wish poetry to be, good lyrics have always said something, too. When a poet like Robert Frost sings—and make no mistake about it, he sings most beautifully—he is not just making agreeable sounds.

It would be difficult to insult Robert more thoroughly and completely than by intimating that he was not always at least trying to say something, even in a couplet. This year, with Mark Van Doren as one of the three judges for the O. Henry, I asked him, as both poet and short story writer, what he thought about the relationship we are discussing, and he answered sagely:—

"The short story should be a little epic, or possibly a little drama, but never a lyric, if lyric suggests the static or merely stated. At its highest, lyric means something narrative or dramatic too; but we don't always find it at its highest. In verse as well as prose it too often degenerates into mere writing and attitudinizing. . . . A great short story is exactly what the name implies: a great little story. But it had better be a story, just as a lyric poem had better be something like a story, too, in the last analysis."

II

Just why have we reached what seems to me a very high plateau—please, not a *peak*—in the development of the American short story? I am firmly convinced that the situation cannot be fully explained by the activities of a few highly talented people. If I did not feel a great fear of using the word genius about a contemporary, I should apply it to Faulkner, Welty, Capote, Boyle, Bowles, and maybe one or two others, who write stories such as nobody else has ever written, or ever will. (Hemingway is not in the list because he long ago abandoned the story for the novel, which seems to me a serious mistake on his part.)

Joseph Henry Jackson, another of this year's O. Henry judges, and a veteran at the job besides being one of the most perceptive reviewers we have, said he thought the explanation lay in the quality of present-day editors—a happy thought indeed. I wish I could agree, but I do not, save for certain exceptions. A little handful of relatively popular magazines publish all the good stories I find outside the literary quarterlies, and some of the very best of these do not at the moment know where next quarter's ink and paper are coming from.

A much more likely explanation, I think, is that there are now actively teaching in all parts of the country some of the best short story writers we have. There is Wallace Stegner, for example, Ray B. West, Jr., and Robert Penn Warren, to mention only three of a considerable number of people who can *do* and who also teach. An even larger number of the up-and-coming younger writers are also teaching creative writing or have had courses under men and women who know what they are talking about, because they have had success with their own stories.

Not all the first-rate teachers of short story writing write stories, too, because some of them are busy running English faculties and taking part in many other campus activities instead of showing that they, too, can do the trick. I think of people like Carroll Towle at the University of New Hampshire, who has had remarkable success with young people; of Hudson Strode at the University of Alabama, whose record is little short of phenomenal as a teacher, but who writes excellent travel books, not fiction.

As a teacher of considerable experience in writers' conferences, I should not be willing to leave these meetings out of consideration, either, in trying to find the explanation for the current spate of good stories. In most cases, short story courses at conferences are taught by people who have written and sold stories themselves. I once saw at a chemical show in New York a silk purse which had actually been made from a sow's ear; but let me pose and then withdraw the question of whether this is easier than trying to teach most people who come to writers' conferences to write anything, including English.

It is unquestionably true, however, that the general improvement in quality in the American short story has been concurrent with the widespread establishment of courses in creative writing and the mush-roomlike growth of writers' conferences. I think Rolfe Humphries summed up the matter for all time when he said: "It is foolish to suppose that you can teach anybody to write, but it is equally foolish to suppose that you cannot teach people a great deal about writing." I have known good teachers at writers' conferences, themselves successful writers, to say that they would have been saved years of trial-and-error by listening to the words of someone who had traveled the path and knew its pitfalls as well as its delights.

I believe I have made it clear that the short story is now in as flourishing a condition artistically as it has ever been, in this country or anywhere else. Perhaps it is safe to say that there are more first-rate and good second-rate stories being written and published right now than at any other time in our history. I wish for everybody's sake one might say with equal veracity that the short story market was as good as the short story quality.

The other side of the coin does not wear a happy expression. A number of the best magazines of the past are dead and buried, the picture books now fill the stands, so that nobody in his right mind would try to start a quality magazine; the quarterlies can at best publish only a handful of stories a year. And the independent "littles" which have always been so useful in this field are hit right where they live during such a period of inflation as we are now in.

Even the quarterlies which enjoy subsidies from universities and colleges are feeling the pinch, since their patrons are also suffering financially; and as such magazines are often regarded as more or less useless trimmings by what are called "practical-minded" trustees, some of the best and wisest editors in the country are now in for long headaches and heartaches. The quarterlies pay from nothing up to the price of a few porterhouse steaks for a story, and they plainly cannot pay more.

The lesson of this is simple: people write quality stories because they must, not because they hope to get rich, or even to make a living, from writing them. The "big slicks" talk glibly about printing the best stories they can, and I have heard some of their editors say they avoided formula stories when possible, but patient reading of what they print convinces me that most of them are kidding themselves. It is true that a magazine like *Collier's* does print a good many borderline stories, but that is the exception. Mass audiences are looking for entertainment, and they must get it from what is printed, if one accepts circulation figures as evidence.

When the short story began to appear in the Annuals, so popular during the thirties and forties of the last century, nobody bothered about mass appeal, because an Annual was something to use for parlor-table decoration, or a culture-symbol, not to be read—except, perhaps, while waiting for Susan to finish lacing up Old Ironsides and dusting her face with flour for her date.

My optimism about the current short story stems from the specimens that are included in the 1951 O. Henry, three of them from this magazine, which has the highest rating in the anthology's records from its inception in 1918, and three of the best, in my judgment. There are two dozen stories in the book, and Mark Van Doren said twelve were absolutely first-rate, while Nancy Hale, the third judge, set the figure at fourteen. Of course, I should say twenty-four. . . .

Both Mr. Jackson and Miss Hale, who follow the short story closely, said it was the best collection in the thirty-three-year history of the O. Henry Memorial, and as its editor for eleven years now, I agree with my eminent colleagues, not even pausing to blush. I ought to say that my wife, who assists me in getting the collection together and who is a far tougher critic than I, casts her ballot with the rest of us. That is why I said *plateau*, not *peak*. How long we shall write as we do and what the next phase will be, I do not care to prophesy, but we have now accomplished something of real moment, in a form peculiarly Ameri-can—of this I am very certain.

For Study and Discussion

1. What short-story writers of the nineteenth and early twentieth centuries does Brickell regard as having exerted key influences on the contemporary short story? What was the contribution of each?

2. What basic similarities does Brickell find between the recent short story and poetry? Are his viewpoints in agreement with those of Mark Van Doren (as stated in the quotation on p. 112)? How different is the position Brickell and Van Doren take on this issue from that taken by Matthews?

3. What does Brickell mean by his statement that the current short story "does not wander so much as a millimeter from its objective"?

4. What influences are primarily responsible, in Brickell's view, for the American short story's being "in as flourishing a condition artistically as it has ever been, in this country or anywhere else"? What might account for the different attitudes taken by Brickell and Lardner toward the teaching of short-story writing?

V. S. PRITCHETT

SHORT STORIES

For a long time the short story was the poor relation of the novel. It was the chapter left over, the anecdote to be tossed off in a spare moment. Even in the hands of genius, like those of Maupassant and Chekhov, the short story was thought to be the *pis aller* of writers who would have written novels if they had only known how, for Chekhov wasted two or three years trying and Maupassant is a failure as a novelist. We now think differently: the originating genius of Poe in America, of these French and Russian writers and (very late) of Kipling in Britain, has turned out to be decisive and, in this century, writers have had the excitement of a new, intensely individual prose art at their disposal. It is a hybrid. It owes much to the quickness, the objectivity and cutting of the cinema; it owes much to the poet on the one hand and the newspaper reporter on the other; something also to the dramatic compression of the theatre, and everything to the restlessness, the alert nerve, the scientific eye and the short breath of contemporary life. It is the art of the short expectation of life. It fulfills Poe's demand that works of art should be short and immediate in effect. It succeeds on condition that it gets off on the right foot and bears in mind what is said to be the motto of the Bank of England: never explain, never apologize.

If the short story is natural to our age, it makes one crucial requirement which many young writers who attempt this form fatally lack. Maxim Gorki, who inherited a natural power of storytelling from his grand-mother, makes it clear in his autobiography that without personality—possibly without the right grandmother—the storyteller is sunk. He describes how his grandmother kept the simple Russian sailors on a ship captivated by her tales. One was about a goblin who ran a splinter in his paw and screamed out, "I can't bear it, little mice, it hurts so much." And, says Gorki, "She lifted her own foot in her hands and rocked comically, screwing up her face as if she actually felt the pain."

The good storyteller knows that, orally or writing, he is putting on a personal, individual act. A novelist can dispense with that. Trollope had almost no personality; quite a number of excellent modern novelists have

Originally published in, and reprinted here from, *Harper's Bazaar*, July 1953, by permission of The Harold Matson Company, Inc. Copyright 1953 by V. S. Pritchett.

an average personality common to them all. The novelist is able, for long periods, to rely on the cumulative weight and diffusion of his material. Not so the storyteller. A miniaturist like Colette, as delicate as a cat, a dramatist of nervous alarm and the inner precipice like Elizabeth Bowen, a reporter like Hemingway, intrepid travelers into the tropics of character like Eudora Welty and Carson McCullers owe the indispensable shock they give to the reader to their personality.

Moralists used to condemn even the greatest novels as dangerous, drugging daydreams. There was something in this argument. Their length, their inclusiveness, their shapelessness—despite all the efforts of Henry James and Flaubert—were bemusing. The story, on the other hand, wakes the reader up. Not only that; it answers the primitive craving for art, the wit, paradox and beauty of shape, the longing to see a dramatic pattern and significance in our experience, the desire for the electric shock. The modern reader is longing for a revival of the tale which the novel, in its complexity and sophistication, has so thoroughly repressed in the brief two hundred and fifty years of its life. But in stressing the "art" of the short story, I do not mean to convey something precious or nicely removed from life. Chekhov's stories form a passionate, indignant yet scientific record of Russian life in his time. Maupassant has described the Normandy peasant forever. All conscience spreads entangled from Conrad's tale of the Captain who hides the refugee in his cabin; all the fatality attending the rebel and the soldier is in Frank O'Connor's tale of the Irishmen playing cards with their British prisoners, while they wait orders to execute them. These stories are not missing chapters or scenarios for novels. Expanded, they would "explain," "apologize" and fail to pierce.

The modern nervous system is keyed up. The very collapse of standards, conventions and values, which has so bewildered the impersonal novelist, has been the making of the story writer who can catch any piece of life as it flies and make his personal performance out of it.

For Study and Discussion

1. What other art forms according to Pritchett have influenced the contemporary short story? Do you agree that it is a "hybrid"? If so, is this fact to be held against the short story?

2. What crucial requirement does the short story impose on the writer?

3. Would Chekhov and Hemingway agree that the personality of the author must show through his story? How valid do you consider the distinction Pritchett draws between the novel and the short story? Must the novelist necessarily be more impersonal than the short-story writer?

4. Summarize the characteristics Pritchett believes the contemporary short story possesses.

FALCON O. BAKER

SHORT STORIES FOR THE MILLIONS

Some time ago Katherine Anne Porter hurled a two-pronged javelin at the popular magazine in an essay called "No Plot, My Dear, No Story." On one prong she dangled the "mercenary author" who dares to write a story with sufficient appeal to entice an editor into paying a goodly sum. On the other she speared the popular magazine editor who, in the exigency of producing a palatable bill of fare for the reader, seeks to corrupt the literary talent of our day.

She said: "Except in emergencies, when you are trying to manufacture a quick trick and make some easy money, you don't really need a plot." Those who pursue such an attempt must be willing "to lose all, including honor"—their eyesight, self-respect, and whatever potentialities they may have. In another essay Miss Porter tells more about her own writing process: ". . . neither praise nor blame affects my actual work, for I am under a compulsion to write as I do." The artist seeks no audience, but only to tell what he has to tell.

Reading this essay, I automatically envisioned some accomplished slick writer, Faith Baldwin perhaps, replying with a parallel essay entitled "No Theme, My Dear, No Story." The essay would satirize those authors so busy picking the dots and commas from their "fragmented visions" that they forgot to tell a story, failed to create interest and suspense. It would advise those wishing to penetrate the mysteries of mankind to resort to philosophy or psychology or sociology, and write papers thereon.

Such an attitude would be as narrow in its vision as the first. Yet neither would be wholly in error. Frequently truth incorporates two extremes, for it turns out that they are not diametrically opposed, but rather two vital parts of the whole. Only the blind can declare that the wrinkled hide or the curling trunk is the true elephant.

I mention this here not because of anything overpoweringly novel in

Originally published in, and reprinted here from, the *Saturday Review*, December 19, 1953, by permission of the publisher; copyright 1953 by The Saturday Review Associates, Inc.

Miss Porter's declaration of "art for sweet art's sake," but merely because she manages to say it a little more vividly than most. During the Depression days of the Thirties we heard the theme emanating from the poetic garret. In the face of hunger such a philosophy of writing helped hold the soul intact. But the war and postwar prosperity made the garret unfashionable. Proponents of this philosophy sought a new home, and found it within ivy walls. The literary quarterlies, published mostly in the universities, furnished the sounding board. An amazing number of the contemporary short-story writers, generally acclaimed as the most promising of the serious authors, have been associated with college English departments. Among them we have such authors as Wallace Stegner, Robert Penn Warren, Peter Taylor, J. F. Powers, Walter Van Tilburg Clark, Jessamyn West, Saul Bellow, Caroline Gordon, Warren Beck, and Mark Schorer.

In the Forties there grew up in the universities a group called the "New Critics."* At first concerned with poetry, they then moved to fiction and in the field of the short story soon dominated modern criticism. Beginning ten years ago after the publication of "Understanding Fiction," by Cleanth Brooks and Robert Penn Warren, there has been a continuing deluge of short-story analysis by the New Critics. . . . It has been said, partly by the New Critics themselves, that this New Criticism has "saved" the American short story from decay. But it is too early to say whether this actually saved the American short story or directed it toward obliteration for lack of an interested audience.

While the garret writers of the Depression era and the university writers of the New Criticism era have in common Miss Porter's desire for truth at the expense of all else, their meaning of "truth" greatly differs. The first group had a driving awareness of social, economic, and political problems. In their exploration of these problems and their revolt against what they believed unjust they found an eager contemporary audience. But the New Critics have objected, among other things, to this creation of a short story with the avowed purpose of presenting truth to illustrate or propagandize a moral. Instead they have resurrected Henry James and set as the criteria of evaluation the internal consistency of the form.

The scope and effect of the New Critics' standard for the short story provide the raw materials for endless discussion. It will suffice here to set forth their dictum that action is not allowed purely for the interest it creates but rather is permitted only when it is the inevitable outgrowth of the balance of character, theme, atmosphere, and structure. With such a noble standard for achieving truth there can be little criticism. Rather

---

*"New Critics" is a term applied to a group of critics who gained recognition in the 1940s. Though they are not an organized group advocating any fixed critical dogma, they do share a common conviction that the meaning and merit of a literary work is properly sought through a close reading and analysis of the text itself rather than in historical and biographical material associated with the work—Eds.

should we look at the end results, the short story that such a goal frequently produces.

The very concern with form and the elaborate details of making every word, every mood, every bit of action internally consistent has a tendency toward the dullness of geometry. Writing without either the consecrated inspiration of a theme or the romantic enthusiasm of action, the "new writers" attempt to explore every facet of a minute point in time and space and truth. The New Critics, wanting total truth in the fragment described, object to the overt selection of incidents and facts around a central purpose directed toward a single point of understanding. Graphically, those who write with what has been termed "creeping preciousness" might be described as $<$, a single point that spreads into infinity; while the theme writer and the action writer would be described as $>$, many incidents that lead to a single conclusion.

This New Critics' approach may be satisfactory in the wide canvas of the novel, where space permits the writer to bring all the many facets back into focus. But in the brief span of the short story the result tends toward a scientific exposition of psychological or philosophical fact. Certainly we cannot call such a presentation of truth, realistically or symbolically, a sin. The reading of psychological case studies is a highly interesting and sometimes profitable pastime. But it does not have the excitement of fiction.

Too frequently, it would seem to the lay reader, the New Critics evaluate in terms of complexity of understanding. The value would be in inverse ratio to the number of people who can be expected to understand. The harder one is forced to dig through the symbols, the myths, and the ironies to ferret the meaning the more successful the story. Reading becomes not an experience but an exercise in mental gymnastics for the critics and the initiated few. To be fair, we must admit that the New Critics view complexity as a means rather than an end. But the results are the same.

While all this cold, technical evaluation has been going on the "little magazines" devoted to publication of serious stories have declined precipitously and the larger magazines directed to the more than casual reader have come to publish less and less fiction. Even the literary quarterlies that have been spawned by many universities in the past decade seem more interested in lengthy debates about who is following whose tradition than in the discovery of good fiction. The audience of these latter magazines is largely confined to university circles and the writing fraternity, and for this reason a predominant concern with critical ideas may be justified. But for the general public there is a great deal more satisfaction in eating a luscious red apple than in hearing a lecture which extols its beauty and flavor.

Fortunately, there has been published a sizable quantity of good short fiction in the popular magazines during the past decade. *Harper's Bazaar,*

Mademoiselle, Esquire, Today's Woman, and *Charm,* to mention a few, have frequently harbored interesting stories. The larger of the popular magazines, such as *Good Housekeeping, Saturday Evening Post,* and *Collier's,* have produced first-rate fiction to an extent not generally realized. Even in the most surprising places good fiction sometimes crops up. *Woman's Day* is found at seven cents a copy sandwiched between loaves of bread and canned vegetables in the A & P grocery. The pick-up circulation, some three million copies, smacks of the height of popularization, and yet the magazine has shown a high level of fiction choice.

At the hint of popular appeal a great many writers and critics automatically begin to simmer. Those gifted writers who repudiate surface action seem to write for a carefully selected clientele: the critics, the college professors, the small audience of the literary quarterlies. These hermits feel secure in the immortality of art, expecting to be discovered in some future age. But is it necessarily dishonest or degrading in so writing that the greatest possible audience, the people who are alive today, may catch the truth, the insight which the author believes himself to possess? Although the purpose of literature provides an unending debate which will never be resolved, a weighty mass of argument can be produced to show that in the final analysis the primary purpose of fiction is not education, not history, not even a portrait of truth, but the entertainment of the reader.

Man is introduced to the short story in the nursery. The tale he hears may have social meaning (it's fun to share toys with brother Jack), it may have educational value (milk makes bones grow strong), and it may even bring him to a psychological understanding of his problems (momma does all those bad things because she loves me). It may be an allegory or a fable. But the story is offered and he listens primarily because of the pleasure he receives in the hearing. He may be intoxicated with that first experience and pursue the short story on up through the juvenile magazines, the slicks, and maybe finally the literary quarterlies. But each step in the journey has been prompted basically by the enjoyment he receives from the reading.

I would not wish to imply that there is only one standard of reading enjoyment. What pleases one may bore another. But the point I would make is that in most discussions of the merits of a short story this vital point of entertainment value is ignored.

Most short stories that have stood the test of time, the stories that today are accepted as masterpieces, have at the base a great deal of surface interest. Regardless of the many cascading levels of meaning, the story can be read entertainingly on a superficial level. All are not reducible to the formula of boy meets girl, pursues girl, marries girl, but they have movement on the surface, an interest created by the skill of the author in making the reader want to discover what is going to happen. Certainly Poe and De Maupassant had a sound basis of surface interest.

The Russian writers Tolstoy, Chekhov, and Bunin made great use of having something actively happen to the characters. Even the symbolic stories of Hawthorne carry a high quotient of surface activity.

Surface plot is the action both by and upon the character which creates a certain suspense for the reader, the abatement of which can be accomplished only by finishing the story. Although it is usually not the real story, it is the vehicle which carries the meaning. It is this surface plot that first catches and holds a great number of readers. It is the primary assumption in Poe's classical definition of a short story, "A skilful literary artist *has construed a tale. . . ."*

Faced with the entertainment value of the short story, many contemporary critics fail in their obligation to the recipient of all literary art: the ordinary reader. Without an audience the *raison d'être* for literature dissolves. No matter how much truth a story may contain, if it is not presented so that a reasonably large audience can understand it then it cannot be a good story.

It would be folly to attempt a defense of the formula story *per se*, yet many critics and editors of short-story anthologies have been so concerned with disparaging the formula story that they have in effect created another formula—the literary formula of the unresolved impasse. This is a psychological era, and the problem is man against himself. As soon as an author attempts to resolve the impasse he has created some critic is lurking around the corner to yell "Formula." A totally unresolved problem *may* be more truthful, but it lacks appeal to the lay reader. By nature Americans are romantic, but there is a certain basic desire for completion and the solution of problems. Stories that achieve the highest level of success have *both* a competent level of meaning and a competent level of surface action. The author has something to say, and he says it with interest and suspense.

The good short story belongs to a larger audience than the university professors, the critics, and the literary quarterlies. Perhaps it is time that the purpose of short-story evaluation be redefined to include the general reader. "Slick" magazines today have shown an eagerness to publish authors who have something to say and are able to say it in a way that will be interesting to a great mass of readers. The phenomenal and continual rise in the general education level of the American public, particularly in the past decade, now makes possible a mass audience for serious short stories. But the pleading notes from editors appearing in the various writing magazines indicate a dearth of such stories. And this dearth exists at a time when there are thousands of college courses, journalism schools, writers' conferences, trade schools, and correspondence courses.

In view of all this, it is astounding that editors are not swamped with publishable fiction. There probably are many answers to this paradox. One might be in the writing schools themselves, which are divided by intent into two categories. One group, exemplified by many of the college "fiction workshops," deals with the short story purely as an experience in truth and meaning, with little regard for surface action; the group exemplified by the correspondence writing schools places all emphasis on plot and suspense. With the intent of writing thus polarized it should not be surprising how infrequently aspiring young writers manage to create a story that really fulfils both requirements of a good story—to be interesting and to say something.

Perhaps a higher mark of esteem is justified for those literary artists, past and present, who have been able to accommodate themselves to the vehicle at hand in order to reach the large public audience. That vehicle for the short-story writer today is the popular magazine. We could find in that vehicle a great abundance of good short fiction if the gifted writer could view the popular magazine as a challenge to his skill rather than as something filled with creeping, crawling things.

For Study and Discussion

1. Baker indicts Katherine Anne Porter's essay, "No Plot, My Dear, No Story," as a "declaration of 'art for sweet art's sake.'" Is this an accurate judgment or an oversimplification of her position? Explain.

2. In his reference to James and the New Critics, what does Baker mean by the "internal consistency" of form and why does he object to it?

3. What has been the influence on the short story of the "New Critics" and "university writers"? Contrast Baker's viewpoint with that of Brickell.

4. What does Baker mean by his statement that "stories that achieve the highest level of success have *both* a competent level of meaning and a competent level of surface action"? On the basis of this criterion, how would you evaluate the stories by James, Anderson, Welty, Kafka, West, and Capote?

5. From among the stories represented in this collection, select one that lacks "surface action" and argue the case for or against its general effectiveness.

TRUMAN CAPOTE

ON PROBLEMS OF FORM AND TECHNIQUE

INTERVIEWER: What did you first write?

CAPOTE: Short stories. And my more unswerving ambitions still revolve around this form. When seriously explored, the short story seems to me the most difficult and disciplining form of prose writing extant. Whatever control and technique I may have I owe entirely to my training in this medium.

INTERVIEWER: What do you mean exactly by "control"?

CAPOTE: I mean maintaining a stylistic and emotional upper hand over your material. Call it precious and go to hell, but I believe a story can be wrecked by a faulty rhythm in a sentence—especially if it occurs toward the end—or a mistake in paragraphing, even punctuation. Henry James is the maestro of the semicolon. Hemingway is a first-rate paragrapher. From the point of view of ear, Virginia Woolf never wrote a bad sentence. I don't mean to imply that I successfully practice what I preach. I try, that's all.

INTERVIEWER: How does one arrive at short-story technique?

CAPOTE: Since each story presents its own technical problems, obviously one can't generalize about them on a two-times-two-equals-four basis. Finding the right form for your story is simply to realize the most *natural* way of telling the story. The test of whether or not a writer has divined the natural shape of his story is just this: after reading it, can you imagine it differently, or does it silence your imagination and seem to you absolute and final? As an orange is final. As an orange is something nature has made just right.

INTERVIEWER: Are there devices one can use in improving one's technique?

CAPOTE: Work is the only device I know of. Writing has laws of perspective, of light and shade, just as painting does, or music. If you are born knowing them, fine. If not, learn them. Then rearrange the rules to

From an interview originally published in the *Paris Review*, Spring-Summer 1957. Reprinted here from *Writers at Work*, First Series, edited by Malcolm Cowley (New York: The Viking Press, 1958), by permission of the publisher. Copyright © 1957, 1958 by The Paris Review, Inc.

suit yourself. Even Joyce, our most extreme disregarder, was a superb craftsman; he could write *Ulysses because* he could write *Dubliners.* Too many writers seem to consider the writing of short stories as a kind of finger exercise. Well, in such cases, it is certainly only their fingers they are exercising. . . .

For Study and Discussion

1. What does Capote mean by "control" in short-story writing and how does the writer maintain it?

2. In Capote's view, what is the "right form" for a story? What test can be applied to determine whether or not a story is cast in the right form? How close in agreement on form is Capote with Anderson? With Saroyan?

3. What does Capote mean when he says that James Joyce "could write *Ulysses because* he could write *Dubliners"*?

FRANK O'CONNOR

ON WRITING THE SHORT STORY

INTERVIEWER: Why do you prefer the short story for your medium?

O'CONNOR: Because it's the nearest thing I know to lyric poetry—I wrote lyric poetry for a long time, then discovered that God had not intended me to be a lyric poet, and the nearest thing to that is the short story. A novel actually requires far more logic and far more knowledge of circumstances, whereas a short story can have the sort of detachment from circumstances that lyric poetry has.

INTERVIEWER: Faulkner has said, "Maybe every novelist wants to write poetry first, finds he can't, and then tries the short story, which is the most demanding form after poetry. And, failing at that, only then does he take up novel writing."* What do you think about this?

O'CONNOR: I'd love to console myself, it's that neat—it sounds absolutely perfect except that it implies, as from a short-story writer, that the novel is just an easy sort of thing that you slide gently into, whereas, in fact, my own experience with the novel is that it was always too difficult for me to do. At least to do a novel like *Pride and Prejudice* requires something more than to be a failed B.A. or a failed poet or a failed short-story writer, or a failed anything else. Creating in the novel a sense of continuing life is the thing. We don't have that problem in the

---

From an interview originally published in the *Paris Review*, Autumn-Winter 1957. Reprinted here from *Writers at Work*, First Series, edited by Malcolm Cowley (New York: The Viking Press, 1958), by permission of the publisher. Copyright © 1957, 1958 by The Paris Review, Inc.

*In *Faulkner in the University*, edited by Frederick L. Gwynn and Joseph L. Blotner (New York: Vintage Books, 1965), p. 207. In response to a question put to him, Faulkner made a similar statement:

Q. Mr. Faulkner, you spoke about *The Sound and the Fury* as starting out to write a short story and it kept growing. Well now, do you think that it's easier to write a novel than a short story?

A. Yes sir. You can be more careless, you can put more trash in it and be excused for it. In a short story that's next to the poem, almost every word has got to be almost exactly right. In the novel you can be careless but in the short story you can't. I mean by that the good short stories like Chekhov wrote. That's why I rate that second—it's because it demands a nearer absolute exactitude. You have less room to be slovenly and careless. There's less room in it for trash. In poetry, of course, there's no room at all for trash. It's got to be absolutely impeccable, absolutely perfect.

short story, where you merely suggest continuing life. In the novel, you have to create it, and that explains one of my quarrels with modern novels. Even a novel like *As I Lay Dying*, which I admire enormously, is not a novel at all, it's a short story. To me a novel is something that's built around the character of time, the nature of time, and the effects that time has on events and characters. When I see a novel that's supposed to take place in twenty-four hours, I just wonder why the man padded out the short story.

INTERVIEWER: Yeats said, "O'Connor is doing for Ireland what Chekhov did for Russia." What do you think of Chekhov?

O'CONNOR: Oh, naturally I admire Chekhov extravagantly, I think every short-story writer does. He's inimitable, a person to read and admire and worship—but never, never, never to imitate. He's got all the most extraordinary technical devices, and the moment you start imitating him without those technical devices, you fall into a sort of rambling narrative, as I think even a good story writer like Katherine Mansfield did. She sees that Chekhov apparently constructs a story without episodic interest, so she decides that if she constructs a story without episodic interest it will be equally good. It isn't. What she forgets is that Chekhov had a long career as a journalist, as a writer for comic magazines, writing squibs, writing vaudevilles, and he had learned the art very, very early of maintaining interest, of creating a bony structure. It's only concealed in the later work. They think they can do without that bony structure, but they're all wrong. . . .

INTERVIEWER: What about working habits? How do you start a story?

O'CONNOR: "Get black on white" used to be Maupassant's advice— that's what I always do. I don't give a hoot what the writing's like, I write any sort of rubbish which will cover the main outlines of the story, then I can begin to see it. When I write, when I draft a story, I never think of writing nice sentences about, "It was a nice August evening when Elizabeth Jane Moriarty was coming down the road." I just write roughly what happened, and then I'm able to see what the construction looks like. It's the design of the story which to me is most important, the thing that tells you there's a bad gap in the narrative here and you really ought to fill that up in some way or another. I'm always looking at the design of a story, not the treatment. Yesterday I was finishing off a piece about my friend A. E. Coppard, the greatest of all the English storytellers, who died about a fortnight ago. I was describing the way Coppard must have written these stories, going around with a notebook, recording what the lighting looked like, what that house looked like, and all the time using metaphor to suggest it to himself, "The road looked like a mad serpent going up the hill," or something of the kind, and "She said so-and-so, and the man in the pub said something else." After he had written them all out, he must have got the outline of his story, and he'd start working in all the details. Now, I could never do that at all. I've got to see what these people did, first of all, and *then* I start thinking of whether it was a nice August evening or a spring evening. I have to wait for the theme before I can do anything.

INTERVIEWER: Do you rewrite?

O'CONNOR: Endlessly, endlessly, endlessly. And keep on rewriting, and after it's published, and then after it's published in book form, I usually rewrite it again. I've rewritten versions of most of my early stories and one of these days, God help, I'll publish these as well.

INTERVIEWER: Do you keep notes as a source of supply for future stories?

O'CONNOR: Just notes of themes. If somebody tells me a good story, I'll write it down in my four lines; that is the secret of the theme. If you make the subject of a story twelve or fourteen lines, that's a treatment. You've already committed yourself to the sort of character, the sort of surroundings, and the moment you've committed yourself, the story is already written. It has ceased to be fluid, you can't design it any longer, you can't model it. So I always confine myself to my four lines. If it won't go into four, that means you haven't reduced it to its ultimate simplicity, reduced it to the fable. . . .

For Study and Discussion

1. Does O'Connor agree with Faulkner (as quoted in the footnote on p. 126) that it is easier to write a novel than a short story? Why does O'Connor regard Faulkner's *As I Lay Dying* as a short story rather than a novel? If you are acquainted with this work by Faulkner, do you consider it a "padded out" short story?

2. How does O'Connor work out the "design" of a story? Why does he limit the statement of the theme of a story to four lines?

3. Why does O'Connor consider Chekhov a writer to "admire and worship—but never, never, never to imitate"?

4. What does he mean by "the bony structure" of a story? Is it the same thing as "design"?

5. Compare O'Connor's method of writing a short story with that of Poe. What are the important similarities and differences between the two?

FLANNERY O'CONNOR

THE FICTION WRITER AND HIS COUNTRY

Among the many complaints made about the modern American novelist, the loudest, if not the most intelligent, has been the charge that he is not speaking for his country. A few seasons back an editorial in *Life* magazine asked grandly, "Who speaks for America today?" and was not able to conclude that our novelists, or at least our most gifted ones, did.

The gist of the editorial was that in the last ten years this country had enjoyed an unparalleled prosperity, that it had come nearer to producing a classless society than any other nation and that it was the most powerful country in the world, but that our novelists were writing as if they lived in packing boxes on the edge of the dump while they awaited admission to the poorhouse. Instead of this, the editorial requested that they give us something that really represented this country, and it ended with a very smooth and slick shift into a higher key and demanded further that the novelist show us the redeeming quality of spiritual purpose, for it said that "what is most missing from our hot-house literature" is "the joy of life itself."

This was irritating enough to provoke answers from many novelists and critics, but I do not know that any of those who answered considered the question specifically from the standpoint of the novelist with Christian concerns, who, presumably, would have an interest at least equal to the editors of *Life* in "the redeeming quality of spiritual purpose."

What is such a writer going to take his "country" to be? The word usually used by literary folk in this connection would be "world," but the word "country" will do; in fact, being homely, it will do better, for it suggests more. It suggests everything from the actual countryside that the novelist describes, on, to, and through the peculiar characteristics of his region and his nation, and on, through, and under all of these to his true country, which the writer with Christian convictions will consider to

Originally published in, and reprinted here from, *The Living Novel: A Symposium*, edited by Granville Hicks (New York: The Macmillan Company, 1957), by permission of the publisher; © 1957 The Macmillan Company.

be what is eternal and absolute. This covers considerable territory, and if one were talking of any other kind of writing than the writing of fiction, one would perhaps have to say "countries," but it is the peculiar burden of the fiction writer that he has to make one country do for all and that he has to evoke that one country through the concrete particulars of a life that he can make believable.

This is first of all a matter of vocation, and a vocation is a limiting factor which extends even to the kind of material that the writer is able to apprehend imaginatively. The writer can choose what he writes about but he cannot choose what he is able to make live, and so far as he is concerned a living deformed character is acceptable and a dead whole one is not. The Christian writer particularly will feel that whatever his initial gift is, it comes from God; and no matter how minor a gift it is, he will not be willing to destroy it by trying to use it outside its proper limits.

The country that the writer is concerned with in the most objective way is, of course, the region that most immediately surrounds him, or simply the country, with its body of manners, that he knows well enough to employ. It's generally suggested that the Southern writer has some advantage here. Most readers these days must be sufficiently sick of hearing about Southern writers and Southern writing and what so many reviewers insist upon calling the "Southern school." No one has ever made plain just what the Southern school is or which writers belong to it. Sometimes, when it is most respectable, it seems to mean the little group of Agrarians that flourished at Vanderbilt in the twenties; but more often the term conjures up an image of Gothic monstrosities and the idea of a preoccupation with everything deformed and grotesque. Most of us are considered, I believe, to be unhappy combinations of Poe and Erskine Caldwell.

At least, however, we are all known to be anguished. The writers of the editorial in question suggest that our anguish is a result of our isolation from the rest of the country. I feel that this would be news to most Southern writers. The anguish that most of us have observed for some time now has been caused not by the fact that the South is alienated from the rest of the country, but by the fact that it is not alienated enough, that every day we are getting more and more like the rest of the country, that we are being forced out, not only of our many sins but of our few virtues. This may be unholy anguish but it is anguish nevertheless.

Manners are of such great consequence to the novelist that any kind will do. Bad manners are better than no manners at all, and because we are losing our customary manners we are probably overly conscious of them; this seems to be a condition that produces writers. In the South there are more amateur authors than there are rivers and streams. In almost every hamlet you'll find at least one lady writing epics in Negro dialect and probably two or three old gentlemen who have impossible historical novels on the way. The woods are full of regional writers, and it is the great horror of every serious Southern writer that he will become one of them.

The writer himself will probably feel that the only way for him to keep from becoming one of them is to examine his conscience and to observe our fierce but fading manners in the light of an ultimate concern; others would say that the way to escape being a regional writer is to widen the region. Don't be a Southern writer; be an American writer. Express this great country—which is enjoying an unparalleled prosperity, which is the strongest nation in the world, and which has almost produced a classless society. How, with all this prosperity and strength and class-lessness staring you in the face, can you honestly produce a literature which doesn't make plain the joy of life?

The writer whose position is Christian, and probably also the writer whose position is not, will begin to wonder at this point if there could not be some ugly correlation between our unparalleled prosperity and the stridency of these demands for a literature that shows us the joy of life. He may at least be permitted to ask if these screams for joy would be quite so piercing if joy were really more abundant in our prosperous society.

The Christian writer will feel that in the greatest depth of vision, moral judgment will be implicit and that when we are invited to represent the country according to survey, what we are asked to do is to separate mystery from manners and judgment from vision, in order to produce something a little more palatable to the modern temper. We are asked to form our consciences in the light of statistics, which is to establish the relative as absolute. For many this may be a convenience, since we don't live in an age of settled belief; but it cannot be a convenience, it cannot even be possible, for the writer who is a Catholic. He will feel that any long-continued service to it will produce a soggy, formless, and senti-mental literature, one that will provide a sense of spiritual purpose for those who connect the spirit with romanticism and a sense of joy for those who confuse that virtue with satisfaction. The storyteller is concerned with what is; but if what is, is what can be determined by survey, then the disciples of Dr. Kinsey and Dr. Gallup are sufficient for the day thereof.

In the greatest fiction, the writer's moral sense coincides with his dramatic sense, and I see no way for it to do this unless his moral judgment is part of the very act of seeing, and he is free to use it. I have heard it said that belief in Christian dogma is a hindrance to the writer, but I myself have found nothing further from the truth. Actually, it frees the storyteller to observe. It is not a set of rules which fixes what he sees in the world. It affects his writing primarily by guaranteeing his respect for mystery.

In the introduction to a collection of his stories called *Rotting Hill*, Wyndham Lewis has written, "If I write about a hill that is rotting, it is because I despise rot." The general accusation passed against writers now is that they write about rot because they love it. Some do, and their works may betray them, but it is impossible not to believe that some write about rot because they see it and recognize it for what it is.

It may well be asked, however, why so much of our literature is apparently lacking in a sense of spiritual purpose and in the joy of life, and if stories lacking such are actually credible. The only conscience I have to examine in this matter is my own, and when I look at stories I have written I find that they are, for the most part, about people who are poor, who are afflicted in both mind and body, who have little—or at best a distorted—sense of spiritual purpose, and whose actions do not apparently give the reader a great assurance of the joy of life.

Yet how is this? For I am no disbeliever in spiritual purpose and no vague believer. I see from the standpoint of Christian orthodoxy. This means that for me the meaning of life is centered in our Redemption by Christ and that what I see in the world I see in its relation to that. I don't think that this is a position that can be taken halfway or one that is particularly easy in these times to make transparent in fiction.

Some may blame preoccupation with the grotesque on the fact that here we have a Southern writer and that this is just the type of imagination that Southern life fosters. I have written several stories which did not seem to me to have any grotesque characters in them at all, but which have immediately been labeled grotesque by non-Southern readers. I find it hard to believe that what is observable behavior in one section can be entirely without parallel in another. At least, of late, Southern writers have had the opportunity of pointing out that none of us invented Elvis Presley and that that youth is himself probably less an occasion for concern than his popularity, which is not restricted to the Southern part of the country. The problem may well become one of finding something that is *not* grotesque and of deciding what standards we would use in looking.

My own feeling is that writers who see by the light of their Christian faith will have, in these times, the sharpest eyes for the grotesque, for the perverse, and for the unacceptable. In some cases, these writers may be unconsciously infected with the Manichaean spirit of the times and suffer the much discussed disjunction between sensibility and belief, but I think that more often the reason for this attention to the perverse is the difference between their beliefs and the beliefs of their audience. Redemption is meaningless unless there is cause for it in the actual life we live, and for the last few centuries there has been operating in our culture the secular belief that there is no such cause.

The novelist with Christian concerns will find in modern life distortions which are repugnant to him, and his problem will be to make these appear as distortions to an audience which is used to seeing them as natural; and he may well be forced to take ever more violent means to get his vision across to this hostile audience. When you can assume that your audience holds the same beliefs you do, you can relax a little and use more normal ways of talking to it; when you have to assume that it does not, then you have to make your vision apparent by shock—to the hard of hearing you shout, and for the almost blind you draw large and startling figures.

Unless we are willing to accept our artists as they are, the answer to the question, "Who speaks for America today?" will have to be: the advertising agencies. They are entirely capable of showing us our unparalleled prosperity and our almost classless society, and no one has ever accused them of not being affirmative. Where the artist is still trusted, he will not be looked to for assurance. Those who believe that art proceeds from a healthy, and not from a diseased, faculty of the mind will take what he shows them as a revelation, not of what we ought to be but of what we are at a given time and under given circumstances; that is, as a limited revelation but a revelation nevertheless.

When we talk about the writer's country we are liable to forget that no matter what particular country it is, it is inside as well as outside him. Art requires a delicate adjustment of the outer and inner worlds in such a way that, without changing their nature, they can be seen through each other. To know oneself is to know one's region. It is also to know the world, and it is also, paradoxically, a form of exile from that world. The writer's value is lost, both to himself and to his country, as soon as he ceases to see that country as a part of himself, and to know oneself is, above all, to know what one lacks. It is to measure oneself against Truth, and not the other way around. The first product of self-knowledge is humility, and this is not a virtue conspicuous in any national character.

St. Cyril of Jerusalem, in instructing catechumens, wrote: "The dragon sits by the side of the road, watching those who pass. Beware lest he devour you. We go to the Father of Souls, but it is necessary to pass by the dragon." No matter what form the dragon may take, it is of this mysterious passage past him, or into his jaws, that stories of any depth will always be concerned to tell, and this being the case, it requires considerable courage at any time, in any country, not to turn away from the storyteller.

A REASONABLE USE OF THE UNREASONABLE

Last fall I received a letter from a student who said she would be "graciously appreciative" if I would tell her "just what enlightenment" I expected her to get from each of my stories. I suspect she had a paper to

Originally a speech made by Flannery O'Connor at Hollins College, Virginia, to introduce a reading of "A Good Man Is Hard to Find" in October 1963. Reprinted here by permission of the publisher from *Mystery and Manners*, selected and edited by Sally and Robert Fitzgerald (New York: Farrar, Straus & Giroux, Inc., 1970), copyright © 1957, 1961, 1963, 1964, 1966, 1967, 1969 by the Estate of Mary Flannery O'Connor. Copyright © 1962 by Flannery O'Connor. Copyright © 1961 by Farrar, Straus & Cudahy, Inc.

write. I wrote her back to forget about the enlightenment and just try to enjoy them. I knew that was the most unsatisfactory answer I could have given because, of course, she didn't want to enjoy them, she just wanted to figure them out.

In most English classes the short story has become a kind of literary specimen to be dissected. Every time a story of mine appears in a Freshman anthology, I have a vision of it, with its little organs laid open, like a frog in a bottle.

I realize that a certain amount of this what-is-the-significance has to go on, but I think something has gone wrong in the process when, for so many students, the story becomes simply a problem to be solved, something which you evaporate to get Instant Enlightenment.

A story really isn't any good unless it successfully resists paraphrase, unless it hangs on and expands in the mind. Properly, you analyze to enjoy, but it's equally true that to analyze with any discrimination, you have to have enjoyed already, and I think that the best reason to hear a story read is that it should stimulate that primary enjoyment.

I don't have any pretensions to being an Aeschylus or Sophocles and providing you in this story with a cathartic experience out of your mythic background, though this story I'm going to read certainly calls up a good deal of the South's mythic background, and it should elicit from you a degree of pity and terror, even though its way of being serious is a comic one. I do think, though, that like the Greeks you should know what is going to happen in this story so that any element of suspense in it will be transferred from its surface to its interior.

I would be most happy if you had already read it, happier still if you knew it well, but since experience has taught me to keep my expectations along these lines modest, I'll tell you that this is the story of a family of six which, on its way driving to Florida, gets wiped out by an escaped convict who calls himself the Misfit. The family is made up of the Grandmother and her son, Bailey, and his children, John Wesley and June Star and the baby, and there is also the cat and the children's mother. The cat is named Pitty Sing, and the Grandmother is taking him with them, hidden in a basket.

Now I think it behooves me to try to establish with you the basis on which reason operates in this story. Much of my fiction takes its character from a reasonable use of the unreasonable, though the reasonableness of my use of it may not always be apparent. The assumptions that underlie this use of it, however, are those of the central Christian mysteries. These are assumptions to which a large part of the modern audience takes exception. About this I can only say that there are perhaps other ways than my own in which this story could be read, but none other by which it could have been written. Belief, in my own case anyway, is the engine that makes perception operate.

The heroine of this story, the Grandmother, is in the most significant position life offers the Christian. She is facing death. And to all appearances she, like the rest of us, is not too well prepared for it. She would like to see the event postponed. Indefinitely.

I've talked to a number of teachers who use this story in class and who tell their students that the Grandmother is evil, that in fact, she's a witch, even down to the cat. One of these teachers told me that his students, and particularly his Southern students, resisted this interpretation with a certain bemused vigor, and he didn't understand why. I had to tell him that they resisted it because they all had grandmothers or great-aunts just like her at home, and they knew, from personal experience, that the old lady lacked comprehension, but that she had a good heart. The Southerner is usually tolerant of those weaknesses that proceed from innocence, and he knows that a taste for self-preservation can be readily combined with the missionary spirit.

This same teacher was telling his students that morally the Misfit was several cuts above the Grandmother. He had a really sentimental attachment to the Misfit. But then a prophet gone wrong is almost always more interesting than your grandmother, and you have to let people take their pleasures where they find them.

It is true that the old lady is a hypocritical old soul; her wits are no match for the Misfit's, nor is her capacity for grace equal to his; yet I think the unprejudiced reader will feel that the Grandmother has a special kind of triumph in this story which instinctively we do not allow to someone altogether bad.

I often ask myself what makes a story work, and what makes it hold up as a story, and I have decided that it is probably some action, some gesture of a character that is unlike any other in the story, one which indicates where the real heart of the story lies. This would have to be an action or a gesture which was both totally right and totally unexpected; it would have to be one that was both in character and beyond character; it would have to suggest both the world and eternity. The action or gesture I'm talking about would have to be on the anagogical level, that is, the level which has to do with the Divine life and our participation in it. It would be a gesture that transcended any neat allegory that might have been intended or any pat moral categories a reader could make. It would be a gesture which somehow made contact with mystery.

There is a point in this story where such a gesture occurs. The Grandmother is at last alone, facing the Misfit. Her head clears for an instant and she realizes, even in her limited way, that she is responsible for the man before her and joined to him by ties of kinship which have their roots deep in the mystery she has been merely prattling about so far. And at this point, she does the right thing, she makes the right gesture.

I find that students are often puzzled by what she says and does here, but I think myself that if I took out this gesture and what she says with it, I would have no story. What was left would not be worth your attention. Our age not only does not have a very sharp eye for the almost imperceptible intrusions of grace, it no longer has much feeling for the nature of the violences which precede and follow them. The devil's greatest wile, Baudelaire has said, is to convince us that he does not exist.

I suppose the reasons for the use of so much violence in modern fiction will differ with each writer who uses it, but in my own stories I have found that violence is strangely capable of returning my characters to reality and preparing them to accept their moment of grace. Their heads are so hard that almost nothing else will do the work. This idea, that reality is something to which we must be returned at considerable cost, is one which is seldom understood by the casual reader, but it is one which is implicit in the Christian view of the world.

I don't want to equate the Misfit with the devil. I prefer to think that, however unlikely this may seem, the old lady's gesture, like the mustard-seed, will grow to be a great crow-filled tree in the Misfit's heart, and will be enough of a pain to him there to turn him into the prophet he was meant to become. But that's another story.

This story has been called grotesque, but I prefer to call it literal. A good story is literal in the same sense that a child's drawing is literal. When a child draws, he doesn't intend to distort but to set down exactly what he sees, and as his gaze is direct, he sees the lines that create motion. Now the lines of motion that interest the writer are usually invisible. They are lines of spiritual motion. And in this story you should be on the lookout for such things as the action of grace in the Grandmother's soul, and not for the dead bodies.

We hear many complaints about the prevalence of violence in modern fiction, and it is always assumed that this violence is a bad thing and meant to be an end in itself. With the serious writer, violence is never an end in itself. It is the extreme situation that best reveals what we are essentially, and I believe these are times when writers are more interested in what we are essentially than in the tenor of our daily lives. Violence is a force which can be used for good or evil, and among other things taken by it is the kingdom of heaven. But regardless of what can be taken by it, the man in the violent situation reveals those qualities least dispensable in his personality, those qualities which are all he will have to take into eternity with him; and since the characters in this story are all on the verge of eternity, it is appropriate to think of what they take with them. In any case, I hope that if you consider these points in connection with the story, you will come to see it as something more than an account of a family murdered on the way to Florida.

For Study and Discussion

1. According to O'Connor in her first essay, what in its fullest definition is the fiction writer's "country"? How does the writer evoke this

country? Why is it that a "writer's value is lost . . . as soon as he ceases to see that country as a part of himself"?

2. O'Connor agrees with the *Life* magazine editorial that Southern writers are "anguished." How does her explanation of why they are "anguished" differ from that given in the editorial?

3. On what basis does she contend that belief in Christian dogma is not a hindrance but an asset to the fiction writer?

4. Why is it that "writers who see by the light of their Christian faith . . . have . . . the sharpest eyes for the grotesque, for the perverse, and for the unacceptable"? What means must the fiction writer adopt to make these distortions "appear as distortions to an audience which is used to seeing them as natural"?

5. To what extent does O'Connor use distortion in "A Good Man Is Hard to Find"? What other contemporary stories in the text make use of similar distortions?

6. What, exactly, does O'Connor mean in her second essay when she says that much of her fiction "takes its character from a reasonable use of the unreasonable"?

7. Is she being reasonable or unreasonable in her assertion that the Grandmother is not only the heroine of "A Good Man Is Hard to Find," but that she has "a good heart" and "a special kind of triumph in this story which instinctively we do not allow to someone altogether bad"?

8. Describe in your own terms the Grandmother's gesture which, according to O'Connor, provides the "intrusion of grace" which touches the heart of this story. What, exactly, does the old lady do and say that can be called an epiphany illuminating her soul? In what sense is she "responsible for the man before her"?

9. What, would you say, are the qualities of personality which both the Misfit and the Grandmother will take with them into eternity as a result of their confrontation?

10. Does the author's explanation convince you that she has achieved literally in this story "a reasonable use of the unreasonable"? Why or why not?

JOYCE CAROL OATES

THE SHORT STORY

> *This is what fools people: a man is always a teller of tales, he lives surrounded by his stories and the stories of others, he sees everything that happens to him through them; and he tries to live his own life as if he were telling a story. . . . But you have to choose: live or tell.*
>
> Sartre, *Nausea*

The distinction between "living" and "telling" is a fascinating one—it is clearly not a distinction that forbids these activities to the same self, but only to the self of a particular time, in a particular fragment of one's life. To make order out of the confusion of history or to suggest in some orderly manner the irremediable confusion of history, one must have experienced it first; so the command is not "live or tell" but "live first then tell." Thrown in the world, as Flaubert says, we are too confused to make sense of it; we must withdraw from the world in order to truly experience it.

In our time, in the Seventies, we are chided for being too intellectual, too clinical, if we do not surrender to the tyranny of the Present. Our art, if it is careful, if it makes a rational and even calculated point, is considered a betrayal of the spontaneous joy of life—living—which is always non-rational or anti-rational, as if only the more primitive levels of our brains are truly human. All this is a mistake. More than that, it is a waste: it is a waste that intelligent people should earnestly deny their intelligence, extolling the impulsive and the sensuous and the "original." In making a blunt distinction between a life of action and a life of reflection, Sartre is insisting that the materials of life cannot become translated immediately into the materials of art; the two belong to entirely different dimensions.

Originally published in, and reprinted here from, the *Southern Humanities Review*, Summer 1971, by permission of the publisher, the author, and Blanche C. Gregory, Inc. Copyright © 1971 by Joyce Carol Oates.

Any remarks about the short story made by a writer of short stories are bound to be autobiographical, if they are at all honest. For me the short story is an absolutely undecipherable fact. Years ago I believed that art was rational, at bottom, that it could be seen to "make sense," that it had a definite relationship with philosophical inquiry, though its aim was not necessarily to resolve philosophical doubt. Now I am not so sure: certain short stories, certain works of fiction, are obviously more rational than others, more reducible to an essence. But others are mysterious and fluid and unpossessible, like certain people. The short story is a dream verbalized, arranged in space and presented to the world, imagined as a sympathetic audience (and not, as the world really is, a busy and indifferent crowd): the dream is said to be some kind of manifestation of desire, so the short story must also represent a desire, perhaps only partly expressed, but the most interesting thing about it is its mystery.

Withdrawing from life does not diminish the mystery of life, as one might think; instead, the mystery is deepened. Anyone who has lived through an upsetting experience can testify that at the time his immediate sensations were too confused to be anything more than superficial—a whirlwind of dots, of pointillistic impressions—and that only through contemplation can any kind of aesthetic or intellectual distance be achieved. Therefore I am in favor of a kind of monastic seclusion for the writer, absurd as that may sound today—when everyone is urged to plunge into life, as into a communal bath at a "sensitivity session"—and though I believe that the basis of the writing of fiction is the unconscious, that oceanic, ungovernable, unfathomable reservoir of human energy, it is still my deepest certainty that art, if not life, requires intelligence and discretion and transcendence, that we must make the choice of living or telling if what we have to tell is worth anyone else's concern.

For Study and Discussion

1. To what extent does Oates qualify Sartre's "live or tell" alternative?

2. Why must we "withdraw from the world in order to truly experience it"? Compare Oates' viewpoint with that of Flannery O'Connor: "To know oneself is to know one's region. It is also to know the world, and it is . . . a form of exile from that world" (p. 133).

3. Why does art seem to betray the "joy of life"?

4. Explain the meaning of Oates' statement that "the short story is a dream verbalized." How does this statement relate to her later one that "the basis of writing fiction is the unconscious . . ."?

TOPICS FOR DISCUSSION AND WRITING

1. According to the writers in this section, in what specific ways does the contemporary short story differ from the nineteenth-century story? On what grounds can these differences be explained? Write an essay pointing out differences (in form, purpose, technique, etc.) between any representative nineteenth-century story and a contemporary story by Flannery O'Connor, Pritchett, West, K. A. Porter, or Oates.

2. Whereas most well-known writers of the nineteenth and early twentieth centuries have lost much of their appeal for today's short-story writers and critics, Chekhov and James are widely regarded as masters still worthy of emulation. Write an essay exploring the reasons for their current popularity and the relative lack of interest in such once-popular writers as Aldrich, Harte, and O. Henry.

3. As Overstreet has noted, a common complaint raised against the contemporary story is that "it specializes in the unpleasant and abnormal." Select a contemporary story against which such a charge might be made and write an essay either justifying or condemning the author's use of the unpleasant or abnormal.

4. In deploring the emphasis placed on psychology in the contemporary story, Baker asserts that "The reading of psychological case studies is a highly interesting and sometimes profitable pastime. But it does not have the excitement of fiction." Overstreet, on the other hand, maintains that "Objective events are necessary for drama in inverse proportion to the psychological charge that a situation carries. If little is thought or felt, much must happen; if much is thought and felt, no elaborate stacking-up of incidents is necessary . . . ." Select two or three modern stories in which psychology plays a prominent role and write an essay explaining whether or not they have "the excitement of fiction."

5. In "The Fiction Writer and His Country," Flannery O'Connor stress-es the importance to the writer of his country—"the region that most immediately surrounds him . . . with its body of manners, that he knows well enough to employ" (p. 130). Using O'Connor's own story or those by Toomer, Faulkner, Taylor, or Oates, write an essay explaining in detail the significance of *place* or *setting* in the story.

6. The critical remarks in Section III advance both optimistic and pessimistic views about the present and future status of the short story. What grounds are there for optimism? For pessimism? Now that you have read representative samples of critical debate covering a century and a half of short-story development, what is your opinion of the present and future status of the short story as a literary form? Develop your views in an essay.

short
stories

Tone: not scary, not frightening.
Not scary. playfull.

WASHINGTON IRVING

THE SPECTRE BRIDEGROOM

A TRAVELLER'S TALE*

> He that supper for is dight,
> He lyes full cold, I trow, this night!
> Yestreen to chamber I him led,
> This night Gray-Steel has made his bed.
> Sir Eger, Sir Grahame and Sir Gray-Steel

On the summit of one of the heights of the Odenwald, a wild and romantic tract of Upper Germany, that lies not far from the confluence of the Main and the Rhine, there stood, many, many years since, the Castle of the Baron Von Landshort. It is now quite fallen to decay, and almost buried among beech trees and dark firs; above which, however, its old watch-tower may still be seen struggling, like the former possessor I have mentioned, to carry a high head, and look down upon a neighboring country.

The baron was a dry branch of the great family of Katzenellenbogen,† and inherited the relics of the property, and all the pride of his ancestors. Though the warlike disposition of his predecessors had much impaired the family possessions, yet the baron still endeavored to keep up some show of former state. The times were peaceable, and the German nobles, in general, had abandoned their inconvenient old castles, perched like eagles' nests among the mountains, and had built more convenient residences in the valleys: still the baron remained proudly drawn up in his little fortress, cherishing, with hereditary inveteracy, all the old family feuds; so that he was on ill terms with some of his nearest

Originally published in the *Sketchbook*, November 1819. Reprinted here from *The Works of Washington Irving*, new edition, revised (New York: G. P. Putnam's Sons, 1860), Vol. II.

*The erudite reader, well versed in good-for-nothing lore, will perceive that the above Tale must have been suggested to the old Swiss by a little French anecdote, a circumstance said to have taken place at Paris.

†*i.e.*, CAT's-ELBOW. The name of a family of those parts very powerful in former times. The appellation, we are told, was given in compliment to a peerless dame of the family, celebrated for her fine arm.

neighbors, on account of disputes that had happened between their great-great-grandfathers.

The baron had but one child, a daughter; but nature, when she grants but one child, always compensates by making it a prodigy; and so it was with the daughter of the baron. All the nurses, gossips, and country cousins, assured her father that she had not her equal for beauty in all Germany; and who should know better than they? She had, moreover, been brought up with great care, under the superintendence of two maiden aunts, who had spent some years of their early life at one of the little German courts, and were skilled in all the branches of knowledge necessary to the education of a fine lady. Under their instructions she became a miracle of accomplishments. By the time she was eighteen, she could embroider to admiration, and had worked whole histories of the saints in tapestry, with such strength of expression in their countenances, that they looked like so many souls in purgatory. She could read without great difficulty, and had spelled her way through several church legends, and almost all the chivalric wonders of the Heldenbuch. She had even made considerable proficiency in writing; could sign her own name without missing a letter, and so legibly, that her aunts could read it without spectacles. She excelled in making little good-for-nothing lady-like nicknacks of all kinds; was versed in the most abstruse dancing of the day; played a number of airs on the harp and guitar; and knew all the tender ballads of the Minnie-lieders by heart.

Her aunts, too, having been great flirts and coquettes in their younger days, were admirably calculated to be vigilant guardians and strict censors of the conduct of their niece; for there is no duenna so rigidly prudent, and inexorably decorous, as a superannuated coquette. She was rarely suffered out of their sight; never went beyond the domains of the castle, unless well attended, or, rather well watched; had continual lectures read to her about strict decorum and implicit obedience; and, as to the men—pah!—she was taught to hold them at such a distance, and in such absolute distrust, that, unless properly authorized, she would not have cast a glance upon the handsomest cavalier in the world—no, not if he were even dying at her feet.

The good effects of this system were wonderfully apparent. The young lady was a pattern of docility and correctness. While others were wasting their sweetness in the glare of the world, and liable to be plucked and thrown aside by every hand, she was coyly blooming into fresh and lovely womanhood under the protection of those immaculate spinsters, like a rose-bud blushing forth among guardian thorns. Her aunts looked upon her with pride and exultation, and vaunted that though all the other young ladies in the world might go astray, yet, thank Heaven, nothing of the kind could happen to the heiress of Katzenellenbogen.

But, however scantily the Baron Von Landshort might be provided with children, his household was by no means a small one; for

Providence had enriched him with abundance of poor relations. They, one and all, possessed the affectionate disposition common to humble relatives; were wonderfully attached to the baron, and took every possible occasion to come in swarms and enliven the castle. All family festivals were commemorated by these good people at the baron's expense; and when they were filled with good cheer, they would declare that there was nothing on earth so delightful as these family meetings, these jubilees of the heart.

The baron, though a small man, had a large soul, and it swelled with satisfaction at the consciousness of being the greatest man in the little world about him. He loved to tell long stories about the stark old warriors whose portraits looked grimly down from the walls around, and he found no listeners equal to those who fed at his expense. He was much given to the marvellous, and a firm believer in all those supernatural tales with which every mountain and valley in Germany abounds. The faith of his guests even exceeded his own; they listened to every tale of wonder with open eyes and mouth, and never failed to be astonished, even though repeated for the hundredth time. Thus lived the Baron Von Landshort, the oracle of his table, the absolute monarch of his little territory, and happy, above all things, in the persuasion that he was the wisest man of the age.

At the time of which my story treats there was a great family gathering at the castle, on an affair of the utmost importance: it was to receive the destined bridegroom of the baron's daughter. A negotiation had been carried on between the father and an old nobleman of Bavaria, to unite the dignity of their houses by the marriage of their children. The preliminaries had been conducted with proper punctilio. The young people were betrothed without seeing each other; and the time was appointed for the marriage ceremony. The young Count Von Altenburg had been recalled from the army for the purpose, and was actually on his way to the baron's to receive his bride. Missives had even been received from him, from Wurtzburg, where he was accidentally detained, mentioning the day and hour when he might be expected to arrive.

The castle was in a tumult of preparation to give him a suitable welcome. The fair bride had been decked out with uncommon care. The two aunts had superintended her toilet, and quarreled the whole morning about every article of her dress. The young lady had taken advantage of their contest to follow the bent of her own taste; and fortunately it was a good one. She looked as lovely as youthful bridegroom could desire; and the flutter of expectation heightened the lustre of her charms.

The suffusions that mantled her face and neck, the gentle heaving of the bosom, the eye now and then lost in reverie, all betrayed the soft tumult that was going on in her little heart. The aunts were continually hovering around her; for maiden aunts are apt to take great interest in affairs of this nature. They were giving her a world of staid counsel how to deport herself, what to say, and in what manner to receive the expected lover.

The baron was no less busied in preparations. He had, in truth, nothing exactly to do: but he was naturally a fuming bustling little man, and could not remain passive when all the world was in a hurry. He worried from top to bottom of the castle with an air of infinite anxiety; he continually called the servants from their work to exhort them to be diligent; and buzzed about every hall and chamber, as idly restless and importunate as a blue-bottle fly of a warm summer's day.

In the mean time the fatted calf had been killed; the forests had rung with the clamor of the huntsmen; the kitchen was crowded with good cheer; the cellars had yielded up whole oceans of *Rhein-wein* and *Ferne-wein*; and even the great Heidelberg tun had been laid under contribution. Every thing was ready to receive the distinguished guest with *Saus und Braus* in the true spirit of German hospitality—but the guest delayed to make his appearance. Hour rolled after hour. The sun that had poured his downward rays upon the rich forest of the Odenwald, now just gleamed along the summits of the mountains. The baron mounted the highest tower, and strained his eyes in hopes of catching a distant sight of the count and his attendants. Once he thought he beheld them; the sound of horns came floating from the valley, prolonged by the mountain echoes. A number of horsemen were seen far below, slowly advancing along the road; but when they had nearly reached the foot of the mountain, they suddenly struck off in a different direction. The last ray of sunshine departed—the bats began to flit by in the twilight—the road grew dimmer and dimmer to the view; and nothing appeared stirring in it but now and then a peasant lagging homeward from his labor.

While the old castle of Landshort was in this state of perplexity, a very interesting scene was transacting in a different part of the Odenwald.

The young Count Von Altenburg was tranquilly pursuing his route in that sober jog-trot way, in which a man travels toward matrimony when his friends have taken all the trouble and uncertainty of courtship off his hands, and a bride is waiting for him, as certainly as a dinner at the end of his journey. He had encountered at Wurtzburg, a youthful companion in arms, with whom he had seen some service on the frontiers; Herman Von Starkenfaust, one of the stoutest hands, and worthiest hearts, of German chivalry, who was now returning from the army. His father's castle was not far distant from the old fortress of Landshort, although an hereditary feud rendered the families hostile, and strangers to each other.

In the warm-hearted moment of recognition, the young friends related all their past adventures and fortunes, and the count gave the whole history of his intended nuptials with a young lady whom he had never seen, but of whose charms he had received the most enrapturing descriptions.

As the route of the friends lay in the same direction, they agreed to perform the rest of their journey together; and, that they might do it more leisurely, set off from Wurtzburg at an early hour, the count having given directions for his retinue to follow and overtake him.

They beguiled their wayfaring with recollections of their military scenes and adventures; but the count was apt to be a little tedious, now and then, about the reputed charms of his bride, and the felicity that awaited him.

In this way they had entered among the mountains of the Odenwald, and were traversing one of its most lonely and thickly-wooded passes. It is well known that the forests of Germany have always been as much infested with robbers as its castles by spectres; and, at this time, the former were particularly numerous, from the hordes of disbanded soldiers wandering about the country. It will not appear extraordinary, therefore, that the cavaliers were attacked by a gang of these stragglers in the midst of the forest. They defended themselves with bravery, but were nearly overpowered, when the count's retinue arrived to their assistance. At sight of them the robbers fled, but not until the count had received a mortal wound. He was slowly and carefully conveyed back to the city of Wurtzburg, and a friar summoned from a neighboring convent, who was famous for his skill in administering to both soul and body; but half of his skill was superfluous; the moments of the unfortunate count were numbered.

With his dying breath he entreated his friend to repair instantly to the castle of Landshort, and explain the fatal cause of his not keeping his appointment with his bride. Though not the most ardent of lovers, he was one of the most punctilious of men, and appeared earnestly solicitous that this mission should be speedily and courteously executed. "Unless this is done," said he, "I shall not sleep quietly in my grave!" He repeated these last words with peculiar solemnity. A request, at a moment so impressive, admitted no hesitation. Starkenfaust endeavored to soothe him to calmness; promised faithfully to execute his wish, and gave him his hand in solemn pledge. The dying man pressed it in acknowledgment, but soon lapsed into delirium—raved about his bride—his engagements—his plighted word; ordered his horse, that he might ride to the castle of Landshort; and expired in the fancied act of vaulting into the saddle.

Starkenfaust bestowed a sigh and a soldier's tear on the untimely fate of his comrade; and then pondered on the awkward mission he had undertaken. His heart was heavy, and his head perplexed; for he was to present himself an unbidden guest among hostile people, and to damp their festivity with tidings fatal to their hopes. Still there were certain whisperings of curiosity in his bosom to see this far-famed beauty of Katzenellenbogen, so cautiously shut up from the world; for he was a passionate admirer of the sex, and there was a dash of eccentricity and enterprise in his character that made him fond of all singular adventure.

Previous to his departure he made all due arrangements with the holy fraternity of the convent for the funeral solemnities of his friend, who was to be buried in the cathedral of Wurtzburg, near some of his illustrious relatives; and the mourning retinue of the count took charge of his remains.

It is now high time that we should return to the ancient family of Katzenellenbogen, who were impatient for their guest, and still more for their dinner; and to the worthy little baron, whom we left airing himself on the watch-tower.

Night closed in, but still no guest arrived. The baron descended from the tower in despair. The banquet, which had been delayed from hour to hour, could no longer be postponed. The meats were already overdone; the cook in an agony; and the whole household had the look of a garrison that had been reduced by famine. The baron was obliged reluctantly to give orders for the feast without the presence of the guest. All were seated at table, and just on the point of commencing, when the sound of a horn from without the gate gave notice of the approach of a stranger. Another long blast filled the old courts of the castle with its echoes, and was answered by the warder from the walls. The baron hastened to receive his future son-in-law.

The drawbridge had been let down, and the stranger was before the gate. He was a tall gallant cavalier, mounted on a black steed. His countenance was pale, but he had a beaming, romantic eye, and an air of stately melancholy. The baron was a little mortified that he should have come in this simple, solitary style. His dignity for a moment was ruffled, and he felt disposed to consider it a want of proper respect for the important occasion, and the important family with which he was to be connected. He pacified himself, however, with the conclusion that it must have been youthful impatience which had induced him thus to spur on sooner than his attendants.

"I am sorry," said the stranger, "to break in upon you thus unseasonably—"

Here the baron interrupted him with a world of compliments and greetings; for, to tell the truth, he prided himself upon his courtesy and eloquence. The stranger attempted, once or twice, to stem the torrent of words, but in vain, so he bowed his head and suffered it to flow on. By the time the baron had come to a pause, they had reached the inner court of the castle; and the stranger was again about to speak, when he was once more interrupted by the appearance of the female part of the family, leading forth the shrinking and blushing bride. He gazed on her for a moment as one entranced; it seemed as if his whole soul beamed forth in the gaze, and rested upon that lovely form. One of the maiden aunts whispered something in her ear; she made an effort to speak; her moist blue eye was timidly raised; gave a shy glance of inquiry on the stranger; and was cast again to the ground. The words died away; but there was a sweet smile playing about her lips, and a soft dimpling of the cheek that showed her glance had not been unsatisfactory. It was impossible for a girl of the fond age of eighteen, highly predisposed for love and matrimony, not to be pleased with so gallant a cavalier.

The late hour at which the guest had arrived left no time for parley. The baron was peremptory, and deferred all particular conversation until the morning, and led the way to the untasted banquet.

It was served up in the great hall of the castle. Around the walls hung the hard-favored portraits of the heroes of the house of Katzenel-lenbogen, and the trophies which they had gained in the field and in the chase. Hacked corselets, splintered jousting spears, and tattered banners, were mingled with the spoils of sylvan warfare; the jaws of the wolf, and the tusks of the boar, grinned horribly among crossbows and battle-axes, and a huge pair of antlers branched immediately over the head of the youthful bridegroom.

The cavalier took but little notice of the company or the entertainment. He scarcely tasted the banquet, but seemed absorbed in admiration of his bride. He conversed in a low tone that could not be overheard—for the language of love is never loud; but where is the female ear so dull that it cannot catch the softest whisper of the lover? There was a mingled tenderness and gravity in his manner, that appeared to have a powerful effect upon the young lady. Her color came and went as she listened with deep attention. Now and then she made some blushing reply, and when his eye was turned away, she would steal a sidelong glance at his romantic countenance, and heave a gentle sigh of tender happiness. It was evident that the young couple were completely enamored. The aunts, who were deeply versed in the mysteries of the heart, declared that they had fallen in love with each other at first sight.

The feast went on merrily, or at least noisily, for the guests were all blessed with those keen appetites that attend upon light purses and mountain air. The baron told his best and longest stories, and never had he told them so well, or with such great effect. If there was any thing marvellous, his auditors were lost in astonishment; and if any thing facetious, they were sure to laugh exactly in the right place. The baron, it is true, like most great men, was too dignified to utter any joke but a dull one; it was always enforced, however, by a bumper of excellent Hochheimer; and even a dull joke, at one's own table, served up with jolly old wine, is irresistible. Many good things were said by poorer and keener wits, that would not bear repeating, except on similar occasions; many sly speeches whispered in ladies' ears, that almost convulsed them with suppressed laughter; and a song or two roared out by a poor, but merry and broad-faced cousin of the baron, that absolutely made the maiden aunts hold up their fans.

Amid all this revelry, the stranger guest maintained a most singular and unseasonable gravity. His countenance assumed a deeper cast of dejection as the evening advanced; and, strange as it may appear, even the baron's jokes seemed only to render him the more melancholy. At times he was lost in thought, and at times there was a perturbed and restless wandering of the eye that bespoke a mind but ill at ease. His conversations with the bride became more and more earnest and mysterious. Lowering clouds began to steal over the fair serenity of her brow, and tremors to run through her tender frame.

All this could not escape the notice of the company. Their gayety was chilled by the unaccountable gloom of the bridegroom; their spirits were infected; whispers and glances were interchanged, accompanied by shrugs and dubious shakes of the head. The song and the laugh grew less and less frequent; there were dreary pauses in the conversation, which were at length succeeded by wild tales and supernatural legends. One dismal story produced another still more dismal, and the baron nearly frightened some of the ladies into hysterics with the history of the goblin horseman that carried away the fair Leonora; a dreadful story, which has since been put into excellent verse, and is read and believed by all the world.

The bridegroom listened to this tale with profound attention. He kept his eyes steadily fixed on the baron, and, as the story drew to a close, began gradually to rise from his seat, growing taller and taller, until, in the baron's entranced eye, he seemed almost to tower into a giant. The moment the tale was finished, he heaved a deep sigh, and took a solemn farewell of the company. They were all amazement. The baron was perfectly thunder-struck.

"What! going to leave the castle at midnight? why, every thing was prepared for his reception; a chamber was ready for him if he wished to retire."

The stranger shook his head mournfully and mysteriously; "I must lay my head in a different chamber to-night!"

There was something in this reply, and the tone in which it was uttered, that made the baron's heart misgive him; but he rallied his forces, and repeated his hospitable entreaties.

The stranger shook his head silently, but positively, at every offer; and, waving his farewell to the company, stalked slowly out of the hall. The maiden aunts were absolutely petrified—the bride hung her head, and a tear stole to her eye.

The baron followed the stranger to the great court of the castle, where the black charger stood pawing the earth, and snorting with impatience. When they had reached the portal, whose deep archway was dimly lighted by a cresset, the stranger paused, and addressed the baron in a hollow tone of voice, which the vaulted roof rendered still more sepulchral.

"Now that we are alone," said he, "I will impart to you the reason of my going. I have a solemn, an indispensable engagement—"

"Why," said the baron, "cannot you send some one in your place?"

"It admits of no substitute—I must attend it in person—I must away to Wurtzburg cathedral—"

"Ay," said the baron, plucking up spirit, "but not until to-morrow—to-morrow you shall take your bride there."

"No! no!" replied the stranger, with tenfold solemnity, "my engagement is with no bride—the worms! the worms expect me! I am a dead man—I have been slain by robbers—my body lies at Wurtzburg—at midnight I am to be buried—the grave is waiting for me—I must keep my appointment!"

He sprang on his black charger, dashed over the drawbridge, and the clattering of his horse's hoofs was lost in the whistling of the nightblast.

The baron returned to the hall in the utmost consternation, and related what had passed. Two ladies fainted outright, others sickened at the idea of having banqueted with a spectre. It was the opinion of some, that this might be the wild huntsman, famous in German legend. Some talked of mountain sprites, of wood-demons, and of other supernatural beings, with which the good people of Germany have been so grievously harassed since time immemorial. One of the poor relations ventured to suggest that it might be some sportive evasion of the young cavalier, and that the very gloominess of the caprice seemed to accord with so melancholy a personage. This, however, drew on him the indignation of the whole company, and especially of the baron, who looked upon him as little better than an infidel; so that he was fain to abjure his heresy as speedily as possible, and come into the faith of the true believers.

But whatever may have been the doubts entertained, they were completely put to an end by the arrival, next day, of regular missives confirming the intelligence of the young count's murder, and his interment in Wurtzburg cathedral.

The dismay at the castle may well be imagined. The baron shut himself up in his chamber. The guests, who had come to rejoice with him, could not think of abandoning him in his distress. They wandered about the courts, or collected in groups in the hall, shaking their heads and shrugging their shoulders, at the troubles of so good a man; and sat longer than ever at table, and ate and drank more stoutly than ever, by way of keeping up their spirits. But the situation of the widowed bride was the most pitiable. To have lost a husband before she had even embraced him—and such a husband! If the very spectre could be so gracious and noble, what must have been the living man? She filled the house with lamentations.

On the night of the second day of her widowhood, she had retired to her chamber, accompanied by one of her aunts, who insisted on sleeping with her. The aunt, who was one of the best tellers of ghost stories in all Germany, had just been recounting one of her longest, and had fallen asleep in the very midst of it. The chamber was remote, and overlooked a small garden. The niece lay pensively gazing at the beams of the rising moon, as they trembled on the leaves of an aspen-tree before the lattice.

The castle clock had just tolled midnight, when a soft strain of music stole up from the garden. She rose hastily from her bed, and stepped lightly to the window. A tall figure stood among the shadows of the trees. As it raised its head, a beam of moonlight fell upon the countenance. Heaven and earth! She beheld the Spectre Bridegroom! A loud shriek at that moment burst upon her ear, and her aunt, who had been awakened by the music, and had followed her silently to the window, fell into her arms. When she looked again, the spectre had disappeared.

Of the two females, the aunt now required the most soothing, for she was perfectly beside herself with terror. As to the young lady, there was something, even in the spectre of her lover, that seemed endearing. There was still the semblance of manly beauty; and though the shadow of a man is but little calculated to satisfy the affections of a love-sick girl, yet, where the substance is not to be had, even that is consoling. The aunt declared that she would never sleep in that chamber again; the niece, for once, was refractory, and declared as strongly that she would sleep in no other in the castle: the consequence was, that she had to sleep in it alone: but she drew a promise from her aunt not to relate the story of the spectre, lest she should be denied the only melancholy pleasure left her on earth—that of inhabiting the chamber over which the guardian shade of her lover kept its nightly vigils.

How long the good old lady would have observed this promise is uncertain, for she dearly loved to talk of the marvellous, and there is a triumph in being the first to tell a frightful story; it is, however, still quoted in the neighborhood, as a memorable instance of female secrecy, that she kept it to herself for a whole week; when she was suddenly absolved from all further restraint by intelligence brought to the breakfast table one morning that the young lady was not to be found. Her room was empty—the bed had not been slept in—the window was open, and the bird had flown!

The astonishment and concern with which the intelligence was received can only be imagined by those who have witnessed the agitation which the mishaps of a great man cause among his friends. Even the poor relations paused for a moment from the indefatigable labors of the trencher; when the aunt, who had at first been struck speechless, wrung her hands, and shrieked out, "The goblin! the goblin! she's carried away by the goblin."

In a few words she related the fearful scene of the garden, and concluded that the spectre must have carried off his bride. Two of the domestics corroborated the opinion, for they had heard the clattering of a horse's hoofs down the mountain about midnight, and had no doubt that it was the spectre on his black charger, bearing her away to the tomb. All present were struck with the direful probability; for events of the kind are extremely common in Germany, as many well authenticated histories bear witness.

What a lamentable situation was that of the poor baron! What a heart-rending dilemma for a fond father, and a member of the great family of Katzenellenbogen! His only daughter had either been rapt away to the grave, or he was to have some wood-demon for a son-in-law, and, perchance, a troop of goblin grandchildren. As usual, he was completely bewildered, and all the castle in an uproar. The men were ordered to take horse and scour every road and path and glen of the Odenwald. The baron himself had just drawn on his jack-boots, girded on his sword, and was about to mount his steed to sally forth on the doubtful quest, when he was brought to a pause by a new apparition. A lady was seen approaching the castle, mounted on a palfrey, attended by a cavalier on horseback. She galloped up to the gate, sprang from her horse, and falling at the baron's feet, embraced his knees. It was his lost daughter, and her companion—the Spectre Bridegroom! The baron was astounded. He looked at his daughter, then at the spectre, and almost doubted the evidence of his senses. The latter, too, was wonderfully improved in his appearance since his visit to the world of spirits. His dress was splendid, and set off a noble figure of manly symmetry. He was no longer pale and melancholy. His fine countenance was flushed with the glow of youth, and joy rioted in his large dark eye.

The mystery was soon cleared up. The cavalier (for, in truth, as you must have known all the while, he was no goblin) announced himself as Sir Herman Von Starkenfaust. He related his adventure with the young count. He told how he had hastened to the castle to deliver the unwelcome tidings, but that the eloquence of the baron had interrupted him in every attempt to tell his tale. How the sight of the bride had completely captivated him, and that to pass a few hours near her, he had tacitly suffered the mistake to continue. How he had been sorely perplexed in what way to make a decent retreat, until the baron's goblin stories had suggested his eccentric exit. How, fearing the feudal hostility of the family, he had repeated his visits by stealth—had haunted the garden beneath the young lady's window—had wooed—had won—had borne away in triumph—and, in a word, had wedded, the fair.

Under any other circumstances the baron would have been inflexible, for he was tenacious of paternal authority, and devoutly obstinate in all family feuds; but he loved his daughter; he had lamented her as lost; he rejoiced to find her still alive; and, though her husband was of a hostile house, yet, thank Heaven, he was not a goblin. There was something, it must be acknowledged, that did not exactly accord with his notions of strict veracity, in the joke the knight had passed upon him of his being a dead man; but several old friends present, who had served in the wars, assured him that every stratagem was excusable in love, and that the cavalier was entitled to especial privilege, having lately served as a trooper.

Matters, therefore, were happily arranged. The baron pardoned the young couple on the spot. The revels at the castle were resumed. The poor relations overwhelmed this new member of the family with loving-kindness; he was so gallant, so generous—and so rich. The aunts, it is true, were somewhat scandalized that their system of strict seclusion, and passive obedience should be so badly exemplified, but attributed all to their negligence in not having the windows grated. One of them was particularly mortified at having her marvellous story marred, and that the only spectre she had ever seen should turn out a counterfeit; but the niece seemed perfectly happy at having found him substantial flesh and blood—and so the story ends.

For Study and Discussion

1. How important to the plot of the story is the baron's "cherishing, with hereditary inveteracy, all the old family feuds"?

2. Are you at any point mystified by the "spectre"? Why or why not? How does the "spectre" contribute to the humor of the story?

3. List and discuss other evidence of Irving's "half-concealed vein of humor" playing throughout the story.

4. Besides these touches of humor, in what other ways does the story fulfill Irving's requirement for a "nicety of execution"?

5. Can you identify in the story any semblance of that "bolus of sound morality" which Irving supposedly pops down the reader's throat?

6. Is the tone of the story consistently spoofing from beginning to end? Which details point most clearly to a whimsically ironic tone? Note especially the characterization of the maiden aunts, poor relations, and the bride herself.

ALEXANDER PUSHKIN

THE SHOT

CHAPTER I

We were stationed in the little town of N——. The life of an officer in the army is well known. In the morning, drill and the riding-school; dinner with the Colonel or at a Jewish restaurant; in the evening, punch and cards. In N—— there was not one open house, not a single marriageable girl. We used to meet in each other's rooms, where, except our uniforms, we never saw anything.

One civilian only was admitted into our society. He was about thirty-five years of age, and therefore we looked upon him as an old fellow. His experience gave him great advantage over us, and his habitual taciturnity, stern disposition and caustic tongue produced a deep impression upon our young minds. Some mystery surrounded his existence; he had the appearance of a Russian, although his name was a foreign one. He had formerly served in the Hussars, and with distinction. Nobody knew the cause that had induced him to retire from the service and settle in a wretched little village, where he lived poorly and, at the same time, extravagantly. He always went on foot, and constantly wore a shabby black overcoat, but the officers of our regiment were ever welcome at his table. His dinners, it is true, never consisted of more than two or three dishes, prepared by a retired soldier, but the champagne flowed like water. Nobody knew what his circumstances were, or what his income was, and nobody dared to question him about them. He had a collection of books, consisting chiefly of works on military matters and a few novels. He willingly lent them to us to read, and never asked for them back; on the other hand, he never returned to the owner the books that were lent to him. His principal amusement was shooting with a pistol.

Originally published under the title, "Vystrel," in *Povesti Pokoinogo Ivana Petrovicha Belkina (The Tales of Belkin)*, 1831. Reprinted here from *The Prose Tales of Alexander Poushkin*, translated by T. Keane (London: G. Bell & Sons, Ltd., 1914), by permission of the publisher.

The walls of his room were riddled with bullets, and were as full of holes as a honeycomb. A rich collection of pistols was the only luxury in the humble cottage where he lived. The skill which he had acquired with his favourite weapon was simply incredible; and if he had offered to shoot a pear off somebody's forage-cap, not a man in our regiment would have hesitated to place the object upon his head.

Our conversation often turned upon duels. Silvio—so I will call him—never joined in it. When asked if he had ever fought, he drily replied that he had; but he entered into no particulars, and it was evident that such questions were not to his liking. We came to the conclusion that he had upon his conscience the memory of some unhappy victim of his terrible skill. Moreover, it never entered into the head of any of us to suspect him of anything like cowardice. There are persons whose mere look is sufficient to repel such a suspicion. But an unexpected incident occurred which astounded us all.

One day, about ten of our officers dined with Silvio. They drank as usual, that is to say, a great deal. After dinner we asked our host to hold the bank for a game at faro. For a long time he refused, for he hardly ever played, but at last he ordered cards to be brought, placed half a hundred ducats upon the table, and sat down to deal. We took our places round him, and the play began. It was Silvio's custom to preserve a complete silence when playing. He never disputed, and never entered into explanations. If the punter made a mistake in calculating, he immediately paid him the difference or noted down the surplus. We were acquainted with this habit of his, and we always allowed him to have his own way; but among us on this occasion was an officer who had only recently been transferred to our regiment. During the course of the game, this officer absently scored one point too many. Silvio took the chalk and noted down the correct account according to his usual custom. The officer, thinking that he had made a mistake, began to enter into explanations. Silvio continued dealing in silence. The officer, losing patience, took the brush and rubbed out what he considered was wrong. Silvio took the chalk and corrected the score again. The officer, heated with wine, play, and the laughter of his comrades, considered himself grossly insulted, and in his rage he seized a brass candlestick from the table, and hurled it at Silvio, who barely succeeded in avoiding the missile. We were filled with consternation. Silvio rose, white with rage, and with gleaming eyes said:

"My dear sir, have the goodness to withdraw, and thank God that this has happened in my house."

None of us entertained the slightest doubt as to what the result would be, and we already looked upon our new comrade as a dead man. The officer withdrew, saying that he was ready to answer for his offence in whatever way the banker liked. The play went on for a few minutes longer, but feeling that our host was no longer interested in the game, we withdrew one after the other, and repaired to our respective quarters, after having exchanged a few words upon the probability of there soon being a vacancy in the regiment.

The next day, at the riding-school, we were already asking each other if the poor lieutenant was still alive, when he himself appeared among us. We put the same question to him, and he replied that he had not yet heard from Silvio. This astonished us. We went to Silvio's house and found him in the courtyard shooting bullet after bullet into an ace pasted upon the gate. He received us as usual, but did not utter a word about the event of the previous evening. Three days passed, and the lieutenant was still alive. We asked each other in astonishment: "Can it be possible that Silvio is not going to fight?"

Silvio did not fight. He was satisfied with a very lame explanation, and became reconciled to his assailant.

This lowered him very much in the opinion of all our young fellows. Want of courage is the last thing to be pardoned by young men, who usually look upon bravery as the chief of all human virtues, and the excuse for every possible fault. But, by degrees, everything became forgotten, and Silvio regained his former influence.

I alone could not approach him on the old footing. Being endowed by nature with a romantic imagination, I had become attached more than all the others to the man whose life was an enigma, and who seemed to me the hero of some mysterious drama. He was fond of me; at least, with me alone did he drop his customary sarcastic tone, and converse on different subjects in a simple and unusually agreeable manner. But after his unlucky evening, the thought that his honour had been tarnished, and that the stain had been allowed to remain upon it in accordance with his own wish, was ever present in my mind, and prevented me treating him as before. I was ashamed to look at him. Silvio was too intelligent and experienced not to observe this and guess the cause of it. This seemed to vex him; at least I observed once or twice a desire on his part to enter into an explanation with me, but I avoided such opportunities, and Silvio gave up the attempt. From that time forward I saw him only in the presence of my comrades, and our confidential conversations came to an end.

The inhabitants of the capital, with minds occupied by so many matters of business and pleasure, have no idea of the many sensations so familiar to the inhabitants of villages and small towns, as, for instance, the awaiting the arrival of the post. On Tuesdays and Fridays our regimental bureau used to be filled with officers: some expecting money, some letters, and others newspapers. The packets were usually opened on the spot, items of news were communicated from one to another, and the bureau used to present a very animated picture. Silvio used to have his letters addressed to our regiment, and he was generally there to receive them.

One day he received a letter, the seal of which he broke with a look of great impatience. As he read the contents, his eyes sparkled. The officers, each occupied with his own letters, did not observe anything.

"Gentlemen," said Silvio, "circumstances demand my immediate departure; I leave to-night. I hope that you will not refuse to dine with me for the last time. I shall expect you, too," he added, turning towards me. "I shall expect you without fail."

With these words he hastily departed, and we, after agreeing to meet at Silvio's, dispersed to our various quarters.

I arrived at Silvio's house at the appointed time, and found nearly the whole regiment there. All his things were already packed; nothing remained but the bare, bullet-riddled walls. We sat down to table. Our host was in an excellent humour, and his gaiety was quickly communicated to the rest. Corks popped every moment, glasses foamed incessantly, and, with the utmost warmth, we wished our departing friend a pleasant journey and every happiness. When we rose from the table it was already late in the evening. After having wished everybody good-bye, Silvio took me by the hand and detained me just at the moment when I was preparing to depart.

"I want to speak to you," he said in a low voice.

I stopped behind.

The guests had departed, and we two were left alone. Sitting down opposite each other, we silently lit our pipes. Silvio seemed greatly troubled; not a trace remained of his former convulsive gaiety. The intense pallor of his face, his sparkling eyes, and the thick smoke issuing from his mouth, gave him a truly diabolical appearance. Several minutes elapsed, and then Silvio broke the silence.

"Perhaps we shall never see each other again," said he; "before we part, I should like to have an explanation with you. You may have observed that I care very little for the opinion of other people, but I like you, and I feel that it would be painful to me to leave you with a wrong impression upon your mind."

He paused, and began to knock the ashes out of his pipe. I sat gazing silently at the ground.

"You thought it strange," he continued, "that I did not demand satisfaction from that drunken idiot R——. You will admit, however, that having the choice of weapons, his life was in my hands, while my own was in no great danger. I could ascribe my forbearance to generosity alone, but I will not tell a lie. If I could have chastised R—— without the least risk to my own life, I should never have pardoned him."

I looked at Silvio with astonishment. Such a confession completely astounded me. Silvio continued:

"Exactly so: I have no right to expose myself to death. Six years ago I received a slap in the face, and my enemy still lives."

My curiosity was greatly excited.

"Did you not fight with him?" I asked. "Circumstances probably separated you."

"I did fight with him," replied Silvio: "and here is a souvenir of our duel."

Silvio rose and took from a cardboard box a red cap with a gold tassel and embroidery (what the French call a *bonnet de police*); he put it on—a bullet had passed through it about an inch above the forehead.

"You know," continued Silvio, "that I served in one of the Hussar regiments. My character is well-known to you: I am accustomed to taking the lead. From my youth this has been my passion. In our time dissoluteness was the fashion, and I was the most outrageous man in the army. We used to boast of our drunkenness: I beat in a drinking bout the famous Bourtsoff,[*] of whom Denis Davidoff[†] has sung. Duels in our regiment were constantly taking place, and in all of them I was either second or principal. My comrades adored me, while the regimental commanders, who were constantly being changed, looked upon me as a necessary evil.

"I was calmly enjoying my reputation, when a young man belonging to a wealthy and distinguished family—I will not mention his name— joined our regiment. Never in my life have I met with such a fortunate fellow! Imagine to yourself youth, wit, beauty, unbounded gaiety, the most reckless bravery, a famous name, untold wealth—imagine all these, and you can form some idea of the effect that he would be sure to produce among us. My supremacy was shaken. Dazzled by my reputation, he began to seek my friendship, but I received him coldly, and without the least regret he held aloof from me. I took a hatred to him. His success in the regiment and in the society of ladies brought me to the verge of despair. I began to seek a quarrel with him; to my epigrams he replied with epigrams which always seemed to me more spontaneous and more cutting than mine, and which were decidedly more amusing, for he joked while I fumed. At last, at a ball given by a Polish landed proprietor, seeing him the object of the attention of all the ladies, and especially of the mistress of the house, with whom I was upon very good terms, I whispered some grossly insulting remark in his ear. He flamed up and gave me a slap in the face. We grasped our swords; the ladies fainted; we were separated; and that same night we set out to fight.

"The dawn was just breaking. I was standing at the appointed place with my three seconds. With inexplicable impatience I awaited my opponent. The spring sun rose, and it was already growing hot. I saw him coming in the distance. He was walking on foot, accompanied by one second. We advanced to meet him. He approached, holding his cap filled with black cherries. The seconds measured twelve paces for us. I had to fire first, but my agitation was so great, that I could not depend upon the steadiness of my hand; and in order to give myself time to become calm, I ceded to him the first shot. My adversary would not

---

[*] A cavalry officer, notorious for his drunken escapades.
[†] A military poet who flourished in the reign of Alexander I.

agree to this. It was decided that we should cast lots. The first number fell to him, the constant favourite of fortune. He took aim, and his bullet went through my cap. It was now my turn. His life at last was in my hands; I looked at him eagerly, endeavouring to detect if only the faintest shadow of uneasiness. But he stood in front of my pistol, picking out the ripest cherries from his cap and spitting out the stones, which flew almost as far as my feet. His indifference annoyed me beyond measure. 'What is the use,' thought I, 'of depriving him of life, when he attaches no value whatever to it?' A malicious thought flashed through my mind. I lowered my pistol.

" 'You don't seem to be ready for death just at present,' I said to him: 'you wish to have your breakfast; I do not wish to hinder you.'

" 'You are not hindering me in the least,' replied he. 'Have the goodness to fire, or just as you please—the shot remains yours; I shall always be ready at your service.'

"I turned to the seconds, informing them that I had no intention of firing that day, and with that the duel came to an end.

"I resigned my commission and retired to this little place. Since then, not a day has passed that I have not thought of revenge. And now my hour has arrived."

Silvio took from his pocket the letter that he had received that morning, and gave it to me to read. Someone (it seemed to be his business agent) wrote to him from Moscow, that a *certain person* was going to be married to a young and beautiful girl.

"You can guess," said Silvio, "who the certain person is. I am going to Moscow. We shall see if he will look death in the face with as much indifference now, when he is on the eve of being married, as he did once with his cherries!"

With these words, Silvio rose, threw his cap upon the floor, and began pacing up and down the room like a tiger in his cage. I had listened to him in silence; strange conflicting feelings agitated me.

The servant entered and announced that the horses were ready. Silvio grasped my hand tightly, and we embraced each other. He seated himself in his *telega*, in which lay two trunks, one containing his pistols, the other his effects. We said good-bye once more, and the horses galloped off.

CHAPTER II

Several years passed, and family circumstances compelled me to settle in the poor little village of M——. Occupied with agricultural pursuits, I ceased not to sigh in secret for my former noisy and careless life. The most difficult thing of all was having to accustom myself to passing the spring and winter evenings in perfect solitude. Until the hour for dinner I managed to pass away the time somehow or other, talking with the bailiff, riding about to inspect the work, or going round to look at the new buildings; but as soon as it began to get dark, I positively did not know what to do with myself. The few books that I had found in the cupboards and store-rooms, I already knew by heart. All the stories that my housekeeper Kirilovna could remember, I had heard over and over again. The songs of the peasant women made me feel depressed. I tried drinking spirits, but it made my head ache; and moreover, I confess I was afraid of becoming a drunkard from mere chagrin, that is to say, the saddest kind of drunkard, of which I had seen many examples in our district.

I had no near neighbours, except two or three topers, whose conversation consisted for the most part of hiccups and sighs. Solitude was preferable to their society. At last I decided to go to bed as early as possible, and to dine as late as possible; in this way I shortened the evening and lengthened out the day, and I found that the plan answered very well.

Four versts from my house was a rich estate belonging to the Countess B——; but nobody lived there except the steward. The Countess had only visited her estate once, in the first year of her married life, and then she had remained there no longer than a month. But in the second spring of my hermitical life, a report was circulated that the Countess, with her husband, was coming to spend the summer on her estate. The report turned out to be true, for they arrived at the beginning of June.

The arrival of a rich neighbour is an important event in the lives of country people. The landed proprietors and the people of their household talk about it for two months beforehand, and for three years afterwards. As for me, I must confess that the news of the arrival of a young and beautiful neighbour affected me strongly. I burned with impatience to see her, and the first Sunday after her arrival I set out after dinner for the village of A——, to pay my respects to the Countess and her husband, as their nearest neighbour and most humble servant.

A lackey conducted me into the Count's study, and then went to announce me. The spacious apartment was furnished with every possible luxury. Around the walls were cases filled with books and surmounted by bronze busts; over the marble mantlepiece was a large mirror; on the floor was a green cloth covered with carpets. Unaccustomed to luxury in my own poor corner, and not having seen the wealth of other people for a long time, I awaited the appearance of the Count with some little trepidation, as a suppliant from the provinces awaits the arrival of the minister. The door opened, and a handsome-looking man, of about thirty-two years of age, entered the room. The Count approached me with a frank and friendly air: I endeavoured to be self-possessed and began to introduce myself, but he anticipated me. We sat down. His conversation, which was easy and agreeable, soon dissipated my awkward bashfulness; and I was already beginning to recover my usual composure, when the Countess suddenly entered, and I became more confused than ever. She was indeed beautiful. The Count presented me. I wished to appear at ease, but the more I tried to assume an air of unconstraint, the more awkward I felt. They, in order to give me time to recover myself and to become accustomed to my new acquaintances, began to talk to each other, treating me as a good neighbour, and without ceremony. Meanwhile, I walked about the room, examining the books and pictures. I am no judge of pictures, but one of them attracted my attention. It represented some view in Switzerland, but it was not the painting that struck me, but the circumstance that the canvas was shot through by two bullets, one planted just above the other.

"A good shot, that!" said I, turning to the Count.

"Yes," replied he, "a very remarkable shot. . . . Do you shoot well?" he continued.

"Tolerably," replied I, rejoicing that the conversation had turned at last upon a subject that was familiar to me. "At thirty paces I can manage to hit a card without fail,—I mean, of course, with a pistol that I am used to."

"Really?" said the Countess, with a look of the greatest interest. "And you, my dear, could you hit a card at thirty paces?"

"Some day," replied the Count, "we will try. In my time I did not shoot badly, but it is now four years since I touched a pistol."

"Oh!" I observed, "in that case, I don't mind laying a wager that Your Excellency will not hit the card at twenty paces: the pistol demands practice every day. I know that from experience. In our regiment I was reckoned one of the best shots. It once happened that I did not touch a pistol for a whole month, as I had sent mine to be mended; and would you believe it, Your Excellency, the first time I began to shoot again, I missed a bottle four times in succession at twenty paces! Our captain, a witty and amusing fellow, happened to be standing by, and he said to me: 'It is evident, my friend, that your hand will not lift itself against the bottle.' No, Your Excellency, you must not neglect to practice, or your hand will soon lose its cunning. The best shot that I ever met used to shoot at least three times every day before dinner. It was as much his custom to do this, as it was to drink his daily glass of brandy."

The Count and Countess seemed pleased that I had begun to talk.

"And what sort of a shot was he?" asked the Count.

"Well, it was this way with him, Your Excellency: if he saw a fly settle on the wall—you smile, Countess, but, before Heaven, it is the truth. If he saw a fly, he would call out: 'Kouzka, my pistol!' Kouzka would bring him a loaded pistol—bang! and the fly would be crushed against the wall."

"Wonderful!" said the Count. "And what was his name?"

"Silvio, Your Excellency."

"Silvio!" exclaimed the Count, starting up. "Did you know Silvio?"

"How could I help knowing him, Your Excellency: we were intimate friends; he was received in our regiment like a brother officer, but it is now five years since I had any tidings of him. Then Your Excellency also knew him?"

"Oh, yes, I knew him very well. Did he ever tell you of one very strange incident in his life?"

"Does Your Excellency refer to the slap in the face that he received from some blackguard at a ball?"

"Did he tell you the name of this blackguard?"

"No, Your Excellency, he never mentioned his name. . . . Ah! Your Excellency!" I continued, guessing the truth: "pardon me . . . I did not know . . . could it really have been you?"

"Yes, I myself," replied the Count, with a look of extraordinary agitation; "and that bullet-pierced picture is a memento of our last meeting."

"Ah, my dear," said the Countess, "for Heaven's sake, do not speak about that; it would be too terrible for me to listen to."

"No," replied the Count: "I will relate everything. He knows how I insulted his friend, and it is only right that he should know how Silvio revenged himself."

The Count pushed a chair towards me, and with the liveliest interest I listened to the following story:

"Five years ago I got married. The first month—the honeymoon—I spent here, in this village. To this house I am indebted for the happiest moments of my life, as well as for one of its most painful recollections.

"One evening we went out together for a ride on horseback. My wife's horse became restive; she grew frightened, gave the reins to me, and returned home on foot. I rode on before. In the courtyard I saw a travelling carriage, and I was told that in my study sat waiting for me a man, who would not give his name, but who merely said that he had business with me. I entered the room and saw in the darkness a man, covered with dust and wearing a beard of several days' growth. He was standing there, near the fireplace. I approached him, trying to remember his features.

"'You do not recognize me, Count?' said he, in a quivering voice.

"'Silvio!' I cried, and I confess that I felt as if my hair had suddenly stood on end.

"'Exactly,' continued he. 'There is a shot due to me, and I have come to discharge my pistol. Are you ready?'

"His pistol protruded from a side pocket. I measured twelve paces and took my stand there in that corner, begging him to fire quickly, before my wife arrived. He hesitated, and asked for a light. Candles were brought in. I closed the doors, gave orders that nobody was to enter, and again begged him to fire. He drew out his pistol and took aim. . . . I counted the seconds. . . . I thought of her. . . . A terrible minute passed! Silvio lowered his hand.

"'I regret,' said he, 'that the pistol is not loaded with cherry-stones . . . the bullet is heavy. It seems to me that this is not a duel, but a murder. I am not accustomed to taking aim at unarmed men. Let us begin all over again; we will cast lots as to who shall fire first.'

"My head went round . . . I think I raised some objection. . . . At last we loaded another pistol, and rolled up two pieces of paper. He placed these latter in his cap—the same through which I had once sent a bullet—and again I drew the first number.

"'You are devilish lucky, Count,' said he, with a smile that I shall never forget.

"I don't know what was the matter with me, or how it was that he managed to make me do it . . . but I fired and hit that picture."

The Count pointed with his finger to the perforated picture; his face glowed like fire; the Countess was whiter than her own handkerchief; and I could not restrain an exclamation.

"I fired," continued the Count, "and, thank Heaven, missed my aim. Then Silvio . . . at that moment he was really terrible. . . . Silvio raised his hand to take aim at me. Suddenly the door opens, Masha rushes into the room, and with a loud shriek throws herself upon my neck. Her presence restored to me all my courage.

"'My dear,' said I to her, 'don't you see that we are joking? How frightened you are! Go and drink a glass of water and then come back to us; I will introduce you to an old friend and comrade.'

"Masha still doubted.

"'Tell me, is my husband speaking the truth?' said she, turning to the terrible Silvio: 'is it true that you are only joking?'

"'He is always joking, Countess,' replied Silvio: 'once he gave me a slap in the face in a joke; on another occasion he sent a bullet through my cap in a joke; and just now, when he fired at me and missed me, it was all in a joke. And now I feel inclined for a joke.'

"With these words he raised his pistol to take aim at me—right before her! Masha threw herself at his feet.

"'Rise, Masha; are you not ashamed!' I cried in a rage: 'and you, sir, will you cease to make fun of a poor woman? Will you fire or not?'

"'I will not,' replied Silvio: 'I am satisfied. I have seen your confusion, your alarm. I forced you to fire at me. That is sufficient. You will remember me. I leave you to your conscience.'

"Then he turned to go, but pausing in the doorway, and looking at the picture that my shot had passed through, he fired at it almost without taking aim, and disappeared. My wife had fainted away; the servants did not venture to stop him, the mere look of him filled them with terror. He went out upon the steps, called his coachman, and drove off before I could recover myself."

The Count was silent. In this way I learned the end of the story, whose beginning had once made such a deep impression upon me. The hero of it I never saw again. It is said that Silvio commanded a detachment of Hetairists during the revolt under Alexander Ipsilanti, and that he was killed in the battle of Skoulana.

For Study and Discussion

1. Which details in the first three paragraphs serve to arouse your curiosity about Silvio?

2. What purpose is served by the card game? Does its outcome lower or intensify your interest in Silvio?

3. Does Silvio's explanation to the narrator concerning his refusal to fight a duel increase or lessen your respect for him?

4. In Chapter II the narrator learns the remainder of Silvio's story from Count B—— instead of from Silvio himself. What is the reason for this shift in narrative method? What is accomplished by it?

5. Why does Silvio refuse a second time to fire at his dueling opponent? Is his renunciation a matter of sheer romantic whimsy? Or is it meant to reveal a fundamental trait of human character?

6. How would you characterize the narrator's attitude toward Silvio?

7. Pushkin and Irving were contemporaries and were among the first significant practitioners of the short-story art in the early nineteenth century. How does "The Shot" differ in tone from "The Spectre Bridegroom"? Despite this difference, do you find any parallelism in the subject matter of the two stories? In the technique? Would "The Shot" fulfill Irving's requirement of "nicety of execution"?

The setting very important. 1.) It is considered a character ..

Stories within stories - frame story.

HONORÉ DE BALZAC

LA GRANDE BRETÈCHE

"Ah! Madame," replied Doctor Horace Bianchon to the lady at whose house he was supping, "it is true that I have many terrible histories in my repertory; but every tale has its due hour in a conversation, according to the clever saying reported by Chamfort and said to the Duc de Fronsac: 'There are ten bottles of champagne between your joke and the present moment.'

"But it is past midnight; what better hour could you have?" said the mistress of the house.

"Yes, tell us, Monsieur Bianchon," urged the assembled company.

At a gesture from the complying doctor, silence reigned.

"About a hundred yards from Vendôme," he said, "on the banks of the Loir, is an old brown house, covered with very steep roofs, and so completely isolated that there is not so much as an evil-smelling tannery, nor a shabby inn such as you see at the entrance of all little towns, in its neighborhood. In front of this dwelling is a garden overlooking the river, where the box edgings, once carefully clipped, which bordered the paths, now cross them and straggle as they fancy. A few willows with their roots in the Loir have made a rapid growth, like the enclosing hedge, and together they half hide the house. Plants which we call weeds drape the bank towards the river with their beautiful vegetation. Fruit-trees, neglected for half a score of years, no longer yield a product, and their shoots and suckers have formed an undergrowth. The espaliers are like a hornbeam hedge. The paths, formerly gravelled, are full of purslain; so that, strictly speaking, there are no paths at all.

"From the crest of the mountain, on which hang the ruins of the old castle of Vendôme (the only spot whence the eye can look down into this enclosure) we say to ourselves that at an earlier period, now difficult to determine, this corner of the earth was the delight of some gentleman devoted to roses and tulips, in a word, to horticulture, but above all possessing a keen taste for good fruits. An arbor is still standing, or

Originally published with "Le Message" under the collective title "Le Conseil," in the second edition of *Scènes de la Vie Privée (Scenes from Private Life)*, 1832. Reprinted here, in a translation by Katharine Prescott Wormeley, from *The Comedy of Human Life* (Boston: Roberts Brothers, 1890), Vol. XXXI *(Fame and Sorrow)*.

rather the remains of one, and beneath it is a table which time has not yet completely demolished.

"From the aspect of this garden, now no more, the negative joys of the peaceful life of the provinces can be inferred, just as we infer the life of some worthy from the epitaph on his tomb. To complete the sad and tender ideas which take possession of the soul, a sundial on the wall bears this inscription, Christian yet bourgeois, 'ULTIMAM COGITA.' The roofs are dilapidated, the blinds always closed, the balconies are filled with swallows' nests, the gates are locked. Tall herbs and grasses trace in green lines the chinks and crevices of the stone portico; the locks are rusty. Sun and moon, summer and winter and snow have rotted the wood, warped the planks, and worn away the paint. The gloomy silence is unbroken save by the birds, the cats, the martens, the rats, the mice, all free to scamper or fly, and to fight, and to eat themselves up.

"An invisible hand has written the word 'MYSTERY' everywhere. If, impelled by curiosity, you wish to look at this house, on the side towards the road you will see a large gate with an arched top, in which the children of the neighborhood have made large holes. This gate, as I heard later, had been disused for ten years. Through these irregular holes you can observe the perfect harmony which exists between the garden side, and the courtyard side of the premises. The same neglect everywhere. Lines of grass surround the paving-stones. Enormous cracks furrow the walls, the blackened eaves of which are festooned with pellitory. The steps of the portico are disjointed, the rope of the bell is rotten, the gutters are dropping apart. What fire from heaven has fallen here? What tribunal has ordained that salt be cast upon this dwelling? Has God been mocked here; or France betrayed? These are the questions we ask as we stand there; the reptiles crawl about but they give no answer.

"This empty and deserted house is a profound enigma, whose solution is known to none. It was formerly a small fief, and is called La Grande Bretèche. During my stay at Vendôme, where Desplein had sent me in charge of a rich patient, the sight of this strange dwelling was one of my keenest pleasures. It was better than a ruin. A ruin possesses memories of positive authenticity; but this habitation, still standing, though slowly demolished by an avenging hand, contained some secret, some mysterious thought,—it betrayed at least a strange caprice.

"More than once of an evening I jumped the hedge, now a tangle, which guarded the enclosure. I braved the scratches; I walked that garden without a master, that property which was neither public nor private; for hours I stayed there contemplating its decay. Not even to obtain the history which underlay (and to which no doubt was due) this strange spectacle would I have asked a single question of any gossiping countryman. Standing there I invented enchanting tales; I gave myself up to debauches of melancholy which fascinated me. Had I known the reason, perhaps a common one, for this strange desertion, I should have lost the unwritten poems with which I intoxicated myself. To me this sanctuary evoked the most varied images of human life darkened by sorrows; sometimes it was a cloister without the nuns; sometimes a graveyard and its peace, without the dead who talk to you in epitaphs; to-day the house of the leper, to-morrow that of the Atrides; but above all was it the provinces with their composed ideas, their hour-glass life.

"Often I wept there, but I never smiled. More than once an involuntary terror seized me, as I heard above my head the muffled whirr of a ringdove's wings hurrying past. The soil is damp; care must be taken against the lizards, the vipers, the frogs, which wander about with the wild liberty of nature; above all, it is well not to fear cold, for there are moments when you feel an icy mantle laid upon your shoulders like the hand of the Commander on the shoulder of Don Juan. One evening I shuddered; the wind had caught and turned a rusty vane. Its creak was like a moan issuing from the house; at a moment, too, when I was ending a gloomy drama in which I explained to myself the monumental dolor of that scene.

"That night I returned to my inn, a prey to gloomy thoughts. After I had supped the landlady entered my room with a mysterious air, and said to me, 'Monsieur, Monsieur Regnault is here.'

"'Who is Monsieur Regnault?'

"'Is it possible that Monsieur doesn't know Monsieur Regnault? Ah, how funny!' she said, leaving the room.

"Suddenly I beheld a long, slim man, clothed in black, holding his hat in his hand, who presented himself, much like a ram about to leap on a rival, and showed me a retreating forehead, a small, pointed head and a livid face, in color somewhat like a glass of dirty water. You would have taken him for the usher of a minister. This unknown personage wore an old coat much worn in the folds, but he had a diamond in the frill of his shirt, and gold earrings in his ears.

"'Monsieur, to whom have I the honor of speaking?' I said.

"He took a chair, sat down before my fire, laid his hat on my table and replied, rubbing his hands: 'Ah! it is very cold. Monsieur, I am Monsieur Regnault.'

"I bowed, saying to myself: *'Il bondo cani!* seek!'

"'I am,' he said, 'the notary of Vendôme.'

"'Delighted, monsieur,' I replied, 'but I am not in the way of making my will,—for reasons, alas, too well-known to me.'

"'One moment!' he resumed, raising his hand as if to impose silence; 'Permit me, monsieur, permit me! I have learned that you sometimes enter the garden of La Grande Bretèche and walk there—'

"'Yes, monsieur.'

"'One moment!' he said, repeating his gesture. 'That action constitutes a misdemeanor. Monsieur, I come in the name and as testamentary executor of the late Comtesse de Merret to beg you to discontinue your visits. One moment! I am not a Turk; I do not wish to impute a crime to you. Besides, it is quite excusable that you, a stranger, should be ignorant of the circumstances which compel me to let the handsomest house in Vendôme go to ruin. Nevertheless, monsieur, as you seem to be a person of education, you no doubt know that the law forbids trespassers on enclosed property. A hedge is the same as a wall. But the state in which that house is left may well excuse your curiosity. I should be only too glad to leave you free to go and come as you liked there, but charged as I am to execute the wishes of the testatrix, I have the honor, monsieur, to request that you do not again enter that garden. I myself, monsieur, have not, since the reading of the will, set foot in that house, which, as I have already had the honor to tell you, I hold under the will of Madame de Merret. We have only taken account of the number of the doors and windows so as to assess the taxes which I pay annually from the funds left by the late countess for that purpose. Ah, monsieur, that will made a great deal of noise in Vendôme!'

"There the worthy man paused to blow his nose. I respected his loquacity, understanding perfectly that the testamentary bequest of Madame de Merret had been the most important event of his life, the head and front of his reputation, his glory, his Restoration. So then, I must bid adieu to my beautiful reveries, my romances! I was not so rebellious as to deprive myself of getting the truth, as it were officially, out of the man of law, so I said,—

"'Monsieur, if it is not indiscreet, may I ask the reason of this singularity?'

"At these words a look which expressed the pleasure of a man who rides a hobby passed over Monsieur Regnault's face. He pulled up his shirt-collar with a certain conceit, took out his snuff-box, opened it, offered it to me, and on my refusal, took a strong pinch himself. He was happy. A man who hasn't a hobby doesn't know how much can be got out of life. A hobby is the exact medium between a passion and a monomania. At that moment I understood Sterne's fine expression to its fullest extent, and I formed a complete idea of the joy with which my Uncle Toby—Trim assisting—bestrode his war-horse.

"'Monsieur,' said Monsieur Regnault, 'I was formerly head-clerk to Maître Roguin in Paris. An excellent lawyer's office of which you have doubtless heard? No! And yet a most unfortunate failure made it, I may say, celebrated. Not having the means to buy a practice in Paris at the price to which they rose in 1816, I came here to Vendôme, where I have relations,—among them a rich aunt, who gave me her daughter in marriage.'

"Here he made a slight pause, and then resumed:—

"'Three months after my appointment was ratified by Monseigneur the Keeper of the Seals, I was sent for one evening just as I was going to bed (I was not then married) by Madame la Comtesse de Merret, then living in her château at Merret. Her lady's-maid, an excellent girl who is now serving in this inn, was at the door with the countess's carriage. Ah! one moment! I ought to tell you, monsieur, that Monsieur le Comte de Merret had gone to die in Paris about two months before I came here. He died a miserable death from excesses of all kinds, to which he gave himself up. You understand? Well, the day of his departure Madame la Comtesse left La Grande Bretèche, and dismantled it. They do say that she even burned the furniture, and the carpets, and all appurtenances whatsoever and wheresoever contained on the premises leased to the said—Ah! beg pardon; what am I saying? I thought I was dictating a lease. Well, monsieur, she burned everything, they say, in the meadow at Merret. Were you ever at Merret, monsieur?'

"Not waiting for me to speak, he answered for me: 'No. Ah! it is a fine spot? For three months, or thereabouts,' he continued, nodding his head, 'Monsieur le Comte and Madame la Comtesse had been living at La Grande Bretèche in a very singular way. They admitted no one to the house; madame lived on the ground-floor, and monsieur on the first floor. After Madame la Comtesse was left alone she never went to church. Later, in her own château she refused to see the friends who came to visit her. She changed greatly after she left La Grande Bretèche and came to Merret. That dear woman (I say dear, though I never saw her but once, because she gave me this diamond),—that good lady was very ill; no doubt she had given up all hope of recovery, for she died without calling in a doctor; in fact, some of our ladies thought she was not quite right in her mind. Consequently, monsieur, my curiosity was greatly excited when I learned that Madame de Merret needed my services; and I was not the only one deeply interested; that very night, though it was late, the whole town knew I had gone to Merret.'

"The good man paused a moment to arrange his facts, and then continued: 'The lady's maid answered rather vaguely the questions which I put to her as we drove along; she did, however, tell me that her mistress had received the last sacraments that day from the curate of Merret, and that she was not likely to live through the night. I reached the château about eleven o'clock. I went up the grand staircase. After passing through a number of dark and lofty rooms, horribly cold and damp, I entered the state bedroom where Madame la Comtesse was lying. In consequence of the many stories that were told about this lady (really, monsieur, I should never end if I related all of them) I expected to find her a fascinating coquette. Would you believe it, I could scarcely see her at all in the huge bed in which she lay. It is true that the only light in that vast room, with friezes of the old style powdered with dust enough to make you sneeze on merely looking at them, was one Argand lamp. Ah! but you say you have never been at Merret. Well, monsieur, the bed was one of those old-time beds with a high tester covered with flowered chintz. A little night-table stood by the bed, and on it I noticed a copy of the "Imitation of Christ."

"'Allow me a parenthesis,' he said, interrupting himself. 'I bought that book subsequently, also the lamp, and presented them to my wife. In the room was a large sofa for the woman who was taking care of Madame de Merret, and two chairs. That was all. No fire. The whole would not have made ten lines of an inventory. Ah! my dear monsieur, could you have seen her as I saw her then, in that vast room hung with brown tapestry, you would have imagined you were in the pages of a novel. It was glacial,—better than that, funereal,' added the worthy man, raising his arm theatrically and making a pause. Presently he resumed:

"'By dint of peering round and coming close to the bed I at length saw Madame de Merret, thanks to the lamp which happened to shine on the pillows. Her face was as yellow as wax, and looked like two hands joined together. Madame la Comtesse wore a lace cap, which, however, allowed me to see her fine hair, white as snow. She was sitting up in the bed, but apparently did so with difficulty. Her large black eyes, sunken no doubt with fever, and almost lifeless, hardly moved beneath the bones where the eyebrows usually grow. Her forehead was damp. Her fleshless hands were like bones covered with thin skin; the veins and muscles could all be seen. She must once have been very handsome, but now I was seized with—I couldn't tell you what feeling, as I looked at her. Those who buried her said afterwards that no living creature had ever been as wasted as she without dying. Well, it was awful to see. Some mortal disease had eaten up that woman till there was nothing left of her but a phantom. Her lips, of a pale violet, seemed not to move when she spoke. Though my profession had familiarized me with such scenes, in bringing me often to the bedside of the dying, to receive their last wishes, I must say that the tears and the anguish of families and friends which I have witnessed were as nothing compared to this solitary woman in that vast building. I did not hear the slightest noise, I did not see the movement which the breathing of the dying woman would naturally give to the sheet that covered her; I myself remained motionless, looking at her in a sort of stupor. Indeed, I fancy I am there still. At last her large eyes moved; she tried to lift her right hand, which fell back upon the bed; then these words issued from her lips like a breath, for her voice was no longer a voice,—'

"'"I have awaited you with impatience."

"'Her cheeks colored. The effort to speak was great. The old woman who was watching her here rose and whispered in my ear: "Don't speak; Madame la Comtesse is past hearing the slightest sound; you would only agitate her." I sat down. A few moments later Madame de Merret collected all her remaining strength to move her right arm and put it, not without great difficulty, under her bolster. She paused an instant; then she made a last effort and withdrew her hand which now held a sealed paper. Great drops of sweat rolled from her forehead.'

"'"I give you my will," she said. "Oh, my God! Oh!"

"'That was all. She seized a crucifix which lay on her bed, pressed it to her lips and died. The expression of her fixed eyes still makes me shudder when I think of it. I brought away the will. When it was opened I found that Madame de Merret had appointed me her executor. She bequeathed her whole property to the hospital of Vendôme, save and excepting certain bequests. The following disposition was made of La Grande Bretèche. I was directed to leave it in the state in which it was at the time of her death for a period of fifty years from the date of her decease; I was to forbid all access to it, by any and every one, no matter who; to make no repairs, and to put by from her estate a yearly sum to pay watchers, if they were necessary, to insure the faithful execution of these intentions. At the expiration of that time the estate was, if the testatrix's will had been carried out in all particulars, to belong to my heirs (because, as monsieur is doubtless well aware, notaries are forbidden by law to receive legacies); if otherwise, then La Grande Bretèche was to go to whoever might establish a right to it, but on condition of fulfilling certain orders contained in a codicil annexed to the will and not to be opened until the expiration of the fifty years. The will has never been attacked, consequently—'

"Here the oblong notary, without finishing his sentence, looked at me triumphantly. I made him perfectly happy with a few compliments.

"'Monsieur,' I said, in conclusion, 'you have so deeply impressed that scene upon me that I seem to see the dying woman, whiter than the sheets; those glittering eyes horrify me; I shall dream of her all night. But you must have formed some conjectures as to the motive of that extraordinary will.'

"'Monsieur,' he replied, with comical reserve, 'I never permit myself to judge of the motives of those who honor me with the gift of a diamond.'

"However, I managed to unloose the tongue of the scrupulous notary so far that he told me, not without long digressions, certain opinions on the matter emanating from the wise-heads of both sexes whose judgments made the social law of Vendôme. But these opinions and observations were so contradictory, so diffuse, that I well-nigh went to sleep in spite of the interest I felt in this authentic story. The heavy manner and monotonous accent of the notary, who was no doubt in the habit of listening to himself and making his clients and compatriots listen to him, triumphed over my curiosity. Happily, he did at last go away.

"'Ha, ha! monsieur,' he said to me at the head of the stairs, 'many persons would like to live their forty-five years longer, but, one moment!'—here he laid the forefinger of his right hand on his nose as if he meant to say, Now pay attention to this!—'in order to do that, to do *that*, they ought to skip the sixties.'

"I shut my door, the notary's jest, which he thought very witty, having drawn me from my apathy; then I sat down in my armchair and put both feet on the andirons. I was plunged in a romance *à la* Radcliffe, based on the notarial disclosures of Monsieur Regnault, when my door, softly opened by the hand of a woman, turned noiselessly on its hinges.

"I saw my landlady, a jovial, stout woman, with a fine, good-humored face, who had missed her true surroundings; she was from Flanders, and might have stepped out of a picture by Teniers.

"'Well, monsieur,' she said, 'Monsieur Regnault has no doubt recited to you his famous tale of La Grande Bretèche?'

"'Yes, Madame Lepas.'

"'What did he tell you?'

"I repeated in a few words the dark and chilling story of Madame de Merret as imparted to me by the notary. At each sentence my landlady ran out her chin and looked at me with the perspicacity of an innkeeper, which combines the instinct of a policeman, the astuteness of a spy, and the cunning of a shopkeeper.

"'My dear Madame Lepas,' I added, in conclusion, 'you evidently know more than that. If not, why did you come up here to me?'

"'On the word, now, of an honest woman, just as true as my name is Lepas—'

"'Don't swear, for your eyes are full of the secret. You knew Monsieur de Merret. What sort of man was he?'

"'Goodness! Monsieur de Merret? well, you see, he was a handsome man, so tall you never could see the top of him,—a very worthy gentleman from Picardy, who had, as you may say, a temper of his own; and he knew it. He paid every one in cash so as to have no quarrels. But, I tell you, he could be quick. Our ladies thought him very pleasant.'

"'Because of his temper?' I asked.

"'Perhaps,' she replied. 'You know, monsieur, a man must have something to the fore, as they say, to marry a lady like Madame de Merret, who, without disparaging others, was the handsomest and the richest woman in Vendôme. She had an income of nearly twenty thousand francs. All the town was at the wedding. The bride was so dainty and captivating, a real little jewel of a woman. Ah! they were a fine couple in those days!'

"'Was their home a happy one?'

"'Hum, hum! yes and no, so far as any one can say; for you know well enough that the like of us don't live hand and glove with the like of them. Madame de Merret was a good woman and very charming, who no doubt had to bear a good deal from her husband's temper; we all liked her though she was rather haughty. Bah! that was her bringing up, and she was born so. When people are noble—don't you see?'

"'Yes, but there must have been some terrible catastrophe, for Monsieur and Madame de Merret to separate violently.'

"'I never said there was a catastrophe, monsieur; I know nothing about it.'

"'Very good; now I am certain that you know all.'

"'Well, monsieur, I'll tell you all I do know. When I saw Monsieur

Regnault coming after you I knew he would tell you about Madame de Merret and La Grande Bretèche; and that gave me the idea of consulting monsieur, who seems to be a gentleman of good sense, incapable of betraying a poor woman like me, who has never done harm to any one, but who is, somehow, troubled in her conscience. I have never dared to say a word to the people about here, for they are all gossips, with tongues like steel blades. And there's never been a traveller who has stayed as long as you have, monsieur, to whom I could tell all about the fifteen thousand francs—'

"'My dear Madame Lepas,' I replied, trying to stop the flow of words, 'if your confidence is of a nature to compromise me, I wouldn't hear it for worlds.'

"'Oh, don't be afraid,' she said, interrupting me. 'You'll see—'

"This haste to tell made me quite certain I was not the first to whom my good landlady had communicated the secret of which I was to be the sole repository, so I listened.

"'Monsieur,' she said, 'when the Emperor sent the Spanish and other prisoners of war to Vendôme I lodged one of them (at the cost of the government),—a young Spaniard on parole. But in spite of his parole he had to report every day to the sub-prefect. He was a grandee of Spain, with a name that ended in *os* and in *dia*, like all Spaniards—Bagos de Férédia. I wrote his name on the register, and you can see it if you like. Oh, he was a handsome young fellow for a Spaniard, who, they tell me, are all ugly. He wasn't more than five feet two or three inches, but he was well made. He had pretty little hands which he took care of—ah, you should just have seen him! He had as many brushes for those hands as a woman has for her head. He had fine black hair, a fiery eye, a rather copper-colored skin, but it was pleasant to look at all the same. He wore the finest linen I ever saw on any one, and I have lodged princesses, and, among others, General Bertrand, the Duc and Duchesse d'Abrantès, Monsieur Decazes and the King of Spain. He didn't eat much; but he had such polite manners and was always so amiable that I couldn't find fault with him. Oh! I did really love him, though he never said four words a day to me; if any one spoke to him, he never answered,—that's an oddity those grandees have, a sort of mania, so I'm told. He read his breviary like a priest, and he went to mass and to all the services regularly. Where do you think he sat? close to the chapel of Madame de Merret. But as he took that place the first time he went to church nobody attached any importance to the fact, though it was remembered later. Besides, he never took his eyes off his prayer-book, poor young man!'

"My jovial landlady paused a moment, overcome with her recollections; then she continued her tale:

"'From that time on, monsieur, he used to walk up the mountain every evening to the ruins of the castle. It was his only amusement, poor man! and I dare say it recalled his own country; they say Spain is all mountains. From the first he was always late at night in coming in. I used to be uneasy at never seeing him before the stroke of midnight; but we got accustomed to his ways and gave him a key to the door, so that we didn't have to sit up. It so happened that one of our grooms told us that one evening when he went to bathe his horses he thought he saw the grandee in the distance, swimming in the river like a fish. When he came in I told him he had better take care not to get entangled in the sedges; he seemed annoyed that any one had seen him in the water. Well, monsieur, one day, or rather, one morning, we did not find him in his room; he had not come in. He never returned. I looked about and into everything, and at last I found a writing in a table drawer where he had put away fifty of those Spanish gold coins called "portugaise," which bring a hundred francs apiece; there were also diamonds worth ten thousand francs sealed up in a little box. The paper said that in case he should not return some day, he bequeathed to us the money and the diamonds, with a request to found masses of thanksgiving to God for his escape and safety. In those days my husband was living, and he did everything he could to find the young man. But, it was the queerest thing! he found only the Spaniard's clothes under a big stone in a sort of shed on the banks of the river, on the castle side, just opposite to La Grande Bretèche. My husband went so early in the morning that no one saw him. He burned the clothes after we had read the letter, and gave out, as Comte Férédia requested, that he had fled. The sub-prefect sent the whole gendarmerie on his traces, but bless your heart! they never caught him. Lepas thought the Spaniard had drowned himself. But, monsieur, I never thought so. I think he was somehow mixed up in Madame de Merret's trouble; and I'll tell you why. Rosalie has told me that her mistress had a crucifix she valued so much that she was buried with it, and it was made of ebony and silver; now when Monsieur de Férédia first came to lodge with us he had just such a crucifix, but I soon missed it. Now, monsieur, what do you say? isn't it true that I need have no remorse about those fifteen thousand francs? are not they rightfully mine?'

"'Of course they are. But how is it you have never questioned Rosalie?' I said.

"'Oh, I have, monsieur; but I can get nothing out of her. That girl is a stone wall. She knows something, but there is no making her talk.'

"After a few more remarks, my landlady left me, a prey to a romantic curiosity, to vague and darkling thoughts, to a religious terror that was something like the awe which comes upon us when we enter by night a gloomy church and see in the distance beneath the arches a feeble light; a formless figure glides before us, the sweep of a robe—of priest or woman—is heard; we shudder. La Grande Bretèche, with its tall grasses, its shuttered windows, its rusty railings, its barred gates, its deserted rooms, rose fantastically and suddenly before me. I tried to penetrate that mysterious dwelling and seek the knot of this most solemn history, this drama which had killed three persons.

"Rosalie became to my eyes the most interesting person in Vendôme. Examining her, I discovered the traces of an ever-present inward thought. In spite of the health which bloomed upon her dimpled face, there was in her some element of remorse, or of hope; her attitude bespoke a secret, like that of devotees who pray with ardor, or that of a girl who has killed her child and forever after hears its cry. And yet her postures were naïve, and even vulgar; her silly smile was surely not criminal; you would have judged her innocent if only by the large neckerchief of blue and red squares which covered her vigorous bust, clothed, confined, and set off by a gown of purple and white stripes. 'No,' thought I; 'I will not leave Vendôme without knowing the history of La Grande Bretèche. I'll even make love to Rosalie, if it is absolutely necessary.'

" 'Rosalie!' I said to her one day.

" 'What is it, monsieur?'

" 'You are not married, are you?'

She trembled slightly.

" 'Oh! when the fancy takes me to be unhappy there'll be no lack of men,' she said, laughing.

"She recovered instantly from her emotion, whatever it was; for all women, from the great lady to the chambermaid of an inn, have a self-possession of their own.

" 'You are fresh enough and taking enough to please a lover,' I said, watching her. 'But tell me, Rosalie, why did you take a place at an inn after you left Madame de Merret? Didn't she leave you an annuity?'

" 'Oh, yes, she did. But, monsieur, my place is the best in all Vendôme.'

"This answer was evidently what judges and lawyers call 'dilatory.' Rosalie's position in this romantic history was like that of a square on a checkerboard; she was at the very centre, as it were, of its truth and its interest; she seemed to me to be tied into the knot of it. The last chapter of the tale was in her, and, from the moment that I realized this, Rosalie became to me an object of attraction. By dint of studying the girl I came to find in her, as we do in every woman whom we make a principal object of our attention, that she had a host of good qualities. She was clean, and careful of herself, and therefore handsome. Some two or three weeks after the notary's visit I said to her, suddenly: 'Tell me all you know about Madame de Merret.'

" 'Oh, no!' she replied, in a tone of terror, 'don't ask me that, monsieur.'

"I persisted in urging her. Her pretty face darkened, her bright color faded, her eyes lost their innocent, liquid light.

" 'Well!' she said, after a pause, 'if you will have it so, I will tell you; but keep the secret.'

"'I'll keep it with the faithfulness of a thief, which is the most loyal to be found anywhere.'

"'If it is the same to you, monsieur, I'd rather you kept it with your own.'

"Thereupon, she adjusted her neckerchief and posed herself to tell the tale; for it is very certain that an attitude of confidence and security is desirable in order to make a narration. The best tales are told at special hours,—like that in which we are now at table. No one ever told a story well, standing or fasting.

"If I were to reproduce faithfully poor Rosalie's diffuse eloquence, a whole volume would scarce suffice. But as the event of which she now gave me a hazy knowledge falls into place between the facts revealed by the garrulity of the notary, and that of Madame Lepas, as precisely as the mean terms of an arithmetical proposition lie between its two extremes, all I have to do is to tell it to you in few words. I therefore give a summary of what I heard from Rosalie.

"The chamber which Madame de Merret occupied at La Grande Bretèche was on the ground-floor. A small closet about four feet in depth was made in the wall, and served as a wardrobe. Three months before the evening when the facts I am about to relate to you happened, Madame de Merret had been so seriously unwell that her husband left her alone in her room and slept himself in a chamber on the first floor. By one of those mere chances which it is impossible to foresee, he returned, on the evening in question, two hours later than usual from the club where he went habitually to read the papers and talk politics with the inhabitants of the town. His wife thought him at home and in bed and asleep. But the invasion of France had been the subject of a lively discussion; the game of billiards was a heated one; he had lost forty francs, an enormous sum for Vendôme, where everybody hoards his money, and where manners and customs are restrained within modest limits worthy of all praise,—which may, perhaps, be the source of a certain true happiness which no Parisian cares anything at all about.

"For some time past Monsieur de Merret had been in the habit of asking Rosalie, when he came in, if his wife were in bed. Being told, invariably, that she was, he at once went to his own room with the contentment that comes of confidence and custom. This evening on returning home, he took it into his head to go to Madame de Merret's room and tell her his ill-luck, perhaps to be consoled for it. During dinner he had noticed that his wife was coquettishly dressed; and as he came from the club the thought crossed his mind that she was no longer ill, that her convalescence had made her lovelier than ever,—a fact he perceived, as husbands are wont to perceive things, too late.

"Instead of calling Rosalie, who at that moment was in the kitchen watching a complicated game of 'brisque,' at which the cook and the coachman were playing, Monsieur de Merret went straight to his wife's room by the light of his lantern, which he had placed on the first step of the stairway. His step, which was easily recognized, resounded under the arches of the corridor. Just as he turned the handle of his wife's door he fancied he heard the door of the closet, which I mentioned to you, shut; but when he entered, Madame de Merret was alone, standing before the fireplace. The husband thought to himself that Rosalie must be in the closet; and yet a suspicion, which sounded in his ears like the ringing of bells, made him distrustful. He looked at his wife, and fancied he saw something wild and troubled in her eyes.

"'You are late in coming home,' she said. That voice, usually so pure and gracious, seemed to him slightly changed.

"Monsieur de Merret made no answer, for at that moment Rosalie entered the room. Her appearance was a thunderbolt to him. He walked up and down the room with his arms crossed, going from one window to another with a uniform movement.

"'Have you heard anything to trouble you?' asked his wife, timidly, while Rosalie was undressing her. He made no answer.

"'You can leave the room,' said Madame de Merret to the maid. 'I will arrange my hair myself.'

"She guessed some misfortune at the mere sight of her husband's face, and wished to be alone with him.

"When Rosalie was gone, or supposed to be gone, for she went no further than the corridor, Monsieur de Merret came to his wife and stood before her. Then he said, coldly:

"'Madame, there is some one in your closet.'

"She looked at her husband with a calm air, and answered, 'No, monsieur.'

"That 'no' agonized Monsieur de Merret, for he did not believe it. And yet his wife had never seemed purer nor more saintly than she did at that moment. He rose and went towards the closet to open the door; Madame de Merret took him by the hand and stopped him; she looked at him with a sad air and said, in a voice that was strangely shaken: 'If you find no one, remember that all is over between us.'

"The infinite dignity of his wife's demeanor restored her husband's respect for her, and suddenly inspired him with one of those resolutions which need some wider field to become immortal.

"'No, Josephine,' he said, 'I will not look there. In either case we should be separated forever. Listen to me: I know the purity of your soul, I know that you lead a saintly life; you would not commit a mortal sin to save yourself from death.'

"At these words, Madame de Merret looked at her husband with a haggard eye.

"'Here is your crucifix,' he went on. 'Swear to me before God that there is no one in that closet and I will believe you; I will not open that door.'

"Madame de Merret took the crucifix and said 'I swear it.'

"'Louder!' said her husband; 'repeat after me,—I swear before God that there is no person in that closet.'

"She repeated the words composedly.

"'That is well,' said Monsieur de Merret, coldly. After a moment's silence he added, examining the ebony crucifix inlaid with silver, 'That is a beautiful thing; I did not know you possessed it; it is very artistically wrought.'

"'I found it at Duvivier's,' she replied; 'he bought it of a Spanish monk when those prisoners-of-war passed through Vendôme last year.'

"'Ah!' said Monsieur de Merret, replacing the crucifix on the wall. He rang the bell. Rosalie was not long in answering it. Monsieur de Merret went quickly up to her, took her into the recess of a window on the garden side, and said to her in a low voice:—

"'I am told that Gorenflot wants to marry you, and that poverty alone prevents it, for you have told him you will not be his wife until he is a master-mason. Is that so?'

"'Yes, monsieur.'

"'Well, go and find him; tell him to come here at once and bring his trowel and other tools. Take care not to wake any one at his house but himself; he will soon have enough money to satisfy you. No talking to any one when you leave this room, mind, or—'

"He frowned. Rosalie left the room. He called her back; 'Here, take my pass-key,' he said.

"Monsieur de Merret, who had kept his wife in view while giving these orders, now sat down beside her before the fire and began to tell her of his game of billiards, and the political discussions at the club. When Rosalie returned she found Monsieur and Madame de Merret talking amicably.

"The master had lately had the ceilings of all the reception rooms on the lower floor restored. Plaster is very scarce at Vendôme, and the carriage of it makes it expensive. Monsieur de Merret had therefore ordered an ample quantity for his own wants, knowing that he could readily find buyers for what was left. This circumstance inspired the idea that now possessed him.

"'Monsieur, Gorenflot has come,' said Rosalie.

"'Bring him in,' said her master.

"Madame de Merret turned slightly pale when she saw the mason.

"'Gorenflot,' said her husband, 'fetch some bricks from the coach-house,—enough to wall up that door; use the plaster that was left over, to cover the wall.'

"Then he called Rosalie and the mason to the end of the room, and, speaking in a low voice, added, 'Listen to me, Gorenflot; after you have done this work you will sleep in the house; and to-morrow morning I will give you a passport into a foreign country, and six thousand francs for the journey. Go through Paris where I will meet you. There, I will secure to you legally another six thousand francs, to be paid to you at the end of ten years if you still remain out of France. For this sum, I demand absolute silence on what you see and do this night. As for you, Rosalie, I give you a dowry of ten thousand francs, on condition that you marry Gorenflot, and keep silence, if not—'

"'Rosalie,' said Madame de Merret, 'come and brush my hair.'

"The husband walked up and down the room, watching the door, the mason, and his wife, but without allowing the least distrust or misgiving to appear in his manner. Gorenflot's work made some noise; under cover of it Madame de Merret said hastily to Rosalie, while her husband was at the farther end of the room: 'A thousand francs annuity if you tell Gorenflot to leave a crevice at the bottom'; then aloud she added, composedly, 'Go and help the mason.'

"Monsieur and Madame de Merret remained silent during the whole time it took Gorenflot to wall up the door. The silence was intentional on the part of the husband to deprive his wife of all chance of saying words with a double meaning which might be heard within the closet; with Madame de Merret it was either prudence or pride.

"When the wall was more than half up, the mason's tool broke one of the panes of glass in the closet door; Monsieur de Merret's back was at that moment turned away. The action proved to Madame de Merret that Rosalie had spoken to the mason. In that one instant she saw the dark face of a man with black hair and fiery eyes. Before her husband turned the poor creature had time to make a sign with her head which meant 'Hope.'

"By four o'clock, just at dawn, for it was in the month of September, the work was done. Monsieur de Merret remained that night in his wife's room. The next morning, on rising, he said, carelessly: 'Ah! I forgot, I must go to the mayor's office about that passport.'

"He put on his hat, made three steps to the door, then checked himself, turned back, and took the crucifix.

"His wife trembled with joy; 'He will go to Duvivier's,' she thought.

"The moment her husband had left the house she rang for Rosalie. 'The pick-axe!' she cried, 'the pick-axe! I watched how Gorenflot did it; we shall have time to make a hole and close it again.'

"In an instant Rosalie had brought a sort of cleaver, and her mistress, with a fury no words can describe, began to demolish the wall. She had knocked away a few bricks, and was drawing back to strike a still more vigorous blow with all her strength, when she saw her husband behind her. She fainted.

"'Put madame on her bed,' said her husband, coldly.

"Foreseeing what would happen, he had laid this trap for his wife; he had written to the mayor, and sent for Duvivier. The jeweller arrived just as the room had been again put in order.

"'Duvivier,' said Monsieur de Merret, 'I think you bought some crucifixes of those Spaniards who were here last year?'

" 'No, monsieur, I did not.'

" 'Very good; thank you,' he said, with a tigerish glance at his wife. 'Jean,' he added to the footman, 'serve my meals in Madame de Merret's bedroom; she is very ill, and I shall not leave her till she recovers.'

"For twenty days that man remained beside his wife. During the first hours, when sounds were heard behind the walled door, and Josephine tried to implore mercy for the dying stranger, he answered, without allowing her to utter a word:—

" 'You swore upon the cross that no one was there.' "

As the tale ended the women rose from table, and the spell under which Bianchon had held them was broken. Nevertheless, several of them were conscious of a cold chill as they recalled the last words.

For Study and Discussion

1. In describing the deserted mansion and gardens, the narrator says: "An invisible hand has written the word 'MYSTERY' everywhere." What specific details are used to develop the feeling of mystery?

2. Early in the story, as the narrator views the decaying mansion, he asks himself, "Has God been mocked here; or France betrayed?" What answer does the story give to this question?

3. In narrating the story, Doctor Bianchon repeats stories told to him by three different persons—Monsieur Regnault, Madame Lepas, and Rosalie. What is the function of each of the three? Why is Rosalie's story presented last and why is it summarized rather than given in her own words?

4. One published translation of this story omits entirely the portion told by Monsieur Regnault. In your opinion, would this omission strengthen or weaken the story as a whole? Why?

5. What uses are made of the crucifix in the story?

6. How are you informed positively that the Spanish grandee is in Madame de Merret's closet?

7. What causes the "cold chill" referred to in the very last line?

8. Balzac, together with Irving and Pushkin, was one of the first significant short-story writers of the early nineteenth century. Do you find his story more or less skillfully written than Irving's or Pushkin's?

9. What major plot situation in the story bears a striking resemblance to the kind Poe was fond of using? If Poe had written this story, how do you suppose his version would have differed from Balzac's?

EDGAR ALLAN POE

THE FALL OF THE HOUSE OF USHER

Son coeur est un luth suspendu;
Sitôt qu'on le touche il résonne. *

De Béranger

During the whole of a dull, dark, and soundless day in the autumn of the year, when the clouds hung oppressively low in the heavens, I had been passing alone, on horseback, through a singularly dreary tract of country; and at length found myself, as the shades of the evening drew on, within view of the melancholy House of Usher. I know not how it was—but, with the first glimpse of the building, a sense of insufferable gloom pervaded my spirit. I say insufferable; for the feeling was unrelieved by any of that half-pleasurable, because poetic, sentiment with which the mind usually receives even the sternest natural images of the desolate or terrible. I looked upon the scene before me—upon the mere house, and the simple landscape features of the domain—upon the bleak walls—upon the vacant eye-like windows—upon a few rank sedges—and upon a few white trunks of decayed trees—with an utter depression of soul which I can compare to no earthly sensation more properly than to the after-dream of the reveller upon opium—the bitter lapse into everyday life—the hideous dropping off of the veil. There was an iciness, a sinking, a sickening of the heart—an unredeemed dreariness of thought, which no goading of the imagination could torture into aught of the sublime. What was it—I paused to think—what was it that so unnerved me in the contemplation of the House of Usher? It was a mystery all insoluble; nor could I grapple with the shadowy fancies that crowded upon me as I pondered. I was forced to fall back upon the unsatisfactory conclusion, that while, beyond doubt, there *are* combinations of very simple natural objects which have the power of thus

---

Originally published in *Burton's Gentleman's Magazine*, September 1839. Reprinted here from *The Complete Works of Edgar Allan Poe*, ed. James A. Harrison (New York: Thomas Y. Crowell and Co., 1902), Vol. III.
*His heart is a suspended lute;
Whenever one touches it, it resounds"—Eds.

affecting us, still the analysis of this power lies among considerations beyond our depth. It was possible, I reflected, that a mere different arrangement of the particulars of the scene, of the details of the picture, would be sufficient to modify, or perhaps to annihilate, its capacity for sorrowful impression; and, acting upon this idea, I reined my horse to the precipitous brink of a black and lurid tarn that lay in unruffled lustre by the dwelling, and gazed down—but with a shudder even more thrilling than before—upon the remodeled and inverted images of the gray sedge, and the ghastly tree-stems, and the vacant and eye-like windows.

Nevertheless, in this mansion of gloom I now proposed to myself a sojourn of some weeks. Its proprietor, Roderick Usher, had been one of my boon companions in boyhood; but many years had elapsed since our last meeting. A letter, however, had lately reached me in a distant part of the country—a letter from him—which, in its wildly importunate nature, had admitted of no other than a personal reply. The MS. gave evidence of nervous agitation. The writer spoke of acute bodily illness—of a mental disorder which oppressed him—and of an earnest desire to see me, as his best, and indeed his only personal friend, with a view of attempting, by the cheerfulness of my society, some alleviation of his malady. It was the manner in which all this, and much more, was said—it was the apparent *heart* that went with his request—which allowed me no room for hesitation; and I accordingly obeyed forthwith what I still considered a very singular summons.

Although, as boys, we had been even intimate associates, yet I really knew little of my friend. His reserve had been always excessive and habitual. I was aware, however, that his very ancient family had been noted, time out of mind, for a peculiar sensibility of temperament, displaying itself, through long ages, in many works of exalted art, and manifested, of late, in repeated deeds of munificent yet unobtrusive charity, as well as in a passionate devotion to the intricacies, perhaps even more than to the orthodox and easily recognisable beauties, of musical science. I had learned, too, the very remarkable fact, that the stem of the Usher race, all time-honored as it was, had put forth, at no period, any enduring branch; in other words, that the entire family lay in the direct line of descent, and had always, with a very trifling and very temporary variation, so lain. It was this deficiency, I considered, while running over in thought the perfect keeping of the character of the premises with the accredited character of the people, and while speculating upon the possible influence which the one, in the long lapse of centuries, might have exercised upon the other—it was this deficiency, perhaps, of collateral issue, and the consequent undeviating transmission, from sire to son, of the patrimony with the name, which had, at length, so identified the two as to merge the original title of the estate in the quaint and equivocal appellation of the "House of Usher"—an appellation which seemed to include, in the minds of the peasantry who used it, both the family and the family mansion.

I have said that the sole effect of my somewhat childish experiment—that of looking down within the tarn—had been to deepen the first singular impression. There can be no doubt that the consciousness of the rapid increase of my superstition—for why should I not so term it?—served mainly to accelerate the increase itself. Such, I have long known, is the paradoxical law of all sentiments having terror as a basis. And it might have been for this reason only, that, when I again uplifted my eyes to the house itself, from its image in the pool, there grew in my mind a strange fancy—a fancy so ridiculous, indeed, that I but mention it to show the vivid force of the sensations which oppressed me. I had so worked upon my imagination as really to believe that about the whole mansion and domain there hung an atmosphere peculiar to themselves and their immediate vicinity—an atmosphere which had no affinity with the air of heaven, but which had reeked up from the decayed trees, and the gray wall, and the silent tarn—a pestilent and mystic vapour, dull, sluggish, faintly discernible, and leaden-hued.

Shaking off from my spirit what *must* have been a dream, I scanned more narrowly the real aspect of the building. Its principal feature seemed to be that of an excessive antiquity. The discoloration of ages had been great. Minute *fungi* overspread the whole exterior, hanging in a fine tangled web-work from the eaves. Yet all this was apart from any extraordinary dilapidation. No portion of the masonry had fallen; and there appeared to be a wild inconsistency between its still perfect adaptation of parts, and the crumbling condition of the individual stones. In this there was much that reminded me of the specious totality of old wood-work which has rotted for long years in some neglected vault, with no disturbance from the breath of the external air. Beyond this indication of extensive decay, however, the fabric gave little token of instability. Perhaps the eye of a scrutinising observer might have discovered a barely perceptible fissure, which, extending from the roof of the building in front, made its way down the wall in a zigzag direction, until it became lost in the sullen waters of the tarn.

Noticing these things, I rode over a short causeway to the house. A servant in waiting took my horse, and I entered the Gothic archway of the hall. A valet, of stealthy step, thence conducted me, in silence, through many dark and intricate passages in my progress to the *studio* of his master. Much that I encountered on the way contributed, I know not how, to heighten the vague sentiments of which I have already spoken. While the objects around me—while the carvings of the ceiling, the sombre tapestries of the walls, the ebon blackness of the floors, and the phantasmagoric armorial trophies which rattled as I strode, were but matters to which, or to such as which, I had been accustomed from my infancy—while I hesitated not to acknowledge how familiar was all this—I still wondered to find how unfamiliar were the fancies which ordinary images were stirring up. On one of the staircases, I met the physician of the family. His countenance, I thought, wore a mingled expression of low cunning and perplexity. He accosted me with trepidation and passed on. The valet now threw open a door and ushered me into the presence of his master.

The room in which I found myself was very large and lofty. The windows were long, narrow, and pointed, and at so vast a distance from the black oaken floor as to be altogether inaccessible from within. Feeble gleams of encrimsoned light made their way through the trellised panes, and served to render sufficiently distinct the more prominent objects around; the eye, however, struggled in vain to reach the remoter angles of the chamber, or the recesses of the vaulted and fretted ceiling. Dark draperies hung upon the walls. The general furniture was profuse, comfortless, antique, and tattered. Many books and musical instruments lay scattered about, but failed to give any vitality to the scene. I felt that I breathed an atmosphere of sorrow. An air of stern, deep, and irredeemable gloom hung over and pervaded all.

Upon my entrance, Usher arose from a sofa on which he had been lying at full length, and greeted me with a vivacious warmth which had much in it, I at first thought, of an overdone cordiality—of the constrained effort of the *ennuyé* man of the world. A glance, however, at his countenance, convinced me of his perfect sincerity. We sat down; and for some moments, while he spoke not, I gazed upon him with a feeling half of pity, half of awe. Surely, man had never before so terribly altered, in so brief a period, as had Roderick Usher! It was with difficulty that I could bring myself to admit the identity of the wan being before me with the companion of my early boyhood. Yet the character of his face had been at all times remarkable. A cadaverousness of complexion; an eye large, liquid, and luminous beyond comparison; lips somewhat thin and very pallid, but of a surpassingly beautiful curve; a nose of a delicate Hebrew model, but with a breadth of nostril unusual in similar formations; a finely moulded chin, speaking, in its want of prominence, of a want of moral energy; hair of a more than web-like softness and tenuity; these features, with an inordinate expansion above the regions of the temple, made up altogether a countenance not easily to be forgotten. And now in the mere exaggeration of the prevailing character of these features, and of the expression they were wont to convey, lay so much of change that I doubted to whom I spoke. The now ghastly pallor of the skin, and the now miraculous lustre of the eye, above all things startled and even awed me. The silken hair, too, had been suffered to grow all unheeded, and as, in its wild gossamer texture, it floated rather than fell about the face, I could not, even with effort, connect its Arabesque expression with any idea of simple humanity.

In the manner of my friend I was at once struck with an incoherence—an inconsistency; and I soon found this to arise from a series of feeble and futile struggles to overcome an habitual trepidancy—an excessive nervous agitation. For something of this nature I had indeed been prepared, no less by his letter, than by reminiscences of certain boyish traits, and by conclusions deduced from his peculiar physical conformation and temperament. His action was alternately vivacious and sullen. His voice varied rapidly from a tremulous indecision (when the animal spirits seemed utterly in abeyance) to that species of energetic concision—that abrupt, weighty, unhurried, and hollow-sounding enunciation, that leaden, self-balanced, and perfectly modulated guttural utterance, which may be observed in the lost drunkard, or the irreclaimable eater of opium, during the periods of his most intense excitement.

It was thus that he spoke of the object of my visit, of his earnest desire to see me, and of the solace he expected me to afford him. He entered, at some length, into what he conceived to be the nature of his malady. It was, he said, a constitutional and a family evil, and one for which he despaired to find a remedy—a mere nervous affection, he immediately added, which would undoubtedly soon pass off. It displayed itself in a host of unnatural sensations. Some of these, as he detailed them, interested and bewildered me; although, perhaps, the terms, and the general manner of the narration had their weight. He suffered much from a morbid acuteness of the senses; the most insipid food was alone endurable; he could wear only garments of certain texture; the odors of all flowers were oppressive; his eyes were tortured by even faint light; and there were but peculiar sounds, and these from stringed instruments, which did not inspire him with horror.

To an anomalous species of terror I found him a bounden slave. "I shall perish," said he, "I *must* perish in this deplorable folly. Thus, thus, and not otherwise, shall I be lost. I dread the events of the future, not in themselves, but in their results. I shudder at the thought of any, even the most trivial, incident, which may operate upon this intolerable agitation of soul. I have, indeed, no abhorrence of danger, except in its absolute effect—in terror. In this unnerved—in this pitiable condition—I feel that the period will sooner or later arrive when I must abandon life and reason together in some struggle with the grim phantasm, FEAR."

I learned, moreover, at intervals, and through broken and equivocal hints, another singular feature of his mental condition. He was enchained by certain superstitious impressions in regard to the dwelling which he tenanted, and whence, for many years, he had never ventured forth—in regard to an influence whose supposititious force was conveyed in terms too shadowy here to be re-stated—an influence which some peculiarities in the mere form and substance of his family mansion, had, by dint of long sufferance, he said, obtained over his spirit—an effect which the *physique* of the gray walls and turrets, and of the dim tarn into which they all looked down, had, at length, brought about upon the *morale* of his existence.

He admitted, however, although with hesitation, that much of the peculiar gloom which thus afflicted him could be traced to a more natural and far more palpable origin—to the severe and long-continued illness—indeed to the evidently approaching dissolution—of a tenderly beloved sister—his sole companion for long years—his last and only relative on earth. "Her decease," he said, with a bitterness which I can never forget, "would leave him (him the hopeless and the frail) the last of the ancient race of the Ushers." While he spoke, the lady Madeline (for so was she called) passed slowly through a remote portion of the apartment, and, without having noticed my presence, disappeared. I regarded her with an utter astonishment not unmingled with dread—and yet I found it impossible to account for such feelings. A sensation of stupor oppressed me, as my eyes followed her retreating steps. When a door, at length, closed upon her, my glance sought instinctively and eagerly the countenance of the brother—but he had buried his face in his hands, and I could only perceive that a far more than ordinary wanness had overspread the emaciated fingers through which trickled many passionate tears.

The disease of the lady Madeline had long baffled the skill of her physicians. A settled apathy, a gradual wasting away of the person, and frequent although transient affections of a partially cataleptical character, were the unusual diagnosis. Hitherto she had steadily borne up against the pressure of her malady, and had not betaken herself finally to bed; but, on the closing in of the evening of my arrival at the house, she succumbed (as her brother told me at night with inexpressible agitation) to the prostrating power of the destroyer; and I learned that the glimpse I had obtained of her person would thus probably be the last I should obtain—that the lady, at least while living, would be seen by me no more.

For several days ensuing, her name was unmentioned by either Usher or myself: and during this period I was busied in earnest endeavours to alleviate the melancholy of my friend. We painted and read together; or I listened, as if in a dream, to the wild improvisations of his speaking guitar. And thus, as a closer and still closer intimacy admitted me more unreservedly into the recesses of his spirit, the more bitterly did I perceive the futility of all attempts at cheering a mind from which darkness, as if an inherent positive quality, poured forth upon all objects of the moral and physical universe, in one unceasing radiation of gloom.

I shall ever bear about me a memory of the many solemn hours I thus spent alone with the master of the House of Usher. Yet I should fail in my attempt to convey an idea of the exact character of the studies, or of the occupations, in which he involved me, or led me the way. An excited and highly distempered ideality threw a sulphureous lustre over all. His long improvised dirges will ring forever in my ears. Among other things, I hold painfully in mind a certain singular perversion and amplification of the wild air of the last waltz of Von Weber. From the paintings over which his elaborate fancy brooded, and which grew, touch by touch, into vaguenesses at which I shuddered the more thrillingly, because I shuddered knowing not why;—from these paintings (vivid as their images now are before me) I would in vain endeavour to educe more than a small portion which should lie within the compass of merely written words. By the utter simplicity, by the nakedness of his designs, he arrested and overawed attention. If ever mortal painted an idea, that mortal was Roderick Usher. For me at least—in the circumstances then surrounding me—there arose out of the pure abstractions which the hypochondriac contrived to throw upon his canvas, an intensity of intolerable awe, no shadow of which felt I ever yet in the contemplation of the certainly glowing yet too concrete reveries of Fuseli.

One of the phantasmagoric conceptions of my friend, partaking not so rigidly of the spirit of abstraction, may be shadowed forth, although feebly, in words. A small picture presented the interior of an immensely long and rectangular vault or tunnel, with low walls, smooth, white, and without interruption or device. Certain accessory points of the design served well to convey the idea that this excavation lay at an exceeding depth below the surface of the earth. No outlet was observed in any portion of its vast extent, and no torch, or other artificial source of light was discernible; yet a flood of intense rays rolled throughout, and bathed the whole in a ghastly and inappropriate splendour.

I have just spoken of that morbid condition of the auditory nerve which rendered all music intolerable to the sufferer, with the exception of certain effects of stringed instruments. It was, perhaps, the narrow limits to which he thus confined himself upon the guitar, which gave birth, in great measure, to the fantastic character of his performances. But the fervid *facility* of his *impromptus* could not be so accounted for. They must have been, and were, in the notes, as well as in the words of his wild fantasias (for he not unfrequently accompanied himself with rhymed verbal improvisations), the result of that intense mental collectedness and concentration to which I have previously alluded as observable only in particular moments of the highest artificial excitement. The words of one of these rhapsodies I have easily remembered. I was, perhaps, the more forcibly impressed with it, as he gave it, because, in the under or mystic current of its meaning, I fancied that I perceived, and for the first time, a full consciousness on the part of Usher, of the tottering of his lofty reason upon her throne. The verses, which were entitled "The Haunted Palace," ran very nearly, if not accurately, thus:

I.

In the greenest of our valleys,
By good angels tenanted,
Once a fair and stately palace—
Radiant palace—reared its head.

In the monarch Thought's dominion—
  It stood there!
Never seraph spread a pinion
  Over fabric half so fair.

II.

Banners yellow, glorious, golden,
  On its roof did float and flow;
(This—all this—was in the olden
  Time long ago)
And every gentle air that dallied,
  In that sweet day,
Along the ramparts plumed and pallid,
  A winged odour went away.

III.

Wanderers in that happy valley
  Through two luminous windows saw
Spirits moving musically
  To a lute's well-tuned law,
Round about a throne, where sitting,
  (Porphyrogene!)
In state his glory well befitting,
  The ruler of the realm was seen.

IV.

And all with pearl and ruby glowing
  Was the fair palace door,
Through which came flowing, flowing, flowing,
  And sparkling evermore,
A troop of Echoes whose sweet duty
  Was but to sing,
In voices of surpassing beauty,
  The wit and wisdom of their king.

V.

But evil things, in robes of sorrow,
  Assailed the monarch's high estate;
(Ah, let us mourn, for never morrow
  Shall dawn upon him, desolate!)
And, round about his home, the glory
  That blushed and bloomed
Is but a dim-remembered story
  Of the old time entombed.

VI.
And travellers now within that valley,
Through the red-litten windows, see
Vast forms that move fantastically
To a discordant melody;
While, like a ghastly rapid river,
Through the pale door,
A hideous throng rush out forever,
And laugh—but smile no more.

I well remember that suggestions arising from this ballad, led us into a train of thought wherein there became manifest an opinion of Usher's which I mention, not so much on account of its novelty, (for other men* have thought thus,) as on account of the pertinacity with which he maintained it. This opinion, in its general form, was that of the sentience of all vegetable things. But, in his disordered fancy, the idea had assumed a more daring character, and trespassed, under certain conditions, upon the kingdom of inorganization. I lack words to express the full extent, or the earnest *abandon* of his persuasion. The belief, however, was connected (as I have previously hinted) with the gray stones of the home of his forefathers. The conditions of the sentience had been here, he imagined, fulfilled in the method of collocation of these stones—in the order of their arrangement, as well as in that of the many *fungi* which overspread them, and of the decayed trees which stood around—above all, in the long undisturbed endurance of this arrangement, and in its reduplication in the still waters of the tarn. Its evidence—the evidence of the sentience—was to be seen, he said (and I here started as he spoke,) in the gradual yet certain condensation of an atmosphere of their own about the waters and the walls. The result was discoverable, he added, in that silent yet importunate and terrible influence which for centuries had moulded the destinies of his family, and which made *him* what I now saw him—what he was. Such opinions need no comment, and I will make none.

Our books—the books which for years had formed no small portion of the mental existence of the invalid—were, as might be supposed, in strict keeping with this character of phantasm. We pored together over such works as the Ververt and Chartreuse of Gresset; the Belphegor of Machiavelli; the Heaven and Hell of Swedenborg; the Subterranean Voyage of Nicholas Klimm by Holberg; the Chiromancy of Robert Flud, of Jean D'Indaginé, and of De la Chambre; the Journey into the Blue Distance of Tieck; and the City of the Sun of Campanella. One favourite volume was a small octavo edition of the *Directorium Inquisitorum*, by

*Watson, Dr. Percival, Spallanzani, and especially the Bishop of Landaff—See "Chemical Essays," vol. v.

the Dominican Eymeric de Gironne; and there were passages in Pomponius Mela, about the old African Satyrs and Ægipans, over which Usher would sit dreaming for hours. His chief delight, however, was found in the perusal of an exceedingly rare and curious book in quarto Gothic—the manual of a forgotten church—the *Vigiliae Mortuorum secundum Chorum Ecclesiæ Maguntinæ.*

I could not help thinking of the wild ritual of this work, and of its probable influence upon the hypochondriac, when, one evening, having informed me abruptly that the lady Madeline was no more, he stated his intention of preserving her corpse for a fortnight, (previously to its final interment,) in one of the numerous vaults within the main walls of the building. The worldly reason, however, assigned for this singular proceeding, was one which I did not feel at liberty to dispute. The brother had been led to his resolution (so he told me) by consideration of the unusual character of the malady of the deceased, of certain obtrusive and eager inquiries on the part of her medical men, and of the remote and exposed situation of the burial-ground of the family. I will not deny that when I called to mind the sinister countenance of the person whom I met upon the staircase, on the day of my arrival at the house, I had no desire to oppose what I regarded as at best but a harmless, and by no means an unnatural, precaution.

At the request of Usher, I personally aided him in the arrangement for the temporary entombment. The body having been encoffined, we two alone bore it to its rest. The vault in which we placed it (and which had been so long unopened that our torches, half smothered in its oppressive atmosphere, gave us little opportunity for investigation) was small, damp, and entirely without means of admission for light; lying, at great depth, immediately beneath that portion of the building in which was my own sleeping apartment. It had been used, apparently, in remote feudal times, for the worst purposes of a donjon-keep, and, in later days, as a place of deposit for powder, or some other highly combustible substance, as a portion of its floor, and the whole interior of a long archway through which we reached it, were carefully sheathed with copper. The door, of massive iron, had been, also, similarly protected. Its immense weight caused an unusually sharp grating sound, as it moved upon its hinges.

Having deposited our mournful burden upon tressels within this region of horror, we partially turned aside the yet unscrewed lid of the coffin, and looked upon the face of the tenant. A striking similitude between the brother and sister now first arrested my attention; and Usher, divining, perhaps, my thoughts, murmured out some few words from which I learned that the deceased and himself had been twins, and that sympathies of a scarcely intelligible nature had always existed between them. Our glances, however, rested not long upon the dead—for we could not regard her unawed. The disease which had thus entombed the lady in the maturity of youth, had left, as usual in all maladies of a strictly cataleptical character, the mockery of a faint blush upon the bosom and the face, and that suspiciously lingering smile upon the lip which is so terrible in death. We replaced and screwed down the lid, and having secured the door of iron, made our way, with toil, into the scarcely less gloomy apartments of the upper portion of the house.

And now, some days of bitter grief having elapsed, an observable change came over the features of the mental disorder of my friend. His ordinary manner had vanished. His ordinary occupations were neglected or forgotten. He roamed from chamber to chamber with hurried, unequal, and objectless step. The pallor of his countenance had assumed, if possible, a more ghastly hue—but the luminousness of his eye had utterly gone out. The once occasional huskiness of his tone was heard no more; and a tremulous quaver, as if of extreme terror, habitually characterized his utterance. There were times, indeed, when I thought his unceasingly agitated mind was labouring with some oppressive secret, to divulge which he struggled for the necessary courage. At times, again, I was obliged to resolve all into the mere inexplicable vagaries of madness, for I beheld him gazing upon vacancy for long hours, in an attitude of the profoundest attention, as if listening to some imaginary sound. It was no wonder that his condition terrified—that it infected me. I felt creeping upon me, by slow yet certain degrees, the wild influences of his own fantastic yet impressive superstitions.

It was, especially, upon retiring to bed late in the night of the seventh or eighth day after the placing of the lady Madeline within the donjon, that I experienced the full power of such feelings. Sleep came not near my couch—while the hours waned and waned away. I struggled to reason off the nervousness which had dominion over me. I endeavoured to believe that much, if not all of what I felt, was due to the bewildering influence of the gloomy furniture of the room—of the dark and tattered draperies, which, tortured into motion by the breath of a rising tempest, swayed fitfully to and fro upon the walls, and rustled uneasily about the decorations of the bed. But my efforts were fruitless. An irrepressible tremour gradually pervaded my frame; and, at length, there sat upon my very heart an incubus of utterly causeless alarm. Shaking this off with a gasp and a struggle, I uplifted myself upon the pillows, and, peering earnestly within the intense darkness of the chamber, hearkened—I know not why, except that an instinctive spirit prompted me—to certain low and indefinite sounds which came, through the pauses of the storm, at long intervals, I knew not whence. Overpowered by an intense sentiment of horror, unaccountable yet unendurable, I threw on my clothes with haste (for I felt that I should sleep no more during the night), and endeavoured to arouse myself from the pitiable condition into which I had fallen, by pacing rapidly to and fro through the apartment.

I had taken but few turns in this manner, when a light step on an adjoining staircase arrested my attention. I presently recognized it as that of Usher. In an instant afterward he rapped, with a gentle touch, at my door, and entered, bearing a lamp. His countenance was, as usual, cadaverously wan—but, moreover, there was a species of mad hilarity in his eyes—an evidently restrained *hysteria* in his whole demeanour. His air appalled me—but anything was preferable to the solitude which I had so long endured, and I even welcomed his presence as a relief.

"And you have not seen it?" he said abruptly, after having stared about him for some moments in silence—"you have not then seen it?—but, stay! you shall." Thus speaking, and having carefully shaded his lamp, he hurried to one of the casements, and threw it freely open to the storm.

The impetuous fury of the entering gust nearly lifted us from our feet. It was, indeed, a tempestuous yet sternly beautiful night, and one wildly singular in its terror and its beauty. A whirlwind had apparently collected its force in our vicinity; for there were frequent and violent alterations in the direction of the wind; and the exceeding density of the clouds (which hung so low as to press upon the turrets of the house) did not prevent our perceiving the life-like velocity with which they flew careering from all points against each other, without passing away into the distance. I say that even their exceeding density did not prevent our perceiving this—yet we had no glimpse of the moon or stars—nor was there any flashing forth of the lightning. But the under surfaces of the huge masses of agitated vapour, as well as all terrestrial objects immediately around us, were glowing in the unnatural light of a faintly luminous and distinctly visible gaseous exhalation which hung about and enshrouded the mansion.

"You must not—you shall not behold this!" said I, shudderingly, to Usher, as I led him with a gentle violence, from the window to a seat. "These appearances, which bewilder you, are merely electrical phenomena not uncommon—or it may be that they have their ghastly origin in the rank miasma of the tarn. Let us close this casement;—the air is chilling and dangerous to your frame. Here is one of your favourite romances. I will read, and you shall listen;—and so we will pass away this terrible night together."

The antique volume which I had taken up was the "Mad Trist" of Sir Launcelot Canning; but I had called it a favourite of Usher's more in sad jest than in earnest; for, in truth, there is little in its uncouth and unimaginative prolixity which could have had interest for the lofty and spiritual ideality of my friend. It was, however, the only book immediately at hand; and I indulged a vague hope that the excitement which now agitated the hypochondriac, might find relief (for the history of mental disorder is full of similar anomalies) even in the extremeness of the folly which I should read. Could I have judged, indeed, by the wild, over-strained air of vivacity with which he hearkened, or apparently hearkened, to the words of the tale, I might well have congratulated myself upon the success of my design.

I had arrived at that well-known portion of the story where Ethelred, the hero of the Trist, having sought in vain for peaceable admission into the dwelling of the hermit, proceeds to make good an entrance by force. Here, it will be remembered, the words of the narrative run thus:

"And Ethelred, who was by nature of a doughty heart, and who was now mighty withal, on account of the powerfulness of the wine which he had drunken, waited no longer to hold parley with the hermit, who, in sooth, was of an obstinate and maliceful turn, but, feeling the rain upon his shoulders, and fearing the rising of the tempest, uplifted his mace outright, and, with blows, made quickly room in the plankings of the door for his gauntleted hand; and now, pulling therewith sturdily, he so cracked, and ripped, and tore all asunder, that the noise of the dry and hollow-sounding wood alarumed and reverberated throughout the forest."

At the termination of this sentence I started, and for a moment, paused; for it appeared to me (although I at once concluded that my excited fancy had deceived me)—it appeared to me that, from some very remote portion of the mansion, there came, indistinctly, to my ears, what might have been, in its exact similarity of character, the echo (but a stifled and dull one certainly) of the very cracking and ripping sound which Sir Launcelot had so particularly described. It was, beyond doubt, the coincidence alone which had arrested my attention; for, amid the rattling of the sashes of the casements, and the ordinary commingled noises of the still increasing storm, the sound, in itself, had nothing, surely, which should have interested or disturbed me. I continued the story:

"But the good champion Ethelred, now entering within the door, was sore enraged and amazed to perceive no signal of the maliceful hermit; but, in the stead thereof, a dragon of a scaly and prodigious demeanour, and of a fiery tongue, which sate in guard before a palace of gold, with a floor of silver; and upon the wall there hung a shield of shining brass with this legend enwritten—

> Who entereth herein, a conqueror hath bin;
> Who slayeth the dragon, the shield he shall win;

And Ethelred uplifted his mace, and struck upon the head of the dragon, which fell before him, and gave up his pesty breath, with a shriek so horrid and harsh, and withal so piercing, that Ethelred had fain to close his ears with his hands against the dreadful noise of it, the like whereof was never before heard."

Here again I paused abruptly, and now with a feeling of wild amazement—for there could be no doubt whatever that, in this instance,

I did actually hear (although from what direction it proceeded I found it impossible to say) a low and apparently distant, but harsh, protracted, and most unusual screaming or grating sound—the exact counterpart of what my fancy had already conjured up for the dragon's unnatural shriek as described by the romancer.

Oppressed, as I certainly was, upon the occurrence of this second and most extraordinary coincidence, by a thousand conflicting sensations, in which wonder and extreme terror were predominant, I still retained sufficient presence of mind to avoid exciting, by any observation, the sensitive nervousness of my companion. I was by no means certain that he had noticed the sounds in question; although, assuredly, a strange alteration had, during the last few minutes, taken place in his demeanour. From a position fronting my own, he had gradually brought round his chair, so as to sit with his face to the door of the chamber; and thus I could but partially perceive his features, although I saw that his lips trembled as if he were murmuring inaudibly. His head had dropped upon his breast—yet I knew that he was not asleep, from the wide rigid opening of the eye as I caught a glance of it in profile. The motion of his body, too, was at variance with this idea—for he rocked from side to side with a gentle yet constant and uniform sway. Having rapidly taken notice of all this, I resumed the narrative of Sir Launcelot, which thus proceeded:

"And now, the champion, having escaped from the terrible fury of the dragon, bethinking himself of the brazen shield, and of the breaking up of the enchantment which was upon it, removed the carcass from out of the way before him, and approached valorously over the silver pavement of the castle to where the shield was upon the wall; which in sooth tarried not for his full coming, but fell down at his feet upon the silver floor, with a mighty great and terrible ringing sound."

No sooner had these syllables passed my lips, than—as if a shield of brass had indeed, at the moment, fallen heavily upon a floor of silver—I became aware of a distinct, hollow, metallic, and clangorous yet apparently muffled reverberation. Completely unnerved, I leaped to my feet; but the measured rocking movement of Usher was undisturbed. I rushed to the chair in which he sat. His eyes were bent fixedly before him, and throughout his whole countenance there reigned a stony rigidity. But, as I placed my hand upon his shoulder, there came a strong shudder over his whole person; a sickly smile quivered about his lips; and I saw that he spoke in a low, hurried, and gibbering murmur, as if unconscious of my presence. Bending closely over him, I at length drank in the hideous import of his words.

"Not hear it?—yes, I hear it, and *have* heard it. Long—long—long—many minutes, many hours, many days, have I heard it—yet I dared not—oh, pity me, miserable wretch that I am!—I dared not—I *dared* not speak! *We have put her living in the tomb!* Said I not that my senses were acute? I *now* tell you that I heard her first feeble movements in the hollow coffin. I heard them—many, many days ago—yet I dared not—*I dared not speak!* And now—to-night—Ethelred—ha! ha!—the breaking of the hermit's door, and the death-cry of the dragon, and the clangour of the shield!—say, rather, the rending of her coffin, and the grating of the iron hinges of her prison, and her struggles within the coppered archway of the vault! Oh whither shall I fly? Will she not be here anon? Is she not hurrying to upbraid me for my haste? Have I not heard her footstep on the stair? Do I not distinguish that heavy and horrible beating of her heart? MADMAN!" here he sprang furiously to his feet, and shrieked out his syllables, as if in the effort he were giving up his soul—"MADMAN! I TELL YOU THAT SHE NOW STANDS WITHOUT THE DOOR!"

As if in the superhuman energy of his utterance there had been found the potency of a spell—the huge antique panels to which the speaker pointed, threw slowly back, upon the instant, their ponderous and ebony jaws. It was the work of the rushing gust—but then without those doors there *did* stand the lofty and enshrouded figure of the lady Madeline of Usher. There was blood upon her white robes, and the evidence of some bitter struggle upon every portion of her emaciated frame. For a moment she remained trembling and reeling to and fro upon the threshold, then, with a low moaning cry, fell heavily inward upon the person of her brother, and in her violent and now final death-agonies, bore him to the floor a corpse, and a victim to the terrors he had anticipated.

From that chamber, and from that mansion, I fled aghast. The storm was still abroad in all its wrath as I found myself crossing the old causeway. Suddenly there shot along the path a wild light, and I turned to see whence a gleam so unusual could have issued; for the vast house and its shadows were alone behind me. The radiance was that of the full, setting, and blood-red moon, which now shone vividly through that once barely-discernible fissure of which I have before spoken as extending from the roof of the building, in a zigzag direction, to the base. While I gazed, this fissure rapidly widened—there came a fierce breath of the whirlwind—the entire orb of the satellite burst at once upon my sight—my brain reeled as I saw the mighty walls rushing asunder—there was a long tumultuous shouting sound like the voice of a thousand waters—and the deep and dank tarn at my feet closed sullenly and silently over the fragments of the "HOUSE OF USHER."

For Study and Discussion

1. What is the full significance of the title of the story? Does it suggest a double meaning after you have finished reading the story? Is there more than a slight hint of allegory in the story?

2. How do the opening passages of description help set the tone and atmosphere of the story? What do you make of the twice-repeated description of the windows as "vacant and eyelike"?

3. How early in the story is the destruction of the house foreshadowed? How many subsequent references can you find that hint at the climax of the story? Make a list and compare them.

4. In the story Poe succeeds in identifying Roderick Usher with the house itself. How does he manage this? By means of what narrative devices?

5. To what extent does the narrator, in turn, become identified with Usher during the course of the story? With whom do you, as reader, become identified? Why?

6. At the end, when Madeline reappears on the scene outside the door, why does Usher address the narrator as "MADMAN"? What sort of reversal occurs at this point?

7. Explain the meaning and function of the poem, "The Haunted Palace," within the context of the story. What other structural details are similarly employed by Poe in the setting and action of the story? List and compare them.

8. What narrative devices does Poe use to make his story seem plausible? Are there any events that seem improbable to you? List these and explain why you found them implausible.

9. How well does "The Fall of the House of Usher" fulfill Poe's prescriptive doctrine for creating an effective short story? Write an essay on this topic.

NATHANIEL HAWTHORNE

THE BIRTHMARK

In the latter part of the last century there lived a man of science, an eminent proficient in every branch of natural philosophy, who not long before our story opens had made experience of a spiritual affinity more attractive than any chemical one. He had left his laboratory to the care of an assistant, cleared his fine countenance from the furnace smoke, washed the stain of acids from his fingers, and persuaded a beautiful woman to become his wife. In those days when the comparatively recent discovery of electricity and other kindred mysteries of Nature seemed to open paths into the region of miracle, it was not unusual for the love of science to rival the love of woman in its depth and absorbing energy. The higher intellect, the imagination, the spirit, and even the heart might all find their congenial aliment in pursuits which, as some of their ardent votaries believed, would ascend from one step of powerful intelligence to another, until the philosopher should lay his hand on the secret of creative force and perhaps make new worlds for himself. We know not whether Aylmer possessed this degree of faith in man's ultimate control over Nature. He had devoted himself, however, too unreservedly to scientific studies ever to be weaned from them by any second passion. His love for his young wife might prove the stronger of the two; but it could only be by intertwining itself with his love of science, and uniting the strength of the latter to his own.

Such a union accordingly took place, and was attended with truly remarkable consequences and a deeply impressive moral. One day, very soon after their marriage, Aylmer sat gazing at his wife with a trouble in his countenance that grew stronger until he spoke.

"Georgiana," said he, "has it never occurred to you that the mark upon your cheek might be removed?"

"No, indeed," said she, smiling; but perceiving the seriousness of his

Originally published in *Pioneer*, March 1843. Reprinted here from *The Complete Works of Nathaniel Hawthorne*, Riverside Edition, ed. George Parsons Lathrop (Boston: Houghton, Mifflin Co., 1883), Vol. II.

manner, she blushed deeply. "To tell you the truth it has been so often called a charm that I was simple enough to imagine it might be so."

"Ah, upon another face perhaps it might," replied her husband; "but never on yours. No, dearest Georgiana, you came so nearly perfect from the hand of Nature that this slightest possible defect, which we hesitate whether to term a defect or a beauty, shocks me, as being the visible mark of earthly imperfection."

"Shocks you, my husband!" cried Georgiana, deeply hurt; at first reddening with momentary anger, but then bursting into tears. "Then why did you take me from my mother's side? You cannot love what shocks you!"

To explain this conversation it must be mentioned that in the centre of Georgiana's left cheek there was a singular mark, deeply interwoven, as it were, with the texture and substance of her face. In the usual state of her complexion—a healthy though delicate bloom—the mark wore a tint of deeper crimson, which imperfectly defined its shape amid the surrounding rosiness. When she blushed it gradually became more indistinct, and finally vanished amid the triumphant rush of blood that bathed the whole cheek with its brilliant glow. But if any shifting motion caused her to turn pale there was the mark again, a crimson stain upon the snow, in what Aylmer sometimes deemed an almost fearful distinctness. Its shape bore not a little similarity to the human hand, though of the smallest pygmy size. Georgiana's lovers were wont to say that some fairy at her birth hour had laid her tiny hand upon the infant's cheek, and left this impress there in token of the magic endowments that were to give her such sway over all hearts. Many a desperate swain would have risked life for the privilege of pressing his lips to the mysterious hand. It must not be concealed, however, that the impression wrought by this fairy sign manual varied exceedingly, according to the difference of temperament in the beholders. Some fastidious persons—but they were exclusively of her own sex—affirmed that the bloody hand, as they chose to call it, quite destroyed the effect of Georgiana's beauty, and rendered her countenance even hideous. But it would be as reasonable to say that one of those small blue stains which sometimes occur in the purest statuary marble would convert the Eve of Powers to a monster. Masculine observers, if the birthmark did not heighten their admiration, contented themselves with wishing it away, that the world might possess one living specimen of ideal loveliness without the semblance of a flaw. After his marriage,—for he thought little or nothing of the matter before,—Aylmer discovered that this was the case with himself.

Had she been less beautiful,—if Envy's self could have found aught else to sneer at,—he might have felt his affection heightened by the prettiness of this mimic hand, now vaguely portrayed, now lost, now stealing forth again and glimmering to and fro with every pulse of emotion that throbbed within her heart; but seeing her otherwise so perfect, he found this one defect grow more and more intolerable with every moment of their united lives. It was the fatal flaw of humanity which Nature, in one shape or another, stamps ineffaceably on all her productions, either to imply that they are temporary and finite, or that their perfection must be wrought by toil and pain. The crimson hand expressed the ineludible gripe in which mortality clutches the highest and purest of earthly mould, degrading them into kindred with the lowest, and even with the very brutes, like whom their visible frames return to dust. In this manner, selecting it as the symbol of his wife's liability to sin, sorrow, decay, and death, Aylmer's sombre imagination was not long in rendering the birthmark a frightful object, causing him more trouble and horror than ever Georgiana's beauty, whether of soul or sense, had given him delight.

At all the seasons which should have been their happiest, he invariably and without intending it, nay, in spite of a purpose to the contrary, reverted to this one disastrous topic. Trifling as it at first appeared, it so connected itself with innumerable trains of thought and modes of feeling that it became the central point of all. With the morning twilight Aylmer opened his eyes upon his wife's face and recognized the symbol of imperfection; and when they sat together at the evening hearth his eyes wandered stealthily to her cheek, and beheld, flickering with the blaze of the wood fire, the spectral hand that wrote mortality where he would fain have worshipped. Georgiana soon learned to shudder at his gaze. It needed but a glance with the peculiar expression that his face often wore to change the roses of her cheek into a deathlike paleness, amid which the crimson hand was brought strongly out, like a bas-relief of ruby on the whitest marble.

Late one night when the lights were growing dim, so as hardly to betray the stain on the poor wife's cheek, she herself, for the first time, voluntarily took up the subject.

"Do you remember, my dear Aylmer," said she, with a feeble attempt at a smile, "have you any recollection of a dream last night about this odious hand?"

"None! none whatever!" replied Aylmer, starting; but then he added, in a dry, cold tone, affected for the sake of concealing the real depth of his emotion, "I might well dream of it; for before I fell asleep it had taken a pretty firm hold of my fancy."

"And you did dream of it?" continued Georgiana, hastily; for she dreaded lest a gush of tears should interrupt what she had to say. "A terrible dream! I wonder that you can forget it. Is it possible to forget this one expression?—'It is in her heart now; we must have it out!' Reflect, my husband; for by all means I would have you recall that dream."

The mind is in a sad state when Sleep, the all-involving, cannot confine her spectres within the dim region of her sway, but suffers them to break forth, affrighting this actual life with secrets that perchance belong to a deeper one. Aylmer now remembered his dream. He had fancied himself with his servant Aminadab, attempting an operation for the removal of the birthmark; but the deeper went the knife, the deeper sank the hand, until at length its tiny grasp appeared to have caught hold of Georgiana's heart; whence, however, her husband was inexorably resolved to cut or wrench it away.

When the dream had shaped itself perfectly in his memory, Aylmer sat in his wife's presence with a guilty feeling. Truth often finds its way to the mind close muffled in robes of sleep, and then speaks with uncompromising directness of matters in regard to which we practise an unconscious self-deception during our waking moments. Until now he had not been aware of the tyrannizing influence acquired by one idea over his mind, and of the lengths which he might find in his heart to go for the sake of giving himself peace.

"Aylmer," resumed Georgiana, solemnly, "I know not what may be the cost to both of us to rid me of this fatal birthmark. Perhaps its removal may cause cureless deformity; or it may be the stain goes as deep as life itself. Again: do we know that there is a possibility, on any terms, of unclasping the firm gripe of this little hand which was laid upon me before I came into the world?"

"Dearest Georgiana, I have spent much thought upon the subject," hastily interrupted Aylmer. "I am convinced of the perfect practicability of its removal."

"If there be the remotest possibility of it," continued Georgiana, "let the attempt be made at whatever risk. Danger is nothing to me; for life, while this hateful mark makes me the object of your horror and disgust,—life is a burden which I would fling down with joy. Either remove this dreadful hand, or take my wretched life! You have deep science. All the world bears witness of it. You have achieved great wonders. Cannot you remove this little, little mark, which I cover with the tips of two small fingers? Is this beyond your power, for the sake of your own peace, and to save your poor wife from madness?"

"Noblest, dearest, tenderest wife," cried Aylmer, rapturously, "doubt not my power. I have already given this matter the deepest thought— thought which might almost have enlightened me to create a being less perfect than yourself. Georgiana, you have led me deeper than ever into the heart of science. I feel myself fully competent to render this dear cheek as faultless as its fellow; and then, most beloved, what will be my triumph when I shall have corrected what Nature left imperfect in her fairest work! Even Pygmalion, when his sculptured woman assumed life, felt not greater ecstasy than mine will be."

"It is resolved, then," said Georgiana, faintly smiling. "And, Aylmer, spare me not, though you should find the birthmark take refuge in my heart at last."

Her husband tenderly kissed her cheek—her right cheek—not that which bore the impress of the crimson hand.

The next day Aylmer apprised his wife of a plan that he had formed whereby he might have opportunity for the intense thought and constant watchfulness which the proposed operation would require; while Georgiana, likewise, would enjoy the perfect repose essential to its success. They were to seclude themselves in the extensive apartments occupied by Aylmer as a laboratory, and where, during his toilsome youth, he had made discoveries in the elemental powers of Nature that had roused the admiration of all the learned societies in Europe. Seated calmly in this laboratory, the pale philosopher had investigated the secrets of the highest cloud region and of the profoundest mines; he had satisfied himself of the causes that kindled and kept alive the fires of the volcano; and had explained the mystery of fountains, and how it is that they gush forth, some so bright and pure, and others with such rich medicinal virtues, from the dark bosom of the earth. Here, too, at an earlier period, he had studied the wonders of the human frame, and attempted to fathom the very process by which Nature assimilates all her precious influences from earth and air, and from the spiritual world, to create and foster man, her masterpiece. The latter pursuit, however, Aylmer had long laid aside in unwilling recognition of the truth—against which all seekers sooner or later stumble—that our great creative Mother, while she amuses us with apparently working in the broadest sunshine, is yet severely careful to keep her own secrets, and, in spite of her pretended openness, shows us nothing but results. She permits us, indeed, to mar, but seldom to mend, and, like a jealous patentee, on no account to make. Now, however, Aylmer resumed these half-forgotten investigations; not, of course, with such hopes or wishes as first suggested them; but because they involved much physiological truth and lay in the path of his proposed scheme for the treatment of Georgiana.

As he led her over the threshold of the laboratory, Georgiana was cold and tremulous. Aylmer looked cheerfully into her face, with intent to reassure her, but was so startled with the intense glow of the birthmark upon the whiteness of her cheek that he could not restrain a strong convulsive shudder. His wife fainted.

"Aminadab! Aminadab!" shouted Aylmer, stamping violently on the floor.

Forthwith there issued from an inner apartment a man of low stature, but bulky frame, with shaggy hair hanging about his visage, which was grimed with the vapors of the furnace. This personage had been Aylmer's underworker during his whole scientific career, and was admirably fitted for that office by his great mechanical readiness, and the skill with which, while incapable of comprehending a single principle, he executed all the details of his master's experiments. With his vast strength, his shaggy hair, his smoky aspect, and the indescribable earthiness that incrusted him, he seemed to represent man's physical nature; while Aylmer's slender figure, and pale, intellectual face, were no less apt a type of the spiritual element.

"Throw open the door of the boudoir, Aminadab," said Aylmer, "and burn a pastil."

"Yes, master," answered Aminadab, looking intently at the lifeless form of Georgiana; and then he muttered to himself, "If she were my wife, I'd never part with that birthmark."

When Georgiana recovered consciousness she found herself breathing an atmosphere of penetrating fragrance, the gentle potency of which had recalled her from her deathlike faintness. The scene around her looked like enchantment. Aylmer had converted those smoky, dingy, sombre rooms, where he had spent his brightest years in recondite pursuits, into a series of beautiful apartments not unfit to be the secluded abode of a lovely woman. The walls were hung with gorgeous curtains, which imparted the combination of grandeur and grace that no other species of adornment can achieve; and as they fell from the ceiling to the floor, their rich and ponderous folds, concealing all angles and straight lines, appeared to shut in the scene from infinite space. For aught Georgiana knew, it might be a pavilion among the clouds. And Aylmer, excluding the sunshine, which would have interfered with his chemical processes, had supplied its place with perfumed lamps, emitting flames of various hue, but all uniting in a soft, impurpled radiance. He now knelt by his wife's side, watching her earnestly, but without alarm; for he was confident in his science, and felt that he could draw a magic circle round her within which no evil might intrude.

"Where am I? Ah, I remember," said Georgiana, faintly; and she placed her hand over her cheek to hide the terrible mark from her husband's eyes.

"Fear not, dearest!" exclaimed he. "Do not shrink from me! Believe me, Georgiana, I even rejoice in this single imperfection, since it will be such a rapture to remove it."

"Oh, spare me!" sadly replied his wife. "Pray do not look at it again. I never can forget that convulsive shudder."

In order to soothe Georgiana, and, as it were, to release her mind from the burden of actual things, Aylmer now put in practice some of the light and playful secrets which science had taught him among its profounder lore. Airy figures, absolutely bodiless ideas, and forms of unsubstantial beauty came and danced before her, imprinting their momentary foot-steps on beams of light. Though she had some indistinct idea of the method of these optical phenomena, still the illusion was almost perfect enough to warrant the belief that her husband possessed sway over the spiritual world. Then again, when she felt a wish to look forth from her seclusion, immediately, as if her thoughts were answered, the procession of external existence flitted across a screen. The scenery and the figures of actual life were perfectly represented, but with that bewitching, yet indescribable difference which always makes a picture, an image, or a shadow so much more attractive than the original. When wearied of this,

Aylmer bade her cast her eyes upon a vessel containing a quantity of earth. She did so, with little interest at first; but was soon startled to perceive the germ of a plant shooting upward from the soil. Then came the slender stalk; the leaves gradually unfolded themselves; and amid them was a perfect and lovely flower.

"It is magical!" cried Georgiana. "I dare not touch it."

"Nay, pluck it," answered Aylmer,—"pluck it, and inhale its brief perfume while you may. The flower will wither in a few moments and leave nothing save its brown seed vessels; but thence may be perpetuated a race as ephemeral as itself."

But Georgiana had no sooner touched the flower than the whole plant suffered a blight, its leaves turning coal-black as if by the agency of fire.

"There was too powerful a stimulus," said Aylmer, thoughtfully.

To make up for this abortive experiment, he proposed to take her portrait by a scientific process of his own invention. It was to be effected by rays of light striking upon a polished plate of metal. Georgiana assented; but, on looking at the result, was affrighted to find the features of the portrait blurred and indefinable; while the minute figure of a hand appeared where the cheek should have been. Aylmer snatched the metallic plate and threw it into a jar of corrosive acid.

Soon, however, he forgot these mortifying failures. In the intervals of study and chemical experiment he came to her flushed and exhausted, but seemed invigorated by her presence, and spoke in glowing language of the resources of his art. He gave a history of the long dynasty of the alchemists, who spent so many ages in quest of the universal solvent by which the golden principle might be elicited from all things vile and base. Aylmer appeared to believe that, by the plainest scientific logic, it was altogether within the limits of possibility to discover this long-sought medium; "but," he added, "a philosopher who should go deep enough to acquire the power would attain too lofty a wisdom to stoop to the exercise of it." Not less singular were his opinions in regard to the elixir vitæ. He more than intimated that it was at his option to concoct a liquid that should prolong life for years, perhaps interminably; but that it would produce a discord in Nature which all the world, and chiefly the quaffer of the immortal nostrum, would find cause to curse.

"Aylmer, are you in earnest?" asked Georgiana, looking at him with amazement and fear. "It is terrible to possess such power, or even to dream of possessing it."

"Oh, do not tremble, my love," said her husband. "I would not wrong either you or myself by working such inharmonious effects upon our lives; but I would have you consider how trifling, in comparison, is the skill requisite to remove this little hand."

At the mention of the birthmark, Georgiana, as usual, shrank as if a redhot iron had touched her cheek.

Again Aylmer applied himself to his labors. She could hear his voice in the distant furnace room giving directions to Aminadab, whose harsh, uncouth, misshapen tones were audible in response, more like the grunt or growl of a brute than human speech. After hours of absence, Aylmer reappeared and proposed that she should now examine his cabinet of chemical products and natural treasures of the earth. Among the former he showed her a small vial, in which, he remarked, was contained a gentle yet most powerful fragrance, capable of impregnating all the breezes that blow across a kingdom. They were of inestimable value, the contents of that little vial; and, as he said so, he threw some of the perfume into the air and filled the room with piercing and invigorating delight.

"And what is this?" asked Georgiana, pointing to a small crystal globe containing a gold-colored liquid. "It is so beautiful to the eye that I could imagine it the elixir of life."

"In one sense it is," replied Aylmer; "or, rather, the elixir of immortality. It is the most precious poison that ever was concocted in this world. By its aid I could apportion the lifetime of any mortal at whom you might point your finger. The strength of the dose would determine whether he were to linger out years, or drop dead in the midst of a breath. No king on his guarded throne could keep his life if I, in my private station, should deem that the welfare of millions justified me in depriving him of it."

"Why do you keep such a terrific drug?" inquired Georgiana in horror.

"Do not mistrust me, dearest," said her husband, smiling; "its virtuous potency is yet greater than its harmful one. But see! here is a powerful cosmetic. With a few drops of this in a vase of water, freckles may be washed away as easily as the hands are cleansed. A stronger infusion would take the blood out of the cheek, and leave the rosiest beauty a pale ghost."

"Is it with this lotion that you intend to bathe my cheek?" asked Georgiana, anxiously.

"Oh, no," hastily replied her husband; "this is merely superficial. Your case demands a remedy that shall go deeper."

In his interviews with Georgiana, Aylmer generally made minute inquiries as to her sensations and whether the confinement of the rooms and the temperature of the atmosphere agreed with her. These questions had such a particular drift that Georgiana began to conjecture that she was already subjected to certain physical influences, either breathed in with the fragrant air or taken with her food. She fancied likewise, but it might be altogether fancy, that there was a stirring up of her system—a strange, indefinite sensation creeping through her veins, and tingling, half painfully, half pleasurably, at her heart. Still, whenever she dared to look into the mirror, there she beheld herself pale as a white rose and with the crimson birthmark stamped upon her cheek. Not even Aylmer now hated it so much as she.

To dispel the tedium of the hours which her husband found it necessary to devote to the processes of combination and analysis, Georgiana turned over the volumes of his scientific library. In many dark old tomes she met with chapters full of romance and poetry. They were the works of the philosophers of the middle ages, such as Albertus Magnus, Cornelius Agrippa, Paracelsus, and the famous friar who created the prophetic Brazen Head. All these antique naturalists stood in advance of their centuries, yet were imbued with some of their credulity, and therefore were believed, and perhaps imagined themselves to have acquired from the investigation of Nature a power above Nature, and from physics a sway over the spiritual world. Hardly less curious and imaginative were the early volumes of the Transactions of the Royal Society, in which the members, knowing little of the limits of natural possibility, were continually recording wonders or proposing methods whereby wonders might be wrought.

But to Georgiana the most engrossing volume was a large folio from her husband's own hand, in which he had recorded every experiment of his scientific career, its original aim, the methods adopted for its development, and its final success or failure, with the circumstances to which either event was attributable. The book, in truth, was both the history and emblem of his ardent, ambitious, imaginative, yet practical and laborious life. He handled physical details as if there were nothing beyond them; yet spiritualized them all, and redeemed himself from materialism by his strong and eager aspiration towards the infinite. In his grasp the veriest clod of earth assumed a soul. Georgiana, as she read, reverenced Aylmer and loved him more profoundly than ever, but with a less entire dependence on his judgment than heretofore. Much as he had accomplished, she could not but observe that his most splendid successes were almost invariably failures, if compared with the ideal at which he aimed. His brightest diamonds were the merest pebbles, and felt to be so by himself, in comparison with the inestimable gems which lay hidden beyond his reach. The volume, rich with achievements that had won renown for its author, was yet as melancholy a record as ever mortal hand had penned. It was the sad confession and continual exemplification of the shortcomings of the composite man, the spirit burdened with clay and working in matter, and of the despair that assails the higher nature at finding itself so miserably thwarted by the earthly part. Perhaps every man of genius in whatever sphere might recognize the image of his own experience in Aylmer's journal.

So deeply did these reflections affect Georgiana that she laid her face upon the open volume and burst into tears. In this situation she was found by her husband.

"It is dangerous to read in a sorcerer's books," said he, with a smile, though his countenance was uneasy and displeased. "Georgiana, there are pages in that volume which I can scarcely glance over and keep my senses. Take heed lest it prove as detrimental to you."

"It has made me worship you more than ever," said she.

"Ah, wait for this one success," rejoined he, "then worship me if you will. I shall deem myself hardly unworthy of it. But come, I have sought you for the luxury of your voice. Sing to me, dearest."

So she poured out the liquid music of her voice to quench the thirst of his spirit. He then took his leave with a boyish exuberance of gayety, assuring her that her seclusion would endure but a little longer, and that the result was already certain. Scarcely had he departed when Georgiana felt irresistibly impelled to follow him. She had forgotten to inform Aylmer of a symptom which for two or three hours past had begun to excite her attention. It was a sensation in the fatal birthmark, not painful, but which induced a restlessness throughout her system. Hastening after her husband, she intruded for the first time into the laboratory.

The first thing that struck her eye was the furnace, that hot and feverish worker, with the intense glow of its fire, which by the quantities of soot clustered above it seemed to have been burning for ages. There was a distilling apparatus in full operation. Around the room were retorts, tubes, cylinders, crucibles, and other apparatus of chemical research. An electrical machine stood ready for immediate use. The atmosphere felt oppressively close, and was tainted with gaseous odors which had been tormented forth by the processes of science. The severe and homely simplicity of the apartment, with its naked walls and brick pavement, looked strange, accustomed as Georgiana had become to the fantastic elegance of her boudoir. But what chiefly, indeed almost solely, drew her attention, was the aspect of Aylmer himself.

He was pale as death, anxious and absorbed, and hung over the furnace as if it depended upon his utmost watchfulness whether the liquid which it was distilling should be the draught of immortal happiness or misery. How different from the sanguine and joyous mien that he had assumed for Georgiana's encouragement!

"Carefully now, Aminadab; carefully, thou human machine; carefully, thou man of clay!" muttered Aylmer, more to himself than his assistant. "Now, if there be a thought too much or too little, it is all over."

"Ho! ho!" mumbled Aminadab. "Look, master! look!"

Aylmer raised his eyes hastily, and at first reddened, then grew paler than ever, on beholding Georgiana. He rushed towards her and seized her arm with a gripe that left the print of his fingers upon it.

"Why do you come hither? Have you no trust in your husband?" cried he, impetuously. "Would you throw the blight of that fatal birthmark over my labors? It is not well done. Go, prying woman, go!"

"Nay, Aylmer," said Georgiana with the firmness of which she possessed no stinted endowment, "it is not you that have a right to complain. You mistrust your wife; you have concealed the anxiety with which you watch the development of this experiment. Think not so unworthily of me, my husband. Tell me all the risk we run, and fear not that I shall shrink; for my share in it is far less than your own."

"No, no, Georgiana!" said Aylmer, impatiently, "it must not be."

" I submit," replied she calmly. "And, Aylmer, I shall quaff whatever draught you bring me; but it will be on the same principle that would induce me to take a dose of poison if offered by your hand."

"My noble wife," said Aylmer, deeply moved, "I knew not the height and depth of your nature until now. Nothing shall be concealed. Know, then, that this crimson hand, superficial as it seems, has clutched its grasp into your being with a strength of which I had no previous conception. I have already administered agents powerful enough to do aught except to change your entire physical system. Only one thing remains to be tried. If that fail us we are ruined."

"Why did you hesitate to tell me this?" asked she.

"Because, Georgiana," said Aylmer, in a low voice, "there is danger."

"Danger? There is but one danger—that this horrible stigma shall be left upon my cheek!" cried Georgiana. "Remove it, remove it, whatever be the cost, or we shall both go mad!"

"Heaven knows your words are too true," said Aylmer, sadly. "And now, dearest, return to your boudoir. In a little while all will be tested."

He conducted her back and took leave of her with a solemn tenderness which spoke far more than his words how much was now at stake. After his departure Georgiana became rapt in musings. She considered the character of Aylmer, and did it completer justice than at any previous moment. Her heart exulted, while it trembled, at his honorable love—so pure and lofty that it would accept nothing less than perfection nor miserably make itself contented with an earthlier nature than he had dreamed of. She felt how much more precious was such a sentiment than that meaner kind which would have borne with the imperfection for her sake, and have been guilty of treason to holy love by degrading its perfect idea to the level of the actual; and with her whole spirit she prayed that, for a single moment, she might satisfy his highest and deepest conception. Longer than one moment she well knew it could not be; for his spirit was ever on the march, ever ascending, and each instant required something that was beyond the scope of the instant before.

The sound of her husband's footsteps aroused her. He bore a crystal goblet containing a liquor colorless as water, but bright enough to be the draught of immortality. Aylmer was pale; but it seemed rather the consequence of a highly-wrought state of mind and tension of spirit than of fear or doubt.

"The concoction of the draught has been perfect," said he, in answer to Georgiana's look. "Unless all my science have deceived me, it cannot fail."

"Save on your account, my dearest Aylmer," observed his wife, "I might wish to put off this birthmark of mortality by relinquishing mortality itself in preference to any other mode. Life is but a sad possession to those who have attained precisely the degree of moral advancement at which I stand. Were I weaker and blinder it might be happiness. Were I stronger, it might be endured hopefully. But, being what I find myself, methinks I am of all mortals the most fit to die."

"You are fit for heaven without tasting death!" replied her husband. "But why do we speak of dying? The draught cannot fail. Behold its effect upon this plant."

On the window seat there stood a geranium diseased with yellow blotches, which had overspread all its leaves. Aylmer poured a small quantity of the liquid upon the soil in which it grew. In a little time, when the roots of the plant had taken up the moisture, the unsightly blotches began to be extinguished in a living verdure.

"There needed no proof," said Georgiana, quietly. "Give me the goblet. I joyfully stake all upon your word."

"Drink, then, thou lofty creature!" exclaimed Aylmer, with fervid admiration. "There is no taint of imperfection on thy spirit. Thy sensible frame, too, shall soon be all perfect."

She quaffed the liquid and returned the goblet to his hand.

"It is grateful," said she with a placid smile. "Methinks it is like water from a heavenly fountain, for it contains I know not what of unobtrusive fragrance and deliciousness. It allays a feverish thirst that had parched me for many days. Now, dearest, let me sleep. My earthly senses are closing over my spirit like the leaves around the heart of a rose at sunset."

She spoke the last words with a gentle reluctance, as if it required almost more energy than she could command to pronounce the faint and lingering syllables. Scarcely had they loitered through her lips ere she was lost in slumber. Aylmer sat by her side, watching her aspect with the emotions proper to a man the whole value of whose existence was involved in the process now to be tested. Mingled with this mood, however, was the philosophic investigation characteristic of the man of science. Not the minutest symptom escaped him. A heightened flush of the cheek, a slight irregularity of breath, a quiver of the eyelid, a hardly perceptible tremor through the frame,—such were the details which, as the moments passed, he wrote down in his folio volume. Intense thought had set its stamp upon every previous page of that volume, but the thoughts of years were all concentrated upon the last.

While thus employed, he failed not to gaze often at the fatal hand, and not without a shudder. Yet once, by a strange and unaccountable impulse, he pressed it with his lips. His spirit recoiled, however, in the very act; and Georgiana, out of the midst of her deep sleep, moved uneasily and murmured as if in remonstrance. Again Aylmer resumed his watch. Nor was it without avail. The crimson hand, which at first had been strongly visible upon the marble paleness of Georgiana's cheek, now grew more faintly outlined. She remained not less pale than ever; but the birthmark, with every breath that came and went, lost somewhat of its former distinctness. Its presence had been awful; its departure was more awful still. Watch the stain of the rainbow fading out of the sky, and you will know how that mysterious symbol passed away.

"By Heaven! it is well-nigh gone!" said Aylmer to himself, in almost irrepressible ecstasy. "I can scarcely trace it now. Success! success! And now it is like the faintest rose color. The lightest flush of blood across her cheek would overcome it. But she is so pale!"

He drew aside the window curtain and suffered the light of natural day to fall into the room and rest upon her cheek. At the same time he heard a gross, hoarse chuckle, which he had long known as his servant Aminadab's expression of delight.

"Ah, clod! ah, earthly mass!" cried Aylmer, laughing in a sort of frenzy, "you have served me well! Matter and spirit—earth and heaven—have both done their part in this! Laugh, thing of the senses! You have earned the right to laugh."

These exclamations broke Georgiana's sleep. She slowly unclosed her eyes and gazed into the mirror which her husband had arranged for that purpose. A faint smile flitted over her lips when she recognized how barely perceptible was now that crimson hand which had once blazed forth with such disastrous brilliancy as to scare away all their happiness. But then her eyes sought Aylmer's face with a trouble and anxiety that he could by no means account for.

"My poor Aylmer!" murmured she.

"Poor? Nay, richest, happiest, most favored!" exclaimed he. "My peerless bride, it is successful! You are perfect!"

"My poor Aylmer," she repeated, with a more than human tenderness, "you have aimed loftily; you have done nobly. Do not repent that with so high and pure a feeling, you have rejected the best the earth could offer. Aylmer, dearest Aylmer, I am dying!"

Alas! it was too true! The fatal hand had grappled with the mystery of life, and was the bond by which an angelic spirit kept itself in union with a mortal frame. As the last crimson tint of the birthmark—that sole token of human imperfection—faded from her cheek, the parting breath of the now perfect woman passed into the atmosphere, and her soul, lingering a moment near her husband, took its heavenward flight. Then a hoarse, chuckling laugh was heard again! Thus ever does the gross fatality of earth exult in its invariable triumph over the immortal essence which, in this dim sphere of half development, demands the completeness of a higher state. Yet, had Aylmer reached a profounder wisdom, he need not thus have flung away the happiness which would have woven his mortal life of the selfsame texture with the celestial. The momentary circumstance was too strong for him; he failed to look beyond the shadowy scope of time, and, living once for all in eternity, to find the perfect future in the present.

For Study and Discussion

1. Georgiana's birthmark is an obvious symbol. What does it stand for, and why does Aylmer want to eradicate it?

2. What symbolic meanings can you detect in Aylmer's dream? In his scientific research, especially his laboratory, its equipment, and the furnace? In his liquid concoctions? In his journal?

3. What fundamental lesson concerning nature and human relationships does Aylmer ignore? Is Georgiana an innocent victim of his self-centered idealism or does she share his guilt? Point out some of the ambiguities in their roles as husband and wife.

4. Discuss Aminadab's role and function in the story. Is a symbolic meaning suggested by his name? By his personality? By his attitude toward both Aylmer and Georgiana?

5. The outcome of Aylmer's experiment is meant to dramatize a basic moral truth. What is it? Can you restate it in your own terms?

6. Does Hawthorne's explicit "moral" at the end enhance or detract from the effectiveness of the story?

7. Does "The Birthmark" fully satisfy Poe's requirement for an "unblemished" story? Does it achieve a "unique or single effect"?

8. Would Poe approve or disapprove of the allegorical elements in "The Birthmark"? Before answering reexamine Poe's remarks about the use of allegory in fiction (p. 14).

9. Compare and contrast the opening paragraphs in "The Birthmark" and "The Fall of the House of Usher." What important differences can you detect in the narrative style and technique in the two stories? Are there any notable similarities?

10. Pick out and compare examples of imagery and figurative language in both stories and show how these affect characterization and action.

IVAN TURGENEV

THE TRYST

I was sitting in a birch grove in autumn, about the middle of
September. A fine drizzling rain had been descending ever since dawn,
interspersed at times with warm sunshine; the weather was inconstant.
Now the sky would be completely veiled in porous white clouds; again,
all of a sudden, it would clear up in spots for a moment, and then, from
behind the parted thunderclouds, the clear and friendly azure would
show itself, like a beautiful eye. I sat, and gazed about me, and listened.
The leaves were rustling in a barely audible manner overhead; from their
sound alone one could tell what season of the year it was. It was not the
cheerful, laughing rustle of springtime, not the soft whispering, not the
long conversation of summer, not the cold and timid stammering of late
autumn, but a barely audible, dreamy chatter. A faint breeze swept feebly
across the treetops. The interior of the grove, moist with the rain, kept
changing incessantly, according to whether the sun shone forth, or was
covered with a cloud; now it was all illuminated, as though everything in
it were suddenly smiling: the slender boles of the not too thickly set
birches suddenly assumed the tender gleam of white silk, the small
leaves which lay on the ground suddenly grew variegated and lighted up
with the golden hue of ducats, and the handsome stalks of the tall, curly
ferns, already stained with their autumnal hue, like the colour of
over-ripe grapes, seemed fairly transparent, as they intertwined interminably and crossed one another before one's eyes; now, of a sudden,
everything round about would turn slightly blue: the brilliant hues were
extinguished for a moment, the birches stood there all white, devoid of
reflections, white as newly fallen snow, which has not yet been touched
by the sparkling rays of the winter sun; and the fine rain began
stealthily, craftily, to sprinkle and whisper through the forest. The
foliage on the trees was still almost entirely green, although it had faded
perceptibly; only here and there stood one, some young tree, all scarlet,

Originally published under the title "Svidanie," in the periodical *Sovremennik (The
Contemporary)*, 1850. Reprinted here, in a translation by Isabel F. Hapgood, from *The
Novels and Stories of Iván Turgénieff* (New York: Charles Scribner's Sons, 1922), Vol. II
(Memoirs of a Sportsman).

or all gold, and you should have seen how brilliantly it flamed up in the sun, when the rays gliding and changing, suddenly pierced through the thick network of the slender branches, only just washed clean by the glittering rain. Not a single bird was to be heard; they had all taken refuge, and fallen silent; only now and then did the jeering little voice of the tom-tit ring out like a tiny steel bell. Before I had come to a halt in this birch-forest I and my dog had traversed a grove of lofty aspens. I must confess that I am not particularly fond of that tree, the aspen, with its pale-lilac trunk, and greyish-green, metallic foliage, which it elevates as high aloft as possible, and spreads forth to the air in a trembling fan; I do not like the eternal rocking of its round, dirty leaves, awkwardly fastened to their long stems. It is a fine tree only on some summer evenings when, rising isolated amid a plot of low-growing bushes, it stands directly in the line of the glowing rays of the setting sun, and glistens and quivers from its root to its crest, all deluged with a uniform reddish-yellow stain,—or when, on a bright, windy day, it is all noisily rippling and lisping against the blue sky, and its every leaf, caught in the current, seems to want to wrench itself free, fly off and whirl away into the distance. But, on the whole, I do not like that tree, and therefore, without halting to rest in that grove, I wended my way to the little birch-coppice, nestled down under one small tree, whose boughs began close to the ground, and, consequently, could protect me from the rain, and after having admired the surrounding view, I sank into that untroubled and benignant slumber which is known to sportsmen alone.

I cannot tell how long I slept, but when I opened my eyes,—the whole interior of the forest was filled with sunlight, and in all directions, athwart the joyously rustling foliage, the bright-blue sky seemed to be sparkling: the clouds had vanished, dispersed by the sportive breeze; the weather had cleared, and in the atmosphere was perceptible that peculiar, dry chill which, filling the heart with a sort of sensation of alertness, almost always is the harbinger of a clear evening after a stormy day. I was preparing to rise to my feet, and try my luck again, when suddenly my eyes halted on a motionless human form. I took a more attentive look; it was a young peasant maiden. She was sitting twenty paces distant from me, with her head drooping thoughtfully, and both arms lying idly on her knees; on one of them, which was half bare, lay a thick bunch of field flowers, which went slipping softly down her plaid petticoat at each breath she drew. Her clean white chemise, unbuttoned at the throat and wrists, fell in short, soft folds about her figure: two rows of large yellow pearl-beads depended from her neck upon her breast. She was very comely. Her thick, fair hair, of a fine ash-blond hue, fell in two carefully brushed semi-circles from beneath a narrow, red band which was pulled down almost on her very brow, as white as ivory; the rest of her face was slightly sunburned to that golden tint which only a fine skin assumes. I could not see her eyes—she did not raise them; but I did see her high, slender eyebrows, her long eyelashes; they were moist, and on one of her cheeks there glittered in the sunlight the dried trace of a tear, that had stopped short close to her lips, which had grown slightly pale. Her whole little head was extremely charming; even her rather thick and rounded nose did not spoil it. I was particularly pleased with the expression of her face: it was so simple and gentle, so sad and so full of childish surprise at its own sadness. She was evidently waiting for some one; something crackled faintly in the forest. She immediately raised her head and looked about her; in the transparent shadow her eyes flashed swiftly before me,—large, clear, timorous eyes, like those of a doe. She listened for several moments, without taking her widely opened eyes from the spot where the faint noise had resounded, sighed, gently turned away her head, bent down still lower than before, and began slowly to sort over her flowers. Her eyelids reddened, her lips moved bitterly, and a fresh tear rolled from beneath her thick eyelashes, halting and glittering radiantly on her cheek. Quite a long time passed in this manner; the poor girl did not stir,—only now and then she moved her hands about and listened, listened still. . . . Again something made a noise in the forest,—she gave a start. The noise did not cease, grew more distinct, drew nearer; at last brisk, decided footsteps made themselves audible. She drew herself up, and seemed to be frightened; her attentive glance wavered, with expectation, apparently. A man's figure flitted swiftly through the thicket. She glanced at it, suddenly flushed up, smiled joyously and happily, tried to rise to her feet, and immediately bent clear over once more, grew pale and confused,—and only raised her palpitating, almost beseeching glance to the approaching man when the latter had come to a halt by her side.

I gazed at him with interest from my ambush. I must confess that he did not produce a pleasant impression on me. From all the signs, he was the petted valet of a young, wealthy gentleman. His clothing betrayed pretensions to taste and foppish carelessness: he wore a short overcoat of bronze hue, probably the former property of his master, buttoned to the throat, a small pink neckerchief with lilac ends, and a black velvet cap, with gold galloon, pulled down to his very eyebrows. The round collar of his white shirt propped up his ears, and ruthlessly sawed his cheeks, and his starched cuffs covered the whole of his hands down to his red, crooked fingers, adorned with gold and silver rings with turquoise forget-me-nots. His fresh, rosy, bold face belonged to the category of visages which, so far as I have been able to observe, almost always irritate men and, unfortunately, very often please women. He was, obviously, trying to impart to his somewhat coarse features a scornful and bored expression; he kept incessantly screwing up his little milky-grey eyes, which were small enough without that, knitting his brows, drawing down the corners of his lips, constrainedly yawning, and with careless, although not quite skilful ease of manner he now adjusted with his hand his sandy, dashingly upturned temple-curls, now plucked at the small yellow hairs which stuck out on his thick upper lip,—in a word, he put on intolerable airs. He began to put on airs as soon as he caught sight of the young peasant girl who was waiting for him; slowly, with a swaggering stride, he approached her, stood for a moment, shrugged his shoulders, thrust both hands into the pockets of his coat, and, barely vouchsafing the poor girl a fugitive and indifferent glance, he dropped down on the ground.

"Well,"—he began, continuing to gaze off somewhere to one side, dangling his foot and yawning:—"hast thou been here long?"

The girl could not answer him at once.

"A long time, sir, Viktór Alexándrovitch,"—she said at last, in a barely audible voice.

"Ah!" (He removed his cap, passed his hand majestically over his thick, tightly curled hair, which began almost at his very eyebrows, and after glancing around him with dignity, he carefully covered his precious head again.) "Why, I came pretty near forgetting all about it. And then, there was the rain, you know!" (He yawned again.)—"I have a lot of things to do: I can't attend to them all, and he scolds into the bargain. To-morrow we are going away. . . ."

"To-morrow?"—ejaculated the girl, and fixed a frightened glance on him.

"Yes, to-morrow. . . . Come, come, come, pray,"—he interposed hastily and with vexation, seeing that she was beginning to tremble, and had softly dropped her head:—"Pray, don't cry, Akulína. Thou knowest that I cannot endure that." (And he wrinkled up his stubby nose.)—"If thou dost, I'll go away instantly. . . . How stupid it is to whimper!"

"Well, I won't, I won't,"—hastily articulated Akulína, swallowing her tears with an effort—"So you are going away to-morrow?"—she added after a short silence:—"When will God grant me to see you again, Viktór Alexándrovitch?"

"We shall see each other again, we shall see each other again. If not next year, then later on. I think the master intends to enter the government service in Petersburg,"—he went on, uttering his words carelessly and somewhat through his nose:—"and perhaps we shall go abroad."

"You will forget me, Viktór Alexándrovitch,"—said Akulína sadly.

"No, why should I? I will not forget thee: only, thou must be sensible, don't make a fool of thyself, heed thy father. . . . And I won't forget thee—no-o-o." (And he calmly stretched himself and yawned again.)

"Do not forget me, Viktór Alexándrovitch," she continued, in a tone of entreaty. "I think that I have loved you to such a degree, it always seems as though for you, I would . . . you say, I must obey my father, Viktór Alexándrovitch. . . . But how am I to obey my father. . . ."

"But why not?" (He uttered these words as though from his stomach, as he lay on his back, with his arms under his head.)

"But what do you mean, Viktór Alexándrovitch . . . you know yourself. . . ."

She stopped short, Viktór toyed with the steel chain of his watch.

"Thou art not a stupid girl, Akulína,"—he began at last:—"therefore, don't talk nonsense. I desire thy welfare, dost understand me? Of course, thou art not stupid, not a regular peasant, so to speak; and thy mother also was not always a peasant. All the same, thou hast no education—so thou must obey when people give thee orders."

"But I'm afraid, Viktór Alexándrovitch."

"I-i, what nonsense, my dear creature! What hast thou to be afraid of? What's that thou hast there,"—he added, moving toward her:— "flowers?"

"Yes,"—replied Akulína, dejectedly.—"I have been plucking some wild tansy,"—she went on, after a brief pause:—"'T is good for the calves. And this here is a good remedy for scrofula. See, what a wonderfully beautiful flower! I have never seen such a beautiful flower in my life. Here are forget-me-nots, and here is a violet. . . . And this, here, I got for you,"—she added, drawing from beneath the yellow tansy a small bunch of blue corn-flowers, bound together with a slender blade of grass:—"Will you take them?"

Viktór languidly put out his hand, took the flowers, smelled of them carelessly, and began to twist them about in his fingers, staring pompously upward. Akulína glanced at him. . . . In her sorrowful gaze there was a great deal of devotion, of adoring submission to him. And she was afraid of him also, and did not dare to cry, and was bidding him farewell and gloating upon him for the last time; but he lay there, sprawling out like a sultan, and tolerated her adoration with magnanimous patience and condescension. I must confess, that I gazed with indignation at his red face, whereon, athwart the feignedly-scornful indifference, there peered forth satisfied, satiated self-conceit. Akulína was so fine at that moment: her whole soul opened confidingly, passionately before him, reached out to him, fawned upon him, and he . . . he dropped the corn-flowers on the grass, pulled a round monocle in a bronze setting from the side-pocket of his paletot, and began to stick it into his eye; but try as he would to hold it fast with his frowning brows, the monocle kept tumbling out and falling into his hand.

"What is that?"—inquired the amazed Akulína at last.

"A lorgnette,"—he replied pompously.

"What is it for?"

"To see better with."

"Pray let me see it."

Viktór frowned, but gave her the monocle.

"Look out, see that thou dost not break it."

"Never fear, I won't break it." (She raised it timidly to her eye.) "I can see nothing,"—she said innocently.

"Why, pucker up thine eye,"—he retorted in the tone of a displeased preceptor. (She screwed up the eye in front of which she was holding the glass.)

"Not that one, not that one, the other one!"—shouted Viktór, and without giving her a chance to repair her mistake, he snatched the lorgnette away from her.

Akulína blushed scarlet, smiled faintly, and turned away.

"Evidently, it is not suited to the like of me,"—said she.

"I should say not!"

The poor girl made no reply, and sighed deeply.

"Akh, Viktór Alexándrovitch; what shall I do without you!"—she suddenly said. Viktór wiped the lorgnette with the tail of his coat, and put it back in his pocket.

"Yes, yes,"—he said at last:—"thou wilt really find it very hard at first." (He patted her condescendingly on the shoulder; she softly removed his hand from her shoulder, and kissed it timidly.)—"Well, yes, yes, thou really art a good girl,"—he went on, with a conceited smile; "but what can one do? Judge for thyself! the master and I cannot remain here; winter will soon be here, and the country in winter—thou knowest it thyself—is simply vile. 'Tis quite another matter in Petersburg! There are simply such marvels there as thou, silly, canst not even imagine in thy dreams. Such houses, such streets, and society, culture—simply astounding! . . . " (Akulína listened to him with devouring attention, her lips slightly parted, like those of a child.)—"But what am I telling thee all this for?"—he added, turning over on the ground. "Of course, thou canst not understand!"

"Why not, Viktór Alexándrovitch? I have understood—I have understood everything."

"Did any one ever see such a girl!"

Akulína dropped her eyes.

"You did not use to talk to me formerly in that way, Viktór Alexándrovitch,"—she said, without raising her eyes.

"Formerly? . . . formerly! Just see there, now! . . . Formerly!"—he remarked, as though vexed.

Both maintained silence for a while.

"But I must be off,"—said Viktór, and began to raise himself on his elbow. . . .

"Wait a little longer,"—articulated Akulína, in a beseeching voice.

"What's the use of waiting? . . . I have already bade thee farewell, haven't I?"

"Wait,"—repeated Akulína.

Viktór stretched himself out again, and began to whistle. Still Akulína never took her eyes from him. I could perceive that she had grown somewhat agitated: her lips were twitching, her pale cheeks had taken on a faint flush. . . .

"Viktór Alexándrovitch,"—she said at last, in a broken voice:—"'t is sinful of you . . . sinful of you, Viktór Alexándrovitch: by heaven, it is!"

"What's sinful?"—he asked, knitting his brows, and he half rose and turned toward her.

" 'T is sinful, Viktór Alexándrovitch. You might at least speak a kind word to me at parting; you might at least say one little word to me, an unhappy orphan. . . ."

"But what am I to say to thee?"

"I don't know; you know that better than I do, Viktór Alexándrovitch. Here you are going away, and not a single word. . . . How have I deserved such treatment?"

"What a queer creature thou art! What can I do?"

"You might say one little word. . . ."

"Come, thou'rt wound up to say the same thing over and over,"—he said testily, and rose to his feet.

"Don't be angry, Viktór Alexándrovitch,"—she added hurriedly, hardly able to repress her tears.

"I'm not angry, only thou art so stupid. . . . What is it thou wantest? I can't marry thee, can I? I can't, can I? Well, then, what is it thou dost want? What?" (He turned his face toward her, as though awaiting an answer, and spread his fingers far apart.)

"I want nothing . . . nothing,"—she replied, stammering, and barely venturing to stretch out to him her trembling arms:—"but yet, if you would say only one little word in farewell. . . ."

And the tears streamed down her face in a torrent.

"Well, there she goes! She's begun to cry," said Viktór coldly, pulling his cap forward over his eyes.

"I want nothing,"—she went on, sobbing, and covering her face with both hands;—"but how do I stand now with my family, what is my position? and what will happen to me, what will become of me, unhappy one? They will marry off the poor deserted one to a man she does not love. . . . Woe is me!"

"O, go on, go on,"—muttered Viktór in an undertone, shifting from foot to foot where he stood.

"And if he would say only one word, just one . . . such as: 'Akulína, I. . . .' "

Sudden sobs, which rent her breast, prevented her finishing her sentence—she fell face downward on the grass, and wept bitterly, bitterly. . . . Her whole body was convulsively agitated, the back of her neck fairly heaved. . . . Her long-suppressed woe had burst forth, at last, in a flood. Viktór stood over her, stood there a while, and shrugged his shoulders, then wheeled round, and marched off with long strides.

Several minutes elapsed. . . . She quieted down, raised her head, glanced around, and clasped her hands; she tried to run after him, but her limbs gave way under her—she fell on her knees. . . . I could not restrain myself, and rushed to her; but no sooner had she glanced at me than strength from some source made its appearance,—she rose to her feet with a faint shriek, and vanished behind the trees, leaving her flowers scattered on the ground.

I stood there for a while, picked up the bunch of corn-flowers, and emerged from the grove into the fields. The sun hung low in the palely-clear sky, its rays, too, seemed to have grown pallid, somehow, and cold: they did not beam, they disseminated an even, almost watery light. Not more than half an hour remained before night-fall, and the sunset glow was only just beginning to kindle. A gusty breeze dashed swiftly to meet me across the yellow, dried-up stubble-field; small, warped leaves rose hastily before it, and darted past, across the road, along the edge of the woods; the side of the grove, turned toward the field like a wall, was all quivering and sparkling with a drizzling glitter, distinct but not brilliant; on the reddish turf, on the blades of grass, on the straws, everywhere around, gleamed and undulated the innumerable threads of autumnal spiders' webs. I halted. . . . I felt sad: athwart the cheerful though chilly smile of fading nature, the mournful terror of not far-distant winter seemed to be creeping up. High above me, cleaving the air heavily and sharply with its wings, a cautious raven flew past, cast a sidelong glance at me, soared aloft and, floating on outstretched wings, disappeared behind the forest, croaking spasmodically; a large flock of pigeons fluttered sharply from the threshing-floor and, suddenly rising in a cloud, eagerly dispersed over the fields—a sign of autumn! Some one was driving past behind the bare hill, his empty cart rumbling loudly. . . .

I returned home; but the image of poor Akulína did not leave my mind for a long time, and her corn-flowers, long since withered, I have preserved to this day. . . .

For Study and Discussion

1. In commenting on descriptions of nature, Chekhov said that "one ought to seize upon the little particulars, grouping them in such a way that, in reading, when you shut your eyes, you get a picture" (p. 21). Do Turgenev's nature descriptions in "The Tryst" meet Chekhov's requirements?

2. Chekhov also said that the description of nature in a story should have "a character of relevance." Is this true of the nature description in "The Tryst"? At what point in the story is there a noticeable shift in the mood of the description? How well does this shift of mood harmonize with the events of the story?

3. How do the bouquet of wild flowers and the monocle function in the development of the contrast between the characters of Akulína and Viktór? Are the flowers and the monocle used symbolically?

4. What effect is produced by this story? How is this effect primarily achieved—through characterization, plot, or theme?

BRET HARTE

THE LUCK OF ROARING CAMP

There was commotion in Roaring Camp. It could not have been a fight, for in 1850 that was not novel enough to have called together the entire settlement. The ditches and claims were not only deserted, but "Tuttle's grocery" had contributed its gamblers, who, it will be remembered, calmly continued their game the day that French Pete and Kanaka Joe shot each other to death over the bar in the front room. The whole camp was collected before a rude cabin on the outer edge of the clearing. Conversation was carried on in a low tone, but the name of a woman was frequently repeated. It was a name familiar enough in the camp,— "Cherokee Sal."

Perhaps the less said of her the better. She was a coarse, and, it is to be feared, a very sinful woman. But at that time she was the only woman in Roaring Camp, and was just then lying in sore extremity, when she most needed the ministration of her own sex. Dissolute, abandoned, and irreclaimable, she was yet suffering a martyrdom hard enough to bear even when veiled by sympathizing womanhood, but now terrible in her loneliness. The primal curse had come to her in that original isolation which must have made the punishment of the first transgression so dreadful. It was, perhaps, part of the expiation of her sin, that, at a moment when she most lacked her sex's intuitive tenderness and care, she met only the half-contemptuous faces of her masculine associates. Yet a few of the spectators were, I think, touched by her sufferings. Sandy Tipton thought it was "rough on Sal," and, in the contemplation of her condition, for a moment rose superior to the fact that he had an ace and two bowers in his sleeve.

It will be seen, also, that the situation was novel. Deaths were by no means uncommon in Roaring Camp, but a birth was a new thing. People had been dismissed from the camp effectively, finally, and with no possibility of return; but this was the first time that anybody had been introduced *ab initio*. Hence the excitement.

Originally published in the *Overland Monthly*, August 1868. Reprinted here from *The Works of Bret Harte* (New York: P. F. Collier and Sons, 1899), Vol. VII.

"You go in there, Stumpy," said a prominent citizen known as "Kentuck," addressing one of the loungers. "Go in there, and see what you kin do. You've had experience in them things."

Perhaps there was a fitness in the selection. Stumpy, in other climes, had been the putative head of two families; in fact, it was owing to some legal informality in these proceedings that Roaring Camp—a city of refuge—was indebted to his company. The crowd approved the choice, and Stumpy was wise enough to bow to the majority. The door closed upon the extempore surgeon and midwife, and Roaring Camp sat down outside, smoked its pipe, and awaited the issue.

The assemblage numbered about a hundred men. One or two of these were actual fugitives from justice, some were criminal, and all were reckless. Physically, they exhibited no indication of their past lives and character. The greatest scamp had a Raphael face, with a profusion of blond hair; Oakhurst, a gambler, had the melancholy air and intellectual abstraction of a Hamlet; the coolest and most courageous man was scarcely over five feet in height, with a soft voice and an embarrassed, timid manner. The term "roughs" applied to them was a distinction rather than a definition. Perhaps in the minor details of fingers, toes, ears, etc., the camp may have been deficient, but these slight omissions did not detract from their aggregate force. The strongest man had but three fingers on his right hand; the best shot had but one eye.

Such was the physical aspect of the men that were dispersed around the cabin. The camp lay in a triangular valley, between two hills and a river. The only outlet was a steep trail over the summit of a hill that faced the cabin, now illuminated by the rising moon. The suffering woman might have seen it from the rude bunk whereon she lay,—seen it winding like a silver thread until it was lost in the stars above.

A fire of withered pine boughs added sociability to the gathering. By degrees the natural levity of Roaring Camp returned. Bets were freely offered and taken regarding the result. Three to five that "Sal would get through with it"; even, that the child would survive; side bets as to the sex and complexion of the coming stranger. In the midst of an excited discussion an exclamation came from those nearest the door, and the camp stopped to listen. Above the swaying and moaning of the pines, the swift rush of the river, and the crackling of the fire rose a sharp, querulous cry—a cry unlike anything heard before in the camp. The pines stopped moaning, the river ceased to rush, and the fire to crackle. It seemed as if Nature had stopped to listen too.

The camp rose to its feet as one man! It was proposed to explode a barrel of gun-powder, but, in consideration of the situation of the mother, better counsels prevailed, and only a few revolvers were discharged; for, whether owing to the rude surgery of the camp, or some other reason, Cherokee Sal was sinking fast. Within an hour she had climbed, as it were, that rugged road that led to the stars, and so passed out of Roaring Camp, its sin and shame forever. I do not think that the announcement disturbed them much, except in speculation as to the fate of the child. "Can he live now?" was asked of Stumpy. The answer was doubtful. The only other being of Cherokee Sal's sex and maternal condition in the settlement was an ass. There was some conjecture as to fitness, but the experiment was tried. It was less problematical than the ancient treatment of Romulus and Remus, and apparently as successful.

When these details were completed, which exhausted another hour, the door was opened, and the anxious crowd, who had already formed themselves into a queue, entered in single file. Beside the low bunk or shelf, on which the figure of the mother was starkly outlined below the blankets, stood a pine table. On this a candle-box was placed, and within it, swathed in staring red flannel, lay the last arrival at Roaring Camp. Beside the candle-box was placed a hat. Its use was soon indicated. "Gentlemen," said Stumpy, with a singular mixture of authority and *ex officio* complacency—"Gentlemen will please pass in at the front door, round the table, and out at the back door. Them as wishes to contribute anything toward the orphan will find a hat handy." The first man entered with his hat on; he uncovered, however, as he looked about him, and so, unconsciously, set an example to the next. In such communities good and bad actions are catching. As the procession filed in, comments were audible,—criticisms addressed, perhaps, rather to Stumpy, in the character of showman,—"Is that him?" "Mighty small specimen"; "Hasn't more'n got the color"; "Ain't bigger nor a derringer." The contributions were as characteristic: A silver tobacco box; a doubloon; a navy revolver, silver mounted; a gold specimen; a very beautifully embroidered lady's handkerchief (from Oakhurst the gambler); a diamond breastpin, a diamond ring (suggested by the pin, with the remark from the giver that he "saw that pin and went two diamonds better"); a slung shot; a Bible (contributor not detected); a golden spur; a silver teaspoon (the initials, I regret to say, were not the giver's); a pair of surgeon's shears; a lancet; a Bank of England note for £5; and about $200 in loose gold and silver coin. During these proceedings Stumpy maintained a silence as impassive as the dead on his left—a gravity as inscrutable as that of the newly-born on his right. Only one incident occurred to break the monotony of the curious procession. As Kentuck bent over the candle-box half curiously, the child turned, and, in a spasm of pain, caught at his groping finger, and held it fast for a moment. Kentuck looked foolish and embarrassed. Something like a blush tried to assert itself in his weather-beaten cheek. "The d——d little cuss!" he said, as he extricated his finger, with, perhaps, more tenderness and care than he might have been deemed capable of showing. He held that finger a little apart from its fellows as he went out, and examined it curiously. The examination provoked the same original remark in regard to the child. In fact, he seemed to enjoy repeating it. "He rastled with my finger," he remarked to Tipton, holding up the member, "the d——d little cuss!"

It was four o'clock before the camp sought repose. A light burnt in the cabin where the watchers sat, for Stumpy did not go to bed that night. Nor did Kentuck. He drank quite freely and related with great gusto his experience, invariably ending with his characteristic condemnation of the newcomer. It seemed to relieve him of any unjust implication of sentiment, and Kentuck had the weaknesses of the nobler sex. When everybody else had gone to bed, he walked down to the river, and whistled reflectingly. Then he walked up the gulch, past the cabin, still whistling with demonstrative unconcern. At a large redwood tree he paused and retraced his steps, and again passed the cabin. Halfway down to the river's bank he again paused, and then returned and knocked at the door. It was opened by Stumpy. "How goes it?" said Kentuck, looking past Stumpy toward the candle-box. "All serene," replied Stumpy. "Anything up?" "Nothing." There was a pause—an embarrassing one—Stumpy still holding the door. Then Kentuck had recourse to his finger, which he held up to Stumpy. "Rastled with it,—the d——d little cuss," he said, and retired.

The next day Cherokee Sal had such rude sepulture as Roaring Camp afforded. After her body had been committed to the hillside, there was a formal meeting of the camp to discuss what should be done with her infant. A resolution to adopt it was unanimous and enthusiastic. But an animated discussion in regard to the manner and feasibility of providing for its wants at once sprung up. It was remarkable that the argument partook of none of those fierce personalities with which discussions were usually conducted at Roaring Camp. Tipton proposed that they should send the child to Red Dog—a distance of forty miles—where female attention could be procured. But the unlucky suggestion met with fierce and unanimous opposition. It was evident that no plan which entailed parting from their new acquisition would for a moment be entertained. "Besides," said Tom Ryder, "them fellows at Red Dog would swap it, and ring in somebody else on us." A disbelief in the honesty of other camps prevailed at Roaring Camp as in other places.

The introduction of a female nurse in the camp also met with objection. It was argued that no decent woman could be prevailed to accept Roaring Camp as her home, and the speaker urged that "they didn't want any more of the other kind." This unkind allusion to the defunct mother, harsh as it may seem, was the first spasm of propriety—the first symptom of the camp's regeneration. Stumpy advanced nothing. Perhaps he felt a certain delicacy in interfering with the selection of a possible successor in office. But when questioned, he averred stoutly that he and "Jinny"—the mammal before alluded to—could manage to rear the child. There was something original, independent, and heroic about the plan that pleased the camp. Stumpy was retained. Certain articles were sent for to Sacramento. "Mind," said the treasurer, as he pressed a bag of gold-dust into the expressman's hand, "the best that can be got—lace, you know, and filigree-work and frills,—d——n the cost!"

Strange to say, the child thrived. Perhaps the invigorating climate of the mountain camp was compensation for material deficiencies. Nature took the foundling to her broader breast. In that rare atmosphere of the Sierra foothills—that air pungent with balsamic odor, that ethereal cordial, at once bracing and exhilarating, he may have found food and nourishment, or a subtle chemistry that transmuted asses' milk to lime and phosphorus. Stumpy inclined to the belief that it was the latter and good nursing. "Me and that ass," he would say, "has been father and mother to him! Don't you," he would add, apostrophizing the helpless bundle before him, "never go back on us."

By the time he was a month old, the necessity of giving him a name became apparent. He had generally been known as "the Kid," "Stumpy's boy," "the Cayote" (an allusion to his vocal powers) and even by Kentuck's endearing diminutive of "the d——d little cuss." But these were felt to be vague and unsatisfactory, and were at last dismissed under another influence. Gamblers and adventurers are generally superstitious, and Oakhurst one day declared that the baby had brought "the luck" to Roaring Camp. It was certain that of late they had been successful. "Luck" was the name agreed upon, with the prefix of Tommy for greater convenience. No allusion was made to the mother, and the father was unknown. "It's better," said the philosophical Oakhurst, "to take a fresh deal all round. Call him Luck, and start him fair." A day was accordingly set apart for the christening. What was meant by this ceremony the reader may imagine, who has already gathered some idea of the reckless irreverence of Roaring Camp. The master of ceremonies was one "Boston," a noted wag, and the occasion seemed to promise the greatest facetiousness. This ingenious satirist had spent two days in preparing a burlesque of the church service, with pointed local allusions. The choir was properly trained, and Sandy Tipton was to stand godfather. But after the procession had marched to the grove with music and banners, and the child had been deposited before a mock altar, Stumpy stepped before the expectant crowd. "It ain't my style to spoil fun, boys," said the little man, stoutly, eyeing the faces around him, "but it strikes me that this thing ain't exactly on the squar. It's playing it pretty low down on this yer baby to ring in fun on him that he ain't goin' to understand. And ef there's going to be any god-fathers round, I'd like to see who's got any better rights than me." A silence followed Stumpy's speech. To the credit of all humorists be it said that the first man to acknowledge its justice was the satirist, thus stopped of his fun. "But," said Stumpy, quickly, following up his advantage, "we're here for a christening, and we'll have it. I proclaim you Thomas Luck, according to the laws of the

United States and the State of California, so help me God." It was the first time that the name of the Deity had been uttered otherwise but profanely in the camp. The form of christening was perhaps even more ludicrous than the satirist had conceived; but strangely enough, nobody saw it and nobody laughed. "Tommy" was christened as seriously as he would have been under a Christian roof, and cried and was comforted in as orthodox fashion.

And so the work of regeneration began in Roaring Camp. Almost imperceptibly a change came over the settlement. The cabin assigned to "Tommy Luck"—or "The Luck," as he was more frequently called—first showed signs of improvement. It was kept scrupulously clean and whitewashed. Then it was boarded, clothed and papered. The rosewood cradle—packed eighty miles by mule—had, in Stumpy's way of putting it, "sorter killed the rest of the furniture." So the rehabilitation of the cabin became a necessity. The men who were in the habit of lounging in at Stumpy's to see "how The Luck got on" seemed to appreciate the change, and, in self-defense, the rival establishment of "Tuttle's grocery" bestirred itself, and imported a carpet and mirrors. The reflections of the latter on the appearance of Roaring Camp tended to produce stricter habits of personal cleanliness. Again Stumpy imposed a kind of quarantine upon those who aspired to the honor and privilege of holding "The Luck." It was a cruel mortification to Kentuck—who, in the carelessness of a large nature and the habits of frontier life, had begun to regard all garments as a second cuticle, which, like a snake's, only sloughed off through decay—to be debarred this privilege from certain prudential reasons. Yet such was the subtle influence of innovation that he thereafter appeared regularly every afternoon in a clean shirt, and face still shining from his ablutions. Nor were moral and social sanitary laws neglected. "Tommy," who was supposed to spend his whole existence in a persistent attempt to repose, must not be disturbed by noise. The shouting and yelling which had gained the camp its infelicitous title were not permitted within hearing distance of Stumpy's. The men conversed in whispers, or smoked with Indian gravity. Profanity was tacitly given up in these sacred precincts, and throughout the camp a popular form of expletive, known as "D——n the luck!" and "Curse the luck!" was abandoned, as having a new personal bearing. Vocal music was not interdicted, being supposed to have a soothing, tranquilizing quality, and one song, sung by "Man-o'-War Jack," an English sailor from Her Majesty's Australian colonies, was quite popular as a lullaby. It was a lugubrious recital of the exploits of "the *Arethusa*, Seventy-four," in a muffled minor, ending with a prolonged dying fall at the burden of each verse, "On b-o-o-o-ard of the *Arethusa*." It was a fine sight to see Jack holding The Luck, rocking from side to side as if with the motion of a ship, and crooning forth this naval ditty. Either through the peculiar rocking of Jack or the length of his song—it contained ninety stanzas, and was continued with conscientious deliberation to the bitter end—the lullaby generally had the desired effect. At such times the men would lie at full length under the trees, in the soft summer twilight, smoking their pipes and drinking in the melodious utterances. An indistinct idea that this was pastoral happiness pervaded the camp. "This 'ere kind o' think," said the Cockney Simmons, meditatively reclining on his elbow, "is 'evingly." It reminded him of Greenwich.

On the long summer days The Luck was usually carried to the gulch, from whence the golden store of Roaring Camp was taken. There, on a blanket spread over pine boughs, he would lie while the men were working in the ditches below. Latterly, there was a rude attempt to decorate this bower with flowers and sweet-smelling shrubs, and generally some one would bring him a cluster of wild honeysuckles, azaleas, or the painted blossoms of Las Mariposas. The men had suddenly awakened to the fact that there were beauty and significance in these trifles, which they had so long trodden carelessly beneath their feet. A flake of glittering mica, a fragment of variegated quartz, a bright pebble from the bed of the creek, became beautiful to eyes thus cleared and strengthened, and were invariably put aside for "The Luck." It was wonderful how many treasures the woods and hillsides yielded that "would do for Tommy." Surrounded by playthings such as never child out of fairyland had before, it is to be hoped that Tommy was content. He appeared to be serenely happy, albeit there was an infantine gravity about him, a contemplative light in his round gray eyes, that sometimes worried Stumpy. He was always tractable and quiet, and it is recorded that once, having crept beyond his "corral"—a hedge of tessellated pine boughs, which surrounded his bed—he dropped over the bank on his head in the soft earth, and remained with his mottled legs in the air in that position for at least five minutes with unflinching gravity. He was extricated without a murmur. I hesitate to record the many other instances of his sagacity, which rest, unfortunately, upon the statements of prejudiced friends. Some of them were not without a tinge of superstition. "I crep' up the bank just now," said Kentuck one day, in a breathless state of excitement, "and dern my skin if he wasn't a talking to a jaybird as was a-sittin on his lap. There they was, just as free and sociable as anything you please, a-jawin at each other just like two cherrybums." Howbeit, whether creeping over the pine boughs or lying lazily on his back, blinking at the leaves above him, to him the birds sang, the squirrels chattered, and the flowers bloomed. Nature was his nurse and playfellow. For him she would let slip between the leaves golden shafts of sunlight that fell just within his grasp; she would send wandering breezes to visit him with the balm of bay and resinous gums; to him the tall redwoods nodded familiarly and sleepily, the bumblebees buzzed, and the rooks cawed a slumbrous accompaniment.

Such was the golden summer of Roaring Camp. They were "flush

times"—and the Luck was with them. The claims had yielded enormously. The camp was jealous of its privileges and looked suspiciously on
strangers. No encouragement was given to immigration, and, to make
their seclusion more perfect, the land on either side of the mountain wall
that surrounded the camp they duly pre-empted. This, and a reputation
for singular proficiency with the revolver, kept the reserve of Roaring
Camp inviolate. The expressman—their only connecting link with the
surrounding world—sometimes told wonderful stories of the camp. He
would say, "They've a street up there in 'Roaring,' that would lay over
any street up there in Red Dog. They've got vines and flowers round
their houses, and they wash themselves twice a day. But they're mighty
rough on strangers, and they worship an Ingin baby."

With the prosperity of the camp came a desire for further improvement. It was proposed to build a hotel in the following spring, and to
invite one or two decent families to reside there for the sake of "The
Luck," who might perhaps profit by female companionship. The sacrifice
that this concession to the sex cost these men, who were fiercely
skeptical in regard to its general virtue and usefulness, can only be
accounted for by their affection for Tommy. A few still held out. But the
resolve could not be carried into effect for three months, and the
minority meekly yielded in the hope that something might turn up to
prevent it. And it did.

The winter of '51 will long be remembered in the foothills. The snow
lay deep on the sierras, and every mountain creek became a river, and
every river a lake. Each gorge and gulch was transformed into a
tumultuous watercourse that descended the hillsides, tearing down giant
trees and scattering its drift and debris along the plain. Red Dog had
been twice under water, and Roaring Camp had been forewarned.
"Water put the gold into them gulches," said Stumpy; "it's been here
once and will be here again!" And that night the North Fork suddenly
leaped over its banks, and swept up the triangular valley of Roaring
Camp.

In the confusion of rushing water, crashing trees, and crackling
timber, and the darkness which seemed to flow with the water and blot
out the fair valley, but little could be done to collect the scattered camp.
When the morning broke, the cabin of Stumpy nearest the river-bank
was gone. Higher up the gulch they found the body of its unlucky owner;
but the pride—the hope—the joy—the Luck—of Roaring Camp had
disappeared. They were returning with sad hearts, when a shout from
the bank recalled them.

It was a relief-boat from down the river. They had picked up, they said,
a man and an infant, nearly exhausted, about two miles below. Did
anybody know them, and did they belong here?

It needed but a glance to show them Kentuck lying there, cruelly
crushed and bruised, but still holding The Luck of Roaring Camp in

his arms. As they bent over the strangely assorted pair, they saw that the child was cold and pulseless. "He is dead," said one. Kentuck opened his eyes. "Dead?" he repeated feebly. "Yes, my man, and you are dying too." A smile lit the eyes of the expiring Kentuck. "Dying!" he repeated, "he's a-taking me with him—tell the boys I've got the Luck with me now"; and the strong man, clinging to the frail babe as a drowning man is said to cling to a straw, drifted away into the shadowy river that flows forever to the unknown sea.

For Study and Discussion

1. Is there any evidence in "The Luck of Roaring Camp" that Harte is covertly "rigging" his presentation of situation and character in order to produce artificial effects? Does he ever falsify a scene in any way in an effort to stir the reader's emotions? If so, point out instances where this occurs.

2. How many specific examples of ironic contrast can you find in the first three pages of the story? Make a list of these and point out whether the effects of these contrasts are humorous or pathetic.

3. Considering Harte's various descriptions of nature, what purpose is served by his treatment of nature in contrast to his characterization of the outlaws? Do you detect any difference in his use of language and imagery in treating these two elements?

4. Modern critics have accused Harte of excessive sentimentality and subjectivity, the same artistic weaknesses condemned by Chekhov (p. 20). Point out evidence of these and other weaknesses caused by the author's intrusion into the story.

5. What evidence of implausibility can you find in the regeneration of Roaring Camp attributed to the presence of "The Luck"?

6. What purpose is served by the flash flood that destroys the camp and its occupants?

7. Are Kentuck's final words logically motivated? If not, why do you suppose Harte has him utter them?

8. Does "The Luck of Roaring Camp" satisfactorily fulfill Harte's own prescription for the American short story? (See his essay, p. 28.) In what sense can the story be praised as an honest attempt to portray "characteristic American life"?

THOMAS BAILEY ALDRICH

MARJORIE DAW

I

DR. DILLON TO EDWARD DELANEY, ESQ., AT THE
PINES, NEAR RYE, N.H.

August 8, 1872

My Dear Sir: I am happy to assure you that your anxiety is without
reason. Flemming will be confined to the sofa for three or four weeks,
and will have to be careful at first how he uses his leg. A fracture of this
kind is always a tedious affair. Fortunately the bone was very skilfully set
by the surgeon who chanced to be in the drugstore where Flemming was
brought after his fall, and I apprehend no permanent inconvenience from
the accident. *Flemming is doing perfectly well physically;* but I must
confess that the irritable and morbid state of mind into which he has
fallen causes me a great deal of uneasiness. He is the last man in the
world who ought to break his leg. You know how impetuous our friend is
ordinarily, what a soul of restlessness and energy, never content unless
he is rushing at some object, like a sportive bull at a red shawl; but
amiable withal. He is no longer amiable. His temper has become
something frightful. Miss Fanny Flemming came up from Newport,
where the family are staying for the summer, to nurse him; but he
packed her off the next morning in tears. He has a complete set of
Balzac's works, twenty-seven volumes, piled up near his sofa, to throw at
Watkins whenever that exemplary serving-man appears with his meals.
Yesterday I very innocently brought Flemming a small basket of lemons.
You know it was a strip of lemon-peel on the curbstone that caused our
friend's mischance. Well, he no sooner set his eyes upon these lemons
than he fell into such a rage as I cannot adequately describe. This is only
one of his moods, and the least distressing. At other times he sits with
bowed head regarding his splintered limb, silent, sullen, despairing.
When this fit is on him—and it sometimes lasts all day—nothing can

Originally published in the *Atlantic Monthly*, April 1873. Reprinted here from *The
Writings of Thomas Bailey Aldrich* (Boston: Houghton, Mifflin Co., 1907), Vol. III.

distract his melancholy. He refuses to eat, does not even read the newspapers; books, except as projectiles for Watkins, have no charms for him. His state is truly pitiable.

Now, if he were a poor man, with a family depending on his daily labor, this irritability and despondency would be natural enough. But in a young fellow of twenty-four, with plenty of money and seemingly not a care in the world, the thing is monstrous. If he continues to give way to his vagaries in this manner, he will end by bringing on an inflammation of the fibula. It was the fibula he broke. I am at my wits' end to know what to prescribe for him. I have anæsthetics and lotions, to make people sleep and to soothe pain; but I've no medicine that will make a man have a little common sense. That is beyond my skill, but maybe it is not beyond yours. You are Flemming's intimate friend, his *fidus Achates*. Write to him, write to him frequently, distract his mind, cheer him up, and prevent him from becoming a confirmed case of melancholia. Perhaps he has some important plans disarranged by his present confinement. If he has you will know, and will know how to advise him judiciously. I trust your father finds the change beneficial? I am, my dear sir, with great respect, etc.

II

EDWARD DELANEY TO JOHN FLEMMING, WEST 38TH
STREET, NEW YORK

August 9, 1872

My Dear Jack: I had a line from Dillon this morning, and was rejoiced to learn that your hurt is not so bad as reported. Like a certain personage, you are not so black and blue as you are painted. Dillon will put you on your pins again in two or three weeks, if you will only have patience and follow his counsels. Did you get my note of last Wednesday? I was greatly troubled when I heard of the accident.

I can imagine how tranquil and saintly you are with your leg in a trough! It is deuced awkward, to be sure, just as we had promised ourselves a glorious month together at the sea-side; but we must make the best of it. It is unfortunate, too, that my father's health renders it impossible for me to leave him. I think he has much improved; the sea air is his native element; but he still needs my arm to lean upon in his walks, and requires some one more careful than a servant to look after him. I cannot come to you, dear Jack, but I have hours of unemployed time on hand, and I will write you a whole post-office full of letters, if that will divert you. Heaven knows, I haven't anything to write about. It isn't as if we were living at one of the beach houses; then I could do you some character studies, and fill your imagination with groups of sea-goddesses, with their (or somebody else's) raven and blond manes hanging down their shoulders. You should have Aphrodite in morning wrapper, in evening costume, and in her prettiest bathing suit. But we are far from all that here. We have rooms in a farm-house, on a cross-road, two miles from the hotels, and lead the quietest of lives.

I wish I were a novelist. This old house, with its sanded floors and high wainscots, and its narrow windows looking out upon a cluster of pines that turn themselves into æolian-harps every time the wind blows, would be the place in which to write a summer romance. It should be a story with the odors of the forest and the breath of the sea in it. It should be a novel like one of that Russian fellow's—what's his name?— Tourguénieff, Turguenef, Turgenif, Toorguniff, Turgénjew—nobody knows how to spell him. Yet I wonder if even a Liza or an Alexandra Paulovna could stir the heart of a man who has constant twinges in his leg. I wonder if one of our own Yankee girls of the best type, haughty and *spirituelle*, would be of any comfort to you in your present deplorable condition. If I thought so, I would hasten down to the Surf House and catch one for you; or, better still, I would find you one over the way.

Picture to yourself a large white house just across the road, nearly opposite our cottage. It is not a house, but a mansion, built, perhaps, in the colonial period, with rambling extensions, and gambrel roof, and a wide piazza on three sides—a self-possessed, high-bred piece of architecture, with its nose in the air. It stands back from the road, and has an obsequious retinue of fringed elms and oaks and weeping willows. Sometimes in the morning, and oftener in the afternoon, when the sun has withdrawn from that part of the mansion, a young woman appears on the piazza with some mysterious Penelope web of embroidery in her hand, or a book. There is a hammock over there—of pineapple fibre, it looks from here. A hammock is very becoming when one is eighteen, and has golden hair, and dark eyes, and an emerald-colored illusion dress looped up after the fashion of a Dresden china shepherdess, and is *chaussée* like a belle of the time of Louis Quartorze. All this splendor goes into that hammock, and sways there like a pond-lily in the golden afternoon. The window of my bedroom looks down on that piazza—and so do I.

But enough of this nonsense, which ill becomes a sedate young attorney taking his vacation with an invalid father. Drop me a line, dear Jack, and tell me how you really are. State your case. Write me a long, quiet letter. If you are violent or abusive, I'll take the law to you.

III

JOHN FLEMMING TO EDWARD DELANEY

August 11, 1872

Your letter, dear Ned, was a godsend. Fancy what a fix I am in—I, who never had a day's sickness since I was born. My left leg weighs three tons. It is embalmed in spices and smothered in layers of fine linen, like a mummy. I can't move. I haven't moved for five thousand years. I'm of the time of Pharaoh.

I lie from morning till night on a lounge, staring into the hot street. Everybody is out of town enjoying himself. The brown-stone-front houses across the street resemble a row of particularly ugly coffins set up on end. A green mould is settling on the names of the deceased, carved on the silver door-plates. Sardonic spiders have sewed up the key-holes. All is silence and dust and desolation—I interrupt this a moment, to take a shy at Watkins with the second volume of César Birotteau. Missed him! I think I could bring him down with a copy of Sainte-Beuve or the Dictionnaire Universel, if I had it. These small Balzac books somehow don't quite fit my hand; but I shall fetch him yet. I've an idea Watkins is tapping the old gentleman's Château Yquem. Duplicate key of the wine-cellar. Hibernian swarries in the front basement. Young Cheops up-stairs, snug in his cerements. Watkins glides into my chamber, with that colorless, hypocritical face of his drawn out long like an accordion; but I know he grins all the way down-stairs, and is glad I have broken my leg. Was not my evil star in the very zenith when I ran up to town to attend that dinner at Delmonico's? I didn't come up altogether for that. It was partly to buy Frank Livingstone's roan mare Margot. And now I shall not be able to sit in the saddle these two months. I'll send the mare down to you at The Pines—is that the name of the place?

Old Dillon fancies that I have something on my mind. He drives me wild with lemons. Lemons for a mind diseased! Nonsense. I am only as restless as the devil under this confinement—a thing I'm not used to. Take a man who has never had so much as a headache or a toothache in his life, strap one of his legs in a section of water-spout, keep him in a room in the city for weeks, with the hot weather turned on, and then expect him to smile and purr and be happy! It is preposterous. I can't be cheerful or calm.

Your letter is the first consoling thing I have had since my disaster, ten days ago. It really cheered me up for half an hour. Send me a screed, Ned, as often as you can, if you love me. Anything will do. Write me more about that little girl in the hammock. That was very pretty, all that about the Dresden china shepherdess and the pond-lily; the imagery a little mixed, perhaps, but very pretty. I didn't suppose you had so much sentimental furniture in your upper story. It shows how one may be familiar for years with the reception-room of his neighbor, and never suspect what is directly under his mansard. I supposed your loft stuffed with dry legal parchments, mortgages and affidavits; you take down a package of manuscript, and lo! there are lyrics and sonnets and can-zonettas. You really have a graphic descriptive touch, Edward Delaney, and I suspect you of anonymous love-tales in the magazines.

I shall be a bear until I hear from you again. Tell me all about your pretty *inconnue* across the road. What is her name? Who is she? Who's her father? Where's her mother? Who's her lover? You cannot imagine how this will occupy me. The more trifling the better. My imprisonment has weakened me intellectually to such a degree that I find your epistolary gifts quite considerable. I am passing into my second child-hood. In a week or two I shall take to India-rubber rings and prongs of coral. A silver cup, with an appropriate inscription, would be a delicate attention on your part. In the mean time, write!

IV

EDWARD DELANEY TO JOHN FLEMMING

August 12, 1872

The sick pasha shall be amused. *Bismillah!* he wills it so. If the story-teller becomes prolix and tedious—the bow-string and the sack, and two Nubians to drop him into the Piscataqua! But, truly, Jack, I have a hard task. There is literally nothing here—except the little girl over the way. She is swinging in the hammock at this moment. It is to me compensation for many of the ills of life to see her now and then put out a small kid boot, which fits like a glove, and set herself going. Who is she, and what is her name? Her name is Daw. Only daughter of Mr. Richard W. Daw, ex-colonel and banker. Mother dead. One brother at Harvard, elder brother killed at the battle of Fair Oaks, ten years ago. Old, rich family, the Daws. This is the homestead, where father and daughter pass eight months of the twelve; the rest of the year in Baltimore and Washington. The New England winter too many for the old gentleman. The daughter is called Marjorie—Marjorie Daw. Sounds odd at first, doesn't it? But after you say it over to yourself half a dozen times, you like it. There's a pleasing quaintness to it, something prim and pansy-like. Must be a nice sort of girl to be called Marjorie Daw.

I had mine host of The Pines in the witness-box last night, and drew the foregoing testimony from him. He has charge of Mr. Daw's vegetable-garden, and has known the family these thirty years. Of course I shall make the acquaintance of my neighbors before many days. It will be next to impossible for me not to meet Mr. Daw or Miss Daw in some of my walks. The young lady has a favorite path to the sea-beach. I shall intercept her some morning, and touch my hat to her. Then the princess will bend her fair head to me with courteous surprise not unmixed with haughtiness. Will snub me, in fact. All this for thy sake, O Pasha of the Snapt Axle-tree! . . . How oddly things fall out! Ten minutes ago I was called down to the parlor—you know the kind of parlors in farm-houses on the coast, a sort of amphibious parlor, with sea-shells on the mantel-piece and spruce branches in the chimney-place—where I found my father and Mr. Daw doing the antique polite to each other. He had come to pay his respects to his new neighbors. Mr. Daw is a tall, slim gentleman of about fifty-five, with a florid face and snow-white mustache and side-whiskers. Looks like Mr. Dombey, or as Mr. Dombey would have looked if he had served a few years in the British Army. Mr. Daw was a colonel in the late war, commanding the regiment in which his son was a lieutenant. Plucky old boy, backbone of New Hampshire granite. Before taking his leave, the colonel delivered himself of an invitation as if he were issuing a general order. Miss Daw has a few friends coming, at 4 P.M., to play croquet on the lawn (parade-ground) and have tea (cold rations) on the piazza. Will we honor them with our company? (or be sent to the guard-house.) My father declines on the plea of ill-health. My father's son bows with as much suavity as he knows, and accepts.

In my next I shall have something to tell you. I shall have seen the little beauty face to face. I have a presentiment, Jack, that this Daw is a *rara avis!* Keep up your spirits, my boy, until I write you another letter—and send me along word how's your leg.

V

EDWARD DELANEY TO JOHN FLEMMING

August 13, 1872

The party, my dear Jack, was as dreary as possible. A lieutenant of the navy, the rector of the Episcopal church at Stillwater, and a society swell from Nahant. The lieutenant looked as if he had swallowed a couple of his buttons, and found the bullion rather indigestible; the rector was a pensive youth, of the daffydowndilly sort; and the swell from Nahant was a very weak tidal wave indeed. The women were much better, as they always are; the two Miss Kingsburys of Philadelphia, staying at the Sea-shell House, two bright and engaging girls. But Marjorie Daw!

The company broke up soon after tea, and I remained to smoke a cigar with the colonel on the piazza. It was like seeing a picture to see Miss Marjorie hovering around the old soldier, and doing a hundred gracious little things for him. She brought the cigars and lighted the tapers with her own delicate fingers, in the most enchanting fashion. As we sat there, she came and went in the summer twilight, and seemed, with her white dress and pale gold hair, like some lovely phantom that had sprung into existence out of the smoke-wreaths. If she had melted into air, like the status of Galatea in the play, I should have been more sorry than surprised.

It was easy to perceive that the old colonel worshipped her, and she him. I think the relation between an elderly father and a daughter just blooming into womanhood the most beautiful possible. There is in it a subtle sentiment that cannot exist in the case of mother and daughter, or that of son and mother. But this is getting into deep water.

I sat with the Daws until half past ten, and saw the moon rise on the sea. The ocean, that had stretched motionless and black against the horizon, was changed by magic into a broken field of glittering ice, interspersed with marvellous silvery fjords. In the far distance the Isles of Shoals loomed up like a group of huge bergs drifting down on us. The Polar Regions in a June thaw! It was exceedingly fine. What did we talk about? We talked about the weather—and *you!* The weather has been disagreeable for several days past—and so have you. I glided from one topic to the other very naturally. I told my friends of your accident; how it had frustrated all our summer plans, and what our plans were. I played quite a spirited solo on the fibula. Then I described you; or, rather, I didn't. I spoke of your amiability, of your patience under this severe affliction; of your touching gratitude when Dillon brings you little presents of fruit; of your tenderness to your sister Fanny, whom you would not allow to stay in town to nurse you, and how you heroically sent her back to Newport, preferring to remain alone with Mary, the cook, and your man Watkins, to whom, by the way, you were devotedly attached. If you had been there, Jack, you wouldn't have known yourself. I should have excelled as a criminal lawyer, if I had not turned my attention to a different branch of jurisprudence.

Miss Marjorie asked all manner of leading questions concerning you. It did not occur to me then, but it struck me forcibly afterwards, that she evinced a singular interest in the conversation. When I got back to my room, I recalled how eagerly she leaned forward, with her full, snowy throat in strong moonlight, listening to what I said. Positively, I think I made her like you!

Miss Daw is a girl whom you would like immensely, I can tell you that. A beauty without affectation, a high and tender nature—if one can read the soul in the face. And the old colonel is a noble character, too.

I am glad the Daws are such pleasant people. The Pines is an isolated spot, and my resources are few. I fear I should have found life here somewhat monotonous before long, with no other society than that of my excellent sire. It is true, I might have made a target of the defenceless invalid; but I haven't a taste for artillery, *moi.*

VI

JOHN FLEMMING TO EDWARD DELANEY

August 17, 1872

For a man who hasn't a taste for artillery, it occurs to me, my friend, you are keeping up a pretty lively fire on my inner works. But go on. Cynicism is a small brass field-piece that eventually bursts and kills the artilleryman.

You may abuse me as much as you like, and I'll not complain; for I don't know what I should do without your letters. They are curing me. I haven't hurled anything at Watkins since last Sunday, partly because I have grown more amiable under your teaching, and partly because

Watkins captured my ammunition one night, and carried it off to the library. He is rapidly losing the habit he had acquired of dodging whenever I rub my ear, or make any slight motion with my right arm. He is still suggestive of the wine-cellar, however. You may break, you may shatter Watkins, if you will, but the scent of the Roederer will hang round him still.

Ned, that Miss Daw must be a charming person. I should certainly like her. I like her already. When you spoke in your first letter of seeing a young girl swinging in a hammock under your chamber window, I was somehow strangely drawn to her. I cannot account for it in the least. What you have subsequently written of Miss Daw has strengthened the impression. You seem to be describing a woman I have known in some previous state of existence, or dreamed of in this. Upon my word, if you were to send me her photograph, I believe I should recognize her at a glance. Her manner, that listening attitude, her traits of character, as you indicate them, the light hair and the dark eyes—they are all familiar things to me. Asked a lot of questions, did she? Curious about me? That is strange.

You would laugh in your sleeve, you wretched old cynic, if you knew how I lie awake nights, with my gas turned down to a star, thinking of The Pines and the house across the road. How cool it must be down there! I long for the salt smell in the air. I picture the colonel smoking his cheroot on the piazza. I send you and Miss Daw off on afternoon rambles along the beach. Sometimes I let you stroll with her under the elms in the moonlight, for you are great friends by this time, I take it, and see each other every day. I know your ways and your manners! Then I fall into a truculent mood, and would like to destroy somebody. Have you noticed anything in the shape of a lover hanging around the colonial Lares and Penates? Does that lieutenant of the horse-marines or that young Stillwater parson visit the house much? Not that I am pining for news of them, but any gossip of the kind would be in order. I wonder, Ned, you don't fall in love with Miss Daw. I am ripe to do it myself. Speaking of photographs, couldn't you manage to slip one of her cartes-de-visite from her album—she must have an album, you know—and send it to me? I will return it before it could be missed. That's a good fellow! Did the mare arrive safe and sound? It will be a capital animal this autumn for Central Park.

O—my leg? I forgot about my leg. It's better.

VII

EDWARD DELANEY TO JOHN FLEMMING

August 20, 1872

You are correct in your surmises. I am on the most friendly terms with our neighbors. The colonel and my father smoke their afternoon cigar together in our sitting-room or on the piazza opposite, and I pass an hour or two of the day or the evening with the daughter. I am more and more struck by the beauty, modesty, and intelligence of Miss Daw.

You ask me why I do not fall in love with her. I will be frank, Jack: I have thought of that. She is young, rich, accomplished, uniting in herself more attractions, mental and personal, than I can recall in any girl of my acquaintance; but she lacks the something that would be necessary to inspire in me that kind of interest. Possessing this unknown quantity, a woman neither beautiful nor wealthy nor very young could bring me to her feet. But not Miss Daw. If we were shipwrecked together on an uninhabited island—let me suggest a tropical island, for it costs no more to be picturesque—I would build her a bamboo hut, I would fetch her bread-fruit and cocoanuts. I would fry yams for her, I would lure the ingenuous turtle and make her nourishing soups, but I wouldn't make love to her,—not under eighteen months. I would like to have her for a sister, that I might shield her and counsel her, and spend half my income on thread-lace and camel's-hair shawls. (We are off the island now.) If such were not my feeling, there would still be an obstacle to my loving Miss Daw. A greater misfortune could scarcely befall me than to love her. Flemming, I am about to make a revelation that will astonish you. I may be all wrong in my premises and consequently in my conclusions; but you shall judge.

That night when I returned to my room after the croquet party at the Daws', and was thinking over the trivial events of the evening, I was suddenly impressed by the air of eager attention with which Miss Daw had followed my account of your accident. I think I mentioned this to you. Well, the next morning, as I went to mail my letter, I overtook Miss Daw on the road to Rye, where the post-office is, and accompanied her thither and back, an hour's walk. The conversation again turned on you, and again I remarked that inexplicable look of interest which had lighted up her face the previous evening. Since then, I have seen Miss Daw perhaps ten times, perhaps oftener, and on each occasion I found that when I was not speaking of you, or your sister, or some person or place associated with you, I was not holding her attention. She would be absent-minded, her eyes would wander away from me to the sea, or to some distant object in the landscape; her fingers would play with the leaves of a book in a way that convinced me she was not listening. At these moments if I abruptly changed the theme—I did it several times as an experiment—and dropped some remark about my friend Flemming, then the sombre blue eyes would come back to me instantly.

Now, is not this the oddest thing in the world? No, not the oddest. The effect which you tell me was produced on you by my casual mention of an unknown girl swinging in a hammock is certainly as strange. You can conjecture how that passage in your letter of Friday startled me. Is it possible, then, that two people who have never met, and who are hundreds of miles apart, can exert a magnetic influence on each other? I have read of such psychological phenomena, but never credited them. I leave the solution of the problem to you. As for myself, all other things being favorable, it would be impossible for me to fall in love with a woman who listens to me only when I am talking of my friend!

I am not aware that any one is paying marked attention to my fair neighbor. The lieutenant of the navy—he is stationed at Rivermouth—sometimes drops in of an evening, and some times the rector from Stillwater; the lieutenant the oftener. He was there last night. I should not be surprised if he had an eye to the heiress; but he is not formidable. Mistress Daw carries a neat little spear of irony, and the honest lieutenant seems to have a particular facility for impaling himself on the point of it. He is not dangerous, I should say; though I have known a woman to satirize a man for years, and marry him after all. Decidedly, the lowly rector is not dangerous; yet, again, who has not seen Cloth of Frieze victorious in the lists where Cloth of Gold went down?

As to the photograph. There is an exquisite ivorytype of Marjorie, in passe-partout, on the drawing-room mantel-piece. It would be missed at once if taken. I would do anything reasonable for you, Jack; but I've no burning desire to be hauled up before the local justice of the peace, on a charge of petty larceny.

P.S.—Enclosed is a spray of mignonette, which I advise you to treat tenderly. Yes, we talked of you again last night, as usual. It is becoming a little dreary for me.

VIII

EDWARD DELANEY TO JOHN FLEMMING

August 22, 1872

Your letter in reply to my last has occupied my thoughts all the morning. I do not know what to think. Do you mean to say that you are seriously half in love with a woman whom you have never seen—with a shadow, a chimera? for what else can Miss Daw be to you? I do not understand it at all. I understand neither you nor her. You are a couple of ethereal beings moving in finer air than I can breathe with my commonplace lungs. Such delicacy of sentiment is something I admire without comprehending. I am bewildered. I am of the earth earthy, and I find myself in the incongruous position of having to do with mere souls, with natures so finely tempered that I run some risk of shattering them in my awkwardness. I am as Caliban among the spirits!

Reflecting on your letter, I am not sure that it is wise in me to continue this correspondence. But no, Jack; I do wrong to doubt the good sense that forms the basis of your character. You are deeply interested in Miss Daw; you feel that she is a person whom you may perhaps greatly admire when you know her: at the same time you bear in mind that the chances are ten to five that, when you do come to know her, she will fall far short of your ideal, and you will not care for her in the least. Look at it in this sensible light, and I will hold back nothing from you.

Yesterday afternoon my father and myself rode over to Rivermouth with the Daws. A heavy rain in the morning had cooled the atmosphere and laid the dust. To Rivermouth is a drive of eight miles, along a winding road lined all the way with wild barberry-bushes. I never saw anything more brilliant than these bushes, the green of the foliage and the pink of the coral berries intensified by the rain. The colonel drove, with my father in front, Miss Daw and I on the back seat. I resolved that for the first five miles your name should not pass my lips. I was amused by the artful attempts she made, at the start, to break through my reticence. Then a silence fell upon her; and then she became suddenly gay. That keenness which I enjoyed so much when it was exercised on the lieutenant was not so satisfactory directed against myself. Miss Daw has great sweetness of disposition, but she can be disagreeable. She is like the young lady in the rhyme, with the curl on her forehead—

"When she is good,
She is very, very good,
And when she is bad, she is horrid!"

I kept to my resolution, however; but on the return home I relented, and talked of your mare! Miss Daw is going to try a side-saddle on Margot some morning. The animal is a trifle too light for my weight. By the bye, I nearly forgot to say that Miss Daw sat for a picture yesterday to a Rivermouth artist. If the negative turns out well, I am to have a copy. So our ends will be accomplished without crime. I wish, though, I could send you the ivorytype in the drawing-room; it is cleverly colored, and would give you an idea of her hair and eyes, which of course the other will not.

No, Jack, the spray of mignonette did not come from me. A man of twenty-eight doesn't enclose flowers in his letters—to another man. But don't attach too much significance to the circumstance. She gives sprays of mignonette to the rector, sprays to the lieutenant. She has even given a rose from her bosom to your slave. It is her jocund nature to scatter flowers, like Spring.

If my letters sometimes read disjointedly, you must understand that I never finish one at a sitting, but write at intervals, when the mood is on me.

The mood is not on me now.

IX

EDWARD DELANEY TO JOHN FLEMMING

August 23, 1872

I have just returned from the strangest interview with Marjorie. She has all but confessed to me her interest in you. But with what modesty and dignity! Her words elude my pen as I attempt to put them on paper; and, indeed, it was not so much what she said as her manner; and that I cannot reproduce. Perhaps it was of a piece with the strangeness of this whole business, that she should tacitly acknowledge to a third party the love she feels for a man she has never beheld! But I have lost, through your aid, the faculty of being surprised. I accept things as people do in dreams. Now that I am again in my room, it all appears like an illusion—the black masses of Rembrandtish shadow under the trees, the fire-flies whirling in Pyrrhic dances among the shrubbery, the sea over there, Marjorie sitting on the hammock!

It is past midnight, and I am too sleepy to write more.

Thursday Morning

My father has suddenly taken it into his head to spend a few days at the Shoals. In the meanwhile you will not hear from me. I see Marjorie walking in the garden with the colonel. I wish I could speak to her alone, but shall probably not have an opportunity before we leave.

X

EDWARD DELANEY TO JOHN FLEMMING

August 28, 1872

You were passing into your second childhood, were you? Your intellect was so reduced that my epistolary gifts seemed quite considerable to you, did they? I rise superior to the sarcasm in your favor of the 11th instant, when I notice that five days' silence on my part is sufficient to throw you into the depths of despondency.

We returned only this morning from Appledore, that enchanted island—at four dollars per day. I find on my desk three letters from you! Evidently there is no lingering doubt in *your* mind as to the pleasure I derive from your correspondence. These letters are undated, but in what I take to be the latest are two passages that require my consideration. You will pardon my candor, dear Flemming, but the conviction forces itself upon me that as your leg grows stronger your head becomes weaker. You ask my advice on a certain point. I will give it. In my opinion you could do nothing more unwise than to address a note to Miss Daw, thanking her for the flower. It would, I am sure, offend her delicacy beyond pardon. She knows you only through me; you are to her an abstraction, a figure in a dream—a dream from which the faintest shock would awaken her. Of course, if you enclose a note to me and insist on its delivery, I shall deliver it; but I advise you not to do so.

You say you are able, with the aid of a cane, to walk about your chamber, and that you purpose to come to The Pines the instant Dillon thinks you strong enough to stand the journey. Again I advise you not to. Do you not see that, every hour you remain away, Marjorie's glamour deepens, and your influence over her increases? You will ruin everything by precipitancy. Wait until you are entirely recovered; in any case, do not come without giving me warning. I fear the effect of your abrupt advent here—under the circumstances.

Miss Daw was evidently glad to see us back again, and gave me both hands in the frankest way. She stopped at the door a moment this afternoon in the carriage; she had been over to Rivermouth for her pictures. Unluckily the photographer had spilt some acid on the plate, and she was obliged to give him another sitting. I have an intuition that something is troubling Marjorie. She had an abstracted air not usual with her. However, it may be only my fancy. . . . I end this, leaving several things unsaid, to accompany my father on one of those long walks which are now his chief medicine—and mine!

XI

EDWARD DELANEY TO JOHN FLEMMING

August 29, 1872

I write in great haste to tell you what has taken place here since my letter of last night. I am in the utmost perplexity. Only one thing is plain—*you* must not dream of coming to The Pines. Marjorie has told her father everything! I saw her for a few minutes, an hour ago, in the garden; and, as near as I could gather from her confused statement, the facts are these: Lieutenant Bradley—that's the naval officer stationed at Rivermouth—has been paying court to Miss Daw for some time past, but not so much to her liking as to that of the colonel, who it seems is an old friend of the young gentleman's father. Yesterday (I knew she was in some trouble when she drove up to our gate) the colonel spoke to Marjorie of Bradley—urged his suit, I infer. Marjorie expressed her dislike for the lieutenant with characteristic frankness, and finally confessed to her father—well, I really do not know what she confessed. It must have been the vaguest of confessions, and must have sufficiently puzzled the colonel. At any rate, it exasperated him. I suppose I am implicated in the matter, and that the colonel feels bitterly towards me. I do not see why: I have carried no messages between you and Miss Daw; I have behaved with the greatest discretion. I can find no flaw anywhere in my proceeding. I do not see that anybody has done anything—except the colonel himself.

It is probable, nevertheless, that the friendly relations between the two houses will be broken off. "A plague o' both your houses," say you. I will keep you informed, as well as I can, of what occurs over the way. We shall remain here until the second week in September. Stay where you are, or, at all events, do not dream of joining me. . . . Colonel Daw is sitting on the piazza looking rather wicked. I have not seen Marjorie since I parted with her in the garden.

XII

EDWARD DELANEY TO THOMAS DILLON, M.D.,
MADISON SQUARE, NEW YORK

August 30, 1872

My Dear Doctor: If you have any influence over Flemming, I beg of you to exert it to prevent his coming to this place at present. There are circumstances which I will explain to you before long, that make it of the first importance that he should not come into this neighborhood. His appearance here, I speak advisedly, would be disastrous to him. In urging him to remain in New York, or to go to some inland resort, you will be doing him and me a real service. Of course you will not mention my name in this connection. You know me well enough, my dear doctor, to be assured that, in begging your secret cooperation, I have reasons that will meet your entire approval when they are made plain to you. We shall return to town on the 15th of next month, and my first duty will be to present myself at your hospitable door and satisfy your curiosity, if I have excited it. My father, I am glad to state, has so greatly improved that he can no longer be regarded as an invalid. With great esteem, I am, etc., etc.

XIII

EDWARD DELANEY TO JOHN FLEMMING

August 31, 1872

Your letter, announcing your mad determination to come here, has just reached me. I beseech you to reflect a moment. The step would be fatal to your interests and hers. You would furnish just cause for irritation to R. W. D.; and, though he loves Marjorie tenderly, he is capable of going to any lengths if opposed. You would not like, I am convinced, to be the means of causing him to treat *her* with severity. That would be the result of your presence at The Pines at this juncture. I am annoyed to be obliged to point out these things to you. We are on very delicate ground, Jack; the situation is critical, and the slightest mistake in a move would cost us the game. If you consider it worth the winning, be patient. Trust a little to my sagacity. Wait and see what happens. Moreover, I understand from Dillon that you are in no condition to take so long a journey. He thinks the air of the coast would be the worst thing possible for you; that you ought to go inland, if anywhere. Be advised by me. Be advised by Dillon.

XIV

TELEGRAMS

September 1, 1872

1—To Edward Delaney

Letter received. Dillon be hanged. I think I ought to be on the ground.

J. F.

2—To John Flemming

Stay where you are. You would only complicate matters. Do not move until you hear from me.

E. D.

3—To Edward Delaney

My being at The Pines could be kept secret. I must see her.

J. F.

4—To John Flemming

Do not think of it. It would be useless. R. W. D. has locked M. in her room. You would not be able to effect an interview.

E. D.

5—To Edward Delaney

Locked in her room. Good God. That settles the question. I shall leave by the twelve-fifteen express.

J. F.

XV

THE ARRIVAL

On the second of September, 1872, as the down express due at 3.40 left the station at Hampton, a young man, leaning on the shoulder of a servant, whom he addressed as Watkins, stepped from the platform into a hack, and requested to be driven to The Pines. On arriving at the gate of a modest farm-house, a few miles from the station, the young man descended with difficulty from the carriage, and, casting a hasty glance across the road, seemed much impressed by some peculiarity in the landscape. Again leaning on the shoulder of the person Watkins, he walked to the door of the farm-house and inquired for Mr. Edward Delaney. He was informed by the aged man who answered his knock, that Mr. Edward Delaney had gone to Boston the day before, but that Mr. Jonas Delaney was within. This information did not appear satisfactory to the stranger, who inquired if Mr. Edward Delaney had left any message for Mr. John Flemming. There *was* a letter for Mr. Flemming, if he were that person. After a brief absence the aged man reappeared with a Letter.

XVI

September 1, 1872

I am horror-stricken at what I have done! When I began this correspondence I had no other purpose than to relieve the tedium of your sick-chamber. Dillon told me to cheer you up. I tried to. I thought you entered into the spirit of the thing. I had no idea, until within a few days, that you were taking matters *au grand sérieux.*

What can I say? I am in sackcloth and ashes. I am a pariah, a dog of an outcast. I tried to make a little romance to interest you, something soothing and idyllic, and, by Jove! I have done it only too well! My father doesn't know a word of this, so don't jar the old gentleman any more than you can help. I fly from the wrath to come—when you arrive! For oh, dear Jack, there isn't any colonial mansion on the other side of the road, there isn't any piazza, there isn't any hammock—there isn't any Marjorie Daw!

For Study and Discussion

1. How much specific information about John Flemming is presented in the first letter, written by Dr. Dillon? How much more is added in Flemming's first letter to his friend, Edward Delaney?

2. Where are the first hints dropped that Marjorie Daw is purely an imaginary person?

3. Is Flemming's intense interest in the girl convincingly developed? What devices does the author employ to persuade the reader to accept his infatuation?

4. How much time elapses between the opening and the close of the Delaney-Flemming correspondence? What is the significance of this time span?

5. What significance can be seen in the fact that all but two of the letters, after the first one, are written by Delaney?

6. Ever since Samuel Richardson wrote his novel *Pamela* (1740) in letter form, the epistolary narrative has been in wide use. What limitations does the writer impose on himself when he elects to tell his story through a sequence of letters? Does Aldrich overcome these limitations in "Marjorie Daw"? Do you think the letter form is an effective method for telling this story?

7. How well does this story meet Matthews' requirements for "compression, originality, . . . ingenuity [and] . . . a touch of fantasy" (p. 34)?

GUY DE MAUPASSANT

THE PIECE OF STRING

It was market-day, and over all the roads around Goderville the peasants and their wives were coming towards the town. The men walked easily, lurching the whole body forward at every step. Their long legs were twisted and deformed by the slow, painful labors of the country:—by bending over to plough, which is what also makes their left shoulders too high and their figures crooked; and by reaping corn, which obliges them for steadiness' sake to spread their knees too wide. Their starched blue blouses, shining as though varnished, ornamented at collar and cuffs with little patterns of white stitch-work, and blown up big around their bony bodies, seemed exactly like balloons about to soar, but putting forth a head, two arms, and two feet.

Some of these fellows dragged a cow or a calf at the end of a rope. And just behind the animal, beating it over the back with a leaf-covered branch to hasten its pace, went their wives, carrying large baskets from which came forth the heads of chickens or the heads of ducks. These women walked with steps far shorter and quicker than the men; their figures, withered and upright, were adorned with scanty little shawls pinned over their flat bosoms; and they enveloped their heads each in a white cloth, close fastened round the hair and surmounted by a cap.

Now a char-à-banc passed by, drawn by a jerky-paced nag. It shook up strangely the two men on the seat. And the woman at the bottom of the cart held fast to its sides to lessen the hard joltings.

In the market-place at Goderville was a great crowd, a mingled multitude of men and beasts. The horns of cattle, the high and long-napped hats of wealthy peasants, the head-dresses of the women, came to the surface of that sea. And voices clamorous, sharp, shrill, made a continuous and savage din. Above it a huge burst of laughter from the sturdy lungs of a merry yokel would sometimes sound, and sometimes a long bellow from a cow tied fast to the wall of a house.

Originally published under the title "La Ficelle," in the periodical *Gaulois*, November 25, 1883. Reprinted here, in a translation by Jonathan Sturges, from *The Odd Number: Thirteen Tales by Guy de Maupassant* (New York: Harper and Brothers, 1889).

It all smelled of the stable, of milk, of hay, and of perspiration, giving off that half-human, half-animal odor which is peculiar to the men of the fields.

Maître Hauchecorne, of Bréauté, had just arrived at Goderville, and was taking his way towards the square, when he perceived on the ground a little piece of string. Maître Hauchecorne, economical, like all true Normans, reflected that everything was worth picking up which could be of any use; and he stooped down—but painfully, because he suffered from rheumatism. He took the bit of thin cord from the ground, and was carefully preparing to roll it up when he saw Maître Malandain, the harness-maker, on his door-step, looking at him. They had once had a quarrel about a halter, and they had remained angry, bearing malice on both sides. Maître Hauchecorne was overcome with a sort of shame at being seen by his enemy looking in the dirt so for a bit of string. He quickly hid his find beneath his blouse; then in the pocket of his breeches; then pretended to be still looking for something on the ground which he did not discover; and at last went off towards the market-place, with his head bent forward, and a body almost doubled in two by rheumatic pains.

He lost himself immediately in the crowd, which was clamorous, slow, and agitated by interminable bargains. The peasants examined the cows, went off, came back, always in great perplexity and fear of being cheated, never quite daring to decide, spying at the eye of the seller, trying ceaselessly to discover the tricks of the man and the defect in the beast.

The women, having placed their great baskets at their feet, had pulled out the poultry, which lay upon the ground, tied by the legs, with eyes scared, with combs scarlet.

They listened to propositions, maintaining their prices, with a dry manner, with an impassible face; or, suddenly, perhaps, deciding to take the lower price which was offered, they cried out to the customer, who was departing slowly:

"All right, I'll let you have them, Maît' Anthime."

Then, little by little, the square became empty, and when the *Angelus* struck mid-day those who lived at a distance poured into the inns.

At Jourdain's the great room was filled with eaters, just as the vast court was filled with vehicles of every sort—wagons, gigs, char-à-bancs, tilburys, tilt-carts which have no name, yellow with mud, misshapen, pieced together, raising their shafts to heaven like two arms, or it may be with their nose in the dirt and their rear in the air.

Just opposite to where the diners were at table the huge fireplace, full of clear flame, threw a lively heat on the backs of those who sat along the right. Three spits were turning, loaded with chickens, with pigeons, and with joints of mutton; and a delectable odor of roast meat, and of gravy gushing over crisp brown skin, took wing from the hearth, kindled merriment, caused mouths to water.

All the aristocracy of the plough were eating there, at Maît' Jourdain's, the innkeeper's, a dealer in horses also, and a sharp fellow who had made a pretty penny in his day.

The dishes were passed round, were emptied, with jugs of yellow cider. Every one told of his affairs, of his purchases and his sales. They asked news about the crops. The weather was good for green stuffs, but a little wet for wheat.

All of a sudden the drum rolled in the court before the house. Every one, except some of the most indifferent, was on his feet at once, and ran to the door, to the windows, with his mouth still full and his napkin in his hand.

When the public crier had finished his tattoo he called forth in a jerky voice, making his pauses out of time:

"Be it known to the inhabitants of Goderville, and in general to all—persons present at the market, that there has been lost this morning, on the Beuzeville road, between—nine and ten o'clock, a pocket-book of black leather, containing five hundred francs and business papers. You are requested to return it—to the mayor's office, at once, or to Maître Fortuné Houlbrèque, of Manneville. There will be twenty francs reward."

Then the man departed. They heard once more at a distance the dull beatings on the drum and the faint voice of the crier.

Then they began to talk of this event, reckoning up the chances which "Maître Houlbrèque had of finding or of not finding his pocket-book again.

And the meal went on.

They were finishing their coffee when the corporal of gendarmes appeared on the threshold.

He asked:

"Is Maître Hauchecorne, of Bréauté, here?"

Maître Hauchecorne, seated at the other end of the table, answered:

"Here I am."

And the corporal resumed:

"Maître Hauchecorne, will you have the kindness to come with me to the mayor's office? M. le Maire would like to speak to you."

The peasant, surprised and uneasy, gulped down his little glass of cognac, got up, and, even worse bent over than in the morning, since the first steps after a rest were always particularly difficult, started off, repeating:

"Here I am, here I am."

And he followed the corporal.

The mayor was waiting for him, seated in an arm-chair. He was the notary of the place, a tall, grave man of pompous speech.

"Maître Hauchecorne," said he, "this morning, on the Beuzeville road, you were seen to pick up the pocket-book lost by Maître Houlbrèque, of Manneville."

The countryman, speechless, regarded the mayor, frightened already by this suspicion which rested on him he knew not why.

"I, I picked up that pocket-book?"

"Yes, you."

"I swear I didn't even know nothing about it at all."

"You were seen."

"They saw me, me? Who is that who saw me?"

"M. Malandain, the harness-maker."

Then the old man remembered, understood, and, reddening with anger:

"Ah! he saw me, did he, the rascal? He saw me picking up this string here, M'sieu' le Maire."

And, fumbling at the bottom of his pocket, he pulled out of it the little end of string.

But the mayor incredulously shook his head:

"You will not make me believe, Maître Hauchecorne, that M. Malandain, who is a man worthy of credit, has mistaken this string for a pocket-book."

The peasant, furious, raised his hand and spit as if to attest his good faith, repeating:

"For all that, it is the truth of the good God, the blessed truth, M'sieu' le Maire. There! on my soul and my salvation I repeat it."

The mayor continued:

"After having picked up the thing in question, you even looked for some time in the mud to see if a piece of money had not dropped out of it."

The good man was suffocated with indignation and with fear:

"If they can say!—if they can say . . . such lies as that to slander an honest man! If they can say!—"

He might protest, he was not believed.

He was confronted with M. Malandain, who repeated and sustained his testimony. They abused one another for an hour. At his own request Maître Hauchecorne was searched. Nothing was found upon him.

At last, the mayor, much perplexed, sent him away, warning him that he would inform the public prosecutor, and ask for orders.

The news had spread. When he left the mayor's office, the old man was surrounded, interrogated with a curiosity which was serious or mocking as the case might be, but into which no indignation entered. And he began to tell the story of the string. They did not believe him. They laughed.

He passed on, button-holed by every one, himself button-holing his acquaintances, beginning over and over again his tale and his protestations, showing his pockets turned inside out to prove that he had nothing.

They said to him:

"You old rogue, va!"

And he grew angry, exasperated, feverish, in despair at not being believed, and always telling his story.

The night came. It was time to go home. He set out with three of his neighbors, to whom he pointed out the place where he had picked up the end of string; and all the way he talked of his adventure.

That evening he made the round in the village of Bréauté, so as to tell every one. He met only unbelievers.

He was ill of it all night long.

The next day, about one in the afternoon, Marius Paumelle, a farm hand of Maître Breton, the market-gardener at Ymauville, returned the pocket-book and its contents to Maître Houlbrèque, of Manneville.

This man said, indeed, that he had found it on the road; but not knowing how to read, he had carried it home and given it to his master.

The news spread to the environs. Maître Hauchecorne was informed. He put himself at once upon the go, and began to relate his story as completed by the *dénouement*. He triumphed.

"What grieved me," said he, "was not the thing itself, do you understand; but it was the lies. There's nothing does you so much harm as being in disgrace for lying."

All day he talked of his adventure, he told it on the roads to the people who passed; at the cabaret to the people who drank; and the next Sunday, when they came out of church. He even stopped strangers to tell them about it. He was easy, now, and yet something worried him without his knowing exactly what it was. People had a joking manner while they listened. They did not seem convinced. He seemed to feel their tittle-tattle behind his back.

On Tuesday of the next week he went to market at Goderville, prompted entirely by the need of telling his story.

Malandain, standing on his door-step, began to laugh as he saw him pass. Why?

He accosted a farmer of Criquetot, who did not let him finish, and, giving him a punch in the pit of his stomach, cried in his face:

"Oh you great rogue, *va!*" Then turned his heel upon him.

Maître Hauchecorne remained speechless, and grew more and more uneasy. Why had they called him "great rogue"?

When seated at table in Jourdain's tavern he began again to explain the whole affair.

A horse-dealer of Montivilliers shouted at him:

"Get out, get out you old scamp; I know all about your string!"

Hauchecorne stammered:

"But since they found it again, the pocket-book!"

But the other continued:

"Hold your tongue, daddy; there's one who finds it and there's another who returns it. And no one the wiser."

The peasant was choked. He understood at last. They accused him of having had the pocket-book brought back by an accomplice, by a confederate.

He tried to protest. The whole table began to laugh.

He could not finish his dinner, and went away amid a chorus of jeers.

He went home, ashamed and indignant, choked with rage, with confusion, the more cast-down since from his Norman cunning, he was, perhaps, capable of having done what they accused him of, and even of boasting of it as a good trick. His innocence dimly seemed to him impossible to prove, his craftiness being so well known. And he felt himself struck to the heart by the injustice of the suspicion.

Then he began anew to tell of his adventure, lengthening his recital every day, each time adding new proofs, more energetic protestations, and more solemn oaths which he thought of, which he prepared in his hours of solitude, his mind being entirely occupied by the story of the string. The more complicated his defence, the more artful his arguments, the less he was believed.

"Those are liar's proofs," they said behind his back.

He felt this; it preyed upon his heart. He exhausted himself in useless efforts.

He was visibly wasting away.

The jokers now made him tell the story of "The Piece of String" to amuse them, just as you make a soldier who has been on a campaign tell his story of the battle. His mind, struck at the root, grew weak.

About the end of December he took to his bed.

He died early in January, and, in the delirium of the death-agony, he protested his innocence, repeating:

"A little bit of string—a little bit of string—see, here it is, M'sieu' le Maire."

For Study and Discussion

1. How important to the story is the opening description of the Normandy peasants and the market scene? Compare the handling of background detail with that of Harte in "The Luck of Roaring Camp."

2. After Hauchecorne has picked up the string, why does he pretend to look for something else? How is this detail important to the story?

3. Why does the return of the pocketbook make things worse for Hauchecorne?

4. How does Maupassant use irony in "The Piece of String"? What does it contribute to the effect of the story?

5. How does Maupassant's treatment of humble people differ from Harte's in "The Luck of Roaring Camp"? Which of the two writers comes nearer to creating realistic characters? Defend your choice. What is the difference in the tone of these two stories?

ANTON CHEKHOV

EASTER EVE

I was standing on the bank of the River Goltva, waiting for the ferry-boat from the other side. At ordinary times the Goltva is a humble stream of moderate size, silent and pensive, gently glimmering from behind thick reeds; but now a regular lake lay stretched out before me. The waters of spring, running riot, had overflowed both banks and flooded both sides of the river for a long distance, submerging vegetable gardens, hayfields and marshes, so that it was no unusual thing to meet poplars and bushes sticking out above the surface of the water and looking in the darkness like grim solitary crags.

The weather seemed to me magnificent. It was dark, yet I could see the trees, the water and the people. . . . The world was lighted by the stars, which were scattered thickly all over the sky. I don't remember ever seeing so many stars. Literally one could not have put a finger in between them. There were some as big as a goose's egg, others tiny as hempseed. . . . They had come out for the festival procession, every one of them, little and big, washed, renewed and joyful, and every one of them was softly twinkling its beams. The sky was reflected in the water; the stars were bathing in its dark depths and trembling with the quivering eddies. The air was warm and still. . . . Here and there, far away on the further bank in the impenetrable darkness, several bright red lights were gleaming. . . .

A couple of paces from me I saw the dark silhouette of a peasant in a high hat, with a thick knotted stick in his hand.

"How long the ferry-boat is in coming!" I said.

"It is time it was here," the silhouette answered.

"You are waiting for the ferry-boat, too?"

Originally published under the title "Svyatoy Noch'yu," in the newspaper *Novoe Vremya*, April 13, 1886. Reprinted here, in a translation by Constance Garnett, from *The Bishop and Other Stories* (1919), Vol. VII of *The Tales of Chekhov* (New York: The Macmillan Co., 1916–1923), by permission of the publisher, David Garnett, and Chatto & Windus, Ltd. Copyright 1919 by The Macmillan Company, renewed 1947 by David Garnett.

"No, I am not," yawned the peasant—"I am waiting for the illumination. I should have gone, but, to tell you the truth, I haven't the five
kopecks for the ferry."

"I'll give you the five kopecks."

"No; I humbly thank you. . . . With that five kopecks put up a candle
for me over there in the monastery. . . . That will be more interesting,
and I will stand here. What can it mean, no ferry-boat, as though it had
sunk in the water!"

The peasant went up to the water's edge, took the rope in his hands,
and shouted: "Ieronim! Ieron—im!"

As though in answer to his shout, the slow peal of a great bell floated
across from the further bank. The note was deep and low, as from the
thickest string of a double bass; it seemed as though the darkness itself
had hoarsely uttered it. At once there was the sound of a cannon shot. It
rolled away in the darkness and ended somewhere in the far distance
behind me. The peasant took off his hat and crossed himself.

"Christ is risen," he said.

Before the vibrations of the first peal of the bell had time to die away in
the air a second sounded, after it at once a third, and the darkness was
filled with an unbroken quivering clamour. Near the red lights fresh
lights flashed, and all began moving together and twinkling restlessly.

"Ieron—im!" we heard a hollow prolonged shout.

"They are shouting from the other bank," said the peasant, "so there
is no ferry there either. Our Ieronim has gone to sleep."

The lights and the velvety chimes of the bell drew one towards
them. . . . I was already beginning to lose patience and grow anxious,
but behold at last, staring into the dark distance, I saw the outline of
something very much like a gibbet. It was the long-expected ferry. It
moved towards us with such deliberation that if it had not been that its
lines grew gradually more definite, one might have supposed that it was
standing still or moving to the other bank.

"Make haste! Ieronim!" shouted my peasant. "The gentleman's tired
of waiting!"

The ferry crawled to the bank, gave a lurch and stopped with a creak. A
tall man in a monk's cassock and a conical cap stood on it, holding the
rope.

"Why have you been so long?" I asked, jumping upon the ferry.

"Forgive me, for Christ's sake," Ieronim answered gently. "Is there
no one else?"

"No one. . . ."

Ieronim took hold of the rope in both hands, bent himself to the figure
of a mark of interrogation, and gasped. The ferry-boat creaked and gave
a lurch. The outline of the peasant in the high hat began slowly
retreating from me—so the ferry was moving off. Ieronim soon drew
himself up and began working with one hand only. We were silent,

gazing towards the bank to which we were floating. There the illumination for which the peasant was waiting had begun. At the water's edge barrels of tar were flaring like huge camp fires. Their reflections, crimson as the rising moon, crept to meet us in long broad streaks. The burning barrels lighted up their own smoke and the long shadows of men flitting about the fire; but further to one side and behind them from where the velvety chime floated there was still the same unbroken black gloom. All at once, cleaving the darkness, a rocket zigzagged in a golden ribbon up the sky; it described an arc and, as though broken to pieces against the sky, was scattered crackling into sparks. There was a roar from the bank like a far-away hurrah.

"How beautiful!" I said.

"Beautiful beyond words!" sighed Ieronim. "Such a night, sir! Another time one would pay no attention to the fireworks, but to-day one rejoices in every vanity. Where do you come from?"

I told him where I came from.

"To be sure . . . a joyful day to-day. . . ." Ieronim went on in a weak sighing tenor like the voice of a convalescent. "The sky is rejoicing and the earth, and what is under the earth. All the creatures are keeping holiday. Only tell me, kind sir, why, even in the time of great rejoicing, a man cannot forget his sorrows?"

I fancied that this unexpected question was to draw me into one of those endless religious conversations which bored and idle monks are so fond of. I was not disposed to talk much, and so I only asked:

"What sorrows have you, father?"

"As a rule only the same as all men, kind sir, but to-day a special sorrow has happened in the monastery: at mass, during the reading of the Bible, the monk and deacon Nikolay died."

"Well, it's God's will!" I said, falling into the monastic tone. "We must all die. To my mind, you ought to rejoice indeed. . . . They say if anyone dies at Easter he goes straight to the kingdom of heaven."

"That's true."

We sank into silence. The figure of the peasant in the high hat melted into the lines of the bank. The tar barrels were flaring up more and more.

"The Holy Scripture points clearly to the vanity of sorrow, and so does reflection," said Ieronim, breaking the silence; "but why does the heart grieve and refuse to listen to reason? Why does one want to weep bitterly?"

Ieronim shrugged his shoulders, turned to me and said quickly:

"If I died, or anyone else, it would not be worth notice, perhaps; but, you see, Nikolay is dead! No one else but Nikolay! Indeed, it's hard to believe that he is no more! I stand here on my ferry-boat and every minute I keep fancying that he will lift up his voice from the bank. He always used to come on the bank and call to me that I might not be afraid on the ferry. He used to get up from his bed at night on purpose for that.

He was a kind soul. My God! how kindly and gracious! Many a mother is not so good to her child as Nikolay was to me! Lord, save his soul!"

Ieronim took hold of the rope, but turned to me again at once.

"And such a lofty intelligence, your honour," he said in a vibrating voice. "Such a sweet and harmonious tongue! Just as they will sing immediately at early matins: 'Oh lovely! oh sweet is Thy Voice!' Besides all other human qualities, he had, too, an extraordinary gift!"

"What gift?" I asked.

The monk scrutinized me, and as though he had convinced himself that he could trust me with a secret, he laughed good-humouredly.

"He had a gift for writing hymns of praise," he said. "It was a marvel, sir; you couldn't call it anything else! You will be amazed if I tell you about it. Our Father Archimandrite comes from Moscow, the Father Sub-Prior studied at the Kazan academy, we have wise monks and elders, but, would you believe it, no one could write them; while Nikolay, a simple monk, a deacon, had not studied anywhere, and had not even any outer appearance of it, but he wrote them! A marvel! a real marvel!" Ieronim clasped his hands and, completely forgetting the rope, went on eagerly:

"The Father Sub-Prior has great difficulty in composing sermons; when he wrote the history of the monastery he worried all the brotherhood and drove a dozen times to town, while Nikolay wrote canticles! Hymns of praise! That's a very different thing from a sermon or a history!"

"Is it difficult to write them?" I asked.

"There's great difficulty!" Ieronim wagged his head. "You can do nothing by wisdom and holiness if God has not given you the gift. The monks who don't understand argue that you only need to know the life of the saint for whom you are writing the hymn, and to make it harmonize with the other hymns of praise. But that's a mistake, sir. Of course, anyone who writes canticles must know the life of the saint to perfection, to the least trivial detail. To be sure, one must make them harmonize with the other canticles and know where to begin and what to write about. To give you an instance, the first response begins everywhere with 'the chosen' or 'the elect.' . . . The first line must always begin with 'the angel.' In the canticle of praise to Jesus the Most Sweet, if you are interested in the subject, it begins like this: 'Of angels Creator and Lord of all powers!' In the canticle to the Holy Mother of God: 'Of angels the foremost sent down from on high,' to Nikolay, the Wonderworker—'an angel in semblance, though in substance a man,' and so on. Everywhere you begin with the angel. Of course, it would be impossible without making them harmonize, but the lives of the saints and conformity with the others is not what matters; what matters is the beauty and sweetness of it. Everything must be harmonious, brief and complete. There must be in every line softness, graciousness and tenderness; not one word should be harsh or rough or unsuitable. It must be written so that the worshipper may rejoice at heart and weep, while his mind is stirred and he is thrown into a tremor. In the canticle to the Holy Mother are the words: 'Rejoice, O Thou too high for human thought to reach! Rejoice, O Thou too deep for angels' eyes to fathom!' In another place in the same canticle: 'Rejoice, O tree that bearest the fair fruit of light that is the food of the faithful! Rejoice, O tree of gracious spreading shade, under which there is shelter for multitudes!'"

Ieronim hid his face in his hands, as though frightened at something or overcome with shame, and shook his head.

"Tree that bearest the fair fruit of light . . . tree of gracious spreading shade . . ." he muttered. "To think that a man should find words like those! Such a power is a gift from God! For brevity he packs many thoughts into one phrase, and how smooth and complete it all is! 'Light-radiating torch to all that be . . .' comes in the canticle to Jesus the Most Sweet. 'Light-radiating!' There is no such word in conversation or in books, but you see he invented it, he found it in his mind! Apart from the smoothness and grandeur of language, sir, every line must be beautified in every way; there must be flowers and lightning and wind and sun and all the objects of the visible world. And every exclamation ought to be put so as to be smooth and easy for the ear. 'Rejoice, thou flower of heavenly growth!' comes in the hymn to Nikolay the Wonder-worker. It's not simply 'heavenly flower,' but 'flower of heavenly growth.' It's smoother so and sweet to the ear. That was just as Nikolay wrote it! exactly like that! I can't tell you how he used to write!"

"Well, in that case it is a pity he is dead," I said; "but let us get on, father, or we shall be late."

Ieronim started and ran to the rope; they were beginning to peal all the bells. Probably the procession was already going on near the monastery, for all the dark space behind the tar barrels was now dotted with moving lights.

"Did Nikolay print his hymns?" I asked Ieronim.

"How could he print them?" he sighed. "And, indeed, it would be strange to print them. What would be the object? No one in the monastery takes any interest in them. They don't like them. They knew Nikolay wrote them, but they let it pass unnoticed. No one esteems new writings nowadays, sir!"

"Were they prejudiced against him?"

"Yes, indeed. If Nikolay had been an elder perhaps the brethren would have been interested, but he wasn't forty, you know. There were some who laughed and even thought his writing a sin."

"What did he write them for?"

"Chiefly for his own comfort. Of all the brotherhood, I was the only one who read his hymns. I used to go to him in secret, that no one else might know of it, and he was glad that I took an interest in them. He would embrace me, stroke my head, speak to me in caressing words as to a little child. He would shut his cell, make me sit down beside him, and begin to read. . . ."

Ieronim left the rope and came up to me.

"We were dear friends in a way," he whispered, looking at me with shining eyes. "Where he went I would go. If I were not there he would miss me. And he cared more for me than for anyone, and all because I used to weep over his hymns. It makes me sad to remember. Now I feel just like an orphan or a widow. You know, in our monastery they are all good people, kind and pious, but . . . there is no one with softness and refinement, they are just like peasants. They all speak loudly, and tramp heavily when they walk; they are noisy, they clear their throats, but Nikolay always talked softly, caressingly, and if he noticed that anyone was asleep or praying he would slip by like a fly or a gnat. His face was tender, compassionate. . . ."

Ieronim heaved a deep sigh and took hold of the rope again. We were by now approaching the bank. We floated straight out of the darkness and stillness of the river into an enchanted realm, full of stifling smoke, crackling lights and uproar. By now one could distinctly see people moving near the tar barrels. The flickering of the lights gave a strange, almost fantastic, expression to their figures and red faces. From time to time one caught among the heads and faces a glimpse of a horse's head motionless as though cast in copper.

"They'll begin singing the Easter hymn directly, . . ." said Ieronim, "and Nikolay is gone; there is no one to appreciate it. . . . There was nothing written dearer to him than that hymn. He used to take in every word! You'll be there, sir, so notice what is sung; it takes your breath away!"

"Won't you be in church, then?"

"I can't; . . . I have to work the ferry. . . ."

"But won't they relieve you?"

"I don't know. . . . I ought to have been relieved at eight; but, as you see, they don't come! . . . And I must own I should have liked to be in the church. . . ."

"Are you a monk?"

"Yes . . . that is, I am a lay brother."

The ferry ran into the bank and stopped. I thrust a five kopeck piece into Ieronim's hand for taking me across, and jumped on land. Immediately a cart with a boy and a sleeping woman in it drove creaking onto the ferry. Ieronim, with a faint glow from the lights on his figure, pressed on the rope, bent down to it, and started the ferry back. . . .

I took a few steps through mud, but a little farther walked on a soft, freshly trodden path. This path led to the dark monastery gates, that looked like a cavern through a cloud of smoke, through a disorderly crowd of people, unharnessed horses, carts and chaises. All this crowd was rattling, snorting, laughing, and the crimson light and wavering shadows from the smoke flickered over it all. . . . A perfect chaos! And in this hubbub the people yet found room to load a little cannon and to sell cakes. There was no less commotion on the other side of the wall in the monastery precincts, but there was more regard for decorum and order. Here there was a smell of juniper and incense. They talked loudly, but there was no sound of laughter or snorting. Near the tombstones and crosses people pressed close to one another with Easter cakes and bundles in their arms. Apparently many had come from a long distance for their cakes to be blessed and now were exhausted. Young lay brothers, making a metallic sound with their boots, ran busily along the iron slabs that paved the way from the monastery gates to the church door. They were busy and shouting on the belfry, too.

"What a restless night!" I thought. "How nice!"

One was tempted to see the same unrest and sleeplessness in all nature, from the night darkness to the iron slabs, the crosses on the tombs and the trees under which the people were moving to and fro. But nowhere was the excitement and restlessness so marked as in the church. An unceasing struggle was going on in the entrance between the inflowing stream and the outflowing stream. Some were going in, others going out and soon coming back again to stand still for a little and begin moving again. People were scurrying from place to place, lounging about as though they were looking for something. The stream flowed from the entrance all round the church, disturbing even the front rows, where persons of weight and dignity were standing. There could be no thought of concentrated prayer. There were no prayers at all, but a sort of continuous, childishly irresponsible joy, seeking a pretext to break out and vent itself in some movement, even in senseless jostling and shoving.

The same unaccustomed movement is striking in the Easter service itself. The altar gates are flung wide open, thick clouds of incense float in the air near the candelabra; wherever one looks there are lights, the gleam and splutter of candles. . . . There is no reading; restless and light-hearted singing goes on to the end without ceasing. After each hymn the clergy change their vestments and come out to burn incense, which is repeated every ten minutes.

I had no sooner taken a place, when a wave rushed from in front and forced me back. A tall thick-set deacon walked before me with a long red candle; the grey-headed archimandrite in his golden mitre hurried after him with the censer. When they had vanished from sight the crowd squeezed me back to my former position. But ten minutes had not passed before a new wave burst on me, and again the deacon appeared. This time he was followed by the Father Sub-Prior, the man who, as Ieronim had told me, was writing the history of the monastery.

As I mingled with the crowd and caught the infection of the universal joyful excitement, I felt unbearably sore on Ieronim's account. Why did they not send someone to relieve him? Why could not someone of less feeling and less susceptibility go on the ferry? "Lift up thine eyes, O Sion, and look around," they sang in the choir, "for thy children have come to thee as to a beacon of divine light from north and south, and from east and from the sea. . . ."

I looked at the faces; they all had a lively expression of triumph, but no one was listening to what was being sung and taking it in, and not one was "holding his breath." Why was not Ieronim released? I could fancy Ieronim standing meekly somewhere by the wall, bending forward and hungrily drinking in the beauty of the holy phrase. All this that glided by the ears of people standing by me he would have eagerly drunk in with his delicately sensitive soul, and would have been spell-bound to ecstasy, to holding his breath, and there would not have been a man happier than he in all the church. Now he was plying to and fro over the dark river and grieving for his dead friend and brother.

The wave surged back. A stout smiling monk, playing with his rosary and looking round behind him, squeezed sideways by me, making way for a lady in a hat and velvet cloak. A monastery servant hurried after the lady, holding a chair over our heads.

I came out of the church. I wanted to have a look at the dead Nikolay, the unknown canticle writer. I walked about the monastery wall, where there was a row of cells, peeped into several windows, and, seeing nothing, came back again. I do not regret now that I did not see Nikolay; God knows, perhaps if I had seen him I should have lost the picture my imagination paints for me now. I imagine that lovable poetical figure, solitary and not understood, who went out at nights to call to Ieronim over the water, and filled his hymns with flowers, stars and sunbeams, as a pale timid man with soft, mild, melancholy features. His eyes must have shone, not only with intelligence, but with kindly tenderness and that hardly restrained childlike enthusiasm which I could hear in Ieronim's voice when he quoted to me passages from the hymns.

When we came out of church after mass it was no longer night. The morning was beginning. The stars had gone out and the sky was a morose greyish blue. The iron slabs, the tombstones and the buds on the trees were covered with dew. There was a sharp freshness in the air. Outside the precincts I did not find the same animated scene as I had beheld in the night. Horses and men looked exhausted, drowsy, scarcely moved, while nothing was left of the tar barrels but heaps of black ash. When anyone is exhausted and sleepy he fancies that nature, too, is in the same condition. It seemed to me that the trees and the young grass were asleep. It seemed as though even the bells were not pealing so loudly and gaily as at night. The restlessness was over, and of the excitement nothing was left but a pleasant weariness, a longing for sleep and warmth.

Now I could see both banks of the river; a faint mist hovered over it in shifting masses. There was a harsh cold breath from the water. When I jumped on to the ferry, a chaise and some two dozen men and women were standing on it already. The rope, wet and as I fancied drowsy, stretched far away across the broad river and in places disappeared in the white mist.

"Christ is risen! Is there no one else?" asked a soft voice.

I recognized the voice of Ieronim. There was no darkness now to hinder me from seeing the monk. He was a tall narrow-shouldered man of five-and-thirty, with large rounded features, with half-closed listless-looking eyes and an unkempt wedge-shaped beard. He had an extraordinarily sad and exhausted look.

"They have not relieved you yet?" I asked in surprise.

"Me?" he answered, turning to me his chilled and dewy face with a smile. "There is no one to take my place now till morning. They'll all be going to the Father Archimandrite's to break the fast directly."

With the help of a little peasant in a hat of reddish fur that looked like the little wooden tubs in which honey is sold, he threw his weight on the rope; they gasped simultaneously, and the ferry started.

We floated across, disturbing on the way the lazily rising mist. Everyone was silent. Ieronim worked mechanically with one hand. He slowly passed his mild lustreless eyes over us; then his glance rested on the rosy face of a young merchant's wife with black eyebrows, who was standing on the ferry beside me silently shrinking from the mist that wrapped her about. He did not take his eyes off her face all the way.

There was little that was masculine in that prolonged gaze. It seemed to me that Ieronim was looking in the woman's face for the soft and tender features of his dead friend.

For Study and Discussion

1. What are the purpose and effect of the opening description—particularly its emphasis on the stars? Compare the description of nature in this story with that in "The Tryst" on the basis of Chekhov's statement that "a true description of Nature should be very brief and have a character of relevance" (p. 20).

2. What is the real cause of Ieronim's grief? How is it related to the celebration taking place on the farther shore?

3. Consider the details used in Ieronim's characterization of his dead friend Nikolay and in his account of Nikolay's artistry as a composer of canticles (pp. 253–256). How do these passages function themati-

cally in the story? What do they disclose about the literary values held by Ieronim himself? By the narrator? How are they related to Chekhov's artistic principles?

4. Examine the nature of the irony in the contrast between the narrator's description of the scene in the church and his preceding experience on the ferry. What is the effect of the irony? What other evidence of effective contrast do you find in this story? Is there any effective implied comparison?

5. When the narrator returns to the river after visiting the church, what changes does he observe and how do these changes alter the mood of the story?

6. Explore the purpose and function of the narrator's last three paragraphs. As a conclusion to the story, do they reveal any significant relationship between the boatman and the meaning of Easter? How would you describe that relationship?

7. Chekhov is said to have taken Maupassant as his model; yet one modern critic finds this hard to believe because, he says, "Their aims and methods are entirely different." Do you find the aims and methods of "Easter Eve" and "The Piece of String" entirely different? If so, in what ways?

RUDYARD KIPLING

AT THE PIT'S MOUTH

> *Men say it was a stolen tide—*
> *The Lord that sent it he knows all.*
> *But in mine ear will aye abide*
> *The message that the bells let fall,*
> *And awesome bells they were to me,*
> *That in the dark rang, 'Enderby.'*

Jean Ingelow

Once upon a time there was a Man and his Wife and a Tertium Quid. All three were unwise, but the Wife was the unwisest. The Man should have looked after his Wife, who should have avoided the Tertium Quid, who, again, should have married a wife of his own, after clean and open flirtations, to which nobody can possibly object, round Jakko or Observatory Hill. When you see a young man with his pony in a white lather, and his hat on the back of his head flying down-hill at fifteen miles an hour to meet a girl who will be properly surprised to meet him, you naturally approve of that young man, and wish him Staff appointments, and take an interest in his welfare, and, as the proper time comes, give them sugar-tongs or side-saddles according to your means and generosity.

The Tertium Quid flew down-hill on horseback, but it was to meet the Man's Wife; and when he flew up-hill it was for the same end. The Man was in the Plains, earning money for his Wife to spend on dresses and four-hundred-rupee bracelets, and inexpensive luxuries of that kind. He worked very hard, and sent her a letter or a postcard daily. She also wrote to him daily, and said that she was longing for him to come up to Simla. The Tertium Quid used to lean over her shoulder and laugh as she wrote the notes. Then the two would ride to the Post-office together.

Originally published in *Under the Deodars*, 1888. Reprinted here from *Wee Willie Winkie, Under the Deodars, The Phantom Rickshaw, and Other Stories*, Library Edition (London: Macmillan and Co., Ltd., 1951).

Now, Simla is a strange place and its customs are peculiar; nor is any man who has not spent at least ten seasons there qualified to pass judgment on circumstantial evidence, which is the most untrustworthy in the Courts. For these reasons, and for others which need not appear, I decline to state positively whether there was anything irretrievably wrong in the relations between the Man's Wife and the Tertium Quid. If there was, and hereon you must form your own opinion, it was the Man's Wife's fault. She was kittenish in her manners, wearing generally an air of soft and fluffy innocence. But she was deadlily learned and evil-instructed; and, now and again, when the mask dropped, men saw this, shuddered and—almost drew back. Men are occasionally particular, and the least particular men are always the most exacting.

Simla is eccentric in its fashion of treating friendships. Certain attachments which have set and crystallised through half a dozen seasons acquire almost the sanctity of the marriage bond, and are revered as such. Again, certain attachments equally old, and, to all appearance, equally venerable, never seem to win any recognised official status; while a chance-sprung acquaintance, not two months born, steps into the place which by right belongs to the senior. There is no law reducible to print which regulates these affairs.

Some people have a gift which secures them infinite toleration, and others have not. The Man's Wife had not. If she looked over the garden wall, for instance, women taxed her with stealing their husbands. She complained pathetically that she was not allowed to choose her own friends. When she put up her big white muff to her lips, and gazed over it and under her eyebrows at you as she said this thing, you felt that she had been infamously misjudged, and that all the other women's instincts were all wrong; which was absurd. She was not allowed to own the Tertium Quid in peace; and was so strangely constructed that she would not have enjoyed peace had she been so permitted. She preferred some semblance of intrigue to cloak even her most commonplace actions.

After two months of riding, first round Jakko, then Elysium, then Summer Hill, then Observatory Hill, then under Jutogh, and lastly up and down the Cart Road as far as the Tara Devi gap in the dusk, she said to the Tertium Quid, 'Frank, people say we are too much together, and people are so horrid.'

The Tertium Quid pulled his moustache, and replied that horrid people were unworthy of the consideration of nice people.

'But they have done more than talk—they have written—written to my hubby—I'm sure of it,' said the Man's Wife, and she pulled a letter from her husband out of her saddle-pocket and gave it to the Tertium Quid.

It was an honest letter, written by an honest man, then stewing in the Plains on two hundred rupees a month (for he allowed his wife eight hundred and fifty), and in a silk banian and cotton trousers. It said that, perhaps, she had not thought of the unwisdom of allowing her name to be so generally coupled with the Tertium Quid's; that she was too much of a child to understand the dangers of that sort of thing; that he, her husband, was the last man in the world to interfere jealously with her little amusements and interests, but that it would be better were she to drop the Tertium Quid quietly and for her husband's sake. The letter was sweetened with many pretty little pet names, and it amused the Tertium Quid considerably. He and She laughed over it, so that you, fifty yards away, could see their shoulders shaking while the horses slouched along side by side.

Their conversation was not worth reporting. The upshot of it was that, next day, no one saw the Man's Wife and the Tertium Quid together. They had both gone down to the Cemetery, which, as a rule, is only visited officially by the inhabitants of Simla.

A Simla funeral with the clergyman riding, the mourners riding, and the coffin creaking as it swings between the bearers, is one of the most depressing things on this earth, particularly when the procession passes under the wet, dank dip beneath the Rockcliffe Hotel, where the sun is shut out, and all the hill streams are wailing and weeping together as they go down the valleys.

Occasionally, folk tend the graves, but we in India shift and are transferred so often that, at the end of the second year, the Dead have no friends—only acquaintances who are far too busy amusing themselves up the hill to attend to old partners. The idea of using a Cemetery as a rendezvous is distinctly a feminine one. A man would have said simply, 'Let people talk. We'll go down the Mall.' A woman is made differently, especially if she be such a woman as the Man's Wife. She and the Tertium Quid enjoyed each other's society among the graves of men and women whom they had known and danced with aforetime.

They used to take a big horse-blanket and sit on the grass a little to the left of the lower end, where there is a dip in the ground, and where the occupied graves stop short and the ready-made ones are not ready. Each well-regulated Indian Cemetery keeps half a dozen graves permanently open for contingencies and incidental wear and tear. In the Hills these are more usually baby's size, because children who come up weakened and sick from the Plains often succumb to the effects of the Rains in the Hills or get pneumonia from their *ayahs* taking them through damp pinewoods after the sun has set. In Cantonments, of course, the man's size is more in request; these arrangements varying with the climate and population.

One day when the Man's Wife and the Tertium Quid had just arrived in the Cemetery, they saw some coolies breaking ground. They had marked out a full-size grave, and the Tertium Quid asked them whether any Sahib was sick. They said that they did not know; but it was an order that they should dig a Sahib's grave.

'Work away,' said the Tertium Quid, 'and let's see how it's done.'

The coolies worked away, and the Man's Wife and the Tertium Quid watched and talked for a couple of hours while the grave was being deepened. Then a coolie, taking the earth in baskets as it was thrown up, jumped over the grave.

'That's queer,' said the Tertium Quid. 'Where's my ulster?'

'What's queer?' said the Man's Wife.

'I have got a chill down my back—just as if a goose had walked over my grave.'

'Why do you look at the thing, then?' said the Man's Wife. 'Let us go.'

The Tertium Quid stood at the head of the grave, and stared without answering for a space. Then he said, dropping a pebble down, 'It is nasty—and cold: horribly cold. I don't think I shall come to the Cemetery any more. I don't think grave-digging is cheerful.'

The two talked and agreed that the Cemetery was depressing. They also arranged for a ride next day out from the Cemetery through the Mashobra Tunnel up to Fagoo and back, because all the world was going to a garden-party at Viceregal Lodge, and all the people of Mashobra would go too.

Coming up the Cemetery road, the Tertium Quid's horse tried to bolt up-hill, being tired with standing so long, and managed to strain a back sinew.

'I shall have to take the mare to-morrow,' said the Tertium Quid, 'and she will stand nothing heavier than a snaffle.'

They made their arrangements to meet in the Cemetery, after allowing all the Mashobra people time to pass into Simla. That night it rained heavily, and, next day, when the Tertium Quid came to the trysting-place, he saw that the new grave had a foot of water in it, the ground being a tough and sour clay.

''Jove! That looks beastly,' said the Tertium Quid. 'Fancy being boarded up and dropped in that well!'

They then started off to Fagoo, the mare playing with the snaffle and picking her way as though she were shod with satin, and the sun shining divinely. The road below Mashobra to Fagoo is officially styled the Himalayan-Tibet Road; but in spite of its name it is not much more than six feet wide in most places, and the drop into the valley below may be anything between one and two thousand feet.

'Now we're going to Tibet,' said the Man's Wife merrily, as the horses drew near to Fagoo. She was riding on the cliff-side.

'Into Tibet,' said the Tertium Quid, 'ever so far from people who say horrid things, and hubbies who write stupid letters. With you—to the end of the world!'

A coolie carrying a log of wood came round a corner, and the mare went wide to avoid him—forefeet in and haunches out, as a sensible mare should go.

'To the world's end,' said the Man's Wife, and looked unspeakable things over her near shoulder at the Tertium Quid.

He was smiling, but, while she looked, the smile froze stiff as it were on his face, and changed to a nervous grin—the sort of grin men wear when they are not quite easy in their saddles. The mare seemed to be sinking by the stern, and her nostrils cracked while she was trying to realise what was happening. The rain of the night before had rotted the drop-side of the Himalayan-Tibet Road, and it was giving way under her. 'What are you doing?' said the Man's Wife. The Tertium Quid gave no answer. He grinned nervously and set his spurs into the mare, who rapped with her forefeet on the road, and the struggle began. The Man's Wife screamed. 'Oh, Frank, get off!'

But the Tertium Quid was glued to the saddle—his face blue and white—and he looked into the Man's Wife's eyes. Then the Man's Wife clutched at the mare's head and caught her by the nose instead of the bridle. The brute threw up her head and went down with a scream, the Tertium Quid upon her, and the nervous grin still set on his face.

The Man's Wife heard the tinkle-tinkle of little stones and loose earth falling off the roadway, and the sliding roar of the man and horse going down. Then everything was quiet, and she called on Frank to leave his mare and walk up. But Frank did not answer. He was underneath the mare, nine hundred feet below, spoiling a patch of Indian corn.

As the revellers came back from Viceregal Lodge in the mists of the evening, they met a temporarily insane woman, on a temporarily mad horse, swinging round the corners, with her eyes and her mouth open, and her head like the head of a Medusa. She was stopped by a man at the risk of his life, and taken out of the saddle, a limp heap, and put on the bank to explain herself. This wasted twenty minutes, and then she was sent home in a lady's 'rickshaw, still with her mouth open and her hands picking at her riding-gloves.

She was in bed through the following three days, which were rainy; so she missed attending the funeral of the Tertium Quid, who was lowered into eighteen inches of water, instead of the twelve to which he had first objected.

For Study and Discussion

1. What does "Tertium Quid" mean? Why is it an appropriate term for Kipling's character?

2. The narrator says that "the least particular men are always the most exacting." How does this statement apply to the Tertium Quid? Does it have any bearing on the story's meaning?

3. Aside from its obvious use in the plot, what purpose is served by having the lovers make the cemetery their rendezvous?

4. Is the catastrophe logically motivated? If so, what preparatory devices does Kipling employ to make it seem inevitable?

5. What sort of ironic effect is achieved by the final paragraph? Is this an appropriate conclusion for the story? If so, why?

6. What is the most impressive single element of this story? Its theme? Action? Characterization? Style? Tone?

Read
also 25-28
for thursday

HENRY JAMES

THE REAL THING

I

When the porter's wife, who used to answer the house-bell, announced "A gentleman and a lady, sir," I had, as I often had in those
days—the wish being father to the thought—an immediate vision of
sitters. Sitters my visitors in this case proved to be; but not in the sense I
should have preferred. There was nothing at first however to indicate
that they mightn't have come for a portrait. The gentleman, a man of
fifty, very high and very straight, with a moustache slightly grizzled and
a dark grey walking-coat admirably fitted, both of which I noted
professionally—I don't mean as a barber or yet as a tailor—would have
struck me as a celebrity if celebrities often were striking. It was a truth of
which I had for some time been conscious that a figure with a good deal
of frontage was, as one might say, almost never a public institution. A
glance at the lady helped to remind me of this paradoxical law: she also
looked too distinguished to be a "personality." Moreover one would
scarcely come across two variations together.

Neither of the pair immediately spoke—they only prolonged the
preliminary gaze suggesting that each wished to give the other a chance.
They were visibly shy; they stood there letting me take them in—which,
as I afterwards perceived, was the most practical thing they could have
done. In this way their embarrassment served their cause. I had seen
people painfully reluctant to mention that they desired anything so gross
as to be represented on canvas; but the scruples of my new friends
appeared almost insurmountable. Yet the gentleman might have said "I
should like a portrait of my wife," and the lady might have said "I should
like a portrait of my husband." Perhaps they weren't husband and
wife—this naturally would make the matter more delicate. Perhaps they
wished to be done together—in which case they ought to have brought a
third person to break the news.

Originally published in *Black and White,* April 16, 1892. Reprinted here from *The Novels
and Tales of Henry James* (New York: Charles Scribner's Sons, 1909), Vol. XVIII.

"We come from Mr. Rivet," the lady finally said with a dim smile that had the effect of a moist sponge passed over a "sunk" piece of painting, as well as of a vague allusion to vanished beauty. She was as tall and straight, in her degree, as her companion, and with ten years less to carry. She looked as sad as a woman could look whose face was not charged with expression; that is her tinted oval mask showed waste as an exposed surface shows friction. The hand of time had played over her freely, but to an effect of elimination. She was slim and stiff, and so well-dressed, in dark blue cloth, with lappets and pockets and buttons, that it was clear she employed the same tailor as her husband. The couple had an indefinable air of prosperous thrift—they evidently got a good deal of luxury for their money. If I was to be one of their luxuries it would behoove me to consider my terms.

"Ah Claude Rivet recommended me?" I echoed; and I added that it was very kind of him, though I could reflect that, as he only painted landscape, this wasn't a sacrifice.

The lady looked very hard at the gentleman, and the gentleman looked round the room. Then staring at the floor a moment and stroking his moustache, he rested his pleasant eyes on me with the remark: "He said you were the right one."

"I try to be, when people want to sit."

"Yes, we should like to," said the lady anxiously.

"Do you mean together?"

My visitors exchanged a glance. "If you could do anything with *me* I suppose it would be double," the gentleman stammered.

"Oh yes, there's naturally a higher charge for two figures than for one."

"We should like to make it pay," the husband confessed.

"That's very good of you," I returned, appreciating so unwonted a sympathy—for I supposed he meant pay the artist.

A sense of strangeness seemed to dawn on the lady. "We mean for the illustrations—Mr. Rivet said you might put one in."

"Put in—an illustration?" I was equally confused.

"Sketch her off, you know," said the gentleman, colouring.

It was only then that I understood the service Claude Rivet had rendered me; he had told them how I worked in black-and-white, for magazines, for storybooks, for sketches of contemporary life, and consequently had copious employment for models. These things were true, but it was not less true—I may confess it now; whether because the aspiration was to lead to everything or to nothing I leave the reader to guess—that I couldn't get the honours, to say nothing of the emoluments, of a great painter of portraits out of my head. My "illustrations" were my pot-boilers; I looked to a different branch of art—far and away the most interesting it had always seemed to me—to perpetuate my fame. There was no shame in looking to it also to make my fortune; but that fortune was by so much further from being made from the moment my visitors wished to be "done" for nothing. I was disappointed; for in the pictorial sense I had immediately *seen* them. I had seized their type—I had already settled what I would do with it. Something that wouldn't absolutely have pleased them, I afterwards reflected.

"Ah you're—you're—a?" I began as soon as I had mastered my surprise. I couldn't bring out the dingy word "models": it seemed so little to fit the case.

"We haven't had much practice," said the lady.

"We've got to *do* something, and we've thought that an artist in your line might perhaps make something of us," her husband threw off. He further mentioned that they didn't know many artists and that they had gone first, on the off-chance—he painted views of course, but sometimes put in figures; perhaps I remembered—to Mr. Rivet, whom they had met a few years before at a place in Norfolk where he was sketching.

"We used to sketch a little ourselves," the lady hinted.

"It's very awkward, but we absolutely *must* do something," her husband went on.

"Of course we're not so *very* young," she admitted with a wan smile.

With the remark that I might as well know something more about them the husband had handed me a card extracted from a neat new pocket-book—their appurtenances were all of the freshest—and inscribed with the words "Major Monarch." Impressive as these words were they didn't carry my knowledge much further; but my visitor presently added: "I've left the army and we've had the misfortune to lose our money. In fact our means are dreadfully small."

"It's awfully trying—a regular strain," said Mrs. Monarch.

They evidently wished to be discreet—to take care not to swagger because they were gentlefolk. I felt them willing to recognise this as something of a drawback, at the same time that I guessed at an underlying sense—their consolation in adversity—that they *had* their points. They certainly had; but these advantages struck me as preponderantly social; such for instance as would help to make a drawing-room look well. However, a drawing-room was always, or ought to be, a picture.

In consequence of his wife's allusion to their age Major Monarch observed: "Naturally it's more for the figure that we thought of going in. We can still hold ourselves up." On the instant I saw that the figure was indeed their strong point. His "naturally" didn't sound vain, but it lighted up the question. "*She* has the best one," he continued, nodding at his wife with a pleasant after-dinner absence of circumlocution. I could only reply, as if we were in fact sitting over our wine, that this didn't prevent his own from being very good; which led him in turn to make answer: "We thought that if you ever have to do people like us we might be something like it. *She* particularly—for a lady in a book, you know."

I was so amused by them that, to get more of it, I did my best to take their point of view; and though it was an embarrassment to find myself appraising physically, as if they were animals on hire or useful blacks, a pair whom I should have expected to meet only in one of the relations in which criticism is tacit, I looked at Mrs. Monarch judicially enough to be able to exclaim after a moment with conviction: "Oh yes, a lady in a book!" She was singularly like a bad illustration.

"We'll stand up, if you like," said the Major; and he raised himself before me with a really grand air.

I could take his measure at a glance—he was six feet two and a perfect gentleman. It would have paid any club in process of formation and in want of a stamp to engage him at a salary to stand in the principal window. What struck me at once was that in coming to me they had rather missed their vocation; they could surely have been turned to better account for advertising purposes. I couldn't of course see the thing in detail, but I could see them make somebody's fortune—I don't mean their own. There was something in them for a waistcoat-maker, an hotel-keeper or a soap-vendor. I could imagine "We always use it" pinned on their bosoms with the greatest effect; I had a vision of the brilliancy with which they would launch a table d'hôte.

Mrs. Monarch sat still, not from pride but from shyness, and presently her husband said to her: "Get up, my dear, and show how smart you are." She obeyed, but she had no need to get up to show it. She walked to the end of the studio and then came back blushing, her fluttered eyes on the partner of her appeal. I was reminded of an incident I had accidentally had a glimpse of in Paris—being with a friend there, a dramatist about to produce a play, when an actress came to him to ask to be entrusted with a part. She went through her paces before him, walked up and down as Mrs. Monarch was doing. Mrs. Monarch did it quite as well, but I abstained from applauding. It was very odd to see such people apply for such poor pay. She looked as if she had ten thousand a year. Her husband had used the word that described her: she was in the London current jargon essentially and typically "smart." Her figure was, in the same order of ideas, conspicuously and irreproachably "good." For a woman of her age her waist was surprisingly small; her elbow moreover had the orthodox crook. She held her head at the conventional angle, but why did she come to *me?* She ought to have tried on jackets at a big shop. I feared my visitors were not only destitute but "artistic"— which would be a great complication. When she sat down again I thanked her, observing that what a draughtsman most valued in his model was the faculty of keeping quiet.

"Oh *she* can keep quiet," said Major Monarch. Then he added jocosely: "I've always kept her quiet."

"I'm not a nasty fidget, am I?" It was going to wring tears from me, I felt, the way she hid her head, ostrich-like, in the other broad bosom.

The owner of this expanse addressed his answer to me. "Perhaps it isn't out of place to mention—because we ought to be quite business-like, oughtn't we?—that when I married her she was known as the Beautiful Statue."

"Oh dear!" said Mrs. Monarch ruefully.

"Of course I should want a certain amount of expression," I rejoined.

"Of *course!*"—and I had never heard such unanimity.

"And then I suppose you know that you'll get awfully tired."

"Oh we *never* get tired!" they eagerly cried.

"Have you had any kind of practice?"

They hesitated—they looked at each other. "We've been photographed—*immensely*," said Mrs. Monarch.

"She means the fellows have asked us themselves," added the Major.

"I see—because you're so good-looking."

"I don't know what they thought, but they were always after us."

"We always got our photographs for nothing," smiled Mrs. Monarch.

"We might have brought some, my dear," her husband remarked.

"I'm not sure we have any left. We've given quantities away," she explained to me.

"With our autographs and that sort of thing," said the Major.

"Are they to be got in the shops?" I enquired as a harmless pleasantry.

"Oh yes, *hers*—they used to be."

"Not now," said Mrs. Monarch, with her eyes on the floor.

II

I could fancy the "sort of thing" they put on the presentation copies of their photographs, and I was sure they wrote a beautiful hand. It was odd how quickly I was sure of everything that concerned them. If they were now so poor as to have to earn shillings and pence they could never have had much of a margin. Their good looks had been their capital, and they had good-humouredly made the most of the career that this resource marked out for them. It was in their faces, the blankness, the deep intellectual repose of the twenty years of country-house visiting that had given them pleasant intonations. I could see the sunny drawing-rooms, sprinkled with periodicals she didn't read, in which Mrs. Monarch had continuously sat; I could see the wet shrubberies in which she had walked, equipped to admiration for either exercise. I could see the rich covers the Major had helped to shoot and the wonderful garments in which, late at night, he repaired to the smoking-room to talk about them. I could imagine their leggings and waterproofs, their knowing tweeds and rugs, their rolls of sticks and cases of tackle and neat umbrellas; and I could evoke the exact appearance of their servants and the compact variety of their luggage on the platforms of country stations.

They gave small tips, but they were liked; they didn't do anything themselves, but they were welcome. They looked so well everywhere; they gratified the general relish for stature, complexion and "form." They knew it without fatuity or vulgarity, and they respected themselves in consequence. They weren't superficial; they were thorough and kept themselves up—it had been their line. People with such a taste for activity had to have some line. I could feel how even in a dull house they could have been counted on for the joy of life. At present something had happened—it didn't matter what, their little income had grown less, it had grown least—and they had to do something for pocket-money. Their friends could like them, I made out, without liking to support them. There was something about them that represented credit—their clothes, their manners, their type; but if credit is a large empty pocket in which an occasional chink reverberates, the chink at least must be audible. What they wanted of me was to help to make it so. Fortunately they had no children—I soon divined that. They would also perhaps wish our relations to be kept secret: this was why it was "for the figure"—the reproduction of the face would betray them.

I liked them—I felt, quite as their friends must have done—they were so simple; and I had no objection to them if they would suit. But somehow with all their perfections I didn't easily believe in them. After all they were amateurs, and the ruling passion of my life was the detestation of the amateur. Combined with this was another perversity—an innate preference for the represented subject over the real one: the defect of the real one was so apt to be a lack of representation. I like things that appeared; then one was sure. Whether they *were* or not was a subordinate and almost always a profitless question. There were other considerations, the first of which was that I already had two or three recruits in use, notably a young person with big feet, in alpaca, from Kilburn, who for a couple of years had come to me regularly for my illustrations and with whom I was still—perhaps ignobly—satisfied. I frankly explained to my visitors how the case stood, but they had taken more precautions than I supposed. They had reasoned out their opportunity, for Claude Rivet had told them of the projected *édition de luxe* of one of the writers of our day—the rarest of the novelists—who, long neglected by the multitudinous vulgar and dearly prized by the attentive (need I mention Philip Vincent?), had had the happy fortune of seeing, late in life, the dawn and then the full light of a higher criticism; an estimate in which on the part of the public there was something really of expiation. The edition preparing, planned by a publisher of taste, was practically an act of high reparation; the wood-cuts with which it was to be enriched were the homage of English art to one of the most independent representatives of English letters. Major and Mrs. Monarch confessed to me they had hoped I might be able to work *them* into my branch of the enterprise. They knew I was to do the first of the books, "Rutland Ramsay," but I had to make clear to them that my participation in the rest of the affair—this first book was to be a test—must depend on the satisfaction I should give. If this should be limited my employers would drop me with scarce common forms. It was therefore a crisis for me, and naturally I was making special preparations, looking about for new people, should they be necessary, and securing the best types. I admitted however that I should like to settle down to two or three good models who would do for everything.

"Should we have often to—a—put on special clothes?" Mrs. Monarch timidly demanded.

"Dear yes—that's half the business."

"And should we be expected to supply our own costumes?"

"Oh no; I've got a lot of things. A painter's models put on—or put off—anything he likes."

"And you mean—a—the same?"

"The same?"

Mrs. Monarch looked at her husband again.

"Oh she was just wondering," he explained, "if the costumes are in *general* use." I had to confess that they were, and I mentioned further that some of them—I had a lot of genuine greasy last-century things—had served their time, a hundred years ago, on living world-stained men and women; on figures not perhaps so far removed, in that vanished world, from *their* type, the Monarchs', *quoi!* of a breeched and bewigged age. "We'll put on anything that *fits*," said the Major.

"Oh I arrange that—they fit in the pictures."

"I'm afraid I should do better for the modern books. I'd come as you like," said Mrs. Monarch.

"She has got a lot of clothes at home: they might do for contemporary life," her husband continued.

"Oh I can fancy scenes in which you'd be quite natural." And indeed I could see the slipshod rearrangements of stale properties—the stories I tried to produce pictures for without the exasperation of reading them—whose sandy tracts the good lady might help to people. But I had to return to the fact that for this sort of work—the daily mechanical grind—I was already equipped: the people I was working with were fully adequate.

"We only thought we might be more like *some* characters," said Mrs. Monarch mildly, getting up.

Her husband also rose; he stood looking at me with a dim wistfulness that was touching in so fine a man. "Wouldn't it be rather a pull sometimes to have—a—to have—?" He hung fire; he wanted me to help him by phrasing what he meant. But I couldn't—I didn't know. So he brought it out awkwardly: "The *real* thing; a gentleman, you know, or a lady." I was quite ready to give a general assent—I admitted that there was a great deal in that. This encouraged Major Monarch to say, following up his appeal with an unacted gulp: "It's awfully hard—we've tried everything." The gulp was communicative; it proved too much for his wife. Before I knew it Mrs. Monarch had dropped again upon a divan and burst into tears. Her husband sat down beside her, holding one of her hands; whereupon she quickly dried her eyes with the other, while I felt embarrassed as she looked up at me. "There isn't a confounded job I haven't applied for—waited for—prayed for. You can fancy we'd be pretty bad first. Secretaryships and that sort of thing? You might as well ask for a peerage. I'd be *anything*—I'm strong; a messenger or a coalheaver. I'd put on a gold-laced cap and open carriage-doors in front of the haberdasher's; I'd hang about a station to carry portmanteaux; I'd be a postman. But they won't *look* at you; there are thousands as good as yourself already on the ground. *Gentlemen*, poor beggars, who've drunk their wine, who've kept their hunters!"

I was as reassuring as I knew how to be, and my visitors were presently on their feet again while, for the experiment, we agreed on an hour. We were discussing it when the door opened and Miss Churm came in with a wet umbrella. Miss Churm had to take the omnibus to Maida Vale and then walk half a mile. She looked a trifle blowsy and slightly splashed. I scarcely ever saw her come in without thinking afresh how odd it was that, being so little in herself, she should yet be so much in others. She was a meagre little Miss Churm, but was such an ample heroine of romance. She was only a freckled cockney, but she could represent everything, from a fine lady to a shepherdess; she had the faculty as she might have had a fine voice or long hair. She couldn't spell and she loved beer, but she had two or three "points," and practice, and a knack, and mother-wit, and a whimsical sensibility, and a love of the theatre, and seven sisters, and not an ounce of respect, especially for the *h*. The first thing my visitors saw was that her umbrella was wet, and in their spotless perfection they visibly winced at it. The rain had come on since their arrival.

"I'm all in a soak; there *was* a mess of people in the 'bus. I wish you lived near a stytion," said Miss Churm. I requested her to get ready as quickly as possible, and she passed into the room in which she always changed her dress. But before going out she asked me what she was to get into this time.

"It's the Russian princess, don't you know?" I answered; "the one with the 'golden eyes,' in black velvet, for the long thing in the *Cheapside*."

"Golden eyes? I *say*!" cried Miss Churm, while my companions watched her with intensity as she withdrew. She always arranged herself, when she was late, before I could turn round; and I kept my visitors a little on purpose, so that they might get an idea, from seeing her, what would be expected of themselves. I mentioned that she was quite my notion of an excellent model—she was really very clever.

"Do you think she looks like a Russian princess?" Major Monarch asked with lurking alarm.

"When I make her, yes."

"Oh if you have to *make* her—!" he reasoned, not without point.

"That's the most you can ask. There are so many who are not makeable."

"Well now, *here's* a lady"—and with a persuasive smile he passed his arm into his wife's—"who's already made!"

"Oh I'm not a Russian princess," Mrs. Monarch protested a little coldly. I could see she had known some and didn't like them. There at once was a complication of a kind I never had to fear with Miss Churm.

This young lady came back in black velvet—the gown was rather rusty and very low on her lean shoulders—and with a Japanese fan in her red hands. I reminded her that in the scene I was doing she had to look over some one's head. "I forget whose it is; but it doesn't matter. Just look over a head."

"I'd rather look over a stove," said Miss Churm; and she took her station near the fire. She fell into position, settled herself into a tall attitude, gave a certain backward inclination to her head and a certain forward droop to her fan, and looked, at least to my prejudiced sense, distinguished and charming, foreign and dangerous. We left her looking so while I went downstairs with Major and Mrs. Monarch.

"I believe I could come about as near it as that," said Mrs. Monarch.

"Oh you think she's shabby, but you must allow for the alchemy of art."

However, they went off with an evident increase of comfort founded on their demonstrable advantage in being the real thing. I could fancy them shuddering over Miss Churm. She was very droll about them when I went back, for I told her what they wanted.

"Well, if *she* can sit I'll tyke to book-keeping," said my model.

"She's very ladylike," I replied as an innocent form of aggravation.

"So much the worse for *you*. That means she can't turn round."

"She'll do for the fashionable novels."

"Oh yes, she'll *do* for them!" my model humorously declared. "Ain't they bad enough without her?" I had often sociably denounced them to Miss Churm.

III

It was for the elucidation of a mystery in one of these works that I first tried Mrs. Monarch. Her husband came with her, to be useful if necessary—it was sufficiently clear that as a general thing he would prefer to come with her. At first I wondered if this were for "propriety's" sake—if he were going to be jealous and meddling. The idea was too tiresome, and if it had been confirmed it would speedily have brought our acquaintance to a close. But I soon saw there was nothing in it and that if he accompanied Mrs. Monarch it was—in addition to the chance of being wanted—simply because he had nothing else to do. When they were separate his occupation was gone and they never *had* been separate. I judged rightly that in their awkward situation their close union was their main comfort and that this union had no weak spot. It was a real marriage, an encouragement to the hesitating, a nut for pessimists to crack. Their address was humble—I remember afterwards thinking it had been the only thing about them that was really professional—and I could fancy the lamentable lodgings in which the Major would have been left alone. He could sit there more or less grimly with his wife—he couldn't sit there anyhow without her.

He had too much tact to try and make himself agreeable when he couldn't be useful; so when I was too absorbed in my work to talk he simply sat and waited. But I liked to hear him talk—it made my work, when not interrupting it, less mechanical, less special. To listen to him was to combine the excitement of going out with the economy of staying at home. There was only one hindrance—that I seemed not to know any of the people this brilliant couple had known. I think he wondered extremely, during the term of our intercourse, whom the deuce I *did* know. He hadn't a stray sixpence of an idea to fumble for, so we didn't spin it very fine; we confined ourselves to questions of leather and even of liquor—saddlers and breeches-makers and how to get excellent claret cheap—and matters like "good trains" and the habits of small game. His lore on these last subjects was astonishing—he managed to interweave the station-master with the ornithologist. When he couldn't talk about greater things he could talk cheerfully about smaller, and since I couldn't accompany him into reminiscences of the fashionable world he could lower the conversation without a visible effort to my level.

So earnest a desire to please was touching in a man who could so easily have knocked one down. He looked after the fire and had an opinion on the draught of the stove without my asking him, and I could see that he thought many of my arrangements not half knowing. I remember telling him that if I were only rich I'd offer him a salary to come and teach me how to live. Sometimes he gave a random sigh of which the essence might have been: "Give me even such a bare old barrack as *this,* and I'd do something with it!" When I wanted to use him he came alone; which was an illustration of the superior courage of women. His wife could bear her solitary second floor, and she was in general more discreet; showing by various small reserves that she was alive to the propriety of keeping our relations markedly professional—not letting them slide into sociability. She wished it to remain clear that she and the Major were employed, not cultivated, and if she approved of me as a superior, who could be kept in his place, she never thought me quite good enough for an equal.

She sat with great intensity, giving the whole of her mind to it, and was capable of remaining for an hour almost as motionless as before a photographer's lens. I could see she had been photographed often, but somehow the very habit that made her good for that purpose unfitted her for mine. At first I was extremely pleased with her ladylike air, and it was a satisfaction, on coming to follow her lines, to see how good they were and how far they could lead the pencil. But after a little skirmishing I began to find her too insurmountably stiff; do what I would with it my drawing looked like a photograph or a copy of a photograph. Her figure had no variety of expression—she herself had no sense of variety. You may say that this was my business and was only a question of placing her. Yet I placed her in every conceivable position and she managed to obliterate their differences. She was always a lady certainly, and into the bargain was always the same lady. She was the real thing, but always the same thing. There were moments when I rather writhed under the serenity of her confidence that she *was* the real thing. All her dealings with me and all her husband's were an implication that this was lucky for *me*. Meanwhile I found myself trying to invent types that approached her own, instead of making her transform itself—in the clever way that was not impossible for instance to poor Miss Churm. Arrange as I would and take the precautions I would, she always came out, in my pictures, too tall—landing me in the dilemma of having represented a fascinating woman as seven feet high, which (out of respect perhaps to my own very much scantier inches) was far from my idea of such a personage.

The case was worse with the Major—nothing I could do would keep *him* down, so that he became useful only for the representation of brawny giants. I adored variety and range, I cherished human accidents, the illustrative note; I wanted to characterise closely, and the thing in the world I most hated was the danger of being ridden by a type. I had quarreled with some of my friends about it; I had parted company with them for maintaining that one *had* to be, and that if the type was beautiful—witness Raphael and Leonardo—the servitude was only a gain. I was neither Leonardo nor Raphael—I might only be a presumptuous young modern searcher; but I held that everything was to be sacrificed sooner than character. When they claimed that the obsessional form could easily *be* character I retorted, perhaps superficially, "Whose?" It couldn't be everybody's—it might end in being nobody's.

After I had drawn Mrs. Monarch a dozen times I felt surer even than before that the value of such a model as Miss Churm resided precisely in the fact that she had no positive stamp, combined of course with the other fact that what she did have was a curious and inexplicable talent for imitation. Her usual appearance was like a curtain which she could draw up at request for a capital performance. This performance was simply suggestive; but it was a word to the wise—it was vivid and pretty. Sometimes even I thought it, though she was plain herself, too insipidly pretty; I made it a reproach to her that the figures drawn from her were monotonously (*bêtement*, as we used to say) graceful. Nothing made her more angry; it was so much her pride to feel she could sit for characters that had nothing in common with each other. She would accuse me at such moments of taking away her "reputytion."

It suffered a certain shrinkage, this queer quantity, from the repeated visits of my new friends. Miss Churm was greatly in demand, never in want of employment, so I had no scruple in putting her off occasionally, to try them more at my ease. It was certainly amusing at first to do the real thing—it was amusing to do Major Monarch's trousers. They *were* the real thing, even if he did come out colossal. It was amusing to do his wife's back hair—it was so mathematically neat—and the particular "smart" tension of her tight stays. She lent herself especially to positions in which the face was somewhat averted or blurred; she abounded in ladylike back views and *profils perdus*. When she stood erect she took naturally one of the attitudes in which court-painters represent queens and princesses; so that I found myself wondering whether, to draw out this accomplishment, I couldn't get the editor of the *Cheapside* to publish a really royal romance, "A Tale of Buckingham Palace." Sometimes however the real thing and the make-believe came into contact; by which I mean that Miss Churm, keeping an appointment or coming to make one on days when I had much work in hand, encountered her invidious rivals. The encounter was not on their part, for they noticed her no more than if she had been the housemaid; not from intentional loftiness, but simply because as yet, professionally, they didn't know how to fraternise, as I could imagine they would have liked—or at least that the Major would. They couldn't talk about the omnibus—they always walked; and they didn't know what else to try—she wasn't interested in good trains or cheap claret. Besides, they must have felt—in the air—that she was amused at them, secretly derisive of their ever knowing how. She wasn't a person to conceal the limits of her faith if she had had a chance to show them. On the other hand Mrs. Monarch didn't think her tidy; for why else did she take pains to say to me—it was going out of the way, for Mrs. Monarch—that she didn't like dirty women?

One day when my young lady happened to be present with my other sitters—she even dropped in, when it was convenient, for a chat—I asked her to be so good as to lend a hand in getting tea, a service with which she was familiar and which was one of a class that, living as I did in a small way, with slender domestic resources, I often appealed to my models to render. They liked to lay hands on my property, to break the sitting, and sometimes the china—it made them feel Bohemian. The next time I saw Miss Churm after this incident she surprised me greatly by making a scene about it—she accused me of having wished to humiliate her. She hadn't resented the outrage at the time, but had seemed obliging and amused, enjoying the comedy of asking Mrs. Monarch, who sat vague and silent, whether she would have cream and sugar, and putting an exaggerated simper into the question. She had tried intonations—as if she too wished to pass for the real thing—till I was afraid my other visitors would take offence.

Oh they were determined not to do this, and their touching patience was the measure of their great need. They would sit by the hour, uncomplaining, till I was ready to use them; they would come back on the chance of being wanted and would walk away cheerfully if it failed. I used to go to the door with them to see in what magnificent order they retreated. I tried to find other employment for them—I introduced them to several artists. But they didn't "take," for reasons I could appreciate, and I became rather anxiously aware that after such disappointments they fell back upon me with a heavier weight. They did me the honour to think me most *their* form. They weren't romantic enough for the painters, and in those days there were few serious workers in black-and-white. Besides, they had an eye to the great job I had mentioned to them—they had secretly set their hearts on supplying the right essence for my pictorial vindication of our fine novelist. They knew that for this undertaking I should want no costume-effects, none of the frippery of past ages—that it was a case in which everything would be contemporary and satirical and presumably genteel. If I could work them into it their future would be assured, for the labour would of course be long and the occupation steady.

One day Mrs. Monarch came without her husband—she explained his absence by his having had to go to the City. While she sat there in her usual relaxed majesty there came at the door a knock which I immediately recognised as the subdued appeal of a model out of work. It was followed by the entrance of a young man whom I at once saw to be a foreigner and who proved in fact an Italian acquainted with no English word but my name, which he uttered in a way that made it seem to include all others. I hadn't then visited his country, nor was I proficient in his tongue; but as he was not so meanly constituted—what Italian is?—as to depend only on that member for expression he conveyed to me, in familiar but graceful mimicry, that he was in search of exactly the employment in which the lady before me was engaged. I was not struck with him at first, and while I continued to draw I dropped few signs of interest or encouragement. He stood his ground however—not importunately, but with a dumb dog-like fidelity in his eyes that amounted to innocent impudence, the manner of a devoted servant—he might have been in the house for years—unjustly suspected. Suddenly it struck me that this very attitude and expression made a picture; whereupon I told him to sit down and wait till I should be free. There was another picture in the way he obeyed me, and I observed as I worked that there were others still in the way he looked wonderingly, with his head thrown back, about the high studio. He might have been crossing himself in Saint Peter's. Before I finished I said to myself "The fellow's a bankrupt orange-monger, but a treasure."

When Mrs. Monarch withdrew he passed across the room like a flash to open the door for her, standing there with the rapt pure gaze of the young Dante spellbound by the young Beatrice. As I never insisted, in

such situations, on the blankness of the British domestic, I reflected that
he had the making of a servant—and I needed one, but couldn't pay him
to be only that—as well as of a model; in short I resolved to adopt my
bright adventurer if he would agree to officiate in the double capacity. He
jumped at my offer, and in the event my rashness—for I had really
known nothing about him—wasn't brought home to me. He proved a
sympathetic though a desultory ministrant, and had in a wonderful
degree the *sentiment de la pose*. It was uncultivated, instinctive, a part of
the happy instinct that had guided him to my door and helped him to
spell out my name on the card nailed to it. He had had no other
introduction to me than a guess, from the shape of my high north
window, seen outside, that my place was a studio and that as a studio it
would contain an artist. He had wandered to England in search of
fortune, like other itinerants, and had embarked, with a partner and a
small green hand-cart, on the sale of penny ices. The ices had melted
away and the partner had dissolved in their train. My young man wore
tight yellow trousers with reddish stripes and his name was Oronte. He
was sallow but fair, and when I put him into some old clothes of my own
he looked like an Englishman. He was as good as Miss Churm, who
could look, when requested, like an Italian.

IV

I thought Mrs. Monarch's face slightly convulsed when, on her
coming back with her husband, she found Oronte installed. It was
strange to have to recognise in a scrap of a lazzarone a competitor to her
magnificent Major. It was she who scented danger first, for the Major
was anecdotically unconscious. But Oronte gave us tea, with a hundred
eager confusions—he had never been concerned in so queer a process—
and I think she thought better of me for having at last an "establishment." They saw a couple of drawings that I had made of the establishment, and Mrs. Monarch hinted that it never would have struck her he
had sat for them. "Now the drawings you make from *us*, they look
exactly like us," she reminded me, smiling in triumph; and I recognised
that this was indeed just their defect. When I drew the Monarchs I
couldn't anyhow get away from them—get into the character I wanted to
represent; and I hadn't the least desire my model should be discoverable
in my picture. Miss Churm never was, and Mrs. Monarch thought I hid
her, very properly, because she was vulgar; whereas if she was lost it was
only as the dead who got to heaven are lost—in the gain of an angel the
more.

By this time I had got a certain start with "Rutland Ramsay," the first
novel in the great projected series; that is I had produced a dozen
drawings, several with the help of the Major and his wife, and I had sent
them in for approval. My understanding with the publishers, as I have

already hinted, had been that I was to be left to do my work, in this particular case, as I liked, with the whole book committed to me; but my connexion with the rest of the series was only contingent. There were moments when, frankly, it *was* a comfort to have the real thing under one's hand; for there were characters in "Rutland Ramsay" that were very much like it. There were people presumably as erect as the Major and women of as good a fashion as Mrs. Monarch. There was a great deal of country-house life—treated, it is true, in a fine fanciful ironical generalised way—and there was a considerable implication of knickerbockers and kilts. There were certain things I had to settle at the outset; such things for instance as the exact appearance of the hero and the particular bloom and figure of the heroine. The author of course gave me a lead, but there was a margin for interpretation. I took the Monarchs into my confidence, I told them frankly what I was about, I mentioned my embarrassments and alternatives. "Oh take *him!*" Mrs. Monarch murmured sweetly, looking at her husband; and "What could you want better than my wife?" the Major enquired with the comfortable candour that now prevailed between us.

I wasn't obliged to answer these remarks—I was only obliged to place my sitters. I wasn't easy in mind, and I postponed a little timidly perhaps the solving of my question. The book was a large canvas, the other figures were numerous, and I worked off at first some of the episodes in which the hero and the heroine were not concerned. When once I had set *them* up I should have to stick to them—I couldn't make my young man seven feet high in one place and five feet nine in another. I inclined on the whole to the latter measurement, though the Major more than once reminded me that *he* looked about as young as any one. It was indeed quite possible to arrange him, for the figure, so that it would have been difficult to detect his age. After the spontaneous Oronte had been with me a month, and after I had given him to understand several times over that his native exuberance would presently constitute an insurmountable barrier to our further intercourse, I waked to a sense of his heroic capacity. He was only five feet seven, but the remaining inches were latent. I tried him almost secretly at first, for I was really rather afraid of the judgement my other models would pass on such a choice. If they regarded Miss Churm as little better than a snare what would they think of the representation by a person so little the real thing as an Italian street-vendor of a protagonist formed by a public school?

If I went a little in fear of them it wasn't because they bullied me, because they had got an oppressive foothold, but because in their really pathetic decorum and mysteriously permanent newness they counted on me so intensely. I was therefore very glad when Jack Hawley came home: he was always of such good counsel. He painted badly himself, but there was no one like him for putting his finger on the place. He had been absent from England for a year; he had been somewhere—I don't remember where—to get a fresh eye. I was in a good deal of dread of any such organ, but we were old friends; he had been away for months and a sense of emptiness was creeping into my life. I hadn't dodged a missile for a year.

He came back with a fresh eye, but with the same old black velvet blouse, and the first evening he spent in my studio we smoked cigarettes till the small hours. He had done no work himself, he had only got the eye; so the field was clear for the production of my little things. He wanted to see what I had produced for the *Cheapside*, but he was disappointed in the exhibition. That at least seemed the meaning of two or three comprehensive groans which, as he lounged on my big divan, his leg folded under him, looking at my latest drawings, issued from his lips with the smoke of the cigarette.

"What's the matter with you?" I asked.

"What's the matter with *you*?"

"Nothing save that I'm mystified."

"You are indeed. You're quite off the hinge. What's the meaning of this new fad?" And he tossed me, with visible irreverence, a drawing in which I happened to have depicted both my elegant models. I asked if he didn't think it good, and he replied that it struck him as execrable, given the sort of thing I had always represented myself to him as wishing to arrive at; but I let that pass—I was so anxious to see exactly what he meant. The two figures in the picture looked colossal, but I supposed this was *not* what he meant, inasmuch as, for aught he knew to the contrary, I might have been trying for some such effect. I maintained that I was working exactly in the same way as when he last had done me the honour to tell me I might do something some day. "Well, there's a screw loose somewhere," he answered; "wait a bit and I'll discover it." I depended upon him to do so: where else was the fresh eye? But he produced at last nothing more luminous than "I don't know—I don't like your types." This was lame for a critic who had never consented to discuss with me anything but the question of execution, the direction of strokes and the mystery of values.

"In the drawings you've been looking at I think my types are very handsome."

"Oh they won't do!"

"I've been working with new models."

"I see you have. *They* won't do."

"Are you very sure of that?"

"Absolutely—they're stupid."

"You mean *I* am—for I ought to get round that."

"You *can't*—with such people. Who are they?"

I told him, so far as was necessary, and he concluded heartlessly: "Ce sont des gens qu'il faut mettre à la porte."

"You've never seen them; they're awfully good"—I flew to their defence.

"Not seen them? Why all this recent work of yours drops to pieces with them. It's all I want to see of them."

"No one else has said anything against it—the *Cheapside* people are pleased."

"Every one else is an ass, and the *Cheapside* people the biggest asses of all. Come, don't pretend at this time of day to have pretty illusions about the public, especially about publishers and editors. It's not for *such* animals you work—it's for those you know, *coloro che sanno;* so keep straight for *me* if you can't keep straight for yourself. There was a certain sort of thing you used to try for—and a very good thing it was. But this twaddle isn't *in* it." When I talked with Hawley later about "Rutland Ramsay" and its possible successors he declared that I must get back into my boat again or I should go to the bottom. His voice in short was the voice of warning.

I noted the warning, but I didn't turn my friends out of doors. They bored me a good deal; but the very fact that they bored me admonished me not to sacrifice them—if there was anything to be done with them—simply to irritation. As I look back at this phase they seem to me to have pervaded my life not a little. I have a vision of them as most of the time in my studio, seated against the wall on an old velvet bench to be out of the way, and resembling the while a pair of patient courtiers in a royal ante-chamber. I'm convinced that during the coldest weeks of the winter they held their ground because it saved them fire. Their newness was losing its gloss, and it was impossible not to feel them objects of charity. Whenever Miss Churm arrived they went away, and after I was fairly launched in "Rutland Ramsay" Miss Churm arrived pretty often. They managed to express to me tacitly that they supposed I wanted her for the low life of the book, and I let them suppose it, since they had attempted to study the work—it was lying about the studio—without discovering that it dealt only with the highest circles. They had dipped into the most brilliant of our novelists without deciphering many passages. I still took an hour from them, now and again, in spite of Jack Hawley's warning: it would be time enough to dismiss them, if dismissal should be necessary, when the rigour of the season was over. Hawley had made their acquaintance—he had met them at my fireside—and thought them a ridiculous pair. Learning that he was a painter they tried to approach him, to show him too that they were the real thing; but he looked at them, across the big room, as if they were miles away: they were a compendium of everything he most objected to in the social system of his country. Such people as that, all convention and patent-leather, with ejaculations that stopped conversation, had no business in a studio. A studio was a place to learn to see, and how could you see through a pair of feather-beds?

The main inconvenience I suffered at their hands was that at first I was shy of letting it break upon them that my artful little servant had begun to sit to me for "Rutland Ramsay." They knew I had been odd enough—they were prepared by this time to allow oddity to artists—to pick a foreign vagabond out of the streets when I might have had a person with whiskers and credentials; but it was some time before they learned how high I rated his accomplishments. They found him in an attitude more than once, but they never doubted I was doing him as an organ-grinder. There were several things they never guessed, and one of them was that for a striking scene in the novel, in which a footman briefly figured, it occurred to me to make use of Major Monarch as the menial. I kept putting this off, I didn't like to ask him to don the livery—besides the difficulty of finding a livery to fit him. At last, one day late in the winter, when I was at work on the despised Oronte, who caught one's idea on the wing, and was in the glow of feeling myself go very straight, they came in, the Major and his wife, with their society laugh about nothing (there was less and less to laugh at); came in like country-callers—they always reminded me of that—who have walked across the park after church and are presently persuaded to stay to luncheon. Luncheon was over, but they could stay to tea—I knew they wanted it. The fit was on me, however, and I couldn't let my ardour cool and my work wait, with the fading daylight, while my model prepared it. So I asked Mrs. Monarch if she would mind laying it out—a request which for an instant brought all the blood to her face. Her eyes were on her husband's for a second, and some mute telegraphy passed between them. Their folly was over the next instant; his cheerful shrewdness put an end to it. So far from pitying their wounded pride, I must add, I was moved to give it as complete a lesson as I could. They bustled about together and got out the cups and saucers and made the kettle boil. I know they felt as if they were waiting on my servant, and when the tea was prepared I said: "He'll have a cup, please—he's tired." Mrs. Monarch brought him one where he stood, and he took it from her as if he had been a gentleman at a party squeezing a crush-hat with an elbow.

Then it came over me that she had made a great effort for me—made it with a kind of nobleness—and that I owed her a compensation. Each time I saw her after this I wondered what the compensation could be. I couldn't go on doing the wrong thing to oblige them. Oh it *was* the wrong thing, the stamp of the work for which they sat—Hawley was not the only person to say it now. I sent in a large number of the drawings I had made for "Rutland Ramsay," and I received a warning that was more to the point than Hawley's. The artistic adviser of the house for which I was working was of opinion that many of my illustrations were not what had been looked for. Most of these illustrations were the subjects in which the Monarchs had figured. Without going into the question of what *had* been looked for, I had to face the fact that at this rate I shouldn't get the other books to do. I hurled myself in despair on Miss Churm—I put her through all her paces. I not only adopted Oronte publicly as my hero, but one morning when the Major looked in to see if

I didn't require him to finish a *Cheapside* figure for which he had begun to sit the week before, I told him I had changed my mind—I'd do the drawing from my man. At this my visitor turned pale and stood looking at me. "Is *he* your idea of an English gentleman?" he asked.

I was disappointed, I was nervous, I wanted to get on with my work; so I replied with irritation: "Oh my dear Major—I can't be ruined for *you!*"

It was a horrid speech, but he stood another moment—after which, without a word, he quitted the studio. I drew a long breath, for I said to myself that I shouldn't see him again. I hadn't told him definitely that I was in danger of having my work rejected, but I was vexed at his not having felt the catastrophe in the air, read with me the moral of our fruitless collaboration, the lesson that in the deceptive atmosphere of art even the highest respectability may fail of being plastic.

I didn't owe my friends money, but I did see them again. They reappeared together three days later, and, given all the other facts, there was something tragic in that one. It was a clear proof they could find nothing else in life to do. They had threshed the matter out in a dismal conference—they had digested the bad news that they were not in for the series. If they weren't useful to me even for the *Cheapside* their function seemed difficult to determine, and I could only judge at first that they had come, forgivingly, decorously, to take a last leave. This made me rejoice in secret that I had little leisure for a scene; for I had placed both my other models in position together and I was pegging away at a drawing from which I hoped to derive glory. It had been suggested by the passage in which Rutland Ramsay, drawing up a chair to Artemisia's piano-stool, says extraordinary things to her while she ostensibly fingers out a difficult piece of music. I had done Miss Churm at the piano before—it was an attitude in which she knew how to take on an absolutely poetic grace. I wished the two figures to "compose" together with intensity, and my little Italian had entered perfectly into my conception. The pair were vividly before me, the piano had been pulled out; it was a charming show of blended youth and murmured love, which I had only to catch and keep. My visitors stood and looked at it, and I was friendly to them over my shoulder.

They made no response, but I was used to silent company and went on with my work, only a little disconcerted—even though exhilarated by the sense that *this* was at least the ideal thing—at not having got rid of them after all. Presently I heard Mrs. Monarch's sweet voice beside or rather above me: "I wish her hair were a little better done." I looked up and she was staring with a strange fixedness at Miss Churm, whose back was turned to her. "Do you mind my just touching it?" she went on—a question which made me spring up for an instant as with the instinctive fear that she might do the young lady a harm. But she quieted me with a glance I shall never forget—I confess I should like to have been able to paint *that*—and went for a moment to my model. She spoke to her softly, laying a hand on her shoulder and bending over her; and as the girl, understanding, gratefully assented, she disposed her rough curls, with a few quick passes, in such a way as to make Miss Churm's head twice as charming. It was one of the most heroic personal services I've ever seen rendered. Then Mrs. Monarch turned away with a low sigh and, looking about her as if for something to do, stooped to the floor with a noble humility and picked up a dirty rag that had dropped out of my paint-box.

The Major meanwhile had also been looking for something to do, and, wandering to the other end of the studio, saw before him my breakfast-things neglected, unremoved. "I say, can't I be useful *here?*" he called out to me with an irrepressible quaver. I assented with a laugh that I fear was awkward, and for the next ten minutes, while I worked, I heard the light clatter of china and the tinkle of spoons and glass. Mrs. Monarch assisted her husband—they washed up my crockery, they put it away. They wandered off into my little scullery, and I afterwards found that they had cleaned my knives and that my slender stock of plate had an unprecedented surface. When it came over me, the latent eloquence of what they were doing, I confess that my drawing was blurred for a moment—the picture swam. They had accepted their failure, but they couldn't accept their fate. They had bowed their heads in bewilderment to the perverse and cruel law in virtue of which the real thing could be so much less precious than the unreal; but they didn't want to starve. If my servants were my models, then my models might be my servants. They would reverse the parts—the others would sit for the ladies and gentlemen and *they* would do the work. They would still be in the studio—it was an intense dumb appeal to me not to turn them out. "Take us on," they wanted to say—"we'll do *anything*."

My pencil dropped from my hand; my sitting was spoiled and I got rid of my sitters, who were also evidently rather mystified and awestruck. Then, alone with the Major and his wife I had a most uncomfortable moment. He put their prayer into a single sentence: "I say, you know—just let *us* do for you, can't you?" I couldn't—it was dreadful to see them emptying my slops; but I pretended I could, to oblige them, for about a week. Then I gave them a sum of money to go away, and I never saw them again. I obtained the remaining books, but my friend Hawley repeats that Major and Mrs. Monarch did me a permanent harm, got me into false ways. If it be true I'm content to have paid the price—for the memory.

For Study and Discussion

1. Why is James' choice of the artist as narrator both appropriate and significant? Could the story be told as effectively from the point of view of one of the five other characters? What effect would be lost if it were told by one of them?

2. After the artist employs Mrs. Monarch and begins to sketch her, what makes him realize that she is, after all, unsatisfactory as a model? Why does he prefer Miss Churm? Is there any irony in his choice?

3. What is gained by bringing the young Italian Oronte into the story? What other qualities do Oronte and Miss Churm have in common besides their ability to pose as artist's models?

4. Is Jack Hawley, the narrator's artist-friend, a necessary element in the story? How does his role strengthen it? What would be lost if he were omitted?

5. In what specific ways do the Monarchs confirm Hawley's harsh judgment of them? Why can't the narrator find out these things for himself?

6. When Mrs. Monarch offers to rearrange Miss Churm's hair during the sitting, what does the narrator mean by confessing that he would "like to have been able to paint *that*"?

7. What conclusions does the story draw concerning art and reality? Are they valid? In what sense is "the real thing . . . so much less precious than the unreal"? Is this notion true only in the realm of art?

8. How would you express the moral judgment implied in the narrator's concluding statement? What price has he paid and what wisdom has he gained?

9. Compare James' technique with Hawthorne's. What similarities, if any, can you detect in their narrative method and style? What significant differences can you detect in their employment of fiction for the purpose of dramatizing a moral sentiment?

10. How closely does "The Real Thing" follow the plans that James outlined for it in his notes? What changes and/or additions did he make? Do all of these changes enhance the story's effectiveness? Which ones, if any, are merely superficial?

11. Did James meet his own original specifications for achieving compactness? Did he succeed in making his story "a little gem of bright, quick, vivid form"? Support your opinion—either way—with illustrations drawn from the story.

W. W. JACOBS

THE MONKEY'S PAW

{ high climax }

Without, the night was cold and wet, but in the small parlor of Laburnam Villa the blinds were drawn and the fire burned brightly. Father and son were at chess, the former, who possessed ideas about the game involving radical changes, putting his king into such sharp and unnecessary perils that it even provoked comment from the white-haired old lady knitting placidly by the fire.

"Hark at the wind," said Mr. White, who, having seen a fatal mistake after it was too late, was amiably desirous of preventing his son from seeing it.

"I'm listening," said the latter, grimly surveying the board as he stretched out his hand. "Check."

"I should hardly think that he'd come to-night," said his father, with his hand poised over the board.

"Mate," replied the son.

"That's the worst of living so far out," bawled Mr. White, with sudden and unlooked-for violence; "of all the beastly, slushy, out-of-the-way places to live in, this is the worst. Pathway's a bog, and the road's a torrent. I don't know what people are thinking about. I suppose because only two houses on the road are let, they think it doesn't matter."

"Never mind, dear," said his wife soothingly; "perhaps you'll win the next one."

Mr. White looked up sharply, just in time to intercept a knowing glance between mother and son. The words died away on his lips, and he hid a guilty grin in his thin gray beard.

"There he is," said Herbert White, as the gate banged to loudly and heavy footsteps came toward the door.

The old man rose with hospitable haste, and opening the door, was heard condoling with the new arrival. The new arrival also condoled with himself, so that Mrs. White said, "Tut, tut!" and coughed gently as her husband entered the room, followed by a tall burly man, beady of eye and rubicund of visage.

Originally published in *Harper's Monthly Magazine*, September 1902. Reprinted here from *The Lady of the Barge and Other Stories* (London and New York: Harper and Brothers, 1902).

"Sergeant-Major Morris," he said, introducing him.

The sergeant-major shook hands, and taking the proffered seat by the fire, watched contentedly while his host got out whisky and tumblers and stood a small copper kettle on the fire.

At the third glass his eyes got brighter, and he began to talk, the little family circle regarding with eager interest this visitor from distant parts, as he squared his broad shoulders in the chair and spoke of strange scenes and doughty deeds, of wars and plagues and strange peoples.

"Twenty-one years of it," said Mr. White, nodding at his wife and son. "When he went away he was a slip of a youth in the warehouse. Now look at him."

"He don't look to have taken much harm," said Mrs. White politely.

"I'd like to go to India myself," said the old man, "just to look round a bit, you know."

"Better where you are," said the sergeant-major, shaking his head. He put down the empty glass and, sighing softly, shook it again.

"I should like to see those old temples and fakirs and jugglers," said the old man. "What was that you started telling me the other day about a monkey's paw or something, Morris?"

"Nothing," said the soldier hastily. "Leastways, nothing worth hearing."

"Monkey's paw?" said Mrs. White curiously.

"Well, it's just a bit of what you might call magic, perhaps," said the sergeant-major off-handedly.

His three listeners leaned forward eagerly. The visitor absentmindedly put his empty glass to his lips and then set it down again. His host filled it for him.

"To look at," said the sergeant-major, fumbling in his pocket, "it's just an ordinary little paw, dried to a mummy."

He took something out of his pocket and proffered it. Mrs. White drew back with a grimace, but her son, taking it, examined it curiously.

"And what is there special about it?" inquired Mr. White, as he took it from his son and, having examined it, placed it upon the table.

"It had a spell put on it by an old fakir," said the sergeant-major, "a very holy man. He wanted to show that fate ruled people's lives, and that those who interfered with it did so to their sorrow. He put a spell on it so that three separate men could each have three wishes from it."

His manner was so impressive that his hearers were conscious that their light laughter jarred somewhat.

"Well, why don't you have three, sir?" said Herbert White cleverly.

The soldier regarded him in the way that middle age is wont to regard presumptuous youth. "I have," he said quietly, and his blotchy face whitened.

"And did you really have the three wishes granted?" asked Mrs. White.

"I did," said the sergeant-major, and his glass tapped against his strong teeth.

"And has anybody else wished?" inquired the old lady.

"The first man had his three wishes, yes," was the reply. "I don't know what the first two were, but the third was for death. That's how I got the paw."

His tones were so grave that a hush fell upon the group.

"If you've had your three wishes, it's no good to you now, then, Morris," said the old man at last. "What do you keep it for?"

The soldier shook his head. "Fancy, I suppose," he said slowly. "I did have some idea of selling it, but I don't think I will. It has caused enough mischief already. Besides, people won't buy. They think it's a fairy tale, some of them, and those who do think anything of it want to try it first and pay me afterward."

"If you could have another three wishes," said the old man, eyeing him keenly, "would you have them?"

"I don't know," said the other. "I don't know."

He took the paw, and dangling it between his front finger and thumb, suddenly threw it upon the fire. White, with a slight cry, stooped down and snatched it off.

"Better let it burn," said the soldier solemnly.

"If you don't want it, Morris," said the old man, "give it to me."

"I won't," said his friend doggedly. "I threw it on the fire. If you keep it, don't blame me for what happens. Pitch it on the fire again, like a sensible man."

The other shook his head and examined his new possession closely. "How do you do it?" he inquired.

"Hold it up in your right hand and wish aloud," said the sergeant-major, "but I warn you of the consequences."

"Sounds like the *Arabian Nights*," said Mrs. White, as she rose and began to set the supper. "Don't you think you might wish for four pairs of hands for me?"

Her husband drew the talisman from his pocket and then all three burst into laughter as the sergeant-major, with a look of alarm on his face, caught him by the arm.

"If you must wish," he said gruffly, "wish for something sensible."

Mr. White dropped it back into his pocket, and placing chairs, motioned his friend to the table. In the business of supper the talisman was partly forgotten, and afterward the three sat listening in an enthralled fashion to a second installment of the soldier's adventures in India.

"If the tale about the monkey paw is not more truthful than those he has been telling us," said Herbert, as the door closed behind their guest, just in time for him to catch the last train, "we shan't make much out of it."

"Did you give him anything for it, father?" inquired Mrs. White, regarding her husband closely.

"A trifle," said he, coloring slightly. "He didn't want it, but I made him take it. And he pressed me again to throw it away."

"Likely," said Herbert, with pretended horror. "Why, we're going to be rich, and famous, and happy. Wish to be an emperor, father, to begin with; then you can't be henpecked."

He darted round the table, pursued by the maligned Mrs. White armed with an antimacassar.

Mr. White took the paw from his pocket and eyed it dubiously. "I don't know what to wish for, and that's a fact," he said slowly. "It seems to me I've got all I want."

"If you only cleared the house, you'd be quite happy, wouldn't you?" said Herbert, with his hand on his shoulder. "Well, wish for two hundred pounds, then; that'll just do it."

His father, smiling shamefacedly at his own credulity, held up the talisman, as his son, with a solemn face somewhat marred by a wink at his mother, sat down at the piano and struck a few impressive chords.

"I wish for two hundred pounds," said the old man distinctly.

A fine crash from the piano greeted the words, interrupted by a shuddering cry from the old man. His wife and son ran toward him.

"It moved," he cried, with a glance of disgust at the object as it lay on the floor. "As I wished it twisted in my hands like a snake."

"Well, I don't see the money," said his son, as he picked it up and placed it on the table, "and I bet I never shall."

"It must have been your fancy, father," said his wife, regarding him anxiously.

He shook his head. "Never mind, though; there's no harm done, but it gave me a shock all the same."

They sat down by the fire again while the two men finished their pipes. Outside, the wind was higher than ever, and the old man started nervously at the sound of a door banging upstairs. A silence unusual and depressing settled upon all three, which lasted until the old couple rose to retire for the night.

"I expect you'll find the cash tied up in a big bag in the middle of your bed," said Herbert, as he bade them good night, "and something horrible squatting up on top of the wardrobe watching you as you pocket your ill-gotten gains."

He sat alone in the darkness, gazing at the dying fire, and seeing faces in it. The last face was so horrible and so simian that he gazed at it in amazement. It got so vivid that, with a little uneasy laugh, he felt on the table for a glass containing a little water to throw over it. His hand grasped the monkey's paw, and with a little shiver he wiped his hand on his coat and went up to bed.

II

In the brightness of the wintry sun next morning as it streamed over the breakfast table he laughed at his fears. There was an air of prosaic wholesomeness about the room which it had lacked on the previous night, and the dirty, shriveled little paw was pitched on the sideboard with a carelessness which betokened no great belief in its virtues.

"I suppose all old soldiers are the same," said Mrs. White. "The idea of our listening to such nonsense! How could wishes be granted in these days? And if they could, how could two hundred pounds hurt you, father?"

"Might drop on his head from the sky," said the frivolous Herbert.

"Morris said the things happened so naturally," said his father, "that you might if you so wished attribute it to coincidence."

"Well, don't break into the money before I come back," said Herbert as he rose from the table. "I'm afraid it'll turn you into a mean, avaricious man, and we shall have to disown you."

His mother laughed, and following him to the door, watched him down the road; and returning to the breakfast table, was very happy at the expense of her husband's credulity. All of which did not prevent her from scurrying to the door at the postman's knock, nor prevent her from referring somewhat shortly to retired sergeant-majors of bibulous habits when she found that the post brought a tailor's bill.

"Herbert will have some more of his funny remarks, I expect, when he comes home," she said, as they sat at dinner.

"I dare say," said Mr. White, pouring himself out some beer; "but for all that, the thing moved in my hand; that I'll swear to."

"You thought it did," said the old lady soothingly.

"I say it did," replied the other. "There was no thought about it; I had just—What's the matter?"

His wife made no reply. She was watching the mysterious movements of a man outside, who, peering in an undecided fashion at the house, appeared to be trying to make up his mind to enter. In mental connection with the two hundred pounds, she noticed that the stranger was well dressed and wore a silk hat of glossy newness. Three times he paused at the gate, and then walked on again. The fourth time he stood with his hand upon it, and then with sudden resolution flung it open and walked up the path. Mrs. White at the same moment placed her hands behind her, and hurriedly unfastening the strings of her apron, put that useful article of apparel beneath the cushion of her chair.

She brought the stranger, who seemed ill at ease, into the room. He gazed furtively at Mrs. White, and listened in a preoccupied fashion as the old lady apologized for the appearance of the room, and her husband's coat, a garment which he usually reserved for the garden. She then waited as patiently as her sex would permit for him to broach his business, but he was at first strangely silent.

"I—was asked to call," he said at last, and stooped and picked a piece of cotton from his trousers. "I come from 'Maw and Meggins.'"

The old lady started. "Is anything the matter?" she asked breathlessly. "Has anything happened to Herbert? What is it? What is it?"

Her husband interposed. "There, there, mother," he said hastily. "Sit down, and don't jump to conclusions. You've not brought bad news, I'm sure, sir"; and he eyed the other wistfully.

"I'm sorry—" began the visitor.

"Is he hurt?" demanded the mother, wildly.

The visitor bowed in assent. "Badly hurt," he said quietly, "but he is not in any pain."

"Oh, thank God!" said the old woman, clasping her hands. "Thank God for that! Thank—"

She broke off suddenly as the sinister meaning of the assurance dawned upon her and she saw the awful confirmation of her fears in the other's perverted face. She caught her breath, and turning to her slower-witted husband, laid her trembling old hand upon his. There was a long silence.

"He was caught in the machinery," said the visitor at length in a low voice.

"Caught in the machinery," repeated Mr. White, in a dazed fashion, "yes."

He sat staring blankly out at the window, and taking his wife's hand between his own, pressed it as he had been wont to do in their old courting-days nearly forty years before.

"He was the only one left to us," he said, turning gently to the visitor. "It is hard."

The other coughed, and rising, walked slowly to the window. "The firm wished me to convey their sincere sympathy with you in your great loss," he said, without looking round. "I beg that you will understand that I am only their servant and merely obeying orders."

There was no reply; the old woman's face was white, her eyes staring, and her breath inaudible; on the husband's face was a look such as his friend the sergeant might have carried into his first action.

"I was to say that Maw and Meggins disclaim all responsibility," continued the other. "They admit no liability at all, but in consideration of your son's services, they wish to present you with a certain sum as compensation."

Mr. White dropped his wife's hand, and rising to his feet, gazed with a look of horror at his visitor. His dry lips shaped the words, "How much?"

"Two hundred pounds," was the answer.

Unconscious of his wife's shriek, the old man smiled faintly, put out his hands like a sightless man, and dropped, a senseless heap, to the floor.

III

In the huge new cemetery, some two miles distant, the old people buried their dead, and came back to a house steeped in shadow and silence. It was all over so quickly that at first they could hardly realize it, and remained in a state of expectation as though of something else to happen—something else which was to lighten this load, too heavy for old hearts to bear.

But the days passed, and expectation gave place to resignation—the hopeless resignation of the old, sometimes miscalled, apathy. Sometimes they hardly exchanged a word, for now they had nothing to talk about, and their days were long to weariness.

It was about a week after that that the old man, waking suddenly in the night, stretched out his hand and found himself alone. The room was in darkness, and the sound of subdued weeping came from the window. He raised himself in bed and listened.

"Come back," he said tenderly. "You will be cold."

"It is colder for my son," said the old woman, and wept afresh.

The sound of her sobs died away on his ears. The bed was warm, and his eyes heavy with sleep. He dozed fitfully, and then slept until a sudden wild cry from his wife awoke him with a start.

"The paw!" she cried wildly. "The monkey's paw!"

He started up in alarm. "Where! Where is it? What's the matter?"

She came stumbling across the room toward him. "I want it," she said quietly. "You've not destroyed it?"

"It's in the parlor, on the bracket," he replied, marveling. "Why?"

She cried and laughed together, and bending over, kissed his cheek.

"I only just thought of it," she said hysterically. "Why didn't I think of it before? Why didn't *you* think of it?"

"Think of what?" he questioned.

"The other two wishes," she replied rapidly. "We've only had one."

"Was not that enough?" he demanded fiercely.

"No," she cried triumphantly; "we'll have one more. Go down and get it quickly, and wish our boy alive again."

The man sat up in bed and flung the bedclothes from his quaking limbs. "Good God, you are mad!" he cried, aghast.

"Get it," she panted; "get it quickly, and wish—Oh, my boy, my boy!"

Her husband struck a match and lit the candle. "Get back to bed," he said unsteadily. "You don't know what you are saying."

"We had the first wish granted," said the old woman feverishly; "why not the second?"

"A coincidence," stammered the old man.

"Go and get it and wish," cried his wife, quivering with excitement.

The old man turned and regarded her, and his voice shook. "He has been dead ten days, and besides he—I would not tell you else, but—I could only recognize him by his clothing. If he was too terrible for you to see then, how now?"

"Bring him back," cried the old woman, and dragged him toward the door. "Do you think I fear the child I have nursed?"

He went down in the darkness, and felt his way to the parlor, and then to the mantelpiece. The talisman was in its place, and a horrible fear that the unspoken wish might bring his mutilated son before him ere he could escape from the room seized upon him, and he caught his breath as he found that he had lost the direction of the door. His brow cold with sweat, he felt his way round the table, and groped along the wall until he found himself in the small passage with the unwholesome thing in his hand.

Even his wife's face seemed changed as he entered the room. It was white and expectant, and to his fears seemed to have an unnatural look upon it. He was afraid of her.

"Wish!" she cried, in a strong voice.

"It is foolish and wicked," he faltered.

"Wish!" repeated his wife.

He raised his hand. "I wish my son alive again."

The talisman fell to the floor, and he regarded it shudderingly. Then he sank trembling into a chair as the old woman, with burning eyes, walked to the window and raised the blind.

He sat until he was chilled with the cold, glancing occasionally at the figure of the old woman peering through the window. The candle-end, which had burnt below the rim of the china candlestick, was throwing pulsating shadows on the ceiling and walls, until, with a flicker larger than the rest, it expired. The old man, with an unspeakable sense of relief at the failure of the talisman, crept back to his bed, and a minute or two afterward the old woman came silently and apathetically beside him.

Neither spoke, but both lay silently listening to the ticking of the clock. A stair creaked, and a squeaky mouse scurried noisily through the wall. The darkness was oppressive, and after lying for some time screwing up his courage, the husband took the box of matches, and striking one, went downstairs for a candle.

At the foot of the stairs the match went out, and he paused to strike another; and at the same moment a knock, so quiet and stealthy as to be scarcely audible, sounded on the front door.

The matches fell from his hand and spilled in the passage. He stood motionless, his breath suspended until the knock was repeated. Then he turned and fled swiftly back to his room, and closed the door behind him. A third knock sounded through the house.

"What's that?" cried the old woman, starting up.

"A rat," said the old man, in shaking tones—"a rat. It passed me on the stairs."

His wife sat up in bed listening. A loud knock resounded through the house.

"It's Herbert!" she screamed. "It's Herbert!"

She ran to the door, but her husband was before her, and catching her by the arm, held her tightly.

"What are you going to do?" he whispered hoarsely.

"It's my boy; it's Herbert!" she cried, struggling mechanically. "I forgot it was two miles away. What are you holding me for? Let go. I must open the door."

"For God's sake don't let it in," cried the old man, trembling.

"You're afraid of your own son," she cried, struggling. "Let me go. I'm coming, Herbert; I'm coming."

There was another knock, and another. The old woman with a sudden wrench broke free and ran from the room. Her husband followed to the landing, and called after her appealingly as she hurried downstairs. He heard the chain rattle back and the bottom bolt drawn slowly and stiffly from the socket. Then the old woman's voice, strained and panting.

"The bolt," she cried loudly. "Come down. I can't reach it."

But her husband was on his hands and knees groping wildly on the floor in search of the paw. If he could only find it before the thing outside got in. A perfect fusillade of knocks reverberated through the house, and he heard the scraping of a chair as his wife put it down in the passage against the door. He heard the creaking of the bolt as it came slowly back, and at the same moment he found the monkey's paw, and frantically breathed his third and last wish.

The knocking ceased suddenly, although the echoes of it were still in the house. He heard the chair drawn back and the door opened. A cold wind rushed up the staircase, and a long loud wail of disappointment and misery from his wife gave him courage to run down to her side, and then to the gate beyond. The street lamp flickering opposite shone on a quiet and deserted road.

For Study and Discussion

1. Is there any point in beginning the story with a chess game rather than with some other activity?

2. How many different devices are employed in Part I to suggest that the monkey's paw really does possess magical powers? Are they convincing?

3. Is Herbert's death a logical result of his father's expressed wish for two hundred pounds? If not, what prior events in the story make it seem so?

4. Is the mother's behavior in Part III logically motivated?

5. How would you characterize the outcome of the story? Is it a surprise ending like that of "Marjorie Daw" or "The Gift of the Magi"? Is there any trickery involved in it? Discuss.

WILLIAM SYDNEY PORTER
(O. HENRY)

THE GIFT OF THE MAGI

One dollar and eighty-seven cents. That was all. And sixty cents of it was in pennies. Pennies saved one and two at a time by bulldozing the grocer and the vegetable man and the butcher until one's cheeks burned with the silent imputation of parsimony that such close dealing implied. Three times Della counted it. One dollar and eighty-seven cents. And the next day would be Christmas.

There was clearly nothing to do but flop down on the shabby little couch and howl. So Della did it. Which instigates the moral reflection that life is made up of sobs, sniffles, and smiles, with sniffles predominating.

While the mistress of the home is gradually subsiding from the first stage to the second, take a look at the home. A furnished flat at $8 per week. It did not exactly beggar description, but it certainly had that word on the lookout for the mendicancy squad.

In the vestibule below was a letter-box into which no letter would go, and an electric button from which no mortal finger could coax a ring. Also appertaining thereunto was a card bearing the name "Mr. James Dillingham Young."

The "Dillingham" had been flung to the breeze during a former period of prosperity when its possessor was being paid $30 per week. Now, when the income was shrunk to $20, the letters of "Dillingham" looked blurred, as though they were thinking seriously of contracting to a modest and unassuming D. But whenever Mr. James Dillingham Young came home and reached his flat above he was called "Jim" and greatly hugged by Mrs. James Dillingham Young, already introduced to you as Della. Which is all very good.

Originally published under the title "Gifts of the Magi," in the New York *Sunday World*, December 10, 1905. Reprinted here from *The Four Million* (New York: Doubleday and Company, 1906), by permission of the publisher. Copyright 1905 by Doubleday and Company, Inc.

Della finished her cry and attended to her cheeks with the powder rag. She stood by the window and looked out dully at a gray cat walking a gray fence in a gray backyard. To-morrow would be Christmas Day, and she had only $1.87 with which to buy Jim a present. She had been saving every penny she could for months, with this result. Twenty dollars a week doesn't go far. Expenses had been greater than she had calculated. They always are. Only $1.87 to buy a present for Jim. Her Jim. Many a happy hour she had spent planning for something nice for him. Something fine and rare and sterling—something just a little bit near to being worthy of the honour of being owned by Jim.

There was a pier-glass between the windows of the room. Perhaps you have seen a pier-glass in an $8 flat. A very thin and very agile person may, by observing his reflection in a rapid sequence of longitudinal strips, obtain a fairly accurate conception of his looks. Della, being slender, had mastered the art.

Suddenly she whirled from the window and stood before the glass. Her eyes were shining brilliantly, but her face had lost its colour within twenty seconds. Rapidly she pulled down her hair and let it fall to its full length.

Now, there were two possessions of the James Dillingham Youngs in which they both took a mighty pride. One was Jim's gold watch that had been his father's and his grandfather's. The other was Della's hair. Had the Queen of Sheba lived in the flat across the airshaft, Della would have let her hair hang out the window some day to dry just to depreciate Her Majesty's jewels and gifts. Had King Solomon been the janitor, with all his treasures piled up in the basement, Jim would have pulled out his watch every time he passed, just to see him pluck at his beard from envy.

So now Della's beautiful hair fell about her, rippling and shining like a cascade of brown waters. It reached below her knee and made itself almost a garment for her. And then she did it up again nervously and quickly. Once she faltered for a minute and stood still while a tear or two splashed on the worn red carpet.

On went her old brown jacket; on went her old brown hat. With a whirl of skirts and with the brilliant sparkle still in her eyes, she fluttered out the door and down the stairs to the street.

Where she stopped the sign read: "Mme. Sofronie. Hair Goods of All Kinds." One flight up Della ran, and collected herself, panting. Madame, large, too white, chilly, hardly looked the "Sofronie."

"Will you buy my hair?" asked Della.

"I buy hair," said Madame. "Take yer hat off and let's have a sight at the looks of it."

Down rippled the brown cascade.

"Twenty dollars," said Madame, lifting the mass with a practised hand.

"Give it to me quick," said Della.

Oh, and the next two hours tripped by on rosy wings. Forget the hashed metaphor. She was ransacking the stores for Jim's present.

She found it at last. It surely had been made for Jim and no one else. There was no other like it in any of the stores, and she had turned all of them inside out. It was a platinum fob chain simple and chaste in design, properly proclaiming its value by substance alone and not by meretricious ornamentation—as all good things should do. It was even worthy of The Watch. As soon as she saw it she knew that it must be Jim's. It was like him. Quietness and value—the description applied to both. Twenty-one dollars they took from her for it, and she hurried home with the 87 cents. With that chain on his watch Jim might be properly anxious about the time in any company. Grand as the watch was, he sometimes looked at it on the sly on account of the old leather strap that he used in place of a chain.

When Della reached home her intoxication gave way a little to prudence and reason. She got out her curling irons and lighted the gas and went to work repairing the ravages made by generosity added to love. Which is always a tremendous task, dear friends—a mammoth task.

Within forty minutes her head was covered with tiny, close-lying curls that made her look wonderfully like a truant schoolboy. She looked at her reflection in the mirror long, carefully, and critically.

"If Jim doesn't kill me," she said to herself, "before he takes a second look at me, he'll say I look like a Coney Island chorus girl. But what could I do—oh! what could I do with a dollar and eighty-seven cents?"

At 7 o'clock the coffee was made and the frying-pan was on the back of the stove hot and ready to cook the chops.

Jim was never late. Della doubled the fob chain in her hand and sat on the corner of the table near the door that he always entered. Then she heard his step on the stair away down on the first flight, and she turned white for just a moment. She had a habit of saying little silent prayers about the simplest everyday things, and now she whispered: "Please God, make him think I am still pretty."

The door opened and Jim stepped in and closed it. He looked thin and very serious. Poor fellow, he was only twenty-two—and to be burdened with a family! He needed a new overcoat and he was without gloves.

Jim stopped inside the door, as immovable as a setter at the scent of quail. His eyes were fixed upon Della, and there was an expression in them that she could not read, and it terrified her. It was not anger, nor surprise, nor disapproval, nor horror, nor any of the sentiments that she had been prepared for. He simply stared at her fixedly with that peculiar expression on his face.

Della wriggled off the table and went for him.

"Jim, darling," she cried, "don't look at me that way. I had my hair cut off and sold it because I couldn't have lived through Christmas without giving you a present. It'll grow out again—you won't mind, will you? I just had to do it. My hair grows awfully fast. Say 'Merry Christmas!' Jim, and let's be happy. You don't know what a nice—what a beautiful, nice gift I've got for you."

"You've cut off your hair?" asked Jim, laboriously, as if he had not arrived at that patent fact yet even after the hardest mental labour.

"Cut it off and sold it," said Della. "Don't you like me just as well, anyhow? I'm me without my hair, ain't I?"

Jim looked about the room curiously.

"You say your hair is gone?" he said, with an air almost of idiocy.

"You needn't look for it," said Della. "It's sold, I tell you—sold and gone, too. It's Christmas Eve, boy. Be good to me, for it went for you. Maybe the hairs of my head were numbered," she went on with a sudden serious sweetness, "but nobody could ever count my love for you. Shall I put the chops on, Jim?"

Out of his trance Jim seemed quickly to wake. He enfolded his Della. For ten seconds let us regard with discreet scrutiny some inconsequential object in the other direction. Eight dollars a week or a million a year—what is the difference? A mathematician or a wit would give you the wrong answer. The magi brought valuable gifts, but that was not among them. This dark assertion will be illuminated later on.

Jim drew a package from his overcoat pocket and threw it upon the table.

"Don't make any mistake, Dell," he said, "about me. I don't think there's anything in the way of a haircut or a shave or a shampoo that could make me like my girl any less. But if you'll unwrap that package you may see why you had me going a while at first."

White fingers and nimble tore at the string and paper. And then an ecstatic scream of joy; and then, alas! a quick feminine change to hysterical tears and wails, necessitating the immediate employment of all the comforting powers of the lord of the flat.

For there lay The Combs—the set of combs, side and back, that Della had worshipped for long in a Broadway window. Beautiful combs, pure tortoise shell, with jewelled rims—just the shade to wear in the beautiful vanished hair. They were expensive combs, she knew, and her heart had simply craved and yearned over them without the least hope of possession. And now, they were hers, but the tresses that should have adorned the coveted adornments were gone.

But she hugged them to her bosom, and at length she was able to look up with dim eyes and a smile and say: "My hair grows so fast, Jim!"

And then Della leaped up like a little singed cat and cried, "Oh, oh!"

Jim had not yet seen his beautiful present. She held it out to him eagerly upon her open palm. The dull precious metal seemed to flash with a reflection of her bright and ardent spirit.

"Isn't it a dandy, Jim? I hunted all over town to find it. You'll have to look at the time a hundred times a day now. Give me your watch. I want to see how it looks on it."

Instead of obeying, Jim tumbled down on the couch and put his hands under the back of his head and smiled.

"Dell," said he, "let's put our Christmas presents away and keep 'em a while. They're too nice to use just at present. I sold the watch to get the money to buy your combs. And now suppose you put the chops on."

The magi, as you know, were wise men—wonderfully wise men—who brought gifts to the Babe in the manger. They invented the art of giving Christmas presents. Being wise, their gifts were no doubt wise ones, possibly bearing the privilege of exchange in case of duplication. And here I have lamely related to you the uneventful chronicle of two foolish children in a flat who most unwisely sacrificed for each other the greatest treasures of their house. But in a last word to the wise of these days let it be said that of all who give gifts these two were the wisest. Of all who give and receive gifts, such as they are wisest. Everywhere they are wisest. They are the magi.

For Study and Discussion

1. What tone is established in the opening section of the story? Is it maintained throughout? Is it appropriate to the events of the story? If not, why did O. Henry use it?

2. By what means does O. Henry make it clear that Della's long hair and Jim's watch are the most prized possessions they have? How does this add to the effect of the story?

3. Does O. Henry prepare the reader for the double-twist of surprise at the end of the story?

4. What "philosophy of life," if any, is embodied in this story? Does O. Henry make it convincing?

5. O. Henry and Aldrich wrote the kinds of tales several of the critics in Section II objected to as magazine stories. What elements in "The Gift of the Magi" and "Marjorie Daw" might have led these critics to make such a judgment? Do you find any of the same qualities in Kipling's "At the Pit's Mouth"? If so, what, nevertheless, makes Kipling's story substantially different from either O. Henry's or Aldrich's?

JAMES JOYCE

ARABY

North Richmond Street, being blind, was a quiet street except at the hour when the Christian Brothers' School set the boys free. An uninhabited house of two storeys stood at the blind end, detached from its neighbours in a square ground. The other houses of the street, conscious of decent lives within them, gazed at one another with brown imperturbable faces.

The former tenant of our house, a priest, had died in the back drawing-room. Air, musty from having been long enclosed, hung in all the rooms, and the waste room behind the kitchen was littered with old useless papers. Among these I found a few paper-covered books, the pages of which were curled and damp: *The Abbot*, by Walter Scott, *The Devout Communicant* and *The Memoirs of Vidocq*. I liked the last best because its leaves were yellow. The wild garden behind the house contained a central apple-tree and a few straggling bushes under one of which I found the late tenant's rusty bicycle-pump. He had been a very charitable priest; in his will he had left all his money to institutions and the furniture of his house to his sister.

When the short days of winter came dusk fell before we had well eaten our dinners. When we met in the street the houses had grown sombre. The space of sky above us was the colour of ever-changing violet and towards it the lamps of the street lifted their feeble lanterns. The cold air stung us and we played till our bodies glowed. Our shouts echoed in the silent street. The career of our play brought us through the dark muddy lanes behind the houses where we ran the gauntlet of the rough tribes from the cottages, to the back doors of the dark dripping gardens where odours arose from the ashpits, to the dark odorous stables where a coachman smoothed and combed the horse or shook music from the buckled harness. When we returned to the street light from the kitchen

Originally published in *Dubliners* (London: Grant Richards, 1914). Reprinted here from *The Portable James Joyce*, edited by Harry Levin (New York: The Viking Press, 1947). Copyright © 1967 by The Estate of James Joyce. All rights reserved. Reprinted by permission of The Viking Press, Inc.

windows had filled the areas. If my uncle was seen turning the corner we hid in the shadow until we had seen him safely housed. Or if Mangan's sister came out on the doorstep to call her brother in to his tea we watched her from our shadow peer up and down the street. We waited to see whether she would remain or go in and, if she remained, we left our shadow and walked up to Mangan's steps resignedly. She was waiting for us, her figure defined by the light from the half-opened door. Her brother always teased her before he obeyed and I stood by the railings looking at her. Her dress swung as she moved her body and the soft rope of her hair tossed from side to side.

Every morning I lay on the floor in the front parlour watching her door. The blind was pulled down to within an inch of the sash so that I could not be seen. When she came out on the doorstep my heart leaped. I ran to the hall, seized my books and followed her. I kept her brown figure always in my eye and, when we came near the point at which our ways diverged, I quickened my pace and passed her. This happened morning after morning. I had never spoken to her, except for a few casual words, and yet her name was like a summons to all my foolish blood.

Her image accompanied me even in places the most hostile to romance. On Saturday evenings when my aunt went marketing I had to go to carry some of the parcels. We walked through the flaring streets, jostled by drunken men and bargaining women, amid the curses of labourers, the shrill litanies of shop-boys who stood on guard by the barrels of pigs' cheeks, the nasal chanting of street-singers, who sang a *come-all-you* about O'Donovan Rossa, or a ballad about the troubles in our native land. These noises converged in a single sensation of life for me: I imagined that I bore my chalice safely through a throng of foes. Her name sprang to my lips at moments in strange prayers and praises which I myself did not understand. My eyes were often full of tears (I could not tell why) and at times a flood from my heart seemed to pour itself out into my bosom. I thought little of the future. I did not know whether I would ever speak to her or not or, if I spoke to her, how I could tell her of my confused adoration. But my body was like a harp and her words and gestures were like fingers running upon the wires.———— *Simile*

One evening I went into the back drawing-room in which the priest had died. It was a dark rainy evening and there was no sound in the house. Through one of the broken panes I heard the rain impinge upon the earth, the fine incessant needles of water playing in the sodden beds. Some distant lamp or lighted window gleamed below me. I was thankful that I could see so little. All my senses seemed to desire to veil themselves and, feeling that I was about to slip from them, I pressed the palms of my hands together until they trembled, murmuring: *"O love! O love!"* many times.

At last she spoke to me. When she addressed the first words to me I was so confused that I did not know what to answer. She asked me was I going to *Araby*. I forgot whether I answered yes or no. It would be a splendid bazaar, she said she would love to go.

"And why can't you?" I asked.

While she spoke she turned a silver bracelet round and round her wrist. She could not go, she said, because there would be a retreat that week in her convent. Her brother and two other boys were fighting for their caps and I was alone at the railings. She held one of the spikes, bowing her head towards me. The light from the lamp opposite our door caught the white curve of her neck, lit up her hair that rested there and, falling, lit up the hand upon the railing. It fell over one side of her dress and caught the white border of a petticoat, just visible as she stood at ease.

"It's well for you," she said.

"If I go," I said, "I will bring you something."

What innumerable follies laid waste my waking and sleeping thoughts after that evening! I wished to annihilate the tedious intervening days. I chafed against the work of school. At night in my bedroom and by day in the classroom her image came between me and the page I strove to read. The syllables of the word *Araby* were called to me through the silence in which my soul luxuriated and cast an Eastern enchantment over me. I asked for leave to go to the bazaar on Saturday night. My aunt was surprised and hoped it was not some Freemason affair. I answered few questions in class. I watched my master's face pass from amiability to sternness; he hoped I was not beginning to idle. I could not call my wandering thoughts together. I had hardly any patience with the serious work of life which, now that it stood between me and my desire, seemed to me child's play, ugly monotonous child's play.

On Saturday morning I reminded my uncle that I wished to go to the bazaar in the evening. He was fussing at the hallstand, looking for the hat-brush, and answered me curtly:

"Yes, boy, I know."

As he was in the hall I could not go into the front parlour and lie at the window. I left the house in bad humour and walked slowly towards the school. The air was pitilessly raw and already my heart misgave me.

When I came home to dinner my uncle had not yet been home. Still it was early. I sat staring at the clock for some time and, when its ticking began to irritate me, I left the room. I mounted the staircase and gained the upper part of the house. The high cold empty gloomy rooms liberated me and I went from room to room singing. From the front window I saw my companions playing below in the street. Their cries reached me weakened and indistinct and, leaning my forehead against the cool glass, I looked over at the dark house where she lived. I may have stood there for an hour, seeing nothing but the brown-clad figure cast by my imagination, touched discreetly by the lamplight at the curved neck, at the hand upon the railings and at the border below the dress.

When I came downstairs again I found Mrs. Mercer sitting at the fire. She was an old garrulous woman, a pawnbroker's widow, who collected used stamps for some pious purpose. I had to endure the gossip of the tea-table. The meal was prolonged beyond an hour and still my uncle did not come. Mrs. Mercer stood up to go: she was sorry she couldn't wait any longer, but it was after eight o'clock and she did not like to be out late, as the night air was bad for her. When she had gone I began to walk up and down the room, clenching my fists. My aunt said:

"I'm afraid you may put off your bazaar for this night of Our Lord."

At nine o'clock I heard my uncle's latchkey in the halldoor. I heard him talking to himself and heard the hallstand rocking when it had received the weight of his overcoat. I could interpret these signs. When he was midway through his dinner I asked him to give me the money to go to the bazaar. He had forgotten.

"The people are in bed and after their first sleep now," he said.

I did not smile. My aunt said to him energetically:

"Can't you give him the money and let him go? You've kept him late enough as it is."

My uncle said he was very sorry he had forgotten. He said he believed in the old saying: "All work and no play makes Jack a dull boy." He asked me where I was going and, when I had told him a second time he asked me did I know *The Arab's Farewell to his Steed*. When I left the kitchen he was about to recite the opening lines of the piece to my aunt.

I held a florin tightly in my hand as I strode down Buckingham Street towards the station. The sight of the streets thronged with buyers and glaring with gas recalled to me the purpose of my journey. I took my seat in a third-class carriage of a deserted train. After an intolerable delay the train moved out of the station slowly. It crept onward among ruinous houses and over the twinkling river. At Westland Row Station a crowd of people pressed to the carriage doors; but the porters moved them back, saying that it was a special train for the bazaar. I remained alone in the bare carriage. In a few minutes the train drew up beside an improvised wooden platform. I passed out on to the road and saw by the lighted dial of a clock that it was ten minutes to ten. In front of me was a large building which displayed the magical name.

I could not find any sixpenny entrance and, fearing that the bazaar would be closed, I passed in quickly through a turnstile, handing a shilling to a weary-looking man. I found myself in a big hall girdled at half its height by a gallery. Nearly all the stalls were closed and the greater part of the hall was in darkness. I recognised a silence like that which pervades a church after a service. I walked into the centre of the bazaar timidly. A few people were gathered about the stalls which were still open. Before a curtain, over which the words *Café Chantant* were written in coloured lamps, two men were counting money on a salver. I listened to the fall of the coins.

Remembering with difficulty why I had come I went over to one of the stalls and examined porcelain vases and flowered tea-sets. At the door of the stall a young lady was talking and laughing with two young gentlemen. I remarked their English accents and listened vaguely to their conversation.

"O, I never said such a thing!"

"O, but you did!"

"O, but I didn't!"

"Didn't she say that?"

"Yes. I heard her."

"O, there's a . . . fib!"

Observing me the young lady came over and asked me did I wish to buy anything. The tone of her voice was not encouraging; she seemed to have spoken to me out of a sense of duty. I looked humbly at the great jars that stood like eastern guards at either side of the dark entrance to the stall and murmured:

simile

"No, thank you."

The young lady changed the position of one of the vases and went back to the two young men. They began to talk of the same subject. Once or twice the young lady glanced at me over her shoulder.

I lingered before her stall, though I knew my stay was useless, to make my interest in her wares seem the more real. Then I turned away slowly and walked down the middle of the bazaar. I allowed the two pennies to fall against the sixpence in my pocket. I heard a voice call from one end of the gallery that the light was out. The upper part of the hall was now completely dark.

Gazing up into the darkness I saw myself as a creature driven and derided by vanity; and my eyes burned with anguish and anger.

For Study and Discussion

1. About how old do you judge the narrator of the story to be?

2. Among the books he found in the dead priest's room, the narrator liked best the one with yellowed pages. What is the importance of this detail? How does it relate to other details in the story such as the narrator's imagining that he bore his "chalice safely through a throng of foes," the tears which spring to his eyes, his murmuring "O love! O love!" etc.?

3. Why is the narrator so determined to go to the bazaar? What delays him? What important discovery does he make about himself while there?

4. Analyze the entire story from the standpoint of Joyce's "epiphany" theory. What exactly is the "epiphany" in "Araby"? (See Joyce's statement in Section III.)

Bazaar
Vases
Eastern Enchantment

SHERWOOD ANDERSON

THE STRENGTH OF GOD

The Reverend Curtis Hartman was pastor of the Presbyterian Church of Winesburg, and had been in that position ten years. He was forty years old, and by his nature very silent and reticent. To preach, standing in the pulpit before the people, was always a hardship for him and from Wednesday morning until Saturday evening he thought of nothing but the two sermons that must be preached on Sunday. Early on Sunday morning he went into a little room called a study in the bell tower of the church and prayed. In his prayers there was one note that always predominated. "Give me strength and courage for Thy work, O Lord!" he plead, kneeling on the bare floor and bowing his head in the presence of the task that lay before him.

The Reverend Hartman was a tall man with a brown beard. His wife, a stout, nervous woman, was the daughter of a manufacturer of underwear at Cleveland, Ohio. The minister himself was rather a favorite in the town. The elders of the church liked him because he was quiet and unpretentious and Mrs. White, the banker's wife, thought him scholarly and refined.

The Presbyterian Church held itself somewhat aloof from the other churches of Winesburg. It was larger and more imposing and its minister was better paid. He even had a carriage of his own and on summer evenings sometimes drove about town with his wife. Through Main Street and up and down Buckeye Street he went, bowing gravely to the people, while his wife, afire with secret pride, looked at him out of the corners of her eyes and worried lest the horse become frightened and run away.

For a good many years after he came to Winesburg things went well with Curtis Hartman. He was not one to arouse keen enthusiasm among the worshippers in his church but on the other hand he made no

Originally published in *Masses*, August 1916. Reprinted here from *Winesburg, Ohio: A Group of Tales of Ohio Small Town Life* (New York: B. W. Huebsch, 1919). Copyright 1919 by B. W. Huebsch, Inc., 1947 by Eleanor Copenhaver Anderson. Reprinted by permission of The Viking Press, Inc.

enemies. In reality he was much in earnest and sometimes suffered prolonged periods of remorse because he could not go crying the word of God in the highways and byways of the town. He wondered if the flame of the spirit really burned in him and dreamed of a day when a strong sweet new current of power would come like a great wind into his voice and his soul and the people would tremble before the spirit of God made manifest in him. "I am a poor stick and that will never really happen to me," he mused dejectedly and then a patient smile lit up his features. "Oh well, I suppose I'm doing well enough," he added philosophically.

The room in the bell tower of the church, where on Sunday mornings the minister prayed for an increase in him of the power of God, had but one window. It was long and narrow and swung outward on a hinge like a door. On the window, made of little leaded panes, was a design showing the Christ laying his hand upon the head of a child. One Sunday morning in the summer as he sat by his desk in the room with a large Bible opened before him, and the sheets of his sermon scattered about, the minister was shocked to see, in the upper room of the house next door, a woman lying in her bed and smoking a cigarette while she read a book. Curtis Hartman went on tiptoe to the window and closed it softly. He was horror stricken at the thought of a woman smoking and trembled also to think that his eyes, just raised from the pages of the book of God, had looked upon the bare shoulders and white throat of a woman. With his brain in a whirl he went down into the pulpit and preached a long sermon without once thinking of his gestures or his voice. The sermon attracted unusual attention because of its power and clearness. "I wonder if she is listening, if my voice is carrying a message into her soul," he thought and began to hope that on future Sunday mornings he might be able to say words that would touch and awaken the woman apparently far gone in secret sin.

The house next door to the Presbyterian Church, through the windows of which the minister had seen the sight that had so upset him, was occupied by two women. Aunt Elizabeth Swift, a grey competent-looking widow with money in the Winesburg National Bank, lived there with her daughter Kate Swift, a school teacher. The school teacher was thirty years old and had a neat trim-looking figure. She had few friends and bore a reputation of having a sharp tongue. When he began to think about her, Curtis Hartman remembered that she had been to Europe and had lived for two years in New York City. "Perhaps after all her smoking means nothing," he thought. He began to remember that when he was a student in college and occasionally read novels, good, although somewhat worldly women, had smoked through the pages of a book that had once fallen into his hands. With a rush of new determination he worked on his sermons all through the week and forgot, in his zeal to reach the ears and the soul of this new listener, both his embarrassment in the pulpit and the necessity of prayer in the study on Sunday mornings.

Reverend Hartman's experience with women had been somewhat limited. He was the son of a wagon maker from Muncie, Indiana, and had worked his way through college. The daughter of the underwear manufacturer had boarded in a house where he lived during his school days and he had married her after a formal and prolonged courtship, carried on for the most part by the girl herself. On his marriage day the underwear manufacturer had given his daughter five thousand dollars and he promised to leave her at least twice that amount in his will. The minister had thought himself fortunate in marriage and had never permitted himself to think of other women. He did not want to think of other women. What he wanted was to do the work of God quietly and earnestly.

In the soul of the minister a struggle awoke. From wanting to reach the ears of Kate Swift, and through his sermons to delve into her soul, he began to want also to look again at the figure lying white and quiet in the bed. On a Sunday morning when he could not sleep because of his thoughts he arose and went to walk in the streets. When he had gone along Main Street almost to the old Richmond place he stopped and picking up a stone rushed off to the room in the bell tower. With the stone he broke out a corner of the window and then locked the door and sat down at the desk before the open Bible to wait. When the shade of the window to Kate Swift's room was raised he could see, through the hole, directly into her bed, but she was not there. She also had arisen and had gone for a walk and the hand that raised the shade was the hand of Aunt Elizabeth Swift.

The minister almost wept with joy at this deliverance from the carnal desire to "peep" and went back to his own house praising God. In an ill moment he forgot, however, to stop the hole in the window. The piece of glass broken out at the corner of the window just nipped off the bare heel of the boy standing motionless and looking with rapt eyes into the face of the Christ.

Curtis Hartman forgot his sermon on that Sunday morning. He talked to his congregation and in his talk said that it was a mistake for people to think of their minister as a man set aside and intended by nature to lead a blameless life. "Out of my own experience I know that we, who are the ministers of God's word, are beset by the same temptations that assail you," he declared. "I have been tempted and have surrendered to temptation. It is only the hand of God, placed beneath my head, that has raised me up. As he has raised me so also will he raise you. Do not despair. In your hour of sin raise your eyes to the skies and you will be again and again saved."

Resolutely the minister put the thoughts of the woman in the bed out of his mind and began to be something like a lover in the presence of his wife. One evening when they drove out together he turned the horse out of Buckeye Street and in the darkness on Gospel Hill, above Waterworks

Pond, put his arm about Sarah Hartman's waist. When he had eaten breakfast in the morning and was ready to retire to his study at the back of his house he went around the table and kissed his wife on the cheek. When thoughts of Kate Swift came into his head, he smiled and raised his eyes to the skies. "Intercede for me, Master," he muttered, "keep me in the narrow path intent on Thy work."

And now began the real struggle in the soul of the brown-bearded minister. By chance he discovered that Kate Swift was in the habit of lying in her bed in the evenings and reading a book. A lamp stood on a table by the side of the bed and the light streamed down upon her white shoulders and bare throat. On the evening when he made the discovery the minister sat at the desk in the study from nine until after eleven and when her light was put out stumbled out of the church to spend two more hours walking and praying in the streets. He did not want to kiss the shoulders and the throat of Kate Swift and had not allowed his mind to dwell on such thoughts. He did not know what he wanted. "I am God's child and he must save me from myself," he cried, in the darkness under the trees as he wandered in the streets. By a tree he stood and looked at the sky that was covered with hurrying clouds. He began to talk to God intimately and closely. "Please, Father, do not forget me. Give me power to go tomorrow and repair the hole in the window. Lift my eyes again to the skies. Stay with me, Thy servant, in his hour of need."

Up and down through the silent streets walked the minister and for days and weeks his soul was troubled. He could not understand the temptation that had come to him nor could he fathom the reason for its coming. In a way he began to blame God, saying to himself that he had tried to keep his feet in the true path and had not run about seeking sin. "Through my days as a young man and all through my life here I have gone quietly about my work," he declared. "Why now should I be tempted? What have I done that this burden should be laid on me?"

Three times during the early fall and winter of that year Curtis Hartman crept out of his house to the room in the bell tower to sit in the darkness looking at the figure of Kate Swift lying in her bed and later went to walk and pray in the streets. He could not understand himself. For weeks he would go along scarcely thinking of the school teacher and telling himself that he had conquered the carnal desire to look at her body. And then something would happen. As he sat in the study of his own house, hard at work on a sermon, he would become nervous and begin to walk up and down the room. "I will go out into the streets," he told himself and even as he let himself in at the church door he persistently denied to himself the cause of his being there. "I will not repair the hole in the window and I will train myself to come here at night and sit in the presence of this woman without raising my eyes. I will not be defeated in this thing. The Lord has devised this temptation as a test of my soul and I will grope my way out of darkness into the light of righteousness."

One night in January when it was bitter cold and snow lay deep on the streets of Winesburg Curtis Hartman paid his last visit to the room in the bell tower of the church. It was past nine o'clock when he left his own house and he set out so hurriedly that he forgot to put on his overshoes. In Main Street no one was abroad but Hop Higgins the night watchman and in the whole town no one was awake but the watchman and young George Willard, who sat in the office of the *Winesburg Eagle* trying to write a story. Along the street to the church went the minister, plowing through the drifts and thinking that this time he would utterly give way to sin. "I want to look at the woman and to think of kissing her shoulders and I am going to let myself think what I choose," he declared bitterly and tears came into his eyes. He began to think that he would get out of the ministry and try some other way of life. "I shall go to some city and get into business," he declared. "If my nature is such that I cannot resist sin, I shall give myself over to sin. At least I shall not be a hypocrite, preaching the word of God with my mind thinking of the shoulders and the neck of a woman who does not belong to me."

It was cold in the room of the bell tower of the church on that January night and almost as soon as he came into the room Curtis Hartman knew that if he stayed he would be ill. His feet were wet from tramping in the snow and there was no fire. In the room in the house next door Kate Swift had not yet appeared. With grim determination the man sat down to wait. Sitting in the chair and gripping the edge of the desk on which lay the Bible he stared into the darkness thinking the blackest thoughts of his life. He thought of his wife and for the moment almost hated her. "She has always been ashamed of passion and has cheated me," he thought. "Man has a right to expect living passion and beauty in a woman. He has no right to forget that he is an animal and in me there is something that is Greek. I will throw off the woman of my bosom and seek other women. I will besiege this school teacher. I will fly in the face of all men and if I am a creature of carnal lusts I will live then for my lusts."

The distracted man trembled from head to foot, partly from cold, partly from the struggle in which he was engaged. Hours passed and a fever assailed his body. His throat began to hurt and his teeth chattered. His feet on the study floor felt like two cakes of ice. Still he would not give up. "I will see this woman and will think the thoughts I have never dared to think," he told himself, gripping the edge of the desk and waiting.

Curtis Hartman came near dying from the effects of that night of waiting in the church, and also he found in the thing that happened what he took to be the way of life for him. On other evenings when he had waited he had not been able to see, through the little hole in the glass, any part of the school teacher's room except that occupied by her bed. In the darkness he had waited until the woman suddenly appeared sitting in the bed in her white night-robe. When the light was turned up she propped herself up among the pillows and read a book. Sometimes she smoked one of the cigarettes. Only her bare shoulders and throat were visible.

On the January night, after he had come near dying with cold and after his mind had two or three times actually slipped away into an odd land of fantasy so that he had by an exercise of will power to force himself back into consciousness, Kate Swift appeared. In the room next door a lamp was lighted and the waiting man stared into an empty bed. Then upon the bed before his eyes a naked woman threw herself. Lying face downward she wept and beat with her fists upon the pillow. With a final outburst of weeping she half arose, and in the presence of the man who had waited to look and to think thoughts the woman of sin began to pray. In the lamplight her figure, slim and strong, looked like the figure of the boy in the presence of the Christ on the leaded window.

Curtis Hartman never remembered how he got out of the church. With a cry he arose, dragging the heavy desk along the floor. The Bible fell, making a great clatter in the silence. When the light in the house next door went out he stumbled down the stairway and into the street. Along the street he went and ran in at the door of the *Winesburg Eagle*. To George Willard, who was tramping up and down in the office undergoing a struggle of his own, he began to talk half incoherently. "The ways of God are beyond human understanding," he cried, running in quickly and closing the door. He began to advance upon the young man, his eyes glowing and his voice ringing with fervor. "I have found the light," he cried. "After ten years in this town, God has manifested himself to me in the body of a woman." His voice dropped and he began to whisper. "I did not understand," he said. "What I took to be a trial of my soul was only a preparation for a new and more beautiful fervor of the spirit. God has appeared to me in the person of Kate Swift, the school teacher, kneeling naked on a bed. Do you know Kate Swift? Although she may not be aware of it, she is an instrument of God, bearing the message of truth."

Reverend Curtis Hartman turned and ran out of the office. At the door he stopped, and after looking up and down the deserted street, turned again to George Willard. "I am delivered. Have no fear." He held up a bleeding fist for the young man to see. "I smashed the glass of the window," he cried. "Now it will have to be wholly replaced. The strength of God was in me and I broke it with my fist."

For Study and Discussion

1. What evidence appears early in the story of the Reverend Hartman's devoutness and earnestness?

2. How does his first seeing the woman lying on the bed and smoking affect the sermon he preaches soon thereafter?

3. Trace, step by step, the seesaw struggle the minister has with himself. What is the climax of his struggle? How does he resolve it—at least momentarily?

4. What significant function in the story does the design on the stained-glass window serve?

5. Does this story fulfill Anderson's own prescription for a story that has "form, not plot" (pp. 70–73)? Would it satisfy Canby's demand for "free fiction" (pp. 51–60)? Explain.

6. Examine closely the words and sentences Anderson employs to characterize the Reverend Hartman in the opening pages. What are some of the distinctive features of this language? How does it suggest the presence of a narrative "voice," a teller reacting to the materials of the tale?

LUIGI PIRANDELLO

MISS HOLLOWAY'S GOAT

There is no doubt of it, Mr. Charles Trockley is always in the right. I
am even disposed to admit that Mr. Charles Trockley could not possibly
be in the wrong, Mr. Trockley and the right being the same thing. Every
gesture of Mr. Charles Trockley's, every glance, every word are rigid and
precise, well-weighed and safe in the assurance that everyone must
immediately recognize the fact it is impossible for Mr. Charles Trockley,
under any circumstances, in connection with any question that may arise
or any incident that may occur, to harbor the wrong opinion or assume
the wrong attitude.

He and I, by way of example, were born in the same year, the same
month and almost on the same day; he in England, I in Sicily. Today,
the fifteenth of June, he is forty-eight; I shall be forty-eight on the
twenty-eighth of June. Very well: how old shall we be, he on the
fifteenth and I on the twenty-eighth of next June? Mr. Charles Trockley
is not baffled by that; he does not hesitate for a moment, but maintains
with assurance that, on the fifteenth and the twenty-eighth, respectively,
of next June, he and I will be just one year older, that is, forty-nine.

Could one think of telling Mr. Charles Trockley that he is wrong?

The years do not go by the same for all. I, in one day, in one hour, may
acquire more damage than he in ten years of his rigorously disciplined
and well-preserved existence. I, owing to the deplorable state of my
mind, may live more than a lifetime in the course of a single year. My
body, weaker and less well-cared-for than his, has, assuredly, aged more
in the past forty-eight years than Mr. Trockley's will in seventy. This is
evidenced by the fact that, while his hair is silvery-white all over, his
lobster-like face displays not the slightest trace of a wrinkle, and he is
still youthfully spry enough to do a little fencing every morning.

But what does it all matter? All these idealistic and matter-of-fact
considerations are, for Mr. Charles Trockley, a waste of time and

Originally published under the title "Il Capretto Nero," in *Un Cavallo nella Luna*, 1918.
Reprinted here, in a translation by Samuel Putnam, from *Horse in the Moon* (New York:
E. P. Dutton and Co., 1932). Copyright 1932, 1960, by E. P. Dutton & Co., Inc., and used
with their permission.

without any reasonable foundation. For reason informs Mr. Charles Trockley that, as a matter of simple fact, on the fifteenth and the twenty-eighth, respectively, of next June, we shall be just one year older than we now are, that is, forty-nine.

Having told you this, I should now like for you to hear what happened to Mr. Charles Trockley recently; and then, ask yourselves whether or not he was in the wrong.

Last April, in following an Italian itinerary that had been mapped out for her by Baedeker, Miss Ethel Holloway, the very young and sprightly daughter of Sir W. H. Holloway, a very rich and highly respected English peer, arrived at Girgenti in Sicily to have a look at the marvelous ruins of the ancient Doric city. Enchanted with the landscape—a sea of white almond-blossoms—at this time of year, white almond-blossoms swaying to the warm zephyrs from off the African sea, she had decided to prolong her one-day stop-over at the big *Hôtel des Temples*, which, ideally situated, stands outside the very steep and squalid city, in the open country.

For twenty-two years, Mr. Charles Trockley has been English vice-consul at Girgenti, and every day for twenty-two years, at sundown, he has taken a walk, striding along at his usual nimble, even pace, from the hillside city down to the ruins of the Acragantian temples, standing airy and majestic upon the sharp ridge at the bottom of a slope, the Acraean hill, where stood of old the haughty marble town, hymned by Pindar as the fairest among the cities of men.

The ancients were in the habit of remarking that the Acragantinians ate every day as if they expected to die the day after, but that they built their houses as if they were never going to die. They eat precious little now; for there is much want in the city and over the countryside; and as for the historic town, after so many wars, after being seven times sacked and as often put to the torch, there no longer remains so much as a trace of its houses. In their place, there stands an almond and olive grove, for this reason known as the *Bosco della Cività*, or Civic Wood. And the long-maned ashen-hued olives, theoretically, run all the way up to the majestic temple columns, and appear to be uttering a requiem on behalf of these abandoned slopes. Under the ridge there flows, when times are propitious, the Acragantas, celebrated by Pindar as being rich in flocks and herds. A few straggling goats now cross the river's stony bed and climb the rocky ridge, to lie down and browse upon the scant pasturage to be found there, in the very shadow of the ancient Temple of Concord, which is still standing. The goat-herd, drowsy and stupid-looking as an Arab, likewise stretches out upon the crumbling steps of the pronaos, and contrives to extract a few lugubrious notes from his reed-flute.

For Mr. Charles Trockley, this invasion of the temple by goats has always seemed a horrible profanation; and times without number, he has lodged a formal complaint with the custodians of monuments, without ever obtaining any other response than an indulgent and philosophic smile or a shrug of the shoulders. Literally trembling with indignation at these smiles and these shoulder-shrugs, Mr. Charles Trockley upon numerous occasions has besought me to accompany him on his daily walk. Now, it often happens that, either in the Temple of Concord, or in the Temple of Hera Lacinia, further up, or in the other one, commonly known as the Temple of the Giants—it often happens that, in one of these places, Mr. Trockley falls in with parties of his countrymen who have come to visit the ruins. And he, thereupon, with that indignation which time cannot wither nor custom stale, calls upon those present to bear witness to the profanation that is being committed: those goats there, stretched out and browsing in the shadow of the temple columns. But not all the British visitors, it must be stated, are inclined to share Mr. Trockley's wrath. Many of them even feel that there is a certain poetic touch in those goats, reclining thus in these temples which have been left standing in an oblivion-wrapped solitude in the midst of the plain. And more than one of the visitors, to Mr. Trockley's great disgust, has gone so far as to remark what an altogether charming sight it was.

Particularly charmed, last April, was the very young and very sprightly Miss Ethel Holloway. And even while the indignant vice-consul was engaged in giving her certain valuable archaeologic information that was not as yet to be found either in Baedeker or in any other guidebook, Miss Holloway was so thoughtless as to turn her back suddenly on Mr. Trockley and run up to a pretty little black kid, only a few days old, which, amid the sprawling goats, was leaping about here and there, as if the dancing sunlight were full of enticing gnats; and then, after these violent exertions, it would stand there as if appalled at what it had done; it was as if every slightest sound, every breath of air, every tiniest shadow in the, for it, as yet uncertain spectacle of life were a cause for fear and trembling.

On that particular day, I was with Mr. Trockley, and I was greatly pleased to see the delight which the little English miss manifested; it was charming to see her fall in love at first sight like that with a little black kid—she was determined to buy it at any cost; but I was also pained to see how poor Mr. Trockley suffered.

"Buy that kid?"

"Yes, yes! buy it, at once, at once!"

The little miss was trembling all over, just like her little black pet; she doubtless did not so much as suspect that she could not have offered Mr. Trockley a greater insult; how was she to know how long and how ferociously he had hated those beasts? It was in vain that Mr. Trockley endeavored to dissuade her, to bring her to see all the trouble that she would have as a result of her purchase. He had to give in, finally, and, out of respect for her father, had to go up to the half-savage goat-herd to dicker over the price of the animal.

Miss Ethel Holloway, having taken out the money from her purse, then informed Mr. Trockley that she wanted the kid turned over to the manager of the *Hôtel des Temples*, and that, as soon as she was back in London, she would telegraph, so that the darling little thing, all expenses paid, could be sent to her at once; and she went back to the hotel in a carriage, with the kid squirming and bleating under her arms.

Against the light of the setting sun—a sun that was going down amid a fantastic fretwork of clouds, flaming above a sea that lay spread out beneath like a boundless golden mirror—I had a glimpse, within that black carriage, of a young blond head, as the slender and ardent Miss Holloway disappeared in a nimbus of gleaming light. I beheld all this; and to me, it was like a dream. And then, I understood that, being so far from her own country and from the accustomed sights and surroundings of her daily life, for her thus to have conceived such a passion for a little black kid could mean but one thing: it must mean that she was without a particle of that solid sense which so gravely governed the acts, thoughts, words, and deeds of Mr. Charles Trockley.

And what, then, did Miss Ethel Holloway have in place of solid sense?

Nothing but gross stupidity, maintained Mr. Charles Trockley, with a rage which it was all he could do to control, a rage that becomes something like a downright affliction with a man like him, who is usually so well-contained.

The reasons for Mr. Trockley's wrath are to be found in the events that followed the purchase of that black kid.

Miss Ethel Holloway left Girgenti the next day. From Sicily, she was bound for Greece, from Greece for Egypt, from Egypt for India.

It is in the nature of a miracle that, having returned safe and sound to London along about the end of November, she should have remembered, after eight months of travel and all the experiences which she surely must have had in the course of so long a trip, the little black kid which she had bought one far-away day, amid the ruins of the Acragantian temples in Sicily. No sooner was she back than she wrote, as she had promised, to Mr. Charles Trockley.

The *Hôtel des Temples* is closed every year from the middle of June to the first of November. The manager, to whom Miss Holloway had entrusted the kid, when he came to leave in the middle of June, had turned it over to the caretaker of the inn, but without any directions as to what was to be done with it; for he had been fed up more than once with all the trouble that the beast had given him. The caretaker waited from day to day for the vice-consul, Mr. Charles Trockley, who, the manager had told him, was to come and get the kid and send it on to England; but when no one showed up, he decided, by way of getting rid of the animal, to turn it over to the same goat-herd who had sold it to Miss Holloway, promising him that he could have it as a gift in case its owner, as seemed likely, was not going to send for it; otherwise, if the vice-consul called for it, the goat-herd was to be reimbursed for its care and keep.

When, after nearly eight months, Miss Holloway's letter arrived from London, the manager of the *Hôtel des Temples*, the caretaker and the goat-herd were all vastly embarrassed; the manager for having entrusted the kid to the caretaker, the caretaker for having turned it over to the goat-herd, and the goat-herd for having in turn given it to another goat-herd with the same promises that had been made to him. And now, nobody knew where this other goat-herd was. They hunted for him for more than a month. At last, one fine day, Mr. Charles Trockley, seated in the vice-consul's office at Girgenti, looked up and saw before him a big overgrown horned beast, very smelly and covered with a scraggly manure-coated, mud-laden fleece of faded reddish hue; the animal, with deep, raucous, quivering bleats, stood there with its head down threateningly, as if demanding what was wanted of it, now that, against its will, they had brought it so far from its accustomed haunts.

But Mr. Charles Trockley was not in the least put out by his unexpected caller; not in the least; not he. He did not waste a moment, but proceeded to calculate rapidly the time that had elapsed between the first of April and the last of December; and he concluded, reasonably enough, that the pretty little black kid could very well be the filthy animal that stood before him. And without the faintest hesitation, he at once sent word to Miss Holloway that he was shipping her the kid, from Porto Empedocle, with the next home-faring British merchantman. And he put around the neck of this horrible beast a tag with Miss Ethel Holloway's address, and ordered it taken down to the port. There, he himself, at great risk to his dignity, led the restive animal by a rope down the quay, followed by a crowd of urchins; he saw it safely aboard the departing steamer, and then returned to Girgenti, quite sure that he had scrupulously fulfilled his duty, not by catering to Miss Holloway's deplorable whim, but by showing the proper respect to her father.

Yesterday, Mr. Charles Trockley came to see me, in such a condition of mind and body that, very much alarmed, I ran up to help him to a chair and had them bring him a glass of water.

"For the love of God, Mr. Trockley, what's happened?"

Still speechless, Mr. Trockley drew from his pocket a letter and handed it to me. It was a letter from Sir W. H. Holloway, British peer, and contained a string of vigorous insults, occasioned by the affront which Mr. Trockley had offered to Sir W. H. Holloway's daughter, Miss Ethel, by sending her that filthy, awful beast.

And this was the thanks that poor Mr. Trockley had for all his trouble.

But what was he to have expected of that utterly stupid Miss Holloway? Did she by any chance think that, after nearly eleven months, she would see arriving at London the same little black kid which she had beheld so timidly leaping about in the sun amid the columns of the ancient Greek Temple in Sicily? Was it possible? It was too much for Mr. Charles Trockley.

Perceiving the state he was in, I did my best to comfort him, assuring him that he was quite right, that Miss Ethel Holloway must be not only an extremely capricious, but an extremely unreasonable creature as well.

"Stupid! Stupid! Stupid!"

"Let us rather say 'unreasonable,' my dear Mr. Trockley. And yet, look, my friend" (I took the liberty of adding) "she left here last April with the pretty picture of that little black kid in her mind's eye; and—let us be fair to her—she could not well have foreseen (however irrational it may appear) that you were suddenly going to confront her with the very image of reason in the form of that monstrous animal you sent her."

"Well, then," and Mr. Trockley bristled up, "what should you say I ought to have done?"

"I cannot say, Mr. Trockley," I replied, hastily and in some embarrassment; "I should not like to appear as unreasonable as that little miss back there in your country; but in your case, Mr. Trockley, do you want to know what I should have done? Either I should have sent word to Miss Ethel Holloway that her pretty little black kid had died of a broken heart; or else, I should have bought another pretty little black kid, very, very small and white, exactly like the one she purchased last April; and I should have sent it to her, quite safe in the assurance that Miss Ethel Holloway would never once give a thought to the fact that her little pet could not possibly be the same after eleven months. All this, my friend, naturally implies, as you see, a recognition of the fact that Miss Ethel Holloway is utterly unreasonable, and that you are absolutely in the right, as always, my dear Mr. Trockley."

For Study and Discussion

1. What kind of person is Mr. Charles Trockley? How does he differ in outlook from the narrator of the story?   The Monarchs

2. Why does the narrator describe the grown-up goat Mr. Trockley sends to Miss Holloway as "the very image of reason"?

3. Was it unreasonable of Miss Holloway's father to react unfavorably to receiving the goat? Or was it unreasonable of Mr. Trockley to send it? Would the narrator's suggestion of substituting another young kid for the goat have been the reasonable solution?

4. What is the meaning of the narrator's comment in the fourth paragraph: "The years do not go by the same for all"?

5. Approximately eleven calendar months pass between Miss Holloway's purchase of the kid and Mr. Trockley's sending the grown animal to England. Relatively, how much time has passed for (1) Miss Holloway, (2) Mr. Trockley, (3) the goat, and (4) the narrator?

FRANZ KAFKA

A HUNGER ARTIST

During these last decades the interest in professional fasting has markedly diminished. It used to pay very well to stage such great performances under one's own management, but today that is quite impossible. We live in a different world now. At one time the whole town took a lively interest in the hunger artist; from day to day of his fast the excitement mounted; everybody wanted to see him at least once a day; there were people who bought season tickets for the last few days and sat from morning till night in front of his small barred cage; even in the nighttime there were visiting hours, when the whole effect was heightened by torch flares; on fine days the cage was set out in the open air, and then it was the children's special treat to see the hunger artist; for their elders he was often just a joke that happened to be in fashion, but the children stood open-mouthed, holding each other's hands for greater security, marveling at him as he sat there pallid in black tights, with his ribs sticking out so prominently, not even on a seat but down among straw on the ground, sometimes giving a courteous nod, answering questions with a constrained smile, or perhaps stretching an arm through the bars so that one might feel how thin it was, and then again withdrawing deep into himself, paying no attention to anyone or anything, not even to the all-important striking of the clock that was the only piece of furniture in his cage, but merely staring into vacancy with half-shut eyes, now and then taking a sip from a tiny glass of water to moisten his lips.

Besides casual onlookers there were also relays of permanent watchers selected by the public, usually butchers, strangely enough, and it was their task to watch the hunger artist day and night, three of them at a time, in case he should have some secret recourse to nourishment. This was nothing but a formality, instituted to reassure the masses, for the initiates knew well enough that during his fast the artist would never in

Originally published under the title "Ein Hungerkünstler," in *In der Strafkolonie (The Penal Colony)* 1919. Reprinted here, in a translation by Willa and Edwin Muir, from *The Penal Colony* (New York: Schocken Books, Inc., 1948). Copyright 1948 by Schocken Books, Inc. Reprinted with their permission.

any circumstances, not even under forcible compulsion, swallow the smallest morsel of food; the honor of his profession forbade it. Not every watcher, of course, was capable of understanding this, there were often groups of night watchers who were very lax in carrying out their duties and deliberately huddled together in a retired corner to play cards with great absorption, obviously intending to give the hunger artist the chance of a little refreshment, which they supposed he could draw from some private hoard. Nothing annoyed the artist more than such watchers; they made him miserable; they made his fast seem unendurable; sometimes he mastered his feebleness sufficiently to sing during their watch for as long as he could keep going, to show them how unjust their suspicions were. But that was of little use; they only wondered at his cleverness in being able to fill his mouth even while singing. Much more to his taste were the watchers who sat close up to the bars, who were not content with the dim night lighting of the hall but focused him in the full glare of the electric pocket torch given them by the impresario. The harsh light did not trouble him at all, in any case he could never sleep properly, and he could always drowse a little, whatever the light, at any hour, even when the hall was thronged with noisy onlookers. He was quite happy at the prospect of spending a sleepless night with such watchers; he was ready to exchange jokes with them, to tell them stories out of his nomadic life, anything at all to keep them awake and demonstrate to them again that he had no eatables in his cage and that he was fasting as not one of them could fast. But his happiest moment was when the morning came and an enormous breakfast was brought them, at his expense, on which they flung themselves with the keen appetite of healthy men after a weary night of wakefulness. Of course there were people who argued that this breakfast was an unfair attempt to bribe the watchers, but that was going rather too far, and when they were invited to take on a night's vigil without a breakfast, merely for the sake of the cause, they made themselves scarce, although they stuck stubbornly to their suspicions.

Such suspicions, anyhow, were a necessary accompaniment to the profession of fasting. No one could possibly watch the hunger artist continuously, day and night, and so no one could produce first-hand evidence that the fast had really been rigorous and continuous; only the artist himself could know that, he was therefore bound to be the sole completely satisfied spectator of his own fast. Yet for other reasons he was never satisfied; it was not perhaps mere fasting that had brought him to such skeleton thinness that many people had regretfully to keep away from his exhibitions, because the sight of him was too much for them, perhaps it was dissatisfaction with himself that had worn him down. For he alone knew, what no other initiate knew, how easy it was to fast. It was the easiest thing in the world. He made no secret of this, yet people did not believe him, at the best they set him down as modest, most of them, however, thought he was out for publicity or else was some kind of cheat who found it easy to fast because he had discovered a way of making it easy, and then had the impudence to admit the fact, more or less. He had to put up with all that, and in the course of time had got used to it, but his inner dissatisfaction always rankled, and never yet, after any term of fasting—this must be granted to his credit—had he left the cage of his own free will. The longest period of fasting was fixed by his impresario at forty days, beyond that term he was not allowed to go, not even in great cities, and there was good reason for it, too. Experience had proved that for about forty days the interest of the public could be stimulated by a steadily increasing pressure of advertisement, but after that the town began to lose interest, sympathetic support began notably to fall off; there were of course local variations as between one town and another or one country and another, but as a general rule forty days marked the limit. So on the fortieth day the flower-bedecked cage was opened, enthusiastic spectators filled the hall, a military band played, two doctors entered the cage to measure the results of the fast, which were announced through a megaphone, and finally two young ladies appeared, blissful at having been selected for the honor, to help the hunger artist down the few steps leading to a small table on which was spread a carefully chosen invalid repast. And at this very moment the artist always turned stubborn. True, he would entrust his bony arms to the outstretched helping hands of the ladies bending over him, but stand up he would not. Why stop fasting at this particular moment, after forty days of it? He had held out for a long time, an illimitably long time; why stop now, when he was in his best fasting form, or rather, not yet quite in his best fasting form? Why should he be cheated of the fame he would get for fasting longer, for being not only the record hunger artist of all time, which presumably he was already, but for beating his own record by a performance beyond human imagination, since he felt that there were no limits to his capacity for fasting? His public pretended to admire him so much, why should it have so little patience with him; if he could endure fasting longer, why shouldn't the public endure it? Besides, he was tired, he was comfortable sitting in the straw, and now he was supposed to lift himself to his full height and go down to a meal the very thought of which gave him a nausea that only the presence of the ladies kept him from betraying, and even that with an effort. And he looked up into the eyes of the ladies who were apparently so friendly and in reality so cruel, and shook his head, which felt too heavy on its strengthless neck. But then there happened yet again what always happened. The impresario came forward, without a word—for the band made speech impossible—lifted his arms in the air above the artist, as if inviting Heaven to look down upon its creature here in the straw, this suffering martyr, which indeed he was, although in quite another sense; grasped him round the emaciated waist, with exaggerated caution, so that the frail condition he was in might be appreciated; and committed him to the care of the blenching ladies, not without secretly giving him a shaking so that his legs and body tottered and swayed. The artist now submitted completely; his head lolled on his breast as if it had landed there by chance; his body was hollowed out; his legs in a spasm of self-preservation clung close to each other at the knees, yet scraped on the ground as if it were not really solid ground, as if they were only trying to find solid ground; and the whole weight of his body, a featherweight after all, relapsed onto one of the ladies, who, looking round for help and panting a little—this post of honor was not at all what she had expected it to be—first stretched her neck as far as she could to keep her face at least free from contact with the artist, then finding this impossible, and her more fortunate companion not coming to her aid but merely holding extended on her own trembling hand the little bunch of knucklebones that was the artist's, to the great delight of the spectators burst into tears and had to be replaced by an attendant who had long been stationed in readiness. Then came the food, a little of which the impresario managed to get between the artist's lips, while he sat in a kind of half-fainting trance, to the accompaniment of cheerful patter designed to distract the public's attention from the artist's condition; after that, a toast was drunk to the public, supposedly prompted by a whisper from the artist in the impresario's ear; the band confirmed it with a mighty flourish, the spectators melted away, and no one had any cause to be dissatisfied with the proceedings, no one except the hunger artist himself, he only, as always.

So he lived for many years, with small regular intervals of recuperation, in visible glory, honored by the world, yet in spite of that troubled in spirit, and all the more troubled because no one would take his trouble seriously. What comfort could he possibly need? What more could he possibly wish for? And if some good-natured person, feeling sorry for him, tried to console him by pointing out that his melancholy was probably caused by fasting, it could happen, especially when he had been fasting for some time, that he reacted with an outburst of fury and to the general alarm began to shake the bars of his cage like a wild animal. Yet the impresario had a way of punishing these outbreaks which he rather enjoyed putting into operation. He would apologize publicly for the artist's behavior, which was only to be excused, he admitted, because of the irritability caused by fasting; a condition hardly to be understood by well-fed people; then by natural transition he went on to mention the artist's equally incomprehensible boast that he could fast for much longer than he was doing; he praised the high ambition, the good will, the great self-denial undoubtedly implicit in such a statement; and then quite simply countered it by bringing out photographs, which were also on sale to the public, showing the artist on the fortieth day of a fast lying in bed almost dead from exhaustion. This perversion of the truth, familiar to the artist though it was, always unnerved him afresh and proved too much for him. What was a consequence of the premature ending of his fast was here presented as the cause of it! To fight against this lack of understanding, against a whole world of nonunderstanding, was impossible. Time and again in good faith he stood by the bars listening to the impresario, but as soon as the photographs appeared he always let go and sank with a groan back on to his straw, and the reassured public could once more come close and gaze at him.

A few years later when the witnesses of such scenes called them to mind, they often failed to understand themselves at all. For meanwhile the aforementioned change in public interest had set in; it seemed to happen almost overnight; there may have been profound causes for it, but who was going to bother about that; at any rate the pampered hunger artist suddenly found himself deserted one fine day by the amusement seekers, who went streaming past him to other more favored attractions. For the last time the impresario hurried him over half Europe to discover whether the old interest might still survive here and there; all in vain; everywhere, as if by secret agreement, a positive revulsion from professional fasting was in evidence. Of course it could not really have sprung up so suddenly as all that, and many premonitory symptoms which had not been sufficiently remarked or suppressed during the rush and glitter of success now came retrospectively to mind, but it was now too late to take any counter-measures. Fasting would surely come into fashion again at some future date, yet that was no comfort for those living in the present. What, then, was the hunger artist to do? He had been applauded by thousands in his time and could hardly come down to showing himself in a street booth at village fairs, and as for adopting another profession, he was not only too old for that but too fanatically devoted to fasting. So he took leave of the impresario, his partner in an unparalleled career, and hired himself to a large circus; in order to spare his own feelings he avoided reading the conditions of his contract.

A large circus with its enormous traffic in replacing and recruiting men, animals and apparatus can always find a use for people at any time, even for a hunger artist, provided of course that he does not ask too much, and in this particular case anyhow it was not only the artist who was taken on but his famous and long-known name as well, indeed considering the peculiar nature of his performance, which was not impaired by advancing age, it could not be objected that here was an artist past his prime, no longer at the height of his professional skill, seeking a refuge in some quiet corner of a circus, on the contrary, the hunger artist averred that he could fast as well as ever, which was entirely credible, he even alleged that if he were allowed to fast as he liked, and this was at once promised him without more ado, he could astound the world by establishing a record never yet achieved, a statement which certainly provoked a smile among the other professionals, since it left out of account the change in public opinion, which the hunger artist in his zeal conveniently forgot.

He had not, however, actually lost his sense of the real situation and took it as a matter of course that he and his cage should be stationed, not in the middle of the ring as a main attraction, but outside, near the animal cages, on a site that was after all easily accessible. Large and gaily painted placards made a frame for the cage and announced what was to be seen inside it. When the public came thronging out in the intervals to see the animals, they could hardly avoid passing the hunger artist's cage and stopping there for a moment, perhaps they might even have stayed longer had not those pressing behind them in the narrow gangway, who did not understand why they should be held up on their way towards the excitements of the menagerie, made it impossible for anyone to stand gazing quietly for any length of time. And that was the reason why the hunger artist, who had of course been looking forward to these visiting hours as the main achievement of his life, began instead to shrink from them. At first he could hardly wait for the intervals; it was exhilarating to watch the crowds come streaming his way, until only too soon—not even the most obstinate self-deception, clung to almost consciously, could hold out against the fact—the conviction was borne in upon him that these people, most of them, to judge from their actions, again and again, without exception, were all on their way to the menagerie. And the first sight of them from the distance remained the best. For when they reached his cage he was at once deafened by the storm of shouting and abuse that arose from the two contending factions, which renewed themselves continuously, of those who wanted to stop and stare at him—he soon began to dislike them more than the others—not out of real interest but only out of obstinate self-assertiveness, and those who wanted to go straight on to the animals. When the first great rush was past, the stragglers came along, and these, whom nothing could have prevented from stopping to look at him as long as they had breath, raced past with long strides, hardly even glancing at him, in their haste to get to the menagerie in time. And all too rarely did it happen that he had a stroke of luck, when some father of a family fetched up before him with his children, pointed a finger at the hunger artist and explained at length what the phenomenon meant, telling stories of earlier years when he himself had watched similar but much more thrilling performances, and the children, still rather uncomprehending, since neither inside nor outside school had they been sufficiently prepared for this lesson—what did they care about fasting?—yet showed by the brightness of their intent eyes that new and better times might be coming. Perhaps, said the hunger artist to himself many a time, things would be a little better if his cage were set not quite so near the menagerie. That made it too easy for people to make their choice, to say nothing of what he suffered from the stench of the menagerie, the animals' restlessness by night, the carrying past of raw lumps of flesh for the beasts of prey, the roaring at feeding times, which depressed him continually. But he did not dare to lodge a complaint with the management; after all, he had the animals to thank for the troops of people who passed his cage, among whom there might always be one here and there to take an interest in him, and who could tell where they might seclude him if he called attention to his existence and thereby to the fact that, strictly speaking, he was only an impediment on the way to the menagerie.

A small impediment, to be sure, one that grew steadily less. People grew familiar with the strange idea that they could be expected, in times like these, to take an interest in a hunger artist, and with this familiarity the verdict went out against him. He might fast as much as he could and he did so; but nothing could save him now, people passed him by. Just try to explain to anyone the art of fasting! Anyone who has no feeling for it cannot be made to understand it. The fine placards grew dirty and illegible, they were torn down; the little notice board telling the number of fast days achieved, which at first was changed carefully every day, had long stayed at the same figure, for after the first few weeks even this small task seemed pointless to the staff; and so the artist simply fasted on and on, as he had once dreamed of doing, and it was no trouble to him, just as he had always foretold, but no one counted the days, no one, not even the artist himself, knew what records he was already breaking, and his heart grew heavy. And when once in a time some leisurely passer-by stopped, made merry over the old figure on the board and spoke of swindling, that was in its way the stupidest lie ever invented by indifference and inborn malice, since it was not the hunger artist who was cheating, he was working honestly, but the world was cheating him of his reward.

Many more days went by, however, and that too came to an end. An overseer's eye fell on the cage one day and he asked the attendants why this perfectly good cage should be left standing there unused with dirty straw inside it; nobody knew, until one man, helped out by the notice board, remembered about the hunger artist. They poked into the straw with sticks and found him in it. "Are you still fasting?" asked the overseer, "when on earth do you mean to stop?" "Forgive me, everybody," whispered the hunger artist; only the overseer, who had his ear to the bars, understood him. "Of course," said the overseer, and tapped his forehead with a finger to let the attendants know what state the man was in, "we forgive you." "I always wanted you to admire my fasting," said the hunger artist. "We do admire it," said the overseer, affably. "But you shouldn't admire it," said the hunger artist. "Well then we don't admire it," said the overseer, "but why shouldn't we admire it?" "Because I have to fast, I can't help it," said the hunger artist. "What a fellow you are," said the overseer, "and why can't you help it?" "Because," said the hunger artist, lifting his head a little and speaking, with his lips pursed, as if for a kiss, right into the overseer's ear, so that no syllable might be lost, "because I couldn't find the food I liked. If I had found it, believe me, I should have made no fuss and stuffed myself like you or anyone else." These were his last words, but in his dimming eyes remained the firm though no longer proud persuasion that he was still continuing to fast.

"Well, clear this out now!" said the overseer, and they buried the hunger artist, straw and all. Into the cage they put a young panther. Even the most insensitive felt it refreshing to see this wild creature leaping around that cage that had so long been dreary. The panther was all right. The food he liked was brought him without hesitation by the attendants; he seemed not even to miss his freedom; his noble body, furnished almost to the bursting point with all that it needed, seemed to carry freedom around with it too; somewhere in his jaws it seemed to lurk; and the joy of life streamed with such ardent passion from his throat that for the onlookers it was not easy to stand the shock of it. But they braced themselves, crowded round the cage, and did not want ever to move away.

For Study and Discussion

1. On the literal level, what events actually occur in this story?

2. Of what does the hunger artist think the world is cheating him? How does his objective in fasting differ from the objective of a hunger striker—say, for example, that of the late Gandhi of India?

3. What is the meaning of the word *impresario?* What specific functions does the impresario in this story perform?

4. For what reason does the hunger artist abandon independent exhibitions, dismiss the impresario, and join a circus?

5. Toward the end of the story, why does the artist ask the circus overseer and attendants to "Forgive me, everybody"?

6. What qualities does the young panther have? How do these dramatically contrast with those of the dead artist? What do you think the panther stands for? Why do the spectators, who were indifferent toward the artist, find the panther irresistible?

7. As with other Kafka stories, "A Hunger Artist" has a number of possible interpretations. The most frequently mentioned is that the fate of the artist in the story symbolically represents the shift in the modern world from spiritual to physical or material values. What evidence do you find in the story to support this interpretation? Can you offer and support an entirely different interpretation?

8. Does the fact that this story can be interpreted in different ways detract from, or add to, its artistic merit? Compare it in this respect with Hawthorne's "The Birthmark" or Mansfield's "The Fly."

Free
"serious"

KATHERINE MANSFIELD's

attitude of the characters is symbolic
of death, & expectations of life.
is a victim of subjected cruelty of one who
is troubled & frustrated.

THE FLY

"Y'are very snug in here," piped old Mr. Woodifield, and he peered out of the great, green leather armchair by his friend the boss's desk as a baby peers out of its pram. His talk was over; it was time for him to be off. But he did not want to go. Since he had retired, since his . . . stroke, the wife and girls kept him boxed up in the house every day of the week except Tuesday. On Tuesday he was dressed up and brushed and allowed to cut back to the City for the day. Though what he did there the wife and girls couldn't imagine. Made a nuisance of himself to his friends, they supposed. . . . Well, perhaps so. All the same, we cling to our last pleasures as the tree clings to its last leaves. So there sat old Woodifield, smoking a cigar and staring almost greedily at the boss, who rolled in his office chair, stout, rosy, five years older than he, and still going strong, still at the helm. It did one good to see him.

Wistfully, admiringly, the old voice added, "It's snug in here, upon my word!"

"Yes, it's comfortable enough," agreed the boss, and he flipped the *Financial Times* with a paperknife. As a matter of fact he was proud of his room; he liked to have it admired, especially by old Woodifield. It gave him a feeling of deep, solid satisfaction to be planted there in the midst of it in full view of that frail old figure in the muffler.

"I've had it done up lately," he explained, as he had explained for the past—how many?—weeks. "New carpet," and he pointed to the bright red carpet with a pattern of large white rings. "New furniture," and he nodded towards the massive bookcase and the table with legs like twisted treacle. "Electric heating!" He waved almost exultantly towards the five transparent, pearly sausages glowing so softly in the tilted copper pan.

But he did not draw old Woodifield's attention to the photograph over the table of a grave-looking boy in uniform standing in one of those

---

Originally published in the *Nation* (London), March 18, 1922. Reprinted here from *The Short Stories of Katherine Mansfield* (New York: Alfred A. Knopf, Inc., 1937), by permission of the publisher and The Society of Authors as the literary representative of the Estate of Katherine Mansfield. Copyright 1922 and renewed 1950 by J. Middleton Murry.

spectral photographers' parks with photographers' storm-clouds behind him. It was not new. It had been there for over six years.

"There was something I wanted to tell you," said old Woodifield, and his eyes grew dim remembering. "Now what was it? I had it in my mind when I started out this morning." His hands began to tremble, and patches of red showed above his beard.

Poor old chap, he's on his last pins, thought the boss. And, feeling kindly, he winked at the old man, and said jokingly, "I tell you what. I've got a little drop of something here that'll do you good before you go out into the cold again. It's beautiful stuff. It wouldn't hurt a child." He took a key off his watch-chain, unlocked a cupboard below his desk, and drew forth a dark, squat bottle. "That's the medicine," said he. "And the man from whom I got it told me on the strict Q.T. it came from the cellars at Windsor Cassel."

Old Woodifield's mouth fell open at the sight. He couldn't have looked more surprised if the boss had produced a rabbit.

"It's whisky, ain't it?" he piped, feebly.

The boss turned the bottle and lovingly showed him the label. Whisky it was.

"D'you know," said he, peering up at the boss wonderingly, "they won't let me touch it at home." And he looked as though he was going to cry.

"Ah, that's where we know a bit more than the ladies," cried the boss, swooping across for two tumblers that stood on the table with the water-bottle, and pouring a generous finger into each. "Drink it down. It'll do you good. And don't put any water with it. It's sacrilege to tamper with stuff like this. Ah!" He tossed off his, pulled out his handkerchief, hastily wiped his moustaches, and cocked an eye at old Woodifield, who was rolling his in his chaps.

The old man swallowed, was silent a moment, and then said faintly, "It's nutty!"

But it warmed him; it crept into his chill old brain—he remembered.

"That was it," he said, heaving himself out of his chair. "I thought you'd like to know. The girls were in Belgium last week having a look at poor Reggie's grave, and they happened to come across your boy's. They're quite near each other, it seems."

Old Woodifield paused, but the boss made no reply. Only a quiver in his eyelids showed that he heard.

"The girls were delighted with the way the place is kept," piped the old voice. "Beautifully looked after. Couldn't be better if they were at home. You've not been across, have yer?"

"No, no!" For various reasons the boss had not been across.

"There's miles of it," quavered old Woodifield, "and it's all as neat as a garden. Flowers growing on all the graves. Nice broad paths." It was plain from his voice how much he liked a nice broad path.

The pause came again. Then the old man brightened wonderfully.

"D'you know what the hotel made the girls pay for a pot of jam?" he piped. "Ten francs! Robbery, I call it. It was a little pot, so Gertrude says, no bigger than a half-crown. And she hadn't taken more than a spoonful when they charged her ten francs. Gertrude brought the pot away with her to teach 'em a lesson. Quite right, too; it's trading on our feelings. They think because we're over there having a look around we're ready to pay anything. That's what it is." And he turned towards the door.

"Quite right, quite right!" cried the boss, though what was quite right he hadn't the least idea. He came around by his desk, followed the shuffling footsteps to the door, and saw the old fellow out. Woodifield was gone.

For a long moment the boss stayed, staring at nothing, while the grey-haired office messenger, watching him, dodged in and out of his cubbyhole like a dog that expects to be taken for a run. Then: "I'll see nobody for half an hour, Macey," said the boss. "Understand? Nobody at all."

"Very good, sir."

The door shut, the firm heavy steps recrossed the bright carpet, the fat body plumped down in the spring chair, and leaning forward, the boss covered his face with his hands. He wanted, he intended, he had arranged to weep. . . .

It had been a terrible shock to him when old Woodifield sprang that remark upon him about the boy's grave. It was exactly as though the earth had opened and he had seen the boy lying there with Woodifield's girls staring down at him. For it was strange. Although over six years had passed away, the boss never thought of the boy except as lying unchanged, unblemished in his uniform, asleep for ever. "My son!" groaned the boss. But no tears came yet. In the past, in the first months and even years after the boy's death, he had only to say those words to be overcome by such grief that nothing short of a violent fit of weeping could relieve him. Time, he had declared then, he had told everybody, could make no difference. Other men perhaps might recover, might live their loss down, but not he. How was it possible? His boy was an only son. Ever since his birth the boss had worked at building up this business for him; it had no other meaning if it was not for the boy. Life itself had come to have no other meaning. How on earth could he have slaved, denied himself, kept going all those years without the promise for ever before him of the boy's stepping into his shoes and carrying on where he left off?

And that promise had been so near being fulfilled. The boy had been in the office learning the ropes for a year before the war. Every morning they had started off together; they had come back by the same train. And what congratulations he had received as the boy's father! No wonder; he had taken to it marvellously. As to his popularity with the staff, every *unnatural sorrow)*

man jack of them down to old Macey couldn't make enough of the boy. And he wasn't in the least spoilt. No, he was just his bright, natural self, with the right word for everybody, with that boyish look and his habit of saying, "Simply splendid!"

But all that was over and done with as though it never had been. The day had come when Macey had handed him the telegram that brought the whole place crashing about his head. "Deeply regret to inform you . . ." And he had left the office a broken man, with his life in ruins.

Six years ago, six years. . . . How quickly time passed! It might have happened yesterday. The boss took his hands from his face; he was puzzled. Something seemed to be wrong with him. He wasn't feeling as he wanted to feel. He decided to get up and have a look at the boy's photograph. But it wasn't a favorite photograph of his; the expression was unnatural. It was cold, even stern-looking. The boy had never looked like that.

At that moment the boss noticed that a fly had fallen into his broad inkpot, and was trying feebly but desperately to clamber out again. Help! help! said those struggling legs. But the sides of the inkpot were wet and slippery; it fell back again and began to swim. The boss took up a pen, picked the fly out of the ink, and shook it on to a piece of blotting-paper. For a fraction of a second it lay still on the dark patch that oozed round it. Then the front legs waved, took hold, and, pulling its small sodden body up it began the immense task of cleaning the ink from its wings. Over and under, over and under, went a leg along a wing, as the stone goes over and under the scythe. Then there was a pause, while the fly, seeming to stand on the tips of its toes, tried to expand first one wing and then the other. It succeeded at last, and, sitting down, it began, like a minute cat, to clean its face. Now one could imagine that the little front legs rubbed against each other lightly, joyfully. The horrible danger was over; it had escaped; it was ready for life again.

But just then the boss had an idea. He plunged his pen back into the ink, leaned his thick wrist on the blotting paper, and as the fly tried its wings down came a great heavy blot. What would it make of that? What indeed! The little beggar seemed absolutely cowed, stunned, and afraid to move because of what would happen next. But then, as if painfully, it dragged itself forward. The front legs waved, caught hold, and, more slowly this time, the task began from the beginning.

He's a plucky little devil, thought the boss, and he felt a real admiration for the fly's courage. That was the way to tackle things; that was the right spirit. Never say die; it was only a question of . . . But the fly had again finished its laborious task, and the boss had just time to refill his pen, to shake fair and square on the new-cleaned body yet another dark drop. What about it this time? A painful moment of suspense followed. But behold, the front legs were again waving; the boss felt a rush of relief. He leaned over the fly and said to it tenderly, *[handwritten margin notes]* The fly ought. of death to cannot putoff death forever. THE BOSS'S LIFE BU!LEAROUND TEStER

"You artful little b . . ." And he actually had the brilliant notion of breathing on it to help the drying process. All the same, there was something timid and weak about its efforts now, and the boss decided that this time should be the last, as he dipped the pen into the inkpot.

It was. The last blot on the soaked blotting-paper, and the draggled fly lay in it and did not stir. The back legs were stuck to the body; the front legs were not to be seen.

"Come on," said the boss. "Look sharp!" And he stirred it with his pen—in vain. Nothing happened or was likely to happen. The fly was dead.

The boss lifted the corpse on the end of the paper-knife and flung it into the waste-paper basket. But such a grinding feeling of wretchedness seized him that he felt positively frightened. He started forward and pressed the bell for Macey.

"Bring me some fresh blotting-paper," he said, sternly, "and look sharp about it." And while the old dog padded away he fell to wondering what it was he had been thinking about before. What was it? It was . . . He took out his handkerchief and passed it inside his collar. For the life of him he could not remember.

For Study and Discussion

1. What purpose is served by the opening scene between old Woodifield and the boss?

2. Where is the central conflict of the story presented? In the opening scene? In the cutback within the boss' memory? In the episode of the fly?

3. What does the struggling fly symbolize?

4. Why does the boss feel wretched and confused after he destroys the fly? What do these feelings have to do with his relationship to his dead son? With the central meaning of the story?

5. At the end of the story, why is it that the boss cannot remember what he had been thinking about?

6. What is the apparent attitude of the author toward the boss?

manus-mal
WHITE agind BlACK "setting is southern"

JEAN TOOMER

BLOOD-BURNING MOON

1

Up from the skeleton stone walls, up from the rotting floor boards and the solid hand-hewn beams of oak of the pre-war cotton factory, dusk came. Up from the dusk the full moon came. Glowing like a fired pine-knot, it illumined the great door and soft showered the Negro shanties aligned along the single street of factory town. The full moon in the great door was an omen. Negro women improvised songs against its spell.

Louisa sang as she came over the crest of the hill from the white folks' kitchen. Her skin was the color of oak leaves on young trees in fall. Her breasts, firm and up-pointed like ripe acorns. And her singing had the low murmur of winds in fig trees. Bob Stone, younger son of the people she worked for, loved her. By the way the world reckons things, he had won her. By measure of that warm glow which came into her mind at thought of him, he had won her. Tom Burwell, whom the whole town called Big Boy, also loved her. But working in the fields all day, and far away from her, gave him no chance to show it. Though often enough of evenings he had tried to. Somehow, he never got along. Strong as he was with hands upon the ax or plow, he found it difficult to hold her. Or so he thought. But the fact was that he held her to factory town more firmly than he thought for. His black balanced, and pulled against, the white of Stone, when she thought of them. And her mind was vaguely upon them as she came over the crest of the hill, coming from the white folks' kitchen. As she sang softly at the evil face of the full moon.

A strange stir was in her. Indolently, she tried to fix upon Bob or Tom as the cause of it. To meet Bob in the canebrake, as she was going to do an hour or so later, was nothing new. And Tom's proposal which she felt on its way to her could be indefinitely put off. Separately, there was no

Originally published in *Cane* (New York: Boni & Liveright, 1923). Reprinted here from the new edition (New York: Harper & Row, 1969) by permission of Liveright Publishers, New York; copyright renewed 1951 by Jean Toomer.

unusual significance to either one. But for some reason, they jumbled when her eyes gazed vacantly at the rising moon. And from the jumble came the stir that was strangely within her. Her lips trembled. The slow rhythm of her song grew agitant and restless. Rusty black and tan spotted hounds, lying in the dark corners of porches or prowling around back yards, put their noses in the air and caught its tremor. They began plaintively to yelp and howl. Chickens woke up and cackled. Intermittently, all over the countryside dogs barked and roosters crowed as if heralding a weird dawn or some ungodly awakening. The women sang lustily. Their songs were cotton-wads to stop their ears. Louisa came down into factory town and sank wearily upon the step before her home. The moon was rising towards a thick cloud-bank which soon would hide it.

> Red nigger moon. Sinner!
> Blood-burning moon. Sinner!
> Come out that fact'ry door.

2

Up from the deep dusk of a cleared spot on the edge of the forest a mellow glow arose and spread fan-wise into the low-hanging heavens. And all around the air was heavy with the scent of boiling cane. A large pile of cane-stalks lay like ribboned shadows upon the ground. A mule, harnessed to a pole, trudged lazily round and round the pivot of the grinder. Beneath a swaying oil lamp, a Negro alternately whipped out at the mule, and fed cane-stalks to the grinder. A fat boy waddled pails of fresh ground juice between the grinder and the boiling stove. Steam came from the copper boiling pan. The scent of cane came from the copper pan and drenched the forest and the hill that sloped to factory town, beneath its fragrance. It drenched the men in circle seated around the stove. Some of them chewed at the white pulp of stalks, but there was no need for them to, if all they wanted was to taste the cane. One tasted it in factory town. And from factory town one could see the soft haze thrown by the glowing stove upon the low-hanging heavens.

Old David Georgia stirred the thickening syrup with a long ladle, and ever so often drew it off. Old David Georgia tended his stove and told tales about the white folks, about moonshining and cotton picking, and about sweet nigger gals, to the men who sat there about his stove to listen to him. Tom Burwell chewed cane-stalk and laughed with the others till someone mentioned Louisa. Till some one said something about Louisa and Bob Stone, about the silk stockings she must have gotten from him. Blood ran up Tom's neck hotter than the glow that flooded from the stove. He sprang up. Glared at the men and said, "She's my gal." Will Manning laughed. Tom strode over to him. Yanked him up and knocked him to the ground. Several of Manning's friends got up to fight for him. Tom whipped out a long knife and would have cut them to shreds if they hadnt ducked into the woods. Tom had had enough. He nodded to Old David Georgia and swung down the path to factory town. Just then, the dogs started barking and the roosters began to crow. Tom felt funny. Away from the fight, away from the stove, chill got to him. He shivered. He shuddered when he saw the full moon rising towards the cloud-bank. He who didnt give a godam for the fears of old women. He forced his mind to fasten on Louisa. Bob Stone. Better not be. He turned into the street and saw Louisa sitting before her home. He went towards her, ambling, touched the brim of a marvelously shaped, spotted, felt hat, said he wanted to say something to her, and then found that he didnt know what he had to say, or if he did, that he couldnt say it. He shoved his big fists in his overalls, grinned, and started to move off.

"Youall want me, Tom?"

"Thats what us wants, sho, Louisa."

"Well, here I am—"

"An here I is, but that aint ahelpin none, all th same."

"You wanted to say something? . ."

"I did that, sho. But words is like th spots on dice: no matter how y fumbles em, there's times when they jes wont come. I dunno why. Seems like th love I feels fo yo done stole m tongue. I got it now. Whee! Louisa, honey, I oughtnt tell y, I feel I oughtnt cause yo is young an goes t church an I has had other gals, but Louisa I sho do love y. Lil gal, Ise watched y from them first days when youall sat right here befo yo door befo th well an sang sometimes in a way that like t broke m heart. Ise carried y with me into th fields, day after day, an after that, an I sho can plow when yo is there, an I can pick cotton. Yassur! Come near beatin Barlo yesterday. I sho did. Yassur! An next year if ole Stone'll trust me, I'll have a farm. My own. My bales will buy yo what y gets from white folks now. Silk stockings and purple dresses—course I dont believe what some folks been whisperin as t how y gets them things now. White folks always did do for niggers what they likes. An they jes cant help alikin yo, Louisa. Bob Stone likes y. Course he does. But not th way folks is awhisperin. Does he, hon?"

"I dont know what you mean, Tom."

"Course y dont. Ise already cut two niggers. Had t hon, t tell em so. Niggers always tryin t make somethin out a nothin. An then besides, white folks aint up t them tricks so much nowadays. Godam better not be. Leastawise not with yo. Cause I wouldnt stand f it. Nassur."

"What would you do, Tom?"

"Cut him jes like I cut a nigger."

"No, Tom—"

"I said I would an there aint no mo to it. But that aint th talk f now.

Sing, honey Louisa, an while I'm listenin t y I'll be makin love."

Tom took her hand in his. Against the tough thickness of his own, hers felt soft and small. His huge body slipped down to the step beside her. The full moon sank upward into the deep purple of the cloud-bank. An old woman brought a lighted lamp and hung it on the common well whose bulky shadow squatted in the middle of the road, opposite Tom and Louisa. The old woman lifted the well-lid, took hold the chain, and began drawing up the heavy bucket. As she did so, she sang. Figures shifted, restless-like, between lamp and window in the front rooms of the shanties. Shadows of the figures fought each other on the gray dust of the road. Figures raised the windows and joined the old woman in song. Louisa and Tom, the whole street, singing:

> Red nigger moon. Sinner!
> Blood-burning moon. Sinner!
> Come out that fact'ry door.

3

Bob Stone sauntered from his veranda out into the gloom of fir trees and magnolias. The clear white of his skin paled, and the flush of his cheeks turned purple. As if to balance this outer change, his mind became consciously a white man's. He passed the house with its huge open hearth which, in the days of slavery, was the plantation cookery. He saw Louisa bent over that hearth. He went in as a master should and took her. Direct, honest, bold. None of this sneaking that he had to go through now. The contrast was repulsive to him. His family had lost ground. Hell no, his family still owned the niggers, practically. Damned if they did, or he wouldnt have to duck around so. What would they think if they knew? His mother? His sister? He shouldnt mention them, shouldnt think of them in this connection. There in the dusk he blushed at doing so. Fellows about town were all right, but how about his friends up North? He could see them incredible, repulsed. They didnt know. The thought first made him laugh. Then, with their eyes still upon him, he began to feel embarrassed. He felt the need of explaining things to them. Explain hell. They wouldnt understand, and moreover, who ever heard of a Southerner getting on his knees to any Yankee, or anyone. No sir. He was going to see Louisa to-night, and love her. She was lovely—in her way. Nigger way. What way was that? Damned if he knew. Must know. He'd known her long enough to know. Was there something about niggers that you couldnt know? Listening to them at church didnt tell you anything. Looking at them didnt tell you anything. Talking to them didnt tell you anything—unless it was gossip, unless they wanted to talk. Of course, about farming, and licker, and craps—but those werent nigger. Nigger was something more. How much more? Something to be afraid of, more? Hell no. Who ever heard of being afraid of a nigger? Tom Burwell. Cartwell had told him that Tom went with Louisa after she reached home. No sir. No nigger had ever been with his girl. He'd like to see one try. Some position for him to be in. Him, Bob Stone, of the old Stone family, in a scrap with a nigger over a nigger girl. In the good old days. . . Ha! Those were the days. His family had lost ground. Not so much, though. Enough for him to have to cut through old Lemon's canefield by way of the woods, that he might meet her. She was worth it. Beautiful nigger gal. Why nigger? Why not, just gal? No, it was because she was nigger that he went to her. Sweet. . . The scent of boiling cane came to him. Then he saw the rich glow of the stove. He heard the voices of the men circled around it. He was about to skirt the clearing when he heard his own name mentioned. He stopped. Quivering. Leaning against a tree, he listened.

"Bad nigger. Yassur, he sho is one bad nigger when he gets started."

"Tom Burwell's been on th gang three times fo cuttin men."

"What y think he's agwine t do t Bob Stone?"

"Dunno yet. He aint found out. When he does— Baby!"

"Aint no tellin."

"Young Stone aint no quitter an I ken tell y that. Blood of th old uns in his veins."

"Thats right. He'll scrap, sho."

"Be gettin too hot f niggers round this away."

"Shut up, nigger. Y dont know what y talkin bout."

Bob Stone's ears burned as though he had been holding them over the stove. Sizzling heat welled up within him. His feet felt as if they rested on red-hot coals. They stung him to quick movement. He circled the fringe of the glowing. Not a twig cracked beneath his feet. He reached the path that led to factory town. Plunged furiously down it. Halfway along, a blindness within him veered him aside. He crashed into the bordering canebrake. Cane leaves cut his face and lips. He tasted blood. He threw himself down and dug his fingers in the ground. The earth was cool. Cane-roots took the fever from his hands. After a long while, or so it seemed to him, the thought came to him that it must be time to see Louisa. He got to his feet and walked calmly to their meeting place. No Louisa. Tom Burwell had her. Veins in his forehead bulged and distended. Saliva moistened the dried blood on his lips. He bit down on his lips. He tasted blood. Not his own blood; Tom Burwell's blood. Bob drove through the cane and out again upon the road. A hound swung down the path before him towards factory town. Bob couldnt see it. The dog loped aside to let him pass. Bob's blind rushing made him stumble over it. He fell with a thud that dazed him. The hound yelped. Answering yelps came from all over the countryside. Chickens cackled. Roosters crowed, heralding the bloodshot eyes of southern awakening. Singers in the town were silenced. They shut their windows down. Palpitant between the rooster crows, a chill hush settled upon the huddled forms of Tom and Louisa. A figure rushed from the shadow and stood before them. Tom popped to his feet.

"Whats y want?"

"I'm Bob Stone."

"Yassur—an I'm Tom Burwell. Whats y want?"

Bob lunged at him. Tom side-stepped, caught him by the shoulder, and flung him to the ground. Straddled him.

"Let me up."

"Yassur—but watch yo doins, Bob Stone."

A few dark figures, drawn by the sound of scuffle, stood about them. Bob sprang to his feet.

"Fight like a man, Tom Burwell, an I'll lick y."

Again he lunged. Tom side-stepped and flung him to the ground. Straddled him.

"Get off me, you godam nigger you."

"Yo sho has started somethin now. Get up."

Tom yanked him up and began hammering at him. Each blow sounded as if it smashed into a precious, irreplaceable soft something. Beneath them, Bob staggered back. He reached in his pocket and whipped out a knife.

"Thats my game, sho."

Blue flash, a steel blade slashed across Bob Stone's throat. He had a sweetish sick feeling. Blood began to flow. Then he felt a sharp twitch of pain. He let his knife drop. He slapped one hand against his neck. He pressed the other on top of his head as if to hold it down. He groaned. He turned, and staggered towards the crest of the hill in the direction of white town. Negroes who had seen the fight slunk into their homes and blew the lamps out. Louisa, dazed, hysterical, refused to go indoors. She slipped, crumbled, her body loosely propped against the woodwork of the well. Tom Burwell leaned against it. He seemed rooted there.

Bob reached Broad Street. White men rushed up to him. He collapsed in their arms.

"Tom Burwell. . . ."

White men like ants upon a forage rushed about. Except for the taut hum of their moving, all was silent. Shotguns, revolvers, rope, kerosene, torches. Two high-powered cars with glaring search-lights. They came together. The taut hum rose to a low roar. Then nothing could be heard but the flop of their feet in the thick dust of the road. The moving body of their silence preceded them over the crest of the hill into factory town. It flattened the Negroes beneath it. It rolled to the wall of the factory, where it stopped. Tom knew that they were coming. He couldnt move. And then he saw the search-lights of the two cars glaring down on him. A quick shock went through him. He stiffened. He started to run. A yell went up from the mob. Tom wheeled about and faced them. They poured down on him. They swarmed. A large man with dead-white face and flabby cheeks came to him and almost jabbed a gun-barrel through his guts.

"Hands behind y, nigger."

Tom's wrists were bound. The big man shoved him to the well. Burn him over it, and when the woodwork caved in, his body would drop to the bottom. Two deaths for a godam nigger. Louisa was driven back. The mob pushed in. Its pressure, its momentum was too great. Drag him to the factory. Wood and stakes already there. Tom moved in the direction indicated. But they had to drag him. They reached the great door. Too many to get in there. The mob divided and flowed around the walls to either side. The big man shoved him through the door. The mob pressed in from the sides. Taut humming. No words. A stake was sunk into the ground. Rotting floor boards piled around it. Kerosene poured on the rotting floor boards. Tom bound to the stake. His breast was bare. Nails scratches let little lines of blood trickle down and mat into the hair. His face, his eyes were set and stony. Except for irregular breathing, one would have thought him already dead. Torches were flung onto the pile. A great flare muffled in black smoke shot upward. The mob yelled. The mob was silent. Now Tom could be seen within the flames. Only his head, erect, lean, like a blackened stone. Stench of burning flesh soaked the air. Tom's eyes popped. His head settled downward. The mob yelled. Its yell echoed against the skeleton stone walls and sounded like a hundred yells. Like a hundred mobs yelling. Its yell thudded against the thick front wall and fell back. Ghost of a yell slipped through the flames and out the great door of the factory. It fluttered like a dying thing down the single street of factory town. Louisa, upon the step before her home, did not hear it, but her eyes opened slowly. They saw the full moon glowing in the great door. The full moon, an evil thing, an omen, soft showering the homes of folks she knew. Where were they, these people? She'd sing, and perhaps they'd come out and join her. Perhaps Tom Burwell would come. At any rate, the full moon in the great door was an omen which she must sing to:

> Red nigger moon. Sinner!
> Blood-burning moon. Sinner!
> Come out that fact'ry door.

For Study and Discussion

1. Pick out specific images of color, sound, and heat in Part 1 which arouse tension and point toward the violent climax in Part 3. Which of these images are repeated predominantly in Parts 2 and 3?

2. What new images involving taste and smell are introduced in Parts 2 and 3? What do they contribute to the unfolding drama involving Louisa, Tom Burwell, and Bob Stone?

3. Comment on the dialogue between Tom and Louisa in Part 2 and the dialogue Bob overhears on his way to meet Louisa in Part 3. Are these passages convincing? How do they prepare you to accept as inevitable the clash between Tom and Bob and the eventual destruction of both men?

4. Louisa is scarcely described at all, yet her character and personality are vividly evoked. In characterizing her, what devices primarily does the author employ to make you accept her as a prize worth fighting and dying for?

5. In what ways are racial tensions used to heighten the development of conflict in this story?

RING LARDNER

HAIRCUT

I got another barber that comes over from Carterville and helps me out Saturdays, but the rest of the time I can get along all right alone. You can see for yourself that this ain't no New York City and besides that, the most of the boys works all day and don't have no leisure to drop in here and get themselves prettied up.

You're a newcomer, ain't you? I thought I hadn't seen you round before. I hope you like it good enough to stay. As I say, we ain't no New York City or Chicago, but we have pretty good times. Not as good, though, since Jim Kendall got killed. When he was alive, him and Hod Meyers used to keep this town in an uproar. I bet they was more laughin' done here than any town its size in America.

Jim was comical, and Hod was pretty near a match for him. Since Jim's gone, Hod tries to hold his end up just the same as ever, but it's tough goin' when you ain't got nobody to kind of work with.

They used to be plenty fun in here Saturdays. This place is jam-packed Saturdays, from four o'clock on. Jim and Hod would show up right after their supper, round six o'clock. Jim would set himself down in that big chair, nearest the blue spittoon. Whoever had been settin' in that chair, why they'd get up when Jim come in and give it to him.

You'd of thought it was a reserved seat like they have sometimes in a theayter. Hod would generally always stand or walk up and down, or some Saturdays, of course, he'd be settin' in this chair part of the time, gettin' a haircut.

Well, Jim would set there a w'ile without openin' his mouth only to spit, and then finally he'd say to me, "Whitey,"—my right name, that is, my right first name, is Dick, but everybody round here calls me Whitey—Jim would say, "Whitey, your nose looks like a rosebud tonight. You must of been drinkin' some of your aw de cologne."

So I'd say, "No, Jim, but you look like you'd been drinkin' somethin' of that kind or somethin' worse."

Originally published in *Liberty Magazine*, March 28, 1925. Reprinted here from *The Love Nest and Other Stories* (New York: Charles Scribner's Sons, 1926) by permission of the publisher. Copyright 1925 by Ellis A. Lardner; renewal copyright 1953.

Jim would have to laugh at that, but then he'd speak up and say, "No, I ain't had nothin' to drink, but that ain't sayin' I wouldn't like somethin'. I wouldn't even mind if it was wood alcohol."

Then Hod Meyers would say, "Neither would your wife." That would set everybody to laughin' because Jim and his wife wasn't on very good terms. She'd of divorced him only they wasn't no chance to get alimony and she didn't have no way to take care of herself and the kids. She couldn't never understand Jim. He *was* kind of rough, but a good fella at heart.

Him and Hod had all kinds of sport with Milt Sheppard. I don't suppose you've seen Milt. Well, he's got an Adam's apple that looks more like a mushmelon. So I'd be shavin' Milt and when I'd start to shave down here on his neck, Hod would holler, "Hey, Whitey, wait a minute! Before you cut into it, let's make up a pool and see who can guess closest to the number of seeds."

And Jim would say, "If Milt hadn't of been so hoggish, he'd of ordered a half a cantaloupe instead of a whole one and it might not of stuck in his throat."

All the boys would roar at this and Milt himself would force a smile, though the joke was on him. Jim certainly was a card!

There's his shavin' mug, settin' on the shelf, right next to Charley Vail's. "Charles M. Vail." That's the druggist. He comes in regular for his shave, three times a week. And Jim's is the cup next to Charley's. "James H. Kendall." Jim won't need no shavin' mug no more, but I'll leave it there just the same for old time's sake. Jim certainly was a character!

Years ago, Jim used to travel for a canned goods concern over in Carterville. They sold canned goods. Jim had the whole northern half of the State and was on the road five days out of every week. He'd drop in here Saturdays and tell his experiences for that week. It was rich.

I guess he paid more attention to playin' jokes than makin' sales. Finally the concern let him out and he come right home here and told everybody he'd been fired instead of sayin' he'd resigned like most fellas would of.

It was a Saturday and the shop was full and Jim got up out of that chair and says, "Gentlemen, I got an important announcement to make. I been fired from my job."

Well, they asked him if he was in earnest and he said he was and nobody could think of nothin' to say till Jim finally broke the ice himself. He says, "I been sellin' canned goods and now I'm canned goods myself."

You see, the concern he'd been workin' for was a factory that made canned goods. Over in Carterville. And now Jim said he was canned himself. He was certainly a card!

Jim had a great trick that he used to play w'ile he was travelin'. For instance, he'd be ridin' on a train and they'd come to some little town like, well, like, we'll say, like Benton. Jim would look out the train window and read the signs on the stores.

For instance, they'd be a sign, "Henry Smith, Dry Goods." Well, Jim would write down the name and the name of the town and when he got to wherever he was goin' he'd mail back a postal card to Henry Smith at Benton and not sign no name to it, but he'd write on the card, well, somethin' like "Ask your wife about that book agent that spent the afternoon last week," or "Ask your Missus who kept her from gettin' lonesome the last time you was in Carterville." And he'd sign the card, "A Friend."

Of course, he never knew what really come of none of these jokes, but he could picture what *probably* happened and that was enough.

Jim didn't work very steady after he lost his position with the Carterville people. What he did earn, doin' odd jobs round town, why he spent pretty near all of it on gin and his family might of starved if the stores hadn't of carried them along. Jim's wife tried her hand at dressmakin', but they ain't nobody goin' to get rich makin' dresses in this town.

As I say, she'd of divorced Jim, only she seen that she couldn't support herself and the kids and she was always hopin' that some day Jim would cut out his habits and give her more than two or three dollars a week.

They was a time when she would go to whoever he was workin' for and ask them to give her his wages, but after she done this once or twice, he beat her to it by borrowin' most of his pay in advance. He told it all round town, how he had outfoxed his Missus. He certainly was a caution!

But he wasn't satisfied with just outwittin' her. He was sore the way she had acted, tryin' to grab off his pay. And he made up his mind he'd get even. Well, he waited till Evans's Circus was advertised to come to town. Then he told his wife and two kiddies that he was goin' to take them to the circus. The day of the circus, he told them he would get the tickets and meet them outside the entrance to the tent.

Well, he didn't have no intentions of bein' there or buyin' tickets or nothin'. He got full of gin and laid round Wright's poolroom all day. His wife and the kids waited and waited and of course he didn't show up. His wife didn't have a dime with her, or nowhere else, I guess. So she finally had to tell the kids it was all off and they cried like they wasn't never goin' to stop.

Well, it seems, w'ile they was cryin', Doc Stair came along and he asked what was the matter, but Mrs. Kendall was stubborn and wouldn't tell him, but the kids told him and he insisted on takin' them and their mother in the show. Jim found this out afterwards and it was one reason why he had it in for Doc Stair.

Doc Stair come here about a year and a half ago. He's a mighty handsome young fella and his clothes always look like he has them made to order. He goes to Detroit two or three times a year and w'ile he's there he must have a tailor take his measure and then make him a suit to order. They cost pretty near twice as much, but they fit a whole lot better than if you just bought them in a store.

For a w'ile everybody was wonderin' why a young doctor like Doc Stair should come to a town like this where we already got old Doc Gamble and Doc Foote that's both been here for years and all the practice in town was always divided between the two of them.

Then they was a story got round that Doc Stair's gal had throwed him over, a gal up in the Northern Peninsula somewheres, and the reason he come here was to hide himself away and forget it. He said himself that he thought they wasn't nothin' like general practice in a place like ours to fit a man to be a good all round doctor. And that's why he'd came.

Anyways, it wasn't long before he was makin' enough to live on, though they tell me that he never dunned nobody for what they owed him, and the folks here certainly has got the owin' habit, even in my business. If I had all that was comin' to me for just shaves alone, I could go to Carterville and put up at the Mercer for a week and see a different picture every night. For instance, they's old George Purdy—but I guess I shouldn't ought to be gossipin'.

Well, last year, our coroner died, died of the flu. Ken Beatty, that was his name. He was the coroner. So they had to choose another man to be coroner in his place and they picked Doc Stair. He laughed at first and said he didn't want it, but they made him take it. It ain't no job that anybody would fight for and what a man makes out of it in a year would just about buy seeds for their garden. Doc's the kind, though, that can't say no to nothin' if you keep at him long enough.

But I was goin' to tell you about a poor boy we got here in town—Paul Dickson. He fell out of a tree when he was about ten years old. Lit on his head and it done somethin' to him and he ain't never been right. No harm in him, but just silly. Jim Kendall used to call him cuckoo; that's a name Jim had for anybody that was off their head, only he called people's head their bean. That was another of his gags, callin' head bean and callin' crazy people cuckoo. Only poor Paul ain't crazy, but just silly.

You can imagine that Jim used to have all kinds of fun with Paul. He'd send him to the White Front Garage for a left-handed monkey wrench. Of course they ain't no such a thing as a left-handed monkey wrench.

And once we had a kind of a fair here and they was a baseball game between the fats and the leans and before the game started Jim called Paul over and sent him way down to Schrader's hardware store to get a key for the pitcher's box.

They wasn't nothin' in the way of gags that Jim couldn't think up, when he put his mind to it.

Poor Paul was always kind of suspicious of people, maybe on account of how Jim had kept foolin' him. Paul wouldn't have much to do with anybody only his own mother and Doc Stair and a girl here in town named Julie Gregg. That is, she ain't a girl no more, but pretty near thirty or over.

When Doc first come to town, Paul seemed to feel like here was a real friend and he hung round Doc's office most of the w'ile; the only time he wasn't there was when he'd go home to eat or sleep or when he seen Julie Gregg doin' her shoppin'.

When he looked out Doc's window and seen her, he'd run downstairs and join her and tag along with her to the different stores. The poor boy was crazy about Julie and she always treated him mighty nice and made him feel like he was welcome, though of course it wasn't nothin' but pity on her side.

Doc done all he could to improve Paul's mind and he told me once that he really thought the boy was gettin' better, that they was times when he was as bright and sensible as anybody else.

But I was goin' to tell you about Julie Gregg. Old Man Gregg was in the lumber business, but got to drinkin' and lost the most of his money and when he died, he didn't leave nothin' but the house and just enough insurance for the girl to skimp along on.

Her mother was a kind of a half invalid and didn't hardly ever leave the house. Julie wanted to sell the place and move somewheres else after the old man died, but the mother said she was born here and would die here. It was tough on Julie, as the young people round this town—well, she's too good for them.

She's been away to school and Chicago and New York and different places and they ain't no subject she can't talk on, where you take the rest of the young folks here and you mention anything to them outside of Gloria Swanson or Tommy Meighan and they think you're delirious. Did you see Gloria in Wages of Virtue? You missed somethin'!

Well, Doc Stair hadn't been here more than a week when he come in one day to get shaved and I recognized who he was as he had been pointed out to me, so I told him about my old lady. She's been ailin' for a couple years and neither Doc Gamble or Doc Foote, neither one, seemed to be helpin' her. So he said he would come out and see her, but if she was able to get out herself, it would be better to bring her to his office where he could make a completer examination.

So I took her to his office and w'ile I was waitin' for her in the reception room, in come Julie Gregg. When somebody comes in Doc Stair's office, they's a bell that rings in his inside office so as he can tell they's somebody to see him.

So he left my old lady inside and come out to the front office and that's the first time him and Julie met and I guess it was what they call love at first sight. But it wasn't fifty-fifty. This young fella was the slickest lookin' fella she'd ever seen in this town and she went wild over him. To him she was just a young lady that wanted to see the doctor.

She'd come on about the same business I had. Her mother had been doctorin' for years with Doc Gamble and Doc Foote and without no results. So she'd heard they was a new doc in town and decided to give him a try. He promised to call and see her mother that same day.

I said a minute ago that it was love at first sight on her part. I'm not only judgin' by how she acted afterwards but how she looked at him that first day in his office. I ain't no mind reader, but it was wrote all over her face that she was gone.

Now Jim Kendall, besides bein' a jokesmith and a pretty good drinker, well, Jim was quite a lady-killer. I guess he run pretty wild durin' the time he was on the road for them Carterville people, and besides that, he'd had a couple little affairs of the heart right here in town. As I say, his wife could of divorced him, only she couldn't.

But Jim was like the majority of men, and women, too, I guess. He wanted what he couldn't get. He wanted Julie Gregg and worked his head off tryin' to land her. Only he'd of said bean instead of head.

Well, Jim's habits and his jokes didn't appeal to Julie and of course he was a married man, so he didn't have no more chance than, well, than a rabbit. That's an expression of Jim's himself. When somebody didn't have no chance to get elected or somethin', Jim would always say they didn't have no more chance than a rabbit.

He didn't make no bones about how he felt. Right in here, more than once, in front of the whole crowd, he said he was stuck on Julie and anybody that could get her for him was welcome to his house and his wife and kids included. But she wouldn't have nothin' to do with him; wouldn't even speak to him on the street. He finally seen he wasn't gettin' nowheres with his usual line so he decided to try the rough stuff. He went right up to her house one evenin' and when she opened the door he forced his way in and grabbed her. But she broke loose and before he could stop her, she run in the next room and locked the door and phoned to Joe Barnes. Joe's the marshal. Jim could hear who she was phonin' to and he beat it before Joe got there.

Joe was an old friend of Julie's pa. Joe went to Jim the next day and told him what would happen if he ever done it again.

I don't know how the news of this little affair leaked out. Chances is that Joe Barnes told his wife and she told somebody else's wife and they told their husband. Anyways, it did leak out and Hod Meyers had the nerve to kid Jim about it, right here in this shop. Jim didn't deny nothin' and kind of laughed it off and said for us all to wait; that lots of people had tried to make a monkey out of him, but he always got even.

Meanw'ile everybody in town was wise to Julie's bein' wild mad over the Doc. I don't suppose she had any idear how her face changed when him and her was together; of course she couldn't of, or she'd of kept away from him. And she didn't know that we was all noticin' how many times she made excuses to go up to his office or pass it on the other side of the street and look up in his window to see if he was there. I felt sorry for her and so did most other people.

Hod Meyers kept rubbin' it into Jim about how the Doc had cut him out. Jim didn't pay no attention to the kiddin' and you could see he was plannin' one of his jokes.

One trick Jim had was the knack of changin' his voice. He could make you think he was a girl talkin' and he could mimic any man's voice. To show you how good he was along this line, I'll tell you the joke he played on me once.

You know, in most towns of any size, when a man is dead and needs a shave, why the barber that shaves him soaks him five dollars for the job; that is, he don't soak *him,* but whoever ordered the shave. I just charge three dollars because personally I don't mind much shavin' a dead person. They lay a whole lot stiller than live customers. The only thing is that you don't feel like talkin' to them and you get kind of lonesome.

Well, about the coldest day we ever had here, two years ago last winter, the phone rung at the house w'ile I was home to dinner and I answered the phone and it was a woman's voice and she said she was Mrs. John Scott and her husband was dead and would I come out and shave him.

Old John had always been a good customer of mine. But they live seven miles out in the country, on the Streeter road. Still I didn't see how I could say no.

So I said I would be there, but would have to come in a jitney and it might cost three or four dollars besides the price of the shave. So she, or the voice, it said that was all right, so I got Frank Abbott to drive me out to the place and when I got there, who should open the door but old John himself! He wasn't no more dead than, well, than a rabbit.

It didn't take no private detective to figure out who had played me this little joke. Nobody could of thought it up but Jim Kendall. He certainly was a card!

I tell you this incident just to show you how he could disguise his voice and make you believe it was somebody else talkin'. I'd of swore it was Mrs. Scott had called me. Anyways, some woman.

Well, Jim waited till he had Doc Stair's voice down pat; then he went after revenge.

He called Julie up on a night when he knew Doc was over in Carterville. She never questioned but what it was Doc's voice. Jim said he must see her that night; he couldn't wait no longer to tell her somethin'. She was all excited and told him to come to the house. But he said he was expectin' an important long distance call and wouldn't she please forget her manners for once and come to his office. He said they couldn't nothin' hurt her and nobody would see her and he just *must* talk to her a little w'ile. Well, poor Julie fell for it.

Doc always keeps a night light in his office, so it looked to Julie like they was somebody there.

Meanw'ile Jim Kendall had went to Wright's poolroom, where they was a whole gang amusin' themselves. The most of them had drank plenty of gin, and they was a rough bunch even when sober. They was always strong for Jim's jokes and when he told them to come with him and see some fun they give up their card games and pool games and followed along.

Doc's office is on the second floor. Right outside his door they's a flight of stairs leadin' to the floor above. Jim and his gang hid in the dark behind these stairs.

Well, Julie come up to Doc's door and rung the bell and they was nothin' doin'. She rung it again and she rung it seven or eight times. Then she tried the door and found it locked. Then Jim made some kind of a noise and she heard it and waited a minute, and then she says, "Is that you, Ralph?" Ralph is Doc's first name.

They was no answer and it must of came to her all of a sudden that she'd been bunked. She pretty near fell downstairs and the whole gang after her. They chased her all the way home, hollerin', "Is that you, Ralph?" and "Oh, Ralphie, dear, is that you?" Jim says he couldn't holler it himself, as he was laughin' too hard.

Poor Julie! She didn't show up here on Main Street for a long, long time afterward.

And of course Jim and his gang told everybody in town, everybody but Doc Stair. They was scared to tell him, and he might of never knowed only for Paul Dickson. The poor cuckoo, as Jim called him, he was here in the shop one night when Jim was still gloatin' yet over what he'd done to Julie. And Paul took in as much of it as he could understand and he run to Doc with the story.

It's a cinch Doc went up in the air and swore he'd make Jim suffer. But it was a kind of a delicate thing, because if it got out that he had beat Jim up, Julie was bound to hear of it and then she'd know that Doc knew and of course knowin' that he knew would make it worse for her than ever. He was goin' to do somethin', but it took a lot of figurin'.

Well, it was a couple days later when Jim was here in the shop again, and so was the cuckoo. Jim was goin' duck-shootin' the next day and had came in lookin' for Hod Meyers to go with him. I happened to know that Hod had went over to Carterville and wouldn't be home till the end of the week. So Jim said he hated to go alone and he guessed he would call it off. Then poor Paul spoke up and said if Jim would take him he would go along. Jim thought a w'ile and then he said, well, he guessed a half-wit was better than nothin'.

I suppose he was plottin' to get Paul out in the boat and play some joke on him, like pushin' him in the water. Anyways, he said Paul could go.

He asked him had he ever shot a duck and Paul said no, he'd never even had a gun in his hands. So Jim said he could set in the boat and watch him and if he behaved himself, he might lend him his gun for a couple of shots. They made a date to meet in the mornin' and that's the last I seen of Jim alive.

Next mornin', I hadn't been open more than ten minutes when Doc Stair come in. He looked kind of nervous. He asked me had I seen Paul Dickson. I said no, but I knew where he was, out duck-shootin' with Jim Kendall. So Doc says that's what he had heard, and he couldn't understand it because Paul had told him he wouldn't never have no more to do with Jim as long as he lived.

He said Paul had told him about the joke Jim had played on Julie. He said Paul had asked him what he thought of the joke and the Doc had told him that anybody that would do a thing like that ought not to be let live.

I said it had been a kind of a raw thing, but Jim just couldn't resist no kind of a joke, no matter how raw. I said I thought he was all right at heart, but just bubblin' over with mischief. Doc turned and walked out.

At noon he got a phone call from old John Scott. The lake where Jim and Paul had went shootin' is on John's place. Paul had came runnin' up to the house a few minutes before and said they'd been an accident. Jim had shot a few ducks and then give the gun to Paul and told him to try his luck. Paul hadn't never handled a gun and he was nervous. He was shakin' so hard that he couldn't control the gun. He let fire and Jim sunk back in the boat, dead.

Doc Stair, bein' the coroner, jumped in Frank Abbott's flivver and rushed out to Scott's farm. Paul and old John was down on the shore of the lake. Paul had rowed the boat to shore, but they'd left the body in it, waitin' for Doc to come.

Doc examined the body and said they might as well fetch it back to town. They was no use leavin' it there or callin' a jury, as it was a plain case of accidental shootin'.

Personally I wouldn't never leave a person shoot a gun in the same boat I was in unless I was sure they knew somethin' about guns. Jim was a sucker to leave a new beginner have his gun, let alone a half-wit. It probably served Jim right, what he got. But still we miss him round here. He certainly was a card!

Comb it wet or dry?

For Study and Discussion

1. What is the effect of having Whitey, the barber, tell the story instead of some other narrator or the author himself?

2. Is Whitey's attitude toward Jim Kendall the same as the author's? How soon in the story do you begin developing a feeling about Jim which is contrary to Whitey's attitude?

3. Do Whitey's "digressions" concerning Doc Stair, Paul Dickson, and Julie Gregg serve more than one purpose in the story? In what ways do they help characterize him and advance the plot at the same time?

4. Cite several examples of (1) irony of statement and (2) irony of event or situation in the story. Which of these two forms of irony is used more extensively?

5. Is the method of narration in "Haircut" similar in any way to James' method in "The Real Thing"? How does Lardner's method differ most conspicuously from James'?

6. Does the story bear any resemblance whatever to the plotting and characterization described in Lardner's essay, "How to Write Short Stories"? Why or why not?

7. Would "Haircut" satisfy Canby's demand for "free fiction"? Would it satisfy Anderson's and Fagin's requirements for the short story? Why or why not? Explain the relationship between theme and form in the story.

ERNEST HEMINGWAY

TEN INDIANS

After one Fourth of July, Nick, driving home late from town in the big wagon with Joe Garner and his family, passed nine drunken Indians along the road. He remembered there were nine because Joe Garner, driving along in the dusk, pulled up the horses, jumped down into the road and dragged an Indian out of the wheel rut. The Indian had been asleep, face down in the sand. Joe dragged him into bushes and got back up on the wagon-box.

"That makes nine of them," Joe said, "just between here and the edge of town."

"Them Indians," said Mrs. Garner.

Nick was on the back seat with the two Garner boys. He was looking out from the back seat to see the Indian where Joe had dragged him alongside of the road.

"Was it Billy Tabeshaw?" Carl asked.

"No."

"His pants looked mighty like Billy."

"All Indians wear the same kind of pants."

"I didn't see him at all," Frank said. "Pa was down into the road and back up again before I seen a thing. I thought he was killing a snake."

"Plenty of Indians'll kill snakes tonight, I guess," Joe Garner said.

"Them Indians," said Mrs. Garner.

They drove along. The road turned off from the main highway and went up into the hills. It was hard pulling for the horses and the boys got down and walked. The road was sandy. Nick looked back from the top of the hill by the schoolhouse. He saw the lights of Petoskey and, off across Little Traverse Bay, the lights of Harbour Springs. They climbed back in the wagon again.

"They ought to put some gravel on that stretch," Joe Garner said. The

Originally published in, and reprinted here from, *Men Without Women* (New York: Charles Scribner's Sons, 1927) by permission of the publisher. Copyright 1927 Charles Scribner's Sons; renewal copyright © 1955 Ernest Hemingway.

wagon went along the road through the woods. Joe and Mrs. Garner sat close together on the front seat. Nick sat between the two boys. The road came out into a clearing.

"Right here was where Pa ran over the skunk."

"It was further on."

"It don't make no difference where it was," Joe said without turning his head. "One place is just as good as another to run over a skunk."

"I saw two skunks last night," Nick said.

"Where?"

"Down by the lake. They were looking for dead fish along the beach."

"They were coons probably," Carl said.

"They were skunks. I guess I know skunks."

"You ought to," Carl said. "You got an Indian girl."

"Stop talking that way, Carl," said Mrs. Garner.

"Well, they smell about the same."

Joe Garner laughed.

"You stop laughing, Joe," Mrs. Garner said. "I won't have Carl talk that way."

"Have you got an Indian girl, Nickie?" Joe asked.

"No."

"He has too, Pa," Frank said. "Prudence Mitchell's his girl."

"She's not."

"He goes to see her every day."

"I don't." Nick, sitting between the two boys in the dark, felt hollow and happy inside himself to be teased about Prudence Mitchell. "She ain't my girl," he said.

"Listen to him," said Carl. "I see them together every day."

"Carl can't get a girl," his mother said, "not even a squaw."

Carl was quiet.

"Carl ain't no good with girls," Frank said.

"You shut up."

"You're all right, Carl," Joe Garner said. "Girls never got a man anywhere. Look at your pa."

"Yes, that's what you would say," Mrs. Garner moved close to Joe as the wagon jolted. "Well, you had plenty of girls in your time."

"I'll bet Pa wouldn't ever have had a squaw for a girl."

"Don't you think it," Joe said. "You better watch out to keep Prudie, Nick."

His wife whispered to him and Joe laughed.

"What you laughing at?" asked Frank.

"Don't you say it, Garner," his wife warned. Joe laughed again.

"Nickie can have Prudence," Joe Garner said. "I got a good girl."

"That's the way to talk," Mrs. Garner said.

The horses were pulling heavily in the sand. Joe reached out in the dark with the whip.

"Come on, pull into it. You'll have to pull harder than this tomorrow."

They trotted down the long hill, the wagon jolting. At the farmhouse everybody got down. Mrs. Garner unlocked the door, went inside, and came out with a lamp in her hand. Carl and Nick unloaded the things from the back of the wagon. Frank sat on the front seat to drive to the barn and put up the horses. Nick went up the steps and opened the kitchen door. Mrs. Garner was building a fire in the stove. She turned from pouring kerosene on the wood.

"Good-by, Mrs. Garner," Nick said. "Thanks for taking me."

"Oh shucks, Nickie."

"I had a wonderful time."

"We like to have you. Won't you stay and eat some supper?"

"I better go. I think Dad probably waited for me."

"Well, get along then. Send Carl up to the house, will you?"

"All right."

"Good-night, Nickie."

"Good-night, Mrs. Garner."

Nick went out the farmyard and down to the barn. Joe and Frank were milking.

"Good-night," Nick said. "I had a swell time."

"Good-night, Nick," Joe Garner called. "Aren't you going to stay and eat?"

"No, I can't. Will you tell Carl his mother wants him?"

"All right. Good-night, Nickie."

Nick walked barefoot along the path through the meadow below the barn. The path was smooth and the dew was cool on his bare feet. He climbed a fence at the end of the meadow, went down through a ravine, his feet wet in the swamp mud, and then climbed up through the dry beech woods until he saw the lights of the cottage. He climbed over the fence and walked around to the front porch. Through the window he saw his father sitting by the table, reading in the light from the big lamp. Nick opened the door and went in.

"Well, Nickie," his father said, "was it a good day?"

"I had a swell time, Dad. It was a swell Fourth of July."

"Are you hungry?"

"You bet."

"What did you do with your shoes?"

"I left them in the wagon at Garner's."

"Come on out to the kitchen."

Nick's father went ahead with the lamp. He stopped and lifted the lid of the ice-box. Nick went on into the kitchen. His father brought in a piece of cold chicken on a plate and a pitcher of milk and put them on the table before Nick. He put down the lamp.

"There's some pie too," he said. "Will that hold you?"

"It's grand."

His father sat down in a chair beside the oil-cloth-covered table. He made a big shadow on the kitchen wall.

"Who won the ball game?"

"Petoskey. Five to three."

His father sat watching him eat and filled his glass from the milk-pitcher. Nick drank and wiped his mouth on his napkin. His father reached over to the shelf for the pie. He cut Nick a big piece. It was huckleberry pie.

"What did you do, Dad?"

"I went out fishing in the morning."

"What did you get?"

"Only perch."

His father sat watching Nick eat the pie.

"What did you do this afternoon?" Nick asked.

"I went for a walk up by the Indian camp."

"Did you see anybody?"

"The Indians were all in town getting drunk."

"Didn't you see anybody at all?"

"I saw your friend, Prudie."

"Where was she?"

"She was in the woods with Frank Washburn. I ran onto them. They were having quite a time."

His father was not looking at him.

"What were they doing?"

"I didn't stay to find out."

"Tell me what they were doing."

"I don't know," his father said. "I just heard them threshing around."

"How did you know it was them?"

"I saw them."

"I thought you said you didn't see them."

"Oh, yes, I saw them."

"Who was it with her?" Nick asked.

"Frank Washburn."

"Were they—were they——"

"Were they what?"

"Were they happy?"

"I guess so."

His father got up from the table and went out the kitchen screen door. When he came back Nick was looking at his plate. He had been crying.

"Have some more?" His father picked up the knife to cut the pie.

"No," said Nick.

"You better have another piece."

"No, I don't want any."

His father cleared off the table.

"Where were they in the woods?" Nick asked.

"Up back of the camp." Nick looked at his plate. His father said, "You better go to bed, Nick."

"All right."

Nick went into his room, undressed, and got into bed. He heard his father moving around in the living room. Nick lay in the bed with his face in the pillow.

"My heart's broken," he thought. "If I feel this way my heart must be broken."

After a while he heard his father blow out the lamp and go into his own room. He heard a wind come up in the trees outside and felt it come in cool through the screen. He lay for a long time with his face in the pillow, and after a while he forgot to think about Prudence and finally he went to sleep. When he awoke in the night he heard the wind in the hemlock trees outside the cottage and the waves of the lake coming in on the shore, and he went back to sleep. In the morning there was a big wind blowing and the waves were running high up on the beach and he was awake a long time before he remembered that his heart was broken.

For Study and Discussion

1. Why do you think Hemingway titled the story "Ten Indians" instead of simply "The Indians," for example? Or, since only the Indian girl receives emphasis in the story, why didn't he title it "The Indian"?

2. In what specific ways does the conversation in the wagon among Nick and the Garner family prepare you for the revelation Nick's father later makes to him? Do the two skunks Nick mentions have any metaphorical significance?

3. How deeply affected do you think Nick is by the knowledge that his Indian girl friend has supplanted him with another lover?

4. In *Death in the Afternoon*, Hemingway wrote: "If a writer of prose knows enough about what he is writing about he may omit things that he knows and the reader, if the writer is writing truly enough, will have a feeling of those things as strongly as though the writer had stated them. The dignity of movement of an ice-berg is due to only one-eighth of it being above water" (p. 192). What, if anything, has been omitted from "Ten Indians"?

5. Do you agree with Eudora Welty's statement that "the atmosphere which surrounds Hemingway's stories is just as thick . . ." as that surrounding D. H. Lawrence's stories (p. 105)? Compare the atmosphere of "Ten Indians" with that of "Two Blue Birds" or of Toomer's "Blood-Burning Moon."

D. H. LAWRENCE

TWO BLUE BIRDS

There was a woman who loved her husband, but she could not live with him. The husband, on his side, was sincerely attached to his wife, yet he could not live with her. They were both under forty, both handsome and both attractive. They had the most sincere regard for one another, and felt, in some odd way, eternally married to one another. They knew each other more intimately than they knew anybody else, they felt more known to one another than to any other person.

Yet they could not live together. Usually, they kept a thousand miles apart, geographically. But when he sat in the greyness of England, at the back of his mind, with a certain grim fidelity, he was aware of his wife, her strange yearning to be loyal and faithful, having her gallant affairs away in the sun, in the south. And she, as she drank her cocktail on the terrace over the sea, and turned her grey, sardonic eyes on the heavy dark face of her admirer, whom she really liked quite a lot, she was actually preoccupied with the clear-cut features of her handsome young husband, thinking of how he would be asking his secretary to do something for him, asking in that good-natured, confident voice of a man who knows that his request will be only too gladly fulfilled.

The secretary, of course, adored him. She was *very* competent, quite young, and quite good-looking. She adored him. But then all his servants always did, particularly his women-servants. His men-servants were likely to swindle him.

When a man has an adoring secretary, and you are the man's wife, what are you to do? Not that there was anything "wrong"—if you know what I mean!—between them. Nothing you could call adultery, to come down to brass tacks. No, no! They were just the young master and his secretary. He dictated to her, she slaved for him and adored him, and the whole thing went on wheels.

Originally published in the *Dial*, April 1927. Reprinted here from *The Woman Who Rode Away and Other Stories* (New York: Alfred A. Knopf, Inc., 1928) by permission of the publisher. Copyright 1928 and renewed 1956 by Frieda Lawrence Ravagli.

He didn't "adore" her. A man doesn't need to adore his secretary. But he depended on her. "I simply rely on Miss Wrexall." Whereas he could never rely on his wife. The one thing he knew finally about *her* was that she didn't intend to be relied on.

So they remained friends, in the awful unspoken intimacy of the once-married. Usually each year they went away together for a holiday, and, if they had not been man and wife, they would have found a great deal of fun and stimulation in one another. The fact that they were married, had been married for the last dozen years, and couldn't live together for the last three or four, spoilt them for one another. Each had a private feeling of bitterness about the other.

However, they were awfully kind. He was the soul of generosity, and held her in real tender esteem, no matter how many gallant affairs she had. Her gallant affairs were part of her modern necessity. "After all, I've got to *live*. I can't turn into a pillar of salt in five minutes, just because you and I can't live together! It takes years for a woman like me to turn into a pillar of salt. At least I hope so!"

"Quite!" he replied. "Quite! By all means put them in pickle, make pickled cucumbers of them, before you crystallise out. That's my advice."

He was like that: so awfully clever and enigmatic. She could more or less fathom the idea of the pickled cucumbers, but the "crystallising out"—what did that signify?

And did he mean to suggest that he himself had been well pickled, and that further immersion was for him unnecessary, would spoil his flavour? Was that what he meant? And herself, was she the brine and the vale of tears?

You never knew how catty a man was being, when he was really clever and enigmatic, withal a bit whimsical. He was adorably whimsical, with a twist of his flexible, vain mouth, that had a long upper lip, so fraught with vanity! But then a handsome, clear-cut, histrionic young man like that, how could he help being vain? The women made him so.

Ah, the women! How nice men would be if there were no other women!

And how nice the women would be if there were no other men! That's the best of a secretary. She may have a husband, but a husband is the mere shred of a man, compared to a boss, a chief, a man who dictates to you and whose words you faithfully write down and then transcribe. Imagine a wife writing down anything her husband said to her! But a secretary! Every *and* and *but* of his she preserves for ever. What are candied violets in comparison!

Now it is all very well having gallant affairs under the southern sun, when you know there is a husband whom you adore dictating to a secretary whom you are too scornful to hate yet whom you rather despise, though you allow she has her good points, away north in the place you ought to regard as home. A gallant affair isn't much good when you've got a bit of grit in your eye. Or something at the back of your mind.

What's to be done? The husband, of course, did not send his wife away.

"You've got your secretary and your work," she said. "There's no room for me."

"There's a bedroom and a sitting-room exclusively for you," he replied. "And a garden and half a motor car. But please yourself entirely. Do what gives you most pleasure."

"In that case," she said, "I'll just go south for the winter."

"Yes, do!" he said. "You always enjoy it."

"I always do," she replied.

They parted with a certain relentlessness that had a touch of wistful sentiment behind it. Off she went to her gallant affairs, that were like the curate's egg, palatable in parts. And he settled down to work. He said he hated working, but he never did anything else. Ten or eleven hours a day. That's what it is to be your own master!

So the winter wore away, and it was spring, when the swallows homeward fly, or northward, in this case. This winter, one of a series similar, had been rather hard to get through. The bit of grit in the gallant lady's eye had worked deeper in the more she blinked. Dark faces might be dark, and icy cocktails might lend a glow; she blinked her hardest to blink that bit of grit away, without success. Under the spicy balls of the mimosa she thought of that husband of hers in his library, and of that neat, competent but *common* little secretary of his, for ever taking down what he said!

"How a man can *stand* it! How *she* can stand it, common little thing as she is, I don't know!" the wife cried to herself.

She meant this dictating business, this ten hours a day intercourse, à *deux*, with nothing but a pencil between them, and a flow of words.

What was to be done? Matters, instead of improving, had grown worse. The little secretary had brought her mother and sister into the establishment. The mother was a sort of cook-housekeeper, the sister was a sort of upper maid—she did the fine laundry, and looked after "his" clothes, and valeted him beautifully. It was really an excellent arrangement. The old mother was a splendid plain cook, the sister was all that could be desired as a *valet-de-chambre*, a fine laundress, an upper parlour-maid, and a table-waiter. And all economical to a degree. They knew his affairs by heart. His secretary flew to town when a creditor became dangerous, and she *always* smoothed over the financial crisis.

"He," of course, had debts, and he was working to pay them off. And, if he had been a fairy prince who could call the ants to help him, he would not have been more wonderful than in securing this secretary and her family. They took hardly any wages. And they seemed to perform the miracle of loaves and fishes daily.

"She," of course, was the wife who loved her husband, but helped him into debt, and she still was an expensive item. Yet when she appeared at her "home," the secretarial family received her with most elaborate attentions and deference. The knight returning from the Crusades didn't create a greater stir. She felt like Queen Elizabeth at Kenilworth, a sovereign paying a visit to her faithful subjects. But perhaps there lurked always this hair in her soup: Won't they be glad to be rid of me again!

But they protested No! No! They had been waiting and hoping and praying she would come. They had been pining for her to be there, in charge: the mistress, "his" wife. Ah, "his" wife!

"His" wife! His halo was like a bucket over her head.

The cook-mother was "of the people," so it was the upper-maid daughter who came for orders.

"What will you order for to-morrow's lunch and dinner, Mrs Gee?"

"Well, what do you usually have?"

"Oh, we want *you* to say."

"No, what do you *usually* have?"

"We don't have anything fixed. Mother goes out and chooses the best she can find, that is nice and fresh. But she thought you would tell her now what to get."

"Oh, I don't know! I'm not very good at that sort of thing. Ask her to go on just the same; I'm quite sure she knows best."

"Perhaps you'd like to suggest a sweet?"

"No, I don't care for sweets—and you know Mr Gee doesn't. So don't make one for me."

Could anything be more impossible! They had the house spotless and running like a dream; how could an incompetent and extravagant wife dare to interfere, when she saw their amazing and almost inspired economy! But they ran the place on simply nothing!

Simply marvellous people! And the way they strewed palm-branches under her feet!

But that only made her feel ridiculous.

"Don't you think the family manage very well?" he asked her tentatively.

"Awfully well! Almost romantically well!" she replied. "But I suppose you're perfectly happy?"

"I'm perfectly comfortable," he replied.

"I can see you are," she replied. "Amazingly so! I never knew such comfort! Are you sure it isn't bad for you?"

She eyed him stealthily. He looked very well, and extremely handsome, in his histrionic way. He was shockingly well-dressed and valeted. And he had that air of easy *aplomb* and good-humour which is so becoming to a man, and which he only acquires when he is cock of his own little walk, made much of by his own hens.

"No!" he said, taking his pipe from his mouth and smiling whimsically round at her. "Do I look as if it were bad for me?"

"No, you don't," she replied promptly: thinking, naturally, as a woman is supposed to think nowadays, of his health and comfort, the foundation, apparently, of all happiness.

Then, of course, away she went on the backwash.

"Perhaps for your work, though, it's not so good as it is for *you*," she said in a rather small voice. She knew he couldn't bear it if she mocked at his work for one moment. And he knew that rather small voice of hers.

"In what way?" he said, bristles rising.

"Oh, I don't know," she answered indifferently. "Perhaps it's not good for a man's work if he is too comfortable."

"I don't know about *that!*" he said, taking a dramatic turn round the library and drawing at his pipe. "Considering I work, actually, by the clock, for twelve hours a day, and for ten hours when it's a short day, I don't think you can say I am deteriorating from easy comfort."

"No, I suppose not," she admitted.

Yet she did think it, nevertheless. His comfortableness didn't consist so much in good food and a soft bed, as in having nobody, absolutely nobody and nothing to contradict him. "I do like to think he's got nothing to aggravate him," the secretary had said to the wife.

"Nothing to aggravate him!" What a position for a man! Fostered by women who would let nothing "aggravate" him. If anything would aggravate his wounded vanity, this would!

So thought the wife. But what was to be done about it? In the silence of midnight she heard his voice in the distance, dictating away, like the voice of God to Samuel, alone and monotonous, and she imagined the little figure of the secretary busily scribbling shorthand. Then in the sunny hours of morning, while he was still in bed—he never rose till noon—from another distance came that sharp insect-noise of the typewriter, like some immense grasshopper chirping and rattling. It was the secretary, poor thing, typing out his notes.

That girl—she was only twenty-eight—really slaved herself to skin and bone. She was small and neat, but she was actually worn out. She did far more work than he did, for she had not only to take down all those words he uttered, she had to type them out, make three copies, while he was still resting.

"What on earth she gets out of it," thought the wife, "I don't know. She's simply worn to the bone, for a very poor salary, and he's never kissed her, and never will, if I know anything about him."

Whether his never kissing her—the secretary, that is—made it worse or better, the wife did not decide. He never kissed anybody. Whether she herself—the wife, that is—wanted to be kissed by him, even that she was not clear about. She rather thought she didn't.

What on earth did she want then? She was his wife. What on earth did she want of him?

She certainly didn't want to take him down in shorthand, and type out again all those words. And she didn't really want him to kiss her; she knew him too well. Yes, she knew him too well. If you know a man too well, you don't want him to kiss you.

What then? What did she want? Why had she such an extraordinary hang-over about him? Just because she was his wife? Why did she rather "enjoy" other men—and she was relentless about enjoyment—without ever taking them seriously? And why must she take him so damn seriously, when she never really "enjoyed" him?

Of course she *had* had good times with him, in the past, before—ah! before a thousand things, all amounting really to nothing. But she enjoyed him no more. She never even enjoyed being with him. There was a silent, ceaseless tension between them, that never broke, even when they were a thousand miles apart.

Awful! That's what you call being married! What's to be done about it? Ridiculous, to know it all and not do anything about it!

She came back once more, and there she was, in her own house, a sort of super-guest, even to him. And the secretarial family devoting their lives to him.

Devoting their lives to him! But actually! Three women pouring out their lives for him day and night! And what did they get in return? Not one kiss! Very little money, because they knew all about his debts, and had made it their life-business to get them paid off! No expectations! Twelve hours' work a day! Comparative isolation, for he saw nobody!

And beyond that? Nothing! Perhaps a sense of uplift and importance because they saw his name and photograph in the newspapers some-times. But would anybody believe that it was good enough?

Yet they adored it! They seemed to get a deep satisfaction out of it, like people with a mission. Extraordinary!

Well, if they did, let them. They were, of course, rather common, "of the people"; there might be a sort of glamour in it for them.

But it was bad for him. No doubt about it. His work was getting diffuse and poor in quality—and what wonder! His whole tone was going down—becoming commoner. Of course it was bad for him.

Being his wife, she felt she ought to do something to save him. But how could she? That perfectly devoted, marvellous secretarial family, how could she make an attack on them? Yet she'd love to sweep them into oblivion. Of course they were bad for him: ruining his work, ruining his reputation as a writer, ruining his life. Ruining him with their slavish service.

Of course she ought to make an onslaught on them! But how *could* she? Such devotion! And what had she herself to offer in their place? Certainly not slavish devotion to him, nor to his flow of words! Certainly not!

She imagined him stripped once more naked of secretary and secretarial family, and she shuddered. It was like throwing the naked baby in the dust-bin. Couldn't do that!

Yet something must be done. She felt it. She was almost tempted to get into debt for another thousand pounds, and send in the bill, or have it sent to him, as usual.

But no! Something more drastic!

Something more drastic, or perhaps more gentle. She wavered between the two. And wavering, she first did nothing, came to no decision, dragged vacantly on from day to day, waiting for sufficient energy to take her departure once more.

It was spring! What a fool she had been to come up in spring! And she was forty! What an idiot of a woman to go and be forty!

She went down the garden in the warm afternoon, when birds were whistling loudly from the cover, the sky being low and warm, and she had nothing to do. The garden was full of flowers: he loved them for their theatrical display. Lilac and snowball bushes, and laburnum and red may, tulips and anemones and coloured daisies. Lots of flowers! Borders of forget-me-nots! Bachelor's buttons! What absurd names flowers had! She would have called them blue dots and yellow blobs and white frills. Not so much sentiment, after all!

There is a certain nonsense, something showy and stagey about spring, with its pushing leaves and chorus-girl flowers, unless you have something corresponding inside you. Which she hadn't.

Oh, heaven! Beyond the hedge she heard a voice, a steady, rather theatrical voice. Oh, heaven!—he was dictating to his secretary in the garden. Good God, was there nowhere to get away from it!

She looked around: there was indeed plenty of escape. But what was the good of escaping? He would go on and on. She went quietly towards the hedge, and listened.

He was dictating a magazine article about the modern novel. "What the modern novel lacks is architecture." Good God! Architecture! He might just as well say: What the modern novel lacks is whalebone, or a teaspoon, or a tooth stopped.

Yet the secretary took it down, took it down, took it down! No, this could not go on! It was more than flesh and blood could bear.

She went quietly along the hedge, somewhat wolf-life in her prowl, a broad, strong woman in an expensive mustard-coloured silk jersey and cream-coloured pleated skirt. Her legs were long and shapely, and her shoes were expensive.

With a curious wolf-like stealth she turned the hedge and looked across at the small, shaded lawn where the daisies grew impertinently. "He" was reclining in a coloured hammock under the pink-flowering horse-chestnut tree, dressed in white serge with a fine yellow-coloured linen shirt. His elegant hand dropped over the side of the hammock and beat a sort of vague rhythm to his words. At a little wicker table the little secretary, in a green knitted frock, bent her dark head over her notebook, and diligently made those awful shorthand marks. He was not difficult to take down, as he dictated slowly, and kept a sort of rhythm, beating time with his dangling hand.

"In every novel there must be one outstanding character with which we always sympathise—with *whom* we always sympathise—even though we recognise its—even when we are most aware of the human frailties——"

Every man his own hero, thought the wife grimly, forgetting that every woman is intensely her own heroine.

But what did startle her was a blue bird dashing about near the feet of the absorbed, shorthand-scribbling little secretary. At least it was a blue-tit, blue with grey and some yellow. But to the wife it seemed blue, that juicy spring day, in the translucent afternoon. The blue bird, fluttering round the pretty but rather *common* little feet of the little secretary.

The blue bird! The blue bird of happiness! Well, I'm blest—thought the wife. Well, I'm blest!

And as she was being blest, appeared another blue bird—that is, another blue-tit—and began to wrestle with the first blue-tit. A couple of blue birds of happiness, having a fight over it! Well, I'm blest!

She was more or less out of sight of the human preoccupied pair. But "he" was disturbed by the fighting blue birds, whose little feathers began to float loose.

"Get out!" he said to them mildly, waving a dark-yellow handkerchief at them. "Fight your little fight, and settle your private affairs elsewhere, my dear little gentlemen."

The little secretary looked up quickly, for she had already begun to write it down. He smiled at her his twisted whimsical smile.

"No, don't take that down," he said affectionately. "Did you see those two tits laying into one another?"

"No!" said the little secretary, gazing brightly round, her eyes half-blinded with work.

But she saw the queer, powerful, elegant, wolf-like figure of the wife, behind her, and terror came into her eyes.

"I did!" said the wife, stepping forward with those curious, shapely, she-wolf legs of hers, under the very short skirt.

"Aren't they extraordinarily vicious little beasts?" said he.

"Extraordinarily!" she re-echoed, stooping and picking up a little breast-feather. "Extraordinarily! See how the feathers fly!"

And she got the feather on the tip of her finger, and looked at it. Then she looked at the secretary, then she looked at him. She had a queer, were-wolf expression between her brows.

"I think," he began "these are the loveliest afternoons, when there's no direct sun, but all the sounds and the colours and the scents are sort of dissolved, don't you know, in the air, and the whole thing is steeped, steeped in spring. It's like being on the inside; you know how I mean, like being inside the egg and just ready to chip the shell."

"Quite like that!" she assented, without conviction.

There was a little pause. The secretary said nothing. They were waiting for the wife to depart again.

"I suppose," said the latter, "you're most awfully busy, as usual?"

"Just about the same," he said, pursing his mouth deprecatingly.

Again the blank pause, in which he waited for her to go away again.

"I know I'm interrupting you," she said.

"As a matter of fact," he said, "I was just watching those two blue-tits."

"Pair of little demons!" said the wife, blowing away the yellow feather from her finger-tip.

"Absolutely!" he said.

"Well, I'd better go, and let you get on with your work," she said.

"No hurry!" he said, with benevolent nonchalance. "As a matter of fact, I don't think it's a great success, working out of doors."

"What made you try it?" said the wife. "You know you never could do it."

"Miss Wrexall suggested it might make a change. But I don't think it altogether helps, do you, Miss Wrexall?"

"I'm sorry," said the little secretary.

"Why should *you* be sorry?" said the wife looking down at her as a wolf might look down half benignly at a little black-and-tan mongrel. "You only suggested it for his good, I'm sure!"

"I thought the air might be good for him," the secretary admitted.

"Why do people like you never think about yourselves?" the wife asked.

The secretary looked her in the eye.

"I suppose we do, in a different way," she said.

"A *very* different way!" said the wife ironically. "Why don't you make *him* think about *you?*" she added slowly, with a sort of drawl. "On a soft spring afternoon like this, you ought to have him dictating poems to you, about the blue birds of happiness fluttering round your dainty little feet. I know *I* would, if I were his secretary."

There was a dead pause. The wife stood immobile and statuesque, in an attitude characteristic of her, half turning back to the little secretary, half averted. She half turned her back on everything.

The secretary looked at him.

"As a matter of fact," he said, "I was doing an article on the Future of the Novel."

"I know that," said the wife. "That's what's so awful! Why not something lively in the life of the novelist?"

There was a prolonged silence, in which he looked pained, and somewhat remote, statuesque. The little secretary hung her head. The wife sauntered slowly away.

"Just where were we, Miss Wrexall?" came the sound of his voice.

The little secretary started. She was feeling profoundly indignant. Their beautiful relationship, his and hers, to be so insulted!

But soon she was veering downstream on the flow of his words, too busy to have any feelings, except one of elation at being so busy.

Tea-time came; the sister brought out the tea-tray into the garden. And immediately, the wife appeared. She had changed, and was wearing a chicory-blue dress of fine cloth. The little secretary had gathered up her papers and was departing, on rather high heels.

"Don't go, Miss Wrexall," said the wife.

The little secretary stopped short, then hesitated.

"Mother will be expecting me," she said.

"Tell her you're not coming. And ask your sister to bring another cup. I want you to have tea with us."

Miss Wrexall looked at the man, who was reared on one elbow in the hammock, and was looking enigmatical, Hamletish.

He glanced at her quickly, then pursed his mouth in a boyish negligence.

"Yes, stay and have tea with us for once," he said. "I see strawberries, and I know you're the bird for them."

She glanced at him, smiled wanly, and hurried away to tell her mother. She even stayed long enough to slip on a silk dress.

"Why, how smart you are!" said the wife, when the little secretary reappeared on the lawn, in chicory-blue silk.

"Oh, don't look at my dress, compared to yours!" said Miss Wrexall. They were of the same colour, indeed!

"At least you earned yours, which is more than I did mine," said the wife, as she poured tea. "You like it strong?"

She looked with her heavy eyes at the smallish, birdy, blue-clad, overworked young woman, and her eyes seemed to speak many inexplicable dark volumes.

"Oh, as it comes, thank you," said Miss Wrexall, leaning nervously forward.

"It's coming pretty black, if you want to ruin your digestion," said the wife.

"Oh, I'll have some water in it, then."

"Better, I should say."

"How'd the work go—all right?" asked the wife, as they drank tea, and the two women looked at each other's blue dresses.

"Oh!" he said. "As well as you can expect. It was a piece of pure flummery. But it's what they want. Awful rot, wasn't it, Miss Wrexall?"

Miss Wrexall moved uneasily on her chair.

"It interested me," she said, "though not so much as the novel."

"The novel? Which novel?" said the wife. "Is there another new one?"

Miss Wrexall looked at him. Not for worlds would she give away any of his literary activities.

"Oh, I was just sketching out an idea to Miss Wrexall," he said.

"Tell us about it!" said the wife. "Miss Wrexall, *you* tell us what it's about."

She turned on her chair, and fixed the little secretary.

"I'm afraid"—Miss Wrexall squirmed—"I haven't got it very clearly myself, yet."

"Oh, go along! Tell us what you *have* got then!"

Miss Wrexall sat dumb and very vexed. She felt she was being baited. She looked at the blue pleatings of her skirt.

"I'm afraid I can't," she said.

"Why are you afraid you can't? You're so *very* competent, I'm sure you've got it all at your finger-ends. I expect you write a good deal of Mr Gee's books for him, really. He gives you the hint, and you fill it all in. Isn't that how you do it?" She spoke ironically, and as if she were teasing a child. And then she glanced down at the fine pleatings of her own blue skirt, very fine and expensive.

"Of course you're not speaking seriously?" said Miss Wrexall, rising on her mettle.

"Of course I am! I've suspected for a long time—at least, for some time—that you write a good deal of Mr Gee's books for him, from his hints."

It was said in a tone of raillery, but it was cruel.

"I should be terribly flattered," said Miss Wrexall, straightening herself, "if I didn't know you were only trying to make me feel a fool."

"Make you feel a fool? My dear child!—why, nothing could be farther from me! You're twice as clever, and a million times as competent as I am. Why, my dear child, I've the greatest admiration for you! I wouldn't do what you do, not for all the pearls in India. I *couldn't*, anyhow——"

Miss Wrexall closed up and was silent.

"Do you mean to say my books read as if——" he began, rearing up and speaking in a harrowed voice.

"I do!" said his wife. "*Just* as if Miss Wrexall had written them from your hints. I *honestly* thought she did—when you were too busy——"

"How very clever of you!" he said.

"Very!" she cried. "Especially if I was wrong!"

"Which you were," he said.

"How very extraordinary!" she cried. "Well, I am once more mistaken!"

There was complete pause.

It was broken by Miss Wrexall, who was nervously twisting her fingers.

"You want to spoil what there is between me and him, I can see that," she said bitterly.

"My dear, but what *is* there between you and him?" asked the wife.

"I was *happy* working with him, working for him! I was *happy* working for him!" cried Miss Wrexall, tears of indignant anger and chagrin in her eyes.

"My dear child!" cried the wife, with simulated excitement, "go *on* being happy working with him, go on being happy while you can! If it makes you happy, why then, enjoy it! Of course! Do you think I'd be so cruel as to want to take it away from you?—working with him? *I* can't do shorthand and typewriting and double-entrance book-keeping, or whatever it's called. I tell you, I'm utterly incompetent. I never earn anything. I'm the parasite on the British oak, like the mistletoe. The blue bird doesn't flutter round my feet. Perhaps they're too big and trampling."

She looked down at her expensive shoes.

"If I *did* have a word of criticism to offer," she said, turning to her husband, "it would be to you, Cameron, for taking so much from her and giving her nothing."

"But he gives me everything, everything!" cried Miss Wrexall. "He gives me everything!"

"What do you mean by everything?" said the wife, turning on her sternly.

Miss Wrexall pulled up short. There was a snap in the air, and a change of currents.

"I mean nothing that *you* need begrudge me," said the little secretary rather haughtily. "I've never made myself cheap."

There was a blank pause.

"My God!" said the wife. "You don't call that being cheap? Why, I should say you got nothing out of him at all, you only give! And if you don't call that making yourself cheap—my God!"

"You see, we see things different," said the secretary.

"I should say we do!—*thank God!*" rejoined the wife.

"On whose behalf are you thanking God?" he asked sarcastically.

"Everybody's, I suppose! Yours, because you get everything for nothing, and Miss Wrexall's, because she seems to like it, and mine because I'm well out of it all."

"You *needn't* be out of it all," cried Miss Wrexall magnanimously, "if you didn't *put* yourself out of it all."

"Thank you, my dear, for your offer," said the wife, rising. "But I'm afraid no man can expect *two* blue birds of happiness to flutter round his feet, tearing out their little feathers!"

With which she walked away.

After a tense and desperate interim, Miss Wrexall cried:

"And *really*, need any woman be jealous of *me*?"

"Quite!" he said.

And that was all he did say.

For Study and Discussion

1. How similar in temperament are the husband and wife?

2. What indications are given early in the story that the wife is jealous of her husband's secretary?

3. Why is it that the wife, so far as her husband is concerned, "didn't intend to be relied on"?

4. Why does the wife, upon returning to her husband's establishment, find his halo "like a bucket over her head"?

5. What is the real reason for the wife's desire to get rid of the secretarial family?

6. Why is the wife described as "wolf-like" when she enters the garden where her husband is dictating to the secretary?

7. How do the bluebirds function as symbols?

8. What important light is shed on the theme of the story by the statement that the wife forgets "that every woman is intensely her own heroine"?

9. How extensively is figurative languge used in the story? Is it used effectively?

10. In her comments on Lawrence, Welty says, "It is the world of the senses that Lawrence writes in, works in, thinks in, takes as his medium" (p. 107). To what extent is "Two Blue Birds" a story of "the world of the senses"?

KATHERINE ANNE PORTER

THEFT

She had the purse in her hand when she came in. Standing in the middle of the floor, holding her bathrobe around her and trailing a damp towel in one hand, she surveyed the immediate past and remembered everything clearly. Yes, she had opened the flap and spread it out on the bench after she had dried the purse with her handkerchief.

She had intended to take the Elevated, and naturally she looked in her purse to make certain she had the fare, and was pleased to find forty cents in the coin envelope. She was going to pay her own fare, too, even if Camilo did have the habit of seeing her up the steps and dropping a nickel in the machine before he gave the turnstile a little push and sent her through it with a bow. Camilo by a series of compromises had managed to make effective a fairly complete set of smaller courtesies, ignoring the larger and more troublesome ones. She had walked with him to the station in a pouring rain, because she knew he was almost as poor as she was, and when he insisted on a taxi, she was firm and said, "You know it simply will not do." He was wearing a new hat of a pretty biscuit shade, for it never occurred to him to buy anything of a practical color; he had put it on for the first time and the rain was spoiling it. She kept thinking, "But this is dreadful, where will he get another?" She compared it with Eddie's hats that always seemed to be precisely seven years old and as if they had been quite purposely left out in the rain, and yet they sat with a careless and incidental rightness on Eddie. But Camilo was far different; if he wore a shabby hat it would be merely shabby on him, and he would lose his spirits over it. If she had not feared Camilo would take it badly, for he insisted on the practice of his little ceremonies up to the point he had fixed for them, she would have said to him as they left Thora's house, "Do go home. I can surely reach the station by myself."

Originally published in the *Gyroscope*, November 1929. Reprinted here from *Flowering Judas and Other Stories* (New York: Harcourt, Brace and Co., 1935) by·permission of Harcourt Brace Jovanovich, Inc. Copyright 1935, renewed 1963, by Katherine Anne Porter.

"It is written that we must be rained upon tonight," said Camilo, "so let it be together."

At the foot of the platform stairway she staggered slightly—they were both nicely set up on Thora's cocktails—and said: "At least, Camilo, do me the favor not to climb these stairs in your present state, since for you it is only a matter of coming down again at once, and you'll certainly break your neck."

He made three quick bows, he was Spanish, and leaped off through the rainy darkness. She stood watching him, for he was a very graceful young man, thinking that tomorrow morning he would gaze soberly at his spoiled hat and soggy shoes and possibly associate her with his misery. As she watched, he stopped at the far corner and took off his hat and hid it under his overcoat. She felt she had betrayed him by seeing, because he would have been humiliated if he thought she even suspected him of trying to save his hat.

Roger's voice sounded over her shoulder above the clang of the rain falling on the stairway shed, wanting to know what she was doing out in the rain at this time of night, and did she take herself for a duck? His long, imperturbable face was streaming with water, and he tapped a bulging spot on the breast of his buttoned-up overcoat: "Hat," he said. "Come on, let's take a taxi."

She settled back against Roger's arm which he laid around her shoulders, and with the gesture they exchanged a glance full of long amiable associations, then she looked through the window at the rain changing the shapes of everything, and the colors. The taxi dodged in and out between the pillars of the Elevated, skidding slightly on every curve, and she said: "The more it skids the calmer I feel, so I really must be drunk."

"You must be," said Roger. "This bird is a homicidal maniac, and I could do with a cocktail myself this minute."

They waited on the traffic at Fortieth Street and Sixth Avenue, and three boys walked before the nose of the taxi. Under the globes of light they were cheerful scarecrows, all very thin and all wearing very seedy snappy-cut suits and gay neckties. They were not very sober either, and they stood for a moment wobbling in front of the car, and there was an argument going on among them. They leaned toward each other as if they were getting ready to sing, and the first one said: "When I get married it won't be jus' for getting married, I'm gonna marry for *love*, see?" and the second one said, "Aw, gwan and tell that stuff to *her*, why n't yuh?" and the third one gave a kind of hoot, and said, "Hell, dis guy? Wot the hell's he got?" and the first one said: "Aaah, shurrup yuh mush, I got plenty." Then they all squealed and scrambled across the street beating the first one on the back and pushing him around.

"Nuts," commented Roger, "pure nuts."

Two girls went skittering by in short transparent raincoats, one green, one red, their heads tucked against the drive of the rain. One of them was saying to the other, "Yes, I know all about *that*. But what about me? You're always so sorry for *him* . . ." and they ran on with their little pelican legs flashing back and forth.

The taxi backed up suddenly and leaped forward again, and after a while Roger said: "I had a letter from Stella today, and she'll be home on the twenty-sixth, so I suppose she's made up her mind and it's all settled."

"I had a sort of letter today too," she said, "making up my mind for me. I think it is time for you and Stella to do something definite."

When the taxi stopped on the corner of West Fifty-third Street, Roger said, "I've just enough if you'll add ten cents," so she opened her purse and gave him a dime, and he said, "That's beautiful, that purse."

"It's a birthday present," she told him, "and I like it. How's your show coming?"

"Oh, still hanging on, I guess. I don't go near the place. Nothing sold yet. I mean to keep right on the way I'm going and they can take it or leave it. I'm through with the argument."

"It's absolutely a matter of holding out, isn't it?"

"Holding out's the tough part."

"Good night, Roger."

"Good night, you should take aspirin and push yourself into a tub of hot water, you look as though you're catching cold."

"I will."

With the purse under her arm she went upstairs, and on the first landing Bill heard her step and poked his head out with his hair tumbled and his eyes red, and he said: "For Christ's sake, come in and have a drink with me. I've had some bad news."

"You're perfectly sopping," said Bill, looking at her drenched feet. They had two drinks while Bill told how the director had thrown his play out after the cast had been picked over twice, and had gone through three rehearsals. "I said to him, 'I didn't say it was a masterpiece, I said it would make a good show.' And he said, 'It just doesn't *play*, do you see? It needs a doctor.' So I'm stuck, absolutely stuck," said Bill, on the edge of weeping again. "I've been crying," he told her, "in my cups." And he went on to ask her if she realized his wife was ruining him with her extravagance. "I send her ten dollars every week of my unhappy life, and I don't really have to. She threatens to jail me if I don't, but she can't do it. God, let her try it after the way she treated me! She's no right to alimony and she knows it. She keeps on saying she's got to have it for the baby and I keep on sending it because I can't bear to see anybody suffer. So I'm way behind on the piano and the victrola, both—"

"Well, this is a pretty rug, anyhow," she said.

Bill stared at it and blew his nose. "I got it at Ricci's for ninety-five dollars," he said. "Ricci told me it once belonged to Marie Dressler, and cost fifteen hundred dollars, but there's a burnt place on it, under the divan. Can you beat that?"

"No," she said. She was thinking about her empty purse and that she could not possibly expect a check for her latest review for another three days, and her arrangement with the basement restaurant could not last much longer if she did not pay something on account. "It's no time to speak of it," she said, "but I've been hoping you would have by now that fifty dollars you promised for my scene in the third act. Even if it doesn't play. You were to pay me for the work anyhow out of your advance."

"Weeping Jesus," said Bill, "you, too?" He gave a loud sob, or hiccough, in his moist handkerchief. "Your stuff was no better than mine, after all. Think of that."

"But you got something for it," she said. "Seven hundred dollars."

Bill said, "Do me a favor, will you? Have another drink and forget about it. I can't, you know I can't, I would if I could, but you know the fix I'm in."

"Let it go, then," she found herself saying almost in spite of herself. She had meant to be quite firm about it. They drank again without speaking, and she went to her apartment on the floor above.

There, she now remembered distinctly, she had taken the letter out of the purse before she spread the purse out to dry.

She had sat down and read the letter over again: but there were phrases that insisted on being read many times, they had a life of their own separate from the others, and when she tried to read past and around them, they moved with the movement of her eyes, and she could not escape them . . . "thinking about you more than I mean to . . . yes, I even talk about you . . . why were you so anxious to destroy . . . even if I could see you now I would not . . . not worth all this abominable . . . the end. . . ."

Carefully she tore the letter into narrow strips and touched a lighted match to them in the coal grate.

Early the next morning she was in the bathtub when the janitress knocked and then came in, calling out that she wished to examine the radiators before she started the furnace going for the winter. After moving about the room for a few minutes, the janitress went out, closing the door very sharply.

She came out of the bathroom to get a cigarette from the package in the purse. The purse was gone. She dressed and made coffee, and sat by the window while she drank it. Certainly the janitress had taken the purse, and certainly it would be impossible to get it back without a great deal of ridiculous excitement. Then let it go. With this decision of her mind, there rose coincidentally in her blood a deep almost murderous anger. She set the cup carefully in the center of the table, and walked steadily downstairs, three long flights and a short hall and a steep short flight into the basement, where the janitress, her face streaked with coal dust, was shaking up the furnace. "Will you please give me back my purse? There isn't any money in it. It was a present, and I don't want to lose it."

The janitress turned without straightening up and peered at her with hot flickering eyes, a red light from the furnace reflected in them. "What do you mean, your purse?"

"The gold cloth purse you took from the wooden bench in my room," she said. "I must have it back."

"Before God I never laid eyes on your purse, and that's the holy truth," said the janitress.

"Oh, well then, keep it," she said, but in a very bitter voice; "keep it if you want it so much." And she walked away.

She remembered how she had never locked a door in her life, on some principle of rejection in her that made her uncomfortable in the ownership of things, and her paradoxical boast before the warnings of her friends, that she had never lost a penny by theft; and she had been pleased with the bleak humility of this concrete example designed to illustrate and justify a certain fixed, otherwise baseless and general faith which ordered the movements of her life without regard to her will in the matter.

In this moment she felt that she had been robbed of an enormous number of valuable things, whether material or intangible: things lost or broken by her own fault, things she had forgotten and left in houses when she moved: books borrowed from her and not returned, journeys she had planned and had not made, words she had waited to hear spoken to her and had not heard, and the words she had meant to answer with; bitter alternatives and intolerable substitutes worse than nothing, and yet inescapable: the long patient suffering of dying friendships and the dark inexplicable death of love—all that she had had, and all that she had missed, were lost together, and were twice lost in this landslide of remembered losses.

The janitress was following her upstairs with the purse in her hand and the same deep red fire flickering in her eyes. The janitress thrust the purse towards her while they were still a half dozen steps apart, and said: "Don't never tell on me. I musta been crazy. I get crazy in the head sometimes, I swear I do. My son can tell you."

She took the purse after a moment, and the janitress went on: "I got a niece who is going on seventeen, and she's a nice girl and I thought I'd give it to her. She needs a pretty purse. I musta been crazy; I thought maybe you wouldn't mind, you leave things around and don't seem to notice much."

She said: "I missed this because it was a present to me from someone . . ."

The janitress said: "He'd get you another if you lost this one. My niece is young and needs pretty things, we oughta give the young ones a chance. She's got young men after her maybe will want to marry her. She oughta have nice things. She needs them bad right now. You're a grown woman, you've had your chance, you ought to know how it is!''

She held the purse out to the janitress saying: "You don't know what you're talking about. Here, take it. I've changed my mind. I really don't want it."

The janitress looked up at her with hatred and said: "I don't want it either now. My niece is young and pretty, she don't need fixin' up to be pretty, she's young and pretty anyhow! I guess you need it worse than she does!''

"It wasn't really yours in the first place," she said, turning away. "You mustn't talk as if I had stolen it from you."

"It's not from me, it's from her you're stealing it," said the janitress, and went back downstairs.

She laid the purse on the table and sat down with the cup of chilled coffee, and thought: I was right not to be afraid of any thief but myself, who will end by leaving me nothing.

For Study and Discussion

1. What is the function in the story of the fragmentary street conversations (that of the three boys, then of the two girls) the woman and Roger overhear when their taxi is blocked by traffic?

2. What is the significance of the letter the woman rereads and then burns?

3. What motive does the janitress have in stealing the purse? How does she attempt to justify the theft?

4. Explain the meaning of the woman's concluding thought, "I was right not to be afraid of any thief but myself, who will end by leaving me nothing."

5. In Porter's ironic essay, "No Plot, My Dear, No Story," she objects to the importance magazine editors frequently attach to plot or to the sequence of action in short stories. How much emphasis does the element of plot receive in "Theft"? Would you describe "Theft" as a story of "form"? Compare the structure of "Theft" with that of West's "Love, Death, and the Ladies' Drill Team."

WILLIAM FAULKNER

MULE IN THE YARD

It was a gray day in late January, though not cold because of the fog. Old Het, just walked in from the poorhouse, ran down the hall toward the kitchen, shouting in a strong, bright, happy voice. She was about seventy probably, though by her own counting, calculated from the ages of various housewives in the town from brides to grandmothers whom she claimed to have nursed in infancy, she would have to be around a hundred and at least triplets. Tall, lean, fog-beaded, in tennis shoes and a long rat-colored cloak trimmed with what forty or fifty years ago had been fur, a modish though not new purple toque set upon her headrag and carrying (time was when she made her weekly rounds from kitchen to kitchen carrying a brocaded carpetbag though since the advent of the ten-cent stores the carpetbag became an endless succession of the convenient paper receptacles with which they supply their customers for a few cents) the shopping-bag, she ran into the kitchen and shouted with strong and childlike pleasure: "Miss Mannie! Mule in de yard!"

Mrs. Hait, stooping to the stove, in the act of drawing from it a scuttle of live ashes, jerked upright; clutching the scuttle, she glared at old Het, then she too spoke at once, strong too, immediate. "Them sons of bitches," she said. She left the kitchen, not running exactly, yet with a kind of outraged celerity, carrying the scuttle—a compact woman of forty-odd, with an air of indomitable yet relieved bereavement, as though that which had relicted her had been a woman and a not particularly valuable one at that. She wore a calico wrapper and a sweater coat, and a man's felt hat which they in the town knew had belonged to her ten years' dead husband. But the man's shoes had not belonged to him. They were high shoes which buttoned, with toes like small tulip bulbs, and in the town they knew that she had bought them new for herself. She and old Het ran down the kitchen steps and into the fog. That's why it was not cold: as though there lay supine and prisoned

Originally published in *Scribner's Magazine*, August 1934. Reprinted here from *The Collected Stories of William Faulkner* (New York: Random House, Inc., 1950) by permission of the publisher. Copyright 1934 and renewed 1962 by William Faulkner.

between earth and mist the long winter night's suspiration of the
sleeping town in dark, close rooms—the slumber and the rousing; the
stale waking thermostatic, by re-heating heat-engendered: it lay like a
scum of cold grease upon the steps and the wooden entrance to the
basement and upon the narrow plank walk which led to a shed building
in the corner of the yard: upon these planks, running and still carrying
the scuttle of live ashes, Mrs. Hait skated viciously.

"Watch out!" old Het, footed securely by her rubber soles, cried
happily. "Dey in de front!" Mrs. Hait did not fall. She did not even
pause. She took in the immediate scene with one cold glare and was
running again when there appeared at the corner of the house and
apparently having been born before their eyes of the fog itself, a mule. It
looked taller than a giraffe. Longheaded, with a flying halter about its
scissorlike ears, it rushed down upon them with violent and apparition-
like suddenness.

"Dar hit!" old Het cried, waving the shopping-bag. "Hoo!" Mrs. Hait
whirled. Again she skidded savagely on the greasy planks as she and the
mule rushed parallel with one another toward the shed building, from
whose open doorway there now projected the static and astonished face
of a cow. To the cow the fog-born mule doubtless looked taller and more
incredibly sudden than a giraffe even, and apparently bent upon charg-
ing right through the shed as though it were made of straw or were
purely and simply mirage. The cow's head likewise had a quality
transient and abrupt and unmundane. It vanished, sucked into invisibili-
ty like a match flame, though the mind knew and the reason insisted that
she had withdrawn into the shed, from which, as proof's burden, there
came an indescribable sound of shock and alarm by shed and beast
engendered, analogous to a single note from a profoundly struck lyre or
harp. Toward this sound Mrs. Hait sprang, immediately, as if by pure
reflex, as though in invulnerable compact of female with female against a
world of mule and man. She and the mule converged upon the shed at
top speed, the heavy scuttle poised lightly in her hand to hurl. Of course
it did not take this long, and likewise it was the mule which refused the
gambit. Old Het was still shouting "Dar hit! Dar hit!" when it swerved
and rushed at her where she stood tall as a stove pipe, holding the
shopping-bag which she swung at the beast as it rushed past her and
vanished beyond the other corner of the house as though sucked back
into the fog which had produced it, profound and instantaneous and
without any sound.

With that unhasteful celerity Mrs. Hait turned and set the scuttle down
on the brick coping of the cellar entrance and she and old Het turned the
corner of the house in time to see the now wraithlike mule at the moment
when its course converged with that of a choleric-looking rooster and
eight Rhode Island Red hens emerging from beneath the house. Then
for an instant its progress assumed the appearance and trappings of an

apotheosis: hell-born and hell-returning, in the act of dissolving completely into the fog, it seemed to rise vanishing into a sunless and dimensionless medium borne upon and enclosed by small winged goblins.

"Dey's mo in de front!" old Het cried.

"Them sons of bitches," Mrs. Hait said, again in that grim, prescient voice without rancor or heat. It was not the mules to which she referred; it was not even the owner of them. It was her whole town-dwelling history as dated from that April dawn ten years ago when what was left of Hait had been gathered from the mangled remains of five mules and several feet of new Manila rope on a blind curve of the railroad just out of town; the geographical hap of her very home; the very components of her bereavement—the mules, the defunct husband, and the owner of them. His name was Snopes; in the town they knew about him too—how he bought his stock at the Memphis market and brought it to Jefferson and sold it to farmers and widows and orphans black and white, for whatever he could contrive—down to a certain figure; and about how (usually in the dead season of winter) teams and even small droves of his stock would escape from the fenced pasture where he kept them and, tied one to another with sometimes quite new hemp rope (and which item Snopes included in the subsequent claim), would be annihilated by freight trains on the same blind curve which was to be the scene of Hait's exit from this world; once a town wag sent him through the mail a printed train schedule for the division. A squat, pasty man perennially tieless and with a strained, harried expression, at stated intervals he passed athwart the peaceful and somnolent life of the town in dust and uproar, his advent heralded by shouts and cries, his passing marked by a yellow cloud filled with tossing jug-shaped heads and clattering hooves and the same forlorn and earnest cries of the drovers; and last of all and well back out of the dust, Snopes himself moving at a harried and panting trot, since it was said in the town that he was deathly afraid of the very beasts in which he cleverly dealt.

The path which he must follow from the railroad station to his pasture crossed the edge of town near Hait's home; Hait and Mrs. Hait had not been in the house a week before they waked one morning to find it surrounded by galloping mules and the air filled with the shouts and cries of the drovers. But it was not until that April dawn some years later, when those who reached the scene first found what might be termed foreign matter among the mangled mules and the savage fragments of new rope, that the town suspected that Hait stood in any closer relationship to Snopes and the mules than that of helping at periodical intervals to drive them out of his front yard. After that they believed that they knew; in a three days' recess of interest, surprise, and curiosity they watched to see if Snopes would try to collect on Hait also.

But they learned only that the adjuster appeared and called upon Mrs.

Hait and that a few days later she cashed a check for eight thousand five hundred dollars, since this was back in the old halcyon days when even the companies considered their southern branches and divisions the legitimate prey of all who dwelt beside them. She took the cash: she stood in her sweater coat and the hat which Hait had been wearing on the fatal morning a week ago and listened in cold, grim silence while the teller counted the money and the president and the cashier tried to explain to her the virtues of a bond, then of a savings account, then of a checking account, and departed with the money in a salt sack under her apron; after a time she painted her house: that serviceable and time-defying color which the railroad station was painted, as though out of sentiment or (as some said) gratitude.

The adjuster also summoned Snopes into conference, from which he emerged not only more harried-looking than ever, but with his face stamped with a bewildered dismay which it was to wear from then on, and that was the last time his pasture fence was ever to give inexplicably away at dead of night upon mules coupled in threes and fours by adequate rope even though not always new. And then it seemed as though the mules themselves knew this, as if, even while haltered at the Memphis block at his bid, they sensed it somehow as they sensed that he was afraid of them. Now, three or four times a year and as though by fiendish concord and as soon as they were freed of the box car, the entire uproar—the dust cloud filled with shouts earnest, harried, and dismayed, with plunging demoniac shapes—would become translated in a single burst of perverse and uncontrollable violence, without any intervening contact with time, space, or earth, across the peaceful and astonished town and into Mrs. Hait's yard, where, in a certain hapless despair which abrogated for the moment even physical fear, Snopes ducked and dodged among the thundering shapes about the house (for whose very impervious paint the town believed that he felt he had paid and whose inmate lived within it a life of idle and queenlike ease on money which he considered at least partly his own) while gradually that section and neighborhood gathered to look on from behind adjacent window curtains and porches screened and not, and from the sidewalks and even from halted wagons and cars in the street—housewives in the wrappers and boudoir caps of morning, children on the way to school, casual Negroes and casual whites in static and entertained repose.

They were all there when, followed by old Het and carrying the stub of a worn-out broom, Mrs. Hait ran around the next corner and onto the handkerchief-sized plot of earth which she called her front yard. It was small; any creature with a running stride of three feet could have spanned it in two paces, yet at the moment, due perhaps to the myopic and distortive quality of the fog, it seemed to be as incredibly full of mad life as a drop of water beneath the microscope. Yet again she did not falter. With the broom clutched in her hand and apparently with a kind of sublime faith in her own invulnerability, she rushed on after the haltered mule which was still in that arrested and wraithlike process of vanishing furiously into the fog, its wake indicated by the tossing and dispersing shapes of the nine chickens like so many jagged scraps of paper in the dying air blast of an automobile, and the madly dodging figure of a man. The man was Snopes; beaded too with moisture, his wild face gaped with hoarse shouting and the two heavy lines of shaven beard descending from the corners of it as though in alluvial retrospect of years of tobacco, he screamed at her: "Fore God, Miz Hait! I done everything I could!" She didn't even look at him.

"Ketch that big un with the bridle on," she said in her cold, panting voice. "Git that big un outen here."

"Sho!" Snopes shrieked. "Jest let um take their time. Jest don't git um excited now."

"Watch out!" old Het shouted. "He headin fer de back again!"

"Git the rope," Mrs. Hait said, running again. Snopes glared back at old Het.

"Fore God, where is ere rope?" he shouted.

"In de cellar fo God!" old Het shouted, also without pausing. "Go roun de udder way en head um." Again she and Mrs. Hait turned the corner in time to see again the still-vanishing mule with the halter once more in the act of floating lightly onward in its cloud of chickens with which, they being able to pass under the house and so on the chord of a circle while it had to go around on the arc, it had once more coincided. When they turned the next corner they were in the back yard again.

"Fo God!" old Het cried. "He fixin to misuse de cow!" For they had gained on the mule now, since it had stopped. In fact, they came around the corner on a tableau. The cow now stood in the centre of the yard. She and the mule faced one another a few feet apart. Motionless, with lowered heads and braced forelegs, they looked like two book ends from two distinct pairs of a general pattern which some one of amateurly bucolic leanings might have purchased, and which some child had salvaged, brought into idle juxtaposition and then forgotten; and, his head and shoulders projecting above the back-flung slant of the cellar entrance where the scuttle still sat, Snopes standing as though buried to the armpits for a Spanish-Indian-American suttee. Only again it did not take this long. It was less than tableau; it was one of those things which later even memory cannot quite affirm. Now and in turn, man and cow and mule vanished beyond the next corner, Snopes now in the lead, carrying the rope, the cow next with her tail rigid and raked slightly like the stern staff of a boat. Mrs. Hait and old Het ran on, passing the open cellar gaping upon its accumulation of human necessities and widowed womanyears—boxes for kindling wood, old papers and magazines, the broken and outworn furniture and utensils which no woman ever throws away; a pile of coal and another of pitch pine for priming fires—and ran on and turned the next corner to see man and cow and mule all vanishing now in the wild cloud of ubiquitous chickens which had once more crossed beneath the house and emerged. They ran on, Mrs. Hait in grim and unflagging silence, old Het with the eager and happy amazement of a child. But when they gained the front again they saw only Snopes. He lay flat on his stomach, his head and shoulders upreared by his outstretched arms, his coat tail swept forward by its own arrested momentum about his head so that from beneath it his slack-jawed face mused in wild repose like that of a burlesqued nun.

"Whar'd dey go?" old Het shouted at him. He didn't answer.

"Dey tightenin' on de curves!" she cried. "Dey already in de back again!" That's where they were. The cow made a feint at running into her shed, but deciding perhaps that her speed was too great, she whirled in a final desperation of despair-like valor. But they did not see this, nor see the mule, swerving to pass her, crash and blunder for an instant at the open cellar door before going on. When they arrived, the mule was gone. The scuttle was gone too, but they did not notice it; they saw only the cow standing in the centre of the yard as before, panting, rigid, with braced forelegs and lowered head facing nothing, as if the child had returned and removed one of the book ends for some newer purpose or game. They ran on. Mrs. Hait ran heavily now, her mouth too open, her face putty-colored and one hand pressed to her side. So slow was their progress that the mule in its third circuit of the house overtook them from behind and soared past with undiminished speed, with brief demon thunder and a keen ammonia-sweet reek of sweat sudden and sharp as a jeering cry, and was gone. Yet they ran doggedly on around the next corner in time to see it succeed at last in vanishing into the fog; they heard its hoofs, brief, staccato, and derisive, on the paved street, dying away.

"Well!" old Het said, stopping. She panted, happily. "Gentlemen, hush! Ain't we had—" Then she became stone still; slowly her head turned, high-nosed, her nostrils pulsing; perhaps for the instant she saw the open cellar door as they had last passed it, with no scuttle beside it. "Fo God I smells smoke!" she said. "Chile, run, git yo money."

That was still early, not yet ten o'clock. By noon the house had burned to the ground. There was a farmers' supply store where Snopes could be usually found; more than one had made a point of finding him there by that time. They told him about how when the fire engine and the crowd reached the scene, Mrs. Hait, followed by old Het carrying her shopping-bag in one hand and a framed portrait of Mr. Hait in the other, emerged with an umbrella and wearing a new, dun-colored, mail-order coat, in one pocket of which lay a fruit jar filled with smoothly rolled banknotes and in the other a heavy, nickel-plated pistol, and crossed the street to the house opposite, where with old Het beside her in another rocker, she had been sitting ever since on the veranda, grim, inscrutable, the two of them rocking steadily, while hoarse and tireless men hurled her dishes and furniture and bedding up and down the street.

"What are you telling me for?" Snopes said. "Hit warn't me that set that ere scuttle of live fire where the first thing that passed would knock hit into the cellar."

"It was you that opened the cellar door, though."

"Sho. And for what? To git that rope, her own rope, where she told me to git it."

"To catch your mule with, that was trespassing on her property. You can't get out of it this time, I. O. There ain't a jury in the county that won't find for her."

"Yes. I reckon not. And just because she is a woman. That's why. Because she is a durn woman. All right. Let her go to her durn jury with hit. I can talk too; I reckon hit's a few things I could tell a jury myself about—" He ceased. They were watching him.

"What? Tell a jury about what?"

"Nothing. Because hit ain't going to no jury. A jury between her and me? Me and Mannie Hait? You boys don't know her if you think she's going to make trouble over a pure acci-dent couldn't nobody help. Why, there ain't a fairer, finer woman in the county than Miz Mannie Hait. I just wisht I had a opportunity to tell her so." The opportunity came at once. Old Het was behind her, carrying the shopping-bag. Mrs. Hait looked once, quietly, about at the faces, making no response to the murmur of curious salutation, then not again. She didn't look at Snopes long either, nor talk to him long.

"I come to buy that mule," she said.

"What mule?" They looked at one another. "You'd like to own that mule?" She looked at him. "Hit'll cost you a hundred and fifty, Miz Mannie."

"You mean dollars?"

"I don't mean dimes nor nickels neither, Miz Mannie."

"Dollars," she said. "That's more than mules was in Hait's time."

"Lots of things is different since Hait's time. Including you and me."

"I reckon so," she said. Then she went away. She turned without a word, old Het following.

"Maybe one of them others you looked at this morning would suit you," Snopes said. She didn't answer. Then they were gone.

"I don't know as I would have said that last to her," one said.

"What for?" Snopes said. "If she was aiming to law something outen me about that fire, you reckon she would have come and offered to pay me money for hit?" That was about one o'clock. About four o'clock he was shouldering his way through a throng of Negroes before a cheap grocery store when one called his name. It was old Het, the now bulging shopping-bag on her arm, eating bananas from a paper sack.

"Fo God I wuz jest dis minute huntin fer you," she said. She handed the banana to a woman beside her and delved and fumbled in the shopping-bag and extended a greenback. "Miz Mannie gimme dis to give you; I wuz jest on de way to de sto whar you stay at. Here." He took the bill.

"What's this? From Miz Hait?"

"Fer de mule." The bill was for ten dollars. "You don't need to gimme no receipt. I kin be de witness I give hit to you."

"Ten dollars? For that mule? I told her a hundred and fifty dollars."

"You'll have to fix dat up wid her yo'self. She jest gimme dis to give ter you when she sot out to fetch de mule."

"Set out to fetch— She went out there herself and taken my mule outen my pasture?"

"Lawd, chile," old Het said, "Miz Mannie ain't skeered of no mule. Ain't you done foun dat out?"

And then it became late, what with the yet short winter days; when she came in sight of the two gaunt chimneys against the sunset, evening was already finding itself. But she could smell the ham cooking before she came in sight of the cow shed even, though she could not see it until she came around in front where the fire burned beneath an iron skillet set on bricks and where nearby Mrs. Hait was milking the cow. "Well," old Het said, "you is settled down, ain't you?" She looked into the shed, neated and raked and swept even, and floored now with fresh hay. A clean new lantern burned on a box, beside it a pallet bed was spread neatly on the straw and turned neatly back for the night. "Why, you is fixed up," she said with pleased astonishment. Within the door was a kitchen chair. She drew it out and sat down beside the skillet and laid the bulging shopping-bag beside her.

"I'll tend dis meat whilst you milks. I'd offer to strip dat cow fer you ef I wuzn't so wo out wid all dis excitement we been had." She looked around her. "I don't believe I sees yo new mule, dough." Mrs. Hait grunted, her head against the cow's flank. After a moment she said,

"Did you give him that money?"

"I give um ter him. He ack surprise at first, lak maybe he think you didn't aim to trade dat quick. I tole him to settle de details wid you later. He taken de money, dough. So I reckin dat's offen his mine en yo'n bofe." Again Mrs. Hait grunted. Old Het turned the ham in the skillet. Beside it the coffee pot bubbled and steamed. "Cawfee smell good too," she said. "I ain't had no appetite in years now. A bird couldn't live on de vittles I eats. But jest lemme git a whiff er cawfee en seem lak hit always whets me a little. Now, ef you jest had nudder little piece o dis ham, now— Fo God, you got company aready." But Mrs. Hait did not even look up until she had finished. Then she turned without rising from the box on which she sat.

"I reckon you and me better have a little talk," Snopes said. "I reckon I got something that belongs to you and I hear you got something that belongs to me." He looked about, quickly, ceaselessly, while old Het watched him. He turned to her. "You go away, aunty. I don't reckon you want to set here and listen to us."

"Lawd, honey," old Het said. "Don't you mind me. I done already had so much troubles myself dat I kin set en listen to udder folks' widout hit worryin me a-tall. You gawn talk whut you came ter talk; I jest set here en tend de ham." Snopes looked at Mrs. Hait.

"Ain't you going to make her go away?" he said.

"What for?" Mrs. Hait said. "I reckon she ain't the first critter that ever come on this yard when hit wanted and went or stayed when hit liked." Snopes made a gesture, brief, fretted, restrained.

"Well," he said. "All right. So you taken the mule."

"I paid you for it. She give you the money."

"Ten dollars. For a hundred-and-fifty-dollar mule. Ten dollars."

"I don't know anything about hundred-and-fifty-dollar mules. All I know is what the railroad paid." Now Snopes looked at her for a full moment.

"What do you mean?"

"Them sixty dollars a head the railroad used to pay you for mules back when you and Hait——"

"Hush," Snopes said; he looked about again, quick, ceaseless. "All right. Even call it sixty dollars. But you just sent me ten."

"Yes. I sent you the difference." He looked at her, perfectly still. "Between that mule and what you owed Hait."

"What I owed——"

—"For getting them five mules onto the tr——"

—"Hush!" he cried. "Hush!" Her voice went on, cold, grim, level.

"For helping you. You paid him fifty dollars each time, and the railroad paid you sixty dollars a head for the mules. Ain't that right?" He watched her. "The last time you never paid him. So I taken that mule instead. And I sent you the ten dollars difference."

"Yes," he said in a tone of quiet, swift, profound bemusement; then he cried: "But look! Here's where I got you. Hit was our agreement that I wouldn't never owe him nothing until after the mules was——"

"I reckon you better hush yourself," Mrs. Hait said.

"—until hit was over. And this time, when over had come, I never owed nobody no money because the man hit would have been owed to wasn't nobody," he cried triumphantly. "You see?" Sitting on the box, motionless, downlooking, Mrs. Hait seemed to muse. "So you just take your ten dollars back and tell me where my mule is and we'll just go back good friends to where we started at. Fore God, I'm as sorry as ere a living man about that fire——"

"Fo God!" old Het said, "hit was a blaze, wuzn't it?"

"—but likely with all that ere railroad money you still got, you just been wanting a chance to build new, all along. So here. Take hit." He put the money into her hand. "Where's my mule?" But Mrs. Hait didn't move at once.

"You want to give it back to me?" she said.

"Sho. We been friends all the time; now we'll just go back to where we left off being. I don't hold no hard feelings and don't you hold none. Where you got the mule hid?"

"Up at the end of that ravine ditch behind Spilmer's," she said.

"Sho. I know. A good, sheltered place, since you ain't got nere barn. Only if you'd a just left hit in the pasture, hit would a saved us both trouble. But hit ain't no hard feelings though. And so I'll bid you goodnight. You're all fixed up, I see. I reckon you could save some more money by not building no house a-tall."

"I reckon I could," Mrs. Hait said. But he was gone.

"Whut did you leave de mule dar fer?" old Het said.

"I reckon that's far enough," Mrs. Hait said.

"Fer enough?" But Mrs. Hait came and looked into the skillet, and old Het said, "Wuz hit me er you dat mentioned something erbout er nudder piece o dis ham?" So they were both eating when in the not-quite-yet accomplished twilight Snopes returned. He came up quietly and stood, holding his hands to the blaze as if he were quite cold. He did not look at any one now.

"I reckon I'll take that ere ten dollars," he said.

"What ten dollars?" Mrs. Hait said. He seemed to muse upon the fire. Mrs. Hait and old Het chewed quietly, old Het alone watching him.

"You ain't going to give hit back to me?" he said.

"You was the one that said to let's go back to where we started," Mrs. Hait said.

"Fo God you wuz, en dat's de fack," old Het said. Snopes mused upon the fire; he spoke in a tone of musing and amazed despair:

"I go to the worry and the risk and the agoment for years and years and I get sixty dollars. And you, one time, without no trouble and no risk, without even knowing you are going to git it, git eighty-five hundred dollars. I never begrudged hit to you; can't nere a man say I did, even if hit did seem a little strange that you should git it all when he wasn't working for you and you never even knowed where he was at and what doing; that all you done to git it was to be married to him. And now, after all these ten years of not begrudging you hit, you taken the best mule I had and you ain't even going to pay me ten dollars for hit. Hit ain't right. Hit ain't justice."

"You got de mule back, en you ain't satisfried yit," old Het said. "Whut does you want?" Now Snopes looked at Mrs. Hait.

"For the last time I ask hit," he said. "Will you or won't you give hit back?"

"Give what back?" Mrs. Hait said. Snopes turned. He stumbled over something—it was old Het's shopping-bag—and recovered and went on.

They could see him in silhouette, as though framed by the two blackened chimneys against the dying west; they saw him fling up both clenched hands in a gesture almost Gallic, of resignation and impotent despair. Then he was gone. Old Het was watching Mrs. Hait.

"Honey," she said. "Whut did you do wid de mule?" Mrs. Hait leaned forward to the fire. On her plate lay a stale biscuit. She lifted the skillet and poured over the biscuit the grease in which the ham had cooked.

"I shot it," she said.

"You which?" old Het said. Mrs. Hait began to eat the biscuit. "Well," old Het said, happily, "de mule burnt de house en you shot de mule. Dat's whut I calls justice." It was getting dark fast now, and before her was still the three-mile walk to the poorhouse. But the dark would last a long time in January, and the poorhouse too would not move at once. She sighed with weary and happy relaxation. "Gentlemen, hush! Ain't we had a day!"

For Study and Discussion

1. Would you describe "old Het" as a major or a minor character? What, precisely, are her functions in the story?

2. How do the heavy fog and the arrangement of the house and yard contribute to the humor of the story?

3. Compare and contrast Mrs. Hait and Snopes on the basis of their moral and ethical qualities. Do you believe that Mrs. Hait is justified in shooting the mule? Why or why not?

4. In "Short Stories for the Millions," Baker contends that stories achieving "the highest level of success have *both* a competent level of meaning and a competent level of action." Does "Mule in the Yard" meet this criterion? If so, what "meaning" does it achieve and how is this meaning related to the action?

5. Is the story primarily comic or humorous in effect? Compare and contrast Faulkner's use of humor with that of Irving, Lardner, and Pirandello.

WILLIAM SAROYAN

THE DARING YOUNG MAN
ON THE FLYING TRAPEZE

I. SLEEP

Horizontally wakeful amid universal widths, practising laughter and mirth, satire, the end of all, of Rome and yes of Babylon, clenched teeth, remembrance, much warmth volcanic, the streets of Paris, the plains of Jericho, much gliding as of reptile in abstraction, a gallery of watercolors, the sea and the fish with eyes, symphony, a table in the corner of the Eiffel Tower, jazz at the opera house, alarm clock and the tap-dancing of doom, conversation with a tree, the river Nile, Cadillac coupe to Kansas, the roar of Dostoyevsky, and the dark sun.

This earth, the face of one who lived, the form without the weight, weeping upon snow, white music, the magnified flower twice the size of the universe, black clouds, the caged panther staring, deathless space, Mr. Eliot with rolled sleeves baking bread, Flaubert and Guy de Maupassant, a wordless rhyme of early meaning, Finlandia, mathematics highly polished and slick as a green onion to the teeth, Jerusalem, the path to paradox.

The deep song of man, the sly whisper of someone unseen but vaguely known, hurricane in the cornfield, a game of chess, hush the queen, the king, Karl Franz, black Titanic, Mr. Chaplin weeping, Stalin, Hitler, a multitude of Jews, tomorrow is Monday, no dancing in the streets.

O swift moment of life: it is ended, the earth is again now.

II. WAKEFULNESS

He (the living) dressed and shaved, grinning at himself in the mirror. Very unhandsome, he said; where is my tie? (He had but one.) Coffee and a gray sky, Pacific Ocean fog, the drone of a passing streetcar, people going to the city, time again, the day, prose and poetry. He

Originally published in *Story*, January 1934. Reprinted here from *The Daring Young Man on the Flying Trapeze and Other Stories* (New York: Modern Age Books, 1934) by permission of the author.

moved swiftly down the stairs to the street and began to walk, thinking suddenly, *It is only in sleep that we may know that we live. There only, in that living death, do we meet ourselves and the far earth, God and the saints, the names of our fathers, the substance of remote moments; it is there that the centuries merge in the moment, that the vast becomes the tiny, tangible atom of eternity.*

He walked into the day as alertly as might be, making a definite noise with his heels, perceiving with his eyes the superficial truth of streets and structures, the trivial truth of reality. Helplessly his mind sang. *He flies through the air with the greatest of ease; the daring young man on the flying trapeze;* then laughed with all the might of his being. It was really a splendid morning: gray, cold, and cheerless, a morning for inward vigor; ah, Edgar Guest, he said, how I long for your music.

In the gutter he saw a coin which proved to be a penny dated 1923, and placing it in the palm of his hand he examined it closely, remembering that year and thinking of Lincoln whose profile was stamped upon the coin. There was almost nothing a man could do with a penny. I will purchase a motorcar, he thought. I will dress myself in the fashion of a fop, visit the hotel strumpets, drink and dine, and then return to the quiet. Or I will drop the coin into a slot and weigh myself.

It was good to be poor, and the Communists—but it was dreadful to be hungry. What appetites they had, how fond they were of food! Empty stomachs. He remembered how greatly he needed food. Every meal was bread and coffee and cigarettes, and now he had no more bread. Coffee without bread could never honestly serve as supper, and there were no weeds in the park that could be cooked as spinach is cooked.

If the truth were known, he was half starved, and yet there was still no end of books he ought to read before he died. He remembered the young Italian in a Brooklyn hospital, a small sick clerk named Mollica, who had said desperately, I would like to see California once before I die. And he thought earnestly, I ought at least to read *Hamlet* once again; or perhaps *Huckleberry Finn.*

It was then that he became thoroughly awake: at the thought of dying. Now wakefulness was a state in the nature of a sustained shock. A young man could perish rather unostentatiously, he thought; and already he was very nearly starved. Water and prose were fine, they filled much inorganic space, but they were inadequate. If there were only some work he might do for money, some trivial labor in the name of commerce. If they would only allow him to sit at a desk all day and add trade figures, subtract and multiply and divide, then perhaps he would not die. He would buy food, all sorts of it: untasted delicacies from Norway, Italy, and France; all manner of beef, lamb, fish, cheese; grapes, figs, pears, apples, melons, which he would worship when he had satisfied his hunger. He would place a bunch of red grapes on a dish beside two black figs, a large yellow pear, and a green apple. He would hold a cut melon to his nostrils for hours. He would buy great brown loaves of French bread, vegetables of all sorts, meat; he would buy life.

From a hill he saw the city standing majestically in the east, great towers, dense with his kind, and there he was suddenly outside of it all, almost definitely certain that he should never gain admittance, almost positive that somehow he had ventured upon the wrong earth, or perhaps into the wrong age, and now a young man of twenty-two was to be permanently ejected from it. This thought was not saddening. He said to himself, sometime soon I must write *An Application for Permission to Live.* He accepted the thought of dying without pity for himself or for man, believing that he would at least sleep another night. His rent for another day was paid; there was yet another tomorrow. And after that he might go where other homeless men went. He might even visit the Salvation Army—sing to God and Jesus (unlover of my soul), be saved, eat and sleep. But he knew that he would not. His life was a private life. He did not wish to destroy this fact. Any other alternative would be better.

Through the air on the flying trapeze, his mind hummed. Amusing it was, astoundingly funny. A trapeze to God, or to nothing, a flying trapeze to some sort of eternity; he prayed objectively for strength to make the flight with grace.

I have one cent, he said. It is an American coin. In the evening I shall polish it until it glows like a sun and I shall study the words.

He was now walking in the city itself, among living men. There were one or two places to go. He saw his reflection in the plate-glass windows of stores and was disappointed with his appearance. He seemed not at all as strong as he felt; he seemed, in fact, a trifle infirm in every part of his body, in his neck, his shoulders, arms, trunk, and knees. This will never do, he said, and with an effort he assembled all his disjointed parts and became tensely, artificially erect and solid.

He passed numerous restaurants with magnificent discipline, refusing even to glance into them, and at last reached a building which he entered. He rose in an elevator to the seventh floor, moved down a hall, and, opening a door, walked into the office of an employment agency. Already there were two dozen young men in the place; he found a corner where he stood waiting his turn to be interviewed. At length he was granted this great privilege and was questioned by a thin, scatterbrained miss of fifty.

Now tell me, she said; what can you do?

He was embarrassed. I can write, he said pathetically.

You mean your penmanship is good? Is that it? said the elderly maiden.

Well, yes, he replied. But I mean that I can write.

Write what? said the miss, almost with anger.

Prose, he said simply.

There was a pause. At last the lady said:

Can you use a typewriter?

Of course, said the young man.

All right, went on the miss, we have your address; we will get in touch with you. There is nothing this morning, nothing at all.

It was much the same at the other agency, except that he was questioned by a conceited young man who closely resembled a pig. From the agencies he went to the large department stores: there was a good deal of pomposity, some humiliation on his part, and finally the report that work was not available. He did not feel displeased, and strangely did not even feel that he was personally involved in all the foolishness. He was a living young man who was in need of money with which to go on being one, and there was no way of getting it except by working for it; and there was no work. It was purely an abstract problem which he wished for the last time to attempt to solve. Now he was pleased that the matter was closed.

He began to perceive the definiteness of the course of his life. Except for moments, it had been largely artless, but now at the last minute he was determined that there should be as little imprecision as possible.

He passed countless stores and restaurants on his way to the Y.M.C.A., where he helped himself to paper and ink and began to compose his *Application*. For an hour he worked on this document, then suddenly, owing to the bad air in the place and to hunger, he became faint. He seemed to be swimming away from himself with great strokes, and hurriedly left the building. In the Civic Center Park, across from the Public Library Building, he drank almost a quart of water and felt himself refreshed. An old man was standing in the center of the brick boulevard surrounded by sea gulls, pigeons, and robins. He was taking handfuls of bread crumbs from a large paper sack and tossing them to the birds with a gallant gesture.

Dimly he felt impelled to ask the old man for a portion of the crumbs, but he did not allow the thought even nearly to reach consciousness; he entered the Public Library and for an hour read Proust, then, feeling himself to be swimming away again, he rushed outdoors. He drank more water at the fountain in the park and began the long walk to his room.

I'll go and sleep some more, he said; there is nothing else to do. He knew now that he was much too tired and weak to deceive himself about being all right, and yet his mind seemed somehow still lithe and alert. It, as if it were a separate entity, persisted in articulating impertinent pleasantries about his very real physical suffering. He reached his room early in the afternoon and immediately prepared coffee on the small gas range. There was no milk in the can, and the half pound of sugar he had purchased a week before was all gone; he drank a cup of the hot black fluid, sitting on his bed and smiling.

From the Y.M.C.A. he had stolen a dozen sheets of letter paper upon which he hoped to complete his document, but now the very notion of writing was unpleasant to him. There was nothing to say. He began to polish the penny he had found in the morning, and this absurd act somehow afforded him great enjoyment. No American coin can be made to shine so brilliantly as a penny. How many pennies would he need to go on living? Wasn't there something more he might sell? He looked about the bare room. No. His watch was gone; also his books. All those fine books; nine of them for eighty-five cents. He felt ill and ashamed for having parted with his books. His best suit he had sold for two dollars, but that was all right. He didn't mind at all about clothes. But the books. That was different. It made him very angry to think that there was no respect for men who wrote.

He placed the shining penny on the table, looking upon it with the delight of a miser. How prettily it smiles, he said. Without reading them he looked at the words, *E Pluribus Unum One Cent United States of America*, and turning the penny over, he saw Lincoln and the words, *In God We Trust Liberty 1923*. How beautiful it is, he said.

He became drowsy and felt a ghastly illness coming over his blood, a feeling of nausea and disintegration. Bewildered, he stood beside his bed, thinking *there is nothing to do but sleep*. Already he felt himself making great strides through the fluid of the earth, swimming away to the beginning. He fell face down upon the bed, saying, I ought first at least to give the coin to some child. A child could buy any number of things with a penny.

Then swiftly, neatly, with the grace of the young man on the trapeze, he was gone from his body. For an eternal moment he was all things at once: the bird, the fish, the rodent, the reptile, and man. An ocean of print undulated endlessly and darkly before him. The city burned. The herded crowd rioted. The earth circled away, and knowing that he did so, he turned his lost face to the empty sky and became dreamless, unalive, perfect.

For Study and Discussion

1. Is there any implied analogy between the young man in the story and the acrobat of the popular song that runs through his mind? If so, what is the intended effect of the parallel? Do you think Saroyan's title is a fitting one for the story? Why?

2. How does Part I prepare you for the events in Part II? Does this jumble of details have any meaning at all?

3. What purpose is served by the penny discovered in the gutter? In what ways does it relate significantly to the young man's predicament?

4. How are the interviews in the employment agencies related to the young man's experience in the park and to his actions at the Y.M.C.A. and later in his own room?

5. Does Saroyan succeed in making you see and feel both the actuality and the pathos of the young hero's death? Point out specific details in the narrative which are intended to produce this dual effect.

6. How would you characterize the irony of this story? Is it bitter? Gentle? Sad? Mocking? Or what? From what source, primarily, does it spring?

7. How fully does this story illustrate Saroyan's viewpoint on the art of the short story, as set forth in his essay, "What Is a Story"?

EUDORA WELTY

A VISIT OF CHARITY

It was mid-morning—a very cold, bright day. Holding a potted plant before her, a girl of fourteen jumped off the bus in front of the Old Ladies' Home, on the outskirts of town. She wore a red coat, and her straight yellow hair was hanging down loose from the pointed white cap all the little girls were wearing that year. She stopped for a moment beside one of the prickly dark shrubs with which the city had beautified the Home, and then proceeded slowly toward the building, which was of whitewashed brick and reflected the winter sunlight like a block of ice. As she walked vaguely up the steps she shifted the small pot from hand to hand; then she had to set it down and remove her mittens before she could open the heavy door.

"I'm a Campfire Girl. . . . I have to pay a visit to some old lady," she told the nurse at the desk. This was a woman in a white uniform who looked as if she were cold; she had close-cut hair which stood up on the very top of her head exactly like a sea wave. Marian, the little girl, did not tell her that this visit would give her a minimum of only three points in her score.

"Acquainted with any of our residents?" asked the nurse. She lifted one eyebrow and spoke like a man.

"With any old ladies? No—but—that is, any of them will do," Marian stammered. With her free hand she pushed her hair behind her ears, as she did when it was time to study Science.

The nurse shrugged and rose. "You have a nice *multiflora cineraria* there," she remarked as she walked ahead down the hall of closed doors to pick out an old lady.

There was loose, bulging linoleum on the floor. Marian felt as if she were walking on the waves, but the nurse paid no attention to it. There was a smell in the hall like the interior of a clock. Everything was silent until, behind one of the doors, an old lady of some kind cleared her

Originally published in, and reprinted here from, *A Curtain of Green and Other Stories* (New York: Harcourt, Brace and Co., 1941) by permission of Harcourt Brace Jovanovich, Inc. Copyright 1941, renewed 1969, by Eudora Welty.

throat like a sheep bleating. This decided the nurse. Stopping in her tracks, she first extended her arm, bent her elbow, and leaned forward from the hips—all to examine the watch strapped to her wrist; then she gave a loud double-rap on the door.

"There are two in each room," the nurse remarked over her shoulder.

"Two what?" asked Marian without thinking. The sound like a sheep's bleating almost made her turn around and run back.

One old woman was pulling the door open in short, gradual jerks, and when she saw the nurse a strange smile forced her old face dangerously awry. Marian, suddenly propelled by the strong, impatient arm of the nurse, saw next the side-face of another old woman, even older, who was lying flat in bed with a cap on and a counterpane drawn up to her chin.

"Visitor," said the nurse, and after one more shove she was off up the hall.

Marian stood tongue-tied; both hands held the potted plant. The old woman, still with that terrible, square smile (which was a smile of welcome) stamped on her bony face, was waiting. . . . Perhaps she said something. The old woman in bed said nothing at all, and she did not look around.

Suddenly Marian saw a hand, quick as a bird claw, reach up in the air and pluck the white cap off her head. At the same time, another claw to match drew her all the way into the room, and the next moment the door closed behind her.

"My, my, my," said the old lady at her side.

Marian stood enclosed by a bed, a washstand and a chair; the tiny room had altogether too much furniture. Everything smelled wet—even the bare floor. She held onto the back of the chair, which was wicker and felt soft and damp. Her heart beat more and more slowly, her hands got colder and colder, and she could not hear whether the old women were saying anything or not. She could not see them very clearly. How dark it was! The window shade was down, and the only door was shut. Marian looked at the ceiling. . . . It was like being caught in a robbers' cave, just before one was murdered.

"Did you come to be our little girl for a while?" the first robber asked.

Then something was snatched from Marian's hand—the little potted plant.

"Flowers!" screamed the old woman. She stood holding the pot in an undecided way. "Pretty flowers," she added.

Then the old woman in bed cleared her throat and spoke. "They are not pretty," she said, still without looking around, but very distinctly.

Marian suddenly pitched against the chair and sat down in it.

"Pretty flowers," the first old woman insisted. "Pretty—pretty . . ."

Marian wished she had the little pot back for just a moment—she had forgotten to look at the plant herself before giving it away. What did it look like?

"Stinkweeds," said the other old woman sharply. She had a bunchy white forehead and red eyes like a sheep. Now she turned them toward Marian. The fogginess seemed to rise in her throat again, and she bleated, "Who—are—you?"

To her surprise, Marian could not remember her name. "I'm a Campfire Girl," she said finally.

"Watch out for the germs," said the old woman like a sheep, not addressing anyone.

"One came out last month to see us," said the first old woman.

A sheep or a germ? wondered Marian dreamily, holding onto the chair.

"Did not!" cried the other old woman.

"Did so! Read to us out of the Bible, and we enjoyed it!" screamed the first.

"Who enjoyed it!" said the woman in bed. Her mouth was unexpectedly small and sorrowful, like a pet's.

"We enjoyed it," insisted the other. "You enjoyed it—I enjoyed it."

"We all enjoyed it," said Marian, without realizing that she had said a word.

The first old woman had just finished putting the potted plant high, high on the top of the wardrobe, where it could hardly be seen from below. Marian wondered how she had ever succeeded in placing it there, how she could ever have reached so high.

"You mustn't pay any attention to old Addie," she now said to the little girl. "She's ailing today."

"Will you shut your mouth?" said the woman in bed. "I am not."

"You're a story."

"I can't stay but a minute—really, I can't," said Marian suddenly. She looked down at the wet floor and thought that if she were sick in here they would have to let her go.

With much to-do the first old woman sat down in a rocking chair—still another piece of furniture!—and began to rock. With the fingers of one hand she touched a very dirty cameo pin on her chest. "What do you do at school?" she asked.

"I don't know . . ." said Marian. She tried to think but she could not.

"Oh, but the flowers are beautiful," the old woman whispered. She seemed to rock faster and faster; Marian did not see how anyone could rock so fast.

"Ugly," said the woman in bed.

"If we bring flowers——" Marian began, and then fell silent. She had almost said that if Campfire Girls brought flowers to the Old Ladies' Home, the visit would count one extra point, and if they took a Bible with them on the bus and read it to the old ladies, it counted double. But the old woman had not listened, anyway; she was rocking and watching the other one, who watched back from the bed.

"Poor Addie is ailing. She has to take medicine—see?" she said, pointing a horny finger at a row of bottles on the table, and rocking so high that her black comfort shoes lifted off the floor like a little child's.

"I am no more sick than you are," said the woman in bed.

"Oh yes you are!"

"I just got more sense than you have, that's all," said the other old woman, nodding her head.

"That's only the contrary way she talks when *you all* come," said the first old lady with sudden intimacy. She stopped the rocker with a neat pat of her feet and leaned toward Marian. Her hand reached over—it felt like a petunia leaf, clinging and just a little sticky.

"Will you hush! Will you hush!" cried the other one.

Marian leaned back rigidly in her chair.

"When I was a little girl like you, I went to school and all," said the old woman in the same intimate, menacing voice. "Not here—another town. . . ."

"Hush!" said the sick woman. "You never went to school. You never came and you never went. You never were anywhere—only here. You never were born! You don't know anything. Your head is empty, your heart and hands and your old black purse are all empty, even that little old box that you brought with you you brought empty—you showed it to me. And yet you talk, talk, talk, talk, talk all the time until I think I'm losing my mind! Who are you? You're a stranger—a perfect stranger! Don't you know you're a stranger? Is it possible that they have actually done a thing like this to anyone—sent them in a stranger to talk, and rock, and tell away her whole long rigmarole? Do they seriously suppose that I'll be able to keep it up, day in, day out, night in, night out, living in the same room with a terrible old woman—forever?"

Marian saw the old woman's eyes grow bright and turn toward her. This old woman was looking at her with despair and calculation in her face. Her small lips suddenly dropped apart, and exposed a half circle of false teeth with tan gums.

"Come here, I want to tell you something," she whispered. "Come here!"

Marian was trembling, and her heart nearly stopped beating altogether for a moment.

"Now, now, Addie," said the first old woman. "That's not polite. Do you know what's really the matter with old Addie today?" She, too, looked at Marian; one of her eyelids drooped low.

"The matter?" the child repeated stupidly. "What's the matter with her?"

"Why, she's mad because it's her birthday!" said the first old woman, beginning to rock again and giving a little crow as though she had answered her own riddle.

"It is not, it is not!" screamed the old woman in bed. "It is not my birthday, no one knows when that is but myself, and will you please be quiet and say nothing more, or I'll go straight out of my mind!" She turned her eyes toward Marian again, and presently she said in the soft, foggy voice, "When the worst comes to the worst, I ring this bell, and the nurse comes." One of her hands was drawn out from under the patched counterpane—a thin little hand with enormous black freckles. With a finger which would not hold still she pointed to a little bell on the table among the bottles.

"How old are you?" Marian breathed. Now she could see the old woman in bed very closely and plainly, and very abruptly, from all sides, as in dreams. She wondered about her—she wondered for a moment as though there was nothing else in the world to wonder about. It was the first time such a thing had happened to Marian.

"I won't tell!"

The old face on the pillow, where Marian was bending over it, slowly gathered and collapsed. Soft whimpers came out of the small open mouth. It was a sheep that she sounded like—a little lamb. Marian's face drew very close, the yellow hair hung forward.

"She's crying!" She turned a bright, burning face up to the first old woman.

"That's Addie for you," the old woman said spitefully.

Marian jumped up and moved toward the door. For the second time, the claw almost touched her hair, but it was not quick enough. The little girl put her cap on.

"Well, it was a real visit," said the old woman, following Marian through the doorway and all the way out into the hall. Then from behind she suddenly clutched the child with her sharp little fingers. In an affected, high-pitched whine she cried, "Oh, little girl, have you a penny to spare for a poor old woman that's not got anything of her own? We don't have a thing in the world—not a penny for candy—not a thing! Little girl, just a nickel—a penny——"

Marian pulled violently against the old hands for a moment before she was free. Then she ran down the hall, without looking behind her and without looking at the nurse, who was reading *Field & Stream* at her desk. The nurse, after another triple motion to consult her wrist watch, asked automatically the question put to visitors in all institutions: "Won't you stay and have dinner with *us?*"

Marian never replied. She pushed the heavy door open into the cold air and ran down the steps.

Under the prickly shrub she stooped and quickly, without being seen, retrieved a red apple she had hidden there.

Her yellow hair under the white cap, her scarlet coat, her bare knees all flashed in the sunlight as she ran to meet the big bus rocketing through the street.

"Wait for me!" she shouted. As though at an imperial command, the bus ground to a stop.

She jumped on and took a big bite out of the apple.

For Study and Discussion

1. Why does Marian, in the room with the two old ladies, feel as if she is "caught in a robbers' cave"?

2. What is the significance of the conflict between the two old ladies?

3. What is the function of the red apple?

4. How effectively is contrast employed in this story? In what ways is it used to contribute to the central meaning?

5. In her essay, Welty says that "the atmosphere in a story may be its chief glory" (p. 104). To what extent is the atmosphere of "A Visit of Charity" its chief glory? What specific details contribute to the creation of the atmosphere?

TRUMAN CAPOTE

A TREE OF NIGHT

It was winter. A string of naked light bulbs, from which it seemed all warmth had been drained, illuminated the little depot's cold, windy platform. Earlier in the evening it had rained, and now icicles hung along the station-house eaves like some crystal monster's vicious teeth. Except for a girl, young and rather tall, the platform was deserted. The girl wore a gray flannel suit, a raincoat, and a plaid scarf. Her hair, parted in the middle and rolled up neatly on the sides, was rich blondish-brown; and, while her face tended to be too thin and narrow, she was, though not extraordinarily so, attractive. In addition to an assortment of magazines and a gray suede purse on which elaborate brass letters spelled Kay, she carried conspicuously a green Western guitar.

When the train, spouting steam and glaring with light, came out of the darkness and rumbled to a halt, Kay assembled her paraphernalia and climbed up into the last coach.

The coach was a relic with a decaying interior of ancient red-plush seats, bald in spots, and peeling iodine-colored woodwork. An old-time copper lamp, attached to the ceiling, looked romantic and out of place. Gloomy dead smoke sailed the air; and the car's heated closeness accentuated the stale odor of discarded sandwiches, apple cores, and orange hulls: this garbage, including Lily cups, soda-pop bottles, and mangled newspapers, littered the long aisle. From a water cooler, embedded in the wall, a steady stream trickled to the floor. The passengers, who glanced up wearily when Kay entered, were not, it seemed, at all conscious of any discomfort.

Kay resisted a temptation to hold her nose and threaded her way carefully down the aisle, tripping once, without disaster, over a dozing fat man's protruding leg. Two nondescript men turned an interested eye as she passed; and a kid stood up in his seat, squalling, "Hey, Mama, look at de banjo! Hey, lady, lemme play ya banjo!" till a slap from Mama quelled him.

Originally published in *Harper's Bazaar*, October 1945. Reprinted here from *Selected Writings of Truman Capote* (New York: Random House, Inc., 1963) by permission of the publisher. Copyright 1945 by Truman Capote.

There was only one empty place. She found it at the end of the car in an isolated alcove occupied already by a man and woman who were sitting with their feet settled lazily on the vacant seat opposite. Kay hesitated a second then said, "Would you mind if I sat here?"

The woman's head snapped up as if she had not been asked a simple question, but stabbed with a needle, too. Nevertheless, she managed a smile. "Can't say as I see what's to stop you, honey," she said, taking her feet down and also, with a curious impersonality, removing the feet of the man who was staring out the window, paying no attention whatsoever.

Thanking the woman, Kay took off her coat, sat down, and arranged herself with purse and guitar at her side, magazines in her lap: comfortable enough, though she wished she had a pillow for her back.

The train lurched; a ghost of steam hissed against the window; slowly the dingy lights of the lonesome depot faded past.

"Boy, what a jerkwater dump," said the woman. "No town, no nothin'."

Kay said, "The town's a few miles away."

"That so? Live there?"

No. Kay explained she had been at the funeral of an uncle. An uncle who, though she did not of course mention it, had left her nothing in his will but the green guitar. Where was she going? Oh, back to college.

After mulling this over, the woman concluded, "What'll you ever learn in a place like that? Let me tell you, honey, I'm plenty educated and I never saw the inside of no college."

"You didn't?" murmured Kay politely and dismissed the matter by opening one of her magazines. The light was dim for reading and none of the stories looked in the least compelling. However, not wanting to become involved in a conversational marathon, she continued gazing at it stupidly till she felt a furtive tap on her knee.

"Don't read," said the woman. "I need somebody to talk to. Naturally, it's no fun talking to *him*." She jerked a thumb toward the silent man. "He's afflicted: deaf and dumb, know what I mean?"

Kay closed the magazine and looked at her more or less for the first time. She was short; her feet barely scraped the floor. And like many undersized people she had a freak of structure, in her case an enormous, really huge head. Rouge so brightened her sagging, fleshy-featured face it was difficult even to guess at her age: perhaps fifty, fifty-five. Her big sheep eyes squinted, as if distrustful of what they saw. Her hair was an obviously dyed red, and twisted into parched, fat corkscrew curls. A once-elegant lavender hat of impressive size flopped crazily on the side of her head, and she was kept busy brushing back a drooping cluster of celluloid cherries sewed to the brim. She wore a plain, somewhat shabby blue dress. Her breath had a vividly sweetish gin smell.

"You do wanna talk to me, don't you, honey?"

"Sure," said Kay, moderately amused.

"Course you do. You bet you do. That's what I like about a train. Bus people are a close-mouthed buncha dopes. But a train's the place for putting your cards on the table, that's what I always say." Her voice was cheerful and booming, husky as a man's. "But on accounta *him*, I always try to get us this here seat; it's more private, like a swell compartment, see?"

"It's very pleasant," Kay agreed. "Thanks for letting me join you."

"Only too glad to. We don't have much company; it makes some folks nervous to be around him."

As if to deny it, the man made a queer, furry sound deep in his throat and plucked the woman's sleeve. "Leave me alone, dearheart," she said, as if she were talking to an inattentive child. "I'm O.K. We're just having us a nice little ol' talk. Now behave yourself or this pretty girl will go away. She's very rich; she goes to college." And winking, she added, "He thinks I'm drunk."

The man slumped in the seat, swung his head sideways, and studied Kay intently from the corners of his eyes. These eyes, like a pair of clouded milky-blue marbles, were thickly lashed and oddly beautiful. Now, except for a certain remoteness, his wide, hairless face had no real expression. It was as if he were incapable of experiencing or reflecting the slightest emotion. His gray hair was clipped close and combed forward into uneven bangs. He looked like a child aged abruptly by some uncanny method. He wore a frayed blue serge suit, and he had anointed himself with a cheap, vile perfume. Around his wrist was strapped a Mickey Mouse watch.

"He thinks I'm drunk," the woman repeated. "And the real funny part is, I am. Oh, shoot—you gotta do something, ain't that right?" She bent closer. "Say, ain't it?"

Kay was still gawking at the man; the way he was looking at her made her squeamish, but she could not take her eyes off him. "I guess so," she said.

"Then let's us have us a drink," suggested the woman. She plunged her hand into an oilcloth satchel and pulled out a partially filled gin bottle. She began to unscrew the cap but, seeming to think better of this, handed the bottle to Kay. "Gee, I forgot about you being company," she said. "I'll go get us some nice paper cups."

So, before Kay could protest that she did not want a drink, the woman had risen and started none too steadily down the aisle toward the water cooler.

Kay yawned and rested her forehead against the windowpane, her fingers idly strumming the guitar: the strings sang a hollow, lulling tune, as monotonously soothing as the Southern landscape, smudged in darkness, flowing past the window. An icy winter moon rolled above the train across the night sky like a thin white wheel.

And then, without warning, a strange thing happened: the man reached out and gently stroked Kay's cheek. Despite the breathtaking delicacy of this movement, it was such a bold gesture Kay was at first too startled to know what to make of it: her thoughts shot in three or four fantastic directions. He leaned forward till his queer eyes were very near her own; the reek of his perfume was sickening. The guitar was silent while they exchanged a searching gaze. Suddenly, from some spring of compassion, she felt for him a keen sense of pity; but also, and this she could not suppress, an overpowering disgust, an absolute loathing: something about him, an elusive quality she could not quite put a finger on, reminded her of—of what?

After a little, he lowered his hand solemnly and sank back in the seat, an asinine grin transfiguring his face, as if he had performed a clever stunt for which he wished applause.

"Giddyup! Giddyup! my little bucker-ROOS . . ." shouted the woman. And she sat down, loudly proclaiming to be, "Dizzy as a witch! Dog tired! Whew!" From a handful of Lily cups she separated two and casually thrust the rest down her blouse. "Keep 'em safe and dry, ha ha ha. . . ." A coughing spasm seized her, but when it was over she appeared calmer. "Has my boy friend been entertaining?" she asked, patting her bosom reverently. "Ah, he's so sweet." She looked as if she might pass out. Kay rather wished she would.

"I don't want a drink," Kay said, returning the bottle. "I never drink: I hate the taste."

"Mustn't be a kill-joy," said the woman firmly. "Here now, hold your cup like a good girl."

"No, please . . ."

"Formercysake, hold it still. Imagine, nerves at your age! Me, I can shake like a leaf, I've got reasons. Oh, Lordy, have I got 'em."

"But . . ."

A dangerous smile tipped the woman's face hideously awry. "What's the matter? Don't you think I'm good enough to drink with?"

"Please, don't misunderstand," said Kay, a tremor in her voice. "It's just that I don't like being forced to do something I don't want to. So look, couldn't I give this to the gentleman?"

"Him? No sirree: he needs what little sense he's got. Come on, honey, down the hatch."

Kay, seeing it was useless, decided to succumb and avoid a possible scene. She sipped and shuddered. It was terrible gin. It burned her throat till her eyes watered. Quickly, when the woman was not watching, she emptied the cup out into the sound hole of the guitar. It happened, however, that the man saw; and Kay, realizing it, recklessly signaled to him with her eyes a plea not to give her away. But she could not tell from his clear-blank expression how much he understood.

"Where you from, kid?" resumed the woman presently.

For a bewildered moment, Kay was unable to provide an answer. The names of several cities came to her all at once. Finally, from this confusion, she extracted: "New Orleans. My home is in New Orleans."

The woman beamed. "N.O.'s where I wanna go when I kick off. One time, oh, say 1923, I ran me a sweet little fortune-telling parlor there. Let's see, that was on St. Peter Street." Pausing, she stooped and set the empty gin bottle on the floor. It rolled into the aisle and rocked back and forth with a drowsy sound. "I was raised in Texas—on a big ranch—my papa was rich. Us kids always had the best; even Paris, France, clothes. I'll bet you've got a big swell house, too. Do you have a garden? Do you grow flowers?"

"Just lilacs."

A conductor entered the coach, preceded by a cold gust of wind that rattled the trash in the aisle and briefly livened the dull air. He lumbered along, stopping now and then to punch a ticket or talk with a passenger. It was after midnight. Someone was expertly playing a harmonica. Someone else was arguing the merits of a certain politician. A child cried out in his sleep.

"Maybe you wouldn't be so snotty if you knew who we was," said the woman, bobbing her tremendous head. "We ain't nobodies, not by a long shot."

Embarrassed, Kay nervously opened a pack of cigarettes and lighted one. She wondered if there might not be a seat in a car up ahead. She could not bear the woman, or, for that matter, the man, another minute. But she had never before been in a remotely comparable situation. "If you'll excuse me now," she said, "I have to be leaving. It's been very pleasant, but I promised to meet a friend on the train. . . ."

With almost invisible swiftness the woman grasped the girl's wrist. "Didn't your mama ever tell you it was sinful to lie?" she stage-whispered. The lavender hat tumbled off her head but she made no effort to retrieve it. Her tongue flicked out and wetted her lips. And, as Kay stood up, she increased the pressure of her grip. "Sit down, dear . . . there ain't any friend . . . Why, we're your only friends and we wouldn't have you leave us for the world."

"Honestly, I wouldn't lie."

"Sit down, dear."

Kay dropped her cigarette and the man picked it up. He slouched in the corner and became absorbed in blowing a chain of lush smoke rings that mounted upward like hollow eyes and expanded into nothing.

"Why, you wouldn't want to hurt his feelings by leaving us, now, would you, dear?" crooned the woman softly. "Sit down—down—now, that's a good girl. My, what a pretty guitar. What a pretty, pretty guitar . . ." Her voice faded before the sudden whooshing, static noise of a second train. And for an instant the lights in the coach went off; in the darkness the passing train's golden windows winked black-yellow-black-yellow-black-yellow. The man's cigarette pulsed like the glow of a firefly, and his smoke rings continued rising tranquilly. Outside, a bell pealed wildly.

When the lights came on again, Kay was massaging her wrist where the woman's strong fingers had left a painful bracelet mark. She was more puzzled than angry. She determined to ask the conductor if he would find her a different seat. But when he arrived to take her ticket, the request stuttered on her lips incoherently.

"Yes, miss?"

"Nothing," she said.

And he was gone.

The trio in the alcove regarded one another in mysterious silence till the woman said, "I've got something here I wanna show you, honey." She rummaged once more in the oilcloth satchel. "You won't be so snotty after you get a gander at this."

What she passed to Kay was a handbill, published on such yellowed, antique paper it looked as if it might be centuries old. In fragile, overly fancy lettering, it read:

LAZARUS

The Man Who Is Buried Alive
A Miracle

SEE FOR YOURSELF
Adults, 25¢—Children, 10¢

"I always sing a hymn and read a sermon," said the woman. "It's awful sad: some folks cry, especially the old ones. And I've got me a perfectly elegant costume: a black veil and a black dress, oh, very becoming. *He* wears a gorgeous made-to-order bridegroom suit and a turban and lotsa talcum on his face. See, we try to make it as much like a bonafide funeral as we can. But shoot, nowadays you're likely to get just a buncha smart alecks come for laughs—so sometimes I'm real glad he's afflicted like he is on accounta otherwise his feelings would be hurt, maybe."

Kay said, "You mean you're with a circus or a side-show or something like that?"

"Nope, us alone," said the woman as she reclaimed the fallen hat. "We've been doing it for years and years—played every tank town in the South: Singasong, Mississippi—Spunky, Louisiana—Eureka, Alabama . . ." these and other names rolled off her tongue musically, running together like rain. "After the hymn, after the sermon, we bury him."

"In a coffin?"

"Sort of. It's gorgeous, it's got silver stars painted all over the lid."

"I should think he would suffocate," said Kay, amazed. "How long does he stay buried?"

"All told it takes maybe an hour—course that's not counting the lure."

"The lure?"

"Uh huh. It's what we do the night before a show. See, we hunt up a store, any ol' store with a big glass window'll do, and get the owner to let *him* sit inside this window, and, well, hypnotize himself. Stays there all night stiff as a poker and people come and look: scares the livin' hell out of 'em . . ." While she talked she jiggled a finger in her ear, withdrawing it occasionally to examine her find. "And one time this ol' bindlestiff Mississippi sheriff tried to . . ."

The tale that followed was baffling and pointless: Kay did not bother to listen. Nevertheless, what she had heard already inspired a reverie, a vague recapitulation of her uncle's funeral; an event which, to tell the truth, had not much affected her since she had scarcely known him. And so, while gazing abstractedly at the man, an image of her uncle's face, white next the pale silk casket pillow, appeared in her mind's eye. Observing their faces simultaneously, both the man's and uncle's, as it were, she thought she recognized an odd parallel: there was about the man's face the same kind of shocking, embalmed, secret stillness, as though, in a sense, he were truly an exhibit in a glass cage, complacent to be seen, uninterested in seeing.

"I'm sorry, what did you say?"

"I said: I sure wish they'd lend us the use of a regular cemetery. Like it is now we have to put on the show wherever we can . . . mostly in empty lots that are nine times outa ten smack up against some smelly fillin' station, which ain't exactly a big help. But like I say, we got us a swell act, the best. You oughta come see it if you get a chance."

"Oh, I should love to," Kay said, absently.

"Oh, I should love to," mimicked the woman. "Well, who ask you? Anybody ask you?" She hoisted up her skirt and enthusiastically blew her nose on the ragged hem of a petticoat. "Bu-leeve me, it's a hard way to turn a dollar. Know what our take was last month? Fifty-three bucks! Honey, you try living on that sometime." She sniffed and rearranged her skirt with considerable primness. "Well, one of these days my sweet boy's sure enough going to die down there; and even then somebody'll say it was a gyp."

At this point the man took from his pocket what seemed to be a finely shellacked peach seed and balanced it on the palm of his hand. He looked across at Kay and, certain of her attention, opened his eyelids wide and began to squeeze and caress the seed in an undefinably obscene manner.

Kay frowned. "What does he want?"

"He wants you to buy it."

"But what is it?"

"A charm," said the woman. "A love charm."

Whoever was playing the harmonica stopped. Other sounds, less unique, became at once prominent: someone snoring, the gin bottle seesaw rolling, voices in sleepy argument, the train wheels' distant hum.

"Where could you get love cheaper, honey?"

"It's nice. I mean it's cute. . . ." Kay said, stalling for time. The man rubbed and polished the seed on his trouser leg. His head was lowered at a supplicating, mournful angle, and presently he stuck the seed between his teeth and bit it, as if it were a suspicious piece of silver. "Charms always bring me bad luck. And besides . . . please, can't you make him stop acting that way?"

"Don't look so scared," said the woman, more flat-voiced than ever. "He ain't gonna hurt you."

"Make him stop, damn it!"

"What can I do?" asked the woman, shrugging her shoulders. "You're the one that's got money. You're rich. All he wants is a dollar, one dollar."

Kay tucked her purse under her arm. "I have just enough to get back to school," she lied, quickly rising and stepping out into the aisle. She stood there a moment, expecting trouble. But nothing happened.

The woman, with rather deliberate indifference, heaved a sigh and closed her eyes; gradually the man subsided and stuck the charm back in his pocket. Then his hand crawled across the seat to join the woman's in a lax embrace.

Kay shut the door and moved to the front of the observation platform. It was bitterly cold in the open air, and she had left her raincoat in the alcove. She loosened her scarf and draped it over her head.

Although she had never made this trip before, the train was traveling through an area strangely familiar: tall trees, misty, painted pale by malicious moonshine, towered steep on either side without a break or clearing. Above, the sky was a stark, unexplorable blue thronged with stars that faded here and there. She could see streamers of smoke trailing from the train's engine like long clouds of ectoplasm. In one corner of the platform a red kerosene lantern cast a colorful shadow.

She found a cigarette and tried to light it: the wind snuffed match after match till only one was left. She walked to the corner where the lantern burned and cupped her hands to protect the last match: the flame caught, sputtered, died. Angrily she tossed away the cigarette and empty folder; all the tension in her tightened to an exasperating pitch and she slammed the wall with her fist and began to whimper softly, like an irritable child.

The intense cold made her head ache, and she longed to go back inside the warm coach and fall asleep. But she couldn't, at least not yet; and there was no sense in wondering why, for she knew the answer very well. Aloud, partly to keep her teeth from chattering and partly because she needed the reassurance of her own voice, she said: "We're in Alabama now, I think, and tomorrow we'll be in Atlanta and I'm nineteen and I'll be twenty in August and I'm a sophomore. . . ." She glanced around at the darkness, hoping to see a sign of dawn, and finding the same endless wall of trees, the same frosty moon, "I hate him, he's horrible and I hate him. . . ." She stopped, ashamed of her foolishness and too tired to evade the truth: she was afraid.

Suddenly she felt an eerie compulsion to kneel down and touch the lantern. Its graceful glass funnel was warm, and the red glow seeped through her hands, making them luminous. The heat thawed her fingers and tingled along her arms.

She was so preoccupied she did not hear the door open. The train wheels roaring clickety-clack-clackety-click hushed the sound of the man's footsteps.

It was a subtle zero sensation that warned her finally; but some seconds passed before she dared look behind.

He was standing there with a mute detachment, his head tilted, his arms dangling at his sides. Staring up into his harmless, vapid face, flushed brilliant by the lantern light, Kay knew of what she was afraid: it was a memory, a childish memory of terrors that once, long ago, had hovered above her like haunted limbs on a tree of night. Aunts, cooks, strangers—each eager to spin a tale or teach a rhyme of spooks and death, omens, spirits, demons. And always there had been the unfailing threat of the wizard man: stay close to the house, child, else a wizard man'll snatch and eat you alive! He lived everywhere, the wizard man, and everywhere was danger. At night, in bed, hear him tapping at the window? Listen!

Holding onto the railing, she inched upward till she was standing erect. The man nodded and waved his hand toward the door. Kay took a deep breath and stepped forward. Together they went inside.

The air in the coach was numb with sleep: a solitary light now illuminated the car, creating a kind of artificial dusk. There was no motion but the train's sluggish sway, and the stealthy rattle of discarded newspapers.

The woman alone was wide awake. You could see she was greatly excited: she fidgeted with her curls and celluloid cherries, and her plump little legs, crossed at the ankles, swung agitatedly back and forth. She paid no attention when Kay sat down. The man settled in the seat with one leg tucked beneath him and his arms folded across his chest.

In an effort to be casual, Kay picked up a magazine. She realized the man was watching her, not removing his gaze an instant: she knew this though she was afraid to confirm it, and she wanted to cry out and waken everyone in the coach. But suppose they did not hear? What if they were not really *asleep!* Tears started in her eyes, magnifying and distorting the print on a page till it became a hazy blur. She shut the magazine with fierce abruptness and looked at the woman.

"I'll buy it," she said. "The charm, I mean. I'll buy it, if that's all—just all you want."

The woman made no response. She smiled apathetically as she turned toward the man.

As Kay watched, the man's face seemed to change form and recede before her like a moon-shaped rock sliding downward under a surface of water. A warm laziness relaxed her. She was dimly conscious of it when the woman took away her purse, and when she gently pulled the raincoat like a shroud above her head.

For Study and Discussion

1. At the opening of the story, the icicles hanging on the station-house are described as being "like some crystal monster's vicious teeth." How is this simile appropriate to the mood of the story? Study the use of figurative language throughout the story in the light of Brickell's remark that the modern short story draws "ever nearer to poetry, in the precise and beautiful use of language" (p. 111).

2. What is the exact function of the symbols in the story, such as the tree of night, the love charm, and the green guitar?

3. To what extent does Kay identify the bizarre couple on the train with her inward or subconscious fears? Are these characters, then, to be regarded as literal or symbolic or both? What is the symbolic significance of the "buried-alive" act the deaf-mute performs?

4. What happens to Kay at the end?

5. In her essay, Overstreet says, "In the twentieth century . . . we are being thrown back upon a study of human nature—human motives, fears, wants, prejudices" (p. 88). In what ways can this statement be applied to "A Tree of Night"?

6. How fully does this story harmonize with the viewpoint Capote expresses in his interview?

7. Compare and contrast the "grotesque" or abnormal characters in the story with those in Flannery O'Connor's "A Good Man Is Hard to Find." Do you think Capote uses such characters for the same reason O'Connor did? See her essays, "The Fiction Writer and His Country" and "A Reasonable Use of the Unreasonable."

V. S. PRITCHETT

THE SAINT

When I was seventeen years old I lost my religious faith. It had been unsteady for some time and then, very suddenly, it went as the result of an incident in a punt on the river outside the town where we lived. My uncle, with whom I was obliged to stay for long periods of my life, had started a small furniture-making business in the town. He was always in difficulties about money, but he was convinced that in some way God would help him. And this happened. An investor arrived who belonged to a sect called the Church of the Last Purification, of Toronto, Canada. Could we imagine, this man asked, a good and omnipotent God allowing His children to be short of money? We had to admit we could not imagine this. The man paid some capital into my uncle's business and we were converted. Our family were the first Purifiers—as they were called—in the town. Soon a congregation of fifty or more were meeting every Sunday in a room at the Corn Exchange.

At once we found ourselves isolated and hated people. Everyone made jokes about us. We had to stand together because we were sometimes dragged into the courts. What the unconverted could not forgive in us was first that we believed in successful prayer and, secondly, that our revelation came from Toronto. The success of our prayers had a simple foundation. We regarded it as "Error"—our name for Evil—to believe the evidence of our senses, and if we had influenza or consumption, or had lost our money or were unemployed, we denied the reality of these things, saying that since God could not have made them they therefore did not exist. It was exhilarating to look at our congregation and to know that what the vulgar would call miracles were performed among us, almost as a matter of routine, every day. Not very big miracles, perhaps; but up in London and out in Toronto we knew that deafness and blindness, cancer and insanity, the great scourges, were constantly vanishing before the prayers of the more advanced Purifiers.

Originally published in *Harper's Magazine,* January 1947. Reprinted here from *Collected Stories* (London: Chatto and Windus, 1956) by permission of The Harold Matson Company, Inc. Copyright © 1956 by V. S. Pritchett.

"What!" said my schoolmaster, an Irishman with eyes like broken glass and a sniff of irritability in the bristles of his nose. "What! Do you have the impudence to tell me that if you fell off the top floor of this building and smashed your head in, you would say you hadn't fallen and were not injured?"

I was a small boy and very afraid of everybody, but not when it was a question of my religion. I was used to the kind of conundrum the Irishman had set. It was useless to argue, though our religion had already developed an interesting casuistry.

"I *would* say so," I replied with coldness and some vanity. "And my head would not be smashed."

"You would not say so," answered the Irishman. "You would not say so." His eyes sparkled with pure pleasure. "You'd be dead."

The boys laughed, but they looked at me with admiration.

Then, I do not know how or why, I began to see a difficulty. Without warning and as if I had gone into my bedroom at night and had found a gross ape seated in my bed and thereafter following me about with his grunts and his fleas and a look, relentless and ancient, scored on his brown face, I was faced with the problem which prowls at the centre of all religious faith. I was faced by the difficulty of the origin of evil. Evil was an illusion, we were taught. But even illusions have an origin. The Purifiers denied this.

I consulted my uncle. Trade was bad at the time and this made his faith abrupt. He frowned as I spoke.

"When did you brush your coat last?" he said. "You're getting slovenly about your appearance. If you spent more time studying books"—that is to say, the Purification literature— "and less with your hands in your pockets and playing about with boats on the river, you wouldn't be letting Error in."

All dogmas have their jargon; my uncle as a business man loved the trade-terms of the Purification. "Don't let Error in," was a favourite one. The whole point about the Purification, he said, was that it was scientific and therefore exact; in consequence it was sheer weakness to admit discussion. Indeed, betrayal. He unpinched his pince-nez, stirred his tea and indicated I must submit or change the subject. Preferably the latter. I saw, to my alarm, that my arguments had defeated my uncle. Faith and doubt pulled like strings round my throat.

"You don't mean to say you don't believe that what our Lord said was true?" my aunt asked nervously, following me out of the room. "Your uncle does, dear."

I could not answer. I went out of the house and down the main street to the river, where the punts were stuck like insects in the summery flash of the reach. Life was a dream, I thought; no, a nightmare, for the ape was beside me.

I was still in this state, half sulking and half exalted, when Mr. Hubert Timberlake came to the town. He was one of the important people from the headquarters of our Church and he had come to give an address on the Purification at the Corn Exchange. Posters announcing this were everywhere. Mr. Timberlake was to spend Sunday afternoon with us. It was unbelievable that a man so eminent would actually sit in our dining-room, use our knives and forks, and eat our food. Every imperfection in our home and our characters would jump out at him. The Truth had been revealed to man with scientific accuracy—an accuracy we could all test by experiment—and the future course of human development on earth was laid down, finally. And here in Mr. Timberlake was a man who had not merely performed many miracles—even, it was said with proper reserve, having twice raised the dead—but who had actually been to Toronto, our headquarters, where this great and revolutionary revelation had first been given.

"This is my nephew," my uncle said, introducing me. "He lives with us. He thinks he thinks, Mr. Timberlake, but I tell him he only thinks he does. Ha, ha." My uncle was a humorous man when he was with the great. "He's always on the river," my uncle continued. "I tell him he's got water on the brain. I've been telling Mr. Timberlake about you, my boy."

A hand as soft as the best-quality chamois leather took mine. I saw a wide upright man in a double-breasted navy-blue suit. He had a pink square head with very small ears and one of those torpid, enamelled smiles which were said by our enemies to be too common in our sect.

"Why, isn't that just fine!" said Mr. Timberlake, who, owing to his contacts with Toronto, spoke with an American accent. "What say we tell your uncle it's funny he thinks he's funny?"

The eyes of Mr. Timberlake were direct and colourless. He had the look of a retired merchant captain who had become decontaminated from the sea and had reformed and made money. His defence of me had made me his at once. My doubts vanished. Whatever Mr. Timberlake believed must be true, and as I listened to him at lunch I thought there could be no finer life than his.

"I expect Mr. Timberlake's tired after his address," said my aunt.

"Tired?" exclaimed my uncle, brilliant with indignation. "How can Mr. Timberlake be tired? Don't let Error in!"

For in our faith the merely inconvenient was just as illusory as a great catastrophe would have been, if you wished to be strict, and Mr. Timberlake's presence made us very strict.

I noticed then that, after their broad smiles, Mr. Timberlake's lips had the habit of setting into a long depressed sarcastic curve.

"I guess," he drawled, "I guess the Al-mighty must have been tired sometimes, for it says He re-laxed on the seventh day. Say, do you know what I'd like to do this afternoon?" he said, turning to me. "While your uncle and aunt are sleeping off this meal, let's you and me go on the river and get water on the brain. I'll show you how to punt."

Mr. Timberlake, I saw to my disappointment, was out to show he understood the young. I saw he was planning a "quiet talk" with me about my problems.

"There are too many people on the river on Sundays," said my uncle uneasily.

"Oh, I like a crowd," said Mr. Timberlake, giving my uncle a tough look. "This is the day of rest, you know." He had had my uncle gobbling up every bit of gossip from the sacred city of Toronto all the morning.

My uncle and aunt were incredulous that a man like Mr. Timberlake should go out among the blazers and gramophones of the river on a Sunday afternoon. In any other member of our Church they would have thought this sinful.

"Waal, what say?" said Mr. Timberlake. I could only murmur.

"That's fixed," said Mr. Timberlake. And on came the smile, as simple, vivid and unanswerable as the smile on an advertisement. "Isn't that just fine!"

Mr. Timberlake went upstairs to wash his hands. My uncle was deeply offended and shocked, but he could say nothing. He unpinched his glasses.

"A very wonderful man," he said. "So human," he apologized.

"My boy," my uncle said. "This is going to be an experience for you. Hubert Timberlake was making a thousand a year in the insurance business ten years ago. Then he heard of the Purification. He threw everything up, just like that. He gave up his job and took up the work. It was a struggle, he told me so himself this morning. 'Many's the time,' he said to me this morning, 'when I wondered where my next meal was coming from.' But the way was shown. He came down from Worcester to London and in two years he was making fifteen hundred a year out of his practice."

To heal the sick by prayer according to the tenets of the Church of the Last Purification was Mr. Timberlake's profession.

My uncle lowered his eyes. With his glasses off, the lids were small and uneasy. He lowered his voice too.

"I have told him about your little trouble," my uncle said quietly with emotion. I was burned with shame. My uncle looked up and stuck out his chin confidently.

"He just smiled," my uncle said. "That's all."

Then we waited for Mr. Timberlake to come down.

I put on white flannels and soon I was walking down to the river with Mr. Timberlake. I felt that I was going with him under false pretences; for he would begin explaining to me the origin of evil and I would have to pretend politely that he was converting me when, already, at the first sight of him, I had believed. A stone bridge, whose two arches were like an owlish pair of eyes gazing up the reach, was close to the landing-stage. I thought what a pity it was the flannelled men and the sunburned girls there did not know I was getting a ticket for *the* Mr. Timberlake who had been speaking in the town that very morning. I looked round for him, and when I saw him I was a little startled. He was standing at the edge of the water looking at it with an expression of empty incomprehension. Among the white crowds his air of brisk efficiency had dulled. He looked middle-aged, out of place and insignificant. But the smile switched on when he saw me.

"Ready?" he called. "Fine!"

I had the feeling that inside him there must be a gramophone record going round and round, stopping at that word.

He stepped into the punt and took charge.

"Now I just want you to paddle us over to the far bank," he said, "and then I'll show you how to punt."

Everything Mr. Timberlake said still seemed unreal to me. The fact that he was sitting in a punt, of all commonplace material things, was incredible. That he should propose to pole us up the river was terrifying. Suppose he fell into the river? At once I checked the thought. A leader of our Church under the direct guidance of God could not possibly fall into a river.

The stream is wide and deep in this reach, but on the southern bank there is a manageable depth and a hard bottom. Over the clay banks the willows hang, making their basket-work print of sun and shadow on the water, while under the gliding boats lie cloudy, chloride caverns. The hoop-like branches of the trees bend down until their tips touch the water like fingers making musical sounds. Ahead in mid-stream, on a day sunny as this one was, there is a path of strong light which is hard to look at unless you half close your eyes, and down this path on the crowded Sundays go the launches with their parasols and their pennants; and also the rowing-boats with their beetle-leg oars, which seem to dig the sunlight out of the water as they rise. Upstream one goes, on and on between the gardens and then between fields kept for grazing. On the afternoon when Mr. Timberlake and I went out to settle the question of the origin of evil, the meadows were packed densely with buttercups.

"Now," said Mr. Timberlake decisively when I had paddled to the other side. "Now I'll take her."

He got over the seat into the well at the stern.

"I'll just get you clear of the trees," I said.

"Give me the pole," said Mr. Timberlake, standing up on the little platform and making a squeak with his boots as he did so. "Thank you, sir. I haven't done this for eighteen years, but I can tell you, brother, in those days I was considered some poler."

He looked around and let the pole slide down through his hands. Then he gave the first difficult push. The punt rocked pleasantly and we moved forward. I sat facing him, paddle in hand, to check any inward drift of the punt.

"How's that, you guys?" said Mr. Timberlake, looking round at our eddies and drawing in the pole. The delightful water sished down it.

"Fine," I said. Deferentially I had caught the word.

He went on to his second and his third strokes, taking too much water on his sleeve, perhaps, and uncertain in his steering, which I corrected, but he was doing well.

"It comes back to me," he said. "How am I doing?"

"Just keep her out from the trees," I said.

"The trees?" he said.

"The willows," I said.

"I'll do it now," he said. "How's that? Not quite enough? Well, how's this?"

"Another one," I said. "The current runs strong this side."

"What? More trees?" he said. He was getting hot.

"We can shoot out past them," I said. "I'll ease us over with the paddle."

Mr. Timberlake did not like this suggestion.

"No, don't do that. I can manage it," he said. I did not want to offend one of the leaders of our Church, so I put the paddle down; but I felt I ought to have taken him farther along away from the irritation of the trees.

"Of course," I said. "We could go under them. It might be nice."

"I think," said Mr. Timberlake, "that would be a very good idea."

He lunged hard on the pole and took us towards the next archway of willow branches.

"We may have to duck a bit, that's all," I said.

"Oh, I can push the branches up," said Mr. Timberlake.

"It is better to duck," I said.

We were gliding now quickly towards the arch, in fact I was already under it.

"I think I should duck," I said. "Just bend down for this one."

"What makes the trees lean over the water like this?" asked Mr. Timberlake. "Weeping willows—I'll give you a thought there. How Error likes to make us dwell on sorrow. Why not call them *laughing* willows?" discoursed Mr. Timberlake as the branch passed over my head.

"Duck," I said.

"Where? I don't see them," said Mr. Timberlake, turning round.

"No, your head," I said. "The branch," I called.

"Oh, the branch. This one?" said Mr. Timberlake, finding a branch just against his chest, and he put out a hand to lift it. It is not easy to lift a willow branch and Mr. Timberlake was surprised. He stepped back as it gently and firmly leaned against him. He leaned back and pushed from his feet. And he pushed too far. The boat went on, I saw Mr. Timberlake's boots leave the stern as he took an unthoughtful step backwards. He made a last-minute grasp at a stronger and higher branch, and then, there he hung a yard above the water, round as a blue damson that is ripe and ready, waiting only for a touch to make it fall. Too late with the paddle and shot ahead by the force of his thrust, I could not save him.

For a full minute I did not believe what I saw; indeed, our religion taught us never to believe what we saw. Unbelieving, I could not move. I gaped. The impossible had happened. Only a miracle, I found myself saying, could save him.

What was most striking was the silence of Mr. Timberlake as he hung from the tree. I was lost between gazing at him and trying to get the punt out of the small branches of the tree. By the time I had got the punt out, there were several yards of water between us and the soles of his boots were very near the water as the branch bent under his weight. Boats were passing at the time, but no one seemed to notice us. I was glad about this. This was a private agony. A double chin had appeared on the face of Mr. Timberlake and his head was squeezed between his shoulders and his hanging arms. I saw him blink and look up at the sky. His eyelids were pale like a chicken's. He was tidy and dignified as he hung there, the hat was not displaced and the top button of his coat was done up. He had a blue silk handkerchief in his breast pocket. So unperturbed and genteel he seemed that as the tips of his shoes came nearer and nearer to the water, I became alarmed. He could perform what are called miracles. He would be thinking at this moment that only in an erroneous and illusory sense was he hanging from the branch of the tree over six feet of water. He was probably praying one of the closely reasoned prayers of our faith which were more like conversations with Euclid than appeals to God. The calm of his face suggested this. Was he, I asked myself, within sight of the main road, the town Recreation Ground and the landing-stage crowded with people, was he about to re-enact a well-known miracle? I hoped that he was not. I prayed that he was not. I prayed with all my will that Mr. Timberlake would not walk upon the water. It was my prayer and not his that was answered.

I saw the shoes dip, the water rise above his ankles and up his socks. He tried to move his grip now to a yet higher branch—he did not succeed—and in making this effort his coat and waistcoat rose and parted from his trousers. One seam of shirt with its pant-loops and brace-tabs broke like a crack across the middle of Mr. Timberlake. It was like a fatal flaw in a statue, an earthquake crack which made the monumental mortal. The last Greeks must have felt as I felt then when they saw a crack across the middle of some statue of Apollo. It was at this moment I realized that the final revelation about man and society on earth had come to nobody and that Mr. Timberlake knew nothing at all about the origin of evil.

All this takes long to describe, but it happened in a few seconds as I paddled towards him. I was too late to get his feet on the boat and the only thing to do was to let him sink until his hands were nearer the level of the punt and then to get him to change hand-holds. Then I would paddle him ashore. I did this. Amputated by the water, first a torso, then a bust, then a mere head and shoulders, Mr. Timberlake, I noticed, looked sad and lonely as he sank. He was a declining dogma. As the water lapped his collar—for he hesitated to let go of the branch to hold the punt—I saw a small triangle of deprecation and pathos between his nose and the corners of his mouth. The head resting on the platter of water had the sneer of calamity on it, such as one sees in the pictures of a beheaded saint.

"Hold on to the punt, Mr. Timberlake," I said urgently. "Hold on to the punt."

He did so.

"Push from behind," he directed in a dry businesslike voice. They were his first words. I obeyed him. Carefully I paddled him towards the bank. He turned and, with a splash, climbed ashore. There he stood, raising his arms and looking at the water running down his swollen suit and making a puddle at his feet.

"Say," said Mr. Timberlake coldly, "we let some Error in that time."

How much he must have hated our family.

"I am sorry, Mr. Timberlake," I said. "I am most awfully sorry. I should have paddled. It was my fault. I'll get you home at once. Let me wring out your coat and waistcoat. You'll catch your death . . ."

I stopped. I had nearly blasphemed. I had nearly suggested that Mr. Timberlake had fallen into the water and that to a man of his age this might be dangerous.

Mr. Timberlake corrected me. His voice was impersonal, addressing the laws of human existence rather than myself.

"If God made water it would be ridiculous to suggest He made it capable of harming His creatures. Wouldn't it?"

"Yes," I murmured hypocritically.

"O.K.," said Mr. Timberlake. "Let's go."

"I'll soon get you across," I said.

"No," he said. "I mean let's go on. We're not going to let a little thing like this spoil a beautiful afternoon. Where were we going? You spoke of a pretty landing-place farther on. Let's go there."

"But I must take you home. You can't sit there soaked to the skin. It will spoil your clothes."

"Now, now," said Mr. Timberlake. "Do as I say. Go on."

There was nothing to be done with him. I held the punt into the bank and he stepped in. He sat like a bursting and sodden bolster in front of me while I paddled. We had lost the pole, of course.

For a long time I could hardly look at Mr. Timberlake. He was taking the line that nothing had happened, and this put me at a disadvantage. I knew something considerable had happened. That glaze, which so many of the members of our sect had on their faces and persons, their minds and manners, had been washed off. There was no gleam for me from Mr. Timberlake.

"What's the house over there?" he asked. He was making conversation. I had steered into the middle of the river to get him into the strong sun. I saw steam rise from him.

I took courage and studied him. He was a man, I realized, in poor physical condition, unexercised and sedentary. Now the gleam had left him one saw the veined empurpled skin of the stoutish man with a poor heart. I remember he had said at lunch:

"A young woman I know said, 'Isn't it wonderful! I can walk thirty miles in a day without being in the least tired.' I said, 'I don't see that bodily indulgence is anything a member of the Church of the Last Purification should boast about.'"

Yes, there was something flaccid, passive and slack about Mr. Timberlake. Bunched in swollen clothes, he refused to take them off. It occurred to me, as he looked with boredom at the water, the passing boats and the country, that he had not been in the country before. That it was something he had agreed to do but wanted to get over quickly. He was totally uninterested. By his questions—what is that church? Are there any fish in this river? Is that a wireless or a gramophone?—I understood that Mr. Timberlake was formally acknowledging a world he did not live in. It was too interesting, too eventful a world. His spirit, inert and preoccupied, was elsewhere in an eventless and immaterial habitation. He was a dull man, duller than any man I have ever known; but his dullness was a sort of earthly deposit left by a being whose diluted mind was far away in the effervescence of metaphysical matters. There was a slightly pettish look on his face as (to himself, of course) he declared he was not wet and that he would not have a heart attack or catch pneumonia.

Mr. Timberlake spoke little. Sometimes he squeezed water out of his sleeve. He shivered a little. He watched his steam. I had planned when we set out to go up as far as the lock, but now the thought of another two miles of this responsibility was too much. I pretended I wanted to go only as far as the bend which we were approaching, where one of the richest buttercup meadows was. I mentioned this to him. He turned and looked with boredom at the field. Slowly we came to the bank.

We tied up the punt and we landed.

"Fine," said Mr. Timberlake. He stood at the edge of the meadow just as he had stood at the landing-stage—lost, stupefied, uncomprehending.

"Nice to stretch our legs," I said. I led the way into the deep flowers. So dense were the buttercups there was hardly any green. Presently I sat down. Mr. Timberlake looked at me and sat down also. Then I turned to him with a last try at persuasion. Respectability, I was sure, was his trouble.

"No one will see us," I said. "This is out of sight of the river. Take off your coat and trousers and wring them out."

Mr. Timberlake replied firmly:

"I am satisfied to remain as I am."

"What is this flower?" he asked, to change the subject.

"Buttercup," I said.

"Of course," he replied.

I could do nothing with him. I lay down full length in the sun; and, observing this and thinking to please me, Mr. Timberlake did the same. He must have supposed that this was what I had come out in the boat to do. It was only human. He had come out with me, I saw, to show me that he was only human.

But as we lay there I saw the steam still rising. I had had enough. "A bit hot," I said, getting up.

He got up at once.

"Do you want to sit in the shade?" he asked politely.

"No," I said. "Would you like to?"

"No," he said. "I was thinking of you."

"Let's go back," I said. We both stood up and I let him pass in front of me. When I looked at him again I stopped dead. Mr. Timberlake was no longer a man in a navy-blue suit. He was blue no longer. He was transfigured. He was yellow. He was covered with buttercup pollen, a fine yellow paste of it made by the damp, from head to foot.

"Your suit," I said.

He looked at it. He raised his eyebrows a little, but he did not smile or make any comment.

The man is a saint, I thought. As saintly as any of those gold-leaf figures in the churches of Sicily. Golden he sat in the punt; golden he sat for the next hour as I paddled him down the river. Golden and bored. Golden as we landed at the town and as we walked up the street back to my uncle's house. There he refused to change his clothes or to sit by a fire. He kept an eye on the time for his train back to London. By no word did he acknowledge the disasters or the beauties of the world. If they were printed upon him, they were printed upon a husk.

Sixteen years have passed since I dropped Mr. Timberlake in the river and since the sight of his pant-loops destroyed my faith. I have not seen him since, and to-day I heard that he was dead. He was fifty-seven. His mother, a very old lady with whom he had lived all his life, went into his bedroom when he was getting ready for church and found him lying on the floor in his shirt-sleeves. A stiff collar with the tie half inserted was in one hand. Five minutes before, she told the doctor, she had been speaking to him.

The doctor who looked at the heavy body lying on the single bed saw a middle-aged man, wide rather than stout and with an extraordinarily box-like thick-jawed face. He had got fat, my uncle told me, in later years. The heavy liver-coloured cheeks were like the chaps of a hound. Heart disease, it was plain, was the cause of the death of Mr. Timberlake. In death the face was lax, even coarse and degenerate. It was a miracle, the doctor said, that he had lived as long. Any time during the last twenty years the smallest shock might have killed him.

I thought of our afternoon on the river. I thought of him hanging from the tree. I thought of him, indifferent and golden, in the meadow. I understood why he had made for himself a protective, sedentary blandness, an automatic smile, a collection of phrases. He kept them on like the coat after his ducking. And I understood why.—though I had feared it all the time we were on the river—I understood why he did not talk to me about the origin of evil. He was honest. The ape was with us. The ape that merely followed me was already inside Mr. Timberlake eating out his heart.

For Study and Discussion

1. Why did the narrator's uncle become a convert to the Church of the Last Purification? What is the basic tenet of the sect?

2. What is the first difficulty the narrator faces with his religious faith?

3. What does the "gross ape" symbolize?

4. When Mr. Timberlake is hanging from the willow branch above the water, why does the narrator pray that Mr. Timberlake will not perform a miracle? How does this fit in with the narrator's further thought, "I realized that the final revelation about man and society on earth had come to nobody"?

5. Why is Mr. Timberlake "a declining dogma" in the view of the narrator?

6. Why does Mr. Timberlake refuse to take off his coat after his ducking in the water?

7. What is the significance of the comparison of Mr. Timberlake—after he gets pollen on his wet suit—with "those gold-leaf figures in the churches of Sicily"?

8. Does the rest of the story confirm the narrator's assertion at the beginning that he has lost his religious faith?

9. In his essay, Pritchett describes a modern short-story writer as "a dramatist of nervous alarm and the inner precipice" (p. 117). Would you say that this description fits the kind of personality that Pritchett seems to project as the author of "The Saint"?

JESSAMYN WEST

LOVE, DEATH, AND
THE LADIES' DRILL TEAM

Emily Cooper, the newest member of the Pocahontas Drill Team, was the first to arrive at the Burnham Building, where the morning practice, called by their drillmaster and team captain, Mrs. Amy Rotunda, was to be held. She stood for a while enjoying the wind—California's warm, dry September wind—before starting up the stairs to Burnham Hall. Burnham Hall was less pretentious than its name, being no more than the drab, unfurnished second floor of the building that housed, on its first floor, Burnham's Hardware, but the only other hall available in the small town of Los Robles was, though its rent was lower, unfortunately located above Sloane & Pierce's Undertaking Parlors.

Emily was halfway up the stairs when she was hailed from the sidewalk below by Mr. Burnham himself, holding a key aloft. "You one of the Pocahontas girls?" he called.

Emily turned about on the stairs and gazed down at the wide-shouldered old man. The wind was lifting his coattails and tossing his white hair about in tufts, like those of the bunch grass she had known as a girl in the Dakotas. She hesitated for a moment before answering. She was a Pocahontas, all right, but "girl" was a different story. She was thirty-six years old, had been married half her life, and had only an hour ago started her youngest off to his first day of school. Then, left without a child in the house for the first time in fifteen years, she had told her passing image in a mirror, "This is the beginning of middle age for you, Emily Cooper." Now "girl."

Mr. Burnham, as if understanding the reason for her hesitation, smiled as she came back down for the key. "My youngest is fifty," he said. Then, perhaps fearing that she might consider such confidences too personal, coming from a stranger, he spoke reassuringly of the weather. "Nice blow we're having—nice touch of wind." He faced about for a second after saying this, to get the full force of the warm, lively agitation, which had everything movable in Los Robles moving.

Originally published, in somewhat different form, in the *New Yorker*, September 22, 1951. Reprinted here from *Love, Death, and the Ladies' Drill Team* (New York: Harcourt, Brace and Co., 1955) by permission of Harcourt Brace Jovanovich, Inc. Copyright 1951 by Jessamyn West.

Actually, this talk of the wind was far more personal to Emily than Mr. Burnham's remark about his children. When he put the key in her hand, she said, "It's wonderful weather. I love the wind." Then she, too, was overtaken by a conviction that there was something unseemly in so much openness with a stranger, and she said a quick thank you and started back up the stairs. As she was unlocking the door, Mr. Burnham called, "Throw open the windows, will you? Modern Woodmen used the hall last night and they're a smoky lot."

Mr. Burnham was right about the Woodmen. Emily felt as if she were stepping into the bowl of a pipe still warm and filled with fumes. There were windows across the entire front of the hall, which faced on Los Robles' Main Street, and she opened them all. Then she pulled a chair up to the middle window and sat down to await the arrival of her team-mates. There was not much to be seen on the street below her. Ten o'clock on a Monday morning is not an hour for shoppers, and the children who yesterday would have been out in the wind, shirt-tails lofted for sails, diving and swooping like birds, but much noisier, were behind closed doors, with shirt-tails tucked in, and speaking only when nodded to by Teacher. She thought of her own Johnny and hoped he was finding school the wonder he had imagined it. He had left her without a tear, without even a backward look, declaring, with the pleasure of a man who has arrived at a goal long deferred, "Now I am a scholar."

Emily leaned out the window to watch a tumbleweed, blown into town from one of the surrounding barley fields, cross Main at Brown, traveling west swiftly and silently. In the vacant lot across the street, the tall, switch-stemmed dust flowers were bent down almost as low as grass. Beneath the window, the Burnham Hardware sign was swinging, and the awning was bellying and snapping with the sound, she supposed, of a ship under full sail. A few merchants were beginning to go up the street to the Gem for their midmorning cups of coffee. Merchants, the wind revealed, had bodies. Inside their usually unyielding tubes of serge and herringbone, their legs were astonishingly thin. As if in restitution for this exposure, the wind parted their coattails to display their firm and stately bottoms. A black cat passed below, its blackness not even skin-deep, for its hair, wind-blown, exposed a skin as white as that of any butcher-shop rabbit. Emily thrust her hands out across the window sill, feeling through her outspread fingers the full force and warmth of the blowing—as if I were the one true gauge, she thought, the one responsive and harmonious harp.

She was leaning thus, and by now almost half out of the room, when Mrs. Rotunda, the drill captain and coach, and Miss Ruby Graves, the team's star performer, arrived. Emily was new not only to the drill team but to the town of Los Robles, and was still able, she thought, to see people as they really were, unlabeled by a knowledge of their professions or reputations. But "Miss" and "Mrs." are in themselves labels, and Mrs. Rotunda's gray hair, elaborately waved and curled, with a fancy off-center part at the back and sculptured bangs arranged with all the finality of marble, said widow, said woman without a husband, filling in an empty and lonesome life with what, in the old, rich days, she would never have wasted time on. While, somewhat contradictorily, Miss Graves's black hair, long and innocent of the slightest ripple, said spinster, said woman without a husband and reconciled to the idea that her hair, curled or uncurled, was never going to be a matter of moment to any man. But without that "Miss" and "Mrs.," without her knowledge that Amy Rotunda was Fred Rotunda's widow, and Ruby Graves was Milton Graves's unmarried daughter and housekeeper, would she have had all this insight about hair? Emily couldn't say.

It was the same with Opal Tetford and Lacey Philips, who arrived next. Mrs. Tetford's husband was an official in the local Bank of America, while Mrs. Philips's husband owned and operated a big grain ranch out on the edge of town. Knowing this, Emily thought Mrs. Tetford's soft opulence was suited to the protection of vaults and burglar alarms, while Mrs. Philips's rawboned frame was right in its austerity for a background of endless barley fields and rolling, cactus-covered hills.

Mrs. Rotunda said, "I am going to demand that the Woodmen do something about this tobacco smoke. Do they think they're the only ones who use this hall?"

Miss Graves, who prided herself on being unprejudiced about men, though with every reason to justify prejudice, said, "I expect they are chain smokers, Amy. One cigarette after another all evening long."

Mrs. Rotunda, who had no need to conjecture, said, "Well, they could at least use a little Air-Wick afterward." She went to a window and leaned out for a breath of uncontaminated air. The other ladies drew up chairs at the windows. Beneath them, Mr. Sloane, of Sloane & Pierce, passed by on his way to the Gem for his mid-morning cup of coffee. Mr. Sloane, like many undertakers, was the picture of rosy durability, an evidence to mourners that though one life had ended, life itself endured.

Mrs. Rotunda withdrew her head from the window and began to pace up and down behind her seated teammates. "No," she declared. "I could never bring myself to do it. Not for a mere two-fifty, any way."

Emily looked inquiringly at Lacey Philips, who was seated next to her. "The Sloane & Pierce hall rents for two-fifty less than this one," Mrs. Philips explained.

"Save two-fifty at the price of drilling back and forth, quite possibly, over the body of your own dead mother? Not I," said Mrs. Rotunda firmly. "It would take a lot more than two-fifty to reconcile me to that."

Ruby Graves, who, in the manner of maiden ladies, combined extreme idealism on some subjects with extreme matter-of-factness on others, said, "If your mother passed away, Amy, wouldn't they hold the services for her down in Anaheim?"

Mrs. Rotunda replied with patience. "Ruby, I was speaking hypotheti-cally. Mother has owned a plot at Rosemead for I don't know how long, and will, of course, be laid to rest there—not be brought up here to the Sloane & Pierce funeral home to be marched across by Odd Fellows and Knights of Pythias and others for whom such things don't matter. But I only mentioned her as an example. I would have exactly the same scruples about marching over *your* mother."

Ruby turned away from the window. "Mother passed away a year ago Labor Day, Amy," she said in a voice that forgave the forgetfulness.

Mrs. Rotunda put her hands to her head. "Ruby, I could bite my tongue out!" she cried. "My point was—anyone. I'd have too much fellow feeling to be willing to meet above the remains."

Emily said, "I think Sloane & Pierce is a good place for Jehovah's Witnesses to meet, though."

"Do they meet there?" Mrs. Tetford asked. Mrs. Tetford had a reputation for asking questions—trained, they said, by Mr. Tetford, who was a man who liked to supply answers.

Emily nodded.

"Why?" Mrs. Tetford asked.

"I don't know," Emily said.

"I mean why do you think it's a good place for them to meet?"

"Oh. Well, that's one of the things a church is for, isn't it?" Emily asked, and, thinking of her children, seeing them already grown and scattered, and herself and John left alone with their memories, she added, "To remind us that all earthly things pass away?"

Mrs. Rotunda, at the words "pass away," stopped her pacing, and the hall had the silence of a room in which a clock suddenly ceases ticking. The women turned toward her and she extended her arms as if about to ask some extraordinary favor. "Oh, girls!" she cried. "My dear girls! Let's not be morbid. Let's not dwell on the inevitable or we'll have no heart for our practice."

Her life is drilling, Emily thought, smiling. The lodge is her husband and we are her children. She admired Mrs. Rotunda and hoped that, should she ever be left alone, she could be as sensible. Mrs. Rotunda came to the window before which Emily and Lacey sat, and perched between them on the window sill. Gazing down into the street, she shook her head. "Poor girl. Poor, poor girl," she said.

"Imola Ramos?" Emily asked, though there was not, at the moment, anyone else in sight who could possibly be called a girl. Imola was a black-haired, brown-skinned woman of about her own age. Her red-flowered dress, which looked as if it might have started life as a window curtain or a tablecloth, was cut like a Mother Hubbard and belted in closely with what appeared, from the second story of the Burnham Building, to be a piece of gray, frayed clothesline. It was plain to be seen that she wore no brassiere—and not much else, for the wind plastered the big red flowers as close to her thighs as if they were tattooed there.

"Ramos!" Mrs. Rotunda said. "Why, Emily, Imola's name's no more Ramos than yours is. Her name's what it's always been—since she was married, anyway. Fetters. She married LeRoy Fetters so young it's hard to remember that she was born a Butterfield. But it's Fetters now. That Mexican never married her. Couldn't, to do him justice, since LeRoy would never divorce her. And anyway why should he have married her? She was willing to live with him."

"Live with him as man and wife," Ruby explained.

"I never knew they weren't married," Emily said. "I've always heard her called Mrs. Ramos."

Mrs. Rotunda excused this. "You haven't been in Los Robles very long. It takes a little time to catch on to these things."

Imola, who was carrying two shopping bags heavy enough to curve her square shoulders, stepped off the sidewalk and into the vacant lot opposite the Burnham Building. There she set the bags down amidst the blue dust flowers, and while the disturbed cicadas one by one ceased shrilling, she hunted in her purse for her cigarettes. By the time she had her cigarette lighted, the cicadas were once again filling Main Street with their country cries, and Imola, her head on one side, appeared to be listening with pleasure to the sound.

"Why did she leave her husband?" Emily asked.

"That is the mystery," Mrs. Rotunda admitted. "There never was a better man on earth, to my mind, than LeRoy Fetters."

"LeRoy used to wash Imola's hair for her, regular as clockwork, every ten days," Mrs. Philips said.

"Why? I always wondered," Mrs. Tetford asked.

"Pride," Ruby said. "Pure pride in that great mane of black hair."

They were all watching Imola, standing at her ease in the vacant lot, the wind outlining her sturdy body—a woman obviously well and happy.

Disagreeing with Ruby, Mrs. Tetford answered her own question. "In my opinion, LeRoy did it to save the price of a beauty parlor."

Contradicted about motives, Ruby took a new tack. "They say, Mrs. Cooper, that this Mexican manhandles her."

Mrs. Rotunda sniffed. "They say," she said. "I *saw*. Just a week ago today, I saw them having breakfast at the Gem, and Imola had black-and-blue spots the size of quarters on her arms."

Ruby said, "Poor Imola."

"What were *you* doing down at the Gem at breakfast time, Amy?" Mrs. Tetford asked.

"Who said anything about its being breakfast time? As a matter of fact, it was three in the afternoon, and I was having a root-beer float. But those two were having fried eggs and hot cakes, bold as brass, not making the least effort to deceive anyone."

"Why?" Ruby asked. "Why were they having breakfast at that hour?"

"You may well ask, Ruby," said Mrs. Rotunda shortly.

"I feel so sorry for Imola," Mrs. Tetford said.

"They live out near our ranch, you know," Mrs. Philips told them. "They're on the edge of the irrigation ditch, in one of those three-room shacks that the water company furnishes its Mexican workers. Two rooms and a lean-to, really, is what they are. Mattress on the floor, in place of a bed. Old, broken-down, rusty oil stove. Chesterfield with its springs half through the upholstery."

"I wonder how Imola's mother *bears* it," Mrs. Rotunda said.

"Do you ever see them?" Mrs. Tetford asked Mrs. Philips.

"Many's the time. Manuel doesn't seem to have any regular working hours, and in the summertime they do a lot of sporting around together, in and out of the water. And the shoe's on the other foot this time so far's washing is concerned. Imola's the one who does the washing now."

"His hair?" asked Ruby.

"Well, just generally," Mrs. Philips answered.

"A Butterfield washing a Mexican! Sunk that low! It doesn't bear thinking about," Mrs. Tetford said.

"I expect he's pretty dark-skinned?" asked Ruby, who evidently could bear thinking about it.

"They both are," Mrs. Philips explained. "After they finish swimming or washing, whichever it is, they lie around in the sun, suntanning. And, like as not, Manuel will play some music for Imola on that instrument of his. That banjo or guitar—I never can tell the two of them apart."

"Fred used to play the clarinet," Mrs. Rotunda said. "He had a natural ear for music and could play anything he'd heard once."

"Is it flat-backed or curved, Lacey?" Mrs. Tetford asked. "This musical instrument."

"I never did notice."

"Big or little, comparatively speaking?"

"Big," Lacey Philips said.

"It's a guitar, then. I thought it would be. That's the Spanish national instrument."

"He is dressed, I suppose, by the time this music-making starts?" Ruby Graves said.

"Dressed!" Mrs. Philips exclaimed. "Why, Ruby, he sits there strumming out melodies and flinching off flies as innocent of clothes as a newborn babe!"

"And Imola?"

"Naked as a jay bird. Lying in the grass kicking up her heels. Sometimes silent, sometimes singing."

Mrs. Tetford shook her head. "The poor girl."

"Play to her, hit her. I guess Imola runs the full gamut with that man," Ruby speculated.

"Speak of the devil," said Mrs. Philips, motioning with her chin up the street.

Emily, who had been watching Imola as she listened to the talk about her, saw her throw away the stub of her cigarette and wave at the man coming up the street toward her. Ramos was a short, stocky man with a strong, toed-in walk and, when he reached Imola, a quick, white smile. Imola stooped down when he turned in at the vacant lot and brought up out of one of her shopping bags an enormous bunch of purple grapes.

"Isabellas," said Mrs. Philips. "First it's a feast, then it's a fast with them, I guess."

"He's a big, burly fellow," Mrs. Rotunda admitted.

"Naked and singing by the irrigation ditch," Ruby marveled as Imola popped grapes alternately into her own mouth and into that of the Mexican.

"LeRoy Fetters was a registered pharmacist," Mrs. Rotunda told Emily. "A very responsible man. He always took a real interest in whether his prescriptions helped."

"Breakfast at three o'clock," Ruby murmured as the feeding below continued, interspersed with considerable affectionate horseplay. "I wonder what it tastes like at that hour."

"Not a thing in the world to keep you from finding out, is there, Ruby?" Mrs. Rotunda asked.

"I doubt it would be the same alone," Ruby said.

Across the street, the grapes finished, Imola, there in the broad daylight of midmorning and in the middle of Los Robles, first kissed the Mexican full on the mouth, then put a cigarette between his lips and, while he shielded it with his hands, lighted it for him.

The ladies were silent for quite a while after this. Finally, Mrs. Tetford said, "Poor Imola! Where is her pride?"

Imola now lighted a cigarette for herself. Emily, watching the two of them at their ease amid the weeds and dust flowers, the wind carrying their cigarette smoke streaming away from them in transparent plumes, said, to her own surprise, "Pride? Why, Mrs. Tetford, pride doesn't enter in. She loves him."

There was another long silence in the hall. A number of additional members of the drill team had arrived, and Emily felt that her unconsidered word was settling among them like a stone in a pond of still water. But just at the moment when she supposed the last ripple had disappeared, Mrs. Rotunda repeated the word, in a voice that lingered and explored. "Love?" she asked. "Love?"

Is she asking me, Emily thought. But evidently she was not, for before Emily could answer, Mrs. Rotunda had turned her back on the window and was calling the team together. "Girls, girls!" she cried. "Let's not moon! We won't wait for the others. Now, hands on shoulders, and remember, an arm's length apart."

Mrs. Rotunda turned them away from the windows and got them

linked together. They reversed by eights, went forward by twos, and formed hollow squares. Emily, still thoughtful, still lingering by the window, saw Imola and the Mexican pick up the shopping bags and proceed, together and equally burdened, down the street. She saw Mr. Sloane return, refreshed, from the Gem to his work. She saw Mr. Burnham out on the edge of the sidewalk, face uplifted as if searching the wind for scents of some lost place or time. She saw how the wind, swooping down off the dry, brown hills, wrapped the soft prints of her drill mates' dresses about their varishaped bodies, so that they moved through the elaborate figures of Mrs. Rotunda's planning like women in some picture of past days. And Mrs. Rotunda's brisk commands—"To the rear by twos!" or "The diamond formation!"—were like a little, inconsequential piping, the way the wind, veering, shrills for a second or two through a crack before resuming its own voice, deep and solemn and prophetic.

For Study and Discussion

1. How much information necessary to the outcome of the story is conveyed in the first four paragraphs?

2. What purpose is served by the emphasis on the wind and its effects upon Mrs. Cooper?

3. How are the ladies' comments about death related to the scene involving Imola, whom they observe from the second-story windows?

4. Discuss whether the ladies' comments about Imola herself are more or less similar, or whether they reveal interesting variations in character and attitude.

5. What is the significance of Mrs. Cooper's pointing out that Imola loves the Mexican?

6. How do Mrs. Cooper's reflections on the wind effectively sum up any meaningful relationships that bind the components of the story together?

7. In what significant ways are love, death, and the ladies' drill team related?

8. Do you think Baker would find this story lacking in "surface action"? (See his essay, pp. 118–123.) If so, do you consider the lack of surface action a defect in the story? Why or why not?

FLANNERY O'CONNOR

A GOOD MAN IS HARD TO FIND

The grandmother didn't want to go to Florida. She wanted to visit some of her connections in east Tennessee and she was seizing at every chance to change Bailey's mind. Bailey was the son she lived with, her only boy. He was sitting on the edge of his chair at the table, bent over the orange sports section of the *Journal*. "Now look here, Bailey," she said, "see here, read this," and she stood with one hand on her thin hip and the other rattling the newspaper at his bald head. "Here this fellow that calls himself The Misfit is aloose from the Federal Pen and headed toward Florida and you read here what it says he did to these people. Just you read it. I wouldn't take my children in any direction with a criminal like that aloose in it. I couldn't answer to my conscience if I did."

Bailey didn't look up from his reading so she wheeled around then and faced the children's mother, a young woman in slacks, whose face was as broad and innocent as a cabbage and was tied around with a green head-kerchief that had two points on the top like rabbit's ears. She was sitting on the sofa, feeding the baby his apricots out of a jar. "The children have been to Florida before," the old lady said. "You all ought to take them somewhere else for a change so they would see different parts of the world and be broad. They never have been to east Tennessee."

The children's mother didn't seem to hear her but the eight-year-old boy, John Wesley, a stocky child with glasses, said, "If you don't want to go to Florida, why dontcha stay at home?" He and the little girl, June Star, were reading the funny papers on the floor.

"She wouldn't stay at home to be queen for a day," June Star said without raising her yellow head.

"Yes and what would you do if this fellow, The Misfit, caught you?" the grandmother asked.

Originally published in, and reprinted here from, *A Good Man Is Hard to Find and Other Stories* (New York: Harcourt, Brace and Co., 1955) by permission of Harcourt Brace Jovanovich, Inc. Copyright 1953 by Flannery O'Connor.

"I'd smack his face," John Wesley said.

"She wouldn't stay at home for a million bucks," June Star said. "Afraid she'd miss something. She has to go everywhere we go."

"All right, Miss," the grandmother said. "Just remember that the next time you want me to curl your hair."

June Star said her hair was naturally curly.

The next morning the grandmother was the first one in the car, ready to go. She had her big black valise that looked like the head of a hippopotamus in one corner, and underneath it she was hiding a basket with Pitty Sing, the cat, in it. She didn't intend for the cat to be left alone in the house for three days because he would miss her too much and she was afraid he might brush against one of the gas burners and accidentally asphyxiate himself. Her son, Bailey, didn't like to arrive at a motel with a cat.

She sat in the middle of the back seat with John Wesley and June Star on either side of her. Bailey and the children's mother and the baby sat in front and they left Atlanta at eight forty-five with the mileage on the car at 55890. The grandmother wrote this down because she thought it would be interesting to say how many miles they had been when they got back. It took them twenty minutes to reach the outskirts of the city.

The old lady settled herself comfortably, removing her white cotton gloves and putting them up with her purse on the shelf in front of the back window. The children's mother still had on slacks and still had her head tied up in a green kerchief, but the grandmother had on a navy blue straw sailor hat with a bunch of white violets on the brim and a navy blue dress with a small white dot in the print. Her collars and cuffs were white organdy trimmed with lace and at her neckline she had pinned a purple spray of cloth violets containing a sachet. In case of an accident, anyone seeing her dead on the highway would know at once that she was a lady.

She said she thought it was going to be a good day for driving, neither too hot nor too cold, and she cautioned Bailey that the speed limit was fifty-five miles an hour and that the patrolmen hid themselves behind billboards and small clumps of trees and sped out after you before you had a chance to slow down. She pointed out interesting details of the scenery: Stone Mountain; the blue granite that in some places came up to both sides of the highway; the brilliant red clay banks slightly streaked with purple; and the various crops that made rows of green lace-work on the ground. The trees were full of silver-white sunlight and the meanest of them sparkled. The children were reading comic magazines and their mother had gone back to sleep.

"Let's go through Georgia fast so we won't have to look at it much," John Wesley said.

"If I were a little boy," said the grandmother, "I wouldn't talk about my native state that way. Tennessee has the mountains and Georgia has the hills."

"Tennessee is just a hillbilly dumping ground," John Wesley said,
~~y state too."

~aid.

"In my time," said the grandmother, folding her thin veined fingers,
"children were more respectful of their native states and their parents
and everything else. People did right then. Oh look at the cute little
pickaninny!" she said and pointed to a Negro child standing in the door
of a shack. "Wouldn't that make a picture, now?" she asked and they all
turned and looked at the little Negro out of the back window. He waved.

"He didn't have any britches on," June Star said.

"He probably didn't have any," the grandmother explained. "Little
niggers in the country don't have things like we do. If I could paint, I'd
paint that picture," she said.

The children exchanged comic books.

The grandmother offered to hold the baby and the children's mother
passed him over the front seat to her. She set him on her knee and
bounced him and told him about the things they were passing. She rolled
her eyes and screwed up her mouth and stuck her leathery thin face into
his smooth bland one. Occasionally he gave her a faraway smile. They
passed a large cotton field with five or six graves fenced in the middle of
it, like a small island. "Look at the graveyard!" the grandmother said,
pointing it out. "That was the old family burying ground. That belonged
to the plantation."

"Where's the plantation?" John Wesley asked.

"Gone With the Wind," said the grandmother. "Ha. Ha."

When the children finished all the comic books they had brought, they
opened the lunch and ate it. The grandmother ate a peanut butter
sandwich and an olive and would not let the children throw the box and
the paper napkins out the window. When there was nothing else to do
they played a game by choosing a cloud and making the other two guess
what shape it suggested. John Wesley took one the shape of a cow and
June Star guessed a cow and John Wesley said, no, an automobile, and
June Star said he didn't play fair, and they began to slap each other over
the grandmother.

The grandmother said she would tell them a story if they would keep
quiet. When she told a story, she rolled her eyes and waved her head and
was very dramatic. She said once when she was a maiden lady she had
been courted by a Mr. Edgar Atkins Teagarden from Jasper, Georgia.
She said he was a very good-looking man and a gentleman and that he
brought her a watermelon every Saturday afternoon with his initials cut
in it, E. A. T. Well, one Saturday, she said, Mr. Teagarden brought the
watermelon and there was nobody at home and he left it on the front
porch and returned in his buggy to Jasper, but she never got the
watermelon, she said, because a nigger boy ate it when he saw the
initials, E. A. T.! This story tickled John Wesley's funny bone and he

giggled and giggled but June Star didn't think it was any good. She said she wouldn't marry a man that just brought her a watermelon on Saturday. The grandmother said she would have done well to marry Mr. Teagarden because he was a gentleman and had bought Coca-Cola stock when it first came out and that he had died only a few years ago, a very wealthy man.

They stopped at The Tower for barbecued sandwiches. The Tower was a part stucco and part wood filling station and dance hall set in a clearing outside of Timothy. A fat man named Red Sammy Butts ran it and there were signs stuck here and there on the building and for miles up and down the highway saying, TRY RED SAMMY'S FAMOUS BARBECUE. NONE LIKE FAMOUS RED SAMMY'S! RED SAM! THE FAT BOY WITH THE HAPPY LAUGH. A VETERAN! RED SAMMY'S YOUR MAN!

Red Sammy was lying on the bare ground outside The Tower with his head under a truck while a gray monkey about a foot high, chained to a small chinaberry tree, chattered nearby. The monkey sprang back into the tree and got on the highest limb as soon as he saw the children jump out of the car and run toward him.

Inside, The Tower was a long dark room with a counter at one end and tables at the other and dancing space in the middle. They all sat down at a board table next to the nickelodeon and Red Sam's wife, a tall burnt-brown woman with hair and eyes lighter than her skin, came and took their order. The children's mother put a dime in the machine and played "The Tennessee Waltz," and the grandmother said the tune always made her want to dance. She asked Bailey if he would like to dance but he only glared at her. He didn't have a naturally sunny disposition like she did and trips made him nervous. The grandmother's brown eyes were very bright. She swayed her head from side to side and pretended she was dancing in her chair. June Star said play something she could tap to so the children's mother put in another dime and played a fast number and June Star stepped out onto the dance floor and did her tap routine.

"Ain't she cute?" Red Sam's wife said, leaning over the counter. "Would you like to be my little girl?"

"No I certainly wouldn't," June Star said. "I wouldn't live in a broken-down place like this for a million bucks!" and she ran back to the table.

"Ain't she cute?" the woman repeated, stretching her mouth politely.

"Arn't you ashamed?" hissed the grandmother.

Red Sam came in and told his wife to quit lounging on the counter and hurry up with these people's order. His khaki trousers reached just to his hip bones and his stomach hung over them like a sack of meal swaying under his shirt. He came over and sat down at a table nearby and let out a combination sigh and yodel. "You can't win," he said. "You can't win," and he wiped his sweating red face off with a gray handkerchief.

"These days you do. I know who to trust," he said. "Ain't that the truth?"

"People are certainly not nice like they used to be," said the grandmother.

"Two fellers come in here last week," Red Sammy said, "driving a Chrysler. It was a old beat-up car but it was a good one and these boys looked all right to me. Said they worked at the mill and you know I let them fellers charge the gas they bought? Now why did I do that?"

"Because you're a good man!" the grandmother said at once.

"Yes'm, I suppose so," Red Sam said as if he were struck with this answer.

His wife brought the orders, carrying the five plates all at once without a tray, two in each hand and one balanced on her arm. "It isn't a soul in this green world of God's that you can trust," she said. "And I don't count nobody out of that, not nobody," she repeated, looking at Red Sammy.

"Did you read about that criminal, The Misfit, that's escaped?" asked the grandmother.

"I wouldn't be a bit surprised if he didn't attact this place right here," said the woman. "If he hears about it being here, I wouldn't be none surprised to see him. If he hears it's two cent in the cash register, I wouldn't be a tall surprised if he. . . ."

"That'll do," Red Sam said. "Go bring these people their Co'-Colas," and the woman went off to get the rest of the order.

"A good man is hard to find," Red Sammy said. "Everything is getting terrible. I remember the day you could go off and leave your screen door unlatched. Not no more."

He and the grandmother discussed better times. The old lady said that in her opinion Europe was entirely to blame for the way things were now. She said the way Europe acted you would think we were made of money and Red Sam said it was no use talking about it, she was exactly right. The children ran outside into the white sunlight and looked at the monkey in the lacy chinaberry tree. He was busy catching fleas on himself and biting each one carefully between his teeth as if it were a delicacy.

They drove off again into the hot afternoon. The grandmother took cat naps and woke up every few minutes with her own snoring. Outside of Toombsboro she woke up and recalled an old plantation that she had visited in this neighborhood once when she was a young lady. She said the house had six white columns across the front and that there was an avenue of oaks leading up to it and two little wooden trellis arbors on either side in front where you sat down with your suitor after a stroll in the garden. She recalled exactly which road to turn off to get to it. She knew that Bailey would not be willing to lose any time looking at an old house, but the more she talked about it, the more she wanted to see it once again and find out if the little twin arbors were still standing. "There was a secret panel in this house," she said craftily, not telling the truth but wishing that she were, "and the story went that all the family silver was hidden in it when Sherman came through but it was never found . . ."

"Hey!" John Wesley said. "Let's go see it! We'll find it! We'll poke all the woodwork and find it! Who lives there? Where do you turn off at? Hey Pop, can't we turn off there?"

"We never have seen a house with a secret panel!" June Star shrieked. "Let's go to the house with the secret panel! Hey Pop, can't we go see the house with the secret panel!"

"It's not far from here, I know," the grandmother said. "It wouldn't take over twenty minutes."

Bailey was looking straight ahead. His jaw was as rigid as a horseshoe. "No," he said.

The children began to yell and scream that they wanted to see the house with the secret panel. John Wesley kicked the back of the front seat and June Star hung over her mother's shoulder and whined desperately into her ear that they never had any fun even on their vacation, that they could never do what THEY wanted to do. The baby began to scream and John Wesley kicked the back of the seat so hard that his father could feel the blows in his kidney.

"All right!" he shouted and drew the car to a stop at the side of the road. "Will you all shut up? Will you all just shut up for one second? If you don't shut up, we won't go anywhere."

"It would be very educational for them," the grandmother murmured.

"All right," Bailey said, "but get this: this is the only time we're going to stop for anything like this. This is the one and only time."

"The dirt road that you have to turn down is about a mile back," the grandmother directed. "I marked it when we passed."

"A dirt road," Bailey groaned.

After they had turned around and were headed toward the dirt road, the grandmother recalled other points about the house, the beautiful glass over the front doorway and the candle-lamp in the hall. John Wesley said that the secret panel was probably in the fireplace.

"You can't go inside this house," Bailey said. "You don't know who lives there."

"While you all talk to the people in front, I'll run around behind and get in a window," John Wesley suggested.

"We'll all stay in the car," his mother said.

They turned onto the dirt road and the car raced roughly along in a swirl of pink dust. The grandmother recalled the times when there were no paved roads and thirty miles was a day's journey. The dirt road was hilly and there were sudden washes in it and sharp curves on dangerous in a red depression with the dust-coated ...

"This place had better turn up in a minute," Bailey said, "or I'm going to turn around."

The road looked as if no one had traveled on it in months.

"It's not much farther," the grandmother said and just as she said it, a horrible thought came to her. The thought was so embarrassing that she turned red in the face and her eyes dilated and her feet jumped up, upsetting her valise in the corner. The instant the valise moved, the newspaper top she had over the basket under it rose with a snarl and Pitty Sing, the cat, sprang onto Bailey's shoulder.

The children were thrown to the floor and their mother, clutching the baby, was thrown out the door onto the ground; the old lady was thrown into the front seat. The car turned over once and landed right-side-up in a gulch off the side of the road. Bailey remained in the driver's seat with the cat—gray-striped with a broad white face and an orange nose—clinging to his neck like a caterpillar.

As soon as the children saw they could move their arms and legs, they scrambled out of the car, shouting, "We've had an ACCIDENT!" The grandmother was curled up under the dashboard, hoping she was injured so that Bailey's wrath would not come down on her all at once. The horrible thought she had had before the accident was that the house she had remembered so vividly was not in Georgia but in Tennessee.

Bailey removed the cat from his neck with both hands and flung it out the window against the side of a pine tree. Then he got out of the car and started looking for the children's mother. She was sitting against the side of the red gutted ditch, holding the screaming baby, but she only had a cut down her face and a broken shoulder. "We've had an ACCIDENT!" the children screamed in a frenzy of delight.

"But nobody's killed," June Star said with disappointment as the grandmother limped out of the car, her hat still pinned to her head but the broken front brim standing up at a jaunty angle and the violet spray hanging off the side. They all sat down in the ditch, except the children, to recover from the shock. They were all shaking.

"Maybe a car will come along," said the children's mother hoarsely.

"I believe I have injured an organ," said the grandmother, pressing her side, but no one answered her. Bailey's teeth were clattering. He had on a yellow sport shirt with bright blue parrots designed in it and his face was as yellow as the shirt. The grandmother decided that she would not mention that the house was in Tennessee.

The road was about ten feet above and they could see only the tops of the trees on the other side of it. Behind the ditch they were sitting in there were more woods, tall and dark and deep. In a few minutes they saw a car some distance away on top of a hill, coming slowly as if the occupants were watching them. The grandmother stood up and waved both arms dramatically to attract their attention. The car continued to come on slowly, disappeared around a bend and appeared again, moving even slower, on top of the hill they had gone over. It was a big black battered hearse-like automobile. There were three men in it.

It came to a stop just over them and for some minutes, the driver looked down with a steady expressionless gaze to where they were sitting, and didn't speak. Then he turned his head and muttered something to the other two and they got out. One was a fat boy in black trousers and a red sweat shirt with a silver stallion embossed on the front of it. He moved around on the right side of them and stood staring, his mouth partly open in a kind of loose grin. The other had on khaki pants and a blue striped coat and a gray hat pulled down very low, hiding most of his face. He came around slowly on the left side. Neither spoke.

The driver got out of the car and stood by the side of it, looking down at them. He was an older man than the other two. His hair was just beginning to gray and he wore silver-rimmed spectacles that gave him a scholarly look. He had a long creased face and didn't have on any shirt or undershirt. He had on blue jeans that were too tight for him and was holding a black hat and a gun. The two boys also had guns.

"We've had an ACCIDENT!" the children screamed.

The grandmother had the peculiar feeling that the bespectacled man was someone she knew. His face was as familiar to her as if she had known him all her life but she could not recall who he was. He moved away from the car and began to come down the embankment, placing his feet carefully so that he wouldn't slip. He had on tan and white shoes and no socks, and his ankles were red and thin. "Good afternoon," he said. "I see you all had you a little spill."

"We turned over twice!" said the grandmother.

"Oncet," he corrected. "We seen it happen. Try their car and see will it run, Hiram," he said quietly to the boy with the gray hat.

"What you got that gun for?" John Wesley asked. "Whatcha gonna do with that gun?"

"Lady," the man said to the children's mother, "would you mind calling them children to sit down by you? Children make me nervous. I want all you all to sit down right together there where you're at."

"What are you telling US what to do for?" June Star asked.

Behind them the line of woods gaped like a dark open mouth. "Come here," said their mother.

"Look here now," Bailey began suddenly, "we're in a predicament! We're in . . ."

The grandmother shrieked. She scrambled to her feet and stood staring. "You're The Misfit!" she said. "I recognized you at once!"

"Yes'm," the man said, smiling slightly as if he were pleased in spite of himself to be known, "but it would have been better for all of you, lady, if you hadn't of reckernized me."

Bailey turned his head sharply and s[...]
shocked even the children. The old la[...]
reddened.

"Lady," he said, "don't you get upset. Sometim[...] [m]an says things
he don't mean. I don't reckon he meant to talk to you thataway."

"You wouldn't shoot a lady, would you?" the grandmother said and
removed a clean handkerchief from her cuff and began to slap at her eyes
with it.

The Misfit pointed the toe of his shoe into the ground and made a little
hole and then covered it up again. "I would hate to have to," he said.

"Listen," the grandmother almost screamed, "I know you're a good
man. You don't look a bit like you have common blood. I know you must
come from nice people!"

"Yes mam," he said, "finest people in the world." When he smiled he
showed a row of strong white teeth. "God never made a finer woman
than my mother and my daddy's heart was pure gold," he said. The boy
with the red sweat shirt had come around behind them and was standing
with his gun at his hip. The Misfit squatted down on the ground. "Watch
them children, Bobby Lee," he said. "You know they make me nervous."
He looked at the six of them huddled together in front of him and he
seemed to be embarrassed as if he couldn't think of anything to say.
"Ain't a cloud in the sky," he remarked, looking up at it. "Don't see no
sun but don't see no cloud neither."

"Yes, it's a beautiful day," said the grandmother. "Listen," she said,
"you shouldn't call yourself The Misfit because I know you're a good
man at heart. I can just look at you and tell."

"Hush!" Bailey yelled. "Hush! Everybody shut up and let me handle
this!" He was squatting in the position of a runner about to sprint
forward but he didn't move.

"I pre-chate that, lady," The Misfit said and drew a little circle in the
ground with the butt of his gun.

"It'll take a half a hour to fix this here car," Hiram called, looking over
the raised hood of it.

"Well, first you and Bobby Lee get him and that little boy to step over
yonder with you," The Misfit said, pointing to Bailey and John Wesley.
"The boys want to ast you something," he said to Bailey. "Would you
mind stepping back in them woods there with them?"

"Listen," Bailey began, "we're in a terrible predicament! Nobody
realizes what this is," and his voice cracked. His eyes were as blue and
intense as the parrots in his shirt and he remained perfectly still.

The grandmother reached up to adjust her hat brim as if she were
going to the woods with him but it came off in her hand. She stood
staring at it and after a second she let it fall on the ground. Hiram pulled
Bailey up by the arm as if he were assisting an old man. John Wesley
caught hold of his father's hand and Bobby Lee followed. They went off
toward the woods and just as they reached the dark edge, Bailey turned

and supporting himself against a gray naked pine trunk, he shouted, "I'll be back in a minute, Mamma, wait on me!"

"Come back this instant!" his mother shrilled but they all disappeared into the woods.

"Bailey Boy!" the grandmother called in a tragic voice but she found she was looking at The Misfit squatting on the ground in front of her. "I just know you're a good man," she said desperately. "You're not a bit common!"

"Nome, I ain't a good man," The Misfit said after a second as if he had considered her statement carefully, "but I ain't the worst in the world neither. My daddy said I was a different breed of dog from my brothers and sisters. 'You know,' Daddy said, 'it's some that can live their whole life out without asking about it and it's others has to know why it is, and this boy is one of the latters. He's going to be into everything!'" He put on his black hat and looked up suddenly and then away deep into the woods as if he were embarrassed again. "I'm sorry I don't have on a shirt before you ladies," he said, hunching his shoulders slightly. "We buried our clothes that we had on when we escaped and we're just making do until we can get better. We borrowed these from some folks we met," he explained.

"That's perfectly all right," the grandmother said. "Maybe Bailey has an extra shirt in his suitcase."

"I'll look and see terrectly," The Misfit said.

"Where are they taking him?" the children's mother screamed.

"Daddy was a card himself," The Misfit said. "You couldn't put anything over on him. He never got in trouble with the Authorities though. Just had the knack of handling them."

"You could be honest too if you'd only try," said the grandmother. "Think how wonderful it would be to settle down and live a comfortable life and not have to think about somebody chasing you all the time."

The Misfit kept scratching in the ground with the butt of his gun as if he were thinking about it. "Yes'm, somebody is always after you," he murmured.

The grandmother noticed how thin his shoulder blades were just behind his hat because she was standing up looking down on him. "Do you ever pray?" she asked.

He shook his head. All she saw was the black hat wiggle between his shoulder blades. "Nome," he said.

There was a pistol shot from the woods, followed closely by another. Then silence. The old lady's head jerked around. She could hear the wind move through the tree tops like a long satisfied insuck of breath. "Bailey Boy!" she called.

"I was a gospel singer for a while," The Misfit said. "I been most everything. Been in the arm service, both land and sea, at home and abroad, been twict married, been an undertaker, been with the railroads, plowed Mother Earth, been in a tornado, seen a man burnt alive oncet," and he looked up at the children's mother and the little girl who were sitting close together, their faces white and their eyes glassy; "I even seen a woman flogged," he said.

"Pray, pray," the grandmother began, "pray, pray . . ."

"I never was a bad boy that I remember of," The Misfit said in an almost dreamy voice, "but somewheres along the line I done something wrong and got sent to the penitentiary. I was buried alive," and he looked up and held her attention to him by a steady stare.

"That's when you should have started to pray," she said. "What did you do to get sent to the penitentiary that first time?"

"Turn to the right, it was a wall," The Misfit said, looking up again at the cloudless sky. "Turn to the left, it was a wall. Look up it was a ceiling, look down it was a floor. I forget what I done, lady. I set there and set there, trying to remember what it was I done and I ain't recalled it to this day. Oncet in a while, I would think it was coming to me, but it never come."

"Maybe they put you in by mistake," the old lady said vaguely.

"Nome," he said. "It wasn't no mistake. They had the papers on me."

"You must have stolen something," she said.

The Misfit sneered slightly. "Nobody had nothing I wanted," he said. "It was a head-doctor at the penitentiary said what I had done was kill my daddy but I known that for a lie. My daddy died in nineteen ought nineteen of the epidemic flu and I never had a thing to do with it. He was buried in the Mount Hopewell Baptist churchyard and you can go there and see for yourself."

"If you would pray," the old lady said, "Jesus would help you."

"That's right," The Misfit said.

"Well then, why don't you pray?" she asked trembling with delight suddenly.

"I don't want no hep," he said. "I'm doing all right by myself."

Bobby Lee and Hiram came ambling back from the woods. Bobby Lee was dragging a yellow shirt with bright blue parrots in it.

"Thow me that shirt, Bobby Lee," The Misfit said. The shirt came flying at him and landed on his shoulder and he put it on. The grandmother couldn't name what the shirt reminded her of. "No, lady," The Misfit said while he was buttoning it up, "I found out the crime don't matter. You can do one thing or you can do another, kill a man or take a tire off his car, because sooner or later you're going to forget what it was you done and just be punished for it."

The children's mother had begun to make heaving noises as if she couldn't get her breath. "Lady," he asked, "would you and that little girl like to step off yonder with Bobby Lee and Hiram and join your husband?"

"Yes, thank you," the mother said faintly. Her left arm dangled helplessly and she was holding the baby, who had gone to sleep, in the other. "Hep that lady up, Hiram," The Misfit said as she struggled to climb out of the 'ditch, "and Bobby Lee, you hold onto that little girl's hand."

"I don't want to hold hands with him," June Star said. "He reminds me of a pig."

The fat boy blushed and laughed and caught her by the arm and pulled her off into the woods after Hiram and her mother.

Alone with The Misfit, the grandmother found that she had lost her voice. There was not a cloud in the sky nor any sun. There was nothing around her but woods. She wanted to tell him that he must pray. She opened and closed her mouth several times before anything came out. Finally she found herself saying, "Jesus, Jesus," meaning, Jesus will help you, but the way she was saying it, it sounded as if she might be cursing.

"Yes'm," The Misfit said as if he agreed. "Jesus thrown everything off balance. It was the same case with Him as with me except He hadn't committed any crime and they could prove I had committed one because they had the papers on me. Of course," he said, "they never shown me my papers. That's why I sign myself now. I said long ago, you get you a signature and sign everything you do and keep a copy of it. Then you'll know what you done and you can hold up the crime to the punishment and see do they match and in the end you'll have something to prove you ain't been treated right. I call myself The Misfit," he said, "because I can't make what all I done wrong fit what all I gone through in punishment."

There was a piercing scream from the woods, followed closely by a pistol report. "Does it seem right to you, lady, that one is punished a heap and another ain't punished at all?"

"Jesus!" the old lady cried. "You've got good blood! I know you wouldn't shoot a lady! I know you come from nice people! Pray! Jesus, you ought not to shoot a lady. I'll give you all the money I've got!"

"Lady," The Misfit said, looking beyond her far into the woods, "there never was a body that give the undertaker a tip."

There were two more pistol reports and the grandmother raised her head like a parched old turkey hen crying for water and called, "Bailey Boy, Bailey Boy!" as if her heart would break.

"Jesus was the only One that ever raised the dead," The Misfit continued, "and He shouldn't have done it. He thown everything off balance. If He did what He said, then it's nothing for you to do but thow away everything and follow Him, and if He didn't, then it's nothing for you to do but enjoy the few minutes you got left the best way you can—by killing somebody or burning down his house or doing some other meanness to him. No pleasure but meanness," he said and his voice had become almost a snarl.

"Maybe He didn't raise the dead," the old lady mumbled, not knowing what she was saying and feeling so dizzy that she sank down in the ditch with her legs twisted under her.

"I wasn't there so I can't say He didn't," The Misfit said. "I wisht I had of been there," he said, hitting the ground with his fist. "It ain't right I wasn't there because if I had of been there I would of known. Listen lady," he said in a high voice, "if I had of been there I would of known and I wouldn't be like I am now." His voice seemed about to crack and the grandmother's head cleared for an instant. She saw the man's face twisted close to her own as if he were going to cry and she murmured, "Why you're one of my babies. You're one of my own children!" She reached out and touched him on the shoulder. The Misfit sprang back as if a snake had bitten him and shot her three times through the chest. Then he put his gun down on the ground and took off his glasses and began to clean them.

Hiram and Bobby Lee returned from the woods and stood over the ditch, looking down at the grandmother who half sat and half lay in a puddle of blood with her legs crossed under her like a child's and her face smiling up at the cloudless sky.

Without his glasses, The Misfit's eyes were red-rimmed and pale and defenseless-looking. "Take her off and thow her where you thown the others," he said, picking up the cat that was rubbing itself against his leg.

"She was a talker, wasn't she?" Bobby Lee said, sliding down the ditch with a yodel.

"She would of been a good woman," The Misfit said, "if it had been somebody there to shoot her every minute of her life."

"Some fun!" Bobby Lee said.

"Shut up, Bobby Lee," The Misfit said. "It's no real pleasure in life."

For Study and Discussion

1. What kind of person is the grandmother? How is her personality related to the outcome of the story? To its meaning?

2. What connection exists between the two main parts of the story—the trip and the meeting with the criminals? How is the scene in The Tower restaurant related to both parts?

3. What do you make of the conversation between the grandmother and The Misfit? Who is more genuinely religious? What does the religious discussion have to do with the story's meaning? What is the significance of the grandmother's last words?

4. Is the story's horror literal, symbolic, or both?

5. Examine the story in the light of O'Connor's essays "The Fiction Writer and His Country" and "A Reasonable Use of the Unreasonable." What importance does she attach to the gesture made by the grandmother in her confrontation with The Misfit? Why does O'Connor call this gesture "an action of grace"? Does her explanation clarify or obscure the meaning of the story?

FRANK O'CONNOR

THE MAN OF THE WORLD

When I was a kid there were no such things as holidays for me and my likes, and I have no feeling of grievance about it because, in the way of kids, I simply invented them, which was much more satisfactory. One year, my summer holiday was a couple of nights I spent at the house of a friend called Jimmy Leary, who lived at the other side of the road from us. His parents sometimes went away for a couple of days to visit a sick relative in Bantry, and he was given permission to have a friend in to keep him company. I took my holiday with the greatest seriousness, insisted on the loan of Father's old travelling bag and dragged it myself down our lane past the neighbours standing at their doors.

"Are you off somewhere, Larry?" asked one.

"Yes, Mrs. Rooney," I said with great pride. "Off for my holidays to the Learys'."

"Wisha, aren't you very lucky?" she said with amusement.

"Lucky" seemed an absurd description of my good fortune. The Learys' house was a big one with a high flight of steps up to the front door, which was always kept shut. They had a piano in the front room, a pair of binoculars on a table near the window, and a toilet on the stairs that seemed to me to be the last word in elegance and immodesty. We brought the binoculars up to the bedroom with us. From the window you could see the whole road up and down, from the quarry at its foot with the tiny houses perched on top of it to the open fields at the other end, where the last gas lamp rose against the sky. Each morning I was up with the first light, leaning out the window in my nightshirt and watching through the glasses all the mysterious figures you never saw from our lane: policemen, railwaymen, and farmers on their way to market.

I admired Jimmy almost as much as I admired his house, and for much the same reasons. He was a year older than I, was well-mannered and well-dressed, and would not associate with most of the kids on the road at all. He had a way when any of them joined us of resting against a wall with his hands in his trousers pockets and listening to them with a sort

Originally published in the *New Yorker*, July 28, 1956. Reprinted here from *Domestic Relations* (New York: Alfred A. Knopf, Inc., 1957) by permission of the publisher. Copyright © 1956 by Frank O'Connor.

of well-bred smile, a knowing smile, that seemed to me the height of elegance. And it was not that he was a softy, because he was an excellent boxer and wrestler and could easily have held his own with them any time, but he did not wish to. He was superior to them. He was—there is only one word that still describes it for me—sophisticated.

I attributed his sophistication to the piano, the binoculars, and the indoor john, and felt that if only I had the same advantages I could have been sophisticated, too. I knew I wasn't, because I was always being deceived by the world of appearances. I would take a sudden violent liking to some boy, and when I went to his house my admiration would spread to his parents and sisters, and I would think how wonderful it must be to have such a home; but when I told Jimmy he would smile in that knowing way of his and say quietly: "I believe they had the bailiffs in a few weeks ago," and, even though I didn't know what bailiffs were, bang would go the whole world of appearances, and I would realize that once again I had been deceived.

It was the same with fellows and girls. Seeing some bigger chap we knew walking out with a girl for the first time, Jimmy would say casually: "He'd better mind himself: that one is dynamite." And, even though I knew as little of girls who were dynamite as I did of bailiffs, his tone would be sufficient to indicate that I had been taken in by sweet voices and broad-brimmed hats, gaslight and evening smells from gardens.

Forty years later I can still measure the extent of my obsession, for, though my own handwriting is almost illegible, I sometimes find myself scribbling idly on a pad in a small, stiff, perfectly legible hand that I recognize with amusement as a reasonably good forgery of Jimmy's. My admiration still lies there somewhere, a fossil in my memory, but Jimmy's knowing smile is something I have never managed to acquire.

And it all goes back to my curiosity about fellows and girls. As I say, I only imagined things about them, but Jimmy knew. I was excluded from knowledge by the world of appearances that blinded and deafened me with emotion. The least thing could excite or depress me: the trees in the morning when I went to early Mass, the stained-glass windows in the church, the blue hilly streets at evening with the green flare of the gas lamps, the smells of cooking and perfume—even the smell of a cigarette packet that I had picked up from the gutter and crushed to my nose—all kept me at this side of the world of appearances, while Jimmy, by right of birth or breeding, was always at the other. I wanted him to tell me what it was like, but he didn't seem to be able.

Then one evening he was listening to me talk while he leant against the pillar of his gate, his pale neat hair framing his pale, good-humoured face. My excitability seemed to rouse in him a mixture of amusement and pity.

"Why don't you come over some night the family is away and I'll show you a few things?" he asked lightly.

"What'll you show me, Jimmy?" I asked eagerly.

"Noticed the new couple that's come to live next door?" he asked with a nod in the direction of the house above his own.

"No," I admitted in disappointment. It wasn't only that I never knew anything but I never noticed anything either. And when he described the new family that was lodging there, I realized with chagrin that I didn't even know Mrs. MacCarthy, who owned the house.

"Oh, they're just a newly married couple," he said. "They don't know that they can be seen from our house."

"But how, Jimmy?"

"Don't look up now," he said with a dreamy smile while his eyes strayed over my shoulder in the direction of the lane. "Wait till you're going away. Their end wall is only a couple of feet from ours. You can see right into the bedroom from our attic."

"And what do they do, Jimmy?"

"Oh," he said with a pleasant laugh, "everything. You really should come."

"You bet I'll come," I said, trying to sound tougher than I felt. It wasn't that I saw anything wrong in it. It was rather that, for all my desire to become like Jimmy, I was afraid of what it might do to me.

But it wasn't enough for me to get behind the world of appearances. I had to study the appearances themselves, and for three evenings I stood under the gas lamp at the foot of our lane, across the road from the MacCarthys', till I had identified the new lodgers. The husband was the first I spotted, because he came from his work at a regular hour. He was tall, with stiff jet-black hair and a big black guardsman's moustache that somehow failed to conceal the youthfulness and ingenuousness of his face, which was long and lean. Usually, he came accompanied by an older man, and stood chatting for a few minutes outside his door—a black-coated, bowler-hatted figure who made large, sweeping gestures with his evening paper and sometimes doubled up in an explosion of loud laughter.

On the third evening I saw his wife—for she had obviously been waiting for him, looking from behind the parlour curtains, and when she saw him she scurried down the steps to join in the conversation. She had thrown an old jacket about her shoulders and stood there, her arms folded as though to protect herself further from the cold wind that blew down the hill from the open country, while her husband rested one hand fondly on her shoulder.

For the first time, I began to feel qualms about what I proposed to do. It was one thing to do it to people you didn't know or care about, but, for me, even to recognize people was to adopt an emotional attitude towards them, and my attitude to this pair was already one of approval. They looked like people who might approve of me, too. That night I remained awake, thinking out the terms of an anonymous letter that would put them on their guard, till I had worked myself up into a fever of eloquence and indignation.

But I knew only too well that they would recognize the villain of the letter and that the villain would recognize me, so I did not write it. Instead, I gave way to fits of anger and moodiness against my parents. Yet even these were unreal because on Saturday night when Mother made a parcel of my nightshirt—I had now become sufficiently self-conscious not to take a bag—I nearly broke down. There was something about my own house that night that upset me all over again. Father, with his cap over his eyes, was sitting under the wall-lamp, reading the paper, and Mother, a shawl about her shoulders, was crouched over the fire from her little wickerwork chair, listening; and I realized that they, too, were part of the world of appearances I was planning to destroy, and as I said good-night I almost felt that I was saying good-bye to them as well.

But once inside Jimmy's house I did not care so much. It always had that effect on me, of blowing me up to twice the size, as though I were expanding to greet the piano, the binoculars, and the indoor toilet. I tried to pick out a tune on the piano with one hand, and Jimmy, having listened with amusement for some time, sat down and played it himself as I felt it should be played, and this, too, seemed to be part of his superiority.

"I suppose we'd better put in an appearance of going to bed," he said disdainfully. "Someone across the road might notice and tell. *They*'re in town, so I don't suppose they'll be back till late."

We had a glass of milk in the kitchen, went upstairs, undressed, and lay down, though we put our overcoats beside the bed. Jimmy had a packet of sweets but insisted on keeping them till later. "We may need these before we're done," he said with his knowing smile, and again I admired his orderliness and restraint. We talked in bed for a quarter of an hour; then put out the light, got up again, donned our overcoats and socks, and tiptoed upstairs to the attic. Jimmy led the way with an electric torch. He was a fellow who thought of everything. The attic had been arranged for our vigil. Two trunks had been drawn up to the little window to act as seats, and there were even cushions on them. Looking out, you could at first see nothing but an expanse of blank wall topped with chimney stacks, but gradually you could make out the outline of a single window, eight or ten feet below. Jimmy sat beside me and opened his packet of sweets, which he laid between us.

"Of course, we could have stayed in bed till we heard them come in," he whispered. "Usually you can hear them at the front door, but they might have come in quietly or we might have fallen asleep. It's always best to make sure."

"But why don't they draw the blind?" I asked as my heart began to beat uncomfortably.

"Because there isn't a blind," he said with a quiet chuckle. "Old Mrs. MacCarthy never had one, and she's not going to put one in for lodgers who may be gone tomorrow. People like that never rest till they get a house of their own."

I envied him his nonchalance as he sat back with his legs crossed, sucking a sweet just as though he were waiting in the cinema for the show to begin. I was scared by the darkness and the mystery, and by the sounds that came to us from the road with such extraordinary clarity. Besides, of course, it wasn't my house and I didn't feel at home there. At any moment I expected the front door to open and his parents to come in and catch us.

We must have been waiting for half an hour before we heard voices in the roadway, the sound of a key in the latch and, then, of a door opening and closing softly. Jimmy reached out and touched my arm lightly. "This is probably our pair," he whispered. "We'd better not speak any more in case they might hear us." I nodded, wishing I had never come. At that moment a faint light became visible in the great expanse of black wall, a faint, yellow stairlight that was just sufficient to silhouette the window frame beneath us. Suddenly the whole room lit up. The man I had seen in the street stood by the doorway, his hand still on the switch. I could see it all plainly now, an ordinary small, suburban bedroom with flowery wallpaper, a coloured picture of the Sacred Heart over the double bed with the big brass knobs, a wardrobe, and a dressing-table.

The man stood there till the woman came in, removing her hat in a single wide gesture and tossing it from her into a corner of the room. He still stood by the door, taking off his tie. Then he struggled with the collar, his head raised and his face set in an agonized expression. His wife kicked off her shoes, sat on a chair by the bed, and began to take off her stockings. All the time she seemed to be talking because her head was raised, looking at him, though you couldn't hear a word she said. I glanced at Jimmy. The light from the window below softly illumined his face as he sucked with tranquil enjoyment.

The woman rose as her husband sat on the bed with his back to us and began to take off his shoes and socks in the same slow, agonized way. At one point he held up his left foot and looked at it with what might have been concern. His wife looked at it, too, for a moment and then swung half-way round as she unbuttoned her skirt. She undressed in swift, jerky movements, twisting and turning and apparently talking all the time. At one moment she looked into the mirror on the dressing-table and touched her cheek lightly. She crouched as she took off her slip, and then pulled her nightdress over her head and finished her undressing beneath it. As she removed her underclothes she seemed to throw them anywhere at all, and I had a strong impression that there was something haphazard and disorderly about her. Her husband was different. Everything he removed seemed to be removed in order and then put carefully where he could find it most readily in the morning. I watched him take out his watch, look at it carefully, wind it, and then hang it neatly over the bed.

Then, to my surprise, she knelt by the bed, facing towards the window, glanced up at the picture of the Sacred Heart, made a large hasty Sign of the Cross, and, covering her face with her hands, buried her head in the bedclothes. I looked at Jimmy in dismay, but he did not seem to be embarrassed by the sight. The husband, his folded trousers in his hand, moved about the room slowly and carefully, as though he did not wish to disturb his wife's devotions, and when he pulled on the trousers of his pyjamas he turned away. After that he put on his pyjama jacket, buttoned it carefully, and knelt beside her. He, too, glanced respectfully at the picture and crossed himself slowly and reverently, but he did not bury his face and head as she had done. He knelt upright with nothing of the abandonment suggested by her pose, and with an expression that combined reverence and self-respect. It was the expression of an employee who, while admitting that he might have a few little weaknesses like the rest of the staff, prided himself on having deserved well of the management. Women, his slightly complacent air seemed to indicate, had to adopt these emotional attitudes, but he spoke to God as one man to another. He finished his prayers before his wife; again he crossed himself slowly, rose, and climbed into bed, glancing again at his watch as he did so.

Several minutes passed before she put her hands out before her on the bed, blessed herself in her wide, sweeping way, and rose. She crossed the room in a swift movement that almost escaped me, and next moment the light went out—it was as if the window through which we had watched the scene had disappeared with it by magic, till nothing was left but a blank black wall mounting to the chimney pots.

Jimmy rose slowly and pointed the way out to me with his flashlight. When we got downstairs we put on the bedroom light, and I saw on his face the virtuous and sophisticated air of a collector who has shown you all his treasures in the best possible light. Faced with that look, I could not bring myself to mention the woman at prayer, though I felt her image would be impressed on my memory till the day I died. I could not have explained to him how at that moment everything had changed for me, how, beyond us watching the young married couple from ambush, I had felt someone else watching us, so that at once we ceased to be the observers and became the observed. And the observed in such a humiliating position that nothing I could imagine our victims doing would have been so degrading.

I wanted to pray myself but found I couldn't. Instead, I lay in bed in the darkness, covering my eyes with my hand, and I think that even then I knew that I should never be sophisticated like Jimmy, never be able to put on a knowing smile, because always beyond the world of appearances I would see only eternity watching.

"Sometimes, of course, it's better than that," Jimmy's drowsy voice said from the darkness. "You shouldn't judge it by tonight."

For Study and Discussion

1. In his interview, O'Connor states that the "design" of the story is most important to him in his writing. How would you describe the "design" of "The Man of the World"?

2. Why does the narrator mention the piano and the indoor toilet along with the binoculars?

3. What does the narrator mean by saying "it wasn't enough for me to get behind the world of appearances"?

4. Why does the narrator feel inferior to his friend Jimmy? How do the two boys differ from each other?

5. How does Jimmy react to the episode of the married couple? What effect does it have on the narrator? On the reader?

6. What is the point of Jimmy's final comment? How does it heighten or intensify the central meaning of the story?

ERNEST J. GAINES

JUST LIKE A TREE

> *I shall not;*
> > *I shall not be moved.*
> *I shall not;*
> > *I shall not be moved.*
> *Just like a tree that's*
> *planted 'side the water.*
> > *Oh, I shall not be moved.*
>
> *I made my home in glory;*
> > *I shall not be moved.*
> *Made my home in glory;*
> > *I shall not be moved.*
> *Just like a tree that's*
> *planted 'side the water.*
> > *Oh, I shall not be moved.*

(from an old Negro spiritual)

CHUCKKIE

Pa hit him on the back and he jeck in them chains like he pulling, but ever'body in the wagon know he ain't, and Pa hit him on the back again. He jeck again like he pulling, but even Big Red know he ain't doing a thing.

"That's why I'm go'n get a horse," Pa say. "He'll kill that other mule. Get up there, Mr. Bascom."

Reprinted here from *Bloodline* (New York: The Dial Press, Inc., 1968) by permission of the publisher. Copyright © 1963, 1964, 1968 by Ernest J. Gaines.

"Oh, let him alone," Gran'mon say. "How would you like it if you was pulling a wagon in all that mud?"

Pa don't answer Gran'mon; he just hit Mr. Bascom on the back again.

"That's right, kill him," Gran'mon say. "See where you get mo' money to buy another one."

"Get up there, Mr. Bascom," Pa say.

"You hear me talking to you, Emile?" Gran'mon say. "You want me hit you with something?"

"Ma, he ain't pulling," Pa say.

"Leave him alone," Gran'mon say.

Pa shake the lines little bit, but Mr. Bascom don't even feel it, and you can see he letting Big Red do all the pulling again. Pa say something kind o' low to hisself, and I can't make out what it is.

I low' my head little bit, 'cause that wind and fine rain was hitting me in the face, and I can feel Mama pressing close to me to keep me warm. She sitting on one side o' me and Pa sitting on the other side o' me, and Gran'mon in the back o' me in her setting chair. Pa didn't want bring the setting chair, telling Gran'mon there was two boards in that wagon already and she could sit on one of 'em all by herself if she wanted to, but Gran'mon say she was taking her setting chair with her if Pa liked it or not. She say she didn't ride in no wagon on nobody board, and if Pa liked it or not, that setting chair was going.

"Let her take her setting chair," Mama say. "What's wrong with taking her setting chair."

"Ehhh, Lord," Pa say, and picked up the setting chair and took it out to the wagon. "I guess I'll have to bring it back in the house, too, when we come back from there."

Gran'mon went and clambed in the wagon and moved her setting chair back little bit and sat down and folded her arms, waiting for us to get in, too. I got in and knelt down 'side her, but Mama told me to come up there and sit on the board 'side her and Pa so I could stay warm. Soon 's I sat down, Pa hit Mr. Bascom on the back, saying what a trifling thing Mr. Bascom was, and soon 's he got some mo' money he was getting rid o' Mr. Bascom and getting him a horse.

I raise my head to look see how far we is.

"That's it, yonder," I say.

"Stop pointing," Mama say, "and keep your hand in your pocket."

"Where?" Gran'mon say, back there in her setting chair.

"'Cross the ditch, yonder," I say.

"Can't see a thing for this rain," Gran'mon say.

"Can't hardly see it," I say. "But you can see the light little bit. That chinaball tree standing in the way."

"Poor soul," Gran'mon say. "Poor soul."

I know Gran'mon was go'n say "poor soul, poor soul," 'cause she had been saying "poor soul, poor soul," ever since she heard Aunt Fe was go'n leave from back there.

EMILE

Darn cane crop to finish getting in and only a mule and a half to do it. If I had my way I'd take that shotgun and a load o' buckshots and—but what's the use.

"Get up, Mr. Bascom—please," I say to that little dried-up, long-eared, tobacco-color thing. "Please, come up. Do your share for God sake—if you don't mind. I know it's hard pulling in all that mud, but if you don't do your share, then Big Red'll have to do his and yours, too. So, please, if it ain't asking you too much to—"

"Oh, Emile, shut up," Leola say.

"I can't hit him," I say, "or Mama back there'll hit me. So I have to talk to him. Please, Mr. Bascom, if you don't mind it. For my sake. No, not for mine; for God sake. No, not even for His'n; for Big Red sake. A fellow mule just like yourself is. Please, come up."

"Now, you hear that boy blaspheming God right in front o' me there," Mama say. "Ehhh, Lord—just keep it up. All this bad weather there like this whole world coming apart—a clap o' thunder come there and knock the fool out you. Just keep it up."

Maybe she right, and I stop. I look at Mr. Bascom there doing nothing, and I just give up. That mule know long 's Mama's alive he go'n do just what he want to do. He know when Papa was dying he told Mama to look after him, and he know no matter what he do, no matter what he don't do, Mama ain't go'n never let me do him anything. Sometimes I even feel Mama care mo' for Mr. Bascom 'an she care for me her own son.

We come up to the gate and I pull back on the lines.

"Whoa up, Big Red," I say. "You don't have to stop, Mr. Bascom. You never started."

I can feel Mama looking at me back there in that setting chair, but she don't say nothing.

"Here," I say to Chuckkie.

He take the lines and I jump down on the ground to open the old beat-up gate. I see Etienne's horse in the yard, and I see Chris new red tractor 'side the house, shining in the rain. When Mama die, I say to myself, Mr. Bascom, you going. Ever'body getting tractors and horses and I'm still stuck with you. You going, brother.

"Can you make it through?" I ask Chuckkie. "That gate ain't too wide."

"I can do it," he say.

"Be sure to make Mr. Bascom pull," I say.

"Emile, you better get back up here and drive 'em through," Leola say. "Chuckkie might break up that wagon."

"No, let him stay down there and give orders," Mama say, back there in that setting chair.

"He can do it," I say. "Come on, Chuckkie boy."

"Come up, here, mule," Chuckkie say.

And soon 's he say that, Big Red make a lunge for the yard, and Mr. Bascom don't even move, and 'fore I can bat my eyes I hear *pow-wow; sagg-sagg; pow-wow*. But above all that noise, Leola up there screaming her head off. And Mama—not a word; just sitting in that chair, looking at me with her arms still folded.

"Pull Big Red," I say. "Pull Big Red, Chuckkie."

Poor little Chuckkie up there pulling so hard till one of his little arms straight out in back; and Big Red throwing his shoulders and ever'thing else in it, and Mr. Bascom just walking there just 's loose and free, like he's suppose to be there just for his good looks. I move out the way just in time to let the wagon go by me, pulling half o' the fence in the yard behind it. I glance up again, and there's Leola still hollering and trying to jump out, but Mama not saying a word—just sitting there in that setting chair with her arms still folded.

"Whoa," I hear little Chuckkie saying. "Whoa up, now."

Somebody open the door and a bunch o' people come out on the gallery.

"What the world—?" Etienne say. "Thought the whole place was coming to pieces there."

"Chuckkie had a little trouble coming in the yard," I say.

"Goodness," Etienne say. "Anybody hurt?"

Mama just sit there about ten seconds, then she say something to herself and start clambing out the wagon.

"Let me help you there, Aunt Lou," Etienne say, coming down the steps.

"I can make it," Mama say. When she get on the ground she look up at Chuckkie. "Hand me my chair there, boy."

Poor little Chuckkie, up there with the lines in one hand, get the chair and hold it to the side, and Etienne catch it just 'fore it hit the ground. Mama start looking at me again, and it look like for at least a' hour she stand there looking at nobody but me. Then she say, "Ehhh, Lord," like that again, and go inside with Leola and the rest o' the people.

I look back at half o' the fence laying there in the yard, and I jump back on the wagon and guide the mules to the side o' the house. After unhitching 'em and tying 'em to the wheels, I look at Chris pretty red tractor again, and me and Chuckkie go inside: I make sure he kick all that mud off his shoes 'fore he go in the house.

LEOLA

Sitting over there by that fireplace, trying to look joyful when ever'body there know she ain't. But she trying, you know; smiling and bowing when people say something to her. How can she be joyful, I ask

you; how can she be? Poor thing, she been here all her li⸺
of it, let's say. 'Fore they moved in this house, they lived⸺
the woods 'bout a mile from here. But for the past twent⸺
years, she been right in this one house. I know ever si⸺
enough to know people I been seeing her right here.

Aunt Fe, Aunt Fe, Aunt Fe, Aunt Fe; the name's been 'ʌ.vɪɪgsɪ us just like us own family name. Just like the name o' God. Like the name of town—the city. Aunt Fe, Aunt Fe, Aunt Fe, Aunt Fe.

Poor old thing; how many times I done come here and washed clothes for her when she couldn't do it herself. How many times I done hoed in that garden, ironed her clothes, wrung a chicken neck for her. You count the days in the year and you'll be pretty close. And I didn't mind it a bit. No, I didn't mind it a bit. She there trying to pay me. Proud—Lord, talking 'bout pride. "Here." "No, Aunt Fe; no." "Here, here; you got a child there, you can use it." "No, Aunt Fe. No. No. What would Mama think if she knowed I took money from you? Aunt Fe, Mama would never forgive me. No. I love doing these thing for you. I just wish I could do more."

And there, now, trying to make 'tend she don't mind leaving. Ehhh, Lord.

I hear a bunch o' rattling round in the kitchen and I go back there. I see Louise stirring this big pot o' eggnog.

"Louise," I say.

"Leola," she say.

We look at each other and she stir the eggnog again. She know what I'm go'n say next, and she can't even look in my face.

"Louise, I wish there was some other way."

"There's no other way," she say.

"Louise, moving her from here's like moving a tree you been used to in your front yard all your life."

"What else can I do?"

"Oh, Louise, Louise."

"Nothing else but that."

"Louise, what people go'n do without her here?"

She stir the eggnog and don't answer.

"Louise, us'll take her in with us."

"You all no kin to Auntie. She go with me."

"And us'll never see her again."

She stir the eggnog. Her husband come back in the kitchen and kiss her on the back o' the neck and then look at me and grin. Right from the start I can see I ain't go'n like that nigger.

"Almost ready, honey?" he say.

"Almost."

He go to the safe and get one o' them bottles of whiskey he got in there and come back to the stove.

"No," Louise say. "Everybody don't like whiskey in it. Add the whiskey after you've poured it up."

"Okay, hon."

He kiss her on the back o' the neck again. Still don't like that nigger. Something 'bout him ain't right.

"You one o' the family?" he say.

"Same as one," I say. "And you?"

He don't like the way I say it, and I don't care if he like it or not. He look at me there a second, and then he kiss her on the ear.

"Un-unnn," she say, stirring the pot.

"I love your ear, baby," he say.

"Go in the front room and talk with the people," she say.

He kiss her on the other ear. A nigger do all that front o' public got something to hide. He leave the kitchen. I look at Louise.

"Ain't nothing else I can do," she say.

"You sure, Louise? You positive?"

"I'm positive," she say.

The front door open and Emile and Chuckkie come in. A minute later Washington and Adrieu come in, too. Adrieu come back in the kitchen, and I can see she been crying. Aunt Fe is her godmother, you know.

"How you feel, Adrieu?"

"That weather out there," she say.

"Y'all walked?"

"Yes."

"Us here in the wagon. Y'all can go back with us."

"Y'all the one tore the fence down?" she ask.

"Yes, I guess so. That brother-in-law o' yours in there letting Chuckkie drive that wagon."

"Well, I don't guess it'll matter too much. Nobody go'n be here, anyhow."

And she start crying again. I take her in my arms and pat her on the shoulder, and I look at Louise stirring the eggnog.

"What I'm go'n do and my nan-nane gone? I love her so much."

"Ever'body love her."

"Since my mama died, she been like my mama."

"Shhh," I say. "Don't let her hear you. Make her grieve. You don't want her grieving, now, do you?"

She sniffs there 'gainst my dress few times.

"Oh, Lord," she say. "Lord, have mercy."

"Shhh," I say. "Shhh. That's what life's 'bout."

"That ain't what life's 'bout," she say. "It ain't fair. This been her home all her life. These the people she know. She don't know them people she going to. It ain't fair."

"Shhh, Adrieu," I say. "Now, you saying things that ain't your business."

She cry there some mo'.

"Oh, Lord, Lord," she say.

Louise turn from the stove.

"About ready now," she say, going to the middle door. "James, tell everybody to come back and get some."

JAMES

Let me go on back here and show these country niggers how to have a good time. All they know is talk, talk, talk. Talk so much they make me buggy round here. Damn this weather—wind, rain. Must be a million cracks in this old house.

I go to that old beat-up safe in that corner and get that fifth of Mr. Harper (in the South now; got to say Mister), give the seal one swipe, the stopper one jerk, and head back to that old wood stove. (Man, like, these cats are primitive—goodness. You know what I mean? I mean like wood stoves. Don't mention TV, man, these cats here never heard of that.) I start to dump Mr. Harper in the pot and Baby catches my hand again and say not all of them like it. You ever heard of anything like that? I mean a stud's going to drink eggnog, and he's not going to put whiskey in it. I mean he's going to drink it straight. I mean, you ever heard anything like that? Well, I wasn't pressing none of them on Mr. Harper. I mean, me and Mr. Harper get along too well together for me to go around there pressing.

I hold my cup there and let Baby put a few drops of this egg stuff in it; then I jerk my cup back and let Mr. Harper run a while. Couple of these cats come over (some of them aren't so lame) and set their cups, and I let Mr. Harper run for them. Then this cat says he's got 'nough. I let Mr. Harper run for this other stud, and pretty soon he says, "Hold it. Good." Country cat, you know. "Hold it. Good." Real country cat. So I raise the cup to see what Mr. Harper's doing. He's just right. I raise the cup again. Just right, Mr. Harper; just right.

I go to the door with Mr. Harper under my arm and the cup in my hand and I look into the front room where they all are. I mean, there's about ninety-nine of them in there. Old ones, young ones, little ones, big ones, yellow ones, black ones, brown ones—you name them, brother, and they were there. And what for? Brother, I'll tell you what for. Just because me and Baby are taking this old chick out of these sticks. Well, I'll tell you where I'd be at this moment if I was one of them. With that weather out there like it is, I'd be under about five blankets with some little warm belly pressing against mine. Brother, you can bet your hat I wouldn't be here. Man, listen to that thing out there. You can hear that rain beating on that old house like grains of rice; and that wind coming through them cracks like it does in those old Charlie Chaplin movies. Man, like you know—like *whooo-ee; whooo-ee.* Man, you talking about some weird cats.

I can feel Mr. Harper starting to massage my wig and I bat my eyes twice and look at the old girl over there. She's still sitting in that funny-looking little old rocking chair, and not saying a word to anybody. Just sitting there looking into the fireplace at them two pieces of wood that aren't giving out enough heat to warm a baby, let alone ninety-nine grown people. I mean, you know, like that sleet's falling out there like all get-up-and-go, and them two pieces of wood are lying there just as dead as the rest of these way-out cats.

One of the old cats—I don't know which one he is—Mose, Sam, or something like that—leans over and pokes in the fire a minute; then a little blaze shoots up, and he raises up, too, looking as satisfied as if he'd just sent a rocket into orbit. I mean, these cats are like that. They do these little bitty things, and they feel like they've really done something. Well, back in these sticks, I guess there just isn't nothing big to do.

I feel Mr. Harper touching my skull now—and I notice this little chick passing by me with these two cups of eggnog. She goes over to the fireplace and gives one to each of these old chicks. The one sitting in that setting chair she brought with her from God knows where, and the other cup to the old chick that Baby and I are going to haul from here sometime tomorrow morning. Wait, man, I mean like, you ever heard of anybody going to somebody else's house with a chair? I mean, wouldn't you call that an insult at the basest point? I mean, now, like tell me what you think of that? I mean—dig—here I am at my pad, and in you come with your own stool. I mean, now, like man, you know. I mean that's an insult at the basest point. I mean, you know . . . you know, like way out. . . .

Mr. Harper, what you trying to do, boy?—I mean, *sir*. (Got to watch myself, I'm in the South. Got to keep watching myself.)

This stud touches me on the shoulder and raise his cup and say, "How 'bout a taste?" I know what the stud's talking about, so I let Mr. Harper run for him. But soon 's I let a drop get in, the stud say, "'Nough." I mean I let about two drops get in, and already the stud's got enough. Man, I mean, like you know. I mean these studs are 'way out. I mean like 'way back there.

This stud takes a swig of his eggnog and say, "Ahhh." I mean this real down-home way of saying "Ahhhh." I mean, man, like these studs—I notice this little chick passing by me again, and this time she's crying. I mean weeping, you know. And just because this old ninety-nine-year-old chick's packing up and leaving. I mean, you ever heard of anything like that? I mean, here she is pretty as the day is long and crying because Baby and I are hauling this old chick away. Well, I'd like to make her cry. And I can assure you, brother, it wouldn't be from leaving her.

I turn and look at Baby over there by the stove, pouring eggnog in all these cups. I mean, there're about twenty of these cats lined up there.

And I bet you not half of them will take Mr. Harper along. Some way-out cats, man. Some way-out cats.

I go up to Baby and kiss her on the back of the neck and give her a little pat where she likes for me to pat her when we're in the bed. She say, "Uh-uh," but I know she likes it anyhow.

BEN O

I back under the bed and touch the slop jar, and I pull back my leg and back somewhere else, and then I get me a good sight on it. I spin my aggie couple times and sight again and then I shoot. I hit it right square in the middle and it go flying over the fireplace. I crawl over there to get it and I see 'em all over there drinking they eggnog and they didn't even offer me and Chuckkie none. I find my marble on the bricks, and I go back and tell Chuckkie they over there drinking eggnog.

"You want some?" I say.

"I want shoot marble," Chuckkie say. "Yo' shot. Shoot up."

"I want some eggnog," I say.

"Shoot up, Ben O," he say. "I'm getting cold staying in one place so long. You feel that draft?"

"Coming from that crack under that bed," I say.

"Where?" Chuckkie say, looking for the crack.

"Over by that bedpost over there," I say.

"This sure's a beat-up old house," Chuckkie say.

"I want me some eggnog," I say.

"Well, you ain't getting none," Gran'mon say, from the fireplace. "It ain't good for you."

"I can drink eggnog," I say. "How come it ain't good for me? It ain't nothing but eggs and milk. I eat chicken, don't I? I eat beef, don't I?"

Gran'mon don't say nothing.

"I want me some eggnog," I say.

Gran'mon still don't say no more. Nobody else don't say nothing, neither.

"I want me some eggnog," I say.

"You go'n get a eggnog," Gran'mon say. "Just keep that noise up."

"I want me some eggnog," I say; "and I 'tend to get me some eggnog tonight."

Next thing I know, Gran'mon done picked up a chip out o' that corner and done sailed it back there where me and Chuckkie is. I duck just in time, and the chip catch old Chuckkie side the head.

"Hey, who that hitting me?" Chuckkie say.

"Move, and you won't get hit," Gran'mon say.

I laugh at old Chuckkie over there holding his head, and next thing I know here's Chuckkie done haul back there and hit me in my side. I jump up from there and give him two just to show him how it feel, and he jump up and hit me again. Then we grab each other and start tussling on the floor.

"You, Ben O," I hear Gran'mon saying. "You, Ben O, cut that out. Y'all cut that out."

But we don't stop, 'cause neither one o' us want be first. Then I feel somebody pulling us apart.

"What I ought to do is whip both o' you," Mrs. Leola say. "Is that what y'all want?"

"No'm," I say.

"Then shake hand."

Me and Chuckkie shake hand.

"Kiss," Mrs. Leola say.

"No, ma'am," I say. "I ain't kissing no boy. I ain't that crazy."

"Kiss him, Chuckkie," she say.

Old Chuckkie kiss me on the jaw.

"Now, kiss him, Ben O."

"I ain't kissing no Chuckkie," I say. "No'm. Uh-uh. You kiss girls."

And the next thing I know, Mama done tipped up back o' me and done whop me on the leg with Daddy belt.

"Kiss Chuckkie," she say.

Chuckkie turn his jaw to me and I kiss him. I almost wipe my mouth. I even feel like spitting.

"Now, come back here and get you some eggnog," Mama say.

"That's right, spoil 'em," Gran'mon say. "Next thing you know, they be drinking from bottles."

"Little eggnog won't hurt 'em, Mama," Mama say.

"That's right, never listen," Gran'mon say. "It's you go'n suffer for it. I be dead and gone, me."

AUNT CLO

Be just like wrapping a chain round a tree and jecking and jecking, and then shifting the chain little bit and jecking and jecking some in that direction, and then shifting it some mo' and jecking and jecking in that direction. Jecking and jecking till you get it loose, and then pulling with all your might. Still it might not be loose enough and you have to back the tractor up some and fix the chain round the tree again and start jecking all over. Jeck, jeck, jeck. Then you hear the roots crying, and then you keep on jecking, and then it give, and you jeck some mo', and then it falls. And not till then that you see what you done done. Not till then you see the big hole in the ground and piece of the taproot still way down in it—a piece you won't never get out no matter if you dig till doomsday. Yes, you got the tree—least got it down on the ground, but did you get the taproot? No. No, sir, you didn't get the taproot. You stand there and look down in this hole at it and you grab yo' axe and jump down in it and start chopping at the taproot, but do you get the taproot? No. You don't get the taproot, sir. You never get the taproot. But, sir, I tell you what you do get. You get a big hole in the ground, sir; and you get another big hole in the air where the lovely branches been all these years. Yes, sir, that's what you get. The holes, sir, the holes. Two holes, sir, you can't never fill no matter how hard you try.

So you wrap yo' chain round yo' tree again, sir, and you start dragging it. But the dragging ain't so easy, sir, 'cause she's a heavy old tree—been there a long time, you know—heavy. And you make yo' tractor strain, sir, and the elements work 'gainst you, too, sir, 'cause the elements, they on her side, too, 'cause she part o' the elements, and the elements, they part o' her. So the elements, they do they little share to discourage you—yes, sir, they does. But you will not let the elements stop you. No, sir, you show the elements that they just elements, and man is stronger than elements, and you jeck and jeck on the chain, and soon she start to moving with you, sir, but if you look over yo' shoulder one second you see her leaving a trail—a trail, sir, that can be seen from miles and miles away. You see her trying to hook her little fine branches in different little cracks, in between pickets, round hills o' grass, round anything they might brush 'gainst. But you is a determined man, sir, and you jeck and you jeck, and she keep on grabbing and trying to hold, but you stronger, sir—course you the strongest—and you finally get her out on the pave road. But what you don't notice, sir, is just 'fore she get on the pave road she leave couple her little branches to remind the people that it ain't her that want leave, but you, sir, that think she ought to. So you just drag her and drag her, sir, and the folks that live in the houses 'side the pave road, they come out on they gallery and look at her go by, and then they go back in they house and sit by the fire and forget her. So you just go on, sir, and you just go and you go—and for how many days? I don't know. I don't have the least idea. The North to me, sir, is like the elements. It mystify me. But never mind, you finally get there, and then you try to find a place to set her. You look in this corner and you look in that corner, but no corner is good. She kind o' stand in the way no matter where you set her. So finally, sir, you say, "I just stand her up here a little while and see, and if it don't work out, if she keep getting in the way, I guess we'll just have to take her to the dump."

CHRIS

Just like him, though, standing up there telling them lies when everybody else feeling sad. I don't know what you do without people like him. And, yet, you see him there, he sad just like the rest. But he just got to be funny. Crying on the inside, but still got to be funny.

He didn't steal it, though; didn't steal it a bit. His grandpa was just like him. Mat? Mat Jefferson? Just like that. Mat could make you die laughing. 'Member once at a wake. Who was dead? Yes—Robert Lewis. Robert Lewis laying up in his coffin dead as a door nail. Everybody sad and droopy. Mat look at that and start his lying. Soon, half o' the place laughing. Funniest wake I ever went to, and yet—

Just like now. Look at 'em. Look at 'em laughing. Ten minutes ago you would 'a' thought you was at a funeral. But look at 'em now. Look at her there in that little old chair. How long she had it? Fifty years—a hundred? It ain't a chair no mo', it's little bit o' her. Just like her arm, just like her leg.

You know, I couldn't believe it. I couldn't. Emile passed the house there the other day, right after the bombing, and I was in my yard digging a water drain to let the water run out in the ditch. Emile, he stopped the wagon there 'fore the door. Little Chuckkie, he in there with him with that little rain cap buckled up over his head. I go out to the gate and I say, "Emile, it's the truth?"

"The truth," he say. And just like that he say it. "The truth."

I look at him there, and he looking up the road to keep from looking back at me. You know, they been pretty close to Aunt Fe ever since they was children coming up. His own mon, Aunt Lou, and Aunt Fe, they been like sisters, there, together.

Me and him, we talk there little while 'bout the cane cutting, then he say he got to get on to the back. He shake the lines and drive on.

Inside me, my heart feel like it done swole up ten times the size it ought to be. Water come in my eyes, and I got to 'mit I cried right there. Yes sir, I cried right there by that front gate.

Louise come in the room and whisper something to Leola, and they go back in the kitchen. I can hear 'em moving things round back there, still getting things together they go'n be taking along. If they offer me anything, I'd like that big iron pot out there in the back yard. Good for boiling water when you killing hog, you know.

You can feel the sadness in the room again. Louise brought it in when she come in and whispered to Leola. Only, she didn't take it out when her and Leola left. Every pan they move, every pot they unhook keep telling you she leaving, she leaving.

Etienne turn over one o' them logs to make the fire pick up some, and I see that boy, Lionel, spreading out his hands over the fire. Watch out, I think to myself, here come another lie. People, he just getting started.

ANNE-MARIE DUVALL

"You're not going?"

"I'm not going," he says, turning over the log with the poker. "And if you were in your right mind, you wouldn't go, either."

"You just don't understand, do you?"

"Oh, I understand. She cooked for your daddy. She nursed you when your mama died."

"And I'm trying to pay her back with a seventy-nine-cents scarf. Is that too much?"

He is silent, leaning against the mantel, looking down at the fire. The fire throws strange shadows across the big, old room. Father looks down at me from against the wall. His eyes do not say go nor stay. But I know what he would do.

"Please go with me, Edward."

"You're wasting your breath."

I look at him a long time, then I get the small package from the coffee table.

"You're still going?"

"I am going."

"Don't call for me if you get bogged down anywhere back there."

I look at him and go out to the garage. The sky is black. The clouds are moving fast and low. A fine drizzle is falling, and the wind coming from the swamps blows in my face. I cannot recall a worse night in all my life.

I hurry into the car and drive out of the yard. The house stands big and black in back of me. Am I angry with Edward? No, I'm not angry with Edward. He's right. I should not go out into this kind of weather. But what he does not understand is I must. Father definitely would have gone if he were alive. Grandfather definitely would have gone, also. And, therefore, I must. Why? I cannot answer why. Only, I must go.

As soon as I turn down that old muddy road, I begin to pray. Don't let me go into that ditch, I pray. Don't let me go into that ditch. Please, don't let me go into that ditch.

The lights play on the big old trees along the road. Here and there the lights hit a sagging picket fence. But I know I haven't even started yet. She lives far back into the fields. Why? God, why does she have to live so far back? Why couldn't she have lived closer to the front? But the answer to that is as hard for me as is the answer to everything else. It was ordained before I—before father—was born—that she should live back there. So why should I try to understand it now?

The car slides towards the ditch, and I stop it dead and turn the wheel, and then come back into the road again. Thanks, father. I know you're with me. Because it was you who said that I must look after her, didn't you? No, you did not say it directly, father. You said it only with a glance. As grandfather must have said it to you, and as his father must have said it to him.

But now that she's gone, father, now what? I know. I know. Aunt Lou, Aunt Clo, and the rest.

The lights shine on the dead, wet grass along the road. There's an old pecan tree, looking dead and all alone. I wish I was a little nigger gal so I could pick pecans and eat them under the big old dead tree.

The car hits a rut, but bounces right out of it. I am frightened for a moment, but then I feel better. The windshield wipers are working well, slapping the water away as fast as it hits the glass. If I make the next half mile all right, the rest of the way will be good. It's not much over a mile now.

That was too bad about that bombing—killing that woman and her two children. That poor woman; poor children. What is the answer? What will happen? What do they want? Do they know what they want? Do they really know what they want? Are they positively sure? Have they any idea? Money to buy a car, is that it? If that is all, I pity them. Oh, how I pity them.

Not much farther. Just around that bend and—there's a water hole. Now what?

I stop the car and just stare out at the water a minute; then I get out to see how deep it is. The cold wind shoots through my body like needles. Lightning comes from towards the swamps and lights up the place. For a split second the night is as bright as day. The next second it is blacker than it has ever been.

I look at the water, and I can see that it's too deep for the car to pass through. I must turn back or I must walk the rest of the way. I stand there a while wondering what to do. Is it worth it all? Can't I simply send the gift by someone tomorrow morning? But will there be someone tomorrow morning? Suppose she leaves without getting it, then what? What then? Father would never forgive me. Neither would grandfather or great-grandfather, either. No, they wouldn't.

The lightning flashes again and I look across the field, and I can see the tree in the yard a quarter of a mile away. I have but one choice: I must walk. I get the package out of the car and stuff it in my coat and start out.

I don't make any progress at first, but then I become a little warmer and I find I like walking. The lightning flashes just in time to show up a puddle of water, and I go around it. But there's no light to show up the second puddle, and I fall flat on my face. For a moment I'm completely blind, then I get slowly to my feet and check the package. It's dry, not harmed. I wash the mud off my raincoat, wash my hands, and I start out again.

The house appears in front of me, and as I come into the yard, I can hear the people laughing and talking. Sometimes I think niggers can laugh and joke even if they see somebody beaten to death. I go up on the porch and knock and an old one opens the door for me. I swear, when he sees me he looks as if he's seen a ghost. His mouth drops open, his eyes bulge—I swear.

I go into the old crowded and smelly room, and every one of them looks at me the same way the first one did. All the joking and laughing has ceased. You would think I was the devil in person.

"Done, Lord," I hear her saying over by the fireplace. They move to the side and I can see her sitting in that little rocking chair I bet you she's had since the beginning of time. "Done, Master," she says. "Child, what you doing in weather like this? Y'all move; let her get to that fire. Y'all move. Move, now. Let her warm herself."

They start scattering everywhere.

"I'm not cold, Aunt Fe," I say. "I just brought you something—something small—because you're leaving us. I'm going right back."

"Done, Master," she says. Fussing over me just like she's done all her life. "Done, Master. Child, you ain't got no business in a place like this. Get close to this fire. Get here. Done, Master."

I move closer, and the fire does feel warm and good.

"Done, Lord," she says.

I take out the package and pass it to her. The other niggers gather around with all kinds of smiles on their faces. Just think of it—a white lady coming through all of this for one old darky. It is all right for them to come from all over the plantation, from all over the area, in all kinds of weather: this is to be expected of them. But a white lady, a white lady. They must think we white people don't have their kind of feelings.

She unwraps the package, her bony little fingers working slowly and deliberately. When she sees the scarf—the seventy-nine-cents scarf—she brings it to her mouth and kisses it.

"Y'all look," she says. "Y'all look. Ain't it the prettiest little scarf y'all ever did see? Y'all look."

They move around her and look at the scarf. Some of them touch it.

"I go'n put it on right now," she says. "I go'n put it on right now, my lady."

She unfolds it and ties it round her head and looks up at everybody and smiles.

"Thank you, my lady," she says. "Thank you, ma'am, from the bottom of my heart."

"Oh, Aunt Fe," I say, kneeling down beside her. "Oh, Aunt Fe."

But I think about the other niggers there looking down at me, and I get up. But I look into that wrinkled old face again, and I must go back down again. And I lay my head in that bony old lap, and I cry and I cry—I don't know how long. And I feel those old fingers, like death itself, passing over my hair and my neck. I don't know how long I kneel there crying, and when I stop, I get out of there as fast as I can.

ETIENNE

The boy come in, and soon, right off, they get quiet, blaming the boy. If people could look little farther than the tip of they nose—No, they blame the boy. Not that they ain't behind the boy, what he doing, but they blame him for what she must do. What they don't know is that the boy didn't start it, and the people that bombed the house didn't start it, neither. It started a million years ago. It started when one man envied another man for having a penny mo' 'an he had, and then the man married a woman to help him work the field so he could get much 's the other man, but when the other man saw the man had married a woman to get much 's him, he, himself, he married a woman, too, so he could still have mo'. Then they start having children—not from love; but so the children could help 'em work so they could have mo'. But even with the children one man still had a penny mo' 'an the other, so the other man went and bought him a ox, and the other man did the same—to keep ahead of the other man. And soon the other man had bought him a slave to work the ox so he could get ahead of the other man. But the other man went out and bought him two slaves so he could stay ahead of the other man, and the other man went out and bought him three slaves. And soon they had a thousand slaves apiece, but they still wasn't satisfied. And one day the slaves all rose and kill the masters, but the masters (knowing slaves was men just like they was, and kind o' expected they might do this) organized theyself a good police force, and the police force, they come out and killed the two thousand slaves.

So it's not this boy you see standing here 'fore you, 'cause it happened a million years ago. And this boy here's just doing something the slaves done a million years ago. Just that this boy here ain't doing it they way. 'Stead of raising arms 'gainst the masters, he bow his head.

No, I say; don't blame the boy 'cause she must go. 'Cause when she's dead, and that won't be long after they get her up there, this boy's work will still be going on. She's not the only one that's go'n die from this boy's work. Many mo' of 'em go'n die 'fore it's over with. The whole place—everything. A big wind is rising, and when a big wind rise, the sea stirs, and the drop o' water you see laying on top the sea this day won't be there tomorrow. 'Cause that's what wind do, and that's what life is. She ain't nothing but one little drop o' water laying on top the sea, and what this boy's doing is called the wind . . . and she must be moved. No, don't blame the boy. Go out and blame the wind. No, don't blame him, 'cause tomorrow, what he's doing today, somebody go'n say he ain't done a thing. 'Cause tomorrow will be his time to be turned over just like it's hers today. And after that, be somebody else time to turn over. And it keep going like that till it ain't nothing left to turn—and nobody left to turn it.

"Sure, they bombed the house," he say; "because they want us to stop. But if we stopped today, then what good would we have done? What good? Those who have already died for the cause would have just died in vain."

"Maybe if they had bombed your house you wouldn't be so set on keeping this up."

"If they had killed my mother and my brothers and sisters, I'd press just that much harder. I can see you all point. I can see it very well. But I can't agree with you. You blame me for their being bombed. You blame me for Aunt Fe's leaving. They died for you and for your children. And I love Aunt Fe as much as anybody in here does. Nobody in here loves her more than I do. Not one of you." He looks at her. "Don't you believe me, Aunt Fe?"

She nods—that little white scarf still tied round her head.

"How many times have I eaten in your kitchen, Aunt Fe? A thousand times? How many times have I eaten tea cakes and drank milk on the back steps, Aunt Fe? A thousand times? How many times have I sat at this same fireplace with you, just the two of us, Aunt Fe? Another thousand times—two thousand times? How many times have I chopped wood for you, chopped grass for you, ran to the store for you? Five thousand times? How many times have we walked to church together, Aunt Fe? Gone fishing at the river together—how many times? I've spent as much time in this house as I've spent in my own. I know every crack in the wall. I know every corner. With my eyes shut, I can go anywhere in here without bumping into anything. How many of you can do that? Not many of you." He looks at her. "Aunt Fe?"

She looks at him.

"Do you think I love you, Aunt Fe?"

She nods.

"I love you, Aunt Fe, much as I do my own parents. I'm going to miss you much as I'd miss my own mother if she were to leave me now. I'm going to miss you, Aunt Fe, but I'm not going to stop what I've started. You told me a story once, Aunt Fe, about my great-grandpa. Remember? Remember how he died?"

She looks in the fire and nods.

"Remember how they lynched him—chopped him into pieces?"

She nods.

"Just the two of us were sitting here beside the fire when you told me that. I was so angry I felt like killing. But it was you who told me get killing out of my mind. It was you who told me I would only bring harm to myself and sadness to the others if I killed. Do you remember that, Aunt Fe?"

She nods, still looking in the fire.

"You were right. We cannot raise our arms. Because it would mean death for ourselves, as well as for the others. But we will do something else—and that's what we will do." He looks at the people standing round him. "And if they were to bomb my own mother's house tomorrow, I would still go on."

"I'm not saying for you not to go on," Louise says. "That's up to you. I'm just taking Auntie from here before hers is the next house they bomb."

The boy look at Louise, and then at Aunt Fe. He go up to the chair where she sitting.

"Good-bye, Aunt Fe," he say, picking up her hand. The hand done shriveled up to almost nothing. Look like nothing but loose skin's covering the bones. "I'll miss you," he say.

"Good-bye, Emmanuel," she say. She look at him a long time. "God be with you."

He stand there holding the hand a while longer, then he nods his head, and leaves the house. The people stir round little bit, but nobody say anything.

AUNT LOU

They tell her good-bye, and half of 'em leave the house crying, or want cry, but she just sit there 'side the fireplace like she don't mind going at all. When Leola ask me if I'm ready to go, I tell her I'm staying right there till Fe leave that house. I tell her I ain't moving one step till she go out that door. I been knowing her for the past fifty some years now, and I ain't 'bout to leave her on her last night here.

That boy, Chuckkie, want stay with me, but I make him go. He follow his mon and paw out the house and soon I hear that wagon turning round. I hear Emile saying something to Mr. Bascom even 'fore that wagon get out the yard. I tell myself, well, Mr. Bascom, you sure go'n catch it, and me not there to take up for you—and I get up from my chair and go to the door.

"Emile?" I call.

"Whoa," he say.

"You leave that mule 'lone, you hear me?"

"I ain't done Mr. Bascom a thing, Mama," he say.

"Well, you just mind you don't," I say. "I'll sure find out."

"Yes'm," he say. "Come up here, Mr. Bascom."

"Now, you hear that boy. Emile?" I say.

"I'm sorry, Mama," he say. "I didn't mean no harm."

They go out in the road, and I go back to the fireplace and sit down again. Louise stir round in the kitchen a few minutes, then she come in the front where we at. Everybody else gone. That husband o' hers, there, got drunk long 'fore midnight, and Emile and them had to put him to bed in the other room.

She come there and stand by the fire.

"I'm dead on my feet," she say.

"Why don't you go to bed," I say. "I'm go'n be here."

"You all won't need anything?"

"They got wood in that corner?"

"Plenty."

"Then we won't need a thing."

She stand there and warm, and then she say good night and go round the other side.

"Well, Fe?" I say.

"I ain't leaving here tomorrow, Lou," she say.

"'Course you is," I say. "Up there ain't that bad."

She shake her head. "No, I ain't going nowhere."

I look at her over in her chair, but I don't say nothing. The fire pops in the fireplace, and I look at the fire again. It's a good little fire—not too big, not too little. Just 'nough there to keep the place warm.

"You want sing, Lou?" she say, after a while. "I feel like singing my 'termination song."

"Sure," I say.

She start singing in that little light voice she got there, and I join with her. We sing two choruses, and then she stop.

"My 'termination for Heaven," she say. "Now—now—"

"What's the matter, Fe?" I say.

"Nothing," she say. "I want get in my bed. My gown hanging over there."

I get the gown for her and bring it back to the firehalf. She get out of her dress slowly, like she don't even have 'nough strength to do it. I help her on with her gown, and she kneel down there 'side the bed and say her prayers. I sit in my chair and look at the fire again.

She pray there a long time—half out loud, half to herself. I look at her kneeling down there, little like a little old girl. I see her making some kind o' jecking motion there, but I feel she crying 'cause this her last night here, and 'cause she got to go and leave ever'thing behind. I look at the fire.

She pray there ever so long, and then she start to get up. But she can't make it by herself. I go to help her, and when I put my hand on her shoulder, she say, "Lou? Lou?"

I say, "What's the matter, Fe?"

"Lou?" she say. "Lou?"

I feel her shaking in my hand with all her might. Shaking, shaking, shaking—like a person with the chill. Then I hear her take a long breath, longest I ever heard anybody take before. Then she ease back on the bed—calm, calm, calm.

"Sleep on, Fe," I tell her. "When you get up there, tell 'em all I ain't far behind."

For Study and Discussion

1. How soon in the series of interior monologues do you learn that the central problem of the story is the departure of Aunt Fe?

2. What methods does the author use to differentiate between the character of Leola and her husband Emile on the one hand and Louise and her husband James on the other?

3. What purpose is served in the story's development by the two young cousins Chuckkie and Ben O? Does their scuffle contribute anything to the tensions shared by the adults?

4. What do the two monologues by Aunt Clo and Chris add to our knowledge of the central theme?

5. Anne-Marie Duvall is the only white person in this story. In what way do her role and her actions serve as a counterpoint to the information provided in Etienne's monologue? Why must Aunt Fe leave the house where her roots are embedded like those of a tree?

6. A good story, regardless of its form, will have a discernible beginning, middle, and end. How and why does the characterization of Aunt Lou fulfill that requirement?

PETER TAYLOR

MRS. BILLINGSBY'S WINE

Shirley Barnes is waiting in Mrs. Billingsby's living room again. This time she is going to see the woman if it means waiting there all afternoon. Shirley lives in one of the new developments out off Summer Avenue, and it isn't often that she gets in to the old part of Memphis, where such well-fixed people as Mrs. Billingsby live. This is the third time she has summoned up the nerve to visit the woman at home, and this time she has come prepared to wait indefinitely. A neighbor is keeping Shirley's two small children, and the meat loaf for supper is already prepared and ready to be popped in the oven.

What healthy-looking houseplants Mrs. Billingsby has! Shirley just can't help wondering who waters them and who sees to setting them out in the sun on good days. They aren't the usual ferns and philodendron. They are unusual plants, which probably require a lot of attention. She can see that the dirt around the grassy-looking thing on the coffee table is rich and rather loose. "Recently repotted and fertilized," she says aloud, quickly putting her fingers over her lips as if to stop herself from speaking again. Then, peering down among the green stalks in a Chinese urn that is on the marble-top end table, she observes that there is a plain earthen pot inside the blue and white urn. "Pots within pots," she whispers through her fingers, and she laughs quietly.

Shirley is beginning to feel rather at home in the room. She even notices that the summer slipcovers have been removed from the chairs since her last call, six weeks ago. (On that occasion, she was allowed to wait for ten or fifteen minutes before being told that Mrs. Billingsby was out of town.) No doubt it would be the butler's duty—the one who admitted her and showed her into the living room just now—to remove the slipcovers on a certain date each fall and to replace them on a date in the spring. No, Shirley decides after considerable thought, that would be

Originally published in the *New Yorker*, October 14, 1967. Reprinted here from *The Collected Stories of Peter Taylor* (New York: Farrar, Straus & Giroux, Inc., 1969) by permission of the publisher. Copyright © 1967, 1969 by Peter Taylor.

the downstairs maid's duty, or whoever the girl is who let her in the last time she came—the one who didn't seem to know that Mrs. Billingsby was out of town. The thought of all Mrs. Billingsby's servants makes Shirley smile to herself. Her own neighbors out there off Summer Avenue would not believe that even people in these huge old houses on Belvedere Street still have servants. How much would you suppose she had to pay them per week? Twenty-five dollars, anyway. Altogether, Shirley reckons, Mrs. Billingsby must pay her servants considerably more than her own Granville clears from his dental practice in a month. Poor Granville, with his eight years of expensive education! Where does Mrs. Billingsby find such servants nowadays, with their efficiency and their polite manners? The only kind of help you can get out there off Summer Avenue aren't worth having. It's better to do your own work and save for the future. Shirley reflects that she has never before really seen such servants—not even in Blackwell, where she and Granville grew up and where both Mr. and Mrs. Billingsby came from originally. That's why Shirley is making this call. She and Mrs. Billingsby are old neighbors, and old neighbors should keep in touch. That's a perfect reason to make a call, no matter what Granville says about it.

She returns to the pleasures of speculation. Would it be the butler or the maid who waters the houseplants? Oh, neither! It would be Mrs. Billingsby herself. Now, all at once, she has a clear image of what Mrs. Billingsby, whom she had only glimpses of as a little girl, is like and what her life is like. She would reserve the watering of her luxuriant house-plants as the one domestic task not to be turned over to her servants. When Mr. Billingsby comes home from his office in the afternoon, that's how he finds her, watering the plants in this room or in the other living room across the hall, or perhaps in the dining room behind the other living room. It is just the reverse of what Shirley does, freshening herself up for Granville's homecoming and sitting in the glider as though she hasn't done a lick of work all day. Mr. Billingsby finds Mrs. Billingsby doing the one useful thing she has done all day, and it gives them both great joy. And that's what it is like to be rich.

Rising from her place on the couch, Shirley strolls across the room toward the wide doorway to the hall. Then she strolls back to the window that overlooks the rose garden. It is really strange how much at home she feels! She positively understands what it is like to be Mrs. Billingsby. Yes, she is standing at the window, which has become her own window, overlooking her rose garden, and she has just this minute come in from a bridge luncheon at the Memphis Country Club. Or perhaps she has come in from lunch at Justine's, with two intimate friends. (But is Justine's open for lunch? It doesn't matter.) And they have stopped by the Helen Shop after lunch, or by Seessel's to pick up some avocados and artichokes. The thought of grocerying so casually at Seessel's evokes a giggle from Shirley. She thinks what it would be like if her children were big now and away in an expensive boarding school—no, one should say "prep school"—or even at an Eastern college. She and Granville are Dr. and Mrs. Granville Barnes, of two hundred and something South Belvedere Street, right next door to the elderly George Billingsbys, with whom they are intimate friends. She envisions a note in one of the society columns that will tell what close friends the two couples are and how they all four began life in the little country town of Blackwell, and even how Mrs. Barnes's and Mrs. Billingsby's families were next-door neighbors there for generations. But it ends there, the newspaper item does, without telling about the ramshackle old cottage Shirley's family lived in, perched right on the sidewalk, or about Mrs. Billingsby's family's big two-story house set so far back in a grove of willow oaks and tulip poplars that in the summertime the two houses weren't visible to each other. None of Mrs. Billingsby's family has really lived in their house since Shirley was born. They went off long ago to Memphis and St. Louis and even Detroit and made or married stacks of money, or went into politics, or became old-maid schoolteachers in exclusive private schools up in Virginia. So far as that family is concerned, the town of Blackwell, Tennessee, could rot! Anyhow, that's what Shirley's mother always said. That family tried to prevent all progress in the town, tried to prevent their putting in street lights and sidewalks even. Shirley's mother once heard Mrs. Billingsby's own mother say, "The only thing Blackwell has left is its natural beauty, and it ought to hold on to that. Otherwise, it's like some poor country girl decked out in a lot of cheap finery." Shirley's old granddaddy, who was a house painter when he wasn't too drunk to hold a brush, always said Mrs. Billingsby's family had never had an eye for anything but money to fill their pockets with. He used to say, "Ever time they seen a dollar they taken after it and they never stopped a-running till they cotched it."

Shirley's dad once owned a little grocery store, but he gave it up to work at the mill—off and on. In the summertime, he would sit on the front porch with his sock feet on the banister rail, and if the subject of Mrs. Billingsby's family came up (in the summertime, some of them would come and stay over there in their house for a few weeks "just out of sentiment for the place"), her dad, with his feet on the banister rail, would say of them, "Them that has gits."

At the end of a summer, when Shirley and her big brothers were bored and were dreading the opening of school, they would skin over the fence and sometimes manage to get inside that big empty house next door. They would break the glass on a picture frame or two and pull some of the loose wallpaper off the walls in the hall or in the parlor. Shirley could remember the smashed glass on a picture of two old-fashioned-looking gunboats. The boats seemed to be firing pink powder puffs at each other over a body of pale-green water. One year, she told her brothers she would like to have the large orange butterfly that was mounted on cotton under glass in the hall. But when they handed the beautiful thing to her, it turned to powder in her hands. Another year, her brothers stole half the bricks from the old walk going up to the house and sold them to a man who came through town buying up old bricks.

Shirley thinks about the work that lies ahead of her on this autumn afternoon when she has finally found Mrs. Billingsby at home. Mrs. Billingsby will be cold to her on this their first visit together, but Shirley will pretend not to notice. She will leave one of her gloves under the cushion on the couch, and when she returns for it, the very next day perhaps, she will bring Mrs. Billingsby an exotic potted plant like none she has ever seen before. Pretty soon the Billingsbys invite the Barneses to a cocktail party, where they meet practically *everybody*. Then Mrs. Billingsby tells people that Shirley's family and hers were old friends in Blackwell and lived next door to each other for generations. Later, at dinner parties at the Billingsbys', the four of them spend whole evenings reminiscing about old times in Blackwell, and they apologize to other people for boring them with their reminiscences. Then there is an emergency in the middle of the night! Granville gets up and gets dressed and meets Mr. Billingsby at his clinic. Granville relieves Mr. Billingsby's pain and saves the tooth! Not long after that, the Barneses are invited to join the Memphis Country Club, and *every*body begins having Granville as their dentist. . . .

By the window overlooking the rose garden, Shirley still stands with her hands folded before her. Suddenly she decides she doesn't really like so many potted plants in a room. It doesn't suit her taste. She saunters casually over to the marble-top end table beside the couch, and her impulse is to remove the big stalky plant there. But she turns away from it. She sees a cut-glass decanter and four glasses on the coffee table. The decanter is half filled with a very dark wine. Shirley shakes her head and says to herself that she doesn't like wine—or doesn't think she does. She glances critically at the stack of magazines and papers lying beside the decanter on the coffee table. She doesn't like magazines and papers lying around in a living room—that much she *knows*. Looking at the end table again, she actually puts out her hand and edges the Chinese urn a little nearer to the center of the table; she experiences a sudden fear that her sleeve may brush against it and knock it off the table and break it. Just as she withdraws her hand, she hears footsteps on the hall stairway. It is Mrs. Billingsby coming down at last. Shirley quickly plops down on the couch. Before her hostess enters, she removes her gloves and sticks one of them underneath the petit-point cushion beside her.

"Now, let me see," says Mrs. Billingsby, extending her hand as she crosses the room to Shirley. "You were the youngest one, weren't you? The one with the dark curls down to her waist."

Shirley rises and offers her hand across the coffee table.

Mrs. Billingsby clasps the hand between her own hands, smiling cordially and peering into Shirley's face. "Yes, it is you," she says. "I do remember your sweet little face. I thought I would if I saw you. Sit down, sit down." She comes round the coffee table and sits beside Shirley on the couch. "I used to catch glimpses of you playing in your yard in the summer, and with your long curls you looked like such an old-fashioned child, so like a little girl from my own generation, that it made me long more than anything else to come back to Blackwell to live."

Shirley finds herself blushing. Why, she *is* going to talk about Blackwell life as though it was something they shared once, as though they really *were* neighbors in the usual, good sense. And what a lovely-looking woman she is, at once so elegant and so natural. Her beautiful hands, now folded in her lap, express the repose and self-assurance that only an elevated mind and spirit can attain. And her blue, blue eyes. How thoroughly you can trust those eyes to see what is best in people and in the world! No wonder one reads in the paper about all the charitable and cultural organizations she heads, and the garden clubs, too, and about her efforts to save the forest trees on North Parkway and the two ante-bellum houses downtown. There is a freshness and vigor about her that make one long to join her and follow her in all her good works. What a joy it is going to be to know her better and better! Even the freshness of her complexion seems good news to Shirley. Mrs. Billingsby really has been napping and is obviously just out of a bath. She has not been trying to deceive Shirley or to postpone their meeting.

"I must tell you at once," she is saying to Shirley now, "how bad I feel about your having to call on *me*. And you've come twice before, you good person you. You came this summer while I was at High Hampton, and you came in the spring when I was so taken up with some silly matters about our old trees in Memphis that I just let all my personal concerns go." As she speaks she bends toward the coffee table and places one hand on the neck of the wine decanter. "But I was not unmindful that you had been here, I want you to know that. Would you join me in a little glass of sherry, or would you rather have coffee? Even before you called the first time, I was not unaware that you and your little family had moved to Memphis. I keep up with the comings and goings of true Blackwellians. Mr. Salisbury still sends me the *Herald* every week. You see, there's a copy there on the table, under those magazines. So many of the names that appear in it now mean nothing to me." She shakes her head sadly. "But a name like Granville Barnes means something. I can assure you, my dear—you're Shirley, aren't you?—I can assure you, my dear Shirley, that it's only because you're a girl still that I left it for you to call on me, instead of myself calling on you." Now she interrupts herself to fill one of the wineglasses and to ask, "Would you much prefer coffee, my dear? You mustn't hesitate to say so if you would."

Shirley is trying to remember what sherry tastes like. Was it sherry or was it claret she had when she and Granville were on their honeymoon in New Orleans? She would give almost anything for a cup of black coffee just now. She frequently has one at this time of day, when Granville is having a highball. Sometimes she has a highball with him, though she is fond of saying it makes her see double and feel single. But she insists to Mrs. Billingsby that a glass of sherry is just what she would like. She accepts the glass, sips it at once, and says, "Ah!"

Shirley thinks it quite beautiful that Mrs. Billingsby has, within the first five minutes, covered all grounds on which her guest might have felt uneasiness. It is how a lady does things, a lady to the manner born. As Mrs. Billingsby goes on to speak of how cold the weather has turned during the past few days, and of winter clothes and of the new hemline and of the *really* best places to shop (Mrs. Billingsby loves Goldsmith's basement and the first floor of Lowenstein's East; she says that any department of any store is only as good as its buyer), Shirley finds her mind going back to the picture glass her brothers broke in Mrs. Billingsby's homeplace, and the butterfly they took from its mounting to give to her, and the mossy bricks they stole from the walk. Oh, why had they been permitted to do that? Suddenly she throws back her head and tosses off her glass of wine.

"And do you and your husband go back to Blackwell often?" she hears Mrs. Billingsby asking.

"The first weekend in every month," Shirley says. "One month we stay with my family, and the next with yours—with Granville's, I mean." How *could* she have made that senseless slip of the tongue? It is because she is so used to talking with Granville, and with no one else, about Blackwell. Or could it be the wine?

"I find it depressing to go back nowadays," says Mrs. Billingsby. She insists on filling Shirley's glass again.

"That's only because none of your family is still there."

"Yes, I suppose so," Mrs. Billingsby consents, with doubt in her voice. "We've all been gone a long time, and it has changed a great deal. There is no social life there of the sort there once was. When I was a girl, Blackwell was such a very gay little place. Yet no parties, I suppose, ever seem as good to anyone as those one went to as a girl."

"That's certainly true," Shirley says. She feels she has spoken too loud and tries to lower her voice. "Granville and I sometimes talk whole evenings away about parties we went to in Blackwell." She knows she should not keep referring to Granville. Mrs. Billingsby has not made one reference to Mr. Billingsby.

"When I was a girl, young people came from all over West and Middle Tennessee to our parties. During the summer, at the time of the June German, every house was full of young lady house guests and young men, too."

Shirley looks at Mrs. Billingsby, not able to imagine what the June German was. She and Granville can never forget the high-school dances of their era, but there were rarely house guests from other towns. Other towns had their own high-school dances. There never seemed any need to import anybody.

As if in response to something, Mrs. Billingsby says, "No doubt it had all changed by the time you came along."

"The first dance I ever went to," Shirley says with enthusiasm, "was in the New Gym at the high school. The New Gym was built in our freshman year—Granville's and mine. Goodness, we had a grand time!"

"You and your husband were in the same class, then?"

"Oh, yes, we went all through school and college together."

"You can't imagine how strange that sounds to the ears of someone of my generation. Mr. Billingsby is nearly ten years older than I. Though we lived within a mile of each other, I didn't really know him till I came back from my year at Miss Merriwether's School."

In a sudden burst of frankness, Shirley says, "Granville and I both worked our way through college, and I worked while he got through dental school. He tells people that I *put* him through, but of course he exaggerates." She is on the verge of confiding in Mrs. Billingsby how hard those years were. But she bites her tongue and tries to think of something else to say. Nothing she thinks of seems appropriate.

"I envy you girls who went to college," Mrs. Billingsby says humbly. "My mother wished to send me and my sister to college, but Father was afraid of what we just might learn there!"

"Still," says Shirley, wondering if her talk of college might have sounded like boasting, "your boarding schools in those days were much better than our high schools today."

"Ah, far better," Mrs. Billingsby agrees—too quickly, it seems to Shirley. "And I don't complain of not going to college, really. Our education prepared us very well indeed. For life, for the good life as it used to be lived in Blackwell. It makes me heartsick to go back and see how it has all changed there. It was a dear old town, with giant trees meeting over the streets, with handsome lawns and superb flower gardens. Even the public square was a charming place before they built that modernistic courthouse in the thirties and ripped down all the coverings over the sidewalks in front of the stores."

Shirley tries to imagine the square with the old courthouse and the sidewalk covers. She tries in vain. Presently she sips at her wine. Then she empties the glass. The room seems to have grown very warm.

"On the hottest day," continues Mrs. Billingsby, "you could walk in shade under those coverings all around the square. And no man spoke to you unless you spoke to him first. But think what it's like now. It's all sun and noise on a summer afternoon. I was there one day this summer. It was incredible. Young girls and boys racing about the sidewalks shouting to each other. And women my age down there on the square in shorts and halters!" (Shirley manages to whisper, "No!") "You couldn't cross the street without one of the young people in a little foreign car—in Blackwell!—blowing a horn at you. They took down those sidewalk coverings I don't know how many years ago, and now the stores—chain stores all of them, of course—have huge, bright-colored plastic fronts to them. It is a blinding spectacle, the square in Blackwell is today! Really ghastly!"

A powerful wave of nostalgia has suddenly swept over Shirley—a nostalgia for the blinding spectacle of Blackwell's public square. She can only remember it the way Mrs. Billingsby has described it in its latter-day, fallen state. That is the way she must think of it. That is the way, she realizes, she *wants* to think of it. It is *her* home town—hers and Granville's. The other town, the old town Mrs. Billingsby described, never existed for her. It probably never existed for her parents, either, she reflects. Who would recognize any town in which only a few of the girls and boys went to parties, so few that they had to invite girls and boys from other towns in order to make it any fun? In their day—hers and Granville's—nobody cared whether the people who came to a party lived on the Mill Hill or on Church Street, whether you lived in one of the big houses set back amid trees or in a ramshackle little place like her dad's. On a Saturday afternoon, she and a bunch of girls would ride around the square in an open roadster while boys called outrageous things to them from other cars or from the uncovered sidewalks. She *loved* the way the square looked as she knew it, without any trees on the courthouse lawn, without any coverings over the sidewalks, and with the bright false fronts to the old stores. That was girlhood. That was when there had been no scraping together dollars to pay fees at the College of Dentistry. That was when there was no scrimping to make time payments on the furniture for the baby's room.

Now she realizes that Mrs. Billingsby's reflections upon Blackwell have somehow wounded her. She eyes the empty glass in her hand and gently sets it on the coffee table. She knows that she must conceal the hurt she feels. And so she does what she knows Granville would say she ought to do—she changes the subject. And as she does so, without being fully conscious of her purpose, she rises from the couch. She is going to leave.

On her feet, she feels a little dizzy. But her speech is clear and firm, giving no evidence of her physical sensations. "Well," she says, "Blackwell is Blackwell, but Granville and I already like Memphis. In fact, we like it very, very much."

"Even Memphis has changed, though," Mrs. Billingsby replies at once, not rising. "It soon won't be the same city—not the city Mr. Billingsby and I came to forty years ago. They're cutting down our trees to make way for superhighways and pulling down famous old mansions to make way for the high-rise apartments and office buildings."

For a moment Shirley hesitates. She is trying to push out thoughts of the smashed picture glass and the stolen bricks. There is the feel of the dry, powdery butterfly between her fingers. She waits until Mrs.

Billingsby has risen and has said, "Must you go so soon?" before she speaks. About Memphis she feels perfectly free to take her stand. "Oh, most of the things they're doing we like," she says. "The new buildings they're putting up are beautiful, we think. And Granville says we're away ahead of most cities in planning for traffic. It is an exciting place to live. Memphis is a wonderful city, Mrs. Billingsby."

Mrs. Billingsby has risen from the couch now and she follows Shirley across the room. In the wide doorway to the hall, she stops and says with a smile, "I'm glad you like Memphis. I can't altogether agree with you about it, but I'm glad you like it. Anyway, we both love Blackwell, don't we?" Standing in the doorway, she looks older—an old lady.

"Yes, we both love Blackwell, Mrs. Billingsby," says Shirley.

"I'm sorry you must go so soon. And I'm sorry I kept you waiting so."

"I just wanted to say hello," Shirley says. Then, suddenly blushing, she adds, "But I believe I've dropped one of my gloves."

"Really?" says Mrs. Billingsby. "I didn't . . ."

Shirley hurries across the room and pulls the glove from under the cushion. "It was on the divan," she says, holding it up for Mrs. Billingsby to see.

For Study and Discussion

1. Shirley's "perfect reason" for calling on Mrs. Billingsby is that of keeping in touch with an "old neighbor." But is that the true reason for her attempting to form an acquaintanceship with Mrs. Billingsby? If not, what is her real motive? How does the author reveal it?

2. How do Shirley's reflections on the house plants and furnishings of Mrs. Billingsby's living room serve to particularize the difference between Shirley's world and Mrs. Billingsby's? What other means does Taylor use to make this contrast specific?

3. What is the significance of Shirley's changing her mind about leaving a glove behind as an excuse to make another call on Mrs. Billingsby?

4. Would the editor who objected to the story Katherine Anne Porter summarized in her essay, "No Plot, My Dear, No Story," also object to this one? Why or why not?

5. In "The Fiction Writer and His Country," Flannery O'Connor says that the fiction writer's country is "inside as well as outside him" and that "art requires a delicate adjustment of the outer and inner worlds in such a way that . . . they can be seen through each other" (p. 133). In the light of this statement, is it possible to describe "Mrs. Billingsby's Wine" as a highly individualized but nevertheless broadly true representation of the urban South? Discuss.

JOYCE CAROL OATES

HOW I CONTEMPLATED THE WORLD FROM THE DETROIT HOUSE OF CORRECTION AND BEGAN MY LIFE OVER AGAIN

Notes for an essay for an English class at Baldwin Country Day School; poking around in debris; disgust and curiosity; a revelation of the meaning of life; a happy ending . . .

I EVENTS

1. The girl (myself) is walking through Branden's, that excellent store. Suburb of a large famous city that is a symbol for large famous American cities. The event sneaks up on the girl, who believes she is herding it along with a small fixed smile, a girl of fifteen, innocently experienced. She dawdles in a certain style by a counter of costume jewelry. Rings, earrings, necklaces. Prices from $5 to $50, all within reach. All ugly. She eases over to the glove counter, where everything is ugly too. In her close-fitted coat with its black fur collar she contemplates the luxury of Branden's, which she has known for many years: its many mild pale lights, easy on the eye and the soul, its elaborate tinkly decorations, its women shoppers with their excellent shoes and coats and hairdos, all dawdling gracefully, in no hurry.

Who was ever in a hurry here?

2. The girl seated at home. A small library, paneled walls of oak. Someone is talking to me. An earnest, husky, female voice drives itself against my ears, nervous, frightened, groping around my heart, saying, "If you wanted gloves, why didn't you say so? Why didn't you ask for them?" That store, Branden's, is owned by Raymond Forrest who lives

Originally published in *Tri-Quarterly*, Spring 1969. Reprinted here from *The Wheel of Love and Other Stories* (New York: Vanguard Press, Inc., 1970) by permission of the publisher. Copyright 1970, 1969, 1968, 1967, 1966, 1965 by Joyce Carol Oates.

on Du Maurier Drive. We live on Sioux Drive. Raymond Forrest. A handsome man? An ugly man? A man of fifty or sixty, with gray hair, or a man of forty with earnest, courteous eyes, a good golf game; who is Raymond Forrest, this man who is my salvation? Father has been talking to him. Father is not his physician; Dr. Berg is his physician. Father and Dr. Berg refer patients to each other. There is a connection. Mother plays bridge with . . . On Mondays and Wednesdays our maid Billie works at . . . The strings draw together in a cat's cradle, making a net to save you when you fall. . . .

3. *Harriet Arnold's*. A small shop, better than Branden's. Mother in her black coat, I in my close-fitted blue coat. Shopping. Now look at this, isn't this cute, do you want this, why don't you want this, try this on, take this with you to the fitting room, take this also, what's wrong with you, what can I do for you, why are you so strange . . . ? "I wanted to steal but not to buy," I don't tell her. The girl droops along in her coat and gloves and leather boots, her eyes scan the horizon, which is pastel pink and decorated like Branden's, tasteful walls and modern ceilings with graceful glimmering lights.

4. Weeks later, the girl at a bus stop. Two o'clock in the afternoon, a Tuesday; obviously she has walked out of school.

5. The girl stepping down from a bus. Afternoon, weather changing to colder. Detroit. Pavement and closed-up stores; grillwork over the windows of a pawnshop. What is a pawnshop, exactly?

II CHARACTERS

1. The girl stands five feet five inches tall. An ordinary height. Baldwin Country Day School draws them up to that height. She dreams along the corridors and presses her face against the Thermoplex glass. No frost or steam can ever form on that glass. A smudge of grease from her forehead . . . could she be boiled down to grease? She wears her hair loose and long and straight in suburban teen-age style, 1968. Eyes smudged with pencil, dark brown. Brown hair. Vague green eyes. A pretty girl? An ugly girl? She sings to herself under her breath, idling in the corridor, thinking of her many secrets (the thirty dollars she once took from the purse of a friend's mother, just for fun, the basement window she smashed in her own house just for fun) and thinking of her brother who is at Susquehanna Boys' Academy, an excellent preparatory school in Maine, remembering him unclearly . . . he has long manic hair and a squeaking voice and he looks like one of the popular teen-age singers of 1968, one of those in a group, *The Certain Forces, The Way*

Out, The Maniacs Responsible. The girl in her turn looks like one of those fieldsful of girls who listen to the boys' singing, dreaming and mooning restlessly, breaking into high sullen laughter, innocently experienced.

2. The mother. A Midwestern woman of Detroit and suburbs. Belongs to the Detroit Athletic Club. Also the Detroit Golf Club. Also the Bloomfield Hills Country Club. The Village Women's Club at which lectures are given each winter on Genet and Sartre and James Baldwin, by the Director of the Adult Education Program at Wayne State University. . . . The Bloomfield Art Association. Also the Founders Society of the Detroit Institute of Arts. Also . . . Oh, she is in perpetual motion, this lady, hair like blown-up gold and finer than gold, hair and fingers and body of inestimable grace. Heavy weighs the gold on the back of her hairbrush and hand mirror. Heavy heavy the candlesticks in the dining room. Very heavy is the big car, a Lincoln, long and black, that on one cool autumn day split a squirrel's body in two unequal parts.

3. The father. Dr.   . He belongs to the same clubs as #2. A player of squash and golf; he has a golfer's umbrella of stripes. Candy stripes. In his mouth nothing turns to sugar, however; saliva works no miracles here. His doctoring is of the slightly sick. The sick are sent elsewhere (to Dr. Berg?), the deathly sick are sent back for more tests and their bills are sent to their homes, the unsick are sent to Dr. Coronet (Isabel, a lady), an excellent psychiatrist for unsick people who angrily believe they are sick and want to do something about it. If they demand a male psychiatrist, the unsick are sent by Dr.   (my father) to Dr. Lowenstein, a male psychiatrist, excellent and expensive, with a limited practice.

4. Clarita. She is twenty, twenty-five, she is thirty or more? Pretty, ugly, what? She is a woman lounging by the side of a road, in jeans and a sweater, hitchhiking, or she is slouched on a stool at a counter in some roadside diner. A hard line of jaw. Curious eyes. Amused eyes. Behind her eyes processions move, funeral pageants, cartoons. She says, "I never can figure out why girls like you bum around down here. What are you looking for anyway?" An odor of tobacco about her. Unwashed underclothes, or no underclothes, unwashed skin, gritty toes, hair long and falling into strands, not recently washed.

5. Simon. In this city the weather changes abruptly, so Simon's weather changes abruptly. He sleeps through the afternoon. He sleeps through the morning. Rising, he gropes around for something to get him going, for a cigarette or a pill to drive him out to the street, where the temperature is hovering around 35°. Why doesn't it drop? Why, why doesn't the cold clean air come down from Canada; will he have to go up

into Canada to get it? will he have to leave the Country of his Birth and sink into Canada's frosty fields . . . ? Will the F.B.I. (which he dreams about constantly) chase him over the Canadian border on foot, hounded out in a blizzard of broken glass and horns . . .?

"Once I was Huckleberry Finn," Simon says, "but now I am Roderick Usher." Beset by frenzies and fears, this man who makes my spine go cold, he takes green pills, yellow pills, pills of white and capsules of dark blue and green . . . he takes other things I may not mention, for what if Simon seeks me out and climbs into my girl's bedroom here in Bloomfield Hills and strangles me, what then . . . ? (As I write this I begin to shiver. Why do I shiver? I am now sixteen and sixteen is not an age for shivering.) It comes from Simon, who is always cold.

III WORLD EVENTS

Nothing.

IV PEOPLE & CIRCUMSTANCES
CONTRIBUTING TO THIS DELINQUENCY

Nothing.

V SIOUX DRIVE

George, Clyde G. 240 Sioux. A manufacturer's representative; children, a dog, a wife. Georgian with the usual columns. You think of the White House, then of Thomas Jefferson, then your mind goes blank on the white pillars and you think of nothing. Norris, Ralph W. 246 Sioux. Public relations. Colonial. Bay window, brick, stone, concrete, wood, green shutters, sidewalk, lantern, grass, trees, blacktop drive, two children, one of them my classmate Esther (Esther Norris) at Baldwin. Wife, cars. Ramsey, Michael D. 250 Sioux. Colonial. Big living room, thirty by twenty-five, fireplaces in living room, library, recreation room, paneled walls wet bar five bathrooms five bedrooms two lavatories central air conditioning automatic sprinkler automatic garage door three children one wife two cars a breakfast room a patio a large fenced lot fourteen trees a front door with a brass knocker never knocked. Next is our house. Classic contemporary. Traditional modern. Attached garage, attached Florida room, attached patio, attached pool and cabana, attached roof. A front door mail slot through which pour *Time Magazine, Fortune, Life, Business Week,* the *Wall Street Journal,* the *New York Times,* the *New Yorker,* the *Saturday Review, M.D., Modern Medicine,*

Disease of the Month . . . and also. . . . And in addition to all this, a
quiet sealed letter from Baldwin saying: *Your daughter is not doing work
compatible with her performance on the Stanford-Binet.* . . . And your son
is not doing well, not well at all, very sad. Where is your son anyway?
Once he stole trick-and-treat candy from some six-year-old kids, he
himself being a robust ten. The beginning. Now your daughter steals. In
the Village Pharmacy she made off with, yes she did, don't deny it, she
made off with a copy of *Pageant Magazine* for no reason, she swiped a roll
of Life Savers in a green wrapper and was in no need of saving her life or
even in need of sucking candy; when she was no more than eight years
old she stole, don't blush, she stole a package of Tums only because it
was out on the counter and available, and the nice lady behind the
counter (now dead) said nothing. . . . Sioux Drive. Maples, oaks, elms.
Diseased elms cut down. Sioux Drive runs into Roosevelt Drive. Slow,
turning lanes, not streets, all drives and lanes and ways and passes. A
private police force. Quiet private police, in unmarked cars. Cruising on
Saturday evenings with paternal smiles for the residents who are
streaming in and out of houses, going to and from parties, a thousand
parties, slightly staggering, the women in their furs alighting from
automobiles bought of Ford and General Motors and Chrysler, very
heavy automobiles. No foreign cars. Detroit. In 275 Sioux, down the
block in that magnificent French-Normandy mansion, lives   himself,
who has the C   account itself, imagine that! Look at where he lives
and look at the enormous trees and chimneys, imagine his many
fireplaces, imagine his wife and children, imagine his wife's hair,
imagine her fingernails, imagine her bathtub of smooth clean glowing
pink, imagine their embraces, his trouser pockets filled with odd coins
and keys and dust and peanuts, imagine their ecstasy on Sioux Drive,
imagine their income tax returns, imagine their little boy's pride in his
experimental car, a scaled-down C   , as he roars around the neighborhood on the sidewalks frightening dogs and Negro maids, oh imagine all
these things, imagine everything, let your mind roar out all over Sioux
Drive and Du Maurier Drive and Roosevelt Drive and Ticonderoga Pass
and Burning Bush Way and Lincolnshire Pass and Lois Lane.

When spring comes, its winds blow nothing to Sioux Drive, no odors
of hollyhocks or forsythia, nothing Sioux Drive doesn't already possess,
everything is planted and performing. The weather vanes, had they
weather vanes, don't have to turn with the wind, don't have to contend
with the weather. There is no weather.

VI   DETROIT

There is always weather in Detroit. Detroit's temperature is always 32°.
Fast-falling temperatures. Slow-rising temperatures. Wind from the

north-northeast four to forty miles an hour, small-craft warnings, partly cloudy today and Wednesday changing to partly sunny through Thursday . . . small warnings of frost, soot warnings, traffic warnings, hazardous lake conditions for small craft and swimmers, restless Negro gangs, restless cloud formations, restless temperatures aching to fall out the very bottom of the thermometer or shoot up over the top and boil everything over in red mercury.

Detroit's temperature is 32°. Fast-falling temperatures. Slow-rising temperatures. Wind from the north-northeast four to forty miles an hour. . . .

VII EVENTS

1. The girl's heart is pounding. In her pocket is a pair of gloves! In a plastic bag! Airproof breathproof plastic bag, gloves selling for twenty-five dollars on Branden's counter! In her pocket! Shoplifted! . . . In her purse is a blue comb, not very clean. In her purse is a leather billfold (a birthday present from her grandmother in Philadelphia) with snapshots of the family in clean plastic windows, in the billfold are bills, she doesn't know how many bills. . . . In her purse is an ominous note from her friend Tykie *What's this about Joe H. and the kids hanging around at Louise's Sat. night? You heard anything?* . . . passed in French class. In her purse is a lot of dirty yellow Kleenex, her mother's heart would break to see such very dirty Kleenex, and at the bottom of her purse are brown hairpins and safety pins and a broken pencil and a ballpoint pen (blue) stolen from somewhere forgotten and a purse-size compact of Cover Girl Make-Up, Ivory Rose. . . . Her lipstick is Broken Heart, a corrupt pink; her fingers are trembling like crazy; her teeth are beginning to chatter; her insides are alive; her eyes glow in her head; she is saying to her mother's astonished face *I want to steal but not to buy.*

2. At Clarita's. Day or night? What room is this? A bed, a regular bed, and a mattress on the floor nearby. Wallpaper hanging in strips. Clarita says she tore it like that with her teeth. She was fighting a barbaric tribe that night, high from some pills; she was battling for her life with men wearing helmets of heavy iron and their faces no more than Christian crosses to breathe through, every one of those bastards looking like her lover Simon, who seems to breathe with great difficulty through the slits of mouth and nostrils in his face. Clarita has never heard of Sioux Drive. Raymond Forrest cuts no ice with her, nor does the C   account and its millions; Harvard Business School could be at the corner of Vernor and 12th Street for all she cares, and Vietnam might have sunk by now into the Dead Sea under its tons of debris, for all the amazement she could show . . . her face is overworked, overwrought, at the age of twenty

(thirty?) it is already exhausted but fanciful and ready for a laugh. Clarita says mournfully to me *Honey somebody is going to turn you out let me give you warning.* In a movie shown on late television Clarita is not a mess like this but a nurse, with short neat hair and a dedicated look, in love with her doctor and her doctor's patients and their diseases, enamored of needles and sponges and rubbing alcohol. . . . Or no: she is a private secretary. Robert Cummings is her boss. She helps him with fantastic plots, the canned audience laughs, no, the audience doesn't laugh because nothing is funny, instead her boss is Robert Taylor and they are not boss and secretary but husband and wife, she is threatened by a young starlet, she is grim, handsome, wifely, a good companion for a good man. . . . She is Claudette Colbert. Her sister too is Claudette Colbert. They are twins, identical. Her husband Charles Boyer is a very rich handsome man and her sister, Claudette Colbert, is plotting her death in order to take her place as the rich man's wife, no one will know because they are *twins.* . . . All these marvelous lives Clarita might have lived, but she fell out the bottom at the age of thirteen. At the age when I was packing my overnight case for a slumber party at Toni Deshield's she was tearing filthy sheets off a bed and scratching up a rash on her arms. . . . Thirteen is uncommonly young for a white girl in Detroit, Miss Brock of the Detroit House of Correction said in a sad newspaper interview for the *Detroit News*; fifteen and sixteen are more likely. Eleven, twelve, thirteen are not surprising in colored . . . they are more precocious. What can we do? Taxes are rising and the tax base is falling. The temperature rises slowly but falls rapidly. Everything is falling out the bottom, Woodward Avenue is filthy, Livernois Avenue is filthy! Scraps of paper flutter in the air like pigeons, dirt flies up and hits you right in the eye, oh Detroit is breaking up into dangerous bits of newspaper and dirt, watch out. . . .

Clarita's apartment is over a restaurant. Simon her lover emerges from the cracks at dark. Mrs. Olesko, a neighbor of Clarita's, an aged white wisp of a woman, doesn't complain but sniffs with contentment at Clarita's noisy life and doesn't tell the cops, hating cops, when the cops arrive. I should give more fake names, more blanks, instead of telling all these secrets. I myself am a secret; I am a minor.

3. My father reads a paper at a medical convention in Los Angeles. There he is, on the edge of the North American continent, when the unmarked detective put his hand so gently on my arm in the aisle of Branden's and said, "Miss, would you like to step over here for a minute?"

And where was he when Clarita put her hand on my arm, that wintry dark sulphurous aching day in Detroit, in the company of closed-down barber shops, closed-down diners, closed-down movie houses, homes, windows, basements, faces . . . she put her hand on my arm and said, "Honey, are you looking for somebody down here?"

And was he home worrying about me, gone for two weeks solid, when they carried me off . . . ? It took three of them to get me in the police cruiser, so they said, and they put more than their hands on my arm.

4. I work on this lesson. My English teacher is Mr. Forest, who is from Michigan State. Not handsome, Mr. Forest, and his name is plain, unlike Raymond Forrest's, but he is sweet and rodentlike, he has conferred with the principal and my parents, and everything is fixed . . . treat her as if nothing has happened, a new start, begin again, only sixteen years old, what a shame, how did it happen?—nothing happened, nothing could have happened, a slight physiological modification known only to a gynecologist or to Dr. Coronet. I work on my lesson. I sit in my pink room. I look around the room with my sad pink eyes. I sigh, I dawdle, I pause, I eat up time, I am limp and happy to be home, I am sixteen years old suddenly, my head hangs heavy as a pumpkin on my shoulders, and my hair has just been cut by Mr. Faye at the Crystal Salon and is said to be very becoming.

(Simon too put his hand on my arm and said, "Honey, you have got to come with me," and in his six-by-six room we got to know each other. Would I go back to Simon again? Would I lie down with him in all that filth and craziness? Over and over again.

a Clarita is being betrayed as in front of a Cunningham Drug Store she is nervously eying a colored man who may or may not have money, or a nervous white boy of twenty with sideburns and an Appalachian look, who may or may not have a knife hidden in his jacket pocket, or a husky red-faced man of friendly countenance who may or may not be a member of the Vice Squad out for an early twilight walk.)

I work on my lesson for Mr. Forest. I have filled up eleven pages. Words pour out of me and won't stop. I want to tell everything . . . what was the song Simon was always humming, and who was Simon's friend in a very new trench coat with an old high school graduation ring on his finger . . . ? Simon's bearded friend? When I was down too low for him, Simon kicked me out and gave me to him for three days, I think, on Fourteenth Street in Detroit, an airy room of cold cruel drafts with newspapers on the floor. . . . Do I really remember that or am I piecing it together from what they told me? Did they tell the truth? Did they know much of the truth?

VIII CHARACTERS

1. Wednesdays after school, at four; Saturday mornings at ten. Mother drives me to Dr. Coronet. Ferns in the office, plastic or real, they look the

same. Dr. Coronet is queenly, an elegant nicotine-stained lady who would have studied with Freud had circumstances not prevented it, a bit of a Catholic, ready to offer you some mystery if your teeth will ache too much without it. Highly recommended by Father! Forty dollars an hour, Father's forty dollars! Progress! Looking up! Looking better! That new haircut is so becoming, says Dr. Coronet herself, showing how normal she is for a woman with an I.Q. of 180 and many advanced degrees.

2. Mother. A lady in a brown suede coat. Boots of shiny black material, black gloves, a black fur hat. She would be humiliated could she know that of all the people in the world it is my ex-lover Simon who walks most like her . . . self-conscious and unreal, listening to distant music, a little bowlegged with craftiness. . . .

3. Father. Tying a necktie. In a hurry. On my first evening home he put his hand on my arm and said, "Honey, we're going to forget all about this."

4. Simon. Outside, a plane is crossing the sky, in here we're in a hurry. Morning. It must be morning. The girl is half out of her mind, whimpering and vague; Simon her dear friend is wretched this morning . . . he is wretched with morning itself . . . he forces her to give him an injection with that needle she knows is filthy, she has a dread of needles and surgical instruments and the odor of things that are to be sent into the blood, thinking somehow of her father. . . . This is a bad morning, Simon says that his mind is being twisted out of shape, and so he submits to the needle that he usually scorns and bites his lip with his yellowish teeth, his face going very pale. *Ah baby!* he says in his soft mocking voice, which with all women is a mockery of love, *do it like this—Slowly*—And the girl, terrified, almost drops the precious needle but manages to turn it up to the light from the window . . . is it an extension of herself then? She can give him this gift then? *I wish you wouldn't do this to me,* she says, wise in her terror, because it seems to her that Simon's danger—in a few minutes he may be dead—is a way of pressing her against him that is more powerful than any other embrace. She has to work over his arm, the knotted corded veins of his arm, her forehead wet with perspiration as she pushes and releases the needle, staring at that mixture of liquid now stained with Simon's bright blood. . . . When the drug hits him she can feel it herself, she feels that magic that is more than any woman can give him, striking the back of his head and making his face stretch as if with the impact of a terrible sun. . . . She tries to embrace him but he pushes her aside and stumbles to his feet. *Jesus Christ*, he says. . . .

5. Princess, a Negro girl of eighteen. What is her charge? She is closed-mouthed about it, shrewd and silent, you know that no one had to wrestle her to the sidewalk to get her in here; she came with dignity. In

the recreation room she sits reading *Nancy Drew and the Jewel Box Mystery*, which inspires in her face tiny wrinkles of alarm and interest: what a face! Light brown skin, heavy shaded eyes, heavy eyelashes, a serious sinister dark brow, graceful fingers, graceful wristbones, graceful legs, lips, tongue, a sugar-sweet voice, a leggy stride more masculine than Simon's and my mother's, decked out in a dirty white blouse and dirty white slacks; vaguely nautical is Princess' style. . . . At breakfast she is in charge of clearing the table and leans over me, saying, *Honey you sure you ate enough?*

6. The girl lies sleepless, wondering. Why here, why not there? Why Bloomfield Hills and not jail? Why jail and not her pink room? Why downtown Detroit and not Sioux Drive? What is the difference? Is Simon all the difference? The girl's head is a parade of wonders. She is nearly sixteen, her breath is marvelous with wonders, not long ago she was coloring with crayons and now she is smearing the landscape with paints that won't come off and won't come off her fingers either. She says to the matron *I am not talking about anything*, not because everyone has warned her not to talk but because, because she will not talk; because she won't say anything about Simon, who is her secret. And she says to the matron, *I won't go home*, up until that night in the lavatory when everything was changed. . . . "No, I won't go home I want to stay here," she says, listening to her own words with amazement, thinking that weeds might climb everywhere over that marvelous $180,000 house and dinosaurs might return to muddy the beige carpeting, but never never will she reconcile four o'clock in the morning in Detroit with eight o'clock breakfasts in Bloomfield Hills . . . oh, she aches still for Simon's hands and his caressing breath, though he gave her little pleasure, he took everything from her (five-dollar bills, ten-dollar bills, passed into her numb hands by men and taken out of her hands by Simon) until she herself was passed into the hands of other men, police, when Simon evidently got tired of her and her hysteria. . . . *No, I won't go home, I don't want to be bailed out*. The girl thinks as a *Stubborn and Wayward Child* (one of several charges lodged against her), and the matron understands her crazy white-rimmed eyes that are seeking out some new violence that will keep her in jail, should someone threaten to let her out. Such children try to strangle the matrons, the attendants, or one another . . . they want the locks locked forever, the doors nailed shut . . . and this girl is no different up until that night her mind is changed for her. . . .

IX   THAT NIGHT

Princess and Dolly, a little white girl of maybe fifteen, hardy however as a sergeant and in the House of Correction for armed robbery, corner her in the lavatory at the farthest sink and the other girls look away and file out to bed, leaving her. God, how she is beaten up! Why is she beaten up? Why do they pound her, why such hatred? Princess vents all the hatred of a thousand silent Detroit winters on her body, this girl whose body belongs to me, fiercely she rides across the Midwestern plains on this girl's tender bruised body . . . revenge on the oppressed minorities of America! revenge on the slaughtered Indians! revenge on the female sex, on the male sex, revenge on Bloomfield Hills, revenge revenge. . . .

X DETROIT

In Detroit, weather weighs heavily upon everyone. The sky looms large. The horizon shimmers in smoke. Downtown the buildings are imprecise in the haze. Perpetual haze. Perpetual motion inside the haze. Across the choppy river is the city of Windsor, in Canada. Part of the continent has bunched up here and is bulging outward, at the tip of Detroit; a cold hard rain is forever falling on the expressways. . . . Shoppers shop grimly, their cars are not parked in safe places, their windshields may be smashed and graceful ebony hands may drag them out through their shatterproof smashed windshields, crying, *Revenge for the Indians!* Ah, they all fear leaving Hudson's and being dragged to the very tip of the city and thrown off the parking roof of Cobo Hall, that expensive tomb, into the river. . . .

XI CHARACTERS WE ARE
FOREVER ENTWINED WITH

1. Simon drew me into his tender rotting arms and breathed gravity into me. Then I came to earth, weighed down. He said, *You are such a little girl,* and he weighed me down with his delight. In the palms of his hands were teeth marks from his previous life experiences. He was thirty-five, they said. Imagine Simon in this room, in my pink room: he is about six feet tall and stoops slightly, in a feline cautious way, always thinking, always on guard, with his scuffed light suede shoes and his clothes that are anyone's clothes, slightly rumpled ordinary clothes that ordinary men might wear to not-bad jobs. Simon has fair long hair, curly hair, spent languid curls that are like . . . exactly like the curls of wood shavings to the touch, I am trying to be exact . . . and he smells of unheated mornings and coffee and too many pills coating his tongue with a faint green-white scum. . . . Dear Simon, who would be panicked in this room and in this house (right now Billie is vacuuming next door in my parents' room; a vacuum cleaner's roar is a sign of all good things), Simon who is said to have come from a home not much different from

this, years ago, fleeing all the carpeting and the polished banisters . . . Simon has a deathly face, only desperate people fall in love with it. His face is bony and cautious, the bones of his cheeks prominent as if with the rigidity of his ceaseless thinking, plotting, for he has to make money out of girls to whom money means nothing, they're so far gone they can hardly count it, and in a sense money means nothing to him either except as a way of keeping on with his life. *Each Day's Proud Struggle*, the title of a novel we could read at jail. . . . Each day he needs a certain amount of money. He devours it. It wasn't love he uncoiled in me with with his hollowed-out eyes and his courteous smile, that remnant of a prosperous past, but a dark terror that needed to press itself flat against him, or against another man . . . but he was the first, he came over to me and took my arm, a claim. We struggled on the stairs and I said, *Let me loose, you're hurting my neck, my face*, it was such a surprise that my skin hurt where he rubbed it, and afterward we lay face to face and he breathed everything into me. In the end I think he turned me in.

2. Raymond Forrest. I just read this morning that Raymond Forrest's father, the chairman of the board at   , died of a heart attack on a plane bound for London. I would like to write Raymond Forrest a note of sympathy. I would like to thank him for not pressing charges against me one hundred years ago, saving me, being so generous . . . well, men like Raymond Forrest are generous men, not like Simon. I would like to write him a letter telling of my love, or of some other emotion that is positive and healthy. Not like Simon and his poetry, which he scrawled down when he was high and never changed a word . . . but when I try to think of something to say, it is Simon's language that comes back to me, caught in my head like a bad song, it is always Simon's language:

> *There is no reality only dreams*
> *Your neck may get snapped when you wake*
> *My love is drawn to some violent end*
> *She keeps wanting to get away*
> *My love is heading downward*
> *And I am heading upward*
> *She is going to crash on the sidewalk*
> *And I am going to dissolve into the clouds*

XII EVENTS

1. Out of the hospital, bruised and saddened and converted, with Princess' grunts still tangled in my hair . . . and Father in his overcoat looking like a prince himself, come to carry me off. Up the expressway and out north to home. Jesus Christ, but the air is thinner and cleaner here. Monumental houses. Heartbreaking sidewalks, so clean.

2. Weeping in the living room. The ceiling is two stories high and two chandeliers hang from it. Weeping, weeping, though Billie the maid is *probably listening*. I will never leave home again. Never. Never leave home. Never leave this home again, never.

3. Sugar doughnuts for breakfast. The toaster is very shiny and my face is distorted in it. Is that my face?

4. The car is turning in the driveway. Father brings me home. Mother embraces me. Sunlight breaks in movieland patches on the roof of our traditional-contemporary home, which was designed for the famous automotive stylist whose identity, if I told you the name of the famous car he designed, you would all know, so I can't tell you because my teeth chatter at the thought of being sued . . . or having someone climb into my bedroom window with a rope to strangle me. . . . The car turns up the blacktop drive. The house opens to me like a doll's house, so lovely in the sunlight, the big living room beckons to me with its walls falling away in a delirium of joy at my return, Billie the maid is *no doubt* listening from the kitchen as I burst into tears and the hysteria Simon got so sick of. Convulsed in Father's arms, I say I will never leave again, never, why did I leave, where did I go, what happened, my mind is gone wrong, my body is one big bruise, my backbone was sucked dry, it wasn't the men who hurt me and Simon never hurt me but only those girls . . . my God, how they hurt me . . . I will never leave home again. . . . The car is perpetually turning up the drive and I am perpetually breaking down in the living room and we are perpetually taking the right exit from the expressway (Lahser Road) and the wall of the rest room is perpetually banging against my head and perpetually are Simon's hands moving across my body and adding everything up and so too are Father's hands on my shaking bruised back, far from the surface of my skin on the surface of my good blue cashmere coat (dry-cleaned for my release). . . . I weep for all the money here, for God in gold and beige carpeting, for the beauty of chandeliers and the miracle of a clean polished gleaming toaster and faucets that run both hot and cold water, and I tell them, *I will never leave home, this is my home, I love everything here, I am in love with everything here.* . . .

I am home.

For Study and Discussion

1. What logic or justification is there for the story's being presented in the form of notes the sixteen-year-old main character makes in preparation for writing an essay for her English class? Do you think the story would be more or less effective if presented in some other form?

2. Why does the young girl leave home? What causes her to return? Do you consider it likely that she will never leave home again, as she affirms at the end of the story?

3. Who is the most important secondary character? Why? List all the minor characters and describe the specific function of each in relation to the main character.

4. How much do you learn about the girl's parents? Does she blame them for her delinquency? If so, should she?

5. How would you describe the girl's mental outlook at the end of the story?

6. In her essay, "The Short Story," Oates defines the short story as "a dream verbalized, arranged in space and presented to the world, imagined as a sympathetic audience" (p. 139). In your opinion, does this story fulfill that definition? Why or why not?

TERM-PAPER TOPICS

Below are twenty topics suitable for paper assignments of various lengths. These topics are not intended as rigidly exclusive but rather as suggested approaches, which may be modified or amplified at the student's or instructor's discretion. Each may be handled without recourse to materials outside this text. Some instructors may, however, prefer to extend their students' literary range by having them consult supplementary library source materials such as those listed in the Selected Bibliography.

1. A contrast and comparison of the nineteenth- and twentieth-century story based on the analysis of one element such as theme, character, plot, setting, style, etc.

2. The use of symbols and/or allegory in the modern short story.

3. The types and functions of humor in the short story.

4. The role of psychology in the modern short story.

5. The use of concrete detail to secure the illusion of reality and lifelikeness.

6. The use of the Joycean "epiphany" principle in the modern short story.

7. Narcissism or self-obsession as a recurring theme in the modern short story.

8. The types and uses of irony as an important element in the short story.

9. The merits of *form* versus *plot* in the short story.

10. The effect the narrative point of view used has on the style and the structure of the story. (Alternate suggestion: The comparable merits and/or limitations of the first-person narrative point of view and those of the unlimited or omniscient point of view.)

11. The merits and limitations of the use of dialect, colloquial language, "disadvantaged" English, and/or other special forms of English in the short story.

12. Poetic style in the contemporary short story (as a point of departure, see particularly the statement on poetic language Herschel Brickell makes in his essay, "What Happened to the Short Story?").

13. The uses and functions of minor characters in developing theme and action.

14. A study of different treatments given to grotesque and abnormal themes and/or characters. (Alternate suggestion: a study of the uses of horror and violence in the short story.)

15. The importance of "atmosphere" in the short story—what it is, how it is secured, what it contributes to stories, etc. (See especially the comments Eudora Welty makes on atmosphere in her essay.)

16. The importance of setting (place and time) in the short story. (Flannery O'Connor's "The Fiction Writer and His Country" will provide some leads into this topic.)

17. The merits and limitations of fictional tricks and devices (such as the surprise ending, the double reversal, etc.) in the short story.

18. Structural devices authors use to secure unity in their stories (such stories as those by Balzac, Oates, and Gaines are among those offering interesting possibilities for this topic).

19. Saints and sinners: A study of good and bad characters.

20. The treatment of characters belonging to minority groups.

BIOGRAPHICAL NOTES

THOMAS BAILEY ALDRICH (1836–1907) was born in New Hampshire but spent most of his early years in New Orleans and New York. After settling in Boston in 1865 as editor of the literary magazine *Every Saturday,* he began writing short stories in the so-called French manner—a style marked by crisp, epigrammatic turns of phrase and surprise endings. The most effective appeared in the collection *Marjorie Daw and Other People* (1873). Aldrich's popularity and influence were later enhanced by other works—notably his autobiographical *Story of a Bad Boy* (1870) and his whimsical essays, *Ponkapog Papers* (1903)—and by his career as editor of the *Atlantic Monthly.*

SHERWOOD ANDERSON (1876–1941) was born in Camden, Ohio, and had little formal education. After a variety of menial jobs, service in the Spanish-American War, and a term at Wittenberg Academy, he became an advertising copywriter in Chicago and then part owner and manager of a paint factory in Elyria, Ohio. In 1912, driven by his urge to write, he left his factory, returned to Chicago, and embarked on a literary career. His first novels, *Windy McPherson's Son* (1916) and *Marching Men* (1917), won little recognition; but *Winesburg, Ohio* (1919), a collection of short stories that departed radically from the prevailing pattern, drew widespread critical attention. Subsequent volumes—*The Triumph of the Egg* (1921), *Horses and Men* (1923), and *Death in the Woods and Other Stories* (1933)—earned him a secure position in the first rank of short-story writers. In 1925 he retired to the small town of Marion, Virginia, where he edited two weekly newspapers, one Republican, one Democratic.

FALCON O. BAKER (1916–   ) has been a member of the Kentucky State Legislature, a tobacco farmer, a department-store manager, a small-town newspaper publisher, and an instructor at the University of Iowa. He has contributed articles to such periodicals as *Saturday Evening Post, Farm Journal, American Mercury,* and *Field and Stream.*

HONORÉ DE BALZAC (1799–1850), one of the greatest writers of France, was born to a prosperous family at Tours. Though trained for the law, he refused to practice and chose to live in poverty in Paris while struggling to achieve success as a writer. He produced a sizable quantity of stories, novels, and plays before finally winning recognition in 1829. During the remaining twenty-one years of his life, he issued more than 350 separate titles in drama and fiction. Writing with furious energy day after day, he depicted the life of his time in minute detail. His *Human Comedy,* a huge complex of some hundred novels and stories, offers a unique panorama of nineteenth-century France and has continued to exert an influence on writers down to the present.

HERSCHEL BRICKELL (1889–1952) divided his career among the activities of editor, author, and lecturer. From 1941 to 1951 he edited the annual volume of *O. Henry Memorial Award Prize Stories.*

HENRY SEIDEL CANBY (1878–1961) won recognition as a teacher, biographer, critic, and editor. A founder of the *Yale Review* (1911) and the *Saturday Review of Literature* (1924), he was for many years professor of writing and literary criticism at Yale University, served as the first chairman of the board of judges of the Book-of-the-Month Club, and wrote numerous biographical and critical studies in American literature. His writings include *The Short Story in English* (1909), *Classic Americans* (1931), *Thoreau* (1939), *Walt Whitman* (1943), and *Turn West, Turn East* (1951).

TRUMAN CAPOTE (1924–   ) was born Truman S. Persons in New Orleans, Louisiana, spent part of his childhood in Alabama, and was encouraged to write by a high-school English teacher in Greenwich, Connecticut. He began publishing stories when he was seventeen, and his first collection, *A Tree of Night and Other Stories,* appeared in 1949. Other works include the novels *Other Voices, Other Rooms* (1948), *The Grass Harp* (1951), *Breakfast at Tiffany's* (1958), and *In Cold Blood* (1965) and books of travel writings. He adapted *The Grass Harp* for the stage in 1952.

ANTON PAVLOVICH CHEKHOV (1860–1904) was born of humble parentage in Taganrog, Russia. Although he earned a degree in medicine at the University of Moscow in 1884, he devoted most of his life to writing. From the successful publication of *Particolored Stories* in 1886 until his death, he developed his short-story technique, reaching the height of his power around 1889 and producing thereafter hundreds of short stories. His influence has been tremendous, particularly in England and the United States, where his vogue has been a dominant one since the 1920s. English translations of his best stories are available in Constance Garnett's *The Tales of Chekhov* (1916–1923) and in other volumes. Chekhov is also internationally famous for such plays as *The Sea Gull* (1896), *Uncle Vanya* (1900), *The Three Sisters* (1901), and *The Cherry Orchard* (1904).

HERBERT ELLSWORTH CORY (1883–1947), educator and scholar, was born in Providence, Rhode Island, and educated at Brown and Harvard universities. He devoted most of his professional career to teaching, first at the University of California and later at the University of Washington. Among the books he wrote are *The Critics of Edmund Spenser* (1911), *Edmund Spenser, A Critical Study* (1917), and *The Intellectuals and the Wage-Workers* (1919).

N[ATHAN] BRYLLION FAGIN (1892–1972), scholar, critic, and teacher, has published such works as *Short Story-Writing: An Art or a Trade?* (1923), *The Phenomenon of Sherwood Anderson: A Study in American Life and Letters* (1927), *William Bartram, Interpreter of the American Landscape* (1933), and *America Through the Short Story* (1936).

WILLIAM FAULKNER (1897–1962) was born in New Albany, Mississippi. At an early age he moved with his family to nearby Oxford, which subsequently became the prototype for the city of Jefferson in his mythical "Yoknapatawpha County," the locale of much of his fiction. He attended public schools in Oxford but never graduated, served for a time in the Royal Canadian Flying Corps, worked in a New York City bookstore and at Oxford in the university post office. After a trip to Europe, he permanently settled down in Oxford to write. In 1924 he published a collection of poems, *The Marble Faun.* Early novels, such as *Soldiers' Pay* (1926), *Mosquitoes* (1927), *Sartoris* (1929), and *The Sound and the Fury* (1929) brought him considerable recognition, but fame and financial success first came with *Sanctuary* (1931). Other important novels include: *Light in August* (1932), *Absalom, Absalom!* (1936), *The Hamlet* (1940), *Intruder in the Dust* (1948), *The Fable* (1954), and *The Reivers* (1962). Among his short-story volumes are *These 13* (1931), *Doctor Martino and Other Stories* (1934), and *The Collected Stories of William Faulkner* (1950). He received the Nobel Prize for literature in 1950. He died of a heart attack and is buried in Oxford in what he once described as "the cedar-bemused" cemetery.

ERNEST J. GAINES (1933–   ), the son of a laborer, was born on a Louisiana plantation where he observed the people and events that he writes about so vividly and movingly. When he was fifteen, Gaines moved to California where he finished high school. After receiving a B.A. from San Francisco State College in 1957, he was awarded a Wallace Stegner Writing Fellowship at Stanford. His writing has appeared in several anthologies of black literature and in the *Sewanee Review* and the *Texas Quarterly.* Among his longer works are four novels, *Catherine Carmier* (1964), *Of Love and Dust* (1967), *The Autobiography of Miss Jane Pittman* (1971), and *A Long Day in November* (1972); and a volume of short stories, *Bloodline* (1968).

[FRANCIS] BRET[T] HARTE (1836–1902) was born in Albany, New York, but rose to fame as a writer while living in California from 1854 to 1870. As editor of the *Overland Monthly* there, he published his story "The Luck of Roaring Camp" (1868), which gained national attention. Two years later *The Luck of Roaring Camp and Other Sketches* won him a commission to write stories for the *Atlantic Monthly*. Harte left the West for good but continued to use his formula for the "wild West" tale in such collections as *Mrs. Skagg's Husbands* (1873), *Tales of the Argonauts* (1875), and *Colonel Starbottle's Client and Some Other People* (1892). Very popular in his own time, he is now considered only a minor regionalist.

NATHANIEL HAWTHORNE (1804–1864) was born in Salem, Massachusetts, of old New England Puritan stock. He was determined to become a writer from his undergraduate days at Bowdoin College; but his first successful collection, *Twice-Told Tales*, did not appear until 1837, and he did not become widely known until after the publication of his masterpiece, *The Scarlet Letter*, in 1850. Later novels such as *The House of the Seven Gables* (1851), *The Blithedale Romance* (1852), and *The Marble Faun* (1860)—together with three other volumes of shorter pieces, the second series of *Twice-Told Tales* (1842), *Mosses from an Old Manse* (1846), and *The Snow Image and Other Twice-Told Tales* (1851)—further established him as one of America's greatest literary geniuses. Hawthorne has grown steadily in reputation since his death; his mastery of symbol and allegory in particular has stimulated much scholarly and critical comment in recent years.

ERNEST HEMINGWAY (1899–1961) was born in Oak Park, Illinois, the second of six children and the eldest son of a physician. Upon graduating from high school, he worked as a cub reporter for the *Kansas City Star,* but soon after volunteered to serve as an ambulance driver in Italy during World War I. Badly wounded in 1918, he spent many months convalescing in hospitals abroad and at home; he subsequently became the Paris correspondent for the *Toronto Star* in 1921. There, encouraged by Gertrude Stein and Ezra Pound, he plunged into a writing career which was to take him to many different countries and culminate in his being awarded the Nobel Prize in 1954 for "forceful and style-making mastery of the art of modern narration." His first two collections of short stories, *In Our Time* (1925) and *Men Without Women* (1926), and his first novel, *The Sun Also Rises* (1926), drew favorable attention, but his first major commercial success was *A Farewell to Arms* (1929). Other significant works include *Death in the Afternoon* (1932), *The Fifth Column* and *First Forty-Nine Stories* (1938), *For Whom the Bell Tolls* (1940), and *The Old Man and the Sea* (1953). He died of a self-inflicted gunshot wound in Ketcham, Idaho.

WASHINGTON IRVING (1783–1859) was born and educated in New York City. Though admitted to the bar in 1806, he preferred literature to the law and in 1809 gained a local reputation as a humorist and literary craftsman with the publication of his *Diedrich Knickerbocker's History of New York.* In 1815 he went to England, where he lived seventeen years, alternately traveling on the Continent and writing the many tales and sketches for which he is best known. The first volume of these, *The Sketch Book* (1819–1820), was an immediate success; similar stories appeared later in *Bracebridge Hall* (1822), *Tales of a Traveller* (1824), and *The Alhambra* (1832). When Irving returned to the United States in 1832, he was internationally famous, having established a prominent position both for himself and for his country in the world of letters. During the rest of his life, he published numerous other volumes of fiction, biography, and history which kept him in the forefront of American literature. Irving has been remembered chiefly, however, as the originator of the American short story.

W[ILLIAM] W[YMARK] JACOBS (1863–1943), the son of a London dock manager, grew up in poverty near the London docks and at sixteen became a clerk in the Civil Service. In 1899, three years after the publication of his first collection, *Many Cargoes,* he left the Civil Service to give all his attention to writing. His work reached the height of its popularity with such collections as *Light Freights* (1901); *The Lady of the Barge and Other Stories* (1902), which contained the famous tale "The Monkey's Paw"; and *Night Watches* (1914).

HENRY JAMES (1843–1916) was born in New York City, the son of wealthy parents and the brother of William James, who was to gain fame as a psychologist and philosopher. He visited Europe frequently in his early years and took up permanent residence in England in 1877. Extending over a half century from the 1860s, his publishing career was marked by excellence in literary criticism as well as in the short story and the novel. His fiction includes eight volumes of short stories; a number of short novels such as *Daisy Miller* (1879), *What Maisie Knew* (1897), and *Turn of the Screw* (1898); and many full-length novels, including *The American* (1877), *The Portrait of a Lady* (1881), *The Wings of the Dove* (1902), *The Ambassadors* (1903), and *The Golden Bowl* (1904). James was a dedicated artist, seeking the ideal of perfection. His prefaces, collected in *The Art of the Novel* (1934), and his *Notebooks* (1947) provide fascinating insights into his methods of solving the difficult writing problems he set for himself.

JAMES JOYCE (1882–1941), born in Dublin, attended Clongowes Wood College and Belvedere College, both Jesuit schools, and then continued his education at University College, Dublin (1899–1902).

After receiving a degree, he went to Paris where he intended to become both a writer and a physician but never fulfilled the latter intention. After turning out numerous essays and book reviews, he began publishing poems and stories in 1904. The same year he also completed a draft of *Stephen Hero* (which contained his famous "epiphany" statement reprinted in this book), which was subsequently reworked and published as *A Portrait of the Artist as a Young Man* (1915). This novel and *Dubliners,* his one collection of short stories, published the year before, brought him no financial security but did achieve literary recognition which in turn won him a British Treasury Fund Grant and periodic support from wealthy patrons. By 1920, Joyce began experiencing severe difficulty with his eyesight, but he continued to write, publishing *Ulysses,* his monumental and widely influential major work, in 1922, and *Finnegans Wake* in 1939. He died in Zurich.

FRANZ KAFKA (1883–1924) was born in Prague of a wealthy Jewish family. In 1908, after earning a doctorate in jurisprudence from the Karls-Ferdinand German University, he secured a government post that provided a good income and also allowed time for writing. Little of his work was published during his lifetime, but Kafka won posthumous fame as a brilliant, highly original author. His collected stories and novels available in translation include *Metamorphosis* (1916, trans. 1937), *The Country Doctor* (1919, trans. 1945), *The Penal Colony* (1919, trans. 1948), *The Trial* (1925, trans. 1937), *The Castle* (1926, trans. 1930), and *Amerika* (1927, trans. 1938).

RUDYARD KIPLING (1865–1936), the son of an English art connoisseur who worked for many years in India, was born in Bombay. Educated in England, Kipling returned to India and at seventeen became subeditor of the Lahore *Civil and Military Gazette.* In 1886 he published *Departmental Ditties,* a volume of light verse, and in 1888 *Plain Tales from the Hills,* a collection of stories. Subsequent works, including *The Light That Failed* (1890), *Barrack Room Ballads* (1892), the two *Jungle Books* (1894, 1895), *Captains Courageous* (1897), and *From Sea to Sea* (1899), made him famous throughout the English-speaking world. Settling finally in England, he wrote such beloved classics as *Kim* (1901) and *Just So Stories* (1902). Kipling received the Nobel Prize for literature in 1907.

RING[GOLD WILMER] LARDNER (1885–1933) was born in Niles, Michigan, and became a sportswriter in Chicago. Attracting national attention with the satiric baseball sketches collected in *You Know Me, Al* (1916), he went on to depict the follies of both metropolitan and small-town life in stories marked by a tone of mordant detachment.

His best work appears in the collections *How to Write Short Stories* (1924), *The Love Nest and Other Stories* (1926), and *Round Up* (1929). Lardner's mastery of American speech rhythms has been considered a major contribution to the art of modern fiction.

D[AVID] H[ERBERT] LAWRENCE (1885–1930), the son of a coal-miner father and a schoolteacher mother, was born in Nottinghamshire, England, and taught school himself until the publication of his first novel, *The White Peacock,* in 1911. Thereafter, despite frail health, he traveled widely and produced not only short stories and novels but also books of travel, criticism, essays, and poetry. His principal works include the novels *Sons and Lovers* (1913), *The Rainbow* (1915), *Women in Love* (1920), *Aaron's Rod* (1922), and *Lady Chatterley's Lover* (1928) and *The Complete Short Stories of D. H. Lawrence* (1955), issued in three volumes.

KATHERINE MANSFIELD (1888–1923) was born Kathleen Beauchamp in Wellington, New Zealand, the daughter of a prominent banker. She began writing as a small child. After completing her education at Queen's College, London, she returned to New Zealand for a short time; but in 1908, with a small allowance from her father, she reestablished herself in London. A few years later she formed a close and lasting association with the critic John Middleton Murry, whom she married in 1918. Intensely self-critical and struggling against illness, she destroyed much of her writing or left it unfinished; but the short stories that reached publication are among the finest in modern English fiction. The best-known appear in *Bliss and Other Stories* (1920), *The Garden Party and Other Stories* (1922), and *The Dove's Nest and Other Stories* (1923). She died in France of tuberculosis.

[JAMES] BRANDER MATTHEWS (1852–1929) was born in New Orleans, Louisiana. A graduate of Columbia College and the Columbia University law school, he served as a professor of literature and then as a professor of dramatic literature at Columbia until 1924. In his long and active career he produced an enormous quantity of writing, including critical articles, plays, short stories, essays, and scholarly books.

GUY DE MAUPASSANT (1850–1893) was born near Dieppe, France. After serving a severe seven-year writing apprenticeship under Gustave Flaubert, his godfather, he won fame in 1880 with "Boule de Suif," still considered one of his best stories. In the next ten years he produced six novels and over three hundred stories, establishing himself as a master of the short-story form. Among his finest stories are "Tellier House" (1881), "Mademoiselle Fifi" (1882), "The Piece of

String" (1883), "Miss Harriet" (1884), "Moonlight" (1884), and "The Horla" (1887). His novels include *Une Vie* (1883), *Bel-Ami* (1885), and *Pierre et Jean* (1888). Afflicted with mental trouble, Maupassant died in a Paris sanitarium.

JOYCE CAROL OATES (1938–   ) was born in Lockport, New York. She received her B.A. from Syracuse University in 1960 and her M.A. from the University of Wisconsin a year later. From 1961 to 1967 she taught English at the University of Detroit; since then she has been on the faculty of the University of Windsor, Ontario, Canada. Oates began publishing stories when she was only twenty-one and brought out her first collection, *By the North Gate,* in 1963. Subsequently, she has published three other collections of stories, *Upon the Sweeping Flood and Other Stories* (1966), *The Wheel of Love and Other Stories* (1970), and *Marriages and Infidelities* (1973); two collections of poetry, *Women in Love and Other Poems* (1968), and *Anonymous Sins and Other Poems* (1969); and six novels, *With Shuddering Fall* (1964), *A Garden of Earthly Delights* (1967), *Expensive People* (1968), *them* (1969), *Wonderland* (1971), and *Do With Me What You Will* (1973). Many of her pieces of short fiction have been reprinted in collections of prize-winning stories, and for her achievements in fiction she won the Rosenthal Award of the National Institute of Arts and Letters in 1968 and the National Book Award in 1970 for *them.*

[MARY] FLANNERY O'CONNOR (1925–1964) was born in Savannah, Georgia, and educated at schools in Savannah, the Georgia State College for Women, and the State University of Iowa, where she earned an M.F.A. degree in 1947. During her fairly brief career, she published two novels, *Wise Blood* (1952) and *The Violent Bear It Away* (1960), and one collection of short stories, *A Good Man Is Hard to Find and Other Stories* (1955). A second important collection of stories, *Everything That Rises Must Converge,* appeared posthumously in 1965. The power and originality of Miss O'Connor's fiction earned her a $10,000 grant from the Ford Foundation in 1959. She died at Milledgeville, Georgia, which was her home.

FRANK O'CONNOR (1903–1966) was born Michael O'Donovan in Cork, Ireland. His earliest work, produced in his school days, was written in Gaelic. While a librarian in Dublin, he contributed stories to English-language periodicals and won high praise from the poet Yeats and other prominent writers. After the publication of his first volume, *Guests of the Nation* (1931), O'Connor issued many volumes of delightful tales. His best stories are available in *Selected Stories* (1946), *The Stories of Frank O'Connor* (1952), *More Stories by Frank O'Connor* (1954), and *Domestic Relations* (1957). He lived and taught in the United States, where many of his stories first appeared.

BONARO [WILKINSON] OVERSTREET (1902–   ) was born in California and received her higher education at the University of California (where she later taught) and at Columbia University. The publication of her first book, *The Poetic Way of Release* (1931), was followed by two volumes of poetry. More recently she has been concerned primarily with psychology and philosophy, authoring such books as *The Search for Self* (1938), *Freedom's People* (1945), and, with her husband Harry Overstreet, *The Mind Goes Forth* (1957).

LUIGI PIRANDELLO (1867–1936), the son of a wealthy mine owner, was born in Girgenti, Sicily, and earned a Ph.D. at the German University of Bonn. He returned to Rome and began writing fiction, publishing his first volume of stories, *Love Without Love,* in 1893. During the next twenty years he published numerous volumes of short stories and four novels, including *The Late Mattia Pascal* (1904). Around 1916 he turned to drama and in 1921–1922 won international fame with the plays *Six Characters in Search of an Author* and *Henry IV.* In 1934 he received the Nobel Prize for literature.

EDGAR ALLAN POE (1809–1849), the son of traveling theatrical parents, was born in Boston. Orphaned at two, he was brought up by John Allan of Richmond, Virginia. Poe attended the University of Virginia for one term, spent two years in the army, and in 1830 entered West Point, only to be dismissed shortly afterwards. In 1832, having already published three books of verse, he broke with Allan and set out to support himself by writing. But though he gained a reputation as an editor, critic, poet, and short-story writer, he was forced to struggle endlessly against poverty and personal misfortune. In 1835 he married frail, thirteen-year-old Virginia Clemm, who died at twenty-six. Poe's death came shortly thereafter, in Baltimore, under mysterious circumstances. His tales influenced the development of the short story at home and abroad.

KATHERINE ANNE PORTER (1894–   ) was born in Indian Creek, Texas, and brought up in Texas and Louisiana. After doing newspaper work in Dallas and Denver, she began publishing short stories; her first collection, *Flowering Judas* (1930, reissued with four additional stories in 1935), won critical acclaim, and subsequent volumes— *Hacienda* (1934), *Noon Wine* (1937), *Pale Horse, Pale Rider* (1939), *The Leaning Tower and Other Stories* (1944), and *Ship of Fools* (1962)—have earned her a respected place in modern fiction. She has received many major literary prizes, including a Ford Foundation award in 1959.

WILLIAM SYDNEY PORTER (1862–1910), known to his readers as O. Henry, was born in Greensboro, North Carolina. He left school at fifteen and in 1882 moved to Texas, where he became a bank clerk. In

1896 he was charged with embezzlement and fled to Honduras, but his wife's fatal illness caused him to return to Austin, where he was sentenced to five years in the federal ward of the Ohio State Penitentiary. Released after three years, he went to New York in 1902 and soon became one of the most popular short-story writers of his day. His many volumes of stories include *The Four Million* (1906), *The Trimmed Lamp* (1907), *The Voice of the City* (1908), and *Whirligigs* (1910).

V[ICTOR] S[AWDON] PRITCHETT (1900–   ) was born in Ipswich, England, and worked as a commercial traveler before beginning his literary career in newspaper work. His first books grew out of his experiences as a correspondent in Spain. He has since published such novels as *Elopement into Exile* (1932) and *Mr. Beluncle* (1951); collections of short stories—*You Make Your Own Life* (1938), *It May Never Happen* (1947), and *Collected Stories* (1956); and volumes of criticism—*The Living Novel* (1947), *Books in General* (1953), and *The Spanish Temper* (1954). Pritchett is particularly well known in the United States for his critical essays and his sprightly lectures.

ALEXANDER SERGEYEVICH PUSHKIN (1799–1837) was born in Moscow. As a member of the aristocracy, he became attached to the ministry of foreign affairs, led a gay social life, and wrote romantic poetry. For his "Ode to Liberty" (1820) and other revolutionary verses, he was sent into exile in southern Russia, where he wrote some of his greatest poetry, including *Boris Godunov* (1826) and the verse-novel *Eugene Onegin* (1823–1831). Later he was restored to favor but was kept under constant surveillance. After 1831 he turned to prose, producing such works as *The Tales of Belkin* (1831), *The Queen of Spades* (1834)—perhaps his most famous story—and *The Captain's Daughter* (1836). Pushkin met his death in a duel.

WILLIAM SAROYAN (1908–   ) was born in Fresno, California, of Armenian parents. At the age of two, following the death of his father, he was placed in an orphanage, where he stayed for five years until he returned to his family. He began trying to break into print while managing a postal telegraph office in San Francisco. His first published story appeared in an Armenian magazine in 1933, and a year later his career was fully launched with the publication of "The Daring Young Man on the Flying Trapeze" in *Story* magazine. This story became the title piece of his first volume (1934). He has written eight novels, including *The Human Comedy* (1942), twelve volumes of short stories, and a dozen plays, one of which, *The Time of Your Life* (1939), won a Pulitzer Prize and the Drama Critics' Circle Award.

HARRY LEE SHAW, JR. (1905–   ) has won respect as an editor, writer, teacher, and lecturer. Besides serving for many years as a teacher of composition and a lecturer on writing at New York University and Columbia University, he has been director of the Federal Writers' Project, New York City (1938) and associate editor and director of research for *Look* magazine (1942–1947). Since 1947 he has served as an editor in various capacities for several major publishers. He is the author of several texts on writing and literature, the most recent being the *Dictionary of Literary Terms* (1972), and has contributed many articles to national magazines.

PETER TAYLOR (1917–   ) was born in Trenton, Tennessee. He received his early education at schools in Nashville, St. Louis, and Memphis, places which often provide the locale for his fiction. After receiving his B.A. from Kenyon College in 1940, he served in the Army during World War II. In 1946, he became a teacher of creative writing at the University of North Carolina at Greensboro. Since then he has taught at many other universities, the most recent being the University of Virginia, where he has been since 1967. Included among the honors accorded him have been a Guggenheim Fellowship in 1950–1951, first prize in the 1950 O. Henry Memorial Awards, and membership in the National Institute of Arts and Letters in 1969. He has published a novel, a play, and five collections of short stories—*A Long Fourth and Other Stories* (1948), *The Widows of Thornton* (1954), *Happy Families Are All Alike* (1959), *Miss Leonora When Last Seen and Other Stories* (1963), and *The Collected Stories of Peter Taylor* (1969).

JEAN TOOMER (1894–1967) was born in Washington, D.C., and educated at the University of Wisconsin and the City College of New York. After publishing minor poems and reviews in several national magazines beginning in 1918, he brought out *Cane* in 1923, a collection of poems, short stories, and sketches based on his brief experience as a schoolteacher in rural Georgia. The book, an intensely lyrical and powerful tribute to his black ancestry in the deep South, was highly praised by other American writers, but it went unnoticed by the public. Although Toomer continued to write, he never again achieved the artistic success of *Cane*. After traveling widely, he finally settled in Bucks County, Pennsylvania, where he died in obscurity.

IVAN SERGEYEVICH TURGENEV (1818–1883) was born of a landowning family at Orel, Russia. He was educated at the universities of Moscow and St. Petersburg and in Berlin, where he studied literature and philosophy. He began publishing poetry in 1837 but achieved his first literary success with the short stories he published between 1847 and 1851—subsequently collected as *A Sportsman's Sketches* (1852). Continuing to work in fiction, he published a number of novels including *Rudin* (1856), *A Nest of Gentle Folk* (1858), *On the Eve*

(1860), *Fathers and Sons* (1862), and *Smoke* (1867). The wide criticism his works provoked in Russia influenced him to live abroad after 1863, first in Germany and later in France, where his work won the admiration of such notable French writers as Flaubert and Zola. Turgenev died at Bougival, near Paris.

EUDORA WELTY (1909–   ) was born in Jackson, Mississippi, and received her higher education at the Mississippi State College for Women, the University of Wisconsin, and Columbia University. In the 1930s she began publishing stories in such magazines as the *Southern Review, Harper's Bazaar,* and the *Atlantic Monthly.* Her first collection of short stories, *A Curtain of Green and Other Stories* (1941), has been followed by three others: *The Wide Net* (1943), *The Golden Apples* (1949), and *The Bride of Innisfallen and Other Stories* (1955). She has also published several novels: *The Robber Bridegroom* (1942), *Delta Wedding* (1946), *The Ponder Heart* (1954), *Losing Battles* (1970), and *The Optimist's Daughter* (1972). Welty continues to reside in Mississippi, which is the setting for most of her fiction.

JESSAMYN WEST (1907–   ) was born in Indiana but has lived in California since she was six. Educated at Whittier College and the University of California, Miss West (Mrs. H. M. McPherson) began publishing with *The Friendly Persuasion* (1945). This series of sketches was followed by *Mirror for the Sky* (1948), an opera script; *The Witch Diggers* (1951), a novel; *Cress Delahanty* (1953), a series of stories of adolescent girlhood; and the short-story collection *Love, Death, and the Ladies' Drill Team* (1955), reissued in 1957 as *Learn to Say Goodbye.* More recent titles include *To See the Dream* (1957), *Love Is Not What You Think* (1959), and *South of the Angels* (1960).

SELECTED BIBLIOGRAPHY

I. HISTORY AND CRITICISM

Austin, Mary. "The Folk Story in America." *South Atlantic Quarterly,* 33 (January 1934): 10–19.

Bader, A. L. "The Structure of the Modern Short Story." *College English,* 7 (November 1945): 86–92.

Baker, Howard. "The Contemporary Short Story." *Southern Review,* 3 (Winter 1938): 576–596.

Bates, H. E. *The Modern Short Story: A Critical Survey.* Boston: The Writer, Inc., 1950.

Beachcroft, T. O. *The Modest Art: A Survey of the Short Story in English.* London: Oxford University Press, 1968.

Beck, Warren. "Art and Formula in the Short Story." *College English,* 5 (November 1943): 55–62.

Bowen, Elizabeth. "The Faber Book of Modern Short Stories." In *Collected Impressions.* New York: Alfred A. Knopf, Inc., 1950, pp. 38–46. This essay was originally published in 1936.

Bowen, James K., and Richard Van Der Beets, eds. *American Short Fiction: Readings and Criticisms.* Indianapolis: Bobbs-Merrill, 1970.

Boyce, Benjamin. "English Short Fiction in the Eighteenth Century: A Preliminary View." *Studies in Short Fiction,* 5 (Winter 1968): 95–112.

Campbell, H. M. "Experiment and Achievement." *Sewanee Review,* 51 (Spring 1943): 305–320.

Canby, Henry S., and Alfred Dashiell. *A Study of the Short Story.* Rev. ed. New York: Henry Holt and Co., Inc., 1935.

Engstrom, A. G. "The Formal Short Story in France and Its Development Before 1850." *Studies in Philology,* 42 (July 1945): 627–639.

Evans, Oliver, and Harry Finestone, *The World of the Short Story: Archetypes in Action.* New York: Alfred A. Knopf, Inc., 1971.

Farrell, James T. "Nonsense and the Short Story" and "The Short Story." In *The League of Frightened Philistines and Other Papers.* New York: The Vanguard Press, Inc., 1945, pp. 72–81; 136–148.

Fitz Gerald, Gregory. "The Satiric Short Story: A Definition." *Studies in Short Fiction,* 5 (Summer 1968): 349–354.

Frakes, James R., and Isadore Traschen. *Short Fiction: A Critical Collection.* Englewood Cliffs, N.J.: Prentice-Hall, Inc., 1969.

Friedman, Norman. "What Makes a Short Story Short?" *Modern Fiction Studies,* 4 (Summer 1958): 103–117.

Frierson, William C. "The Maupassant School in England." In *The*

English Novel in Transition: 1885–1940. Norman: University of Oklahoma Press, 1942, pp. 48–59.

Geismar, Maxwell. "The American Short Story Today." *Studies on the Left,* 4 (Spring 1964): 21–27.

George, Albert J. *Short Fiction in France: 1800–1850.* Syracuse, N.Y.: Syracuse University Press, 1964.

Gerould, Katherine. "The American Short Story." *Yale Review,* NS 13 (July 1924): 642–663.

Gillespie, Gerald. "Novella, Nouvelle, Novelle, Short Novel?—A Review of Terms." *Neophilologus,* 51 (April 1967): 117–127; part II, 51 (July 1967): 225–230.

Gold, Herbert, ed. *Fiction of the Fifties: A Decade of American Writing.* New York: Doubleday & Co., Inc., 1959, pp. 7–15.

Grabo, Carl H. *The Art of the Short Story.* New York: Charles Scribner's Sons, 1913.

Gullason, Thomas A. "The Short Story: An Underrated Art." *Studies in Short Fiction,* 2 (Fall 1964): 13–31.

Harris, Wendell V. "English Short Fiction in the 19th Century." *Studies in Short Fiction,* 6 (Fall 1968): 1–93.

Hartley, L. P. "In Defence of the Short Story." In *The Novelist's Responsibility.* London: Hamish Hamilton, 1967, pp. 157–159.

Hinckley, Henry Barrett. "The Framing-Tale." *Modern Language Notes,* 49 (February 1934): 69–80.

Howells, W. D. "Some Anomalies of the Short Story." *North American Review,* 173 (September 1901): 422–432.

Janeway, Elizabeth, et al. "Is the Short Story Necessary?" In *The Writer's World.* Ed. Elizabeth Janeway. New York: McGraw-Hill Book Co., Inc., 1969, pp. 251–273.

Jarrell, Randall. "Stories." In *A Sad Heart at the Supermarket: Essays & Fables.* New York: Atheneum Publishers, 1962, pp. 140–159.

Joselyn, Sister M., O.S.B. "Edward Joseph O'Brien and the American Short Story." *Studies in Short Fiction,* 3 (Fall 1965): 1–15.

Kempton, Kenneth Payson. *The Short Story.* Cambridge: Harvard University Press, 1947.

Kenner, Hugh, ed. *Studies in Change: A Book of the Short Story.* Englewood Cliffs, N.J.: Prentice-Hall, Inc., 1965.

Kostelanetz, Richard. "The Short Story in Search of Status." *Twentieth Century,* 174 (Autumn 1965): 65–69.

Leal, Luis. "The New Mexican Short Story." *Studies in Short Fiction,* 8 (Winter 1971), 9–19.

Maugham, W. Somerset. "The Short Story." In *Points of View: Five Essays.* Garden City, N.Y.: Doubleday & Co., Inc., 1959, pp. 163–212.

Mayo, Robert D. "The Gothic Short Story in the Magazines." *Modern Language Review,* 37 (October 1942): 448–454.

McKenzie, Barbara, ed. *The Process of Fiction: Contemporary Stories and Criticism.* New York: Harcourt Brace Jovanovich, Inc., 1969.

Mercier, Vivian. "The Irish Short Story and Oral Tradition." In *The Celtic Cross: Studies in Irish Culture and Literature.* Eds. Ray B. Browne, William John Roscelli, and Richard Loftus. Lafayette, Ind.: Purdue University Studies, 1964, pp. 98–116.

Mirrielees, E. R. "The American Short Story." *Atlantic Monthly,* 167 (June 1941): 714–722.

Moffett, James. "Telling Stories: Methods of Abstraction in Fiction." *ETC.: A Review of General Semantics,* 21 (December 1964): 425–450.

Newman, Frances. "The American Short Story in the First Twenty-five Years of the Twentieth Century." *Bookman,* 63 (April 1926): 186–193.

O'Brien, D. J. *The Advance of the American Short Story.* Rev. ed. New York: Dodd, Mead and Co., 1931.

O'Connor, Flannery. "Writing Short Stories." In *Mystery and Manners.* Eds. Sally and Robert Fitzgerald. New York: Farrar, Straus & Giroux, Inc., 1969, pp. 87–106.

O'Connor, Frank. *The Lonely Voice: A Study of the Short Story.* Cleveland and New York: The World Publishing Co., 1963.

O'Connor, William Van, ed. *The Forms of Modern Fiction.* Minneapolis: University of Minnesota Press, 1948.

O'Faolain, Sean. *The Short Story.* New York: The Devin-Adair Co., 1951.

Onis, Harriet de. "The Short Story in the Caribbean Today." In *The Caribbean: Peoples, Problems, and Prospects.* Ed. A. Curtis Wilgus. Gainesville: University of Florida Press, 1952, pp. 123–134.

Pattee, Fred Lewis. *The Development of the American Short Story.* New York: Harper and Brothers, 1923.

Peden, William. *The American Short Story: Front Line in the National Defense of Literature.* Boston: Houghton Mifflin Co., 1964.

Pelzie, Bernard E. "Teaching Meaning Through Structure in the Short Story." *English Journal,* 55 (September 1966): 703–709, 719.

Penzoldt, Peter. *The Supernatural in Fiction.* New York: Humanities Press, 1965. Originally published in 1952 as *The English Short Story of the Supernatural.*

Perry, Bliss. "The Short Story." In *A Study of Prose Fiction.* Rev. ed. Boston: Houghton Mifflin Co., 1920.

Pochmann, Henry A. "Germanic Materials and Motifs in the Short Story." In *German Culture in America: Philosophical and Literary Influences: 1600–1900.* Madison: The University of Wisconsin Press, 1957, pp. 367–408.

Pupo-Walker, Enrique. "The Contemporary Short Fiction of Spanish America: An Introductory Note." *Studies in Short Fiction,* 8 (Winter 1971), 1–8.

Ross, Danforth. *The American Short Story.* Minneapolis: University of Minnesota Press, 1961.

Sayers, Raymond S. "Twenty-Five Years of Portuguese Short Fiction." *Studies in Short Fiction,* 3 (Winter 1966): 253–264.

Scherer-Virski, Olga. *The Modern Polish Short Story.* The Hague: Mouton & Co., 1955.

Schlauch, Margaret. "English Short Fiction in the 15th and 16th Centuries." *Studies in Short Fiction,* 3 (Summer 1966): 393–434.

Shepherd, Esther. "The Tall Tale in American Literature." *Pacific Review,* 2 (December 1921): 402–414.

Smith, Horatio E. "The Development of Brief Narrative in Modern French Literature: A Statement of the Problem." *PMLA,* 32 (1917), 583–597.

Stanford, Derek. "A Larger Latitude: Three Themes in the 'Nineties Short Story." *Contemporary Review,* 210 (February 1967): 96–104.

Stead, Christina, et al. "The International Symposium on the Short Story." *Kenyon Review,* 30, no. 4 (1968): 443–490; part II, 31, no. 1 (1969): 58–94; part III, 31, no. 4 (1969): 450–503.

Stegner, Wallace. *Teaching the Short Story. U. of Calif., Davis, Pubs. in English,* no. 2 (Fall 1965).

Strong, L. A. G. "The Art of the Short Story." In *Essays by Divers Hands: Being the Transactions of the Royal Society of Literature of the United Kingdom,* NS 23. Ed. Hon. Harold Nicholson. London: Geoffrey Cumberlege, Oxford University Press, 1947, pp. 37–51.

Stroud, Theodore A. "A Critical Approach to the Short Story." *Journal of General Education,* 9 (January 1956): 91–100.

Symons, Julian. *The Detective Story in Britain.* London: Longmans, Green and Co., 1962.

Taylor, J. Chesley. *The Short Story: Fiction in Transition.* New York: Charles Scribner's Sons, 1969.

Taylor, J. Golden. "The Western Short Story." *South Dakota Review,* 2 (Autumn 1964): 37–55.

Thompson, Stith. *The Folktale.* New York: The Dryden Press, 1946.

Thurston, Jarvis. "Analyses of Short Fiction: A Checklist." Special issue of *Perspective: A Quarterly of Literature and the Arts* (Summer 1953).

———, et al. *Short Fiction Criticism—A Checklist of Interpretation Since 1925 of Stories and Novelettes (American, British, Continental) 1800–1958.* Denver: Alan Swallow, 1960.

Vlach, Robert. "Modern Slavic Short Fiction." *Studies in Short Fiction,* 3 (Winter 1966): 126–137.

Waidson, H. M. "The German Short Story as a Literary Form." *Modern Languages,* 40 (December 1959): 121–127.

Welty, Eudora. *Short Stories.* New York: Harcourt, Brace and Co., 1950.

West, Ray B., Jr. *The Short Story in America: 1900–1950.* Chicago: Henry Regnery Co., 1952. (Paperback—Gateway Editions, Henry Regnery Co., 1956.)

Wharton, Edith. "Telling a Short Story." In *The Writing of Fiction.* New York: Charles Scribner's Sons, 1925, pp. 38–58.

Wright, Austin McGiffert. *The American Short Story in the Twenties.* Chicago: The University of Chicago Press, 1961.

II. ANTHOLOGIES*

Barroll, J. Leeds, III, and Austin M. Wright, eds. *The Art of the Short Story: An Introductory Anthology.* Boston: Allyn and Bacon, Inc., 1969.

Bates, Sylvia Chatfield, ed. *Twentieth Century Short Stories.* New York: Houghton Mifflin Co., 1933.

Baumbach, Jonathan, and Arthur Edelstein, eds. *Moderns and Contemporaries.* New York: Random House, 1968.

Booth, Michael R., and Clinton S. Burhans, Jr., eds. *31 Stories.* Englewood Cliffs, N.J.: Prentice-Hall, Inc., 1960.

Brewster, Dorothy, ed. *A Book of Contemporary Short Stories.* New York: The Macmillan Co., 1936.

Brooks, Cleanth, Jr., and Robert Penn Warren, eds. *Understanding Fiction.* 2nd ed. New York: Appleton-Century-Crofts, Inc., 1959.

————. *The Scope of Fiction.* New York: Appleton-Century-Crofts, Inc., 1960.

Brown, Leonard, ed. *Modern Short Stories.* New York: Harcourt, Brace and Co., 1937.

Buckler, William E., and Arnold B. Sklare, eds. *Stories from Six Authors.* New York: McGraw-Hill Book Co., Inc., 1960.

Burrell, John A., and Bennett Cerf, eds. *An Anthology of Famous American Stories.* New York: Random House, 1953.

Casty, Alan, ed. *The Shape of Fiction.* Boston: D. C. Heath, 1967.

Cerf, Bennett, ed. *Modern American Short Stories.* Cleveland: World Publishing Co., 1945.

Crane, Milton, ed. *50 Great Short Stories.* New York: Bantam Books, Inc., 1952. (Paperback.)

Cross, Ethan Allen, ed. *A Book of the Short Story.* New York: American Book Co., 1934.

Current-García, Eugene, and Walton R. Patrick, eds. *American Short Stories: 1820 to the Present.* Chicago: Scott, Foresman and Company, 1952; rev. ed., 1964.

————. *Short Stories of the Western World.* Chicago: Scott, Foresman and Company, 1969.

Felheim, Marvin, F. B. Newman, and W. R. Steinhoff, eds. *Modern Short Stories.* New York: Oxford University Press, 1951.

Flores, Angel, ed. *Nineteenth-Century French Tales.* Garden City, N.Y.: Doubleday and Co., Inc., 1960. Anchor Book (Paperback).

————. *Nineteenth-Century German Tales.* Garden City, N.Y.: Doubleday and Co., Inc., 1959. Anchor Book (Paperback).

Frederick, John T., comp. *Thirty-four Present-Day Stories.* New York: Charles Scribner's Sons, 1941.

---

*For a nearly complete list of major anthologies published through 1969, see *Studies in Short Fiction*, 7 (Winter 1970).

Geist, Stanley, ed. *French Stories and Tales.* New York: Alfred A. Knopf, Inc., 1954.

Gordon, Caroline, and Allen Tate, eds. *The House of Fiction: An Anthology of the Short Story with Commentary.* 2nd ed. New York: Charles Scribner's Sons, 1960.

Greet, T. Y., et al., eds. *The Worlds of Fiction.* Boston: Houghton Mifflin, 1964.

Gullason, T. A., and Leonard Casper, eds. *The World of Short Fiction.* 2nd ed. New York: Harper and Row, 1971.

Hardy, John E., ed. *The Modern Talent.* New York: Holt, Rinehart, and Winston, 1964.

Heilman, Robert B., ed. *Modern Short Stories.* New York: Harcourt, Brace and Co., 1950.

Howes, Barbara, and Gregory J. Smith, eds. *Sea-green Horse: A Collection of Short Stories.* New York: Macmillan Co., 1970.

James, Charles L., ed. *From the Roots: Short Stories by Black Americans.* New York: Dodd, Mead & Co., 1970.

Jessup, Alexander, ed. *Representative Modern Short Stories.* New York: The Macmillan Co., 1944.

Kempton, Kenneth Payson, ed. *Short Stories for Study.* Cambridge: Harvard University Press, 1953.

Kielty, Bernadine, ed. *A Treasury of Short Stories.* New York: Simon and Schuster, Inc., 1947.

Lin Yutang. *Famous Chinese Short Stories.* New York: The John Day Co., Inc., 1952. (Also published by Pocket Books, Inc.)

Male, Roy, ed. *Types of Short Fiction.* Belmont, California: Wadsworth Publishing Co., 1962.

Maugham, W. Somerset, ed. *Tellers of Tales.* New York: Doubleday, Doran and Co., 1939.

McClennen, Joshua, comp. *Masters and Masterpieces of the Short Story.* 2nd ser. New York: Henry Holt and Co., Inc., 1960.

Mitchell, Edward, and Rainer Schulte, eds. *Continental Short Stories.* New York: W. W. Norton & Co., Inc., 1968.

Mizener, Arthur, ed. *Modern Short Stories.* 3rd ed. New York: W. W. Norton, 1971.

Mott, F. L., ed. *Good Stories.* New York: The Macmillan Co., 1936.

Neider, Charles, ed. *Great Short Stories from the World's Literature.* New York: Rinehart and Co., Inc., 1950.

Oates, Joyce Carol, ed. *Scenes from American Life: Contemporary Short Fiction.* New York: Random House, 1973.

O'Brien, E. J., ed. *50 Best American Short Stories, 1915–1939.* Boston: Houghton Mifflin Co., 1939.

———. *The Short Story Case Book.* New York: Farrar and Rinehart, 1935.

O'Faolain, Sean, ed. *The Short Story.* New York: Devin-Adair Co., 1951.

Pattee, Fred Lewis, ed. *American Short Stories.* New York: Duffield and Co., 1925.

Rehder, Jesse, ed. *The Story at Work.* New York: Odyssey Press, 1963.

Scarborough, Dorothy, ed. *Selected Short Stories of Today.* New York: Farrar and Rinehart, 1935.

Schorer, Mark, ed. *The Story: A Critical Anthology.* New York: Prentice-Hall, Inc., 1950.

Short, Raymond W., and Richard B. Sewall, eds. *Short Stories for Study.* 3rd ed. New York: Henry Holt and Co., Inc., 1956.

Simpson, Claude M., ed. *The Local Colorists—American Short Stories, 1857–1900.* New York: Harper and Brothers, 1960.

Stanton, Robert, ed. *The Short Story and the Reader.* New York: Henry Holt and Co., Inc., 1960.

Stegner, Wallace, and Mary Stegner, eds. *Great American Short Stories.* New York: Dell Publishing Co., Inc., 1958. (Paperback)

Stegner, Wallace, et al., eds. *The Writer's Art: A Collection of Short Stories.* Boston: D. C. Heath and Co., 1950.

Thurston, J. A., ed. *Reading Modern Short Stories.* Chicago: Scott, Foresman and Company, 1955.

Timko, Michael, and Clinton F. Oliver, eds. *38 Short Stories.* New York: Alfred A. Knopf, 1968.

Turner, Arlin, ed. *Southern Stories.* New York: Holt, Rinehart and Winston, Inc., 1960.

Warren, Robert Penn, ed. *A Southern Harvest: Short Stories by Southern Writers.* Boston: Houghton Mifflin Co., 1937.

———, and Albert Erskine, eds. *A New Southern Harvest.* New York: Bantam Books, Inc., 1957. (Paperback.)

West, Ray B., Jr., ed. *American Short Stories.* New York: Thomas Y. Crowell Co., 1960.

———, and Robert W. Stallman, eds. *The Art of Modern Fiction.* New York: Rinehart and Co., Inc., 1949.

West, Theodora L., ed. *The Continental Short Story.* New York: Odyssey Press, 1969.

III. INDIVIDUAL AUTHORS

THOMAS BAILEY ALDRICH

Bowen, E. W. "Thomas Bailey Aldrich, a Decade After." *Methodist Review,* 99 (May 1917): 379–390.

Carpenter, Frederic I. "The Genteel Tradition: A Re-interpretation." *New England Quarterly,* 15 (September 1942): 427–443.

Howells, W. D. "Mr. Aldrich's Fiction." *Atlantic Monthly,* 32 (November 1880): 695–698.

Pattee, Fred Lewis. "Following the Civil War." In *The Development of the American Short Story.* New York: Harper & Brothers, 1923, pp. 211–216, 219.

Samuels, Charles E. *Thomas Bailey Aldrich.* New York: Twayne Publishers, 1965.

SHERWOOD ANDERSON

Abcarian, Richard. "Innocence and Experience in *Winesburg, Ohio.*" *University Review,* 35 (Winter 1968): 95–105.

Anderson, David D. *Sherwood Anderson: An Introduction and Interpretation.* New York: Barnes & Noble, Inc., 1967.

Browning, Chris. "Kate Swift: Sherwood Anderson's Creative Eros." *Tennessee Studies in Literature,* 13 (1968): 141–148.

Burbank, Rex. *Sherwood Anderson.* New York: Twayne Publishers, 1964.

Fagin, N. B. "Sherwood Anderson, the Liberator of Our Short Story." *English Journal,* 16 (April 1927): 271–279.

Faulkner, William. "Sherwood Anderson: An Appreciation." *Atlantic Monthly,* 191 (June 1953): 27–29.

Fussell, Edwin. "'Winesburg, Ohio': Art and Isolation." *Modern Fiction Studies,* 6 (Summer 1960): 106–114.

Gold, Herbert. "The Purity and Cunning of Sherwood Anderson." *Hudson Review,* 10 (Winter 1957–58): 548–557.

Howe, Irving. *Sherwood Anderson.* New York: William Sloane Associates, 1951; reissued by Stanford University Press, 1966.

Joselyn, Sister M., O.S.B. "Sherwood Anderson and the Lyric Story." In *The Twenties: Poetry and Prose.* Eds. Richard E. Langford and William E. Taylor. Deland, Florida: Everett Edwards Press, 1966, pp. 70–73.

Love, Glen A. "*Winesburg, Ohio* and the Rhetoric of Silence." *American Literature,* 40 (March 1968): 38–57.

Mahoney, John J. "An Analysis of *Winesburg, Ohio.*" *Journal of Aesthetics and Art Criticism,* 15 (December 1956), 245-252.

McAleer, John J. "Christ Symbolism in *Winesburg, Ohio.*" *Discourse: A Review of the Liberal Arts,* 4 (Summer 1961): 168–181.

McDonald, Walter R. "*Winesburg, Ohio*: Tales of Isolation." *University Review,* 35 (Spring 1969): 237–240.

Mellard, James M. "Narrative Forms in *Winesburg, Ohio.*" *PMLA,* 83 (October 1968): 1304–1312.

Murphy, George D. "The Theme of Sublimation in Anderson's *Winesburg, Ohio.*" *Modern Fiction Studies,* 13 (Summer 1967): 237–246.

Phillips, William L. "How Sherwood Anderson Wrote *Winesburg, Ohio.*" *American Literature,* 23 (March 1951): 7–30.

Rideout, Walter B. "The Simplicity of *Winesburg, Ohio.*" *Shenandoah,* 13 (Spring 1962): 20–31.

San Juan, Epifanio, Jr. "Vision and Reality: A Reconsideration of Sherwood Anderson's *Winesburg, Ohio.*" *American Literature,* 35 (May 1963): 137–155.

Thurston, Jarvis. "Anderson and 'Winesburg': Mysticism and Craft." *Accent,* 16 (Spring 1956): 107–128.

Trilling, Lionel. "Sherwood Anderson." *Kenyon Review,* 3 (Summer 1941): 293–302; revised and reprinted in Trilling's *The Liberal Imagination.* New York: The Viking Press, Inc., 1950, pp. 22–33.

Walcutt, Charles C. "Sherwood Anderson: Impressionism and the Buried Life." In *American Literary Naturalism, A Divided Stream.* Minneapolis: University of Minnesota Press, 1956, pp. 222–239.

White, Ray L., ed. *The Achievement of Sherwood Anderson: Essays in Criticism.* Chapel Hill: University of North Carolina Press, 1966.

Winther, S. K. "The Aura of Loneliness in Sherwood Anderson." *Modern Fiction Studies,* 5 (Summer 1959): 145–152.

HONORÉ DE BALZAC

Bertault, Philippe. *Balzac and the Human Comedy.* New York: New York University Press, 1963.

Dargan, E. P., ed. *The Evolution of Balzac's Comedie Humaine.* Chicago: University of Chicago Press, 1942.

Dedinsky, Brucia. *Development of the Scheme of the "Comedie Humaine": Distribution of the Stories.* Chicago: University of Chicago Press, 1943.

Hunt, Herbert J. *Honoré de Balzac: A Biography.* London: University of London, Athlone Press, 1957.

Royce, William H. *Balzac As He Should Be Read.* New York: Auguste Giraldi, 1946; 2nd ed., Fair Lawn, N.J.: Essential Books, Inc., 1957.

TRUMAN CAPOTE

Aldridge, John W. *After the Lost Generation.* New York: McGraw-Hill, 1951.

———."The Metaphorical World of Truman Capote." *Western Review,* 15 (Summer 1951): 247–260.

Levine, Paul. "Truman Capote: The Revelation of the Broken Image." *Virginia Quarterly Review,* 34 (Fall 1958): 600–617.

Malin, Irving, ed. *Truman Capote's "In Cold Blood": A Critical Handbook.* Belmont, Cal.: Wadsworth, 1968, pp. 163–176, 176–186, 239–269.

Norden, Eric. "*Playboy* Interview: Truman Capote." *Playboy,* 15 (March 1968): 51–53, 56, 58–62, 160–162, 164–170.

ANTON CHEKHOV

Brewster, Dorothy. "Chekhov in America and England." *Masses and Mainstream,* 7 (July 1954): 35–41.

Buford, W. H. *Anton Chekhov.* New Haven: Yale University Press, 1957.

Friedland, Louis S., ed. *Anton Chekhov's Letters on the Short Story, the Drama, and Other Literary Topics.* New York: Blom, 1968.

Gerhardi, William. *Anton Chekhov: A Critical Study.* New York: Duffield, 1923.

Hagan, John. "Chekhov's Fiction and the Ideal of 'Objectivity.'" *PMLA,* 81 (March 1966): 409–417.

Hingley, Ronald. *Chekhov: A Biographical and Critical Study.* New York: Macmillan, 1950; rev. ed., 1966.

Jackson, Robert L., ed. *Chekhov: A Collection of Critical Essays.* Englewood Cliffs, N.J.: Prentice-Hall, 1967.

McConkey, James. "In Praise of Chekhov." *Hudson Review,* 20 (Winter 1968): 417–428.

Simmons, E. J. *Chekhov.* Boston: Little, Brown, 1962.

Winner, Thomas. *Chekhov and His Prose.* New York: Holt, Rinehart and Winston, 1966.

WILLIAM FAULKNER

Adams, Richard P. "The Apprenticeship of William Faulkner." *Tulane Studies in English,* 12 (1962): 113–156.

———. *Faulkner: Myth and Motion.* Princeton, N.J.: Princeton University Press, 1968.

Arthos, John. "Ritual and Humor in the Writing of William Faulkner." *Accent 9* (Autumn 1948): 17–30.

Backman, Melvin. *Faulkner: The Major Years: A Critical Study.* Bloomington and London: Indiana University Press, 1966.

Beach, Joseph Warren. "William Faulkner: The Haunted South" and "William Faulkner: Virtuoso." In *American Fiction: 1920–1940.* New York: Russell and Russell, 1960, pp. 123–143, 147–169.

Brooks, Cleanth. "William Faulkner: Vision of Good and Evil." In *The Hidden God: Studies in Hemingway, Faulkner, Yeats, Eliot, and Warren.* New Haven: Yale University Press, 1963, pp. 22–43.

———. *William Faulkner: The Yoknapatawpha Country.* New Haven: Yale University Press, 1963.

Brown, Calvin S. "Faulkner's Use of the Oral Tradition." *Georgia Review,* 22 (Summer 1968): 160–169.

Everett, Walter K. *Faulkner's Art and Characters.* Woodbury, N.Y.: Barron's Educational Series, 1969.

Hoffman, Frederick J., and Olga W. Vickery, eds. *William Faulkner: Three Decades of Criticism.* Lansing: Michigan State University Press, 1960.

Holmes, Edward M. *Faulkner's Twice Told Tales: His Re-use of His Material.* The Hague: Mouton & Co., 1966.

Howe, Irving. *William Faulkner: A Critical Study.* New York: Random House, 1952; 2nd ed., New York: Vintage Books, 1962.

Howell, Elmo. "William Faulkner's Mule: A Symbol of the Post-War South." *Kentucky Folklore Record,* 15 (1969), 81-86.

Kazin, Alfred. "William Faulkner: The Short Stories." In *Contemporaries.* Boston: Little, Brown, 1962, pp. 154–158.

Kirk, Robert W., and Marvin Klotz. *Faulkner's People: A Complete Guide and Index to the Characters in the Fiction of William Faulkner.* Berkeley: University of California Press, 1963.

Litz, Walton. "William Faulkner's Moral Vision." *Southwest Review,* 37 (Summer 1952): 200–209.

Millgate, Michael. *The Achievement of William Faulkner.* New York: Random House, 1966.

Richardson, H. Edward. *William Faulkner: The Journey to Self-Discovery.* Columbia: University of Missouri Press, 1970.

Waggoner, Hyatt H. *William Faulkner: From Jefferson to the World.* Lexington: University of Kentucky Press, 1959.

Warren, Robert Penn, ed. *Faulkner: A Collection of Critical Essays.* Englewood Cliffs, N.J.: Prentice-Hall, Inc., 1966.

ERNEST J. GAINES

Blackburn, Sara. Review of *Bloodline. Nation,* 207 (September 9, 1968): 221.

Contemporary Authors. Detroit: Gale Research Company, 1965. Vol. XI-XII, p. 141.

Dollen, Charles. Review of *Bloodline. Best Sellers,* 28 (August 15, 1968): 207.

Gross, R. A. Review of *Bloodline. Newsweek* (June 16, 1969): 96-98.

Hicks, Granville. "Sounds of Soul." *Saturday Review,* 51 (August 17, 1968): 19–20.

LaFore, Laurence. Review of *Bloodline. New York Times Book Review* (September 29, 1968): 57.

Review of *Bloodline. Booklist,* 65 (November 1, 1968): 289.

BRET HARTE

Boggan, J. R. "The Regeneration of 'Roaring Camp'," *Nineteenth-Century Fiction,* 22 (December 1967): 271–280.

Brooks, Cleanth, and Robert Penn Warren. *The Scope of Fiction.* New York: Appleton-Century-Crofts, 1960, pp. 161–165.

Brown, Allen B. "The Christian Motif in 'The Luck of Roaring Camp'." *Papers of the Michigan Academy of Science, Arts, and Letters,* 16 (1961), 629–633.

Chesterton, G. K. "American Humor and Bret Harte." *Critic,* 12 (August 1902): 170–174.

Harrison, Joseph B., ed. *Bret Harte: Representative Selections,* with introduction, bibliography, and notes. New York: American Book Co., 1941.

O'Connor, Richard. *Bret Harte.* Boston: Little, Brown, 1966.

Pattee, Fred L. "Bret Harte." In *The Development of the American Short Story.* New York: Harper & Brothers, 1923. pp. 220–224.

NATHANIEL HAWTHORNE

Abel, Darrel. "Giving Lustre to Gray Shadows: Hawthorne's Potent Art." *American Literature,* 40 (November 1969): 373–388.

Baym, Nina. "The Head, the Heart, and the Unpardonable Sin." *New England Quarterly,* 40 (March 1967): 31–47.

Belden, H. M. "Poe's Criticism of Hawthorne." *Anglia,* 23 (1901): 376–404.

Bush, Sargent, Jr. "Bosom Serpents Before Hawthorne: The Origins of a Symbol." *American Literature,* 43 (May 1971), 181–199.

Clay, Edward M. "The 'Dominating' Symbol in Hawthorne's Last Phase." *American Literature,* 39 (January 1968): 506–516.

Crews, Frederick C. *The Sins of the Fathers: Hawthorne's Psychological Themes.* New York: Oxford University Press, 1966.

Dusenbery, Robert. "Hawthorne's Merry Company: The Anatomy of Laughter in the Tales and Short Stories." *PMLA,* 82 (May 1967): 285–288.

Erlich, Gloria Chasson. "Deadly Innocence: Hawthorne's Dark Women." *New England Quarterly,* 41 (June 1968): 163–179.

Fogle, R. H. "Weird Mockery: An Element of Hawthorne's Style." *Style,* 2 (Fall 1968): 191–202.

Heilman, R. B. "Hawthorne's 'The Birthmark': Science as Religion." *South Atlantic Quarterly,* 48 (October 1949): 575–583.

Horne, Lewis B. "The Heart, the Hand, and 'The Birthmark'." *American Transcendental Quarterly,* 1 (I Quarter 1969): 38–41.

Martin, Terence. *Nathaniel Hawthorne.* New York: Twayne Publishers, 1965.

Miller, James E., Jr. "Hawthorne and Melville: The Unpardonable Sin." *PMLA,* 70 (March 1955): 91–114.

Regan, Robert. "Hawthorne's 'Plagiary'; Poe's Duplicity." *Nineteenth-Century Fiction,* 25 (December 1970), 281–298.

Reid, Alfred S. "Hawthorne's Humanism: 'The Birthmark' and Sir Kenelm Digby." *American Literature,* 38 (November 1966): 337–351.

Thompson, W. R. "Aminadab in Hawthorne's 'The Birthmark'." *Modern Language Notes,* 70 (June 1955): 413–415.

Warren, Austin. *Nathaniel Hawthorne: Representative Selections,* with introduction, bibliography, and notes. New York: American Book Co., 1934.

ERNEST HEMINGWAY

Aiken, William. "Hemingway's 'Ten Indians'." *The Explicator,* 28 (December 1969): item 31.

Baker, Carlos, ed. and introd. *Hemingway and His Critics: An International Anthology.* New York: Hill and Wang, Inc., 1961.

———. *Hemingway: The Writer As Artist.* 3rd ed. Princeton, N.J.: Princeton University Press, 1963.

Brooks, Cleanth. "Ernest Hemingway: Man on His Moral Uppers." In *The Hidden God: Studies in Hemingway, Faulkner, Yeats, Eliot, and Warren.* New Haven: Yale University Press, 1963, pp. 6–21.

Carpenter, Frederic I. "Hemingway Achieves the Fifth Dimension." *PMLA,* 69 (September 1954): 711–718.

DeFalco, Joseph. *The Hero in Hemingway's Short Stories.* Pittsburgh: University of Pittsburgh Press, 1963.

Fenton, Charles A. *The Apprenticeship of Ernest Hemingway: The Early Years.* New York: Farrar, Straus & Giroux, Inc., 1954.

Flanagan, John T. "Hemingway's Debt to Sherwood Anderson." *Journal of English and Germanic Philology,* 54 (October 1955): 507–520.

Graham, John. "Ernest Hemingway: The Meaning of Style." *Modern Fiction Studies,* 6 (Winter 1960–1961): 298–313.

Grebstein, Sheldon N. *Hemingway's Craft.* Carbondale: Southern Illinois University Press, 1973.

Halliday, E. M. "Hemingway's Ambiguity: Symbolism and Irony." *American Literature,* 28 (March 1956): 1–22.

Knieger, Bernard. "The Concept of Maturity in Hemingway's Short Stories." *CLA Journal,* 8 (December 1964): 149–156.

Levin, Harry. "Observations on the Style of Ernest Hemingway." *Kenyon Review,* 13 (Autumn 1951): 581–609.

Lewis, Robert W., Jr. *Hemingway on Love.* Austin & London: University of Texas Press, 1965.

Rovit, Earl. *Ernest Hemingway.* New York: Twayne Publishers, 1963.

Stein, William Bysshe. "Love and Lust in Hemingway's Short Stories." *Texas Studies in Literature and Language,* 3 (Summer 1961): 234–242.

Walker, Warren S. "Ernest Hemingway." In *Twentieth-Century Short Story Explication.* Hamden, Conn.: The Shoe String Press, 1961, pp. 146–160.

Wilson, Edmund. "Hemingway: Gauge of Morale." In *The Wound and the Bow: Seven Studies in Literature.* New York: Oxford University Press, 1947, pp. 214–242.

Wylder, Delbert E. *Hemingway's Heroes.* Albuquerque: University of New Mexico Press, 1969.

Young, Philip. *Ernest Hemingway: A Reconsideration.* Rev. ed. University Park, Pa.: The Pennsylvania State University Press, 1966.

WASHINGTON IRVING

Current-García, E. "Irving Sets the Pattern: Professionalism and the Art of the Short Story." *Studies in Short Fiction,* 10 (Fall 1973): 326–340.

Hedges, William L. *Washington Irving: An American Study, 1802–1832.* Baltimore: The John Hopkins Press, 1965.

Pochmann, Henry A. "Germanic Materials and Motifs in the Short Story: Washington Irving." In *German Culture in America.* Madison: University of Wisconsin Press, 1961, pp. 367–381, 696–705.

———. "Irving's German Sources in *The Sketch Book.*" *Studies in Philology,* 27 (July 1930): 477–507.

———. "Irving's German Tour and Its Influence on His Tales." *PMLA,* 45 (December 1930): 1150–1187.

———. *Washington Irving: Representative Selections,* with introduction, bibliography, and notes. New York: American Book Company, 1934.

———. "Washington Irving: Amateur or Professional?" In *Essays on American Literature in Honor of Jay B. Hubbell.* Durham, N.C.: Duke University Press, 1967, pp. 63–76.

Reed, Kenneth T. "'Oh, These Women! These Women!': Irving's Shrews and Coquettes." *American Notes and Queries,* 8 (June 1970), 147–150.

Reichert, Walter A. *Washington Irving and Germany.* Ann Arbor: University of Michigan Press, 1957.

Ringe, Donald A. "New York and New England: Irving's Criticism of American Society." *American Literature,* 38 (January 1966): 455–467.

Snell, George. "Washington Irving: A Revaluation." *Modern Language Quarterly,* 7 (Summer 1946): 303–310.

HENRY JAMES

Anderson, Quentin. *The American Henry James.* New Brunswick, N.J.: Rutgers University Press, 1957.

Bewley, Marius. "Henry James and 'Life'" and "Henry James and the Economic Age." In *The Eccentric Design: Form in the Classic American Novel.* New York: Columbia University Press, 1959, pp. 220–244, 245–258.

Clair, John A. *The Ironic Dimension in the Fiction of Henry James.* Pittsburgh, Pa.: Duquesne University Press, 1965.

Dupee, F. W. *Henry James.* New York: William Sloane Associates, 1951. Rev. ed. New York: Dell, 1965.

Edel, Leon. *Henry James: 1882–1895: The Middle Years.* Philadelphia and New York: J. B. Lippincott Co., 1962.

Gale, Robert L. *The Caught Image: Figurative Language in the Fiction of Henry James.* Chapel Hill: The University of North Carolina Press, 1964.

Horne, Helen. "Henry James: 'The Real Thing' (1890): An Attempt at Interpretation." *Die Neueren Sprachen,* 2 (1959), 214–219.

Kehler, Harold. "James's 'The Real Thing'." *The Explicator,* 25 (May 1967): item 79.

Matthiessen, F. O., and Kenneth B. Murdock, eds. *The Notebooks of Henry James.* New York: Oxford University Press, 1947.

McElderry, Bruce R., Jr. *Henry James.* New York: Twayne Publishers, 1965.

Reilly, Robert J. "Henry James and the Morality of Fiction." *American Literature,* 39 (March 1967): 1–30.

Short, R. W. "The Sentence Structure of Henry James." *American Literature,* 18 (May 1946): 71–88.

Stone, Edward, ed. *Henry James: Seven Stories and Studies.* New York: Appleton-Century-Crofts, Inc., 1961.

Thorberg, Raymond. "Henry James and 'The Real Thing': 'The Beldonald Holbein'." *Southern Humanities Review,* 3 (1968), 78–85.

Toor, David. "Narrative Irony in Henry James' 'The Real Thing'." *University Review,* 34 (Winter 1967): 95–99.

Ward, J. A. *The Imagination of Disaster: Evil in the Fiction of Henry James.* Lincoln: University of Nebraska Press, 1961.

———. *The Search for Form: Studies in the Structure of James's Fiction.* Chapel Hill: The University of North Carolina Press, 1967.

Wright, Walter F. "'The Real Thing'." *Research Studies of the State College of Washington,* 25 (1957): 85–90.

———. *The Madness of Art: A Study of Henry James.* Lincoln: University of Nebraska Press, 1962.

JAMES JOYCE

Beck, Warren. *Joyce's Dubliners: Substance, Vision, and Art.* Durham, N.C.: Duke University Press, 1969.

Carrier, Warren. "*Dubliners:* Joyce's Dantean Vision." *Renascence,* 17 (Summer 1965): 211–215.

Collins, Ben L. "Joyce's 'Araby' and the 'Extended Simile'." *James Joyce Quarterly,* 4 (1967): 84–90.

Cooke, M. G. "From Comedy to Terror: On *Dubliners* and the Development of Tone and Structure in the Modern Short Story." *Massachusetts Review,* 9 (Spring 1968): 331–343.

Ellmann, Richard. *James Joyce.* New York: Oxford University Press, 1959.

Freimarck, John. "'Araby': A Quest for Meaning." *James Joyce Quarterly,* 7 (1969), 366–368.

Friedman, Stanley. "Joyce's 'Araby'." *The Explicator,* 24 (January 1966): item 43.

Friedrich, Gerhard. "The Perspective of Joyce's *Dubliners.*" *College English* 26 (March 1965): 421–426.

Ghiselin, Brewster. "The Unity of Joyce's *Dubliners.*" *Accent,* 16 (Spring 1956): 75–88; (Summer 1956): 196–213.

Gibbons, T. H. "*Dubliners* and the Critics." *Critical Quarterly,* 9 (Summer 1967): 179–187.

Going, William T. "Joyce's 'Araby'." *The Explicator,* 26 (January 1968): item 39.

Hart, Clive, ed. *James Joyce's* Dubliners: *Critical Essays.* New York: The Viking Press, Inc., 1969.

Levin, Harry. *James Joyce: A Critical Introduction.* Rev. ed. New York: New Directions Paperbook, 1960.

Levin, Richard, and Charles Shattuck. "First Flight to Ithaca: A New Reading of Joyce's *Dubliners.*" *Accent,* 4 (Winter 1944): 75–99.

Magalaner, Marvin. "The Evolution of *Dubliners.*" In *Time of Apprenticeship: The Fiction of Young James Joyce.* London, New York: Abelard-Schuman Ltd., 1959, pp. 72–96.

Moseley, Virginia. *Joyce and the Bible.* De Kalb: Northern Illinois University Press, 1967.

Roberts, Robert P. "'Araby' and the Palimpsest of Criticism." *Antioch Review,* 26 (Winter 1966–1967): 469–489.

Scholes, Robert, and Florence L. Walzl. "The Epiphanies of Joyce." *PMLA,* 82 (March 1967): 152–154.

Silverman, O. A., introd. and notes. *James Joyce: EPIPHANIES.* Buffalo, N.Y.: Lockwood Memorial Library (University of Buffalo), 1956.

Walzl, Florence L. "Pattern of Paralysis in Joyce's *Dubliners:* A Study of the Original Framework." *College English,* 22 (January 1961): 221–228.

FRANZ KAFKA

Arendt, Hannah. "Franz Kafka: A Revaluation." *Partisan Review,* 11 (Fall 1944): 412–422.

Asher, J. A. "Turning-Points in Kafka's Stories." *Modern Language Review,* 57 (January 1962): 47–52.

Burgum, Edwin Berry. "Franz Kafka and the Bankruptcy of Faith." In *The Novel and the World's Dilemma.* New York: Oxford University Press, 1947, pp. 72–94.

Camus, Albert. "Hope and the Absurd in the Work of Franz Kafka." In *The Myth of Sisyphus and Other Essays.* Translated by Justin O'Brien. New York: Alfred A. Knopf, Inc., 1955, pp. 124–138.

Carrouges, Michael. *Kafka Versus Kafka.* Translated by Emmett Parker. University, Ala.: University of Alabama Press, 1968.

Collignon, Jean. "Kafka's Humor." *Yale French Studies,* no. 16 (Winter 1955–56), 53–62.

Flores, Angel, and Homer Swander, eds. *Franz Kafka Today.* Madison: University of Wisconsin Press, 1958.

Foulkes, A. P. *The Reluctant Pessimist: A Study of Franz Kafka.* The Hague: Mouton & Co., 1967.

——. "Kafka's Cage Image." *Modern Language Notes,* 82 (October 1967): 462–471.

Gordon, Caroline. "Notes on Hemingway and Kafka." *Sewanee Review,* 57 (Spring 1949): 215–226.

Gray, Ronald D., ed. *Kafka: A Collection of Critical Essays.* Englewood Cliffs, N.J.: Prentice-Hall, 1962.

Greenberg, Martin. *The Terror of Art: Kafka and Modern Literature.* New York: Basic Books, Inc., 1968.

Moyer, Patricia. "Time and the Artist in Kafka and Hawthorne." *Modern Fiction Studies,* 4 (Winter 1958–59): 295–306.

Neider, Charles. *The Frozen Sea: A Study of Franz Kafka.* New York: Oxford University Press, 1948.

Newmeyer, Peter F. "Franz Kafka, Sugar Baron." *Modern Fiction Studies,* 17 (Spring 1971), 5–36.

Osborne, Charles. *Kafka.* New York: Barnes & Noble, Inc., 1967.

Politzer, Heinz. "Franz Kafka's Language." *Modern Fiction Studies,* 8 (Spring 1962):16–22.

Rubinstein, William C. "Franz Kafka: A Hunger Artist." *Monatshefte,* 44 (January 1952):13–19.

Russell, Francis. *Three Studies in Twentieth-Century Obscurity.* Chester Springs, Pa.: Dufour Editions, 1961, pp. 45–65.

Sandbank, S. "Action as Self-Mirror: On Kafka's Plots." *Modern Fiction Studies,* 17 (Spring 1971), 21–29.

——. "Structures of Paradox in Kafka." *Modern Language Quarterly,* 28 (December 1967): 462–472.

Seyppel, Joachim H. "The Animal Theme and Totemism in Franz Kafka." *Literature and Psychology,* 4 (September 1954): 49–63.

Stallman, R. W. "A Hunger Artist." In *Franz Kafka Today.* Eds. Angel Flores and Homer Swander. Madison: University of Wisconsin Press, 1958, pp. 61–70.

Wilson, Edmund. "A Dissenting Opinion on Kafka." *New Yorker,* 23 (July 26, 1947): 58, 61–64.

RUDYARD KIPLING

Bayley, John. "The Kipling Conundrum." *Encounter,* 25 (December 1965):24–31.

Beachcroft, T. O. *The Modest Art: A Survey of the Short Story in English.* London: Oxford University Press, 1968, pp. 130–148.

Bodelsen, C. A. *Aspects of Kipling's Art.* New York: Barnes & Noble, 1964.

Cook, Richard. "Rudyard Kipling and George Orwell." *Modern Fiction Studies,* 7 (Summer 1961): 125–135.

Croft-Cooke, Rupert. *Rudyard Kipling.* Denver: Alan Swallow, 1948.

Dobree, Bonamy. *Rudyard Kipling: Realist and Fabulist.* London: Oxford University Press, 1967.

Gilbert, Elliot L., ed. and introd. *Kipling and the Critics.* New York: New York University Press, 1965.

Hart, Walter Morris. *Kipling: The Story Writer.* Berkeley: University of California Press, 1918.

Jarrell, Randall. "On Preparing to Read Kipling." In *The Best Short Stories of Rudyard Kipling.* Garden City, N.Y.: Hanover House, 1961, pp. vii–xix.

Kaufman, Ester. "Kipling and the Technique of Action." *Nineteenth-Century Fiction,* 6 (September 1951): 107–120.

Mirrielees, Edith. "Time and Mr. Kipling." *Virginia Quarterly Review,* 11 (January 1935): 37–46.

Rao, K. Bhaskara. *Rudyard Kipling's India.* Norman: University of Oklahoma Press, 1967.

Rutherford, Andrew, ed. *Kipling's Mind and Art: Selected Critical Essays.* Stanford, Cal.: Stanford University Press, 1964.

Tompkins, J. M. S. *The Art of Rudyard Kipling.* London: Methuen & Co., 1959.

Wilson, Edmund. "The Kipling That Nobody Read." In *The Wound and the Bow: Seven Studies in Literature.* New York: Oxford University Press, 1947, pp. 105–181.

RING LARDNER

Berryman, John. "The Case of Ring Lardner." *Commentary,* 22 (November 1956): 416–423.

Elder, Donald. *Ring Lardner, A Biography.* Garden City, N.Y.: Doubleday & Co., 1956.

Kasten, M. C. "The Satire of Ring Lardner." *English Journal,* 36 (April 1947): 192–195.

Mencken, Henry L. "Lardner." In *Prejudices, Fifth Series.* New York: Knopf, 1926.

———. "A Humorist Shows His Teeth." *American Mercury,* 8 (June 1926): 354–355.

Patrick, Walton R. *Ring Lardner.* New York: Twayne Publishers, 1963.

Seldes, Gilbert. "Editor's Introduction." In *The Portable Ring Lardner.* New York: Viking Press, 1946.

————. "Mr. Dooley, Meet Mr. Lardner." In *The Seven Lively Arts.* New York: Harper and Brothers, 1957, pp. 111–129.

Van Doren, Carl. "Beyond Grammar: Ring Lardner, Philologist Among the Low-Brows." *Century,* 106 (July 1923): 471–475.

Webb, Howard W., Jr. "The Meaning of Ring W. Lardner's Fiction: A Reevaluation." *American Literature,* 31 (January 1960): 434–445.

Wilson, Edmund. "Mr. Lardner's American Characters." *Dial,* 77 (July 1924), 69–72; reprinted in Wilson's, *A Literary Chronicle: 1920–1950.* Garden City, N.Y.: Doubleday (Anchor): pp. 37–40.

D. H. LAWRENCE

Bates, H. E. "Lawrence and the Writers of To-day." In *The Modern Short Story: A Critical Survey.* Boston: The Writer, Inc., 1961, pp. 194–213.

Ford, George H. *Double Measure: A Study of the Novels and Stories of D. H. Lawrence.* New York: Holt, Rinehart, and Winston, Inc., 1965.

Garrett, Peter K. "D. H. Lawrence: The Revelation of the Unconscious." In *Scene and Symbol from George Eliot to James Joyce: Studies in Changing Fictional Mode.* New Haven: Yale University Press, 1969, pp. 181–213.

Hoffman, Frederick J., and Harry T. Moore, eds. *The Achievement of D. H. Lawrence.* Norman: University of Oklahoma Press, 1953.

Moore, Harry T., ed. *A D. H. Lawrence Miscellany.* Carbondale: Southern Illinois University Press, 1959.

————. *D. H. Lawrence: His Life and Works.* Rev. ed. New York: Twayne Publishers, 1964.

Spilka, Mark. "Lawrence's Quarrel with Tenderness." *Critical Quarterly,* 9 (Winter 1967): 363–377.

Stavrou, Constantine N. "D. H. Lawrence's 'Psychology' of Sex." *Literature and Psychology,* 6 (August 1956): 90–95.

Vickery, John B. "Myth and Ritual in the Shorter Fiction of D. H. Lawrence." *Modern Fiction Studies,* 5 (Spring 1959): 65–82.

Vivas, Eliseo. *D. H. Lawrence: The Failure and Triumph of Art.* Evanston: Northwestern University Press, 1960.

Widmer, Kingsley. "Birds of Passion and Birds of Marriage in D. H. Lawrence." *University of Kansas City Review,* 25 (October 1958): 73–79.

————. *The Art of Perversity: D. H. Lawrence's Shorter Fictions.* Seattle: University of Washington Press, 1962.

KATHERINE MANSFIELD

Assad, Thomas J. "Mansfield's 'The Fly'." *The Explicator,* 14 (November 1955): item 10.

Baldeshwiler, Eileen. "Katherine Mansfield's Theory of Fiction." *Studies in Short Fiction,* 7 (Summer 1970): 421–432.

Bell, Pauline B. "Mansfield's 'The Fly'." *The Explicator,* 19 (December 1960): item 20.

Berkman, Sylvia. *Katherine Mansfield: A Critical Study.* New Haven: Yale University Press, 1951.

Bledsoe, Thomas A. "Mansfield's 'The Fly'." *The Explicator,* 5 (May 1947): item 53.

Boyle, Ted E. "The Death of the Boss: Another Look at Katherine Mansfield's 'The Fly'." *Modern Fiction Studies,* 11 (Summer 1965): 183–186.

Gateau, Andre-Marie. "Katherine Mansfield, Impressioniste, II." *Caliban,* 6 (January 1969): 33–48.

Greenfield, Stanley B. "Mansfield's 'The Fly'." *The Explicator,* 17 (October 1958): item 2.

Hagopian, John V. "Capturing Mansfield's 'Fly'." *Modern Fiction Studies,* 9 (Winter 1963–64): 385–390.

Hormasji, Nariman. *Katherine Mansfield: An Appraisal.* Auckland and London: Collins, 1967.

Jacobs, Willis D. "Mansfield's 'The Fly'." *The Explicator,* 5 (February 1947): item 32.

Rea, J. "Mansfield's 'The Fly'." *The Explicator.* 23 (May 1965): item 68.

Schahevitch, B. "From Simile to Short Story: On K. Mansfield's 'The Fly'." *Hasifrut: Quarterly for the Study of Literature,* 1 (1968): 368–377.

Stallman, R. W. "Mansfield's 'The Fly'." *The Explicator,* 3 (April 1945): item 49.

Thomas, J. D. "Symbol and Parallelism in 'The Fly'." *College English,* 22 (January 1961): 256–262.

Wright, Celeste T. "Genesis of a Short Story," *Philological Quarterly.* 34 (January 1955): 91–96.

———. "Mansfield's 'The Fly'," *The Explicator.* 12 (February 1954): item 27.

GUY DE MAUPASSANT

Artinian, Artine. "Maupassant As Seen by American and English Writers of Today." *French Review,* 17 (October 1943): 9–14.

Atkins, Ernest G. "The Supernaturalism of Maupassant." *PMLA,* 42 (March 1927): 185–220.

Freimanis, Dzintars. "Maupassant As a Romantic." *Romanic Review,* 54 (December 1963): 274–280.

Galantière, Lewis, ed. "Introduction." In *The Portable Maupassant.* New York: The Viking Press, Inc., 1947, pp. 1–24.

Hainsworth, G. "Pattern and Symbol in the Work of Maupassant," *French Studies.* 5 (January 1951): 1–17.

Ignotus, Paul. *The Paradox of Maupassant.* New York: Funk & Wagnalls Co., 1968.

James, Henry. "Guy de Maupassant." In *Partial Portraits.* London and New York: Macmillan, 1888, pp. 243–287.

Kempton, Kenneth P. *The Short Story.* Cambridge: Harvard University Press, 1947, pp. 107–109.

Matthews, J. H. "Theme and Structure in Maupassant's Short Stories." *Modern Languages,* 42 (December 1962): 136–144.

O'Faolain, Sean. *The Short Story.* New York: The Devin-Adair Co., 1951, pp. 106–143.

Steegmuller, Francis. *Maupassant: A Lion in the Path.* New York: Random House, Inc., 1949.

Sullivan, Edward D. *Maupassant: The Short Stories.* Great Neck, N.Y.: Barron's Educational Series, Inc., 1962.

Turnell, Martin. "Maupassant." In *The Art of French Fiction.* New York: New Directions, 1959, pp. 197–220.

JOYCE CAROL OATES

Clemons, Walter. "Joyce Carol Oates at Home." *New York Times Book Review,* (September 28, 1969): 4–6, 48.

Dalton, Elizabeth. "Joyce Carol Oates: Violence in the Head." *Commentary,* 49 (June 6, 1970): 75–77.

DeMott, Benjamin. "The Necessity in Art of a Reflective Intelligence." *Saturday Review,* 52 (November 22, 1969): 71–73, 89.

Kuehl, Linda. "An Interview with Joyce Carol Oates." *Commonweal,* 91 (December 5, 1969): 307–310.

Madden, David. "The Violent World of Joyce Carol Oates." In *The Poetic Image in 6 Genres.* Carbondale and Edwardsville, Illinois: Southern Illinois University Press, 1969, pp. 25–46.

FLANNERY O'CONNOR

Brittain, Joan Tucker. "O'Connor's 'A Good Man Is Hard to Find'." *The Explicator,* 26 (September 1967): item 1.

Browning, Preston M., Jr. "Flannery O'Connor and the Grotesque Recovery of the Holy." In *Adversity and Grace: Studies in Recent American Literature.* Ed. Nathan Scott. Chicago: University of Chicago Press, 1968, pp. 133–161.

Burns, Stuart L. "'Torn by the Lord's Eye': O'Connor's Use of Sun Imagery." *Twentieth Century Literature,* 13 (October 1967): 154–166.

Carlson, Thomas M. "Flannery O'Connor: The Manichaean Dilemma." *Sewanee Review,* 77 (Spring 1969): 254–276.

Carter, Thomas H. "Rhetoric and Southern Landscapes." *Accent,* 15 (Autumn 1955): 293–297.

Detweiler, Robert. "The Curse of Christ in Flannery O'Connor's Fiction." *Comparative Literature Studies,* 3, no. 2 (1966): 235–245.

Dowell, Bob. "The Moment of Grace in the Fiction of Flannery O'Connor." *College English,* 27 (December 1965): 235–239.

Drake, Robert. "'The Bleeding Stinking Mad Shadow of Jesus' in the Fiction of Flannery O'Connor." *Comparative Literature Studies,* 3, no. 2 (1966): 183–196.

———. "The Paradigm of Flannery O'Connor's True Country." *Studies in Short Fiction,* 6 (Summer 1969): 433–442.

Duhamel, P. A. "Flannery O'Connor's Violent View of Reality." *Catholic World,* 190 (February 1960): 280–285.

Feeley, Sister M. Kathleen. "Thematic Imagery in the Fiction of Flannery O'Connor." *Southern Humanities Review,* 3 (Winter 1969): 14–32.

Friedman, Melvin J., and Lewis A. Lawson, eds. *The Added Dimension: The Art and Mind of Flannery O'Connor.* New York: Fordham University Press, 1966.

Griffith, Albert J. "Flannery O'Connor's Salvation Road." *Studies in Short Fiction,* 3 (Spring 1966): 329–333.

Hendin, Josephine. *The World of Flannery O'Connor.* Bloomington: Indiana University Press, 1970.

Lorch, Thomas M. "Flannery O'Connor: Christian Allegorist." *Critique: Studies in Modern Fiction,* 10, no. 2 (1968): 69–80.

Marks, W. S., III. "Advertisements for Grace: Flannery O'Connor's 'A Good Man Is Hard to Find'." *Studies in Short Fiction,* 4 (Fall 1966): 19–27.

Martin, Sister M., O.P. "O'Connor's 'A Good Man Is Hard to Find'." *The Explicator,* 24 (October 1965): item 19.

Montgomery, Marion. "Beyond Symbol and Surface: The Fiction of Flannery O'Connor." *Georgia Review,* 22 (Summer 1968): 188–193.

———. "In Defense of Flannery O'Connor's Dragon." *Georgia Review,* 25 (Fall 1971): 302–316.

———. "Flannery O'Connor and the Natural Man." *Mississippi Quarterly,* 21 (Fall 1968): 235–242.

———. "Flannery O'Connor's 'Leaden Tract Against Complacency and Contraception'." *Arizona Quarterly,* 24 (Summer 1968): 133–146.

———. "Flannery O'Connor's Territorial Center." *Critique: Studies in Modern Fiction,* 11, no. 2 (1969): 5–10.

———. "Miss O'Connor and the Christ-Haunted." *Southern Review,* NS 4 (Summer 1968): 665–672.

Oates, Joyce Carol. "The Visionary Art of Flannery O'Connor." *Southern Humanities Review,* 8 (Summer 1973): 235–246.

O'Brien, John T. "The Un-Christianity of Flannery O'Connor." *Listening,* 5 (Winter 1971): 71–82.

Orvell, Miles D. "Flannery O'Connor." *Sewanee Review,* 78 (Winter 1970): 184–192.

Quinn, Sister M. Bernetta. "View from a Rock: The Fiction of Flannery

O'Connor and J. F. Powers." *Critique: Studies in Modern Fiction,* 2 (Fall 1958): 21–22.

Rubin, Louis D., Jr. "Flannery O'Connor: A Note on Literary Fashions." *Critique: Studies in Modern Fiction,* 2 (Fall 1958): 15–18.

————. "Two Ladies of the South." *Sewanee Review,* 63 (Autumn 1955): 671–681.

Shinn, Thelma J. "Flannery O'Connor and the Violence of Grace." *Contemporary Literature* (formerly *Wisconsin Studies in Contemporary Literature*), 9 (Winter 1968): 58–73.

Smith, J. Oates. "Ritual and Violence in Flannery O'Connor." *Thought,* 41 (Winter 1966): 545–560.

Snow, Ollye Tine. "The Functional Gothic of Flannery O'Connor." *Southwest Review,* 50 (Summer 1965): 286–299.

Stephens, Martha. "Flannery O'Connor and the Sanctified Tradition." *Arizona Quarterly,* 24 (Autumn 1968): 223–239.

Sullivan, Walter. "The Achievement of Flannery O'Connor." *Southern Humanities Review,* 2 (Summer 1968): 303–309.

Taylor, Henry. "The Halt Shall Be Gathered Together: Physical Deformity in the Fiction of Flannery O'Connor." *Western Humanities Review,* 22 (Autumn 1968): 325–328.

FRANK O'CONNOR

Cooke, Michael G. "Frank O'Connor and the Fiction of Artlessness." *University Review* (Dublin), 5 (Spring 1968): 87–102.

Johnston, Denis. "If You Like Them Short." *Saturday Review,* 40 (September 21, 1967): 17.

McAleer, Edward C. "Frank O'Connor's Oedipus Trilogy." *Hunter College Studies* (New York), 2 (1964): 33–40.

Prosky, Murray. "The Pattern of Diminishing Certitude in the Stories of Frank O'Connor." *Colby Library Quarterly,* ser. 9 (June 1971): 311–331.

Saul, George Brandon. "A Consideration of Frank O'Connor's Short Stories." *Colby Library Quarterly,* ser. 6 (December 1963): 329–342.

Smith, W. J. "Calm Wise Stories of the Human Comedy." *Commonweal,* 67 (October 25, 1957): 101–102.

Weiss, Daniel. "Freudian Criticism: Frank O'Connor as Paradigm." *Northwest Review,* 2 (Spring 1959): 5–14.

Whittier, Anthony. "The Art of Fiction XIX: Frank O'Connor." *Paris Review,* 5 (Autumn-Winter 1957): 43–64.

LUIGI PIRANDELLO

Hughes, M. Y. "Pirandello's Humor." *Sewanee Review,* 35 (April 1927): 175–186.

Leo, Ulrich. "Pirandello Between Fiction and Drama." In *Pirandello: A Collection of Critical Essays.* Ed. Glauco Cambon. Englewood Cliffs, N.J.: Prentice-Hall, Inc., 1967, pp. 83–90.

May, Frederick. "Introduction." In *Luigi Pirandello: Short Stories.* London: Oxford University Press, 1965, pp. ix–xxx.

Pirandello, Luigi. "On Humor." Trans. Teresa Novel. *Tulane Drama Review,* 10 (Spring 1966): 46–59.

Poggioli, Renato. "Pirandello in Retrospect." In *The Spirit of the Letter: Essays in European Literature.* Cambridge, Mass.: Harvard University Press, 1965, pp. 146–170.

Ragusa, Olga. *Luigi Pirandello.* New York and London: Columbia University Press, 1968.

Starkie, Walter. *Luigi Pirandello: 1867–1936.* 3rd ed. Berkeley and Los Angeles: University of California Press, 1965.

Tilgher, Adriano. "Life Versus Form." In *Pirandello: A Collection of Critical Essays.* Ed. Glauco Cambon. Englewood Cliffs, N.J.: Prentice-Hall, Inc., 1967, pp. 19–34.

EDGAR ALLAN POE

Abel, Darrel. "A Key to the House of Usher." *University of Toronto Quarterly,* 18 (January 1949): 176–185.

Bailey, J. O. "What Happens in 'The Fall of the House of Usher'?" *American Literature,* 35 (January 1964): 445–466.

Beebe, Maurice. "The Universe of Roderick Usher." *The Personalist,* 37 (Spring 1956): 147–160.

Belden, H. M. "Poe's Criticism of Hawthorne." *Anglia,* (1901): 376–404.

Blair, Walter. "Poe's Conception of Incident and Tone in the Tale." *Modern Philology,* 41 (May 1944): 228–240.

Cecil, L. M. "Poe's 'Arabesque'." *Comparative Literature,* 18 (Winter 1966): 55–70.

Davidson, Edward H. *Poe: A Critical Study.* Cambridge: Harvard University Press, 1957, pp. 196–198, 281.

Garrison, Joseph M., Jr. "The Function of Edgar Allan Poe." *American Quarterly,* 18 (Summer 1966): 136–150.

Goodwin, K. L. "Roderick Usher's Overrated Knowledge." *Nineteenth-Century Fiction,* 16 (September 1961): 173–175.

Hartley, Lodwick. "From Crazy Castle to the House of Usher: A Note Toward a Source." *Studies in Short Fiction,* 2 (Spring 1965): 256–261.

Howarth, William L., ed. *Twentieth-Century Interpretations of Poe's Tales.* Englewood Cliffs, N.J.: Prentice-Hall, Inc., 1971.

Kendall, Lyle H., Jr. "The Vampire Motif in 'The Fall of the House of Usher'." *College English,* 24 (March 1963): 450–452.

Lawrence, D. H. *Studies in Classic American Literature.* Garden

City, N.Y.: Doubleday and Co., Inc., 1953 (Anchor Book Paperback), pp. 85–90.

Lawson, Lewis A. "Poe's Conception of the Grotesque." *Mississippi Quarterly,* 19 (Fall 1966): 200–205.

Mabbott, T. O. "Poe's 'The Fall of the House of Usher'." *The Explicator,* 15 (November 1956): item 7.

Moldenhauer, Joseph J. "Murder as a Fine Art: Basic Connections Between Poe's Aesthetics, Psychology, and Moral Vision." *PMLA,* 83 (May 1968): 284–297.

Olson, Bruce. "Poe's Strategy in 'The Fall of the House of Usher'." *Modern Language Notes,* 75 (November 1960): 556–559.

Phillips, William L. "Poe's 'The Fall of the House of Usher'." *The Explicator,* 9 (February 1951): item 29.

Quinn, Patrick F. *The French Face of Edgar Poe.* Carbondale: Southern Illinois University Press, 1957, pp. 54–55, 237–252.

Smith, Herbert F. "Usher's Madness and Poe's Organicism: A Source." *American Literature,* 39 (November 1967): 379–389.

Spitzer, Leo. "A Reinterpretation of 'The Fall of the House of Usher'." *Comparative Literature,* 4 (Fall 1952): 351–363.

Stein, William Bysshe. "The Twin Motif in 'The Fall of the House of Usher'," *Modern Language Notes,* 75 (February 1960): 109–110.

Thompson, G. R. "Unity, Death, and Nothingness—Poe's 'Romantic Skepticism'," *PMLA,* 85 (March 1970): 297–300.

Woodson, Thomas, ed. *Twentieth-Century Interpretations of "The Fall of the House of Usher."* Englewood Cliffs, N.J.: Prentice-Hall, Inc., 1969.

KATHERINE ANNE PORTER

Aldridge, John W. "Art and Passion in Katherine Anne Porter." In *Time to Murder and Create: The Contemporary Novel in Crisis.* New York: David McKay Co., Inc., 1966, pp. 178–184.

Baker, Howard. "The Upward Path: Notes on the Work of Katherine Anne Porter." *Southern Review,* NS 4 (January 1968): 1–19.

Curley, Daniel. "Katherine Anne Porter: The Larger Plan." *Kenyon Review,* 25 (Autumn 1963): 671–695.

Givner, Joan. "A Re-reading of Katherine Anne Porter's 'Theft'." *Studies in Short Fiction,* 6 (Summer 1969): 463–465.

Hartley, Lodwick. "Katherine Anne Porter." *Sewanee Review,* 48 (April-June 1940): 206–216.

———, and George Core, eds. *Katherine Anne Porter: A Critical Symposium.* Athens: University of Georgia Press, 1969, pp. 89, 94, 106.

Hendrick, George. *Katherine Anne Porter.* New York: Twayne Publishers, Inc., 1965, pp. 100–103.

Johnson, James William. "Another Look at Katherine Anne Porter." *Virginia Quarterly Review,* 36 (Autumn 1960): 598–613.

Joselyn, Sister M., O.S.B. "Animal Imagery in Katherine Anne Porter's Fiction." In *Myth and Symbol: Critical Approaches and Applications.* Ed. Bernice Slote. Lincoln: University of Nebraska Press, 1963, pp. 101–115.

Marsden, Malcolm M. "Love as Threat in Katherine Anne Porter's Fiction." *Twentieth Century Literature,* 13 (April 1967): 29–38.

Mooney, Harry John, Jr. *The Fiction and Criticism of Katherine Anne Porter.* Rev. ed. Pittsburgh: University of Pittsburgh Press, 1962.

Nance, William L., S.M. *Katherine Anne Porter & the Art of Rejection.* Chapel Hill: University of North Carolina Press, 1964, pp. 29–36.

Ryan, Marjorie. "*Dubliners* and the Stories of Katherine Anne Porter." *American Literature,* 31 (January 1960): 464–473.

Schwartz, Edward. "The Fictions of Memory." *Southwest Review,* 45 (Summer 1960): 204–215.

Thompson, Barbara. "The Art of Fiction XXIX: Katherine Anne Porter: An Interview." *Paris Review,* 8 (Winter-Spring 1963): 87–114.

Warren, Robert Penn. "Irony with a Center: Katherine Anne Porter." In *Selected Essays.* New York: Random House, Inc., 1958, pp. 136–156.

———. "Uncorrupted Consciousness: The Stories of Katherine Anne Porter." *Yale Review,* 55 (December 1965): 280–290.

Welty, Eudora. "The Eye of the Story." *Yale Review,* 55 (December 1965): 265–274.

West, Ray B., Jr. "Katherine Anne Porter and 'Historic Memory'." In *The Writer in the Room: Selected Essays.* Lansing: Michigan State University Press, 1968, pp. 212–225.

Young, Vernon A. "The Art of Katherine Anne Porter." *New Mexico Quarterly Review,* 15 (Autumn 1945): 326–341.

Zyl, John Van. "Surface Elegance, Grotesque Content—A Note on the Short Stories of Katherine Anne Porter." *English Studies in Africa,* 9 (September 1966): 168–175.

WILLIAM SYDNEY PORTER (O. HENRY)

Current-García, E. "O. Henry's Southern Heritage." *Studies in Short Fiction,* 2 (Fall 1964): 1–12.

———. *O. Henry.* New York: Twayne Publishers, Inc., 1965.

Echols, Edward C., "O. Henry's Shaker of Attic Salt." *Classical Journal,* 43 (1947–48): 488–489; 44 (1948–49): 209–210.

Gallegly, J. S. "Backgrounds and Patterns of O. Henry's Texas Barman Stories." *Rice Institute Pamphlets,* no. 42 (October 1955): 1–37.

Long, E. Hudson. "O. Henry as a Regional Artist." In *Essays on American Literature in Honor of Jay B. Hubbell.* Ed. Clarence Gohdes. Durham, N.C.: Duke University Press, 1967, pp. 229–240.

Pattee, Fred Lewis. "O. Henry and the Handbooks." In *The Development of the American Short Story.* New York: Harper and Brothers, 1923, pp. 357–379.

Saroyan, William. "O What a Man Was O. Henry." *Kenyon Review,* 24 (November 1967), 671–675.

ALEXANDER PUSHKIN

Beckwith, Martha Warren, et al. *Pushkin: The Man and the Artist.* New York: Paisley Press, 1937.

Cross, Samuel H., ed. *Centennial Essays for Pushkin.* New York: Russell and Russell, 1967.

Magarshack, David. *Pushkin.* New York: Grove Press, 1968.

Troyat, Henri. *Pushkin: A Biography.* New York: Pantheon Books, Inc., 1950.

Vickery, Walter N. *Alexander Pushkin.* New York: Twayne Publishers, Inc., 1970.

WILLIAM SAROYAN

Angoff, Charles. "William Saroyan: Some Footnotes." In *The Tone of the Twenties and Other Essays.* New York: Barnes, 1966, pp. 203–208.

Burgum, E. B. "The Lonesome Young Man on the Flying Trapeze." *Virginia Quarterly Review,* 20 (Summer 1944): 392–403.

Floan, Howard R. *William Saroyan.* New York: Twayne Publishers, Inc., 1966.

Kherdian, David. *A Bibliography of William Saroyan: 1934–1964.* San Francisco: Roger Beacham, 1965.

Nathan, G. J. "Saroyan: Whirling Dervish of Fresno." *American Mercury,* 51 (November 1940): 303–308.

PETER TAYLOR

Blum, Morgan. "Peter Taylor: Self-Limitation in Fiction." *Sewanee Review,* 70 (Autumn 1962): 559–578.

Brown, Ashley. "The Early Fiction of Peter Taylor." *Sewanee Review,* 70 (Autumn 1962): 588–602.

Cathey, Kenneth Clay. "Peter Taylor: An Evaluation." *Western Review,* 18 (Autumn 1953): 9–19.

Griffith, Albert J. *Peter Taylor.* New York: Twayne Publishers, Inc., 1970.

Peden, William. *The American Short Story.* Boston: Houghton, Mifflin, 1964, pp. 61–68.

———. "A Hard and Admirable Toughness: The Stories of Peter Taylor." *The Hollins Critic,* 7 (February 1970), 1–9.

Schuler, Sister Cor Mariae [Barbara]. "The House of Peter Taylor." *Critique: Studies in Modern Fiction,* 9, no. 3 (1967): 6–18.

Smith, James P. "Narration and Theme in Taylor's *A Woman of Means.*" *Critique: Studies in Modern Fiction,* 9, no. 3 (1967): 19–30.

Warren, Robert Penn. "Introduction." In *A Long Fourth and Other Stories.* New York: Harcourt, Brace & Co., 1948, pp. vii–x.

JEAN TOOMER

Ackley, Donald G. "Theme and Vision in Jean Toomer's *Cane.*" *Studies in Black Literature,* 1 (Spring 1970): 45–65.

Cancel, Rafael A. "Male and Female Interrelationship in Toomer's *Cane.*" *Negro American Literature Forum,* 5 (1971): 25–31.

Chase, Patricia. "The Women in *Cane.*" *CLA Journal,* 14 (1971): 259–273.

Durham, Frank. "Jean Toomer's Vision of the Southern Negro." *Southern Humanities Review,* 6 (Winter 1972): 13–22.

Frank, Waldo. Forward to *Cane.* New York: Boni and Liverwright, 1923.

Grant, Mary Kathryn. "Images of Celebration in *Cane.*" *Negro American Literature Forum,* 4 (1970): 62–63.

Kraft, James. "Jean Toomer's *Cane.*" *Markham Review,* 2 (October 1970): 61–63.

Reilly, John M. "The Search for Black Redemption: Jean Toomer's *Cane.*" *Studies in the Novel,* 2 (1970): 312–324.

Stein, Marian L. "The Poet-Observer and 'Fern' in Jean Toomer's *Cane.*" *Markham Review,* 2 (October 1970): 64–65.

Turner, Darwin T. *In a Minor Chord: Three Afro-American Writers and Their Search for Identity.* Carbondale: Southern Illinois University Press, 1971.

Welburn, Ron. "Reissues of Afro-American Literature" [on *Cane*]. *Southwest Review,* 54 (Spring 1970): 217–221.

IVAN TURGENEV

Gettman, Royal. *Turgenev in England and America.* Urbana: University of Illinois Press, 1941.

Harrison, W. Introduction to *A Sportsman's Sketches.* Chicago: Russian Language Specialties, 1965.

Magarshack, David. *Turgenev: A Life.* New York: Grove Press, 1954.

Yarmolinsky, A. *Turgenev: The Man, His Art and His Age.* London: Hodder and Stoughton, 1926; New York: Century Company, 1926.

EUDORA WELTY

Bradham, Jo Allen. "'A Visit of Charity': Menippean Satire." *Studies in Short Fiction,* 1 (Summer 1964): 258–263.

Daniel, Robert. "The World of Eudora Welty." *Hopkins Review,* 7 (Winter 1953): 49–58; reprinted in *The Southern Renascence.* Eds. Louis Rubin and Robert D. Jacobs. Baltimore: Johns Hopkins Press, pp. 306–315.

Glenn, Eunice. "Fantasy in the Fiction of Eudora Welty." *A Southern Vanguard.* Ed. Allen Tate. New York: Prentice-Hall, Inc., 1947, pp. 78–91.

Hardy, John Edward. "The Achievement of Eudora Welty." *Southern Humanities Review,* 2 (Summer 1968): 269–278.

Hartley, Lodwick. "Proserpina and the Old Ladies." *Modern Fiction Studies,* 3 (Winter 1957–58): 350–354.

Jones, Alun R. "The World of Love: The Fiction of Eudora Welty." In *The Creative Present.* Eds. Nona Balakian and Charles Simmons. Garden City, N.Y.: Doubleday and Company, 1963, pp. 175–192.

Jones, William M. "Name and Symbol in the Prose of Eudora Welty." *Southern Folklore Quarterly,* 22 (December 1958): 173–185.

Masserand, Anne M. "Eudora Welty's Travellers: The Journey Theme in Her Short Stories." *Southern Literary Journal,* 3 (Spring 1971): 39–48.

May, Charles E. "The Difficulty of Loving in 'A Visit of Charity'." *Studies in Short Fiction,* 6 (Spring 1969): 338–341.

Palmer, Melvin Delmar. "Welty's 'A Visit of Charity'." *The Explicator,* 22 (May 1964): item 69.

Rubin, Louis D., Jr. "Two Ladies of the South." *Sewanee Review,* 63 (Autumn 1955): 671–681.

Toole, William B., III. "The Texture of 'A Visit of Charity'." *Mississippi Quarterly,* 20 (Winter 1966–67): 43–46.

Vande Kieft, Ruth M. *Eudora Welty.* New York: Twayne Publishers, 1962.

Warren, Robert Penn. "The Love and the Separateness in Miss Welty." *Kenyon Review,* 6 (Spring 1944): 246–259.

JESSAMYN WEST

Katope, Christopher G. "West's 'Love, Death, and the Ladies' Drill Team'." *The Explicator,* 23 (December 1964): item 27.

Smith, Harrison. "Many-Dimensioned Beings." *Saturday Review,* 38 (December 3, 1955): 27.

Feb 1, 1944

144-250
3-4
28-32

March 22, 1977
P 345 - Faulkner

2 3 4 5 6 7 8 9 10 11 12 13 14 15 –KP– 85 84 83 82 81 80 79 78 77 76 75 74